Samuel Pepys

Samuel Pepys

The Unequalled Self

CLAIRE TOMALIN

VIKING
an imprint of
PENGUIN BOOKS

VIKING

Published by the Penguin Group
Penguin Books Ltd, 80 Strand, London WC2R ORL, England
Penguin Putnam Inc., 375 Hudson Street, New York, New York 10014, USA
Penguin Books Australia Ltd, 250 Camberwell Road,
Camberwell, Victoria 3124, Australia
Penguin Books Canada Ltd, 10 Alcorn Avenue, Toronto, Ontario, Canada M4V 3B2
Penguin Books India (P) Ltd, 11 Community Centre,
Panchsheel Park, New Delhi – 110 017, India
Penguin Books (NZ) Ltd, Cnr Rosedale and Airborne Roads,
Albany, Auckland, New Zealand
Penguin Books (South Africa) (Pty) Ltd, 24 Sturdee Avenue,
Rosebank 2196, South Africa

Penguin Books Ltd, Registered Offices: 80 Strand, London WC2R ORL, England

www.penguin.com

First published 2002

4

Copyright © Claire Tomalin, 2002
Maps copyright © Andrew Farmer, 2002

The moral right of the author has been asserted

The acknowledgements on p. 470 constitute an extension of this copyright page

Set in 12/14.75pt Monotype Bembo
Typeset by Rowland Phototypesetting Ltd, Bury St Edmunds, Suffolk
Printed in Great Britain by Clays Ltd, St Ives plc

A CIP catalogue record for this book is available from the British Library

ISBN 0-670-88568-1

The whole book, if you will but look at it in that way, is seen to be a work of art to Pepys's own address. Here, then, we have the key to that remarkable attitude preserved by him throughout his diary, to that unflinching – I had almost said, that unintelligent – sincerity which makes it a miracle among human books . . . Whether he did ill or well, he was still his own unequalled self; still that entrancing *ego* of whom alone he cared to write.

– Robert Louis Stevenson, 'Samuel Pepys'

Un livre est le produit d'un autre moi que celui que nous manifestons dans nos habitudes, dans la société, dans nos vices.

– Marcel Proust, *Contre Sainte-Beuve*

[There is] in every one, two men, the wise and the foolish, and . . . each of them must be allowed his turn. If you would have the wise, the grave, the serious, always to rule and have sway, the fool would grow so peevish and troublesome, that he would put the wise man out of order, and make him fit for nothing: he must have his times of being let loose to follow his fancies, and play his gambols, if you would have your business go on smoothly.

– Anthony Ashley Cooper, Lord Shaftesbury, to John Locke

Contents

List of Illustrations

★

Acknowledgements

My first thanks go to the master and fellows of Magdalene College, Cambridge, for their hospitality and for allowing me the privilege of working in the Pepys Library. Richard Luckett, Pepys librarian, encouraged me from the start. Mrs Aude Fitzsimons, assistant librarian, has borne with my many prolonged visits and given me every sort of assistance; I have profited greatly by her kindness, and by the good advice and help of Dr Charles S. Knighton, deputy editor of the Pepys Library Catalogue.

Thanks to the Earl and Countess of Sandwich for support, help and encouragement; and to Brian Crichton for his generosity.

I am grateful to Robin Harcourt Williams, archivist at Hatfield House, for sparing a day to give me his advice and taking me on an instructive and enjoyable tour of the Woodhall area; also to Mrs Sally Timson of the Cottage, Woodhall Farm, Hatfield, for showing me her house; and to Mr H. W. Gray for answering my queries about St Ethelreda's, Hatfield.

Lady McAlpine was good enough to allow me to visit the present house at Durdans, where Ray Rudman went to considerable trouble to give me information about the history of the place and previous houses there.

Hoare's Bank kindly allowed me to examine and photocopy their records of Pepys's account with them.

Thanks to John Cronin, curator of Hinchingbrooke School, Huntingdon, for taking me over the building and the grounds, and to Mr and Mrs Julian Curtis for showing me the Pepys house at Brampton. Also to J. H. L. Puxley for showing me his family portraits and allowing them to be photographed.

Thanks to Sir Oliver Millar, GCVO, FBA, FSA, for help in tracking down portraits; to Dr Frances Harris for general guidance and especially for talking to me about John Evelyn; to Simon May, archivist at St Paul's School, for his help; to Nicolas Barker; to Mrs Rhona Mitchell, archivist of Christ's Hospital; to Julian Mitchell, who sent me his paper on John Creed's brother Richard; to Robin Hyman for checking my account of the publishing history of the Diary, and for allowing plates from his Braybrooke edition to be photographed; to David Wickham, archivist of the Clothworkers' Company; to Canon Graham Corneck of St Nicholas, Deptford; to Revd John Cowling of St Olave, Hart Street; to Nicholas Monck for making a new translation of Daniel Skinner's Latin letter to Pepys; to Sheila Russell for information about Impington Manor; to Mrs Dagtoglou for sending me G. R. Balleine's account of Sir George Carteret; to Robin Gibson for lending me his copy of the catalogue to the National Portrait Gallery's Pepys exhibition of 1970; and to Andrew Howard for showing me over 12 Buckingham Street.

Also to Professor Gordon Campbell, to Dr Timothy Graham, to Professor R. I. Page, to Christopher de Hamel and to Professor B. S. Capp, all of whom gave me advice and suggestions for further reading; and to Professor John Bossy for his elucidation of the topography of Salisbury Court.

On medical questions I have been advised by Dr Patrick French, FRCP, consultant in genito-urinary medicine, Mortimer Market Centre, London; also by Milo Keynes, who sent me his paper on Pepys's health; R. Goodwin, MA, Msc, FRCS, and H. N. Whitfield; and by the Real Tennis Club of Cambridge, where I was given the dimensions of the real tennis ball, which the stone removed from Pepys equalled in size.

I am grateful to the staff of the following libraries for their assistance: the Wellcome Library of Medical History, the Library of the Royal Society of London, the British Library, the London Library, the Bodleian Library, the National Maritime Museum, Greenwich, the Public Record Office, the Guildhall Library, the National Portrait Gallery archives, the Liddle Hart archives held at King's College, the London National Meteorological Library and in particular Ian MacGregor, library and archives services manager, who sent me Gordon Manley's weather charts for the seventeenth century; the Huntingdon County Record Office and Public Library, and the Hertfordshire Record Office.

As always, particular thanks to Tony Lacey, Charles Elliot and Donna Poppy for their questions, suggestions and help; also to Keith Taylor, Dinah Drazin, and to Diana Lecore, who made the index.

And finally to my husband, who first went to Huntingdon and Brampton with me, who has walked from Bermondsey to Greenwich and from Fleet Street to the Tower and back with me on a number of occasions, and who put up with my virtual disappearance into the seventeenth century for several years with patience and good humour.

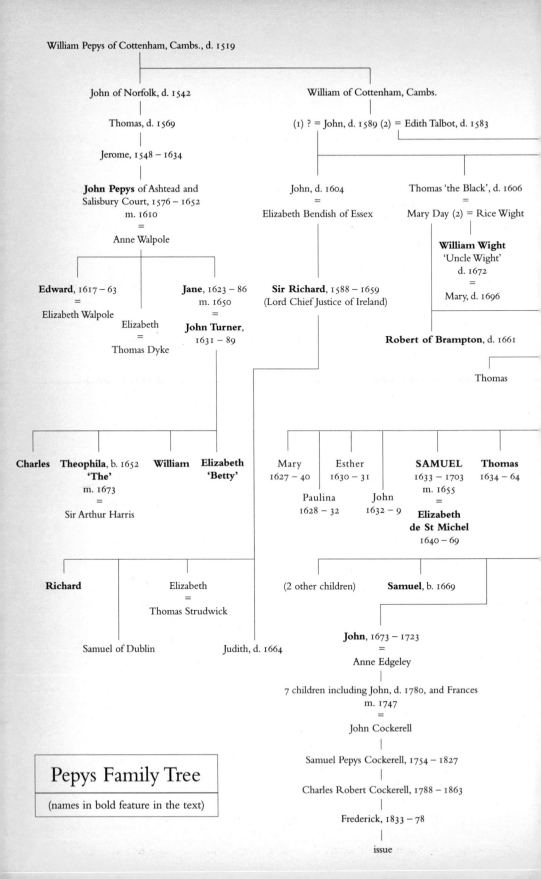

William Pepys of Cottenham, Cambs., d. 1519

John of Norfolk, d. 1542

William of Cottenham, Cambs.

Thomas, d. 1569

(1) ? = John, d. 1589 (2) = Edith Talbot, d. 1583

Jerome, 1548 – 1634

John Pepys of Ashtead and
Salisbury Court, 1576 – 1652
m. 1610
=
Anne Walpole

John, d. 1604
=
Elizabeth Bendish of Essex

Thomas 'the Black', d. 1606
=
Mary Day (2) = Rice Wight

William Wight
'Uncle Wight'
d. 1672
=
Mary, d. 1696

Edward, 1617 – 63
=
Elizabeth Walpole

Elizabeth
=
Thomas Dyke

Jane, 1623 – 86
m. 1650
=
John Turner,
1631 – 89

Sir Richard, 1588 – 1659
(Lord Chief Justice of Ireland)

Robert of Brampton, d. 1661

Thomas

Charles **Theophila**, b. 1652
'The'
m. 1673
=
Sir Arthur Harris

William **Elizabeth**
'Betty'

Mary
1627 – 40

Esther
1630 – 31

Paulina
1628 – 32

John
1632 – 9

SAMUEL
1633 – 1703
m. 1655
=
**Elizabeth
de St Michel**
1640 – 69

Thomas
1634 – 64

Richard

Elizabeth
=
Thomas Strudwick

(2 other children) **Samuel**, b. 1669

Samuel of Dublin

Judith, d. 1664

John, 1673 – 1723
=
Anne Edgeley

7 children including John, d. 1780, and Frances
m. 1747
=
John Cockerell

Samuel Pepys Cockerell, 1754 – 1827

Charles Robert Cockerell, 1788 – 1863

Frederick, 1833 – 78

issue

Pepys Family Tree

(names in bold feature in the text)

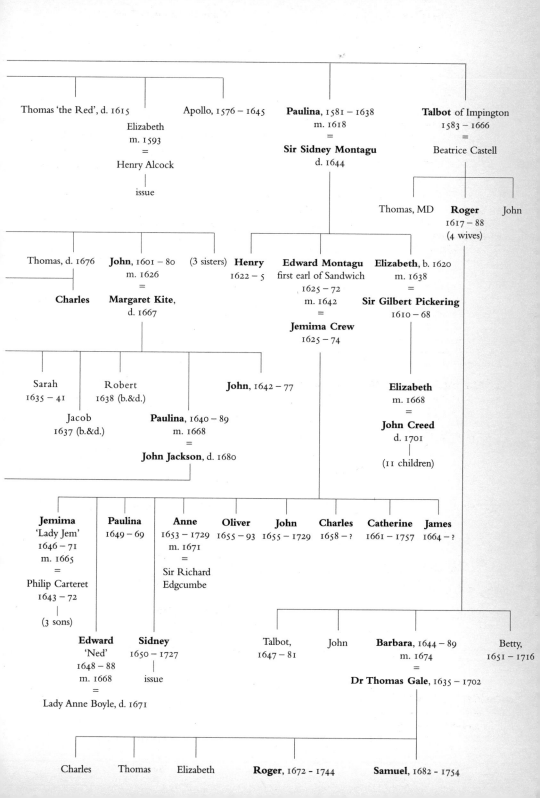

Thomas 'the Red', d. 1615   Apollo, 1576 – 1645   **Paulina**, 1581 – 1638   **Talbot** of Impington

Elizabeth
m. 1593
=
Henry Alcock
|
issue

m. 1618
=
Sir Sidney Montagu
d. 1644

1583 – 1666
=
Beatrice Castell

Thomas, MD   **Roger**   John
1617 – 88
(4 wives)

Thomas, d. 1676   **John**, 1601 – 80   (3 sisters) **Henry**   **Edward Montagu**   **Elizabeth**, b. 1620

               m. 1626   1622 – 5   first earl of Sandwich   m. 1638
Charles   **Margaret Kite**,   1625 – 72   =
          d. 1667   m. 1642   **Sir Gilbert Pickering**
                                          =   1610 – 68
                                      Jemima Crew
                                      1625 – 74

Sarah   Robert   **John**, 1642 – 77   **Elizabeth**
1635 – 41   1638 (b.&d.)   m. 1668
Jacob   **Paulina**, 1640 – 89   =
1637 (b.&d.)   m. 1668   **John Creed**
                =   d. 1701
        John Jackson, d. 1680   (11 children)

Jemima   **Paulina**   **Anne**   **Oliver**   **John**   **Charles**   **Catherine**   **James**
'Lady Jem'   1649 – 69   1653 – 1729 1655 – 93 1655 – 1729 1658 – ?   1661 – 1757 1664 – ?
1646 – 71   m. 1671
m. 1665   =
=   Sir Richard
Philip Carteret   Edgcumbe
1643 – 72
|
(3 sons)

Edward   Sidney   Talbot,   John   **Barbara**, 1644 – 89   Betty,
'Ned'   1650 – 1727   1647 – 81   m. 1674   1651 – 1716
1648 – 88 | =
m. 1668   issue   **Dr Thomas Gale**, 1635 – 1702
=
Lady Anne Boyle, d. 1671

Charles   Thomas   Elizabeth   **Roger**, 1672 - 1744   **Samuel**, 1682 - 1754

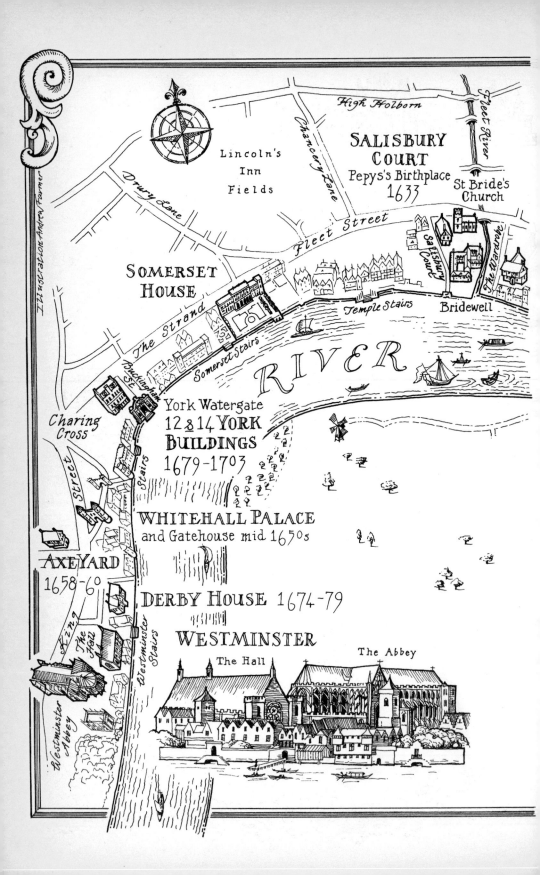

Illustration: Andrew Farmer

High Holborn

Chancery Lane

Fleet River

SALISBURY
COURT
Pepys's Birthplace
1633

St Bride's
Church

Lincoln's
Inn
Fields

Drury Lane

Fleet Street

Salisbury Court

The Wardrobe

SOMERSET
HOUSE

The Strand

Temple Stairs

Bridewell

Somerset Stairs

RIVER

Buckingham St.

York Watergate
12 & 14 YORK
BUILDINGS
1679–1703

Charing
Cross

Stairs

Street

WHITEHALL PALACE
and Gatehouse mid 1650s

AXE YARD
1658-60

King St

DERBY HOUSE 1674–79

Westminster Stairs

WESTMINSTER

The Hall

The Abbey

Westminster Abbey

The Hall

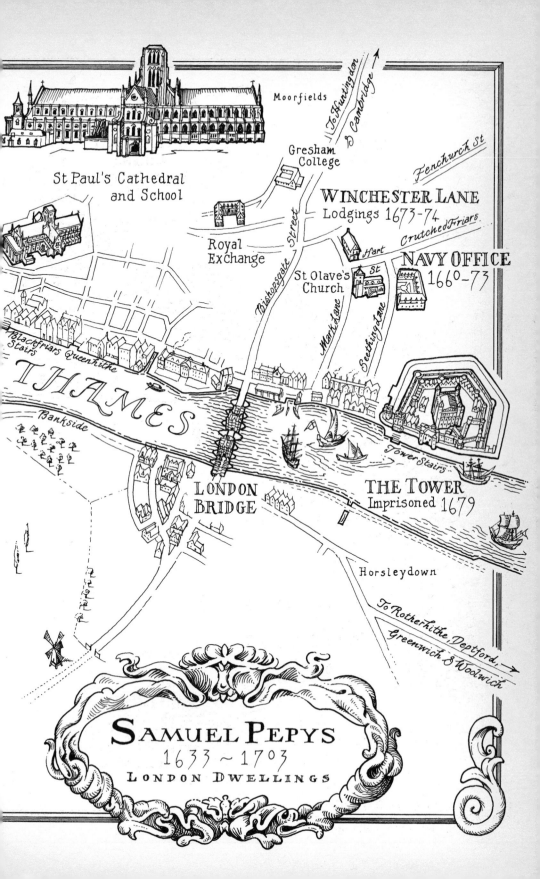

Moorfields

St Paul's Cathedral
and School

Gresham
College

WINCHESTER LANE
Lodgings 1673-74

To Huntingdon
& Cambridge

Fenchurch St

Crutched Friars

Royal
Exchange

Bishopsgate Street

Hart

NAVY OFFICE
1660-73

St Olave's
Church

St

Mark Lane

Seething Lane

Blackfriars Stairs Queenhithe

THAMES

Bankside

LONDON
BRIDGE

Tower Stairs

THE TOWER
Imprisoned 1679

Horsleydown

To Rotherhithe, Deptford,
Greenwich & Woolwich

SAMUEL PEPYS
1633 ~ 1703
LONDON DWELLINGS

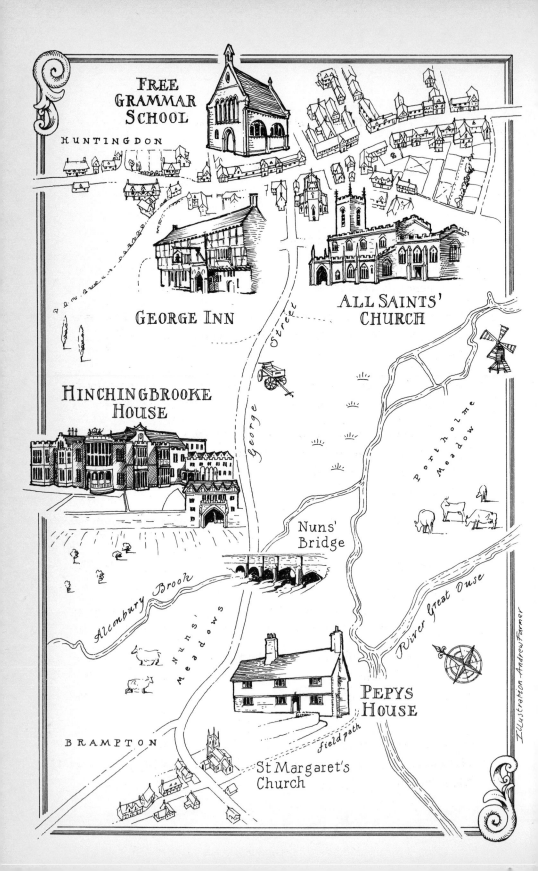

FREE
GRAMMAR
SCHOOL

HUNTINGDON

GEORGE INN

ALL SAINTS'
CHURCH

HINCHINGBROOKE
HOUSE

George Street

Portholme Meadow

Nuns'
Bridge

Alconbury Brook

Nuns' Meadows

River Great Ouse

PEPYS
HOUSE

BRAMPTON

field path

St Margaret's
Church

Illustration Andrew Farmer

List of Principal Figures

SP stands for Samuel Pepys; EP for Elizabeth Pepys.

Albemarle, duke of, *see* George Monck.

Mary Ashwell, teacher in girls' school before becoming EP's companion; skilful singer, dancer and card-player.

William Bagwell, ship's carpenter at Deptford, encouraged wife to offer herself to SP, which she did, in order to win promotion. Her first name is unknown.

Sir John Banks, financier; SP on friendly terms with his family in 1670s; he testified before the House of Commons that SP was not a Catholic.

Sir William Batten, West Country sea captain of humble origins who rose to be surveyor of the navy before the civil war and, despite shifts of allegiance, was reappointed to the Navy Board in 1660, becoming SP's colleague and neighbour.

Thomas Betterton, actor–manager, the greatest of his time, much admired by SP.

Jane Birch, SP's first and favourite maid, worked for him on and off from the age of fourteen, married his clerk Tom Edwards, helped by SP when widowed. Her younger brother, Wayneman Birch, worked for SP, sacked by him for bad behaviour and sent to the plantations.

Robert Blackborne, powerful secretary to the Admiralty commissioners under the commonwealth, lost job at Restoration, introduced his nephew Will Hewer to SP. Later secretary to the East India Co., and stood bail for SP in 1690.

Sir Francis Boteler, Hertfordshire landowner, of the Woodhall estate adjoining Hatfield House; with his second wife, Elizabeth, brought up her niece Mary Skinner.

Robert Bowyer, Exchequer official. He and his wife Elizabeth were both kind and hospitable to the young SP and EP. Sometimes called 'father Bowyer' by SP.

William Brouncker, second viscount, royalist mathematician and scientist with interest in music, first president of the Royal Society and SP's admired senior colleague at the Navy Board; also his neighbour, with his mistress Abigail Williams, of whom SP disapproved.

Sir William Buck, baronet, Lincolnshire landowner, husband of Frances Skinner, Mary's sister.

Buckingham, duke of, *see* George Villiers.

Josiah Burchett, clerk to SP, sacked by him but later secretary to the Admiralty.

Sir George Carteret, royalist, treasurer of the navy from 1660 and as such SP's boss. Married his son Philip to Jemima Montagu.

Castlemaine, countess of, *see* Barbara Villiers.

Catherine of Braganza, Portuguese princess, Charles II's queen.

Charles II: SP took a detached and mostly unfavourable view of him while appreciating that his own career depended on pleasing him, and enjoying the effects of his patronage of theatre, music and painting.

Dr Arthur Charlett, master of University College, Oxford, friend and correspondent of SP in later years.

Clarendon, first earl of, *see* Edward Hyde.

Clarendon, second earl of, *see* Henry Hyde.

John Closterman, German portrait painter settled in England, painted SP in old age.

Captain George Cocke, merchant, drinking companion of SP and his associate during episode of prize goods.

Sir Robert Coke, son of Chief Justice Edward Coke who employed John Pepys of Ashtead; Sir Robert and his wife, Lady Theophila (née Berkeley), entertained SP as a child at their house in Surrey, Durdans.

Anthony Ashley Cooper, later first earl of Shaftesbury, served Cromwell, made peace with Charles II and was given office and title by him. Known to

SP through Montagu and the Tangier Committee. Sought to exclude duke of York from succession to throne, attacked SP as duke of York's man and accused him of Catholicism, leading to SP's imprisonment during Popish Plot.

William Coventry, later Sir William, royalist, statesman, secretary to duke of York and admired friend to SP at Navy Board; left royal service disillusioned in 1667 but continued to serve in parliament.

John Creed, puritan, contemporary and rival of SP, at first in service of Montagu; married Montagu's niece Elizabeth Pickering.

John Crew, father of Jemima and father-in-law of Edward Montagu, moderate parliamentarian, created Baron Crew 1661; friendly and hospitable to SP.

Samuel Cromleholme, surmaster of St Paul's School during SP's schooldays, book collector, his library destroyed in the fire.

Richard Cromwell, son of Oliver, succeeded him briefly as protector.

Oliver Cromwell, general, statesman, lord protector; neighbour and friend of Edward Montagu.

Richard Cumberland, like SP a Salisbury Court tailor's son, went to St Paul's and Magdalene; friend of SP, scholar, became bishop of Peterborough.

Samuel Daniel, naval lieutenant whose wife solicited commission for him from SP.

Dartmouth, first Baron, *see* George Legge.

Sir William D'Avenant, dramatist and actor–manager, ran the Duke's Company.

Anthony Deane, later Sir Anthony, outstanding ship designer, son of Harwich mariner; close friend of SP, their careers rising and falling together.

George Downing, later Sir George, SP's first official employer, at the Exchequer; rose to high office under Cromwell, changed sides adroitly and rose again under Charles II. Downing Street is named for the house he built for himself on land given him by the king.

John Dryden, poet and dramatist, known to SP from Cambridge; friendship revived in the 1690s.

Tom Edwards, chorister at the Chapel Royal, joined Pepys household when his voice broke, making music, working in the house and at the Navy Office. Married Jane Birch, SP godfather to their son.

John Evelyn, gentleman-scholar of many talents, gardener, writer, planner, health administrator, diarist, became SP's greatly loved friend and correspondent in later life.

Captain Robert Ferrer, Montagu's cornet, then his master of horse; dashing, drinker and gambler, friendly to SP, dangerous to EP.

Dr Thomas Gale, cousin by marriage (*see* Cambridge Pepyses), valued friend and correspondent of SP in later life; scholar, high master of St Paul's School, dean of York.

Sir Denis Gauden, victualler to navy under the commonwealth and after the Restoration, working closely with SP. Owner of fine country house in Clapham acquired by Will Hewer when Gauden was bankrupted.

Richard Gibson, chief clerk and friend to SP. Served in commonwealth navy from age of thirteen and had low opinion of 'gentlemen' officers of the Restoration. Advised SP and wrote many papers on naval questions.

Nell Gwyn, actress who delighted SP; he did favours for her after the death of Charles II.

James Harrington, met by SP at the Rota Club; author of *Oceana*, programme for republican reform of England; imprisoned 1660, never recovered.

Samuel Hartlib, Prussian exile, friend of Milton and Petty, neighbour of SP in Axe Yard; his son Samuel, a government clerk, one of SP's early circle.

John Hayls, portrait painter patronized by SP.

Thomas Hayter, navy clerk under the commonwealth, employed by SP in 1660; Nonconformist, defended by SP when attacked; succeeded SP as clerk of the acts in 1673.

Arthur Herbert, later earl of Torrington, admiral detested by SP; went over to William of Orange in 1688 and in charge of the invasion fleet.

William Hewer, puritan lad, son of a stationer and nephew of Robert Blackborne, became SP's clerk in 1660 and developed into his closest associate and friend, becoming extremely rich.

Dr George Hickes, Anglo-Saxon scholar and dean of Worcester, friend of SP; after 1688 a nonjuror (i.e., refused oath of allegiance to William III). Obliged to live in hiding; visited James II secretly in France; attended SP on his deathbed and conducted his funeral.

Thomas Hill, musical friend of SP, son of commonwealth civil servant and brother of Abraham, founding member of the Royal Society, also known to SP. Employed by the Houblons as a merchant in Lisbon, where he found Cesare Morelli for SP.

Richard and James Hoare, founders of the bank where SP had an account.

Thomas Hollier, surgeon who operated on SP to remove the stone from his bladder.

Robert Hooke, outstanding scientist, architect and secretary of the Royal Society; admired by SP. Kept diary. Possibly designed the building at Magdalene College, Cambridge, in which SP's Diary is housed.

Houblon family, French Protestant merchants who settled in London at end of the sixteenth century and became exceedingly rich. SP's particular friends were James, knighted in 1691, and his wife, Sarah. He and two of his brothers were directors of the Bank of England; another was director of the East India Company.

John and Elizabeth Hunt, neighbours in Axe Yard, he in the Excise Office, she connected to the Cromwells; friends during the Diary period.

Anne Hyde, first wife of James, duke of York, and mother of the future queens Mary and Anne; daughter of Edward Hyde.

Edward Hyde, first earl of Clarendon, chief adviser to Charles II before the Restoration and his chancellor afterwards; sacked and exiled by him after the Dutch attack on the Medway. Known to SP and liked by him.

Henry Hyde, second earl of Clarendon, son of the above, close friend of SP in later life.

John Jackson, SP's younger nephew who became his protégé; sent to Cambridge and on Grand Tour. SP's principal heir.

Samuel Jackson, SP's elder nephew.

James, duke of York, later King James II, lord high admiral in 1660. He and SP had a common interest in the navy that led to a close relationship, strengthened by attacks made on both by political opponents. James did his best for SP, and SP maintained a stubborn loyalty to him.

John James, butler to SP, dismissed by him; gave false evidence against him during Popish Plot, which he withdrew on his deathbed.

Sir John Kempthorne, formidable Devon-born sea commander, fought Algerian pirates in the Mediterranean; became commissioner for Portsmouth and had many dealings with SP and with Will Hewer.

Thomas Killigrew, dramatist, theatre manager, courtier; discussed theatre history with SP.

Colonel Percy Kirke, commander-in-chief of Tangier garrison, disliked by SP, promoted by William III.

Joshua Kirton, bookseller to SP, ruined in the fire.

Sir Godfrey Kneller, court painter well known to SP, produced portraits of and for him.

Elizabeth Knipp, actress, married to a horse dealer; admired by SP and intimate with him.

Betty Lane, later Martin, Nottingham girl who kept a linen stall in Westminster Hall and maintained a casual affair with SP. Her sister Doll provided back-up services.

John Langley, high master of St Paul's School during SP's years there: strongly puritan and parliamentarian.

George Legge, first Baron Dartmouth, led expedition to Tangier in which SP took part; as commander-in-chief of the navy failed to prevent the landing of William of Orange in 1688.

Sir Peter Lely, Dutch painter in England from 1641, painted Cromwell, became favourite court painter of Charles II. Visited and admired by SP.

Paul Lorrain, French Protestant clerk to SP, worked on cataloguing library; ordained and became chaplain at Newgate Prison.

Peter Luellin, early 'clubbing' friend of SP, died of plague.

John Matthews, Huntingdon schoolmaster and distant cousin of SP, cared for and educated his sister's sons, Sam and John Jackson.

Sir John Mennes, old fighting royalist and poet, comptroller of navy from 1661 until his death ten years later. SP despaired of his incompetence but enjoyed his wit.

Mary Mercer, companion to EP for two years, much liked by SP, remained family friend.

Betty Michell, daughter of Westminster Hall stallholders, wife of spirit-seller; hotly pursued by SP.

Daniel Mills, rector of St Olave's, Hart Street, where SP and other members of the Navy Office worshipped; not much liked by SP but attended EP on her deathbed and provided certificate of regular attendance for SP when he was accused of Catholicism.

John Milton, poet; like SP, St Paul's and Cambridge educated; commonwealth official and apologist for the execution of Charles I; life spared in 1660 but regarded as a 'diabolical rebel' thereafter. Mary Skinner's brother Daniel worked as his amanuensis.

George Monck, duke of Albemarle, having served Charles I and then Cromwell, became chiefly responsible for the Restoration. SP disliked him, and he was critical of the Navy Office.

Edward Montagu, later earl of Sandwich; son of Sir Sidney Montagu and his wife Paulina, née Pepys, sister to Talbot Pepys and great-aunt to SP; the crucial figure in SP's life, his benefactor and patron. Montagu broke with his royalist father to support Cromwell, whom he served as colonel, general-at-sea and holder of many offices of state and a peerage. Disillusioned by the anarchy following the death of Cromwell, he helped to bring about the Restoration and was created first earl of Sandwich by Charles II.

Montagu's wife *Jemima* was born into the parliamentary and puritan family of the Crews; she was always 'My Lady' to SP, who loved and respected her. Their ten children, all known to SP, were Jemima (Jem), Edward (Ned), Paulina, Sidney, Anne, the twins Oliver and John, Charles, Catherine and James – the names of the last five neatly illustrate Montagu's changing politics.

Lady Mordaunt (Betty), 'young and pretty rich and good-natured', family connection, close to SP during the 1670s; also her sister Mrs Steward.

Cesare Morelli, musician and linguist, Italian Catholic employed by SP as his household musician.

Samuel Morland, later Sir Samuel, SP's tutor at Cambridge, envoy and intelligence expert during the commonwealth, went over to Charles before the Restoration. Mathematician and inventor of water engines and pumps; remained poor and SP had a low opinion of him.

Sir Christopher Myngs, naval commander of modest background, hostile to Sandwich, killed in action, his funeral attended by SP.

Isaac Newton, later Sir Isaac, the great scientist in many fields including optics and gravitation, author of *Principia Mathematica* published by the Royal Society when SP was president. SP consulted him about the appointment of a mathematics master at Christ's Hospital.

Samuel Newton, mathematics master at Christ's Hospital recommended by Isaac Newton (no relation); complained to SP of the system of sending boys to sea too young.

Titus Oates, squalid but effective villain responsible for the Popish Plot; used by Shaftesbury for his own political ends.

James Pearse, naval surgeon whose career started under Montagu during the commonwealth. After 1660 employed at court and SP's chief source of gossip. He and wife Elizabeth were close friends of SP.

Sir William Penn, SP's *bête noire*, another West Country sea captain trained by Sir William Batten, served in Cromwell's Dutch war, but made peace with Charles II and was appointed to the Navy Board in 1660. Father of William Penn the younger, a Quaker and the founder of Pennsylvania: he became SP's friend under James II, who took up Penn for his own political purposes.

John Pepys, SP's father. London tailor living and working in Salisbury Court off Fleet Street, married Margaret Kite; of their eleven children four survived into adult life, the eldest of whom was SP. The other three were Tom, unenthusiastic and unsuccessful tailor, John, who followed SP to St Paul's and Cambridge, and Paulina – Pall – disliked by SP, who married John Jackson, a farmer, and had two sons who survived into adult life.

John Pepys of Ashtead and Salisbury Court, third cousin once removed of SP's father, made his fortune working for the great jurist Edward Coke; a friend to the boy SP. His daughter Jane also a good friend to SP, married lawyer John Turner and was the mother of 'The' (Theophila).

Richard Pepys, first cousin of SP's father, lord chief justice of Ireland under Cromwell and the father of 'cousin Richard' whom SP met in 1660 after a fourteen-year-absence in America.

Robert Pepys, elder brother of SP's father, bailiff on the Hinchingbrooke estate in Huntingdonshire and owner of a house still standing at Brampton.

Four generations of *Cambridge Pepyses*: Talbot, lawyer and MP, great-uncle to SP; his son Roger, also lawyer and friend of SP; Roger's daughter Barbara ('Babs') who married Dr Thomas Gale, scholar and high master of St Paul's and close friend of SP in later life; among their sons, Roger and Samuel (SP's godson) became antiquarians.

Pett family, leading shipbuilders over several generations. SP knew best Peter Pett, who built ships for the commonwealth and Charles II, and was made the scapegoat when the Dutch launched their attack on the Medway. He retired to his Chatham villa that, said Evelyn, resembled 'some villa about Rome'.

Sir William Petty, physician, economist, statistician, social theorist, founding member of the Royal Society; a great man and greatly admired by SP.

Sir Gilbert Pickering, Northamptonshire landowner, husband of Edward Montagu's sister Elizabeth, chamberlain to Cromwell, pardoned at the Restoration through the intervention of Montagu; cousin of Dryden; daughter Elizabeth married John Creed.

Thomas Povey, son of an Exchequer official, rich and hospitable, promoter of trading and colonial ventures under the commonwealth; at the Restoration treasurer to the duke of York's household. Known to SP through the Tangier Committee.

Dr John Radcliffe, physician to SP and Mary Skinner in later years.

Prince Rupert, cousin of Charles II, brave and effective soldier and sea commander. Regarded with hostility by SP, especially when accused by Rupert and Albemarle of inefficiency in supplying the fleet during the

Dutch war. Rupert opposed SP's reform obliging naval lieutenants to sit an examination.

Balthasar de St Michel, brother of Elizabeth, perpetually dependent on SP's patronage and charity; twice married, his first wife, Esther, dying from the birth of their eighth child.

Elizabeth de St Michel, daughter of a French father and an English mother; partly educated in Paris; married SP at fourteen.

Sandwich, earl of, *see* Edward Montagu.

John Scott, colonel, confidence man working schemes in America, England and on the Continent. Claimed to own a castle called Mornamont. Paid by Buckingham to trap SP with false accusations of treason.

Sir Charles Sedley, poet and playwright whose wit SP admired and envied; reputedly the lover of Mrs Knipp.

Thomas Shadwell, playwright, friend of SP, Sedley and Dryden. SP was godfather to his son John, who became a physician and attended SP in his last illness.

Shaftesbury, earl of, *see* Anthony Ashley Cooper.

Henry Sheeres, later Sir Henry, engineer who worked on the Tangier 'mole', and for whom EP had a soft spot; became lifelong friend of SP; a Jacobite.

Richard Sherwyn, commonwealth official who signed SP's civil marriage certificate. SP observed him reduced to clerking after the Restoration.

Mary Skinner, daughter of City merchant but brought up by her aunt Dame Elizabeth Boteler in Hatfield; became SP's mistress after the death of EP and remained with him until the end of his life, accepted by his friends and her family as his consort.

Skinner family: Daniel Skinner, City merchant and his wife Frances (née Corbet) attended the same church as SP; among his children, Daniel, amanuensis to Milton, sought SP's help in his career; other sons including Peter and Corbet did likewise; for daughter Mary, see above.

Hans Sloane, later Sir Hans, physician who attended SP and performed the autopsy on him.

Dr Thomas Smith, keeper of the Cotton Library, nonjuror, Jacobite sympathizer; friend and correspondent of SP in old age.

Southampton, earl of, *see* Thomas Wriothesley.

Sir Robert Southwell, MP, diplomat, president of the Royal Society, friend and correspondent of SP.

Frances Stuart, duchess of Richmond, court beauty admired by SP.

Will Symons, government clerk and early 'clubbing' friend of SP.

Frances Tooker, probably daughter or niece of John Tooker, who was appointed shipping agent by SP: 'a pretty child', sexually abused by SP with the connivance of her mother.

Torrington, earl of, *see* Arthur Herbert.

John Turner, Yorkshire lawyer husband of SP's friendly cousin Jane.

Antonio Verrio, Italian painter popular in England and employed by SP to paint a mural for Christ's Hospital, in which SP figures among the benefactors.

Barbara Villiers, countess of Castlemaine, later duchess of Cleveland, principal mistress of Charles II for many years, admired by SP for her beauty and her reputation for erotic tricks.

George Villiers, second duke of Buckingham, son of the favourite of Charles I and brought up with the future Charles II; rich, brilliant, handsome, irresponsible and vile. While associate of Shaftesbury became paymaster of John Scott, who falsely accused SP of treason.

Vines family, living in New Palace Yard, father Christopher worked for the Exchequer, sons George and Dick drank, played cards and made music with the young SP.

Dr John Wallis, mathematician and member of the Royal Society whose portrait SP commissioned from Kneller for the University of Oxford.

Humfrey Wanley, brilliant young palaeographer befriended by SP in old age.

Sir William Warren, rich Nonconformist timber merchant who successfully wooed SP for contracts, acquiring a virtual monopoly; later suffered severe losses through fires at his yards.

Jane Welsh, worked for SP's wig-maker and briefly took SP's fancy.

Bulstrode Whitelocke, lawyer and diplomat, prominent in Cromwell's service; purchased pardon from king; diarist.

Bishop John Wilkins, inventor, secretary of the Royal Society, interested in universal language, foretold space travel, admired by SP.

Deborah Willet, EP's maid/companion with whom SP fell in love.

Sir Joseph Williamson, SP's contemporary and acquaintance with a similar but more successful career curve: scholarships, public service, MP, court favour, president of the Royal Society, late, grand marriage, weathered 1688 revolution, served William III as zealously as he had his predecessors.

Thomas Wriothesley, fourth earl of Southampton, lord treasurer, son of Shakespeare's patron, known to SP through the Navy Board and the Tangier Committee.

York, duke of, *see* James, duke of York.

Prologue

At seven o'clock on a January morning, as the sky over London was growing light, a row broke out in a bedroom between a husband and wife. They had been to the theatre the night before, and afterwards had to wait nearly an hour for a cab. When they finally reached home, rather than going to bed, he insisted on returning to his office – it was across the yard – to finish some work. So although he was usually the first awake and out of bed on a weekday, on this particular day he was sleeping in; or at least he was hoping to. Instead he was woken by an angry and tearful wife.

Still lying in bed and only half awake, he began to take in what she was saying. At first it was a complicated complaint about a maid they had recently dismissed who was spreading stories, accusing her of giving away his money to her family. He had no intention of arguing about this and tactfully calmed her until they seemed to be friends again; but at that point her real grievance appeared, and turned out to be something different and worse. What was really upsetting her, she said, was that she was lonely. She suffered so much from loneliness that she had written him a letter expressing her unhappiness, she reminded him, and handed it to him two months ago. But he had refused to read it and burnt it without even glancing at her carefully chosen words.[1]

Now she told him she had kept a copy – it was something she must have learnt from his meticulous office habits – and she called their maid Jane into the bedroom, gave her the keys of her trunk and told her to fetch the bundle of papers she kept locked inside. Jane, who knew both of them well and had witnessed many scenes, brought the papers and discreetly left the room again. Elizabeth Pepys began to read the letter aloud to her husband. The scene is played out in front of us on the page of his Diary: it is Friday, 9 January 1663.

His wife's letter impressed Pepys so much that he began to worry about its falling into anyone else's hands. It was 'picquant, and wrote in English and most of it true' – he specified English because French came as naturally to her – and it would reflect badly on him. He asked her to tear it up, and when she did not respond he ordered her to do so. She refused. He snatched it from her along with the whole bundle of her private papers; then he got out of bed in his nightshirt and stuffed them all into the large pockets of his breeches, which were lying by the bed. He had to struggle into the breeches and put on his stockings and gown, defending himself from her attempts to retrieve her property. When he was half dressed, he started pulling the papers out again one by one and tearing them up, while she cried and begged to have them back. By now she was more distressed than she had been at the start of their talk, and he was in a rage. He let his anger flare up so fiercely that when he came to his own love letters he began to tear them up too. Then he tore the copy of the will he had written and given her, in which he had left her all he had.

Yet all the time a corner of himself was calm enough to notice and set aside certain papers. There was a bond and their marriage licence: money and the law must be respected. He also spared the first letter he had ever sent her; and, when he felt he had gone far enough to make his point, he took all the papers, the ones he had torn and the ones he had spared, into his own room and considered whether he should burn them. He put aside the pieces of his will and of her letter to him that had started the trouble, and all the papers he had left intact. Everything else went on the fire. After that he finished dressing and departed for the office, 'troubled in mind'.

We know all this because he described it himself. In writing it down, he detached himself from the self who acted out the scene. He watched himself just as he watched Elizabeth, or Jane; just as he had watched the players and the audience in the theatre the night before. His conflicting emotions – indignation and anger, pity for her and acknowledgement that she was justified in what she had done – make this as absorbing as a scene in a play or novel. It is life, but as he writes it down it becomes art; and it is the art of a diarist of genius, one who does not choose to give himself the *beau rôle*. Later in his career Pepys sometimes stood greatly on his dignity, but here in the pages of his own Diary he assumes none of the gravitas we should all like to claim for ourselves in a bedroom row. He struggles into his breeches, he behaves unjustly and cruelly, he offers no justification of any kind for his behaviour except his anger and fear of being blamed. This is what he had seen and what he had felt, transmuted into words.

The quarrel was made up in the evening, but the morning scene was a painful landmark in the marriage. To both husband and wife the written word was of great importance. Both were readers, and destruction of the written evidence of their love and its history was a symbolic act. The marriage, which had never been calm, became increasingly stormy after this. In the long run even the torn pieces of Elizabeth's letter failed to survive, and not a single line of her writing has reached us among all the masses of papers he preserved. His heirs, rather than Pepys himself, may have been responsible for this; and, in any case, if he himself controlled the record by destroying her complaint and leaving only his version, it is also true that his version was one she would probably have accepted as accurate and fair.

Other diaries of the seventeenth century were devoted to the spiritual life, to politics or to accounts of travel and sightseeing, and even those that do give some details of domestic life are discreet about marital disagreements. It would not be too surprising to find that Pepys, as a busy government administrator, kept notes about his work and contacts, even his reading and theatregoing. What is extraordinary is that he went into areas no one else considered recording, looked at himself with as much curiosity as he looked at the exterior world, weighing himself and the world equally in the balance. Sometimes he divided himself as he wrote to report on his own condition: 'a great joy it is to me to see myself in a good disposition to business', he remarked on the first day of March 1666, having found himself guilty of backsliding with a woman on the last day of February. The shamelessness of his self-observation deserves to be called scientific. Just about every aspect of his behaviour is set out, from his working practices and his professional and moral struggles to his bowel movements and ejaculations. He knows how to shape his material, where to linger, where to give a piece of direct speech, where to hurry on. He is also singular in having the steady application needed to write regularly and at the same time a romantic and tempestuous nature that made almost every day an adventure of the spirit and the senses. It took the eye and application of a scientist and the pen of an artist to catch for ever in his tidy shorthand that cold midwinter morning in the bedroom in Seething Lane, in the heart of the City.

And much more. The Diary is best known for his reporting of the national disasters that struck England while he was keeping it: the great plague of 1665, the great fire of London in 1666, the Dutch attack on the Medway in 1667. The record of these and other public events is used by historians and read with enjoyment by school-children, because his reporter's eye was as keenly trained on them as it was on his private experience. What he was doing in such reporting was more significant than may appear at first glance, because the censorship imposed by the government of Charles II ensured that there were no newspapers at this period except for a single govern-ment-controlled information sheet, the *London Gazette*. It meant that no proper record of public events was being kept, and even parliamentary debates were not allowed to be reported. Pepys was performing a unique public function. He had grown up in the 1640s and 1650s when there was no censorship, and pamphlets and papers appeared at a great rate, sometimes as many as three a day, making a better-informed public than there had ever been. He was formed by that culture, with its faith in the power of the written word. He lived with it as a schoolboy at St Paul's and as a student at Cambridge, and saw it hailed as a sign of national strength by his predecessor at St Paul's and Cambridge, John Milton. It was after Cromwell imposed censorship again in 1655 that Pepys began to compose private news-letters for his patron and cousin, Edward Montagu, keeping him abreast of what was going on in London. The few of those letters to survive give all the evidence one could want of his abilities as a journalist. It was a natural step to proceed from composing newsletters to making his own record of events. The Diary gives both a cool critique of Charles II's performance in the House of Commons and a panoramic account of London and its people – in political turmoil, at work and at play, in celebration and at war, and enduring disease, death and destruction.

As well as being a diarist, Pepys is regarded as one of the most important naval administrators in England's history. He rose to a position of eminence and power and was proud of his work in organizing, disciplining and developing the navy, and in insisting that shipbuilding must be properly funded. Those who most admire the administrator are sometimes ambivalent about the Diary. The great Pepys scholar John Tanner wrote that 'At certain points in the Diary we can see the great official maturing, but in the main the intimate self-revelation of a human being seems far removed from official life.

It is the combination of qualities that is so astounding, and those who regard Pepys only as "the most amusing and capable of our seventeenth-century diarists" – a mere literary performer making sport for us – do little justice to a great career.'[2] Tanner was careful not to endorse the idea that Pepys is 'a mere literary performer', but he did describe the Diary as 'an indiscretion of his youth', and underlying his remarks was a preference for dwelling on the 'great career' and an assumption – which others have shared – that official life and intimate experience are indeed far removed from one another.

The truth is that the Diary demonstrates precisely how close and interdependent they are. Both the account of his working life and the great set-pieces of reporting insist on telling us this truth. Pepys lets us know that each of us inhabits a perpetually fluctuating environment, and that we are changed, moved and sometimes controlled by our inner tides and weather fronts even when we are most engaged in official functions. Committee meetings, office life and relations with colleagues are laid out in all their bristling competitiveness, jealousies, fears, pomposities, backbiting and disappointments. It makes high entertainment, and at the same time provides real insight into how administrative procedures work, good enough to be applied to today as well as to three hundred years ago. I don't doubt that, had the Diary continued as frankly into the years in which he was secretary to the navy, we should have learnt much more.

But it did not, and his literary gifts were specific to the Diary and the unofficial letters. When, with much encouragement from his friend John Evelyn, he embarked on a history of the navy his genius deserted him. The single volume he published in 1690, *Memoires Relating to the State of the Royal Navy of England*, is a curiosity, of interest to naval historians only, its value disputed even by them.[3] He must have felt unhappy with it himself, because the mass of materials he collected towards writing more naval history remained in note form, suggesting that, once he had tested himself as a historian, he understood that his skills did not lie there. He knew that the burden of his work as a civil servant had stood in the way of becoming more of a scholar and a writer, of developing what he called his 'liberal genius', and he sometimes regretted it was so.[4]

It is tantalizing to think that a less successful career might have given us more volumes of the Diary. His reason for abandoning it was fear that his eyesight was failing; yet his eyes, although they troubled him, served him to the end of his life. Why did he not return to it? It may have been that the break in his circumstances at the end of 1669, as though a line had been drawn under one part of his life, determined him not to revive it. Or that, like some other writers, he knew he could never equal what he had already written and decided he had done enough. He did keep two brief journals later, one of them an intermittent daily record of the early months of 1680, another in the autumn of 1683, known as the Tangier Diary.[5] They are useful and informative but have none of the qualities of the first Diary. Something essential was missing – some grit that had caused him to produce his pearl. There were at least two sorts of grit at work in the great Diary. One was his determination to prove himself, to show what he was capable of, and how much better gifted and qualified to a position of power than almost everyone placed above him. The other grit was Elizabeth, to whom he was bound emotionally and imaginatively. The tension between his day-to-day relations with 'my wife' and what he wrote down and kept secret from her is palpable; her presence or absence, her provocations and her anger, are shown over and over again as touching his deepest self. The Diary could hardly have existed without his sense that he and Elizabeth were inextricably joined.

Yet it allows us to experience the world from inside his skin, and for all its huge, Shakespearean cast of characters, it is always essentially a rhapsody on himself at the centre. This is the controlling force throughout the work. Whatever the tensions with others, he is in love with his own nature, and the adventures each day brings must revolve round that adored, although often uncomfortable, self. When he behaves outrageously, his gift for comedy makes it easy for us to collude with him, and even as we sweat guiltily alongside him it is hard not to laugh. Shocked, but also sympathetic, we share in financial scandal and sexual farce, turning the rigid oughts and ought nots of life upside down for a couple of hours.

The politician Tony Benn has said that he writes his diary in order to experience everything three times, once as lived, once in the writing down, once in the later reading of what he has written. It is a good explanation, and there is a further reason, which is to offer yourself to posterity. Whether Pepys had any idea that he was embarking on a unique project when he began to keep his Diary on

1 January 1660, he must soon have come to see that he had done so. Yet he was alone in knowing this, and he lived and died alone in the knowledge. He made his reputation in the world in a wholly different way, as a naval administrator, a friend and colleague of the powerful and learned, an influential figure in the running of charitable foundations, a man of substance and virtue. The Diary keeper, his own young self, was only setting out on his career, and one of the basic principles of the Diary was that he allowed himself not a shred of dignity. When he was an old man, highly respected and respectable, he had to decide whether to destroy or preserve its six volumes. Happily he chose not only to preserve them but to bequeath and protect them in such a way that they were going to be discovered and read by posterity. 'The greatness of his life was open, yet he longed to communicate its smallness also.'[6] The greatest thing about Pepys, after the composition of the Diary, was his decision to preserve it. How such a man was formed and developed, and in what circumstances he came to embark on his Diary, are the themes of the first part of this book.

PART ONE
1633–1660

1. The Elected Son

He was born in London, above the shop, just off Fleet Street, in Salisbury Court, where his father John Pepys ran a tailoring business, one of many serving the lawyers living in the area. The house backed on to the parish church of St Bride's, where all the babies of the family were christened and two were already buried in the churchyard; when he was a man, Pepys still kept the thought in his mind of 'my young brothers and sisters' laid in the ground outside the house of his youth.[1] Salisbury Court was an open space surrounded by a mixture of small houses like John Pepys's and large ones, once the abodes of bishops and ambassadors, with gardens; it was entered through narrow lanes, one from Fleet Street opposite Shoe Lane, another in the south-west corner leading into Water Lane and so down to the Thames and river steps fifty yards below.[2] The south-facing slope above the river was a good place to live; people had been settled here since Roman times, and when Pepys was born in 1633 a Christian church had stood on the spot for at least five hundred years.[3] A block to the east was the Fleet River, with the pink brick crenellated walls of Bridewell rising beside it; it had been built as a palace by King Henry VIII and deteriorated into a prison for vagrants, homeless children and street women, known to the locals as 'Bridewell Birds'. A footbridge spanned the Fleet between Fleet Street and Ludgate Hill, and from St Bride's you could look across its deep valley – much deeper then than it is today – with houses crammed up both sides in a maze of courts and alleys, to old St Paul's rising on its hill above the City.

This was the western edge of the City, and Pepys's first playground. The City was proud of being the most populous in the world; it had something like 130,000 inhabitants, and in the whole country there were only about five million.[4] If you went west from Salisbury Court along Fleet Street, you came to the gardens of the Temple lawyers, with their groves of trees, formal beds and walks, and further west along the Strand you were out of the City, on the way to Whitehall and Westminster. To the east was the only bridge – London Bridge, almost as old as St Bride's Church, with its nineteen arches and its spikes on which traitors' heads were stuck – and then the Tower. The river, without embankments, was very wide, with a sloping shore at low tide, a place for children to explore; and the great houses of the aristocracy were strung along the riverside, each with its own watergate. The best way to get about fast in London was by boat.

The Pepys house centred round the shop and cutting room, with their shelves, stools and drawers, cutting board and looking-glass. At the back the kitchen opened into a yard, and in the cellar were the washing tubs and coal hole, with a lock-up into which troublesome children or maids might be put for punishment. The stairs to the living quarters went up at the back. Timber-framed, tall and narrow, with a jetty sticking out over the street at the front, set tight against its neighbours, with a garret under the steeply pitched roof: this was the pattern of ordinary London houses. On the first floor the parlour doubled as dining room. Above there were two bedrooms, each with a small closet or study opening off it, and high beds with red or purple curtains. In one of these Pepys was born and spent his first weeks. Older children, maids and apprentices slept on the third floor – Pepys mentions 'the little chamber, three storeys high' – or in the garret, or in trundle beds, kept in most of the rooms, including the shop and the parlour; sometimes they bedded down in the kitchen for warmth.[5]

In one of the bedrooms was a virginals, the neat, box-like harpsi-chord of the period. John Pepys was musical: he played the bass viol, and his eldest daughter, six-year-old Mary, could have started at the keyboard by the time Sam was born. Singing and musical instruments – viol, violin, lute, virginals, flageolet (a recorder of sorts) – were an essential part of family life, and music became the child's passion.[6] Music was not only in the family but literally in the air for many months during the first year of Sam's life. It came from one of the large houses in Salisbury Court, in which a young and ambitious lawyer, Bulstrode Whitelocke, was preparing a masque to be per-formed before King Charles and his queen. Whitelocke and Edward Hyde, together representing the Middle Temple, had joined with members of the other three Inns of Court in a plan to celebrate Candlemas in a great masque to be produced before the Court at Whitehall, and Whitelocke, who had some skill as a composer, was in charge of the music. He assembled a large group of singers, including some from the Queen's Chapel, and 'caused them all to meet in practise at his house in Salisbury Court where he . . . had sometimes 40 lutes, besides other instruments and voices, in consort together'. The noise must have been terrific. On the day of the performance, 2 February 1634, three weeks before Pepys's first birthday, the masquers, in costumes of silver, crimson and blue, some riding plumed horses draped in cloth of silver, some carrying flaming torches, processed along Holborn and Chancery Lane, through Temple Bar to Charing Cross and so to the Banqueting House. Inigo Jones was the designer, and the poet Thomas Carew wrote the words.[7] The event was such a success that Queen Henrietta Maria asked for a repeat performance at the Merchant Taylors' Hall in the City. This was done, and gave 'great contentment to their Majesties and no less to the Citizens, especially the younger sort of them'.[8] It may be too much to imagine the infant Pepys held up to enjoy the festivities among the many Londoners agog at the sound of the music and the brilliant show of the young lawyers; but music, theatre, celebration, processions, ritual and fine clothes delighted him throughout his life.

A tailor's family was likely to be well dressed. There was a looking-glass upstairs, in which the children could look at themselves in imitation of the customers below and make themselves fine with scraps of cloth. But clothes, fine or plain, were hard to keep clean in London. Every household burnt coal brought from Newcastle by sea in its fireplaces and cooking ranges. So did the brewers and dyers, the brick-makers up the Tottenham Court Road, the ubiquitous soap and salt boilers. The smoke from their chimneys made the air dark, covering every surface with sooty grime. There were days when a cloud of smoke half a mile high and twenty miles wide could be seen over the city from the Epsom Downs. Londoners spat black.[9] Wall hangings, pictures and clothes turned yellow and brown like leaves in autumn, and winter undervests, sewn on for the season against the cold, were the colour of mud by the time spring arrived. Hair was expected to look after itself; John Evelyn made a special note in his diary in August 1653 that he was going to experiment with an 'annual hair wash'. But every house, every family enjoyed its own smell, to which father, mother, children, apprentices, maids and pets all contributed, a rich brew of hair, bodies, sweat and other emissions, bedclothes, cooking, whatever food was lying about, whatever dirty linen had been piled up for the monthly wash, whatever chamber pots were waiting to be emptied into yard or street. Home meant the familiar reek which everyone breathed. The smell of the house might strike a new maid as alien, but she would quickly become part of the atmosphere herself. When Pepys wrote of his 'family', meaning not blood relations but everyone who lived in his household – the Latin word *familia* has this sense – we understand that, as a group sharing the same rooms, they also comfortably shared the same smell.

His mother was a connoisseur of dirty linen, having worked as a washmaid in a grand household before her marriage. It was not a bad preparation for eleven children in fourteen years; the babies followed one another so fast that she was always either nursing or expecting one, and each made its contribution to the monthly washing day. Samuel was her fifth, hardly more than a year after John. Paulina and Esther, who preceded him, were both dead before he was born, but by the time he was five there would be four more, Thomas, Sarah, Jacob and Robert, of whom only Tom would live to grow up. God's system was inefficient and depressing. A doctor writing in 1636 regretted that humans did not reproduce like trees, without the 'trivial and vulgar way of coition'.[10] This was Sir Thomas Browne. He might have added a further expression of regret at the wearing out of so much health and happiness, but he failed to, and instead overcame his distaste at the triviality of the act often enough to father twelve children on his wife. Pepys's mother must have been always busy, tired, distracted or grieving for the deaths of his brothers and sisters when he was a child: soon worn out, physically and emotionally.

Pepys's birthday was on 23 February and his baptism by the vicar of St Bride's, James Palmer, is recorded on 3 March 1632/3, 'Samuell sonn to John Peapis wyef Margaret'.[11] The same year, in October, the queen gave birth across town at St James's Palace to her second son, James. After his christening, he was given the title of duke of York. He had a staff of officials paid to rock his cradle; and, unthinkable as it would have seemed then, he was destined to become one of Sam Pepys's close associates. Another boy who grew up to influence Sam's life, Anthony Ashley Cooper, was also living off Fleet Street, in Three Cranes Court, from 1631 to 1635.[12] Sam's brother Tom was born in the summer of 1634, making a trio of little Pepys boys, John, Sam and

Tom, and a sister Sarah the following summer. Other tailoring families in the district produced playmates. There were the Cumberlands, also in Salisbury Court, with three boys, Richard and his younger brothers William and John; Richard would go to school with Pepys later, and to college, and become a bishop. Another tailor, Russell, in St Bride's Churchyard, was landlord to a bachelor scholar, poet and school-master, John Milton, who had his eight-year-old nephew Johnny living with him when Pepys was six. Here was an outstanding and conveniently placed teacher; but there is no sign that the tailor's sons took any lessons with him.[13]

Who did teach the little Pepys children? The learned and leisured John Evelyn coached his eldest son into reading and writing at the age of two, but John Pepys, who had left his native Cambridgeshire for London at fourteen to be apprenticed, was only just literate himself, and if his wife could write at all she left no trace of it. Manuals for parents of the period recommended they should start their children's education at home by playing with them at mealtimes or when sitting by the fire before they started school; but John and Margaret Pepys were unlikely readers of manuals.[14] The household must have been in a perpetual scramble between babies and apprentices, and what energy there was to spare was for music-making. Sam put nothing on record about early lessons. Instead he recalled boys' games in the backyard; being carried by one of his father's workers into one of the Temple Halls, to see the law students gambling with dice at Christmas; and street activities such as 'beating the bounds', when the children of the parish went in procession, carrying broomsticks and shepherded by the constable and churchwarden, had water poured over them from the windows of their neighbours and were playfully beaten before being rewarded with bread and cheese and a drink – the whole ancient ritual intended to fix the limits of their own parish in their memories.[15]

Contemporary books of manners for children give some idea of what was expected of them at home. There was advice on how to set the table for family dinner, with trenchers (wooden plates), napkins, salt and bread; glasses should be placed well away from the edge of the table to avoid knocking them off. Children should not crumble their bread into 'mammocks' but cut it up properly; salt was taken with the knife, and they should not overload their spoons with 'pottage', which might spill on the cloth. A polite child would volunteer to remove and fold up the cloth after the meal, and bring a jug of water, basin and towel for parents to wash their hands.[16] Since there was no dining room in the Pepys household, only a folding table in the parlour, meals can rarely have risen to such elegance; but it was something to which Sam paid attention later in life, when he could hardly bring himself to eat food served by a woman with greasy hands, and was sharp with his wife about the presentation of dinner in his own house. Children were also told to keep their clothes in decent order at all times:

> Let not thy privy members be
> Layd open to be view'd
> It is most shamefull and abhord,
> Detestable and rude.

Four adjectives seem a lot for one small privy member, but children had to be given a sense of its sinfulness.

When he was six, in 1639, his closest brother, seven-year-old John, fell ill and died.[17] Two years later a second John was born, never much liked by Sam, perhaps because he missed the first so much; but he had a strong sense of duty towards his siblings. He was now top of the hierarchy, as the eldest boy in the family. Tom, who was closest to him, was not clever; he learnt to write but not much better than his father, and he struggled with a speech impediment; Sam was always protective towards him.[18] Mary, at twelve, was almost grown up, one of the solid loving presences in his world; but Mary failed to grow up. When she was thirteen, at Christmas 1640, a year after John's death, she sickened and died. The next year Sarah, who had reached five, followed her to the grave; so did the family maid Barbara. Sam was left with only Tom, besides the two new babies, Paulina, or Pall the second, born in October 1640, just before Mary's death, and John the second.

Sam must have wondered when his turn was coming, the more so since his own health was not good. Looking back from middle age, he wrote that he could not remember any period of his early life without pain. He meant the pain of the stone in his kidneys. The condition was so bad that he often passed blood – as he put it, made 'bloody water upon any extraordinary motion'.[19] The ebullient Pepys of the Diary sorts oddly with the pain-racked childhood. It seems to have taught him physical stoicism – there were no painkillers – and given him his determination to seize and enjoy everything he could while life lasted. You see it again later, in his elated response to the plague year when, with death all around, he grabbed at whatever there was to enjoy. Andrew Marvell's lines about lovers tearing their

> . . . Pleasures with rough strife,
> Thorough the Iron gates of Life

fit this Pepys, with his greed for life's pleasures sharpened by pain and fear.

His mother suffered from the stone too; whether this made her more or less anxious, more or less sympathetic to him, we don't know, but he was sent away from time to time, with Tom to keep him company, for the good of their health, into the fresh air outside London. An aunt Ellen, his mother's sister, was working in Newington Green as a servant, and a nurse was found for the boys in the nearby hamlet of Kingsland, surrounded by open fields. He remembered her as Goody Lawrence, and she did well by him, for he was boarded out with her for several summers. Again, he remembered the physical activities, the pleasure of playing with his bow and arrows in the fields around Hackney.[20] Other memories were of his father taking the family for jaunts to the King's Head in rural Islington, where they were served with 'cakes and ale'.[21]

Cakes and ale might keep pain at bay for half an hour. The other thing he noticed about his body was that it seemed hotter than other people's. He claimed quite seriously that it was usually only just below fever point. Whether he was right about this or not, he felt it was something that marked him out. Families may elect one of their children on whom their hopes are placed, traditionally the eldest son; or one of the children may elect himself, sometimes against the odds. Charles Dickens, who saw his parents prefer his sister while they consigned him to the blacking factory, elected himself in this way, worked with superhuman energy to prove his claim and rose to greatness, as well as taking over lifelong responsibility for his parents and siblings. The John Pepyses, like the John Dickenses, had little standing in the world; one of the childhood memories of which Sam was ashamed was of being sent round to deliver clothes to his father's high and mighty customers. It may have felt like a mini-version of the blacking factory to a boy eager to achieve something, and knowing himself capable.[22] Luckily for him, his abilities were noticed. John Pepys had relatives who were in a position to give a helping hand to this obstinately surviving and clever son.

Among these relatives was cousin John Pepys from Norfolk, prosperous and affable, with a wife and three children of his own, a house in Salisbury Court and another large country place at Ashtead in Surrey. This other John Pepys had done very well indeed. He had served the greatest lawyer and legal writer of the age, Sir Edward Coke, as confidential secretary and man of business. In his time Coke defied King James I and Charles I, was imprisoned in the Tower and had his papers seized by the crown; he was a hero to those who believed in common law and a strong parliament for his insistence that 'the King is under God and the law'.[23] At Coke's death in 1634 John Pepys of Norfolk was one of his executors, and he went on to work for Coke's son Robert. Sir Robert Coke was the husband of Lady Theophila Berkeley, and they lived splendidly in a country house belonging to her family, Durdans, near Epsom. It was at Durdans that Sam Pepys, carried off to Surrey by John Pepys and his wife Anne, was co-opted by the Cokes to play a part in a private production of Beaumont and Fletcher's romantic comedy *Philaster, or Love Lies a-Bleeding*. He was asked to take a leading role, as Arethusa. The daughter of a usurper, Arethusa is loved by the rightful heir, Philaster, but her father intends her for another. Philaster places his page Bellario in her service – but Bellario is really a woman, and after many turns of plot she is left single while Philaster and Arethusa marry. The play was a wonderful concoction of love, fine words, confusion and cross-dressing. 'What a ridiculous thing it would have been for me to have acted a beautiful woman,' wrote Pepys in 1668.[24] But what an adventure for a small boy – he can't have been more than nine – to find himself singled out, made much of, invited to show off in a star part in a great house. He learnt his part so well that he could still remember almost every word twenty-five years later.

Durdans impressed itself on him and set him a standard, with its formal gardens, its fountain and statues, its terraces and bosky wood rising towards the Downs, its long gallery, newly built by the Cokes in classical style as an addition to the Jacobean mansion, its comfortable and charming rooms that included a fine, well-stocked library: a place to remember, 'where I have been very merry when I was a little boy' and again, 'where I have seen so much mirth'.[25] As well as delighting in gardens and architecture, Lady Theophila read French, Italian, Latin and Greek; she had been educated with Princess Elizabeth and a bridesmaid at her wedding to Frederick, king of Bohemia. Durdans introduced Sam into a world of splendour and civilized enjoyment. It gave him confidence too, to be chosen, first by his Pepys uncle and then by Sir Robert and Lady Theophila, for his charm and his talents. He could read and master a part, he felt he was full of promise; he saw for the first time that he might aspire to something more than the cutting room in Salisbury Court. He made several visits to Surrey before everybody's lives – and *Philaster* too – were disrupted by the outbreak of the civil war in 1642; and he always remembered Ashtead as 'my old place of pleasure'.[26]

The other cousins who were to play a crucial part in shaping his life were based in East Anglia. Sam's Cambridgeshire grandfather had a sister, Paulina Pepys, who was orphaned young and married late, at thirty-seven – late but splendidly. Considering that she was then already middle aged, with a fortune of no more than £200, her marriage to Sir Sidney Montagu, distinguished younger son of an aristocratic and gifted family, suggests she was an outstanding woman and had wisely waited for the right husband. He was educated at Cambridge and the Middle Temple and had served as an MP in the time of Queen Elizabeth; one brother was an earl, another a bishop. Paulina's marriage in 1618 made her cousin to a score of grandees. Her glory was acknowledged in Salisbury Court, where two of Sam's sisters were named for her. A daughter and a son were born to the Montagus, but at three the boy, playing beside the moat, fell into the water and was drowned. His grieving parents had to take consolation in the birth of a third and last child, another boy, Edward, in 1625. With little Edward they moved to Hinchingbrooke, a great house outside Huntingdon.

Hinchingbrooke had been an abbey until King Henry evicted the holy ladies and sold it to Sir Richard Cromwell; the Cromwells rebuilt it, and James I stayed there more than once and even considered buying it for himself. Sir Sidney paid £3,000 for it, and there Edward grew up, knowing the estate would be his one day, and went to the grammar school along the road in Huntingdon where their neighbour Oliver Cromwell had been a pupil. A cousin of his mother lived in his own modest farmhouse at Brampton, two miles from Hinching-brooke, and worked as a bailiff for the Montagus. He was Robert Pepys, elder brother of Sam's father, and this was the family connection that in due course brought Sam to the grammar school at Huntingdon, to lodge at Brampton and to be welcome at Hinchingbrooke, not as an equal to be sure, but as a cousin who could be useful and might deserve some help on his way.[27]

Edward Montagu was put down for the Middle Temple when he was ten and Sam was three. But nothing went according to plan. His mother, Paulina, died when he was twelve. His father withdrew into melancholy, and by the time he was seventeen the country was at war. Instead of becoming a law student, Edward found himself in command of a regiment. Sir Sidney would not turn against the King, but Edward was a passionate parliamentarian, like his sister's husband, Sir Gilbert Pickering; both were admirers and personal friends of Cromwell. In the excitement and impending danger of war Edward fell in love and decided to marry. He and his bride were both seventeen. Jemima was the daughter of a rich Northamptonshire MP and parliamentarian, John Crew, and the womanly virtues admired in her father's family can be judged from the names of her grandmother and aunts, Temperance, Patience, Prudence and Silence.[28] Jemima's personal virtues included a warm heart, good humour and a straight-forward disposition, some of which can be made out in an early miniature of her, which shows a tip-tilted nose and open, friendly face. She and Edward were married at St Margaret's, Westminster, on 7 November 1642. Five days later King Charles's nephew, Prince Rupert, sacked Brentford and the people of London braced themselves to defend Turnham Green, Westminster and the City against the forces of the King. Edward Montagu's career was set on course as a fighting man.

Pepys's early life has to be explained in terms of families but it has also to be set against the political turmoil of the years leading up to the civil war. As a London boy, he saw in the streets the effects of debates he could not yet understand, played out with passion, cruelty, violence and reversals of fortune to equal anything in the theatre. 'The war was begun in our streets before the King or the Parliament had any armies,' wrote one wise observer, and Sam had the chance to see this in action, the propaganda fixed on the City walls, the rioting apprentices and sailors, attacks on suspected Roman Catholics, crowds surging to welcome their heroes and threaten their enemies, or assembling to watch the executions of detested figures.[29]

In November 1640, for example, when he was seven, two men without ears rode into London at Charing Cross with branches of rosemary in their hands, escorted by crowds, 'every man on horseback or on foot having bays and rosemary in their hats and hands, and the people on either side of the street strewing the way as they passed with herbs and such other greens as the season afforded, and expressing great joy for their return'.[30] This extraordinary piece of street drama was for William Prynne and Henry Burton, a lawyer and a preacher, whose ears had been cut off publicly in Palace Yard, Westminster, four years earlier, before another large and sympathetic crowd. They had been punished – Prynne was also branded and sentenced to life imprisonment – for offending the king and Archbishop Laud. Now they were released by the power of the House of Commons. A week later there was second triumphal return, with trumpets playing at the windows for Dr Bastwick, their fellow martyr to freedom of conscience and speech. Early the next year the king's two most hated servants, Laud and the earl of Strafford, were taken to the Tower. City mobs agitated for Strafford's execution, collected signatures demanding his death and posted up in the street the names of those MPs who opposed it. Shops were shut while a large and well-organized group of armed citizens accompanied the MPs who went to the king to urge him to sign the Bill of Attainder that would allow Strafford to be beheaded.[31] The crowd that watched the execution in May 1641 included many soberly dressed women; there was more enthusiasm for this than for the wedding of two royal children, nine-year-old Princess Mary to the twelve-year-old Prince of Orange, which had taken place a few days before the execution.[32]

The two passions fuelling parliament and people were religious fervour and the fear that the king, egged on by his Catholic wife, was aiming to become an absolute ruler. The religious rollercoaster of the previous century, when successive Tudor monarchs first overthrew the Catholic Church, set up Protestantism, restored Catholicism and then settled into uneasy compromise under Elizabeth, had left a legacy of fierce hatred of the Catholics and a burgeoning of Protestant sects. The movement came to be called puritanism, and the puritans, disliking the established Church with its bishops and tithes that bore harshly on the poor, became the allies of the political opponents of the king. Margaret Pepys, like a great many of her neighbours, seems to have veered towards puritanism, although she still attended St Bride's church and had her own pew.[33] Her boys grew accustomed to hearing puritan preachers in the street. In 1640 a local leather-seller called Praisegod Barebones set up his Baptist congregation right outside, in Fleet Street. Baptist ministers saw no need for church buildings, supported themselves by working at other jobs and welcomed women as preachers; and more Baptist congregations were begun in other parts of town.[34] The City apprentices who gathered in Westminster in the winter of 1641 shouted 'No Bishops'; there was some fighting, and in the days after Christmas the same boys blocked the river stairs to prevent the bishops newly appointed by the king from taking their seats in the House of Lords, and went on to attack them in their coaches. When the bishops protested, parliament found grounds for impeaching them and sent them to prison, at which the apprentices rang the City churchbells joyfully and made bonfires in the streets. The king then moved to impeach his chief enemies in parliament.

Pepys was quite old enough to be on the streets when on 4 January 1642 the king pursued the five MPs he was trying to arrest from the House of Commons into the City. He was mobbed by huge numbers of tradesmen, apprentices and seamen, all shouting 'privilege of Parliament, privilege of Parliament' – a difficult mouthful for a mob, but they made it sound frightening. Although the king was not harmed, he was thoroughly scared. This was a spectacular moment in English history, and a week later Charles left London with his family. He was not seen there again until his execution in Whitehall, five years later, when an approving Pepys was by his own account standing in the crowd.

On the day after the king left, the five MPs he had threatened made a triumphal journey on the Thames from the City to Westminster, escorted by a flotilla of beribboned boats loaded with cheering and waving Londoners, while citizen soldiers marched along the Strand with drums and flags to meet them as they came ashore. These soldiers, known as the trained bands, were ordinary townsmen organized into fighting groups, their effectiveness depending more on enthusiasm than discipline. The next big street show was the execution in late January of two Catholic priests in front of an approving crowd. In March parliament began to raise its own army, and in May the City's regiments were reviewed on Finsbury Fields in front of the assembled MPs. In June Londoners were asked for money by parliament and they responded generously, even though times were hard for tradesmen in the absence of the court. John Pepys's lawyer customers had fewer clients and less to spend; and the prospect of civil war promised worse to come, as their one-time neighbour, lawyer Whitelocke, now in parliament, warned, saying the country was 'at the pit's brink, ready to plunge ourselves into an ocean of troubles and miseries . . . What the issue of it will be no man alive can tell. Probably few of us now here may live to see the end of it.'[35] In July the royalist Mayor Gurney was impeached in parliament and sent to the Tower, where he remained almost until his death five years later. A puritan was appointed as mayor in his place. Milton called the City 'the mansion house of liberty', and as such it had to prepare to defend itself against the gathering forces of the king, who raised his standard at Nottingham on 22 August 1642.

This was the official start of the civil war. It was brought about essentially by the king's refusal to accept the limitations parliament was determined to set upon his power, and by parliament's refusal to accept his supremacy. The war split the nation, dividing families, cities, counties and social classes as well as the great bodies and institutions, the navy, the universities, the legal and medical professions; and the religious rift between those who held to the established Church of England and those who rejected it sharpened the bitterness of the fight. Within seven years the country would rid itself of king, lords and bishops; and though these reforms were reversed, it was never again ruled for any length of time without the cooperation of the elected House of Commons. From the English revolution came much of the inspiration for both the American and the French revolutions of the next century. The intellectual revolution that accompanied the war was as important as the war itself, so that 'it is difficult for us to conceive how men thought before it was made'.[36] Both the political and intellectual aspects of the revolution were to have a profound effect upon Pepys.

Meanwhile parliament ordered the digging of trenches and building of ramparts and forts to close all the main roads into London. Islington, the fields round St Pancras Church, Mile End, Rotherhithe and Wapping were the sites of some of the twenty-four forts. A huge workforce was needed. It was found among the people of the City and the suburbs, women and children included; Sam and Tom Pepys may well have taken part. When announcements were made in the churches, citizens turned out with 'baskets, spades and such like instruments, for digging of trenches and casting up of breast-works from one fort to another'. More than 20,000 people were said to have worked on the defences, a sixth of the population. They were directed by sailors and officers of the trained bands, and their effectiveness was observed with surprise and respect by the Venetian ambassador among others. John Evelyn, a supporter of the king, also came to view the 'so much celebrated line of communication'.[37] The work was in full swing in the autumn of 1642, the season of Edward Montagu's marriage to Jemima Crew in Westminster and of Prince Rupert's sacking of Brentford, which inspired John Milton to write his sonnet 'When the assault was intended to the city'. It was addressed to the expected royalist invaders, 'Captain or Colonel, or Knight in Arms', and suggested they would be well advised to spare a poet.

Milton's plea proved unnecessary. The royalists were kept from London. They were tired after a long march, and short of supplies, and their nerve failed. The earl of Essex, with 24,000 of the trained bands, held Turnham Green for parliament. The London troops had good supplies, including the baskets of food brought to them by their wives and sweethearts. The success of the London trained bands was decisive, and the royalists never threatened the capital again. But the fear remained that Rupert would return and sack the City, and the work on the defences continued until the following summer of 1643.[38]

These were the first ten years of Pepys's life. They brought him bodily pain and the loss of his dearest playmates. Flesh, he learnt, was vulnerable as well as shameful, but also capable of taking intense pleasure: in music, in running about the streets, in playing with bows and arrows, in country trips and in cakes and ale. Child of a washmaid and a tailor, he found himself the exceptional, elected son and as such was given glimpses of a way of life other than the constricted one in the house off Fleet Street. This other life was luxurious, artistic and seductive. At Durdans he not only took part in acting, he delighted in the gardens and walked in the woods with a woman who gave him his 'first sentiments of love and pleasure in a woman's company, discourse and taking her by the hand'. Her name was Mrs Hely, and the impression she made on him was so strong that he remembered and wrote it down when he was thirty.[39] So the private Samuel Pepys began to develop and yearn.

At the same time he was a London boy through and through, eyes alert for every detail of a street scene that offered constant excitement, and quick-witted enough to be sent on awkward errands about town. For instance, while he was still a 'little boy', his mother dispatched him for word of his father, who had gone to Holland and left them without news. He had to go a long way, across the river to Horsley-down in Bermondsey, to get information out of the men at St Saviour's Dock where the ships came in. Whatever his father was doing abroad, he turned up again safely and went on quietly with his tailoring. He may have been trying to do some business, although the tailoring trade seems an unlikely reason for travelling in wartime; and it may also be that Edward Montagu, already one of Cromwell's lieutenants, used his cousin as a courier to the Dutch, since Dutch engineers were brought over early in 1643 to advise on the London fortifications.[40] And maybe it was at this time that Montagu first noticed Sam, and thought of doing something for him.

The London defences were still being worked on in the summer of 1643. In May the Venetian ambassador reported, 'The forts round the city are now completed and admirably designed. They are now beginning the connecting lines. As they wish to complete them speedily and the circuit is most vast, they have gone through the city with drums beating and flags flying, to enlist the men and women volunteers for the work. Although they only give them their bare food, without any pay, there has been an enormous rush of people even of some rank, who believe they are serving God by assisting in the pious work, as they deem it.'[41] But with summer also came the plague. There was nothing new about this, it had been making irregular appearances for years: there had been a very bad outbreak in 1625, when one City father noted that 'three score children died out of one alley', and there were lesser ones in 1630, 1636 and 1642.[42] Fear of the plague would have been a good reason for sending Sam and Tom out of town to Kingsland and Hackney, and may now have contributed to the decision to send Sam away again. This time it was neither to Hackney nor to Surrey, but to somewhere quite strange to him, sixty miles north-east of London: into the misty fens of Huntingdonshire.

2. A Schoolboy's War: Huntingdon and St Paul's

Ordinary people travelling from London to Huntingdon went with the carrier, who arrived in London every Wednesday and set off homewards again on Thursday from Cripplegate, the northernmost of the City gates. The journey took two days of steady plod with load and passengers, through Kingsland, Enfield, Ware, Puckeridge, Royston and Caxton, little towns of two or three streets each clustered round a church, along the track of the old Roman road that was to become deeply familiar to Pepys.[1] Once out of London the road was liable to disappear beneath mud or water, or simply to lose any definition; and outside London the world was very empty, very quiet and very dark at night. All this he already knew, but he liked travelling, he was always curious, and the carrier was not going to get lost. Sam was on his way to visit his uncle Robert and to attend the 'Free Grammar School' in Huntingdon.

In principle it was free only to the sons of burgesses of the town, but it was the school where Edward Montagu had been a pupil a few years before, and since he was also the local landowner he may have got Sam a free place, or even paid for him.[2] Edward was now soldiering and on the move, but Sir Sidney had formally given over Hinchingbrooke to the young couple, and Jemima is likely to have been there in charge of the household.[3] The house stands just outside Huntingdon, on a high point looking over a vast expanse of idyllic water-meadows bordering the River Ouse and its tributaries. Sam's uncle Robert was employed as an agent on the Hinchingbrooke estate and lived only a mile from the big house, across the meadows in the village of Brampton. He had prospered enough to acquire some land, which he leased out to small tenant farmers, and he owned a small but solidly built house, two storeys high, with six low-ceilinged rooms. He served in the local militia as Captain Pepys – no doubt recruited by Edward Montagu and loyal to his parliamentary allegiance – and he had a wife but no children of his own. He took to his brother's boy, strongly enough to decide to make him his heir; and the Brampton house became an important element in Sam's life.[4]

Like Hinchingbrooke, it is still standing, still with a large garden and surrounded by open fields.[5] A footpath round the back of the garden leads to the church, and to the Bull Inn, both well known to Sam.[6] Captain Pepys must have got his nephew on to a horse and riding like a country boy, because when he was a man Sam thought nothing of riding a hired horse from London to Huntingdon in a day. But whether he spent more time at Brampton or at Hinchingbrooke is an open question: great houses maintained large numbers of servants and dependants and easily absorbed an odd boy into the family; and long afterwards, when Sam was married and had his own home, he still behaved as though he belonged to the Montagu family, dropping in uninvited for meals with the other servants and staying overnight whenever he felt like it.

As a boy with a sense of his own worth, whose schooling so far had been meagre, he must have been avid for education; and serious teaching is what you got at a grammar school, all day long, from seven in the morning until five in the afternoon. Two hours were allowed for lunch in the middle of the day, time to walk to Brampton and back, although the Hinchingbrooke kitchens would have been handier. Huntingdon School had a reputation, made under its headmaster Thomas Beard, who had sent his best pupils on to Cambridge, Oliver Cromwell among them. Latin was the chief subject, and the master's job was to put Latin into the heads of the boys, so forcefully that they could think and write in Latin as easily as in English.[7] Very little else was studied except for some Greek by those who did well with their Latin and a bit of basic Hebrew for the exceptional pupil. Mathematics was hardly mentioned, beyond learning the Roman numerals, which took precedence over the Arabic ones, and Pepys had to learn his multiplication tables when he was twenty-nine.

Once past elementary grammar and vocabulary, Latin was taught largely by translating classical texts into English and then back into Latin, the object being to finish as close to the original as you could. It was common for boys to be punished if they failed to talk to one another in Latin, and parents occasionally complained of their sons forgetting how to read English.[8] In any case they did not study English writers – no Chaucer, Bacon, Shakespeare, Jonson or Donne. They learnt instead to compose verses, essays and letters in Latin, and became familiar with a list of ancient authors that included Cicero, Virgil, Horace, Ovid, Terence, Juvenal and Livy. The aim was admirable for anyone who wanted to correspond with foreigners, since Latin was used by all educated Europeans; Milton was appointed 'Latin secretary' to Cromwell when he became lord protector, in order to compose diplomatic correspondence for him in that language. Pepys was a good scholar, able to read Latin for pleasure all his life; and that very skill may have helped to leave his English free and uncluttered for the Diary, the language of life as opposed to the elaborately constructed formulations of the classroom and study.

By the time Sam arrived at Huntingdon School Cromwell's teacher Thomas Beard was no longer in charge, and his successor, Henry Cooke, was not interested in the job. He paid a substitute £10 a year to teach the boys, and it was this nameless and no doubt penniless scholar who gave Sam a good-enough grounding to allow him to go on to St Paul's School in London, and to do well there.[9] How long he was at Huntingdon School we don't know. It may have been only a year, possibly two, but only one friend from the school puts in an appearance later, Tom Alcock, whom he met again in the spring of 1660, remarking that he had not seen him for sixteen years, i.e., since 1644.[10] The headmaster of St Paul's, John Langley, particularly disliked taking pupils over the age of eleven, on the grounds that the school suffered from boys 'who have been tossed about from schole to schole until 13 or 14 yeares of age and then come fitted for nothing but knavery and Idlenesse and soe drawe lesser and more towardly children by their example into rudeness and idlenesse'.[11] If Langley was serious about this, Sam may have been back in London and attending St Paul's before he was twelve in February 1645. But not before he had plenty of time to get to know Huntingdon, with its four churches, its ancient bridge over the Ouse, its straggling half-mile of high street and its green surrounding territory.

The other good thing Sam found at Huntingdon was Hinchingbrooke House. Even if any meals he ate there were taken with the servants in the kitchen, the grandeur of the place, with its wide windows and high-ceilinged rooms, must have reminded him of Durdans. And with Jemima Montagu presiding over the place, its appeal would have been even greater. A boy of ten, far from his family and with a precocious susceptibility to women, could play Cherubino to my Lady, a young bride, also separated from her family, with her husband away at the wars, and no baby yet in prospect. If so, it was the beginning of an intimacy that persisted into his adult life, when she always looked on him 'like one of her own family', entrusted her children to his care, scolded him, joked with him, borrowed money from him, consulted him and confided in him. And he reciprocated with devoted admiration and respect; for him she was always the model of what a woman should be.

Hinchingbrooke, Brampton and Huntingdon are all remarkably little changed by the passing of the centuries since Pepys knew them. The nuns placed their abbey very well on one of the few areas of high ground above the water-meadows, and when they were evicted the cloister became a courtyard, the chapel a library, the refectory part of a great hall; the chapter-house entrance was simply bricked up, coming to light again only at the end of the twentieth century.[12] Two magnificent bay windows were brought from Ramsey Abbey, as well as a triple-arched gatehouse sporting the figure of a Green Man; and another big semicircular two-storey stone bay was added to the façade. The mixture of medieval grey stone and rich Tudor red brick, the jumble of outbuildings, the parade of tall chimneys, the formally planted gardens and trees all added to Hinchingbrooke's charm. It was 'old, spacious, irregular, yet not vast or forlorn'.[13] The terrace, face to the sun, offered spectacular views over the flat countryside below, and the park sloped down to one of the Ouse's tributary streams and a series of wide, glinting ponds.

You can still walk from Robert Pepys's house in Brampton, past Hinchingbrooke and on to Huntingdon and, traffic apart, enjoy most of the sights past which Sam trudged in the 1640s: the Nuns' Meadows on the left, and on the right the huge expanse of Portholme Meadow, supposed to be the biggest in England; it has lost its windmills and watermill and taken in a railway embankment, but is otherwise very much the same as when it was described as 'the largest and most flowery spot the sun ever beheld'.[14] A dip in the path takes the walker across Alconbury Brook by the Nuns' Bridge, and up what is still the old lane along the edge of Hinchingbrooke Park and beneath the wall of the terrace, then on past the gatehouse and close to the windows of the house itself. This is about halfway between Brampton and the centre of Huntingdon, and the road continues straight on into what was George Street in the seventeenth century – named for St George – and still bears the same name. Today the town starts with the railway station, a row of nineteenth-century villas and almshouses, and there is a ring road to cross, but after that you are again alongside buildings well known to Pepys: the George Inn on the left, All Saints' Church on the right, with the market place beyond it, all facing on to the high street ahead. The school building, in his day encased in red brick, now shorn away to reveal its original medieval stone, is on the other side of the high street.[15]

As a grown man, Pepys's opinion of life in the country veered between condescension towards the poverty and ignorance of ordinary rural people and occasional bursts of appreciation of the scenery and the quiet life that could be lived there. He wrote about how much he enjoyed a walk in Portholme Meadow with his father in the summer of 1661, and the following year the same meadow inspired him to one of his most lyrical passages: 'with my father took a melancholy walk to Portholme, seeing the country-maids milking their Cowes there (they being now at grasse) and to see with what mirth they come all home together in pomp with their milk, and sometimes they have musique go before them'.[16] The 'sometimes' tells you this was not the first time he had watched and listened to the milkmaids; and of course it was not, because he must have seen and heard them often when he was a boy.

But cows and milkmaids were of less moment at Brampton and at Hinchingbrooke in 1644, when the talk would have centred around the war that was being fought, bitterly and confusedly, all over England. News of the military campaigns and the part played in the fighting by the young master of Hinchingbrooke – Sam's own kin – was eagerly awaited. Montagu, tall and as handsome as his enemy Prince Rupert, and with the same shoulder-length curls, was only eight years older than Sam, and he was galloping about the country risking his life, and often at the side of a still greater local hero. Not only had Hinchingbrooke belonged to Cromwell's grandfather, half the gentry of Huntingdonshire were Cromwells when Oliver Cromwell was born in the town, and he had been elected its MP in 1628. It did not prevent the town from being politically divided, in the same way the Montagu family was divided. Sir Sidney remained unbudgeably loyal to the king, refused a levy made by parliament and was imprisoned briefly in the Tower; he then remained in retirement in Northamptonshire, no doubt nursing some bitter feelings about his son and his son-in-law Gilbert Pickering, as well as their cousin, the earl of Manchester, who became major-general in charge of all the parliamentary forces in East Anglia in August 1643. Edward found in Cromwell a hero, a friend and perhaps a surrogate father, and so he remained for fifteen years, during which he fought beside him, participated in his government of the country and accepted high appointments from him. A few months before Cromwell's death he expressed his continuing strong personal attachment to him.[17] He also shared Cromwell's religious faith: it is strongly expressed in his letters during these early years.

Edward was given a commission to raise a regiment in Cambridgeshire and the Isle of Ely in the autumn of 1643. In the winter he was in Bedford, raising more men and horses. Early in 1644 he went with Manchester to Cambridge to purge the university of senior members suspected of royalist sympathies; eleven of the sixteen heads of the colleges were turned out and replaced by puritan scholars.[18] After this came his first experience of battle at the storming of Hillesden House under Cromwell's leadership in March. The summer of 1644 was spent fighting gloriously in the north. He led his men in hand-to-hand combat in the assault on Lincoln in May, fought in the thick of Marston Moor in July and received the surrender of York on behalf of the earl of Manchester soon afterwards, when he was just nineteen. After this proud moment he was back recruiting again in Huntingdon in the autumn – once the harvest had been brought in – and was at Hinchingbrooke to tell his battle stories and receive the admiration of his household. That September his father died, as far as we know unreconciled.

At this point the earl of Manchester began to have doubts about the cause. Accused by parliament of dragging his feet, he told Cromwell, 'If we beat the king ninety and nine times, yet he is king still and so will his posterity be after him; but if the king beat us once, we shall all be hanged, and our posterity made slaves.' To which Cromwell replied, 'My Lord, if this be so, why did we take up arms at first?'[19] Montagu took Cromwell's side in the argument and joined in public criticism of the earl; and Manchester gave up his command in the spring of 1645, when the New Model Army was being formed. Montagu was made governor of Henley, where he had to put down mutinous, because unpaid, troops, and in the summer he was fighting in the West Country.

Cromwell was now established as a great figure in the eyes of the whole nation, enemies as well as friends. Prince Rupert called him 'Old Ironsides', and his soldiers became Ironsides too. When he went recruiting for his New Model Army in the Isle of Ely in June 1645, men flocked to join him. Among their thirty-seven officers, seven had risen from non-gentry families, a signal that the whole social order was open to change.[20] Alongside these plain men Montagu fought at Naseby, not fifty miles from Huntingdon, in June 1645; and at Naseby the king's infantry was effectively destroyed. Five hundred royalist officers were taken among the 5,000 prisoners, most of whom were marched to London and paraded through the streets of the City in front of triumphant crowds. Montagu went on to take part in the storming of Bristol in September, and with his brother-in-law John Pickering received Prince Rupert's surrender. Sam, with his City background and watching his cousin's dazzling military successes, could not fail to be a fervent enemy of the king. He may have been back in the City to see the procession of prisoners from Naseby, or if he was still in Huntingdon in August he would have witnessed what happened when the king himself rode into the town after a skirmish, and his men fell to plundering. By then Jemima Montagu was expecting her first child – conceived in May, between battles – and her husband was with Cromwell in the west. The king was welcomed by the mayor – either loyal or obsequious – but his troops proceeded to terrorize the people on whom they were billeted. On being told that four of his soldiers had stolen from a glove-maker, the king 'caused lots to be cast . . . and one to be hanged therefore, and, at his departure, gave the town and county thanks for their kind entertainment of him'. This account from a parliamentarian source adds that the soldiers 'knocked off the irons of all the felons and other prisoners in Huntingdon Gaol', all of whom at once joined the cavalier army. But it also acknowledges that the county was still divided between royalists and parliamentarians. 'One providence is observable, that divers of the best affected to the Parliament have escaped with the least loss,' it says, suggesting that Hinchingbrooke did not suffer badly. Some accounts say Charles lodged there – he had stayed at the house more than once in the past – while others put him at the George Inn, which seems more likely. Jemima Montagu would have received the king with perfect politeness, but he knew her husband was fighting against his forces. And she must have shared in the distress and indignation of the local people at the damage and losses they suffered, her agent Captain Pepys of Brampton among them: the departing cavaliers drove off all the cattle and horses from the fields round Huntingdon for their own use.[21]

The autumn of 1645 brought Colonel Montagu to London to receive the thanks of parliament for his victory at Bristol. Within a month he had a seat in the House and was appointed to the Army Committee.[22] With this his fighting days were over for the time being. In February 1646 he became a father; his first child, a daughter, was given her mother's name. The war effectively ended in March, although there was mopping up until June, when Oxford was taken, the king fled to the dubious protection of the Scots and the thirteen-year-old duke of York (James) was handed over to parliament and held prisoner in St James's Palace with his younger brother and sister. In September the earl of Essex, who had led the parliamentary forces in the early stages of the war and held Turnham Green against the cavaliers, died at his house in the Strand. Parliament decreed a splendid funeral, and Sam was taken to see the embalmed body lying in state in Essex House.[23]

At home with his parents again, Sam was already the best educated member of the family, with a mental world he could hardly share with them. The divide would grow steadily greater. Now his daily walk took him across the Fleet ditch instead of the Alconbury Brook, towards St Paul's School beside the cathedral. The boys put in a six-day week, with a free afternoon on Thursdays. All 150 of them sat in one room sixty feet long, with high windows on which the words AUT DOCE, AUT DISCE, AUT DISCEDE ('Either teach, or study, or leave') were inscribed. They had benches, not desks. At one end sat the high master, John Langley, beneath the bust of John Colet, the school's founder, and at the other the surmaster, although he spent more time walking about to supervise. There were eight classes, and the pupils were divided by achievement, not age: a boy might be still in the Second Form at thirteen or already in the Seventh at twelve. Since Pepys was still at school in 1650, when he was seventeen, he had clearly made steady, rather than spectacular, progress. Greek was started in the Sixth Form, Hebrew in the Eighth. The day began with Latin prayers and a chapter of the Bible, which, judging from the sparse biblical allusions in the Diary, did not take his fancy. All the boys learnt to speak as well as to write; they had to undergo regular oral examinations and also to deliver their own compositions, in Latin, like so many young Roman orators. It was a good training and made Sam into an effective speaker in adult life, as well as a stern critic of those who were not. They included his cousin Montagu and the future king Charles II, about whose poor public performance he was particularly scathing.[24]

His fellow pupils came from widely different levels of society, ranging from the sons of baronets and MPs, through country parsons, to booksellers, soap-boilers and drapers; Sam was not the only tailor's son, and one boy's father was a humble carrier. Poor boys could win awards for going on to a university, as Sam did in due course. Langley had a particularly good record for getting his pupils into Cambridge; the Cambridge to Oxford ratio was three to one. Cambridge possessed a powerful Calvinist body of teachers, and St Paul's was the most strongly puritan of the London schools at this time. Approving Calvinist preachers sent their sons to be educated by Langley, who had been persecuted by Laud and got his revenge by testifying against him before the House of Lords Committee in 1644 (Laud was executed on Tower Hill in January 1645). Langley wanted the abolition of bishops, and saw it achieved the next year. The irony of fate, and no doubt the effect of his excellent teaching, meant that several of his pupils went on to become bishops when episcopacy was brought back in the 1660s; but by then Langley was dead too, albeit from natural causes.[25]

Langley's reputation as a strongly religious man, a scholar and an antiquarian was backed by 'a very awful presence and speech that struck a mighty respect and fear into his scholars, which however wore off after they were a little used to him; and the management of himself towards them was such that they both loved and feared him'.[26] No doubt he beat his boys, as every schoolmaster was expected to do; Sam grew up quite ready to beat in their turn the children who worked for him, although he sometimes hurt himself more than his intended victim in the process, never acquiring the easy schoolmasterly swish. Langley's boys became lord mayors, bankers, engineers, academics, booksellers, MPs, administrators – and of course writers. St Paul's was responsible for the education of two of the great writers of the century, Milton – under an earlier high master, Alexander Gill – and Pepys. The fact that both have been found shocking is in itself a tribute to the quality of the education they got there.[27]

When Pepys was thirteen a new surmaster, Samuel Cromleholme, arrived. Not yet thirty, he was an enthusiastic book collector who impressed his young namesake with his learning and rose to become high master in his turn. Pepys regarded St Paul's with pride and affection after he left, presented books to the library, dropped in to see whether they were keeping up the standards of his day and was pleased to have his brother John follow him at the school. Tom had no chance of St Paul's at all, with his speech problem and slowness; he was set to learn tailoring in their father's shop, though he showed little talent or enthusiasm for that. The one thing Tom had an aptitude for seems to have been French, which he managed to speak fluently. So did Sam: another mystery, for where did they learn it? Not at school. Good French grammars were printed and sold in London, but Tom at least seems more likely to have picked it up directly. It is possible the Pepyses had a French lodger, since anyone with spare rooms and an uncertain income took in lodgers, as Tom himself did when he was in charge at Salisbury Court later.[28]

They did have a visitor from America this year, in the shape of cousin Richard Pepys, just returned from Boston. He had left England for religious reasons and returned with the abolition of the hated bishops; his lawyer father was soon to be appointed lord chief justice of Ireland by Cromwell. Another returning American emigrant in 1646 was George Downing, who began by finding work as an army preacher in the regiment of a Colonel Okey, from which he made a rapid rise through Cromwell's administration. Within a few years he, like Montagu, exerted a crucial influence on Sam Pepys's life, because when Sam put in for a leaving exhibition at St Paul's, Downing was chairman of the judges who awarded it to him, and so played a crucial part in helping him to go on to Cambridge to continue his studies.[29]

★

The sharp pain of the stone was still part of Sam's life, but he did not let it prevent him from profiting by what St Paul's had to offer. Boys were expected to work steadily and hard. Pepys took to this regime, and it gave him a lifelong belief in the power of education, as well as a model for his later working practice. In that large, light schoolroom he learnt how to apply himself vigorously to a subject and how to keep orderly notes, two things that helped to make him into the committed and meticulous administrator he became. Still, it is surprising that the school did so well by him, given what was going on all around. Outside, London was in almost continuous turmoil. There must have been days when it was difficult for boys even to make their way to and from St Paul's, and others when it was impossible not to be distracted by the sights to be seen in the streets. During this period the cathedral itself was partly used as a shopping precinct and sometimes for stabling horses for the army. Twice – in the summer of 1647, when Sam was fourteen and again in November 1648 – the New Model Army marched in and occupied the City. The spectacle of 18,000 troops tramping through the streets and across London Bridge with Cromwell at their head was intended to overawe the citizens and must have drawn admiring schoolboys like a magnet.

There was plenty to look at, and yet more to avoid. Rioting was endemic, and if you did not want to be caught up in it you had to keep out of the way. The London prentices – Tom Pepys became an apprentice in 1648, when he was fourteen – were usually ready to turn out, supported by the watermen and any sailors who happened to be ashore; there were times when they were joined by members of the trained bands, and other times when they were attacked by them. Plenty of ordinary citizens were also ready to swell the numbers of the rioters when feelings rose high enough. Milton might see the City as the mansion house of liberty, but the crowd's view of what constituted liberty shifted wildly and unpredictably. In July 1647, for instance, a mob from the City kicked in the doors of the House of Commons, terrorized the MPs, held the speaker prisoner and forced a vote inviting the king to London.

There was always a royalist element inside the predominantly anti-royalist City, just as there was always among the puritan majority a group who yearned for a return to the established form of church service, and who deplored the destruction of stained glass and statues and the removal of cherished landmarks like the old stone cross at Charing Cross, taken down in 1647 as an idolatrous object and sadly missed. The Pepys who wrote the Diary had become on the whole hostile to puritanism and necessarily a royalist, but the St Paul's boy was a puritan and a republican. Religion made bitter divisions: parliament and army struggled against one another, parliament and City, and City and army. Outside London the king was moved about like a piece on a chessboard, alternately threatening and threatened. For the first six months of 1647, after the Scots handed him over to parliament, he was held in Northamptonshire, where Jemima Montagu's father, John Crew, was one of those responsible for his custody. In June the army sent Cornet Joyce to abduct him into their power, and as a prisoner of the army he again visited Hinchingbrooke, probably still escorted by Crew. It was reported that he was 'nobly treated' by his hostess, Mistress Montagu – this was Jemima. She was, as it happens, again three months' pregnant, and her husband was away attending parliament in London.[30] From Huntingdon the king went on to Hampton Court; and in November he escaped to the Isle of Wight. After this parliament became reluctant to continue their negotiations with him.[31]

Christmas brought more trouble in the City when the branches of rosemary and bays that were traditional decorations appeared mysteriously in the churches, and a group of apprentices decked a pump in Cornhill with holly and ivy, all in defiance of the puritan ban on seasonal festivities. Troops sent to remove the offending greenery were driven back by angry crowds, and there was deep resentment against soldiers entering private houses to check on Sunday observance as well as to prevent the celebration of Christmas. Then there was the matter of the theatre. The Globe had been pulled down in 1644, but during the winter of 1647/8, some actor–managers, observing that the ordinance forbidding theatrical performances was due to run out on 1 January, got up plays and opened their doors on New Year's Day. At once the streets were jammed with the carriages of eager theatregoers, all those men and women who had grown up with a tradition of playgoing and were now eager to resume it. Parliament furiously slapped down penalties, ordering the destruction of 'all stage-galleries, seats and boxes', the fining of spectators and the public flogging of actors, who were further required to promise to give up their profession for good. But the persecution was never entirely effective. It is impossible to unmake an actor, and a public reared on Shakespeare and Jonson was too enthusiastic to be denied. John Evelyn notes that he saw 'a Tragie Comedie' acted in London in February that year. There was also a tradition that the boys of St Paul's put on plays, although their puritan high master must now have forbidden anything of that kind. Pepys, who had tasted the pleasures of amateur acting and developed a passion for playgoing as soon as he had the chance, either had to pretend indifference or, under Langley's influence, went through his own phase of sanctimonious disapproval.

Another fracas occurred in the City in the spring, when royalists made bonfires in the streets to celebrate the anniversary of the king's accession on 31 March, and forced passers-by to stop and drink his health. This was followed by an incident in which puritan intolerance provoked a full-scale royalist riot. On a fine Sunday in April a group of small boys was playing at tip-cat on the open green space of Moorfields. The game was a popular and harmless one, the 'cat' nothing more than a sharpened stick to be sent flying; but, because it was Sunday, the lord mayor sent a detachment from the trained bands to stop the sport. A crowd of apprentices decided to defend the children's freedom to play games. Soon the apprentices were stoning the soldiers and went on to disarm them. By then a crowd several thousand strong had gathered, which proceeded to march along Fleet Street and the Strand, shouting 'Now for King Charles'. Cromwell was in London, and he ordered out the cavalry and charged the crowd, killing two and injuring more. Very early next morning the apprentices secured the City gates at Ludgate and Newgate and fired shots through the lord mayor's windows. He prudently took refuge in the Tower, and by 8 a.m. – when Sam should have been at school – the City was in the hands of the rioters. The army then moved round the walls and brought troops in through Moorgate. Some of the rioters were killed, those suspected of being ringleaders were taken to prison, everyone else dispersed. Law-abiding citizens breathed a sigh of relief, and lessons were taken up again at St Paul's.

George Downing, who was in London at this point and making himself noticed by Cromwell, wrote a good account of 'the great divisions among us' – 'us' meaning the army, parliament and the puritans – to his uncle in America:

One cryes out, settle church government, punish errours and blasphemyes . . .; another, remember your often declarations for liberty for tender consciences; one, bring home the King according to the covenant; another, it can't stand with the preservation of the true religion and liberty, etc., and thus for want of a downright playne understanding of the foundation of this warre . . . we have been likely often to have been embroyled in a more bloody, and by our quarrellings to give occasion to any third party to devoure all . . . What the issue will be the Lord only knows, only he seems to be shaking the great ones of the earth.[32]

Shaken as they were, parliament even considered giving the crown to their fourteen-year-old captive, James, duke of York; but at the end of April he made his escape during a game of hide-and-seek in the park of St James's Palace. He got away disguised as a girl, with a wig, a cloak and a specially made dress of 'mixed mohair' with scarlet under-petticoat, and in this humiliating get-up was whisked aboard a barge bound for Gravesend and so to Holland.[33]

In May the City churches remained almost empty when thanksgiving services were held for the defeat of royalist risings in Wales, and later in the month there were serious riots when Surrey petitioners marched through town shouting 'For God and King Charles'. In the fighting outside the House of Commons the demonstrators threw lumps of coal and brickbats, the soldiers fired on them and at least eight were dead by the end of the day.[34] After this parliament and the City decided they must get on to better terms, and the army was persuaded to remove its garrison from the Tower and allow the City to install its own militia again.

Outside London similar conflicts were being enacted in 1648. There was a riot about a maypole at Bury St Edmunds. Edward Montagu was held prisoner briefly by a group of royalists while trying to suppress their gatherings in Huntingdonshire; in July he successfully put down others in St Neots.[35] This was what is known as the Second Civil War, during which Colchester was besieged and a parliamentary vice-admiral, William Batten, took his ship *The Constant Warwick* out to join the prince of Wales off Yarmouth and was knighted by him, but was back serving parliament within months: he and Pepys became colleagues twelve years later. Cromwell went north and defeated the invading Scottish army at Preston. In November the English army marched into London again under its commander-in-chief Fairfax, who had written to the lord mayor warning him that he expected to collect £40,000 'arrears' from the City to pay his men. He quartered his troops in the citizens' houses for a few days, long enough to persuade them of the wisdom of paying up.

Other elements of the army were now preparing to bring the king captive to London; they had decided that his deviousness made him impossible to negotiate with any longer. But he was still the king, and a substantial number of MPs voiced a hope that it might be possible to reopen discussions with him after all. To prevent any such move, a group of republican officers went into the House of Commons, arrested 45 MPs and sent away another 186 whom they judged unlikely to support their plans for getting rid of Charles. This decisive intervention, known as 'Pride's Purge' – a Colonel Thomas Pride took a leading part – happened in December 1648 (those MPs who were permitted to remain became known as the 'Rump' parliament). Among the purged MPs were John Crew and Edward Montagu, neither of whom was enthusiastic about putting the king on trial. Montagu took himself quietly back to Hinchingbrooke and family life. In the Lords the earl of Manchester urged that to try the king was in contradiction with fundamental principles of law, and the plan was unanimously rejected. It made no difference but sealed the fate of the House of Lords, abolished shortly afterwards.

Cromwell returned to London, and the stage was set for the trial of the king. A special court was set up, and 135 commissioners were appointed to act as combined jury and judges. No more than 68 ever appeared to carry out their duties. Fairfax, whose name was among them, did not attend, and when the trial began his wife, openly royalist in her sympathies, made her own interventions. This was the true theatrical performance of 1649, for the court was held in Westminster Hall and open to the public. Troops stood on guard inside, but people came in freely through the entrance at the north end of the hall, and there were galleries set up in the corners for ladies and privileged persons. The king was seated in a crimson velvet chair. There he heard himself accused of a 'wicked design' to subvert the ancient laws and liberties of the nation, and there he refused to acknowledge the legitimacy of the court. He found he was not without supporters. When Fairfax's name was read out, Lady Fairfax called from the gallery, 'He has more wit than to be here.' Later, on hearing the king accused of being a traitor to his country, she shouted that, on the contrary, it was Oliver Cromwell who was the traitor. When her taunting grew too strong, an officer threatened to order his men to shoot into the gallery. She was persuaded to leave, but she had made her point. The soldiers shouted 'Justice! Justice!' when the king left the hall, but it was answered by 'God save the King!' from many of the civilian spectators.[36]

We know from Pepys's own account how strongly republican he was at this point. He was fifteen, and his sympathies were entirely against the king; in this way he was far more radical than his cousin Montagu, who chose to stay away during the trial. Sam may well have got himself into Westminster Hall for a glimpse of the king in his crimson chair; he was certainly present at his execution. Since it happened on a Tuesday – 30 January – either St Paul's sent the boys home or he made his own decision to go to Whitehall and take the consequences. The Westminster schoolboys were kept locked in for the day to prevent them from attending.[37] He must have set off early, because the crowd was dense and there were lines of soldiers posted to prevent disturbances. The king walked across St James's at ten in the morning, showing a dignity and courage that impressed itself even on his enemies, and entered the Banqueting Hall, where he said his prayers and from which he emerged through a tall window on to the scaffold just before two in the afternoon. Soldiers were positioned between the scaffold and the crowd to make it difficult for anyone to hear his last words. Philip Henry, an Oxford undergraduate a little older than Pepys, was present and has left a description of the moment when the executioner struck off the royal head: 'The blow I saw given and can truly say with a sad heart, at the instant whereof, I remember well, there was such a grone by the Thousands then present as I never heard before and desire I may never hear again.' Henry goes on to describe how two troops of soldiers were set to march in opposite directions between Westminster and Charing Cross in order to disperse the people; but there was no trouble in London that day, and in some respects life continued in its normal course, with the shops open and people going about their business.[38] Pepys may even have gone back to school, because he remembers telling his friends there that if he had to preach a sermon on the king, his text would

be, 'The memory of the wicked shall rot.' It is the only time he
imagined himself in the pulpit, and he recalled it a shade nervously
when, in 1660, a man he had known at St Paul's reminded him that
he had been 'a great roundhead' at school.[39] Elsewhere in his Diary
he remained studiously non-committal in what he had to say of the
execution; for instance, when he witnessed the hanging, drawing and
quartering of Thomas Harrison, one of those who had signed the
death warrant of the king, he only commented, 'Thus it was my
chance to see the King beheaded at Whitehall and to see the first
blood shed in revenge for the blood of the King at Charing cross.'[40]
The grown man was not going to express a grief he did not feel, or
any remorse for the satisfaction he had felt.

The king was dead, but the king was also alive, since his son was
immediately proclaimed as Charles II in his exile in Holland, and
became the new focus for royalists everywhere. On Jersey George
Carteret waved his hat, shouting, 'Long live King Charles II.' In
England, however, a republic was declared. Monarch, bishops and
lords were now all abolished or, as Evelyn put it, 'Un-king-ship
proclaim'd, & his Majesties Statues throwne downe at St Paules
Portico, & Exchange'.[41] And Evelyn went to Paris to kiss the new
king's hands, and to observe his mistress, Mrs Barlow, 'browne,
beautiful, bold but insipid' and mother of the martyred king's grandchild, the infant duke of Monmouth. London became more peaceful
for a while, with only the odd incident like the shooting dead of a
young trooper thought to be a Leveller in St Paul's Churchyard, the
beheading of a group of royalists outside Westminster Hall and the
arrest, imprisonment and ejection from his office of Mayor Reynolds
for refusing to proclaim the Act abolishing the kingly office. John
Lilburne was also arrested and tried for publishing pamphlets in
defiance of the censorship laws. He fought his own case and was
acquitted by the jury to rejoicing and more bonfires all over the City.
This was in October, and Cromwell was now fighting in Ireland.

Pepys had another year at school, some of it spent negotiating his
entrance to the university of Cambridge. Sam was a good bit older
than many undergraduates: fourteen was quite usual, but he did not
start his Cambridge studies until he was eighteen. There was no
question of his father financing him, so he had to find support in

other places. It came from some powerful Cromwellians. George
Downing's part in the award of his first exhibition in February 1650
has already been mentioned. Five months after this Pepys's name was
entered at Trinity Hall. This was the college of his great-uncle Talbot
Pepys, now recorder, or chief magistrate, of Cambridge and very
active in raising taxes for Cromwell's army.[42] Talbot was also Edward
Montagu's uncle. Trinity Hall was a legal college, so there may have
been thought of Sam becoming a lawyer. But that plan was given up
– he may have disliked the idea, or it may have been too expensive
to pursue – and the place at Trinity Hall was not taken up. He was
admitted instead, in October, to Magdalene College. As it happened,
Magdalene had just lost its master who, summoned to London to take
the 'Engagement' of loyalty to the commonwealth by the commission
for the universities, refused on grounds of conscience. His offer to
live quietly was not good enough and he was replaced. The newly
appointed master was John Sadler, another successful lawyer in Chancery, a town clerk of London, much favoured by Cromwell, who had
already offered him the position of chief justice of Munster, which he
turned down. As it happened, Sadler lived in Salisbury Court.[43]
Montagu's patronage probably came into it too; his chaplain had
a Magdalene connection, and Samuel Morland, who claimed his
friendship, had just been appointed to a fellowship there and became
Pepys's tutor. Later, Morland and Downing were both chosen by
Cromwell to go on diplomatic missions, and he appointed Colonel
Edward Montagu as visitor to both Cambridge and Oxford, although
he had attended neither university. The appointment made him
responsible for inspecting, supervising and removing abuses from the
universities.

Oxford and Cambridge were obvious battlegrounds for the minds
of the younger generation, and seen as such by the government. There
was talk in parliament of abolishing both universities and setting up
alternative ones in other cities – York, London and Durham were all
mentioned – and although these ideas were dropped, the purging of
the old guard of Oxbridge masters and fellows was vigorously pursued.
It was necessary to build up a body of graduates sympathetic to the
commonwealth, something that helps to explain why Sam Pepys,
with his proclaimed views and politically correct connections, was

thought worth helping. In November he was awarded a second leaving exhibition by St Paul's, and within a month of starting his studies at Cambridge he picked up another scholarship.

3. Cambridge and Clerking

Cambridge is a cold and beautiful place, and was certainly as cold and possibly as beautiful in the 1650s as it is today. But Evelyn did not enthuse when he came in 1654 to see the great colleges, St John's, Trinity and King's, on to whose chapel roof he ascended to survey the views of Ely, Royston, Newmarket and many miles of field and fenland stretching to the horizon; the town was, he said, 'situated in a low dirty unpleasant place, the streetes ill paved, the aire thick, as infested by the fenns'. He observed that Clare College was being elegantly rebuilt to a 'new and noble design', but that the work had been brought to a halt by the war; and he did not so much as mention Magdalene, perhaps because it was out of the way, the only college set on the north side of the River Cam, where the Huntingdon road started.[1] Originally built for Benedictine monks, it was one of the smallest and least well-endowed foundations; but the modest red-brick court of two storeys, topped by attics with dormer windows, was and still is attractive, with its riverside gardens and, in Pepys's time, open country beyond.

Pepys, at eighteen short, dark, with slightly protruding eyes and fleshy cheeks, nose and lips, finally put on his Cambridge gown at Magdalene in March 1651.[2] He was not going to impress his fellow students by either his looks or his social standing, since he went as a sizar, that is, a student whose teaching is paid for by the college; one shilling and sixpence a week seems to have been the rate. Undergraduate numbers were in any case low because of the war. When Pepys arrived there were only thirty in residence in the college, and he was one of eleven freshmen. Each of them had to put in £5.5s. a year towards their 'commons' – shared provisions – and pay twelve shillings a year for washing and ten shillings for his bed-maker, who had to be either a man or an old woman, since young women were formally forbidden entry to any college.[3] Here was the smell of an all-male community, and with minimal washing arrangements. Pepys mentions more than one of his Cambridge 'chamber fellows' in his Diary, and there are still sets of rooms in the oldest part of Magdalene that show how things were arranged, with bedrooms and living rooms shared but separate rooms for study: work at least was seen as a private activity. The day started with chapel at six; the new master had moved it forward from five, as much for his own sake as the scholars', no doubt. Breakfast followed, then classes all morning, and dinner at noon in the college hall. Until 1643 Magdalene's chapel and hall were embellished by forty 'superstitious pictures', including a piece of old stained glass in which 'Joseph and Mary stood to be espoused in the Windowes', something we know about from records kept by the enthusiastic vandal who destroyed them in 1643, following an edict from parliament.[4]

College rules were strict, in theory at any rate. The young men were not allowed to wander about the Cambridge streets or linger in the market place, and certainly not to enter taverns. As at school, they were expected to talk together in Latin, or Greek, or Hebrew. They were forbidden to play cards or dice, or to have irreligious books in their rooms, or to attend dances, boxing matches or cock-fights; and they were not officially allowed anywhere near the famous Sturbridge Fair that was set up in an encampment of booths and tents every September outside the town. It had existed before the university, and it brought trade and visitors from all over Europe. Wool, wine, tin, lead, hops and linen were the serious business, but there were secondhand bookstalls too, haberdashery and even fish for sale; and it attracted numerous 'vagabonds, naughtie and joly persons'.[5] The university was at the height of its puritanism when Pepys was there, and, although he was a good student, he managed to be reprimanded formally for drunkenness at least once. The college register for 21 October 1653 reads, in the hand of his tutor Samuel Morland, 'Peapys and Hind were solemnly admonished by myself and Mr Hill for having been scandalously overserved with drink the night before. This was done in the presence of the Fellows then resident, in Mr Hill's Chamber.' That is all we know of his drinking history at the university. Less heroically, he used to purchase stewed prunes from a woman known as Goody Mulliner living opposite Magdalene, whose son served – and perhaps sometimes overserved – in the college buttery, where the students went to buy ale as well as food.

Sam, who never enjoyed single-sex living, also hung about various young women, including Betty Archer, whom he remembered tenderly, and her sister Mary, who married a college friend. There was also the less respectable Elizabeth Aynsworth, who kept an inn and taught him a very lewd song called 'Full Forty Times Over'; she was later banished from Cambridge.[6] And if he did not own any irreligious books, he wrote one, or part of one, in the shape of a novel or romance that he called 'Love a Cheate.' Maddeningly for us, he destroyed his own manuscript ten years later in a fit of tidiness, or 'humour of making all things even and clear in the world'; worse, in 'reading it over tonight, I liked it very well and wondered a little at myself at my vein at that time when I wrote it, doubting that I cannot do so well now if I would try'.[7] The disappearance of this first evidence of Pepys's literary ambition, and of his early narrative voice, is lamentable; but it is worth knowing that he was trying his hand at fiction when he was twenty, because it tells us that the skills displayed in the Diary were built on something he had already worked at. He also enjoyed playing games with words, anagrams, for instance, on the names of young women he admired, including one Elizabeth Whittle living in Salisbury Court, where she lodged in a house belonging to another Montagu connection. If Pepys's anagrams were meant to woo, they failed to soften her heart towards him, and in 1654 she married an able young man, Stephen Fox, with whom he had friendly professional dealings later.[8]

Shorthand was another extracurricular enthusiasm. Thomas Shelton's *Short Writing*, first published in 1626, had been improved and renamed *Tachygraphy*, and was republished by the Cambridge University Press in 1635. It was not too difficult to master, and there was something of a craze for it among young men and women who used it for taking notes on sermons; there were two reprints during the pious and talkative 1640s.[9] It looks as though Pepys learnt it during his undergraduate years, because by the time he started to use it for his Diary he was a practised shorthand writer, although there is no evidence that he took down sermons. Shelton's system uses a symbol for each consonant and double consonant, as well as for many suffixes and prefixes; the vowels are indicated by positioning the following consonant or by a dot in one of five places; and there are 300 whole word symbols to be memorized – e.g., the symbol for the letter *g* is also the symbol for the word *God*, the symbol for *k* also stands for *king* and *l* for *lord*. It is not a fast system by the standards of later shorthand, but, although Pepys used it on occasion to take down speech, speed was not his object in the Diary.[10]

Students usually took eight or nine weeks' holiday in the summer, when Pepys would have gone home to Salisbury Court, and might remain in residence for the rest of the year.[11] The official Cambridge curriculum had for centuries concentrated on logic, philosophy and rhetoric, but under the commonwealth the dominance of puritan teaching meant that the classical curriculum was pushed aside by many in favour of religious studies. Oliver Heywood, a Trinity contemporary of Pepys, described how his 'time and thoughts were more employed in practical divinity' and how he preferred the sermons of Calvinist preachers and prayers in his tutor's rooms to the study of Aristotle and Plato. He and his friends were more inclined to read the works of English divines, and he names Sibbes, Perkins, Bolton and Preston. The titles of their books indicate their preoccupations: *A Garden of Spiritual Flowers*; *The Saint's Cordials*; *A Treatise of Mans Imaginations, Showing His Naturall Evill Thoughts*; *The Sinfulnesse of Sin*; *An Elegant Description of Spiritual Life and Death*; and *Sinnes Overthrow, or a Treatise of Mortification*.[12] I doubt if Pepys spent much time with these. He preferred Bacon and Erasmus among modern writers, Cicero among the ancients, and was keenly interested in English history. Rhetoric came naturally to him, and he is likely to have performed well at the disputations required of students, which involved formal public debates on subjects such as 'Was Julius Caesar justly put to death?' or 'Whether a lettered or an unlettered wife be preferable?'. There were also declamations to be prepared. These were the equivalent of the modern weekly essay, papers to be read aloud, in Latin and ideally larded with quotations from classical authors diligently collected by the student in a commonplace book.[13] Grammar and ethics, the latter involving some study of history, must also have been to Sam's taste. Poetry too, whether ancient or modern. John Dryden, already with a reputation for his verse, was an acquaintance – he was at Trinity, where he got into trouble for 'contumacy', much as you might expect of a young poet – and later in life he and Pepys corresponded and shared an admiration for Chaucer.[14] Then there was music, always pre-eminent for Pepys. Although King's College Chapel had lost its organ and choristers to the puritan ban on such delights, there was still domestic music to be made. A family of musicians called Saunders lived in Green Street in the centre of town, and Pepys referred to one of the Saunderses later as 'the only Viallin in my time'. On another occasion he talked of meeting 'Mr Nicholson, my old fellow-student at Magdalen, and we played three or four things upon violin and Basse', which suggests they were continuing an established practice.[15] There is a story of a Cambridge student taking his viol into a philosophy class and defending the position of 'sol, fa, mi, la' against three opponents, whom he routed, at which the teacher exclaimed, '*Ubi desinit philosophus, ibi incipit musicus*', meaning, roughly, that music begins where philosophy ends. If he heard of it, it must have pleased Pepys, who always insisted on the importance of musical studies.[16]

He was a good walker too, and it is hard not to think he made the fourteen-mile walk to Brampton and Hinchingbrooke several times during his time at Cambridge, to see his uncle Robert and to pay his respects to my Lady – Jemima Montagu – now with four small children tumbling about her skirts. After little Jem came Edward, then Paulina, and, in July 1650, Sidney. But nothing is known of such visits, only of much shorter Cambridge walks. He took pleasure, he said, in going frequently to Chesterton church – St Andrew's, with its Doomsday painting above the chancel arch – and on to the ruined remains of Barnwell Abbey on the Newmarket road, then across the river with the ferry, and so back along Jesus Lane.[17] Another walk, clearly etched in his memory because of its after-effects, was made with a group of friends who set out in good spirits on a sweltering summer's day to what they chose to call Aristotle's Well. Pepys, always sensitive to heat, gulped down such quantities of its cold water that the sheer weight in his system, he believed, gave him several exceedingly unpleasant days before a stone was washed out of his kidney and into his bladder. The result was that his already painful condition became worse. From then on, he wrote, 'I lived under a constant succession of fits of stone in the bladder'. His account, which describes how he put up with the condition for several years after leaving Cambridge, until the pain became more than he could bear, suggests that his student days were not all busy, cheerful activity, declamations, drinking, music-making and reading, but had their darker side too. There was always a degree of pain to be dealt with, and days and nights when it flared up and he suffered miserably in the room he shared with his chamber fellows. Bladder problems and the passing of bloody water are uncomfortable, humiliating and frightening. Pepys depended on his charm and conviviality to make and keep friends at Cambridge; the fact that he had a chronic illness makes it the more striking that he kept up his spirits and his friendships as he did.

His great-uncle Talbot Pepys, the Cambridge family connection, was less important in the university than in the town, where his position as recorder gave him considerable influence and control over civil and criminal jurisdiction. He had been its MP three decades earlier; now he was in his sixties and married to his fourth wife, with grown-up sons who had followed him into the law; and he was still very active. He lived in the large manor house at Impington, a few miles north of Cambridge, where Pepys noted that the country people all rose to their feet respectfully as his uncle Talbot entered the church. His political stance is perfectly clear, since he was a leading figure in the raising of taxes to finance Cromwell's armies during the 1640s and 1650s. He was also appointed to a body meant to ensure that there was 'godly and religious' – meaning puritan – preaching in the non-university churches of the area.[18]

In the 1650s the university felt the force of Cromwell's will. During Sam's college years the earl of Manchester was dismissed as chancellor for refusing to take the oath of loyalty to the commonwealth and replaced by Lord Chief Justice Oliver St John, a Huntingdon man who happened to be married to Cromwell's cousin. This was in the autumn of 1651, and the following May Cromwell himself became high steward of Cambridge. It was a good thing for the university, because he wrote a stern letter forbidding the quartering of troops on the colleges.[19] In 1654 his son Henry Cromwell became MP for Cambridge. Sam Pepys had only to look about to see how thoroughly everything was being reorganized, opponents got rid of, key positions filled by supporters of the new system, and good behaviour rewarded. This may have been the biggest lesson of his college years, that the world is changed by efficient administrators. When he completed his studies in the mid 1650s, the legal system, the headships of the once royalist colleges, the curriculum, Church appointments and the raising of taxes were all in the hands of Cromwellians; it was just after he left that Colonel Edward Montagu was appointed to the powerful position of visitor to both universities, along with Sir Gilbert Pickering and Bulstrode Whitelocke.[20]

What could Pepys expect once he had a degree? The majority of his contemporaries were bound for careers in the Church – Charles Carter, John Powell, Theophilus Hooke, John Castell, Richard Cumberland, Clement Sankey, Thomas Meriton, all of whose names can be gleaned from the Diary – but the Church clearly made no appeal to him. So little religious feeling did he possess that even at Cambridge he took the sacrament only 'once or twice' – he was not sure which – and then not again for more than ten years.[21] Charles Anderson, one of his high-spirited chamber fellows, went on to become a doctor, as did John Hollins. Others progressed to the law, including Robert Sawyer, another who shared rooms with Pepys.[22] Sam's lack of interest in a legal career is puzzling because it was such an obvious path to success for someone in his situation, poor and able. Instead, after being awarded another scholarship in October 1653, during his last year as a student, and taking his BA degree in March 1654, it appears that he simply went home to his parents. He was not offered a fellowship. It may be that the problems with his health were barring his ambitions; he had little to say later about this period of his life, and this could be as much to do with illness as a wish to gloss over his lowly and uncertain start on a London career. What is certain is that he was proud of having been at Cambridge, and was always pleased to return and show off its sights to others – his wife, his friends, even his maidservants.

But the best clue to what happened next is to be found in what was taking place in Montagu's life. For three years, from 1650 to 1653, he had lived quietly at Hinchingbrooke with his family. During this time Cromwell subdued Ireland, crushed the young Charles II and his army at Worcester and forced him to flee abroad again; defeated the Dutch in a trade war fought at sea; and dissolved parliament. Montagu played no part in any of this, but during Sam's last summer at Cambridge, in 1653, he re-emerged into London politics as an MP in the short-lived parliament known as Barebones (so called by its enemies after Praisegod Barebones, the Fleet Street preacher, whom Cromwell had summoned to sit in the House). As soon as Colonel Montagu took his place in the House, Cromwell invited him to sit on his Council of State. Within months he was also made a commissioner of the Treasury, which brought him £1,000 a year, and put on the committee for Foreign Affairs, as well as a number of smaller committees. In November he was appointed lord president of the Council of State. In December parliament dissolved itself – Montagu helped to engineer this – and Cromwell became lord protector. The position was elective, but election was by the Council of State, and Cromwell himself had the final say in its membership. At twenty-eight Edward Montagu was suddenly a great man, one of the makers of the protectorate and a clear favourite of the protector.

Cromwell now took up his residence in Whitehall, and Montagu was given substantial lodgings within the palace. They were at the western end of the great complex of buildings and extended over the King Street gate. The birth of another daughter, Anne, probably kept Jemima at Hinchingbrooke that winter, while Edward was busy in London. Until then he had been a soldier and a country squire; now he had to master economics, politics and foreign affairs. Early in the new year he was in Huntingdonshire fighting an election at which both royalists and republicans gave trouble; but he and Henry Cromwell prevailed, winning the two county seats. In London again, he entertained the French and Dutch ambassadors, and attended the celebrations that marked the end of the first war with the Dutch. On this occasion, in April 1654, Oliver Cromwell presided over a performance of instrumental music and psalm singing. In June Montagu was praised by Milton in his *Defensio Secunda*, alongside Cromwell, Bradshaw, Fairfax and Pickering; they were men of 'highest ability and of the best culture and accomplishments'.[23] Given his many new responsibilities, Montagu needed clerks and helpers, and this is where Sam Pepys became useful. Sam's position was hardly more than that of a family dogsbody – a seventeenth-century Figaro now – who might equally be asked to order riding coats, caps or toys for the children, sort out problems with domestic servants or keep Montagu informed by letter of what was going on in London when he was at Hinchingbrooke; and although Montagu sometimes took a peremptory tone with his servant, he clearly trusted him, both to be discreet and also with the handling of substantial sums of money. Pepys was often at the house of Jemima Montagu's father, John Crew, in Lincoln's Inn Fields, where he was well liked; and he was in and out of Montagu's Whitehall lodgings. He was treated as family there and soon found himself a corner to bed down in; it was more convenient, and more congenial too than being at home with parents and siblings with whom he had ever less in common. To live in a palace, even as a servant among the other servants, would have appealed greatly to Sam's sense of place and history.

Dates are in short supply for his life during these years. We don't know when he started working for Montagu. The earliest extant letter between them is dated March 1656, but it is clear that Sam was by then well established in his service. And in 1656 he acquired another job, and a more formal one, for which he had to thank George Downing. Downing's career had prospered famously. He was now MP for Edinburgh and spoke often and confidently in the House; he had also acquired an aristocratic wife. When Cromwell decided to revive the government department of the Exchequer, which had become moribund during the wars, Downing was given a position within it; he must have remembered the St Paul's boy to whom he had awarded an exhibition and offered him one of the many clerkships in his gift. There was another link with the Exchequer: in 1654 Richard Pepys, first cousin to Sam's father, was made both lord chief justice of Ireland and baron of the Exchequer by Cromwell.[24]

Pepys had only to walk along King Street from the Montagu lodgings to find himself at the Exchequer, another great complex of buildings on the east side of New Palace Yard, within the palace of Westminster; and Whitehall and Westminster, linked by King Street, with its old timber-built houses and taverns, became the territory in which he felt at home for the rest of his life, the very heart of the political and administrative machinery of the nation, where even the humblest clerk knew the glamour of being at the centre of things; where he passed great men in the street every day, and took delight in being so well informed about what was going on.[25] Pepys gives us a glimpse in the early pages of his Diary of the lives of the young government clerks who became his colleagues and friends, with whom he went 'clubbing' – his word – in Cromwell's time.[26] Collectively, he calls them 'the old Crew' – he has known them for some years by then – and he shows us the anxieties and manoeuvres of their working lives as well as their convivial meetings in taverns and cookhouses: Wood's in Pall Mall, Marsh's in Whitehall, Harper's and the Fox in King Street, the Westminster Swan and the Half Moon in the Strand, and a great many more. They gathered to talk politics in coffee houses like Miles's in New Palace Yard. They enjoyed card games and musical evenings; they exchanged ridiculous bets – on whether the meat they were eating was veal or lamb – and gambled gently. A game called 'Selling a Horse for a Dish of Eggs and Herrings' is mentioned, and another called 'Handicap'. They tried out new drinking places, and borrowed and lent small sums of money to one another. They gossiped about the great and made knowing jokes. Some lived with their parents, some with friends or in lodgings, others were already married to young wives. Some had rich uncles in the background, and most kept a keen eye on promotion possibilities. From Pepys's scattered descriptions we get the first account ever written of how young men with meagre jobs, sharp wits and an appetite for experience live and work in a modern city, and we can see that it has not changed all that much over the centuries. You can find something similar going on in Keats's letters, and in what Dickens conveys of his anxious, hard-working but enjoyable years as a parliamentary reporter; there is even a physical link in that Garraway's Coffee House, which opened in 1658, was still in business when Dickens wrote the *Pickwick Papers*. The flash boys and girls working the stock market in the City of London in the 1990s and 2000s are distant descendants of the friends with whom Pepys went clubbing. Pepys, here as in so many places, has led the way with his account.

We can glean a little more about his colleagues and friends from official papers. For instance, we know that in 1654 the seven under-clerks to Cromwell's council, working directly under John Milton as the chief secretary, were paid by the day, at six shillings and eight pence; they included Will Symons, who became a good friend of Pepys, and the Leigh (or Lea) brothers Matthew and Thomas, also known to him; there was a Ewers too, and two Frost brothers, more names that link themselves with the Diary. The council sat from nine until one from Monday to Thursday, and all day Friday; Saturdays were free, so that although Sundays were strictly for churchgoing and not for pleasure, they did get a weekend break; but it looks as though they could not expect to earn much more than £1 a week. This fits with the £50 a year Pepys was getting when he first recorded his salary as an Exchequer clerk six years later. The job of the council clerks was to take minutes of the meetings, sometimes chaired by Cromwell, where Montagu sat with, among others, his brother-in-law Gilbert Pickering, Sir Anthony Ashley Cooper and Henry Cromwell. Milton's eyesight was failing, but he still attended the meetings; in April 1655 Montagu was present when Milton's salary was discussed, and lowered, while that of Henry Scobell, chief clerk, was raised to £500 a year. Scobell was the uncle of Will Symons, and you can see how clerkships went naturally to family members and friends.[27] All these clerks except the Lea brothers were sacked in January 1660, when the political situation was changing fast, and another lot appointed. But there seems to have been little resentment: Symons, who was out, continued to drink with Peter Luellin, who was in. He was the son of an under-keeper at Windsor with a good claim to be a royalist, and a drinker and teller of rude stories that made them all laugh. The one about the friend who persuaded a gullible pretty woman to let him handle her private parts by pretending to be a doctor impressed Pepys so much that he went out looking for the woman. A real woman he and his fellow clerks got to know was Betty Lane, who worked in Westminster Hall, where a well-established community of stallholders sold linen, gloves, books and newspapers, and she ran a draper's stall from which he sometimes bought his linen. Betty was a Nottingham lass who had come south to conduct her own business; she took a cheerful, pagan view of sex and its possibilities, she liked Pepys, and he was fascinated by her.

In 1658 Milton's nephew Edward Phillips, just such a young man about town as Pepys had become, published a book of advice to those eager to get on with girls. Its frontispiece shows the outfits of the day: smart young men wore their own hair, often down to their shoulders in curls; tall-crowned, wide-brimmed hats, short jackets, breeches to the knee with stockings below and neat shoes tied with laces. Phillips's book was called *The Mysteries of Love and Eloquence; or, the Arts of Wooing and Complementing,* and it includes specimens of dialogue between the sexes, set in places such as the Spring Gardens at Charing Cross or Hyde Park, 'a la mode Pastimes', verses and plenty of indecorous jokes. It also includes some delightful proverbs: 'He that hath a Woman by the waste, hath a wet Eel by the tail' and 'Love though blind can smell', followed by its explanation: 'This is the reason, that a man that runs passionately after a Woman, is said to have his nose in her tail, and is call'd a smell-smock.' Suitors are advised, on outings to the park, to buy their sweethearts cheese-cakes, tarts, wine and sugar, and baskets of cherries, which were believed to be diuretic and so likely to send girls into the bushes. Gentlemen's conversations run along questions like how many positions he knows, how many times he can lie with a woman in one night, how many mistresses he has and how many children he dares not own. There are dialogues between an apprentice and a young lady at a boarding school, who is wooed with food because she gets short commons from the mistress; and between a seamstress and a gentleman 'lolling over the counter'. A lawyer's clerk strikes lucky with his master's daughter, who turns out to be the girl of every clerk's dreams with her 'Come, Robin, Clerk me no Clerks, I love thee: and if my father do compel me to marry another, yet Robin, thou knowst there are private corners in London . . . What do you think of a little horse-play in the mean time? . . . I love tumbling dearly.' But a gentleman usher who asks his colleague, a waiting gentlewoman, to comb his head for him is fobbed off because she has a sweetheart already, a barber in Fleet Street. Hair combing, much enjoyed by Pepys, was an acknowleged erotic pastime.

Phillips's verses go straight to the point: 'Dorothy this Ring is thine/And now thy bouncing body's mine.' 'Ellen, all men commend thy eyes/Onely I commend thy thighs.' 'Katie I chose with hair so red,/For the fine tricks she plays in bed.' And so on. Edward Phillips was reacting against everything his uncle Milton stood for. His book was a deliberately frivolous, even cynical, exercise, but it gives a feeling for what made some young Londoners laugh in the last years of the commonwealth period – young men like his uncle's under-clerks and others with whom Pepys spent his leisure time. Beneath the harsh and troubled political surface there were still pleasant undercurrents of life to be enjoyed.[28]

During 1655, the year Pepys was twenty-two, the political surface was exceptionally rough. The country was being governed by ordinance, without parliament and with censorship of newspapers; there were frequent attempts to suppress ale houses, gaming houses and houses of ill fame, together with horse racing, cock-fighting, theatres (yet again) and bear-baiting: the seven bears of the Hope Theatre on the south bank were finally shot by Colonel Pride a year later to save them from their torments.[29] Major-generals were appointed to rule over the regions, and travel was policed in an effort to keep down royalist activities. The naval dockyards built a great ship, the *Naseby*, with the figure of Cromwell trampling down six nations at its prow. There was much talk of whether Cromwell would take the crown, and some of the old republicans were either kept under guard or imprisoned. In April news came of a massacre of the Vaudois Protestants, a harmless and pious people living in the mountains of Piedmont; all Protestant Europe was appalled, and Cromwell took immediate action, raising money to help the survivors and sending letters drafted by Milton and carried by Pepys's old tutor Samuel Morland to the French king, Louis XIV, and the duke of Savoy, Charles Emmanuel. George Downing followed Morland as a special envoy and achieved some successful negotiation on behalf of the persecuted Protestants; and in October an Anglo-French treaty was signed. Whether this meant anything to the fourteen-year-old French girl, lately of Paris and currently living in the parish of St Martin-in-the-Fields, whose parentage was as mixed as her religious ideas, there is no way of knowing. Her name was Elizabeth Marchant de St Michel, and she was about to become the bride of Sam Pepys. Neither had a penny to their name.

4. Love and Pain

Pepys wooed the woman who was to be his wife with passion. Thirteen years after his wooing, he relived what he had felt during that time in a moment of intense, recaptured emotion. It came to him as he listened to music in the theatre. The music, he wrote in his Diary, was 'so sweet . . . that it made me really sick, just as I have formerly been when in love with my wife'. Memory and music had merged into one another. 'It ravished me' and 'wrapped up my soul' and 'I remained all night transported so as I could not believe that ever any music hath that real command over the soul of a man as this did upon me'.[1] The music that brought about this magical effect was played, improbably perhaps to some modern ears, on recorders, and, although he does not say so, it accompanied the appearance of Nell Gwyn, as she made a carefully stage-managed descent from the flies to the stage, bearing a basket of fruit and flowers and playing the part of a winged angel. In Pepys's collection of prints there is one of Nell Gwyn wearing little more than a pair of wings, and, though she would have worn rather more on the stage, there was no hiding the fact that she was the most celebrated erotic icon of the London theatre.[2] The angel in Dekker and Massinger's *The Virgin Martyr*, the play Pepys was attending, comes on disguised as a boy during the first four acts and appears in heavenly form only in the last; and it could be that her provokingly desirable appearance, as well as the music, was responsible for plunging Pepys into the past in this Proustian way, and reheating the memory of his old love and longing for the body of his Elizabeth.

The sickness of love and the sickness of the stone were the two preoccupations of his early twenties. To speak of love as a mixture of sweetness and sickness as he did is a striking conceit; clearly for him, at twenty-two, it had been an overpowering experience. So much so that it led him to fly in the face of what every intelligent clerk about town knew: that marriage was meant to be a step on the social ladder, and that a bride should bring some money and a worthwhile family alliance; it should not simply be a matter of running passionately after a woman with your nose in her smock. Pepys lost his good sense in his desire for Elizabeth. Nothing is known of how they met, whether in a bookshop or any other sort of shop, or through a friend; he may simply have got into conversation with her in the street. She was pretty enough to catch the eye, with her bright, definite face surrounded by curls, prominent eyes and expressive mouth; and she was a lively talker in two languages, which may have been what first caught the fancy of a man who loved to practise his own skills as a linguist. In the year he met her he bought himself a French *Nouveau Testament*.[3] Being foreign marked her off from other young women. She had lived in Paris, her father was French, and both her parents could boast of a higher social standing than Pepys himself. Alexandre le Marchant de St Michel came of a noble family in the Anjou, and her English mother also had grandly connected, landowning parents. All this sounded impressive, although in fact they were virtually destitute and friendless when Pepys met her.

Never mind that. He wanted Elizabeth for herself. The pain of his illness, and the question mark it set over his future, can only have sharpened his determination to possess her as soon as he could. If life was to give him no more than this, then at least he would have had her. Whether his wooing was an honourable one from the start or not, it became so. He persuaded himself that he could support a bride on his scant earnings, take her to live in the Montagu lodgings in Whitehall and put everything else out of his mind. He did not discuss his marital intentions with his employer or, it would seem, in any serious manner with her family or his own. There was no question on either side of a marriage settlement.

Elizabeth was fourteen, the same age as his sister Pall, but the two girls were as unlike as it was possible to be and notably failed to become friends, then or at any later time. Pall was only just literate and, according to her brother, far from lovely, 'full of Freckles and not handsome in face', whereas Elizabeth was vivacious as well as attractive, took trouble with her appearance and her clothes, and had acquired some education and polish in spite of her parents' difficulties – she was a reader as well as a talker.[4] Sam took trouble with his love letters; although none survive, the words of a young Cambridge contemporary wooing his future wife suggest the style of the times:

Endeared Sweetheart, When I was last with you there fell into my Bosom such a spark of Love that nothing will quench it but Yourself. The Nature of this Love, is, I hope sincere, the measure of it great, and as far as I know my own Heart it is right and genuine. The very bare probability of success ravished my Heart with Joy . . . I hope the Lord has given You in part your father's Spirit, and has made You all glorious within, he has beautified your Body, very pleasant are You to me. You are in my Heart to live and die in waiting on You; and I extremely please Myself in loving You, and I like my Affections the better because they tell me they are only placed upon You . . . sweet Mrs Betty as I have given my Heart to You, You ought in return to give me Yours, and You cannot in Equity deny it me.

Whether or not Pepys wrote love letters as frank and delightful as this one, Elizabeth found him an eloquent and persuasive lover, and she was ready to be wooed and won.[5]

They were married at St Margaret's, Westminster, on 1 December 1655. Religious ceremonies had been declared invalid since August 1653, but churches were still used for the civil ceremonies that replaced them, and this one was presided over by a senior administrative figure, Richard Sherwyn, secretary to the Treasury commissioners and justice of the peace for Westminster.[6] The notice of the civil ceremony on 1 December reads 'Samuel Peps of this parish gent and Elizabeth March-ant De Snt. Michell, of Martin's in the ffields Spinster. Published october 15th, 22, 29 And were married by Richard Sherwyn Esq. one of Justices of the Peace of the Cittie and lyberties of Westm. December 1st Ri. Sherwyn.' But the Westminster ceremony was entirely eclipsed in the minds of the bride and groom by what they always remembered as their proper wedding, which took place on 10 October. This was the anniversary they celebrated with merriment and, when it came to the tenth year, with dancing.[7] What they recalled was their wedding *night*, meaning the consummation, and the obvious explanation is that they went through a private – and unrecorded – religious ceremony on that day, which allowed Pepys to bed his so much desired bride. This was for them the real thing.

It was also two weeks before her fifteenth birthday, which fell on 23 October. If this makes Elizabeth a child bride in our eyes, child brides were common enough; marriage was legal for girls at the age of twelve. The gentle and civilized John Evelyn, for instance, married his wife (in 1647) when he was twenty-six and she was twelve; and although he did not begin to cohabit with her until she was fourteen, she had a miscarriage at fifteen and her first full-term child two years later.[8] Pepys bought a ring from a goldsmith near the new Exchange in the Strand – so perhaps the wedding took place in this part of town – and Elizabeth wore a petticoat adorned with gold lace.[9] Bride and groom both showed what he called 'bridal respect' and 'kindness' towards one another.[10] Afterwards they celebrated at a tavern in Old Fish Street in the City, not necessarily with family, because weddings were rarely large affairs, and the families may not have been inclined to rejoice much, the Pepyses regretting Sam's romantic folly, the St Michels regarding a poor clerk as an unsatisfactory match for the daughter of a noble French house.[11] And after the meal the poor clerk must have taken her back to his servant's room in the attics of Whitehall. Arthur Bryant wrote of this moment, 'And perhaps, than what was theirs at that moment, life offers nothing better'; but his tender view is hardly borne out by what happened next.[12]

Since neither the St Michels nor the Pepyses were in a position to help the young couple, they were left to get on with their life as best they could. Things did not go well for them. The living was not easy, with one room not really their own and up a great many stairs, which Pepys sometimes referred to as his 'turret'. They had almost no money, his health was poor, she was adolescent, with her head full of the French romances she enjoyed reading. It was not that she was impractical or idle: 'How she used to make coal fires, and wash my foul clothes with her own hand for me, poor wretch! in my little room,' he remembered later.[13] But she could also weep, scold and storm, and her periods were monthly dramas that needed help and comfort he had no idea how to give. She was a virgin when they married, and he may have been just about one too, given how nervous he was of catching diseases from loose-living girls. No doubt he had engaged in much fumbling, but neither knew much about sex, and he was desperate for it. He needed help and comfort too, for his own agonies and embarrassments. The symptoms of the stone grew worse all the time, and by now he was probably suffering some pain and difficulty in urinating, and tenderness in those parts; while she, by dreadful coincidence, developed what he called boils on 'the lip of her *chose*'.[14] She was suffering from a condition well known to modern doctors but untreatable then, in which the glands at the entrance to the vagina become blocked and a cyst is formed, producing abscesses that are not only painful but also make sexual intercourse virtually impossible at times.[15] He was in no way to blame, but she may have suspected he was. It would be hard to imagine a worse recipe for a honeymoon.

The Montagus knew nothing about the extra presence among the servants in the Whitehall lodgings. Pepys seems to have kept Elizabeth out of their way very efficiently, because it was not until November 1660 that his cousin took notice of her for the first time.[16] In any case Montagu had many important things on his mind, and Jemima was about to give birth again at Hinchingbrooke. In October 1655 he was appointed an Admiralty commissioner, and in December she presented him with twin sons. One was loyally named Oliver, the other given the family name of John. No sooner were they baptized than the great Oliver directed Montagu's career in a new direction, appointing him general-at-sea and joint commander, with Blake, of the English battle fleet. This was in January 1656, and he prepared to set sail for the Mediterranean almost at once, with instructions to seek a permanent station there for the English. As a complete novice at sea, he took navigation manuals and models of rigged ships to study in his cabin aboard his flagship, the *Naseby*. Pepys saw him off from Lambeth when he embarked.[17]

Then Pepys returned to his discontented bride. The basic trouble must have been their medical problems, but whatever else started them quarrelling – her disappointment in the daily reality of marriage, his disappointment in her response to his attempts at love-making, his jealousy when she smiled too sunnily at his cheerful and doubtless flirtatious friends, or hers when he stayed out late – both had tempers that flared up into violent rows. Had she become pregnant, they would have faced serious practical difficulties, but she would at least have been absorbed in preparing for the child. Only there was no sign of pregnancy. Pepys's failure to father children has always been attributed to the effects of the surgery he underwent in 1658, so it is worth pointing out that none were forthcoming in the three preceding years.[18] Love in a turret was not what either of them had imagined or hoped, and she was wretched. She simmered with resentment and complained to sympathetic friends; and then one day she simply walked out and did not come back. The message to her husband was as clear as could be. He had failed.

Pepys was not accustomed to failure – he was the success of the family, the boy who did well and won scholarships – and the separation from Elizabeth, which lasted for many months, was terrible to him. He felt it as a wound, an insult, an affront to his dignity as man and lover. Afterwards, he took care to destroy all the letters relating to this episode and hated any mention of it.[19] Years later he would still brood unforgivingly if something reminded him of what she had done; while she used it as a weapon against him, knowing she could wound merely by mentioning it. It had been her grand gesture, and became her way of holding her own in the battle of their marriage, with the implied threat of a repeat performance. The humiliation in front of his friends and family was cruel, and the loss of his bedmate, so ardently wooed, almost too much to bear. Like Milton, he had married in a glow of expectation, only to be forced back into miserable chastity.[20]

Classically, an injured wife goes home to her parents, and this may be what Elizabeth did, to begin with at any rate. Not much was to be expected of them beyond affection, since they notably lacked any grasp of the practical side of life. Her father was a quixotic figure full of ingenious schemes – perpetual-motion machines and smoke-free chimneys – and her brother Balthasar had been reared to give himself the airs of a gentleman, with no resources to back them. The father's story filters down to us through Balthasar's not entirely reliable pen, which described him as 'a Gentleman, Extreamely well-bread', born a Catholic and converted to the Protestant faith. The conversion came about in his youth, while he was fighting as a professional soldier in Germany, and it allegedly lost him his inheritance in France. He next got himself a position in the suite of Princess Henrietta Maria as gentleman carver – a superior attendant at table in the formal court life of the day – when she travelled to England in 1625 to become Charles I's queen. This job he lost after a dispute with one of the queen's friars turned into a fight. Silence then, until he appeared in Ireland in 1639, and there won the hand of Dorothea, thirty-year-old widow of a gentleman of Cork and daughter of Sir Francis Kingsmill. The marriage was not approved by her family, and things went downhill for the couple from the start. Balthasar and Elizabeth were apparently both born in 1640, in Devon, where their mother had inherited land.[21] But this and everything else they possessed was lost in various unlucky episodes. They wandered from England to France, from Flanders to Germany; sometimes he served as a soldier, once he was imprisoned. He claimed to have fought under Cromwell in Ireland, from where his wife fled to Flanders without him, having first pawned whatever they had to finance her flight – so running away from husbands was something Elizabeth learnt from her mother.

In 1652 Madame de St Michel was alone in Paris with her two children. She was persuaded to hand them over to Catholic friends, who placed Elizabeth in an Ursuline convent and Balthasar as page to the papal nuncio, a recollection that provoked him to a flash of wit: with such a start, he told Pepys, he might have ended up as either a cardinal or a catamite. The children were rescued by their indignant father, who carried the whole family off to London; this was shortly before Elizabeth met Pepys.[22] The timing of Balthasar's story is vague and the accuracy doubtful, since he wrote it down with the specific intention of proving that his sister was a staunch Protestant, whereas it is clear from Pepys's own account that the Catholic faith never lost its hold on her: when, for instance, he bought a mass book for himself in 1660 and sat up late reading it, it gave 'great pleasure to my wife to hear that that she long ago was so well acquainted with'.[23] The circumstances of her upbringing suggest why she was in some ways mature for her age, and also restless and flighty. She seems to have moved on from her parents to stay with friends called Palmer, whose name crops up when Pepys mentioned what he always called his 'differences' with her. Palmer was a lawyer and may have pointed out to her the difficulties of the situation of a separated wife, and encouraged a reconciliation.

The St Michel parents present another puzzle in Pepys's life. During the whole period of the Diary he never once visited them or received them in his house. Elizabeth went to see them and took them gifts, money and old clothes, and even small jobs to do for Pepys, but he went to almost farcical lengths to avoid speaking to her father: once, for instance, when he saw him in Westminster Hall after dropping Elizabeth, he sent a porter with an anonymous message across the Hall to St Michel, remaining at a safe distance to observe his baffled response.[24] Elizabeth was equally resistant to their coming face to face.

Family arrangements are often puzzling to outsiders, and this is more bizarre than most. Perhaps the St Michels failed to encourage her to return to Pepys when she left him, and he furiously resented the fact. Perhaps he took a vow not to forgive them, since taking vows was a habit of his, and this became one of the vows he kept. Later, when questioned by Jemima Montagu about 'how I did treate my wife's father and mother', he gave her 'a good account', but did not elaborate further – understandably, given the actual situation.[25]

During this barely documented and unhappy period of Sam's life we must assume he went on living in the Whitehall attics and attending to whatever instructions he received from his cousin and patron, General Montagu. His orders from aboard the *Naseby* to 'my Servant Samuell Pepys at my Lodginges in Whitehalle' were short and sharp: 'You are upon sight hereoff . . .' and 'Hereoff you are not to faile'; and Pepys's letters were formal and respectful, as was to be expected, addressing his employer as 'your Honour', 'my honoured maister' and 'My Lord'. And, whatever his personal troubles, he kept a keen eye on public events and was ready to report discreetly on the struggle between the army republicans, who distrusted Cromwell, and those who wanted to give him greater power, of whom Montagu was one. Another of Cromwell's keenest supporters was George Downing, now a well-established diplomat, MP and highly placed figure at the Exchequer; and about this time Pepys found himself his second and more official job as one of Downing's clerks. The improvement in his income must have been very welcome as a way of impressing Elizabeth.

Downing saw that Pepys was talented, but Pepys, though always respectful of Downing's intellectual powers, never liked him. You can understand why. An example of his brutality came in the winter of 1656, when the case of James Naylor, a Quaker accused of blasphemy, was brought before the House. It excited Downing particularly. Pronouncing that 'We are God's executioners, and ought to be tender of his honour,' he urged that if Naylor escaped the death penalty, he should at least be pilloried, whipped – in the event he received 310 strokes – and branded, and his tongue bored through with a hot iron for good measure. 'You ought to do something with that tongue that has bored through God. You ought to bore his tongue through,' insisted the religious Downing.[26] Sir Gilbert Pickering proposed that hard labour and imprisonment would be enough punishment, and Cromwell himself attempted to intervene, but the savage sentences were carried out, while Naylor expressed forgiveness of his tormentors, and the crowd who watched him branded and bored stood bare-headed and silent in sympathy. Downing's combination of bigotry and cruelty was far removed from Pepys's tolerance and what has been called his 'miscellaneous religious enjoyment'.[27]

His other employer was back in England in the autumn. Montagu had justified Cromwell's confidence in him and brought with him treasure captured from the Spanish fleet on its return from South America. Although it had actually been taken by another commander, the poet Edmund Waller greeted the new general-at-sea's homecoming with the spoils of battle in an elegant couplet:

> With these returns victorious MONTAGU
> With laurels in his hand, and half Peru.[28]

The cargoes of the captured Spanish ships were thought to be worth £600,000 – one estimate put it at a million – and the money was desperately needed to pay for the war with Spain. Montagu wrote piously to Cromwell's secretary of state, John Thurloe, ascribing the triumph to God: 'Blessed be his name who hath looked upon the low condition of the nation, and hath turned the reproaches of wicked men with shame upon their own faces . . . Indeed, my heart is very much warmed with the apprehension of the singular providence of God in bringing this about'.[29] But the singular providence of God did not prevent the treasure from being plundered on its way to London, and by the time it arrived to be counted half of it had disappeared. 'A private captain, they say, hath got to his own share £60,000, and many private mariners £10,000 a man; and this is so universal amongst the seamen and taken in the heat of fight, that it is not possible to get it again, or any part of it.' This was Thurloe's account, and, while it may have exaggerated the figures, it acknowledged the real problem, which was the assumption by both officers and men that they were entitled to help themselves to a large part of what they had risked their lives for – the more so since most of them were owed many months of pay.[30] Montagu was personally blameless; it was his first experience of the troubles associated with prizes (ships seized at sea carrying valuable cargoes) that were to plague him later. For the present, in spite of the disappointment, he was thanked in parliament, and there was a day of official thanksgiving on 5 November. He remained long enough in London to attend some scientific meetings where there was also political talk, with Pepys at his side.[31] Then he went home to Hinchingbrooke, leaving Pepys to sort out practical problems connected with prize goods.

Pepys's letters to his master, the earliest of his writings to survive, offer cool glimpses of what was happening in London without venturing opinions of his own. He wrote about the debate over whether Cromwell should be succeeded by an elected ruler or one of his own family; he described rehearsals of a song with Latin words, specially written in Cromwell's honour, giving the fatuous text without comment. A thumbnail sketch of the behaviour of Mr Feake, a preacher from the extreme religious sect of the Fifth Monarchists, newly released from prison, describes Feake preaching from a window, being silenced by order of the lord mayor and responding by saying he knows neither why he was imprisoned nor why released, and further, that 'the Spirit which warranted him to speake was above Mr Protectors command, and therefore much more Mr Mayors'.[32] There is just enough satirical edge in Pepys's account to suggest he is more impressed by Feake's wit than by the heavy hand of authority. More comedy inspired by religious differences came in a later letter, which tells how Cromwell, on being shown some 'popish vestments' confiscated from Jesuits, got his gentlemen to dress up in them, 'causing abundance of mirth'.[33]

The whole year of 1657, so privately wretched for Pepys, was crammed with public events. In January Downing, speaking in the House, urged the crown on Cromwell. In March Montagu was in London to bear the sword of state when Cromwell gave an audience to parliament in the Banqueting Hall. Over the next months Cromwell was repeatedly urged to take the title of 'King' and repeatedly declined on grounds of conscience. He described kingship as 'a mere feather in a man's hat'; in the end he went close to taking the feather. In a ceremony in Westminster Hall in late June, with the coronation stone in place beneath the royal chair of Scotland, he put on a robe of purple lined with ermine and a sword of state, and swore the new lord protector's oath of office, sceptre in hand. He took the title of 'Highness' for himself and his wife, and his sons became lords. There was a great deal of velvet and gold, there were prayers and shouts, trumpets and hurrahs. Montagu was at Cromwell's side and accompanied him in the coach that drove him through the crowds to Whitehall.[34] No doubt all the clerks of Whitehall and Westminster were in the streets for the occasion. Montagu's ascent continued. Cromwell appointed him to his new Advisory Council. In August Admiral Blake died and was given a hero's burial in the Abbey; it left Montagu as sole general-at-sea. At the end of the year he was offered, and accepted, one of Cromwell's new peerages. He was now Baron Montagu.

Pepys's lowly work continued meanwhile. He busied himself with dispatching goods, running errands to Lady Montagu's family, the Crews, in Lincoln's Inn and the management of servants in the Whitehall household. In December he was in trouble about a maid who had left to be married, without asking permission, to a fellow she had met at a cookhouse. Pepys, who had also omitted to ask permission for his marriage, defended himself from any complicity in her behaviour and claimed that he was never out at night himself except on Sundays, after dining at his father's house. When immediate forgiveness was not forthcoming, he abased himself: 'The losse of your Honours good word I am too sure will prove as much my undoing, as hitherto it hath beene my best friend.'[35] He did not lose his position, but the gap between the situations of the two cousins remained wide and sometimes humiliating.

One trouble improved before the end of the year, while another got worse. A bare mention of his housekeeping expenses in a December letter indicates that things were at least partly patched up between him and Elizabeth: 'my selfe and my wife' were spending four shillings a week on their food.[36] He had at least come clean to his employer about being married. But he was hardly able to enjoy Elizabeth's return, since the pain produced by the stone had become too bad to endure. The bitter cold of that winter aggravated it, and he took the decision to seek a surgeon. He saw it as his only hope of escaping from 'a condition of constant and dangerous and most painful sickness and low condition and poverty'.[37]

Surgery was not an easy choice. It was known to be a hideously unpleasant procedure and a gamble besides. 'In this great and dangerous Operation, life and death doe so wrastle together, that no man can tell which will have the victory,' warned one treatise for surgeons, and patients were recommended to make their peace with God before undergoing it.[38] Yet, in spite of the risk, the operation was always in demand, because of the 'scarce credible' pain caused by the stone.[39] Pepys chose as his surgeon Thomas Hollier of St Thomas's and Bart's, a staunch Cromwellian who had been operating for thirty years and had besides stitched up the wounds of many commonwealth fighters. The operation was not to take place in what was called the 'cutting ward' of the hospital, however. Pepys was to be a private patient and was happy enough to find himself an ideal arrangement. His cousin Jane, née Pepys and now Turner, his friend since the boyhood visits to her father at Ashtead, offered to nurse him in her house in Salisbury Court. Her husband was a successful lawyer, she had one or two small children, and she was an active, cheerful and generous woman. Unhesitatingly she put herself and her house at his disposal. Her offer meant he would be near his anxious parents. Pepys's father went about mobilizing as many members of the family as he could to pray for Sam during his ordeal; the prayers of one maternal aunt, a 'poor, religious, well-meaning, good humble soul', 'did do me good among the many good souls that did by my father's desires pray for me when I was cut of the stone, and which God did hear'.[40] No doubt Elizabeth prayed too; at least one hopes so.

Patients were advised to have the operation in the spring. Both cold and heat were considered unfavourable, and the surgeon hoped to have bright sunlight to help him to see what he was doing. Pepys duly settled on the end of March. The preparations took some time. The sick person was advised to cultivate a calm frame of mind and to avoid anger or sadness; he should feel confidence in the surgeon, even affection (all this modern-sounding advice comes from contemporary manuals). And surgeons were encouraged to give their patients an honest account of what they were to undergo. Wine was not allowed during the preparatory weeks, only sweet drinks made from almond, cucumber and melon, and a diet of fresh meat, chicken, pigeon, eggs, butter, barley and water-gruel. In the days before the operation Pepys would have been given warm baths – possibly an unprecedented experience – and kept in a warm bed. His belly would be rubbed with unguents, he would be bled in the arm and given gentle purges, until the final day, when he was left in peace and simply served with a good meal.

The operation was performed in the patient's bedroom. On the day of the surgery a lightly boiled egg was recommended, and a talk with a religious adviser. For Sam, whether he ate the egg or spoke with a clergyman, the day was 26 March. He had a last bath, was dried, told to take a turn or two about the room and offered a specially prescribed drink made of liquorice, marshmallow, cinnamon, milk, rosewater and the whites of fifteen eggs – six ounces to be swallowed with an ounce of syrup of althea and other herbs, a large dose for a nervous man to swallow.[41] After this he was asked to position himself on a table, possibly covered with a straw-filled bag into which he could be settled while the process of binding him up began. Some surgeons thought it wise to say a few reassuring words at this point, because the binding was terrifying to many patients. They were trussed like chickens, their legs up, a web of long linen strips wound round legs, neck and arms that was intended to hold them still and keep their limbs out of the surgeon's way. The instructions for the binding alone take up several pages of one manual; and when it was done the patient was further bound to the table. He was shaved around his privy parts, and a number of strong men were positioned to hold him fast: 'two whereof may hold him by the knees, and feet, and two by the Arme-holes, and hands . . . The hands are also sometimes tyed to the knees, with a particular rowler, or the knees by themselves, by the help of a pulley fastened into the table.'[42] Meanwhile the surgeon lubricated his instruments with warm water and oil or milk of almonds: the catheter, the probe, the itinerarium, the specular, the pincers, small hooks and so forth; he also had powder to stop bleeding, sponges and cordial waters to hand. There were no anaesthetics, and alcohol was certainly not allowed to a patient undergoing surgery to the bladder.

The surgeon got to work. First he inserted a thin silver instrument, the itinerarium, through the penis into the bladder to help position the stone. Then he made the incision, about three inches long and a finger's breadth from the line running between scrotum and anus, and into the neck of the bladder, or just below it. The patient's face was sponged as the incision was made. The stone was sought, found and grasped with pincers; the more speedily it could be got out the better. Once out, the wound was not stitched – it was thought best to let it drain and cicatrize itself – but simply washed and covered with a dressing, or even kept open at first with a small roll of soft cloth known as a tent, dipped in egg white. A plaster of egg yolk, rose vinegar and anointing oils was then applied.[43]

Pepys, no doubt by now fainting with shock and pain, was unbound and moved to his warmed bed. A cold syrup of lemon juice, radishes and marshmallow was ready for him to drink.[44] The first dressing was left for twelve hours, and the thighs were kept tied to help the wound heal naturally. There was no question of getting out of bed for a week. Broth, cinnamon water and soothing drinks were given during the first day of recovery, and when he felt like something more an austere vegetable diet of succory (chicory), endive and spinach was recommended. There was further anointing of his belly with oils; oil of earthworms was held in readiness against possible convulsions, and a purge given if necessary, but only after two weeks. Fever, insomnia and pain were all to be expected, and above all, you would think, acute anxiety. Was the bladder healing? How soon might he expect it to function normally again? If he moved, would he tear the just healing wound open? Had the surgeon missed the prostate, something the manual worried about? Pepys was the type of patient who is likely to have read it for himself. We know that he sought information and anatomical explanations from the doctors who attended him, as he recalled when he saw a corpse dissected at the Surgeons' Hall in 1663, and took a particular interest in the bladder and kidneys.[45]

Recovery, for those who did not succumb to secondary infection, was expected to take thirty to forty days. Pepys made it in thirty-five. It was a triumph. By his own account he was himself again by 1 May: exactly two years later he wrote in his Diary for 1 May 1660: 'This day I do count myself to have had full two years of perfect cure for the stone.' Hollier could be proud of his work, especially considering the size of Pepys's stone, described as 'very great' by his medical colleagues; it was as big as a tennis ball, according to Evelyn, who saw it later. Real tennis, the only kind then played, uses very slightly smaller balls than modern lawn tennis, but still with a diameter of about 2¼ inches; the stone must have been exceedingly awkward to get hold of and extract through a three-inch incision.[46] Fortunately Hollier was at the height of his powers as a lithotomist; that year alone he operated successfully on thirty patients. The following year, 1659, was not so good; his first four died, presumably because his instruments had picked up some infectious matter that no warm water or milk of almonds could clear.

Pepys's joy was great, and he declared his intention of celebrating the anniversary of the operation with a dinner for the rest of his life, a plan that proved over-ambitious, but showed how seriously he felt that without the operation he could have expected nothing but sickness and poverty. He also preserved the stone carefully and, when he could afford it, had a special 'Stone-case' made for it, costing twenty-five shillings, in which he displayed it to others who might be considering the operation.[47] His mother, who suffered from the same trouble, although less severely, was lucky enough to void a stone spontaneously two years later; she disposed of hers by tossing it into the fireplace.[48] Nothing marks the difference in their characters more clearly: the tough old woman, incurious, sluttish even, and her neat, purposeful son, intent on understanding, mastering, classifying and teaching. For Sam, with his curiosity and optimism, his stone was something to be investigated, treated, boxed, labelled and shown to anyone interested, and doubtless to some who were not.

He came out of his ordeal with a revival of confidence and energy, and set about putting his life on a new footing. He had kept his two jobs, and both his employers were in high favour, which promised well for his own future. They were also out of town, conveniently enough, while he was recovering and re-establishing himself. Downing was in the Hague as Cromwell's ambassador and part of his intelligence service, and Montagu was at sea, blockading Dunkirk in alliance with the French. While there Montagu invited Cardinal Mazarin to a magnificent banquet aboard the *Naseby* and gave him a tour of the ship. Mazarin was delighted and impressed not only by the ship but also by the young English general, and in particular by his personal devotion to Cromwell; he described him as 'un des gentilhommes du monde le plus franc et mieux intentionné et le plus attaché à la personne de M. le Protecteur'. His attachment was well known; it was also mutual. Cromwell signed himself to Montagu, 'your very affectionate friend Oliver P'.[49] Cromwell's power had never seemed stronger or more stable. The latest royalist conspiracies had been put down and punished, and his name was respected and feared all over Europe. Pepys knew he was serving men close to the very centre of this power. He saw old acquaintances from Cambridge improving their situations in its orbit. One of them, John Dryden, arrived in town and was found some clerking to do for his cousin Pickering, lord chamberlain to Cromwell's household. Another was Pepys's one-time tutor, Samuel Morland, who got himself a place in the intelligence service. Pepys himself needed to shake off the condition of a living-in servant and find a house of his own; and this he set about doing.

5. A House in Axe Yard

Pepys could afford to rent only half a house – 'my poor little house' he still called it after he'd taken over the other half later – but he had an eye for where to live, and perhaps a helping hand from one or the other of his powerful employers, and it was as well placed as could be. Axe Yard was a cul-de-sac in the heart of Westminster. Today government buildings cover the whole area, leaving no trace of the old street pattern, but in 1658 there were twenty-five houses along the length of the Yard, the larger ones inhabited by rich and well-connected families.[1] Its narrow entrance in King Street, where the Axe tavern stood, was only a step away from the King Street gate into Whitehall Palace; and the Yard ran to the edge of St James's Park, giving the houses at that end airy views over the green space.

Whitehall, although it was called a palace, was really nothing more than a vast jumble of houses jostled together between the Thames and St James's Park and cut across by the main road from Charing Cross to Westminster; its most modern building was Inigo Jones's Banqueting House, built for James I and the scene of Charles I's execution. The old buildings were said to consist of something like two thousand rooms, some done up as residences for the ruler – currently Cromwell – and his family; otherwise apartments were awarded to the most favoured servants of the state, Edward Montagu among them. As in the college courtyards of Cambridge or Oxford, you reached people's rooms through a multitude of separate doorways and stairs. There were three acres of garden and two of bowling green – an orchard in Henry VIII's time – as well as a great hall, a council chamber, a chapel, guard rooms and several long galleries used for exercise and conversation; and there was a wharf, since provisions came mostly by water, and several sets of stairs to the river.

If you turned right where Axe Yard joined King Street you were soon at Westminster Palace, another jumble of buildings, halls and chapels in which parliament sat, both commons and lords, as well as various courts of law. The Painted Chamber was here, and the Great

Hall, where booksellers and other shopkeepers put up their stalls; it opened on to New Palace Yard. The offices of the Exchequer were also housed in Westminster Palace, which made Axe Yard especially convenient for an Exchequer clerk; and in fact Pepys's boss George Downing had a house of his own in Axe Yard, in which Pepys's colleague and friend John Hawley was currently living. To Downing he was 'my clerk and servant', to Pepys 'my brother Hawley'.[2]

So, to the right the Exchequer, the Great Hall with its friendly shopkeepers, and parliament; to the left the gate into Whitehall in which the Montagu lodgings were situated, where Pepys lived until he acquired his Axe Yard house and still thought of as a second home, because some of his books remained there in 1660.[3] It can have taken no more than a hand cart to bring his few other belongings across from his room. He and Elizabeth had something like twenty shillings a week to live on, out of which there was the rent and taxes to pay, and he expected her to keep daily accounts 'even to a bunch of carrot and a ball of whiteing'.[4] At this stage they could have owned little more by way of furniture than a table and a few chairs, a bed big enough for the two of them and a small bed for the maid, because, in shaking off the condition of living-in servant himself, Pepys had become for the first time the employer of a servant of his own.

In August 1658 he accordingly installed his 'family' of three, himself, his wife, who had reached the mature age of seventeen, and their servant, Jane Birch: a trio where they had been a duet, and perhaps the trio form suited them better. They had five rooms and a yard in which they bred pigeons. It was a great deal more spacious than the single room he and Elizabeth had shared at the start of their marriage; but still, when master, mistress and maid were together in half a small house with its rooms opening straight into each other, it meant that a bad mood, an illness or a hangover headache was likely to involve all three of them. And since tact was not the foremost quality of either Sam or Elizabeth, much was expected of Jane.

She was fourteen. Her job was to make the fires and clean the grates, sweep and wash the floors, fetch water and empty slops, do much of the family laundry – sometimes rising at two in the morning to get started on it – shop for provisions, give a hand with cooking and clear and clean up after meals. Beyond this, she must help in keeping the peace. We know from Pepys that she turned out good cakes and refused point blank to kill a turkey, or chickens or pigeons. She seems to have been able to read, because she owned a book, something unusual for a country girl, as Jane was.[5] In the country she had left behind a mother, to whom she was attached, and a small brother, Wayneman; and she had an elder one already settled in London as a groom, and married. Pepys paid her about £2 year. He felt free to beat her with a broom when he was displeased, although this was not often.[6] Intelligent, merry and discreet, she was destined to play a long and important part in his life, and he in hers.

A web of friends and colleagues surrounded the Pepyses in their new home. Recovered from his operation, he had taken up with his old clubbing set again; they talked, they drank, they sang and swapped rude stories and played cards in the taverns. Harper's was close to the Axe Yard, and Wilkinson's Cookshop, also in King Street, served food and drink. The names of the friends with whom he passed the time of day and night crop up in the early pages of the diary: Dick Scobell, Will Symons, Peter Luellin, James Chetwynd, Tom Doling, Matthew and Tom Lea, Sam Samford, the Ashwell cousins, George and Dick Vines, Sam Hartlib, Robin Shaw, Jack Spicer, John Hawley, Will Bowyer. These are the clerks of Cromwell's London, and we can imagine them busy at their office desks, standing in doorways, hurrying through the streets, worrying about their lodgings, some idling, some joking, some lazy, some ambitious, rising or at least hopeful young men in the great man's administration, proud to be where the action was, their jobs mostly secured through family connections and recommendations. Will Bowyer was only a door-keeper, but his father Robert was an usher at the Exchequer, and he prided himself on keeping a paternal eye on the clerks and often invited them home to his houseful of daughters in Westminster, and sometimes to his country place in Buckinghamshire. He and his wife made friends with Elizabeth, and Sam sometimes called him 'father Bowyer'. The Vines household was another hospitable place, also headed by a long-established Exchequer officer living in New Palace Yard; the sons were musical, and Sam could take his fiddle round to play with them in the evening. There was more music to be had in Axe Yard, at the house of Mrs Crisp, a friend of the Montagus who played the harpsichord and was teaching her son Laud to sing; her house was large and grandly furnished. The house next to hers belonged to Samuel Hartlib, scholar and refugee from Prussia and a close friend of John Milton, now quite blind and living near Cripplegate in the City; young Hartlib was a government clerk and one of Pepys's circle. Sir Edward Widdrington, related both to the speaker of the House and the public orator at Cambridge, was another Axe Yard resident; so was Thomas Wade, a naval administrator. Other neighbours who quickly became friends were John and Elizabeth Hunt, young like the Pepyses and still without children; they came from East Anglia, and she had a family connection with the Cromwells that may have helped her husband to his job with the Excise Office.

At the centre of Whitehall was 'His Highness the Lord Protector' himself. Cromwell was fifty-nine this year and his authority appeared incontestable. He had vigorously put down and punished the latest royalist conspiracies; he had won Dunkirk and Jamaica for England and defeated Spain decisively. In Europe he was acknowledged and respected as a great leader, and at home his government was strong and stable; but many problems remained, one being the disaffection of former colleagues who held to the Good Old Cause of true republicanism. Another was finance: every official at the Exchequer knew that the army and the navy were clamouring for money, and that the soldiers and sailors went unpaid month after month, sometimes to the point of mutinous outbreaks. Reforming the financial system had to be Cromwell's next task. But even as the Pepys family was settling into Axe Yard, Cromwell was moving away from both his problems and his triumphs. The illness and death of his favourite daughter caused him a profound, distracting grief. He was with her at Hampton Court when she died in early August, and four days later had her buried in Westminster Abbey. He returned to Whitehall, and, through his shock and sorrow, became aware that he himself was unwell. On 26 August he dined with his old friend Bulstrode Whitelocke and admitted as much. And now it was suddenly obvious to everyone who saw him. The alarming news spread, and on Sunday, 29 August, prayers for the lord protector were said in the churches. On the Monday a hurricane blew over England. It was a common belief that a high wind heralded the death of a great person, one shared by Pepys, who alluded to it more than once in his Diary. Now it was seen as a portent of the end of an era, and so Andrew Marvell described the winds:

Out of the binder's hand the sheaves they tore,
And thrashed the harvest in the airy floor;
Or of huge trees, whose growth with his did rise,
The deep foundations opened to the skies . . .
And as through air his wasting spirits flowed,
The universe laboured beneath their load.[7]

But it also marked the beginning of a new era, for, as the hurricane blew, a Lincolnshire schoolboy called Isaac Newton amused himself computing its force by noting the difference in the distances he could jump, first with, and then against, the wind.[8]

On 2 September a council meeting was called. Edward Montagu had returned to London from his ship to be there. Cromwell was too ill to attend; in any case he had understood that he was not going to recover. When his attendant encouraged him to drink a cordial to help him sleep, he replied, 'It is not my design to drink or to sleep, but my design is to make what haste I can to be gone.' In the afternoon of the next day he died. Death had come upon him with terrible speed, reaching him on the anniversary of two of his greatest battles, Dunbar and Worcester, at which he had crushed Charles Stuart. The country was stunned, much as it had been in January 1649 at the death of Charles I. Thurloe wrote to Downing in the Hague that Cromwell 'died more lamented than any man hath done in this or the generations past. His name is and will be precious to all generations, and is now even to those who murmured at him in his life tyme.'[9] Downing put his household in Holland into mourning and prepared to travel to London for the funeral.

Edward Montagu immediately signed the proclamation supporting the appointment of Richard Cromwell to succeed his father, while the republican army leaders prepared to oppose him. Montagu also drew up his own declaration of loyalty to Richard – the two men were much of an age – and expressed his confidence that he would 'carry on the glorious work of liberty and reformation' begun by his father; and he pledged loyalty to government by a single person, two houses of parliament and a commonwealth, repudiating republicans and royalists alike. He led a deputation of naval officers to present this to the new protector, who received them with obvious pleasure and offered to pay special attention to naval affairs.[10] As a gesture of personal friendship, Richard Cromwell also appointed Montagu colonel of a regiment of horse. Pepys felt the benefit, because the new colonel made him regimental muster-master and secretary, for which he was handsomely paid at £50 a quarter without, in his own words, 'taking any care in the world for'.[11] It was his first direct experience of how government funds were distributed through patronage. A man who received one well-paid sinecure could simply hand out further sinecures to chosen underlings. The principle was stored away in Pepys's mental filing system for future use.

Montagu kept his servant and secretary hard at work during the next months as the new protector's supporters faced his republican opponents across the council table. In October he went to sea with a squadron from Portsmouth to deal with privateers off Dunkirk, but he was back in November for Council of State and Treasury business. The preparations for Cromwell's state funeral were under way. It was staged like that of a king and directly modelled on James I's. Ironically, there was a suggestion that royalists should be ordered out of London as a security measure, but Montagu opposed this, saying there was no fear of disturbance.[12] Cost was not spared, and the preparations took so long that the ceremony had to be postponed from 9 November until the 23rd, twelve weeks after the death. Cromwell's body had been buried privately much earlier, but now six horses drew his effigy – crowned, with a sceptre and clothed in royal robes – from Somerset House, where it had lain in state, accompanied by a procession of mourners; the most important of these had been summoned to be there by eight in the morning, ticket in hand. The start was delayed because of disputes about precedence among the foreign ambassadors.

All were on foot, and they proceeded very slowly along the Strand and past Charing Cross, turning south into King Street, and through Whitehall and on to the Abbey. Drummers and trumpeters, banners and horses decorated with plumes and escutcheons, went with them. Pickering held up the train of Lord Fleetwood, Cromwell's son-in-law and chief mourner. Republicans and their enemies walked together. Montagu himself was among Cromwell's peers, his baron's train carried behind him, and Downing, who must have been staying in Axe Yard, was in the procession as teller of the Exchequer. He was a friend of Milton, who was there leaning on the arm of Hartlib, and two younger poets, Marvell and Dryden, were also in the line, with all the time in the world to meditate their ceremonial verses on the death.[13] Bulstrode Whitelocke was one of the twelve pallbearers. A group of Cromwell's favourite musicians was there. Mr Secretary Thurloe was among the high officials, and General Monck had come from Scotland. All along the way railings had been put up and infantry in new red coats trimmed with black stood two deep against them. Pepys's 'father Bowyer' was there as usher of the Exchequer, and his old tutor Samuel Morland as clerk of the Signet, and Henry Scobell, clerk to the House of Lords and uncle of Pepys's friend Dick; and Mr Creed, secretary to the general-at-sea, Montagu, probably Richard Creed, whose younger brother John was to become Pepys's close associate and rival. Among all these, where was Pepys? It is inconceivable that he was not keeping a keen eye on the show, and even possible he was admitted to the procession as one of Montagu's servants, since numbers of such lowly figures were allowed to take their places among the great ones.

Most of those present must have known that Cromwell's body had already been buried, and one hostile witness noted that 'there was none that Cried', and that the soldiers were drinking and taking tobacco in the streets as the procession passed: this was John Evelyn, but even he observed that there were 'innumerable mourners'.[14] They processed for most of the short winter day, and when they reached the abbey the effigy was carried by ten gentlemen to the east end and installed in a magnificent structure; ticket holders were admitted, but there was no further ceremony, and the mourners dispersed, by now certainly eager for something to eat.[15]

Richard Cromwell was a reluctant successor, with none of the instincts of a leader or even a politician. As one harsh chronicler put it, 'The old Vulture died, and out of his ashes rose a Titmouse.'[16] His council was split from the start between hostile republicans, mostly army officers, and supporters, among them Montagu. Montagu was at Hinchingbrooke for Christmas and to greet another newborn son, his fifth: rather strikingly for a declared anti-royalist, he named the boy Charles. While he was at home there were elections, and although as a peer he was not concerned in them directly, he helped Thurloe, another of the new protector's supporters, to win Huntingdon. The absence of any letters from Pepys in London to Hinchingbrooke this winter – there are letters for 1657 and 1659 – suggests that Montagu may have summoned him to come down and lend a hand with the election, allowing him to pay his respects to his Lady and to visit his uncle Robert at Brampton at the same time. It is obvious from the way he mentions the Huntingdon gentry in the early part of his Diary that he was used to seeing them, recognized them in church and knew all their names. It is also clear that a relationship of trust and friendship was well established between Pepys and Jemima Montagu, who showed him 'extraordinary love and kindness' when she came to London in 1660.[17]

Montagu took up his duties as general-at-sea again and sailed for the Baltic in March 1659 to take command of the fleet supporting the Swedes against the Danes in their long-running quarrel. On leaving he told Richard Cromwell he would rather see him in his grave than that he should give way to the republican plots being hatched against him.[18] Montagu anchored off Elsinore in April. He was there to ensure that the Baltic should be kept open to English trade, something the Dutch alliance with the Danes threatened. From the Hague, Downing was writing advice on naval matters to Thurloe, recommending that the English should adopt the convoy system for all their trade. But naval policy was the last thing anyone in London was concentrating on, as the army leaders applied every sort of pressure to make Richard Cromwell submit to their will. In April a despondent Whitelocke left London; in May he was accused of corresponding with Charles Stuart and had to defend himself stoutly. Evelyn noted 'Anarchy & confusion' in his diary; but Evelyn also managed to attend a performance of an opera by William D'Avenant at the Cockpit in Drury Lane in May, finding it 'prodigious, that in a time of such a publique Consternation, such a Vanity should be kept up or permitted; I being ingag'd with company, could not decently resist the going to see it, though my heart smote me for it'.[19] However Evelyn's heart smote him, the persistence of art, music and poetry was one of the few encouraging aspects of the times; Milton, still officially a servant of the state, had begun to write *Paradise Lost*.

Pepys, music lover as he was, is unlikely to have been at D'Avenant's opera for the good reason that he too was preparing to go to sea. His activities emerge from obscurity and guesswork in May, when Montagu summoned him to the Baltic as a messenger who could be trusted to carry private papers. Pepys himself said he had no idea what he was taking to his master, though it has been conjectured that he took letters from both Richard Cromwell and the republican army leader Charles Fleetwood, each asking for the support of the fleet.[20] But it was too late for Richard, and on 24 May he signed a paper promising to retire. By now Pepys was well on his way north aboard a ketch, the *Hind*. He made friends with Captain Richard Country – 'my little Captain that I loved', he called him later – and on the 26th he handed his packet of letters to Montagu, who gave no indication at all of what they contained or what his response to them might be.[21] He simply had Pepys courteously entertained aboard the *Naseby* by his lieutenant, David Lambert, then sent him straight back to London.[22]

Pepys was home in Axe Yard on 8 June 1659, in time for Richard Cromwell's formal abdication. Behind the scenes furious plotting was under way. Thurloe had been sacked and had written to Downing to ask him if he wished to continue as English envoy at the Hague under the new government. Downing chose to remain at the Hague, where he was considering his position carefully. Samuel Morland, who had been intercepting letters for Thurloe, provided Charles Stuart with a written account of Montagu's character, describing him as a man of sweet and candid disposition, but extremely cautious, and intimate with very few. 'As for his affection,' he went on, 'he was wholly devoted to old Noll, his country man, and for his sake a great lover of all his family, but a perfect hater of the men that now rule, as he has often told me privately: and I have it from very good hands, that he is at this time very deeply discontented at the present change; insomuch that I verily believe if he ever be gained it is in this conjuncture.' But, Morland warned the king, Montagu had estates, income, wife and many children to consider.[23] Armed with this information, Charles sent his own messengers to the Baltic in July, with a letter offering Montagu great rewards – an earldom, a fortune, whatever he desired – in exchange for his, and the fleet's, support. Montagu replied that the time was not yet ripe. His prudence was well judged, not least because the arrival of the royal envoys coincided with that of Algernon Sidney, a republican MP and councillor sent out to supervise and spy on Montagu by the new republican government in London.

Montagu saw Sidney as a 'mortal enemy', and indeed Sidney charged him with negotiating secretly with Charles, an act of treachery deserving of death.[24] Montagu later told Pepys that he had made up his mind to support Charles that August, but told nobody.[25] Discreet as he was, in London the council stripped him of his peerage, his colonelcy and his place on the council, announced they were reclaiming his Whitehall lodgings and seized many of his private papers. Although Pepys knew nothing, he was in a difficult situation: he could only keep his head down. His discretion at this time was enough to convince Montagu that he could be relied on absolutely and marked him out for serious promotion once the moment came – but Pepys himself had no idea of this. Montagu determined to take the fleet home, informing Sidney that lack of provisions and sickness among the men made it necessary. His captains shared his view, and most of them sailed with him. When he reached the Suffolk coast he was met by the news that a royalist rising in Cheshire had been put down, and two icy and inquisitorial Admiralty commissioners were waiting to come aboard and insist he went straight to London. In London he was questioned further. An informant alleged he was engaged to bring Charles Stuart over. No evidence was found, but the command of the navy effectively passed to its republican vice-admiral, John Lawson. Richard Cromwell wrote to commiserate and suggest that 'out of town' was 'the most proper place for persons that are out of employment'. Montagu agreed, and, since there were no grounds for keeping him in London, he was allowed to go home to Hinchingbrooke.[26]

And there he remained during the last months of 1659, while Pepys kept him informed of what was happening in London. He could not have had a better pair of eyes and ears at his service than this dedicated rover of the streets with a keen interest in events in Whitehall. After the republican major-general John Lambert surrounded Westminster Hall with his soldiers on 13 October and excluded the speaker and most of the MPs, Pepys was able to report the despairing departure from London of the parliamentary leader Arthur Haslerig and Admiralty commissioner Herbert Morley, and to list the members of the new Committee of Safety – yet another government for a nation bewildered and exhausted by conflict and change. He kept to a discreetly non-committal tone himself, but he also parcelled up other people's comments for Montagu: 'I have adventured to send your

Lordshipp the enclosed pamphlets for your diversion.'[27] He was finding his own *métier* as a writer, and in December produced a sequence
of letters on the crisis that are classics of reporting.

In the first he sets the scene: the City apprentices are busy with a
petition for the removal of the army from their streets, so that 'a rising
was expected last night, and many indeed have been the affronts
offered from the apprentices to the Red-coats of late. Late last night
was likewise a proclamation made up and down the town, to prohibit
the contriving or Subscribing any such petitions or papers for the
future.' This was on 3 December. On the 5th there was a 'fray' in
which the apprentices went forward with their petition, the council
saw this as the start of an insurrection, and many more soldiers, foot
and horse, were sent into the City. The shops were shut, the people
hooted at the soldiers,

boys flung stones, tiles, turnips &c . . . some they disarmed and kicked,
others abused the horses with stones and rubbish they flung at them . . . in
some places the apprentices would get a football (it being a hard frost) and
drive it among the soldiers on purpose, and they either darst not (or prudently
would not) interrupt them; in fine, many soldiers were hurt with stones,
and one I see was very near having his brains knocked out with a brickbat
flung from the top of an house at him. On the other side, the soldiers
proclaimed the proclamation against any subscriptions, which the boys
shouted at in contempt, which some could not bear but let fly their muskets
and killed in several places (whereof I see one in Cornhill shot through the
head) 6 or 7. [*sic*] and several wounded.[28]

Pepys is giving his description of a scene that has been played and
replayed all over the world from that century to this, one we have
seen on our television screens so that every point is familiar. It is the
first eyewitness account of an urban riot, young people clashing with
armed soldiers, since the Jewish historian Josephus; and it shows how
good he was at taking the pulse of the streets and fixing on essential
details, the rubbish thrown at the horses, the football in the frosty
street, the stones thrown from rooftops and the soldiers unable to bear
the contempt of the boys and so shooting them dead.

On 8 December Pepys continued with this story, taking it into
court now at the Old Bailey:

The present posture of the City is very dangerous, who I believe will never be quiet till the Soldiers have absolutely quitted the town. These circumstances (my Lord) may give your Lordship the best guess of the City's condition. viz. The Coroner's inquest upon the death of those that were slain on Monday have given it in Murder and place it upon Colonel Huson [Hewson], who gave his Soldiers order to fire. The Grand Jury at the Sessions this week in the Old Bailey desired of my Lord Mayor that the Soldiers might be removed out of the town, who answering that he knew not well with the safety of the City how to do it, they offered in open Court to indict their officers and undertake to bring them before his Lordship . . . One passage more I shall add, that in the common council house upon the reading of the Prentices' petition, Brandrith [Henry Brandreth, member of the Committee of Safety] stood up and inveighed highly against the Insolence of the boys to meddle in such businesses, whereupon he was hissed down by the whole Council and answered by Wilde the Recorder, who particularly defended the whole petition with a general applause. This is the present fate of the City, who are informed how the army have sent in Granados [grenades] to Pauls [St Paul's Cathedral] and the Tower to fire the City upon an extremity (which is certain) and I am confident will not rest but in chasing away the soldiers out of town.

Another letter, posted later on the same day, ended, 'Never was there (my Lord) so universal a fear and despair as now.' Londoners were anxious and exhausted, but Pepys's vitality still bubbled: his postscript, about a family debt due at Christmas, reminds us that even during weeks of fear and despair people need to keep accounts. He also made time to look into London's only synagogue and found the Portuguese Jews lamenting the death of one of their merchants following his operation for the stone. It had been carried out by Pepys's surgeon, Hollier, and must have given him pause, to pity the victim and congratulate himself on his own good luck. This was a piece of news he thought worth passing on to those who cared for him at Hinchingbrooke.

At home in Axe Yard, Elizabeth believed herself pregnant at last. She had not had a period since before the great funeral. Lady Montagu sent the Pepyses some brawn from Hinchingbrooke at Christmas, and her husband put it about that he was ill, 'confined to my chamber by a distemper'. He also stalled when asked to sign a proclamation prepared by Lawson asserting the navy's republican loyalties, and waited, while Lawson brought the fleet into the Thames and Monck moved his army slowly south to the Scottish border.[29] Neither Downing nor Montagu discussed his difficulties with Pepys. Both had made their careers through friendship with Cromwell, and it was precisely the power Cromwell had given them that put them in a position to have something valuable to offer Charles Stuart when they thought the time had come to do so. Montagu was driven by dismay and disgust at what had happened since Cromwell's death, and, like most of the nation, he feared the prospect of anarchy and renewed civil war. Downing was altogether more cynical and opportunistic. Both were sharp enough to know they must judge exactly when to jettison their loyalty to the remnants of Cromwell's regime and to make their submission to the king, and then to make it so acceptably that he would reward them for it. The year 1659 ended in political confusion and uncertainty for everyone; and on the last day of the year Elizabeth found she was not after all pregnant – a fact we know for the one very good reason that it appears on the first page of the Diary Pepys started to keep on 1 January 1660.

6. A Diary

When Pepys was in Cornhill on 5 December 1659, the day he saw an apprentice shot through the head by soldiers, the shops had their shutters up against the violence in the streets. On another day before the end of the year he was in Cornhill again, and this time he went into the stationer's shop at the sign of the Globe, where John Cade sold paper and pens as well as the prints and maps Pepys loved to leaf through; and there he bought himself a paper-covered notebook, too fat to go into his pocket, and carried it home to Axe Yard. Over the next days he ruled neat margins in red ink down the left-hand side and across the top of each plain white page: seven inches down, five inches across. It was a long task, given that there were 282 pages, and he did not number them. This was his preparation for 1 January and the start of his Diary. That first notebook brought home from Cornhill still exists, bound into leather and with gilding on the edges of the pages, otherwise exactly as he wrote it. Now, together with its five successor volumes, it has become one of the great literary manuscripts of the world and is priceless – a change in value that would have appealed greatly to Pepys.

What made him embark on a diary? It is just possible he knew and was impressed by the fact that both his employers kept journals, although they, as high officials serving the state, had good reason to keep records of their meetings and travel, while he had no reason at all, coming of an undistinguished family, poor and without prospects. Whatever sense of destiny he had as a boy had culminated in a Cambridge degree and then failed to carry him any further. He had not begun to justify his education or fulfil his promise. Marriage had if anything made his situation worse. The times were uncertain and threatening. It was an unpromising moment to embark on a record of his daily activities, and the activities themselves were nothing to boast about.

Yet set against this was the very fact that he had no important, interesting or demanding work to absorb him and take up his energy.

In preparing to keep a journal he was giving himself a task, and his temperament and training meant he was going to take the task seriously. The idea that he was singled out by fate was encouraged when he survived the stone operation, and, even if he had no idea of what he might achieve, he appears to have seen himself as a man who might do something in the world. Without his enthusiasm for himself, the Diary would hardly have begun to take shape as it did.

He was a passionate reader and cared for good writing. He had already tried his hand as a novelist and discovered a flair for reporting history in the making. Like many others, Pepys started off wanting to write something without quite knowing what it was, and the Diary could be a way of finding out. He may have seen it as a source book for something grander to be undertaken later. The high drama of the world in which he had grown up, the still continuing conflict between republic and monarchy, the heroic figures set against one another, paralleled the conflicts of the ancient world he had studied in classical texts. And principally there was his curiosity about himself, which made him see his own mental and physical nature as not merely a legitimate but a valuable and glorious subject for exploration. He did not yet know Montaigne's essays, and his circumstances and status were as different as could be from those of Montaigne, who was born into a prosperous landed family in France; but he breathed the same intellectual air.[1] He may have read Francis Bacon's recommendation to keep a diary, although that was specifically aimed at travellers: 'It is a strange thing that in sea voyages, where there is nothing to be seen but sky and sea, men should make diaries, but in land travel, wherein so much is to be observed, for the most part they omit it; as if chance were fitter to be registered than observation. Let diaries therefore be brought in use.'[2]

Whatever nourished the idea of the Diary in his mind, he took care over its physical appearance and condition. It was to be written in ink, black or brown as it came to hand, with a quill pen, sharp when newly cut and even when blunt good enough to allow him to form shorthand symbols no more than two millimetres square. He spaced the lines evenly, with between twenty and thirty to a page. He gave curly ornamentations to the capital letters for the name of the month at the head of each page – very occasionally forgetting it was a new month, so that he had to delete 'December' and put in 'January'.

September and October were given particularly lush capitals, and February's *F* always came out looking scratchy with its straight double up-and-down strokes. Some pages have browned to a pale toast colour with the years, but more have remained a fresh, almost chalky white; there are thin, fragile pages, and others that feel downy, almost velvety to the touch. Pepys was a fine calligrapher when he made time to write slowly, as he did for his Diary, and his pages are as beautiful as pieces of embroidery, with their neatly spaced symbols, the curly, the crotchety and the angular, interspersed with longhand for names, places and any other words that took his fancy, on one page a dozen, as many as forty on another. The longhand leaps out at you tantalizingly as you turn the pages, each word suggesting its own stories – Axe-yard, Mr Downing, Jane, Hinchingb., Deptfd, White-hall, Monke, Easterday, emerods, venison pasty, pigions, Uncle Robert is dead, Uncles corps, Queen, DY [Duke of York], Robes, papists, Clergy, conventicles, tumults, subsidys, Justice, Sessions, Sr WP, gentleman, yellow plume, petty coate, drawers, summer, amours – small packets of meaning surrounded by the elegant, impenetrable shorthand.

The shorthand made the Diary inaccessible to casual curiosity, which was obviously his intention, although Shelton's system was popular – at least one of his clerks learnt it.[3] In any case Pepys guarded it carefully, and says he mentioned its existence to only two people, Lieutenant Lambert, the young naval officer he first met in the Baltic, to whom he showed 'my manner of keeping a Journall' in the spring of 1660, and much later a discreet and trusted senior colleague, William Coventry.[4] At first he wrote it at home in Axe Yard, and on one occasion, in February 1660, he mentions Elizabeth being in the room while he set down 'of this day its passages' before going to bed, standing up to write.[5] But if she knew what he was doing, the subject did not come up in any recorded conversation between them; in any case, she knew no shorthand; and it was not long before his circumstances changed and he could be sure of privacy when he wrote. It is clear that he made up his mind from the start that each day was to have its entry. He kept to this plan, and when he was not able to write on the day he would catch up, as he often explains he is doing in the text, occasionally expressing his pleasure in the process. He maintained the separation of each day on all but a handful of entries where one carries over into the next because he has been up all night or travelling. Sometimes he kept loose written notes to draw on, and there is also mention of a 'by-book' in which he put down material to be transferred later.[6] More important, he trained his memory and shaped passages in his mind, a process he describes: 'enter all my Journall since the 28th of October, having every day's passage well in my head, though it troubles me to remember it; and what I was forced to, being kept from my lodging, where my books and papers are, for several days'.[7] Plainly there was an element of mental exercise as well as literary skill in the process.

He intended from the start to cover public events but also made it clear from the first page that it was to be a chronicle of intimate experience. For this he had no model. Montagu's and Downing's journals, supposing he got a glimpse of one or the other, were largely official and impersonal and altogether different from what Pepys was about to embark on.[8] As for other examples, there was a wave of enthusiasm for diary-keeping in England in the seventeenth century – it is the earliest period from which diaries have been preserved in considerable numbers – and Pepys may well have had an inkling that others were recording their lives; but he cannot have seen any them, since almost all remained unpublished until the nineteenth or twentieth century.[9] If he was in fashion, he hardly knew it. It has been suggested that he may have encountered at Cambridge puritan divines who recommended Christian diary-keeping as a valuable exercise, a form of moral accounting that encouraged the individual to watch and discipline himself. And he may have looked at John Beadle's *The Journal or Diary of a Thankful Christian*, published in 1656, which also approved the keeping of a diary and suggested it should include both public events and private experience.[10] Supposing Pepys pondered any of this, he took his time and formed a very different view of what constituted the interest of private life from that of Beadle, who suggests listing experience of divine assistance, moments of calling, deliverance from danger, answers to prayers and the commemoration of parents, schoolmasters and benefactors. Nothing could be further from what we find in Pepys, whose private themes were to be not spiritual but intensely human: work, ambition, avarice, worldly pleasure in all its forms, jealousy, friendship, gossip, cheating and broken vows. Beadle's likening of the diary to a tradesman's shop book or merchant's account book, a lawyer's book of precedents or physician's of experiments, or even state records, could well have appealed to Pepys, but his inspiration was all his own, and from the first page he produced a narrative with an entirely individual and wholly worldly point of view.

A look at some of his contemporaries' diaries, with their various emphases on political, public and spiritual experience, family life, science and travel, underlines the originality and pre-eminence of his achievement.[11] Among those from a generation older than his, Bulstrode Whitelocke, born in 1605 – the young man who organized the music for a masque from his house in Salisbury Court when Pepys was a baby – produced one of the fullest and most informative records of a successful career in public life during the interregnum; he started his diary in 1644 and wrote up the earlier parts of his life only after 1660, when his political fall made him anxious to justify himself.

The Jersey sea captain, George Carteret, who was to be Pepys's colleague later, wrote a journal of his adventurous voyage to Africa in 1638.[12] The royalist and scholarly John Evelyn's immense diary, also begun in the 1640s when he was in his twenties, was a conscientious record of travels, sights, public events, work undertaken, sermons, family matters and meetings with important people. Evelyn started 'in imitation of what I had seene my Father do', his father being a methodical man of affairs, and after many years noted his own belief in the 'infinite benefit of daily Examination; comparing to a Merchant keeping his books, to see whether he thrived, or went backward; & how it would facilitate our reckonings, & what a Comfort on our death bed'.[13] Both Evelyn and Whitelocke cover wide areas of interest and are crammed with information, but neither has Pepys's candour or immediacy, and neither engages the reader in his narrative as strongly as Pepys does. Another of their generation, Nehemiah Wallington, a London tradesman with little formal education, kept a commonplace book in which he recorded great events such as the escape of Pym and Hampden from arrest by the king: 'tell it to your children', he wrote, 'that they may tell it to their children, how God did miraculously deliver his servants'. His political and religious passions are vividly conveyed, and he also set down private matters; like Evelyn, he mourned in his diary the death of a beloved child: 'The grief for this child was so great that I forgot myself so much that I did offend God.' But he is without Pepys's curiosity about himself.

Ralph Josselin, an Essex clergyman, farmer and schoolteacher, born in 1616, kept a diary steadily from the mid 1640s until the year of his death, 1683. It is a remarkable record by an intelligent man: like Pepys, Josselin studied at Cambridge, read and collected books, took an interest in public and foreign affairs and gave an account of his domestic life. He was a Nonconformist, served as a chaplain to the parliamentary army, rejoiced at Naseby yet did not approve the execution of the king. But although he records a dream in which he was secretary and adviser to Cromwell, it was only a dream, and he lived out his days in a small village, chiefly preoccupied with the weather, the state of the crops and his own health. His children, once past the age when they were always falling into fires or down stairs, gravitated towards London, and London stirred him to his only aphorism: 'On good and bad of London: they must be good that miscarry not, there are so many temptations, and very bad that miscarry, so many opportunities for good' – a countryman's view that might have amused Pepys. Josselin's diary becomes dull, partly because his experience is so confined, and still more because his language is weighed down with routine religious phrases. Hardly a day goes by without him thanking the Lord for being gracious to him, or seeking to understand why the Lord has punished him with a bad leg or a disobedient son. Josselin is Pepys's contemporary, but, compared with Josselin's fixed habits of thought, Pepys's curiosity and scepticism, expressed in vivid, flexible and varied prose, take his Diary into what feels like the modern world.

Philip Henry, Pepys's close contemporary, also kept a lifelong diary covering domestic and parish activities as a Nonconformist clergyman. Henry was a sweet-tempered and scrupulous man, devoted to his wife and children. He never ceased to grieve for the firstborn son full of promise who died at five, but he ensured that his daughters received unusually good educations, including classical studies. Oliver Heywood, another Nonconformist minister, also born in the 1630s, kept journals recording his work as well as his private struggles – he was greatly tormented by what he named, in a phrase of Shakespearean gorgeousness, 'my darling and dalilah lusts'. He wrote of his brief happy marriage, the death of his young wife and the bringing up of their children with the help of a chaste maidservant. Yet another of Pepys's contemporaries, the greatly gifted scientist and architect

Robert Hooke, secretary of the Royal Society, recorded the facts of his daily life and work in the driest and most secular of diaries – no token churchgoing, hardly even any naming of God – its laconic entries also allowing a disconcerting view into his domestic arrangements. He was known to Pepys and will be discussed later.[14] From women there are no known diaries, although Anne Fanshawe and Lucy Hutchinson, both of Pepys's generation, would have been quite capable of keeping them, and each wrote spirited memoirs, from opposing political standpoints.

Philip Henry comes closest to Pepys in his origins and formation. Born in London to an educated mother and a father who was servant to a courtier, he was sent to Westminster School and Oxford. Like Pepys he was present at the execution of Charles I, but, unlike him, was shocked by it; and he settled in the remote provinces, in Shropshire, and reared his family there. His diaries were written in pocket almanacs, four inches by two, and in longhand. He was a braver and a simpler soul than Pepys. He refused to conform when his religious practice was proscribed, and he routinely gave one tenth of all his earnings to charity. The acquisition of a new suit caused him to write, 'lord, clothe me with thy Righteousness, which is a comely costly lasting everlasting Garment'. He agonized about accepting interest on a small sum of money left to his children and about attending the performance of a play put on by the same children; in both cases good sense happily prevailed over religious scruples. He noted many public events, the Turks at Vienna, the plague and the fire of London, and warmly approved the war against the Dutch, giving as good reasons the fishing dispute and their refusal to acknowledge British rights in the Channel, and only lamenting 'they are Protestants, *hinc illae lachrymae*'. He was credulous about divine intervention in human life, especially when death struck drunken or ill-behaved neighbours, like most puritans finding it hard not to look to heaven for direct rewards and punishments. Gentle, pious Henry and Pepys, streetwise and sceptical, are like the town and the country mouse: the purity of the country is admirable, but we shall have a better time in the company of the town mouse.

Pepys's Diary is from its first pages doing so many things at once that it can be daunting. It lists places visited and people encountered, without explaining where or who they are. It chronicles contemporary history: Londoners building bonfires to proclaim good riddance to a detested parliament, the ecstatic festivities accompanying the coronation of the restored king. It provides the first full and direct account ever of a man starting uncertainly on a professional career and finding, to his own surprise, that work is one of the major pleasures of life. It supplies much of the detail of his working practice, and also of his daily domestic experience. It is full of music, theatre, sermons, paintings, books and scientific devices. It is a tale of ambition and acquisition, and money is one of its obsessive themes: how it is made, how borrowed and lent, how spent, how saved, how hidden. Money in all its forms runs through the pages, as pieces of gold and bags of silver, shiploads of spices and silks, bribes, wages, debts, loans, payments, inheritances, Exchequer tallies (hazelwood sticks on which the amount of every loan to the government was notched) and the first paper promissory notes. When the Diary starts, Pepys has hardly £25 to his name; when it ends less than ten years later he has a fortune of £10,000.

Within a few months from the start there is the joyous sense of the momentum of a young man's life at last getting under way, the surprise of good luck, success, riches and the power of patronage all coming at once. In the first pages the Pepyses are too poor to keep their house warm in winter, and are driven out to get their Sunday dinner with his parents on the other side of town; by the end of the year he is enjoying a barrel of oysters pressed on him by a colleague whom he takes home to enjoy the piece of excellent roast beef he has at the fire for dinner. It was the sort of contrast he delighted in.

And although in its pages Pepys delights in remembering the past and in planning the future, he is always conscious that *now* must be the best time to enjoy life. This is why he conveys pleasure so memorably, pleasure in the lengthening of the days and spring and in summer weather, in journeys out of town, in music made and listened to, and in the theatre, with great acting like Thomas Betterton's and the astounding first appearance on the English stage of women to play women. He gives an unblushing account of the satisfactions of becoming successful and important; and prizes his own physical toughness and good health all the more because sickness had spoilt his boyhood and youth.

The Diary is history – on the whole reliable history – and it is comedy, of which Pepys was also a master. Parts of it read like a novel, parts like a farce. Its near literary relation is the fiction of Chaucer, whom he admired so much, another Londoner who worked in colloquial language three hundred years before him. Chaucer put his anatomy of English society into poetry without ever losing the zest of common speech and displayed his characters at their lewd and rude worst much as Pepys showed himself. What Pepys does not do is explain, or fill in the background of what is happening. He rarely writes a character of a man or woman, just as he hardly ever asks himself why his wife might be behaving as she is. He gives scurrilous stories and gossip, especially about those he dislikes, but most of his circle of acquaintance are touched in with only the smallest strokes as occasion arises; there are no formal portraits such as we find in Evelyn. This lack of ceremony towards others is partly due to his curiosity being so squarely centred on himself, on 'that entrancing *ego* of whom alone he cared to write', in Robert Louis Stevenson's phrase.[15] The famous and obscure, the loved and the hated, everyone else revolved round him in his place at the centre of the universe. He is also, for the moment at any rate, talking to himself.

One other thing about the Diary: as it opens, and at those moments when he puts in a summary of his current condition, or remarks on the state of the nation at the conclusion of a month or a year, it looks as though part of his intention in writing is to try to make order and clarity in his life, like a good accountant drawing up a balance sheet of profits and losses. But the totality of the Diary defeats any such aim. It becomes instead a demonstration of how impossible it is to make a tidy account of any one life. What we become most aware of is the bursting, disorganized, uncontrollable quality of his experience.

Pepys started his Diary with some formal statements. The opening words thank God for his health, restored by the operation for the stone, clear evidence that he regarded this as the most significant event in his life so far. God continues to receive occasional thanks throughout the Diary; moments of guilty feeling bring on a 'God forgive me', and a serious crisis will drive Pepys to prayer, which is about as far as his relations with the deity go. For although he thought swearing on God's name unbecoming, defended the Church of Eng-

1. A distant view of St Paul's and the City from rural Islington, where Pepys's father took his children for outings, with 'cakes and ale' at the King's Head. Hollar's etching of 1665 shows what was left of the civil war fortifications.

by Milford Staires.

London

2. The Thames was the main thoroughfare for Londoners, and the many water stairs on the banks acted rather like bus stops. At Milford Stairs there was a public convenience, mentioned by Pepys on 30 May 1661. This Hollar drawing is from the 1640s.

3. Pepys encountered a world of high culture and luxury for the first time when he was taken as a child to Durdans in Surrey by his uncle John, who served the Coke family. Here Sir Robert and Lady Theophila Coke presided over a fine house with a library and elegantly laid-out gardens; they newly built, in classical style, a long gallery as an addition to the Jacobean mansion. One of their pleasures was to put on plays, and they took to little Sam Pepys so well that he was invited to act a leading part, as the Princess Arethusa in Beaumont and Fletcher's *Philaster; or, Love Lies a-Bleeding*.

4. With the civil war came the destruction by puritan zealots of stained glass, statues and crosses, the banning of Sunday sports and the closing of all theatres.

5, 6, 7. The great house of Hinchingbrooke outside Huntingdon, home of Edward Montagu, keen supporter of Cromwell. His mother had been a Pepys, and he married Jemima Crew, from a puritan family, at the outbreak of the civil war, when both were seventeen. He took Lincoln, stormed Bristol, and fought at Marston Moor and Naseby.

8. The modest house at Brampton, near Hinchingbrooke, belonging to Pepys's uncle Robert, bailiff to the Montagus. Pepys came here early in the civil war to attend the Free Grammar School at Huntingdon. Both Hinchingbrooke and this house are still standing.

9. Thousands in the City had petitioned for the impeachment of Charles I's chief adviser, Strafford. Hollar shows the scene at Tower Hill on 12 May 1641, as men and women crowded into every inch of space to witness the execution of the man they hated.

OLIVERIVS CROMWELL
GENERALIS LOCVM TENENS ET GVBERNATOR
Parliamento Reipublicae Anglicana
consecratur omni Victorum

EXERCITVM ANGLIÆ REIPVBLICÆ DVX
HIBERNIÆ OXONIENSIS ACADEMIÆ CANCELLAR
Hanc sui Ducis effigiem offert Petat
nuncupatur Petrus Lombardus

10. A powerful and dignified print of Cromwell from Pepys's own collection, in which he placed the Cromwells among the Royal Families of England.

11. The execution of Charles I outside the Banqueting House in Whitehall, on Tuesday, 30 January 1649. Fifteen-year-old Pepys played truant from St Paul's School to be there, and expressed his approval by telling his friends that, if he were to preach about it, he would take as his text 'The memory of the wicked shall rot.'

12. Hollar's 1644 view of New Palace Yard from the river end shows, left, Westminster Hall, right, the Clock Tower, and behind it the Gatehouse. St Stephen's Chapel, where the House of Commons met, is out of sight behind the Hall. As well as being the political heart of the country, Palace Yard was a shopping centre and general meeting place.

13, 14, 15. Samuel Morland, painted by Lely in 1659 (*left*), was Pepys's tutor at Magdalene College, Cambridge. He and George Downing (*right*) were powerful figures during the commonwealth, acting as foreign envoys and intelligence experts. Downing noticed Pepys early and set him to make ciphers. Both Morland and Downing also became double agents, timing their switch to the Stuarts so well that they were rewarded with knighthoods. Morland went on to work as an engineer, inventing a calculating machine and water pumps, while Downing applied his abilities at the Treasury: Downing Street is named after him. The print below shows Magdalene in 1690, after the construction of the building at the back, in which the Pepys Library is housed.

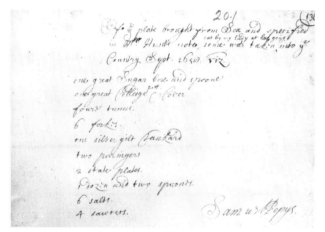

16. Pepys's neatly written list of household items made while he was a servant to the Montagu family in the late 1650s, lodged in a turret room in one of the Whitehall gatehouses. He notes that some of the plate 'was taken out by my lady at her going into the country Sept. 1658'.

17. Frontispiece of a book of 'à la mode Pastimes', jokes, proverbs – 'He that hath a Woman by the waste, hath a wet Eel by the tail' – and advice to young men like Pepys and his 'clubbing' friends on how to succeed with girls, compiled by Edward Phillips, Milton's nephew, during the 1650s. 'Dorothy this Ring is thine / And now thy bouncing body's mine,' reads one rhyme. Poor as Pepys was, he wooed and married his bouncing fourteen-year-old bride in 1655.

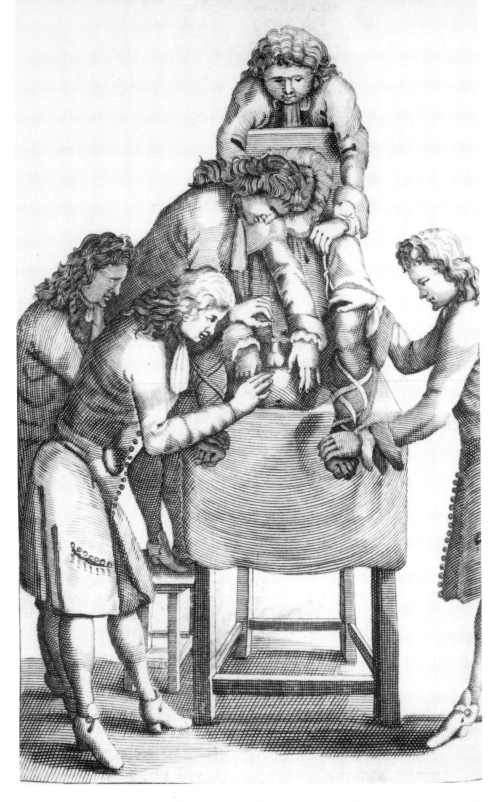

18. Engraving from 1683 English edition of Tolet's surgical text, showing a patient bound and held in preparation for the removal of a bladder stone, the operation Pepys underwent in 1658.

land – 'the Religion I was born in', he tells his mother firmly in the course of an argument – and enjoyed commenting on sermons, neither his Anglicanism nor his wider religious sense can be called enthusiastic on the evidence of the Diary.[16] He takes family prayers on Sunday evenings, but rarely prays by himself, scarcely refers to the Bible, attends church irregularly, works on Sunday when he finds it necessary and never takes communion. God's name comes up in his pages as a tic of usage, routine rather than reverential, except when Pepys is thanking him for his recovered health, when a note of sincere gratitude does sound; but when, in the course of the first year of the Diary, Montagu tells him that he is 'wholly Scepticall' in matters of religion, Pepys expresses his agreement privately with an 'as well as I'.[17] And when he found a thin congregation at the Abbey, he wrote, 'I see religion, be it what it will, is but a humour, and so the esteem of it passeth as other things do.'[18]

After God and his health, his next sentence places himself as the occupant of his house in Axe Yard and as the head of a family of three, flanked by his wife, whose name he does not find it necessary to give, and their servant, who is named as Jane. He goes straight on to the dashing of his hopes of his wife being with child by noting that, on the last day of the old year, she had what he calls her 'terms'. Elizabeth's monthly periods become a sad repeated message tolling through the years of the Diary under many different names, her menses, her months, her being unwell, *ses mois, ceux-la, moys, mois* – no doubt her own usage was French – or simply 'those'. But for now they are just one of the features of his life that requires to be set down. And from this he turns to the condition of the state. It makes a striking start, this direct yoking of the private and public, of Elizabeth's period and news of General Monck with his army in Scotland. In fact it is so striking that until 1970 no edition of the Diary printed the complete text. Elizabeth's period was simply removed, and Pepys's clear sign-posting of the intended scope of his Diary went for nothing.[19]

This is what he wrote in the opening paragraphs:

Blessed be God, at the end of last year I was in very good health, without any sense of my old pain but upon taking of cold.

I lived in Axe yard, having my wife and servant Jane, and no more in family then us three.

My wife, after the absence of her terms for seven weeks, gave me hopes of her being with child, but on the last day of the year she hath them again. The condition of the State was thus. *Viz.* the Rump, after being disturbed by my Lord Lambert, was lately returned to sit again. The officers of the army all forced to yield. Lawson lies still in the River and Monke is with his army in Scotland. Only my Lord Lambert is not yet come in to the Parliament; nor is it expected that he will, without being forced to it.

The new Common Council of the City doth speak very high; and hath sent to Monke their sword-bearer, to acquaint him with their desires for a free and full Parliament, which is at present the desires and the hopes and expectation of all – 22 of the old secluded members having been at the House door the last week to demand entrance; but it was denied them, and it is believed that they nor the people will not be satisfied till the House be filled.

As he wrote, he was still living in the world in which he had grown up, a republican state, but it was now in terminal confusion, with rival groups fighting and scheming for the upper hand and a fourth civil war very likely, an unbearable prospect for the exhausted population. The effect was that the first few months make a prologue distinct from the main body of the Diary, during which he does not know where either of his employers stands, and no one else knows who is friend and who enemy. The first page sketches the situation in a few cautious sentences. Essentially, it was this: the Rump parliament, residue of the Long parliament voted in nearly twenty years before and from which many MPs have been excluded, has become wholly ineffective. It had been suspended by an army junta in October and then recalled in December when the army leaders fell out among themselves; and it has now ordered the republican General Lambert to disband his troops in the north of England. But he has disobeyed them, because he and the junta want to re-establish a republican and puritan government.

In Scotland General Monck, who has disavowed the army junta, is hovering with his troops on the border with England, his intentions mysterious. And if the 'universal fear and despair' Pepys reported to Montagu in December has given way to any glimmer of hope at all, it is being offered by the City Council, which has asked for 'a free and full Parliament', by which they mean a newly elected one. Pepys says this is desired, hoped and expected by all, but this is still wishful thinking; it has to be remembered that Pepys's parents, and many of his cousins, are dwellers and workers in the City. The City Council has also sent a message to Monck asking for his support. Meanwhile troops continue to occupy the City, and Vice-Admiral Lawson, who is confusingly against the army and in favour of the Rump, has brought the fleet into the Thames and looks as though he might be preparing to blockade London, cutting off the coal and corn on which it depends; he has his own programme of republican reform that he has submitted to the City and had rudely rejected.[20] The City Council, the Rump, the army junta, Monck and Lawson are all pursuing different and unclear objects, while in the background the exiled royalists stir, plot and hope.

Pepys did not know that Montagu was waiting for the right moment to declare his support for the exiled Charles II, although he may have had his suspicions; he was certainly unaware of the fact that 'Mr Downing, master of my office', who appears at the end of his introduction to the Diary, was also considering how he could ingratiate himself with Charles. Neither Pepys nor anyone else could be sure what Monck or Lawson had in mind, because neither was sure himself yet; both had explicitly repudiated the idea of support for a restored monarchy, and Montagu suspected Monck of wanting power for himself and went on thinking this as late as March 1660.[21] Bulstrode Whitelocke, until very recently one of the most influential men of the government and keeper of the Great Seal, had delivered up the seal and gone into hiding under the disguise of a grey wig on the last day of 1659, despairing of the future; he would come creeping out again, but meanwhile his wife destroyed as many of his papers as she could find. So it is not surprising that Pepys was cautious about expressing political opinions of his own, even in the private pages of his insignificant Diary, and that he concluded his introductory remarks with the reflection that his own position was 'somewhat uncertain'.

Yet what he does over these first months of the Diary is to cover with rare effectiveness one of the key periods in history when a whole population is changing its allegiance. It was a movement comparable to the political wave that swept Communism out of Eastern Europe in 1989, and like that wave it came out of a surge of feeling that had built up over a long period until it became an irresistible force. The feeling was very widespread, but everyone had to work out for himself individually what compromises or betrayals he must be prepared to make to keep afloat as republicanism and puritanism were thrown out. Some heads were bound to roll, and some rich rewards were to be won. Hard decisions had to be made, and the most delicate timing was required.

PART TWO

1660–1669

7. Changing Sides

Pepys's luck was that both his employers, Edward Montagu and George Downing, each of whom had made his career through Cromwell's army and government departments, negotiated their tricky changes of coat with perfect finesse. The Diary tells us that throughout January 1660 'Mr Downing, master of my office', staunch official of the commonwealth and servant of the Rump, was in his Westminster house. He kept Pepys busy, and not only on Exchequer business. Downing liked to entertain lavishly at a local French restaurant, and Pepys was sent out with dinner invitations to his friends and important contacts among the parliamentary leaders; one was Arthur Haslerig, who had been Downing's colleague since they served together in the army in the 1640s. Pepys was on call at all hours: mealtimes, late at night and early in the morning, when he took instructions standing by his master's bed. He was also set to making ciphers, which Downing needed in preparation for his return to the Hague as the government's envoy. Pepys obliged – he was good at ciphers – but when Downing flatteringly asked him if he would like to accompany him back to Holland, he did not take up the offer; he had the excuse of his obligations to Montagu, and Downing did not press him. He was civil to Pepys on leaving and offered to do him any service that lay in his power; and Pepys, a shade nervous of this formidable boss, suddenly thought a parting present might be in order. He sent a porter to fetch his own fur hat, but the hat was brought too late. This was at the end of January. Downing left without giving a sign that he had anything in mind but the continuation of his diplomatic service to the existing government of England. Known to the exiled royalists as 'the fearful gentleman', he was particularly loathed for having persuaded the Dutch to drive Charles out of Holland. They hoped either to assassinate or to hang him.[1]

To Pepys's considerable surprise, the next time he saw Downing, on 22 May, he had become Sir George, his knighthood conferred by Charles himself. With his inside knowledge of the commonwealth's intelligence network, Downing had been trading his secrets for a royal pardon since March – no doubt using Pepys's ciphers – and by May he had given away enough to be rewarded with the knighthood.[2] His was a spectacularly successful conversion. Having come from puritan America to preach and fight for the commonwealth, he had served in its parliament, acted as Cromwell's envoy in Europe, and been at the heart of the financial and diplomatic affairs of the republic. By 1660 he may have had enough of near-anarchy in England; he was also clear in his mind that he cared more for power and money than for any principle, and saw that he could sell his abilities to whoever was in a position to bid for them.

Montagu's position was different, in that he had been negotiating with the royalists since the summer, although Pepys was equally in the dark about his intentions. Lying low at Hinchingbrooke throughout January and February, he relied on him for regular accounts of public events and gossip circulating in London, but gave away nothing in return. Pepys's ignorance left him free to indulge his own political curiosity. In the early pages of the Diary he shows himself exploring ideological currents. In mid January he joined a republican club, the Rota, and went along to hear political theory discussed by a group of serious radicals. The founder, James Harrington, had published a book, *Oceana*, proposing a republic with a rotating senate, property limitations and a much extended franchise; another strikingly original member of the club was William Petty, physician, social planner, scientist and economist, who went on to become a founder member of the Royal Society and a good friend of Pepys. Cyriack Skinner, Milton's pupil and friend, attended meetings, as did the one-time Leveller John Wildman and John Aubrey, at this date an enthusiastic republican; and there were other assorted politicians, City merchants, MPs and journalists who came to debate.[3] They met at the Turk's Head Coffee House in New Palace Yard to discuss current issues and political theory, taking a vote on topics such as how effectively ancient Rome had been governed. What made their meetings significant, and heady, was that they demonstrated a belief that discussion and argument were the best way of finding solutions to political problems. Pepys was intrigued and impressed; but the club did not last for more than a few weeks after he joined its sessions. Outside it, he observed that public opinion veered and shifted from day to day.

'Strange, the difference of men's talk,' he wrote, almost with a shrug, as the news of General Monĉk marching south, General Fairfax laying down his arms in Yorkshire and General Lambert attempting to block Monck reached London. Later, he said he had discussed the exiled king's prospects with friends, and even drunk a covert cup to him in mid February at Harper's; if so, he was too cautious to put it in his Diary at the time. The Rota fizzled out in February, and most of its members gave up theorizing, or at least kept their heads down. Not quite far enough down in the case of Harrington, who was considered dangerous after the Restoration, arrested and imprisoned; but, though his health was destroyed in prison, his book survived, and Pepys did not forget him.[4]

The political uncertainty affected everyone's lives in London during the early months of 1660. Several of Pepys's friends among the clerks of the council lost their jobs in January, victims of power struggles at higher levels. The Diary, with its tumbling stream of information, is a reminder that the moods and demands of daily life easily blot out politics. Lack of cash was a more pressing problem for Pepys than any possible change of regime. He found himself so short of money in January that he had to borrow from Downing's office to pay his rent, and was then forced to repay the loan by borrowing again from an obliging steward in the household of Lady Montagu's father, John Crew. Pepys and his friend Peter Luellin agreed over a drink how much pleasanter their lives would be if only they owned estates and commanded private incomes. Instead, Pepys was kept busy visiting the Montagus' eldest child, fourteen-year-old Jemima, under treatment at the house of a surgeon who had promised to straighten her crooked neck, and escorting her younger brother Ned to his boarding school at Twickenham. Their father might or might not be planning the overthrow of the state, but the children's needs must still be seen to. Lady Montagu kept him supplied from Hinchingbrooke at Christmas.

The Montagus' Whitehall lodgings were still subject to dispute: Pepys had to negotiate with Sir Anthony Ashley Cooper, who had his eye on them. When Ashley Cooper gracefully gave way, Pepys was entrusted with the keys and felt free to throw a dinner party of his own there to impress his parents and friends. Elizabeth cooked, his brother Tom came, and his new friend James Pearse, who had been Montagu's surgeon aboard the *Naseby*, brought his wife, noted for her beauty. After the guests had left, and Pepys had put in some work on Downing's ciphers, he and Elizabeth sat luxuriating in the heat thrown out by the great log in the palace fireplace. It made a fine contrast to their meagre fires in Axe Yard.

There were other evenings when he stayed at home, knocking nails into the wall for hats and cloaks, or reading the poet Francis Quarles, whose *Emblems* offered delicious dialogues between Eve and the Serpent, and the Flesh and the Spirit. There was a difficult day when Elizabeth's scissors and Jane's book were both missing after a visit from his sister Pall, and Pepys had to go to Salisbury Court to speak sharply to her. Pall was set to be a troublesome presence, and another was Elizabeth's brother, Balthasar, who enters the Diary bringing a present of a pretty black dog and goes away without asking for anything in return – uncharacteristically, as Pepys's note implies. On that same day Pepys was at Salisbury Court again and heard that his brother John had won an exhibition from St Paul's, but that he had also angered their uncle Robert at Brampton. This was regrettable, since uncle Robert had an estate to leave and must be kept in good humour. Pepys and his father went downstairs to the kitchen to talk undisturbed about the prospects of uncle Robert's will.

Neither Pepys's days nor his weeks had a regular pattern. He carried out business for Downing and Montagu as they required it, and took his meals at home or out as it pleased him on the spur of the moment. Elizabeth would have been wasting her time had she tried to plan meals in advance. He might breakfast with friends at Harper's, where cold goose and turkey pie were on offer, dine out in the middle of the day with a friend met by chance – and Westminster and Whitehall were small enough to make such meetings more likely than not – and stay out in the evening too, enjoying pot venison and ale till midnight with Will Symons, Peter Luellin and his friend Jeremiah Mount, who had his own bachelor room in the palace.

These easy-going ways were interrupted on 2 February when Pepys had his first sight of Monck's troops in the Strand. His immediate response was to take his small stock of cash to be hidden at Montagu's Whitehall lodgings. From there, peering out of an upstairs window, he saw foot soldiers bawling for a free parliament and money, and threatening a confrontation with some cavalry; when the dispute resolved itself, Pepys took his money home again. The next morning he was out playing his pipe in St James's Park in the sunshine and spent a good deal of the day agreeably with his Cambridge cousin Roger Pepys, son of Talbot; Roger was a good-humoured barrister about to celebrate his third marriage. A few days later the sight of soldiers treating Quakers roughly upset Sam again; he disliked religious intolerance and hated persecution. He had to go round to reassure Lady Jem, who was frightened by the arrival of the troops in London and still under doctor's treatment. But what he mostly did was to walk the streets, eyes missing nothing, ears alert as he threaded his way east, west and east again, sometimes alone, more often with a friend, from Westminster and Whitehall to Charing Cross, from Somerset House to London Bridge, from St James's to Fleet Street, from Gray's Inn to St Paul's, from the Temple to Aldgate, from Lincoln's Inn Fields back to Whitehall. He knew the territory as well as an animal knows its runs.

The first set-piece of the Diary comes on 11 February with his account of the rejoicing in the City when Monck made his decisive move against the Rump parliament and humiliated Haslerig and its leaders by insisting that it was unrepresentative and that a free election must be called. Pepys gives several pages to a running description of his own long day from noon, when he went into Westminster Hall, heard that a letter from Monck had been delivered to parliament and saw the faces of the men in the Hall outside changed with joy. An angry Haslerig was plucked by the arm by a Quaker as he left and told, 'Thou must fall.' After this Pepys tells how he walked dinnerless with his friend James Chetwynd towards the City, and with some difficulty found a pullet ready-roasted at Temple Bar; how they went to Chetwynd's law office, where Pepys sang some cheerful songs; on then to the Guildhall, and there, after much standing about and drinking, saw with his own eyes Monck greeted with a great cry of 'God bless your Excellence'; and how the people pressed drink and money on Monck's soldiers, and Pepys stopped at the Star Tavern to write a hurried letter to Montagu; and how the church bells began to ring all over the City. By ten o'clock that night he could count thirty-one bonfires from the spot in the Strand where he stood. 'Indeed, it was past imagination, both the greatness and the suddenness of it.' And when he got home at last and found John Hunt sitting with Elizabeth, he took her out again to show her the fires.

You can't read these pages without being moved as Pepys becomes one with the crowd and its excitement and relief at Monck's determination to break the political deadlock, and at the same time impressed by his capacity to watch, listen and take in everything. The entry may look as though it wrote itself, but the effects are worked with skill, the rhythm of the long sentences leading you through the streets, their momentum occasionally broken by pauses – marked by semicolons – to drink, observe or talk. The three pieces of direct speech used to punctuate the passage raise the sense of immediacy, the warning to Haslerig, the greeting to Monck and the 'God bless them's of the people to the soldiers. Pepys is lucky enough, or skilful enough, to find Monck's secretary Lock; he takes him to a tavern, extracts the substance of Monck's letter to parliament directly from him and writes down its six points. This is businesslike stuff, but he also lets us feel how his own awareness of the importance of the day through which he is living expands and permeates everything as the hours go by: 'But the common joy that was everywhere to be seen!' he exclaims, as Bow bells start to ring. He has the good reporter's gift for being in the right place at the right moment, and the structure and rhythm of his sentences show how well he has mastered his medium.

After this he sent off volleys of letters, many to Hinchingbrooke and one to Downing in Holland. The excitement in London gave no guarantees about the future, and he still committed himself to no direct expression of opinion in his Diary. On 20 February he mentions reading what he described as a well-written pamphlet in praise of the old form of monarchy. Later in the same day he went with Will Symons to the Rota Club and got the impression it would not meet any more; if it did, Pepys did not attend again. Visiting his parents in Salisbury Court, he noticed that the republican Praisegod Barebones had his windows broken in Fleet Street – *again*, he writes. John Crew urged Pepys to send for his master from Hinchingbrooke, since he was now assured of government employment again, and two days later, on Pepys's twenty-seventh birthday, Montagu was indeed elected to the Council of State. Pepys decided to ride with his brother John, just starting his Cambridge studies, and to go on to Hinchingbrooke. But his communications were bad. He hired a horse and set off, only to learn in Cambridge that Montagu was already on his way to London.[5]

At Magdalene, Pepys observed that the fellows of his old college spoke in new voices: they had abandoned the puritan twang he remembered from his undergraduate days. The change amused him, and he joined in their toasts to the king and the royal family, still made strictly in the privacy of their rooms. Then he hurried back to London. He was not yet in Montagu's confidence. On 2 March he observed that 'Great is talk of a single person [as ruler], and that it would now be Charles [Stuart], George [Monck], or Richard [Cromwell] again.' On the same day, Whitelocke's diary entry is 'Monck & Montagu voted to be Generals at Sea, both fit for the intended design.'[6] Montagu was replacing Lawson as commander of the fleet, a crucial appointment at this juncture, but he was still uncertain about Monck's ultimate intentions. On 5 March Pepys committed himself to 'Great hopes of the King's coming again'.

At last, on 6 March, Montagu opened his mind to Pepys and asked him, with exquisite politeness, if he could, 'without too much inconvenience', go to sea with him as his secretary, since he was going to need someone he could trust. He told him he believed the king would be restored and laid great stress on the affection of the people and the City – 'at which I was full glad'. There were still republicans and adherents of Richard Cromwell about, and Montagu stressed that the king would have to carry himself 'very soberly and well' if he were to succeed, but for the first time, Pepys wrote, people felt free to drink the king's health openly. And since this was good enough for 'my Lord', he would happily go with him to sea.

He had been to sea only once, on his dash to the Baltic the previous year. Then Montagu had a secretary called John Creed. Now Creed lost his job to Pepys. There was nothing wrong with Creed's abilities, only his politics and religion. He was known as a committed puritan, while his elder brother Richard was an important commonwealth official who had been clerk to the Admiralty Committee from 1653 and deputy-treasurer to the fleet from 1657, and served both under Montagu and under Major-General Harrison, zealot and regicide. Richard Creed, ordered to leave London in March, refused to do so and was imprisoned in the Tower for several months.[7] So the name of Creed would have been a liability to Montagu, while Pepys's discretion, personal loyalty and open-mindedness recommended him. John Creed's ambitions turned out to be stronger than his convictions, and he adapted to the changing circumstances with impressive speed, although he was not quite quick enough to keep his job as secretary. He did, however, manage to remain in Montagu's service, and he and Pepys maintained from then on an awkward relationship, part rivals, part friends. Pepys frequently expressed his dislike of Creed's meanness and deviousness in the Diary, and even plotted to do him out of his job again; yet the two of them spent many hours and days together over the coming years, swapping stories and advice, sometimes collaborating, and pacing one another with beady eyes up the career ladder.[8] Some of Pepys's mockery of Creed is patently unfair – for instance, when they took a Sunday drink in a tavern together, a year after the Restoration, Pepys's gibe was 'Mr Creed, who twelve months ago might have been got to hang himself almost, as soon as to go to a drinking-house on a Sunday'.[9] The change in Creed was of course part of the general change that affected everyone, including their master Montagu and Pepys himself. But although Creed tried hard, it took him time to lose the smell of his past, and five years later he was still talked of as 'a fanatic and a false fellow'.[10]

Almost the first advice Pepys got when his promotion was known was from a sea captain telling him how to fiddle his expenses by listing five or six non-existent servants when he went on board and claiming pay for them all. It made an interesting introduction to the workings of the navy.[11] When he went to the Admiralty offices he met anxious officials who had served the commonwealth for many years. Robert Blackborne, a man of influence as secretary both to the naval commissioners and to the customs, expressed his fear that the king would come in and 'all good men and good things' be discouraged; he did not expect to keep either of his positions.[12] There was nothing Pepys could say to this. He had become overnight a person with the power to hire or fire, and found himself courted by men who hoped for jobs and offered presents – wine, a rapier, a silver hatband, a gown for his wife. On top of this dream-like change of circumstances he also heard that his uncle Robert had just declared he was making him his heir. One day in the not too distant future he would come into his own country estate at Brampton. It was exactly the good fortune he and Luellin had wished for a few weeks before.

With the news of uncle Robert's will fresh in his mind, he sat down to write his own before setting off to sea. Everything was to go to Elizabeth except his books, which were bequeathed to John, although any books in French were to be hers. During his absence he arranged for her to go to the Bowyer family in Buckinghamshire. He wrote to inform Downing he was going to sea and suggested a substitute to take over his work. After this he spent a sleepless night worrying about the change in his circumstances and made a vow to give up drinking for a week. Meanwhile the Rump dissolved itself, elections were called, 'and now they begin to talk loud of the King'.[13] Monck began a purge of army officers and gave Montagu his support by moving troops out of Huntingdon, with the idea of pleasing the townspeople before the election.

Pepys took a short, melancholy leave of his parents, expressing the fear that he might never see his mother again; she had nothing worse than a cold, but he was in a heightened state of emotion. His leave-taking of his friends among the clerks was longer and jollier, and on 23 March he took a barge at the Tower and boarded the *Swiftsure* with a group of Montagu's servants and his own clerk and boy to serve him, the first he ever employed. There was a gun salute for Montagu, and a busy time began. Pepys had to compile lists of ships and men and write out orders and letters to the council and abroad. Soon a personal letter came to him from Blackborne, addressed as he had never been addressed before, to Samuel Pepys, Esquire, 'of which, God knows, I was not a little proud'. A few days later the astute writer appeared in person and surprised Pepys further by commending Charles Stuart as 'a sober man' whom he would be happy to serve. Sobriety was evidently the quality new royalists most wanted to see in the king: Montagu had said he would need it, Blackborne claimed it for him, and when Pepys saw Charles for the first time a few weeks later he also described him as 'a very sober man'.[14]

From this point two stories are being told in the Diary. One is a breezy account of shipboard life, in which Pepys enjoyed his snug cabin, set out to learn sea terms, walked on the deck to keep sickness at bay as they put out to sea and bravely dealt with rain blowing in and soaking his berth. He was always prepared to make the best of things. He made music with Montagu's clerk Will Howe, consumed pickled oysters and radishes and, leaning out of a porthole, appreciated the sight of some handsome women aboard a passing East Indiaman through a friendly lieutenant's telescope – there were no women aboard his ship. He relished the drama of rattling guns and dense clouds of smoke that enveloped the whole fleet when they exchanged salutes with the three coastal forts of Walmer, Deal and Sandown. He played ninepins on deck; and he argued pleasurably with the ship's chaplain, who, unlike Pepys, believed in extempore prayers. He explored below decks to see the 'massy timbers' and the storerooms where wine and provisions were kept. The insides of fighting ships were painted red, and the sailors lived among the powder magazines and stores, slinging their hammocks between decks less than a man's height deep and inured to the stink made up of the bilge in the hold, their own sweat and the supplies of living chickens and meat that started the voyage fresh but was soon high: beef and pork were what seamen expected to eat. The officers were fed more delicately in their finely panelled quarters; Montagu had his own fireplace, a surprising arrangement in a wooden ship. Officers paid visits from one ship to another, dining one another and drinking well, and Montagu encouraged music-making, joining in himself on occasion, one evening with a rude song against the Rump.

The other story that emerges from the Diary is the political one. From the *Swiftsure* Montagu and his party transferred to the *Naseby*, his former and much loved flagship, with the figure of Cromwell treading down six nations on its prow. He could hardly go to greet the king from a ship so decorated, and carpenters were summoned to start transforming its appearance. In London Blackborne busied himself arranging for new flags of acceptably royalist design to be rushed to the fleet.[15] The ship's decorations were not the only problem. Montagu started going through the list of his senior officers, getting rid of radicals and religious zealots, and dispatching others to far-off destinations to keep them out of the way. Most must have been personally known to him from the days when they fought together. It was a delicate and painful business, and he was nervous. He told Pepys he had doubts about even his own flag-captain's loyalty. A gun salute that blew out many of the windows of his ship as he joined Lawson's squadron at Tilbury may have increased his anxiety: was it enthusiastic greeting or warning? As it turned out, Lawson had decided to make his accommodation with the new regime, and his submission sent a useful message to all the other officers. Blackborne's eagerness to serve Montagu reinforced Lawson's signal to the captains who had been his friends for years that, if they hoped to go on working, they too had better change their coats.

Everything was moving in Montagu's direction. Word arrived that he was elected to parliament for Weymouth, with both Dover and Cambridge also eager to have him as their MP. After this came the most important news, from London, where the newly elected parliament received a 'Declaration' from Charles in Breda. It was drawn up by his chief adviser, Edward Hyde, a subtle diplomat, and promised a free and general pardon to all who within forty days claimed it and asserted their loyalty – the only exceptions to be those parliament chose to exempt. Liberty of conscience was also promised; parliament was to decide what should happen to sequestered royalist estates; and Monck's troops and the navy would have their arrears paid. Hyde's master stroke was to leave all contentious matters to be settled by parliament – later. Charles himself asserted his devotion to the Protestant faith and asked for divine blessings on parliament. On receiving the Declaration, parliament voted £50,000 for the king. This was on 1 May, and the news reached Montagu, and Pepys, the next day in a letter from Thurloe.[16] Hearing that Londoners were drinking the king's health on their knees in the streets, Pepys remarked that this was a little too much – in the privacy of his Diary. The same kneeling was going on in Deal, and maypoles, prohibited for so long, were being raised, topped with the royal flag.

Montagu instructed Pepys to read out Charles's Declaration to the assembled officers and to follow it with the loyal response he had carefully written out for them. And although Pepys felt that 'many in their hearts were against it', they agreed to it formally; they were not going to make trouble now.[17] As for the seamen, they had no reservations at all and shouted 'God bless King Charles' with genuine joy when Pepys spoke to them, no doubt throwing their caps in the air as they did so. Everyone had become a royalist. The state's arms were to be removed from every ship, painters sent for from Dover to replace them with the king's.

Visitors came and went ceaselessly in small boats, admirals and Admiralty commissioners, rejoicing royalists and nervous grandees eager to prove their perfect enthusiasm for the return of Charles

Stuart. 'General Penn', the formidable sea captain who had fought alongside Blake and against Prince Rupert, lately appointed an Admiralty commissioner by Monck, came to dine with Montagu on his way to Holland and the king. Lord St John, a neighbour of the Montagus in Huntingdonshire, one-time lord chief justice and ennobled by Cromwell, arrived seeking a passage to Flushing, eager to justify himself to Charles. A triumphant Penn returned with a knighthood, but St John got the thumbs-down and crept back reduced to plain Mr St John, his career finished, to retire to the country and later into exile.

Ashley Cooper, who had been in correspondence with Charles since March, made the crossing and said enough to be pardoned and made a privy councillor, and soon a peer. Pepys's old tutor Samuel Morland took himself to Breda and got his knighthood on 20 May.[18] Lesser men schemed to get on board just as eagerly, one of them Pepys's brother-in-law, Balthasar, who came with a bold request to be taken on as a 'reformado' (it meant serving at sea without a formal commission, but allowed the status of an officer). Since Balty was a wholly inexperienced twenty-year-old, this was awkward, and, although Montagu was civil to him at dinner and promised to put in a word for him, he was sent back to London with nothing more than a small loan from Pepys and letters to Elizabeth. Peter Luellin also turned up for a week, supped with Pepys in 'the great cabin below' and shared his breakfast oysters; and John Creed appeared, made himself useful and remained.

On 10 May Montagu's eldest son, Ned, came aboard, and on the same day a message from Monck arrived, urging Montagu to fetch the king at once rather than hang about waiting for instructions from parliament. It would do him no harm with the king, and if it made him some enemies too, they were of no account. Montagu took the advice, and sailed on the 12th, leaving strict orders with the ships he left off the English coast to bring over no one but his cousin, his wife's cousin and his brother-in-law. The importance of associating his own family with the great enterprise was something he kept steadily in mind. He had already written to the king asking him to look favourably on his father-in-law, John Crew, fearful that his political and religious affiliations would tell against him.[19]

Pepys was responsible for procuring the 'rich barge' that would be used to bring Charles ashore, and the professional musicians, trumpeters and fiddlers who joined the already crowded ship. The painters were still at work, and tailors were cutting out crowns and stitching flags, as well as preparing gold and silver embroidered clothes for Montagu to wear when he met the king. They anchored at Scheveningen, the port for the Hague, on 14 May. Letters were sent to inform Charles of Montagu's arrival, carried ashore by his nephew Edward Pickering, who accompanied an official delivering a trunk containing £10,000 for the king from parliament. Pickering told Pepys that they found Charles and his attendants dressed in cheap and shabby clothes, and that when he saw the money he became 'so joyful, that he called the Princess Royal and Duke of York to look upon it as it lay in the Portmanteau before it was taken out'. The scene tells everything about the conditions of his exile and explains a good deal of his conduct afterwards.

Over the next ten days Pepys made sightseeing trips ashore, days of intense experience in which he absorbed architecture and pictures, shopped for presents – small baskets for Elizabeth and Mrs Pearse, books for himself – lost and found young Ned, gawped like everyone at the king and assorted members of the royal family and at a gout-stricken Hyde receiving visitors from his bed, who spoke 'very merrily' to Pepys and Ned. Pepys contrived to kiss one fashionably dressed Dutchwoman in a coach and failed to make headway with another in a guest house where, by Dutch custom, men and women shared bedrooms; although, he wrote frankly, 'I had a month's mind to her'.[20] There were other adventures, singing with a musical friend from Cambridge at the Princess Dowager's country house, 'a haven of pleasure in a strange country', where there was an echo to increase the enjoyment; and a visit to a village famous for its thirteenth-century countess, who had given birth to 365 children at one delivery.[21] Pepys was a determined tourist, and he was not going to miss anything on offer if he could help it.

Back on board, he heard more news from London. The new speaker of the House had proposed that all who had held arms against Charles I should be excluded from pardon. This was an absurdity, given that half the nation had opposed him. The speaker was reproved, but the House went on to exclude from pardon all who had taken any part in the king's trial. It ordered the seizure of their estates, the closure of ports to prevent their escape and their arrest. Montagu knew that his brother-in-law Gilbert Pickering was one of those named, but there was nothing he could do at present. Pepys saw that the court party at the Hague was 'growing high', the clergymen among them sure of the restoration of all the Church lands; there was now nothing 'to hinder them and the king from doing what they have a mind'. It was a shrewd account of the situation, since Charles was being restored without any formal conditions or limitations on his power.

For Charles, men such as Montagu, who had held arms against his father and him for years, had redeemed themselves by their change of heart and the help they were giving him now. Pepys asked Montagu in his cabin when he had been converted to the king's cause and was told it was in the summer of 1659, in the Baltic, when he realized what sort of treatment he was likely to get from the commonwealth. He did not add that this was also when he was approached by Charles's envoys with promises of great rewards if he would change his allegiance.[22] Now, after so many months of danger and caution, the time had come for his rewards; and during the next days and weeks King Charles, with a proper sense of obligation to the man who had delivered the fleet to him, conferred these. He received an earldom, lands with a value of £4,000 a year and the Order of the Garter; he was also made a privy councillor, a Treasury commissioner, master of the Wardrobe and vice-admiral of the navy, under the new lord high admiral, who was to be the king's brother James, duke of York.

Much of this was announced when the king came on board, on the same day that he formally renamed the ships. The *Naseby* became the *Royal Charles*, the *Richard* became the *James*, and the *Dunbar* became the *Henry*, named for the king's youngest brother. Walking on the deck of his new *Royal Charles*, Charles told stories of his escape from England after the battle of Worcester. Pepys, standing within earshot, was moved by his account of the hardship he had endured and wrote down a summary immediately afterwards.[23]

Before the royal party left the ship at Dover, Pepys managed to get a word with the duke of York, who told him his name was already known and promised future favour. Then the royal party swept on to the shore. Montagu was 'almost transported with joy' at the perfect success of all his arrangements, while Pepys, casting himself in a favourite role as the plain man, expressed his pleasure at the behaviour of the king's pet dog 'which shit in the boat, which made us laugh and me think that a King and all that belong to him are but just as others are'.[24]

Pepys heard from Elizabeth, who had returned to London, that some cousins were suggesting he might be knighted by the king; he brushed aside the idea. 'We must have a little patience and we will rise together,' Montagu told him, following this elegant forecast with a more down-to-earth, 'In the meantime I will do you all the good Jobbs I can.'[25] It was his way of making clear to Pepys that he had proved himself efficient, intelligent, discreet and loyal in his duties, and would be rewarded.

He arrived back in London on 9 June. Things were in such turmoil that he did not return to Axe Yard for nearly two weeks, camping out instead at his parents' house. 'At my father's found my wife' was all he had time to write about their reunion, on Whitsunday, as he hurried round town for Montagu in the hot weather. Blackborne was assiduous in his attendance, Creed was much in evidence also, and Pepys managed a couple of meetings with his old friends from clerking days. Balty irritated him by asking him again to find him 'a place for a gentleman that may not stain his family' – when, as Pepys complained, 'God help him, he wants bread.'[26] There were more important matters to attend to. Montagu was hesitating over his choice of titles and visiting the new Admiralty offices installed at Whitehall Palace by the duke of York. 'Court attendance infinite tedious,' noted Pepys after accompanying him there one evening. Another was spent at Montagu's elbow, looking over his list of captains and marking more of those he intended to put out of naval service as politically unreliable.

They were not the only ones for whom the times were difficult. Montagu's sister, Elizabeth Pickering, 'desired my assistance with my Lord, and did give me, wrapped up in paper, £5 in silver': her husband was in danger – perhaps already in custody – and she was reduced to this humiliating procedure to reach her brother.[27] Montagu did help, and Sir Gilbert Pickering became one of the very few who had sat at the trial of Charles I who escaped a death penalty, saved by his brother-in-law and £5 for Pepys.[28] Some were contriving to escape abroad, some were in hiding, others gave themselves up, trusting to a pardon. Haslerig was already in the Tower; so was Thomas Harrison, who had fought at Marston Moor and Naseby alongside Montagu.[29]

Another of his old colleagues, Bulstrode Whitelocke, spent the month of June suing for mercy – not a heroic story but an instructive one. First his wife went to the MP and lawyer William Prynne, once an ally and the hero of the parliamentarians, who treated her 'more like a kitchin wench than a gentlewoman'. Then he approached Monck and was dismissed brutally. Next he was dunned for £500 by a peer who told him he would make sure he was excluded from the general pardon if he did not pay up. He paid and then, at the cost of £250 to the man who arranged it, had an interview with the king, to whom he kneeled for pardon. Two years' income from his estates were said to be the royal price. Finally, to his former friend Edward Hyde, now lord chancellor, he paid another £250, plus (he noted carefully) £32.18s.8d. in legal fees for an official pardon, written out and sealed. His life was effectively saved by money, helped along by his willingness to accept humiliation. It was not the end of his troubles, but he felt able take up his legal practice once more.[30]

Montagu, appointed master of the Wardrobe, a government department responsible for all the furniture, liveries and robes required by the court, took Pepys along to inspect the building that came with the job. It stood at Blackfriars, near Puddle Dock – where Queen Victoria Street is today, close to the church of St Andrew-by-the-Wardrobe – and they learnt that for the past eleven years, since 1649, it had been run by a charitable body in the City as an orphanage and training school for needy children. A group of the children now came to Montagu, dressed in their tawny-coloured uniforms, to sing to him and present him with a petition in which they asked not to be turned out. But turned out they were. 'My Lord did bid me give them five pieces of gold at his going away,' wrote Pepys, and that was that.[31]

By the end of the month, Montagu was able to tell Pepys that he had secured him the job of clerk of the acts with the Navy Board, at a salary of £350 a year. And if Pepys had little idea what was involved in terms of work and was not even sure whether he wanted to keep the job or trade it in, he began to find out at once that it was worth more than the salary, as offers of money came in from people hoping to profit from his good fortune. He resigned his clerkship at the

Exchequer, calling Downing a 'stingy fellow' in the process. The new position came to him solely through family patronage, making it an appointment of exactly the sort Pepys himself objected to later; as George Aylmer, historian of the seventeenth-century civil service, has written, 'on one view the Restoration delayed serious administrative reforms for 150 years'.[32]

A house came with the Navy Board job, and the story of how Pepys moved into his house, like so much that was happening all around, is both entertaining and shameful. The Navy Office houses were in Seething Lane, just west of Tower Hill, in a very large, rambling building divided into five substantial residences and office accommodation, with a courtyard and a communal garden stretching north-west to the edge of Tower Hill. There was an entry gate, shut at night by the resident porter, making it an early gated community.[33] Pepys liked the place so much when he went to take a look on 4 July that he began to worry in case he was not allotted a house as promised, but excluded, or 'shuffled out'. He was back with two of his new bosses two days later to take possession of the office, and he spent the next day there making an inventory of papers. Some of the officers of the departing regime were naturally still about, and his new clerk, Tom Hayter, was in fact one of the existing clerks. A week after Pepys's first visit, he was annoyed to see a 'busy fellow' arrive, apparently to select the best house for Lord Berkeley, one of the new commissioners. Pepys reacted swiftly. He hurried home to Axe Yard, collected a pair of sheets and invited Hayter to accompany him back to Seething Lane, where he knocked at the door of the house he wanted. It was inhabited by Major Francis Willoughby, a commissioner since 1653 and a friend of Blackborne; Willoughby had visited the *Naseby* in April, as Pepys had noted in his Diary. Perhaps this made him less abashed at announcing that he wanted to spend the night in Willoughby's house. Willoughby courteously agreed, Pepys enjoyed a good night's sleep, and two days later asserted his right to the house. He received permission to start on some alterations and showed Elizabeth over 'my house' – a breathless sequence that leaves you impressed by his determination and effectiveness, if not by his sensitivity.

Few could allow themselves sensitive feelings in the great change-over. On the same day he observed that Major-General Whalley's house was now the property of Madam Palmer – Barbara Villiers – already established as the king's mistress. Houses and jobs were changing hands, and it was better to be moving in than out. And on the 17th, after a day's delay caused by rain, he moved with his family into Seething Lane, just thirteen days after first seeing the house. He expressed a little disappointment when Major Willoughby sent for his own things nine days later. Not surprisingly, Willoughby chose to return to New England, from where he, like Downing, had come to serve the republic.[34]

In July Pepys recorded his patron's entry into the House of Lords. He was too tactful to recall that Montagu had been there before, as a baron, among Cromwell's lords. His reinstallation was as the earl of Sandwich, with the further titles of Viscount Hinchingbrooke and Baron Montagu of St Neots. From then on he was known as Lord Sandwich, and will now become Sandwich in this book. Titles make confusion for us, but the new name must have been welcome not only for the honour but also for drawing a distinct line under one life as he embarked on another. He was thirty-five in July, halfway through the span allotted by the Bible, and it made a good moment to leave behind the young man he had been, pious parliamentarian, fellow officer, friend, neighbour and servant of the Cromwells. Enter instead the courtier, soon to be dispatched to fetch the queen mother, Henrietta Maria, from France, for a ceremonial visit to the country from which he had helped to drive her out. His son, little Ned, became Lord Hinchingbrooke, and a year later he and his brother Sidney would both be sent to France to receive the polished education that their father considered appropriate. Their mother was now countess of Sandwich; she remained in the country with the younger children through all the turmoil of the king's return and did not see her husband until he joined her for a fortnight in August. Meanwhile he received the thanks of the Commons, who decreed that his service in bringing over the king should be recorded in their journal, 'there to remain for your Honour so long as this World endures'.[35] Pepys knew he owed every part of his good fortune to Lord Sandwich and rejoiced with him. How could he do otherwise? The world had turned over, and he had come out on top. The nation showed its joy at the restoration of the king with such a show of unanimity that

Charles himself joked that 'it was his own fault that he had been abroad so long, for he saw nobody that did not protest he had ever wished for his return' – and Pepys rejoiced with the nation, and with his personal triumph.[36]

Sandwich secured him a second job, at the Privy Seal, where all petitioners to the crown went to have their documents signed, usually for a fee; Pepys had only to go in when he could, sign petitions and collect his fees. The money was useful, but it was tedious, and kept him busier than he liked to be. He complained that he had no time left to read newspapers or keep up with public affairs: 'For this month or two, it is not imaginable how busy my head hath been.'[37] He could not ride the crest of the wave all the time. Balty kept clamouring for a share in the good fortune, and even Pepys's father pestered him for a job at the Wardrobe, with such persistence that he took to avoiding him. Pepys also had his moments of doubt about it all. In early August he was reluctant to give up the lease of his house in Axe Yard, 'for fear of a turn'. He meant, in case of the overthrow of the monarchy and a return to a republic. He had seen enough turns in his lifetime to be able to imagine another easily enough.

Sandwich necessarily remained the most important figure in his life, and the two men were in almost daily contact when he was in town. They were brought together by public business, Navy Board meetings, the Privy Seal Office and a new task of receiving the oaths of allegiance to the crown, required from every naval employee. Pepys also continued his old work of preparing 'my Lord's' accounts and running his errands. And he respectfully noted many of Sandwich's dinner engagements: with the king at the Tower, with Chancellor Hyde, about to become the earl of Clarendon, in Kensington with this lord or that, or at a supper with General Monck and the royal family. He kept watch on Sandwich's health too, giving even a slight cold three mentions in the Diary. He noted when Sandwich sent him half a buck from Hinchingbrooke, 'smelling a little strong', it was true, but Pepys passed it on to his mother. All the while their intimacy grew, as they sometimes walked and talked in the Whitehall gardens, or attended the Whitehall chapel together. Churchgoing was expected, but Sandwich continued to declare himself without faith. In July he called himself a 'Stoick and a Sceptic', in October Pepys wrote, 'I perceive my Lord is grown a man very indifferent in all matters of Religion', and two weeks later Sandwich again asserted his perfect scepticism.[38] The earl's disavowal of the faith of his youth was understandable, since for him and his former party religion had failed. The people had turned against their puritan zeal, except for those who had tried to make it into a political instrument, and that had failed too. Sandwich began to remember that his father had been favoured by royalty – James I made him a knight of the Bath – and told Pepys it was his sense of gratitude for that royal favour that had brought him back to obedience to the present king.[39] It was a neat piece of justification.

This new Sandwich began to utter the kind of opinions aristocrats were expected to deliver and to make jokes like a man of the world. He thought sermons should be replaced in the churches by homilies that admonished the people to political obedience; no doubt he could recall many stirring sermons from his youth, given by radical puritans like Hugh Peters, now under arrest.[40] The king asked Sandwich to bring his sister, Princess Mary, over from Holland – Pepys was impressed by the royal hug of farewell as he set off – and when he got back he invited Pepys to dine with him alone to discuss his great expenses and need for more money, adding, however, that 'he believed he might have anything that he would ask of the King'.[41] A few days later he again entertained Pepys, this time on a Sunday, with stories of the duke of York getting Chancellor Hyde's daughter Anne with child after falsely promising her marriage. Pepys was riveted by the juicy gossip, relayed in French to keep it from the servants, but he was also somewhat disconcerted by this new aspect of my Lord's talk and put it down to his indifference to religion. Manfully, he wrote down Sandwich's version of a saying of his father's, that a man who gets a wench with child 'and marries her afterward it is as if a man should shit in his hat and then clap it upon his head'.[42]

The robustness of Sandwich's conversation must have been partly a distraction from the painful aspects of his new position. The trials of those held responsible for the execution of Charles I were due in October, and he was required to sit on the bench, because these were show trials in which loyalty to the new regime must be displayed. It was a frightful situation for him, considering that some of the so-called regicides had been his friends and all of them his colleagues. The day before the trials began, Sandwich took to his bed, feeling unwell. He also sent for his wife; her loyal and undemanding presence would be a comfort. Then he took his place on the bench. Ashley Cooper, who had done his best to protect former colleagues, was in the same situation.

Others who faced the imminent prospect of their old comrades being hanged, drawn and quartered took to drink. Blackborne uncharacteristically sat drinking healths one after another with Creed and Pepys at the Rhenish winehouse in King Street on the day some of the sentences were passed. Pepys himself went on 13 October to see the first execution, that of Thomas Harrison, who behaved with flawless courage. He had protested at his trial that he had been kept closely confined for six months and not allowed any counsel. 'If I had been minded to run away I might have had many opportunities,' he said, truthfully, for he had chosen to give himself up. 'But being so clear in the thing, I durst not turn my back nor step a foot out of the way by reason I had been engaged in the service of so glorious and great a God.'[43] He had begun his army career under the earl of Essex and fought at all the great battles; now, sustained by his faith, he endured the procedure of being first hanged and then cut down, still alive, and chopped to pieces. When executions are public, crowds gather to see them, drawn mostly by the deep ghoulish streak that exists in all of us. For some there was also the wish to witness and learn from another man's courage at the end. Pepys, in one of his most famous formulations, wrote that Major-General Harrison looked 'as cheerfully as any man could do in that condition'. Coolly impersonal, even perky, the remark may seem, but it was not just perkiness; Pepys had been under the knife and at risk of death himself, and he had a proper respect for courage. He added, distancing himself from the behaviour of the people, that they gave great shouts of joy when the head and heart were shown, and he went straight on to report respectfully Harrison's, and Mrs Harrison's, declared trust in the judgement of Christ.

Pepys did not devote the rest of his day to higher thoughts any more than one of us, turning from famine or child murder on television, remains sombre an hour later. Other ideas supervene, we even try to cheer ourselves up, as Pepys did. He collected two friends from Whitehall and took them to a tavern for oysters. Then he went home and lost his temper with Elizabeth for leaving things lying about, and kicked and broke the little basket he had brought her from the Hague. After this he withdrew and put up shelves in his study. The flat account of what he did is more powerful than any attempt to moralize or lament.

There were more days on the bench for Sandwich, and more executions. He sent for Pepys on the evening of that of Cromwell's brother-in-law John Jones and 'seemed to be in a melancholy humour'.[44] His servant Will Howe put this down to large losses at cards, enough to upset a man no doubt, but there were more painful reasons. A few days later his spirits bounced up again to an almost manic high as he boasted to Pepys over dinner about how he would have a French cook and a master of his horse, and put his lady and child into black patches, the latest fashion fad, which Pepys found particularly surprising. 'But he is become a perfect Courtier,' he wrote in the Diary afterwards.[45] Lady Sandwich was present at the dinner, and made the mistake of saying she would like to marry their daughter Jem to a good merchant, unleashing a scornful comment from her husband, who told her he would rather see Jem with a pedlar's pack at her back than let her marry a common citizen. The countess had displayed the values of the puritan household in which she was reared and was being told unceremoniously to adjust to her new rank and the new society that had supplied it. Pepys went home thoughtfully, noticing on the way the limbs of some of the dead men set on Aldersgate, 'which was a sad sight to see; and a bloody week this and the last have been'.[46] In November he read a book justifying the trials, which calmed some of his feelings about them.[47]

The navy treasurer, Sir George Carteret, who had known Charles for many years, assured Pepys that he was so compassionate that, left to himself, he would acquit all the regicides, and it is true that he had no liking for the executions – of the twenty-nine condemned that autumn, only ten were put to death. But many languished to slow deaths in prison, prices were put on the heads of some who escaped abroad – £300 for Ludlow, for instance – and there were more victims to come.[48] The king took no pleasure in cruelty, but he did not flinch from killing his enemies. This was made clear when a tiny group of about fifty Nonconformist rebels invoking 'the heads upon the gates', i.e., the executed regicides, and expecting King Jesus to arrive, rose up in London the following January: fourteen were executed, and their heads set up on London Bridge. And Pepys was horrified when he learnt that the bodies of Cromwell, Ireton and Bradshaw were to be dug up and hanged on a gallows on the anniversary of Charles I's execution. In the Diary he called Cromwell 'Oliver', as he had been known in the days of his protectorship, and deplored 'that a man of so great courage as he was should have that dishonour' – adding carefully, as if in fear of an eye over his shoulder, 'though otherwise he might deserve it enough'.[49] Sandwich was away, escorting Henrietta Maria back to France, when the ghastly exhumation took place, and Pepys kept away from it, but Elizabeth was among the thousands who went to watch the show. For sixpence you got a good close look at the body of Cromwell in his coffin. His head was cut off and set up on a pole at the south end of Westminster Hall, next to the houses of parliament and the most important public meeting place in London, where Pepys inevitably saw it in the course of his work within a few days. Every man, woman and child was bound to see it sooner or later; because there it remained, as a warning against rebellion and republicanism, throughout the twenty-five years of Charles II's reign.[50] Pepys kept his own counsel, but it is worth remarking that when, towards the end of his life, he put together a collection of prints showing the royal families of England, he included Cromwell among them – not one but several portraits, all representing him as a great ruler – and Richard Cromwell too, as well as the arms of the commonwealth.

Sir George Downing displayed his change of heart and mind with particular dedication. In January 1662, when he was again acting as English envoy in the Hague, he got news that three old commonwealth associates who had escaped abroad at the Restoration were in Germany and might be lured to Delft. They were Sir John Barkstead, one of Cromwell's major-generals; Miles Corbet, a lawyer of manifest integrity; and John Okey, in whose regiment Downing had served as chaplain when he first came to England. All three were implicated in the trial and execution of Charles I. Downing bribed a Dutchman whom they believed to be their friend to lay a trap for them and wrote his own cool description of their capture. He went himself with some armed men to the house where they were lodging, knocked and rushed in as the door was opened. The three were sitting by a fyere side with a pipe of tobacco and a cup of beere, immediately they started to have gott out at a back Doore but it was too late, the Roome was in a moment fulle. They made many excuses, the one to have gott liberty to have fetcht his coate and another to goe to privy but all in vayne. Corbet did not lodge in that house but had that night supped with Barkstead and . . . had we come a moment later hee had beene gone, . . . but fynding himself thus seized on, his body fell to purging upwards and downwards in the very roome afer a most strange manner.[51]

After some difficulties with the Dutch, Downing had his victims shipped to London, where they were held in the Tower, tried and sentenced to the usual penalty for traitors. They said they had sought only to serve God and their country, and on the scaffold Okey forgave his former chaplain 'that did pursue me to the very death'. Downing was rewarded with a baronetcy.

There is no doubt that the overwhelming majority of the nation wanted to see Charles II on the throne. They had had enough of fighting, they had never approved the execution of the king, they resented the puritan suppression of Christmas and Mayday festivals, dancing, the theatre and children's games on Sunday. Men like Sandwich and Ashley Cooper, who had admired and supported Cromwell, were appalled by the disorder that followed his death and by the power of the military commanders. They came to believe that the restoration of the Stuarts was the best course, and they helped to bring it about as peacefully and as honourably as possible; and they also did very well out of the settlement that was reached. But there was a price to pay, in the betrayal of friends and principles; and although Charles gave them a warm welcome and heaped rewards on them, they carried the mark of men who had changed their loyalties, and were never allowed to forget it. In the next decades this would bring Sandwich to tragedy and lead Ashley Cooper into a fierce struggle against Charles; and in both these episodes Pepys would find himself involved.

8. Families

Whatever Pepys's private feelings when he passed the protector's head in Westminster Hall, and whatever his fears that there might be another political 'turn', he did not let himself forget that he owed his advance to the new regime that had put it there. In January 1661 he was in a 'handsome and thriving condition' and well settled at Seething Lane.[1] For Pepys, the new house was the outward sign of his progress; it became almost the emblem of himself. Even though it was not his own freehold, he was from the start obsessed with altering, decorating and improving the place. If he was not rebuilding the staircase he was enlarging a window, adding an extra storey, putting in a new chimney piece, inserting a door where no door had been before or smartening up the cellar. It was rarely free of workmen in all the time he lived in it; the Diary is crammed with references to joiners, plasterers, painters and upholsterers, and the decorations grew more sumptuous from year to year. Even in the first months he refloored, redecorated and installed gilded leather hangings in the dining room. 'I pray God keep me from setting my mind too much upon it,' he wrote of his feeling for his precious house, but such prayers were formalities, and nothing was going to wean him from his passion.[2] For the next twelve years Seething Lane was the centre of his life. It was to be not just clean, orderly and comfortable but elegantly laid out as to staircases and entrance hall, luxuriously decorated, with displays of pictures and maps; with silver and damask in the dining room, books for both husband and wife arranged on well-built shelves and rooms arranged for entertaining – dinners and card parties – as well as for music-making and quiet private study.

Of course, like every house at that time, it smelt of bodies and hair not often washed, of the frequently overflowing 'house of office' underneath the building, either his own or the neighbours', which needed emptying regularly; and of the chamber pots that had to be carried up and down and were, not surprisingly, sometimes spilt, a cause of merriment to Elizabeth as she cleared up the mess.[3] But it bore no resemblance either to the house in which he had grown up or to the narrow farm house at Brampton. There may have been memories of rooms at Durdans and Hinchingbrooke in his head, and he was inspired above all by his sense of himself as a man of 'liberal genius' – that is, one temperamentally attached to gentlemanly pursuits and studies.[4] He might be working on figures, contracts and estimates across the courtyard at the Navy Board, or tramping along the river to Deptford to inspect the shipyards; he might not have the elegant appearance or bearing of an aristocrat; but his inner self was that of an aesthete and an artist, and the house represented his aspiration to live by higher cultural values.

Within months of moving in he doubled the size of his household; they were now a family of six. This must have been a relief to Jane, who had helped them single-handedly through the move from Axe Yard. She persuaded Pepys to take her younger brother Wayneman on as his boy servant, after he had made a brief trial of another and sacked him. Wayneman was between ten and twelve years old, and she had to teach him his duties, how to put his master to bed, tidying away his clothes and fetching nightgown and cap, and how to comb his hair, the bedtime procedure Pepys enjoyed so much and sometimes made an occasion for horseplay: Jane may have been relieved to delegate this too. Pepys thought him a nice-looking boy and was pleased to find he could just about read, and might be taught to do better; he liked teaching as well as having his hair combed.[5] Wayneman was provided with a livery, and sometimes called 'young Pepys' by the neighbours.[6] As for a child of their own: a room was set aside hopefully to become the nursery.[7]

Pall was also offered a place in the household. She was still living at Salisbury Court with her parents, and, to make sure she had no illusions about the position they expected her to occupy with them, she was told bluntly that she was to come, 'not as a sister in any respect but as a servant'. The tears she shed, Pepys decided, were brought on by her joy at the prospect of working for them; and perhaps she did expect to have more fun with Elizabeth and Jane than with her mother, and accepted that a brother who had risen to such heights of success might be entitled to forget to be civil to his own sister.[8] She arrived early in January 1661 and, to emphasize what had already been said, was forbidden to sit down at table with her brother and sister-in-law on her first day in the house.[9]

The third new member of the family came to them through Pepys's friendship with Blackborne. The Diary is studded with references to drinks, meals and other meetings between the two men, as Blackborne, intent on salvaging something from the wreck of his past career, put his knowledge, contacts and advice at Pepys's disposal; in exchange he got his sister's young son William Hewer a job with Pepys, in the combined roles of personal servant and clerk. It was a master stroke for a man faced with the end of the regime in which he had flourished, to get his nephew into the organization from which he himself had been ejected – a Darwinian coup, ensuring that his family genes retained their influence. And Will Hewer succeeded beyond any dream Blackborne can have had. Pepys noted his arrival at the house in Seething Lane but omitted any account of how he came to employ him other than that he was Blackborne's nephew.[10]

Will, the son of Thomas Hewer, a stationer, was an unfledged, fair-haired boy of seventeen, and Pepys felt free to bully him and box his ears, sometimes reducing him to tears.[11] But he learnt to defend himself and to argue back. Over the next few years he even managed to misbehave with some style. He stayed out late. He became too friendly with the maids, corrupting them, according to Pepys, although it seems to have meant little more than discussing their employer with them behind his back. He got drunk. He refused to go to church. He wore his hat in the house and flung his cloak dramatically over his shoulder in the street 'like a Ruffian'.[12] He said he would not be treated like a slave.[13] In short, he did his best to become the son Pepys failed to beget. He was only ten years younger than his master, but you would hardly guess that from Pepys's treatment of him. Pepys complained of Will's behaviour to his uncle Blackborne more than once, and the point was even reached when he angrily turned him out of the house – though not out of his clerkship – and told him he must live in lodgings. Will was much too good at his work to be sacked, and Pepys defended him when he was attacked by others. In January 1662, for instance, there was a complaint from the highest official of the Navy Board that Will was telling office business to his parliamentarian uncle, Blackborne, described as 'a rogue', and Pepys was advised to sack him. Though troubled, Pepys did no such thing. He simply had a cautionary word with Will, who took the warning and presumably became more discreet in visiting his uncle Blackborne. Nothing more was heard of the matter.[14]

The arrival of this clever, good-natured young man enriched the emotional possibilities within the household. He was only two years younger than Elizabeth, and if he took on the role of son to Pepys, he also seems to have given his heart to her. It was an innocent passion as such things go, and also a definitive one. When some years later Pepys tried to persuade him to marry Pall, Will made it clear that this was out of the question, adding that he had no intention of marrying anyone. He never went back on this resolve. At Christmas 1667 he offered Elizabeth a diamond locket, which she kept for some weeks before showing it to her husband, who insisted on her returning it: since Will was earning only £30 a year, and the locket was worth £40, he had obviously already learnt how to profit from his position in the office. Pepys had no objection to that, but suffered from twinges of jealousy over his friendship with Elizabeth; she often invited Will to escort her when she went out or to keep her company at home when her perpetually busy husband was absent.[15]

But at the beginning, in the summer of 1660 when Will arrived, he was nothing more than a bright, shy boy, ready to make himself useful. He read Latin with his master, learnt to use his shorthand when Pepys asked him to; and he could soon turn out accounts every bit as neatly and nimbly. Another thing they had in common was a name that defeated almost everyone who tried to write it down. Will Hewer's appeared in variations ranging exotically through Ewre, Ewere and Eure to Hewers, Hewest, Yewers and Youar, though he seems to have stuck to 'Hewer' himself, as Pepys did to Pepys, although he appeared as Pepies, Paypes, Pepes, Peeps, Peppiss, Peipes, Peepys, Pypss and more.[16] Hewer's intellectual and business abilities, his even temper, his central position in the household as friend to both husband and wife and the way he withstood Pepys's bullying made him not only a surrogate son but, as the years went by, his closest friend.

The lease of the house in Axe Yard ('my poor little house') was got rid of in the autumn of 1660, although not before Pepys had taken advantage of its emptiness to entertain two different young women there: his old friend Betty Lane, with whom he was 'exceeding free' and she 'not unfree to take it'; and Diana, daughter of Mrs Crisp, his neighbour in the Yard. He had suspected Diana of being not as good as she should be over drinks at her mother's house one evening, when her brother Laud was leaving to serve Lord Sandwich; when Pepys got her alone he found her surprisingly compliant, and for the first time resorted to a foreign language in the Diary to record his success: '*nulla puella negat*', he wrote in Latin, meaning 'the girl refused nothing'.[17] He salved his conscience towards Elizabeth by taking her out and buying her a pearl necklace costing £4.10s. the following day. This was a variant on his system of moral accounting, in which he made vows – to abstain from drink or theatregoing, for instance – and paid money into the poor box to atone for each broken vow; by spending money on his wife he compensated for his infidelity.

He had now become, in addition to his other offices, a justice of the peace, his rising path crossing with that of Richard Sherwyn, the JP who had presided over his wedding five years before: Sherwyn was then secretary to the Treasury commissioners and a valued colleague of Downing; now he was out, reduced to finding what work he could as a humble clerk.[18] Pepys's new status was full of these surprises. He found himself receiving a five-gun salute when he escorted Lord Sandwich to his ship. He was invited to dine by the lord mayor. He was able to escort his wife into the presence room at court to observe the queen mother at close quarters: 'a very little plain old woman and nothing more' is what he saw.[19] Men who would not have deigned to speak to him a year ago now came cap in hand, as he noted with relish, and sea captains were so deferential that he had to learn 'how to receive so much reverence, which at the begining I could not tell how to do'.[20] It took time for him to believe in himself as a gentleman; on the death of his uncle Robert in the summer of 1661 he exaggerated the value of his Brampton inheritance to his colleagues at the Navy Office, because he felt he must try to impress them.[21]

He was the youngest of the officers there, the poorest, the least experienced and one of the few without a title. The two he got to know first, because they were also his new neighbours in Seething Lane, Sir William Batten and Sir William Penn, were naval commanders of long service with distinguished fighting records; the Pepyses gave their first dinner party for them in January 1661. Penn had taken Jamaica for the English, and Batten, a man of sixty, had been surveyor of the navy under Charles I and knew everything there was to know about the naval yards where ships were built. To a junior colleague who had been to sea only twice and had no knowledge of ships, they were potentially alarming figures. Both were West Country men who had gone to sea as boys; Batten had trained Penn, who was a generation younger, not yet forty. Both had served the commonwealth and made good money, and Penn had acquired estates in Ireland. Both owned fine country houses at Walthamstow. Penn had risen to vice-admiral under Cromwell. Blackborne told Pepys that Penn had put on a 'pretence of sanctity' in order to get promotion; but puritan piety had been required when he was young and was standard at the time, as Sandwich's history bore witness.[22] Penn had fought against the Dutch alongside Blake and Monck, and pursued Prince Rupert furiously in the Mediterranean. In 1652 he claimed he had not set foot on land for a whole year; but he was not just brawn and bluster, for he had drawn up a code of naval tactics for Cromwell and served as a commissioner on his Navy Board. He had also had some inconclusive contact with the exiled Charles and been briefly imprisoned by Cromwell; yet he had accepted a knighthood from Richard Cromwell. With Monck's support he made another approach to Charles, which explained his favourable reception and second knighthood in 1660, and his reappointment as a commissioner to the new Navy Board.

In short, like the majority of his fellow countrymen, he had changed and adapted with time and circumstance. Batten too had gone over to Charles for a while in the early 1650s – he had received his knighthood from him then – and then thought better of it; and finally both men had contrived to be on the right side at the right time. When Pepys, drinking at the Dolphin with them, listened to them 'betwitt' and reproach one another with their behaviour under the commonwealth, he said he felt ashamed to hear them; but there must have been a lot of this sort of talk going on, and Pepys's remark seems oddly inappropriate given his own patrons' history.[23] Batten bought some commonwealth ships' carvings and coats of arms that were being sold off, some to be made into garden ornaments, others to burn on the night of Charles II's coronation, which suggests he didn't take these things too seriously.[24] He had been reappointed surveyor to the board, and Pepys observed that he lived like a prince with his young second wife in their Walthamstow house. Penn's half-Dutch wife came from their Irish estates to join him in London; Pepys described her as 'an old Dutchwoman'. They had a daughter Pegg, and two sons, the elder, William, at Oxford, just getting into trouble for his Nonconformity: he became a Quaker, to his father's initial fury, and was the future founder of Pennsylvania.[25] Pepys was snobbish about both families, which he had no right to be; his only claim to superiority was his university education, but it allowed him to look down his nose at them for not being gentlemen. The truth was they were exactly the sort of naval officers he came to approve of, 'tarpaulins' who had worked their way up from boyhood and knew all the ropes, as opposed to the gentlemen officers who expected to be given commands without knowing anything of the discipline of the sea. Penn in particular was an energetic and intelligent man, and soon drew up a new version of his code of tactics that became standard, put out as 'The Duke of York's Sailing and Fighting Instructions'. 'Vieux Pen', as the duke called him in 1665 when he was forty-three, went to sea against the Dutch again, although ill with gout, was appointed 'Captain of the Fleet' and fought bravely.[26]

The two Sir Williams were sociable and hospitable neighbours, entertaining Pepys and Elizabeth with meals, theatre expeditions and visits to Walthamstow. Pepys was intrigued by the black domestic servants each of them owned, Mingo and Jack, slaves from the African trade; it was fashionable for officers to own one, and Sandwich had also acquired a little Turk and a Negro boy for his family.[27] Batten invited the Pepyses to celebrate his election to parliament at Rochester with an outing and a festive dinner, and his third wedding anniversary with some fancy pies; on another occasion Penn invited them to *his* eighteenth wedding anniversary, at which eighteen mince pies were served. The three men arranged to watch the pre-coronation procession together. There were occasional fallings out of the kind neighbours have – Lady Batten felt that Mrs Pepys did not show her all the respect she should – but there was a great deal of conviviality and cooperation too. Pepys and Batten collaborated on having new top floors for their houses constructed in the shipyards at Deptford. Pepys joined in bawdy songs with Penn, but he also listened carefully when he talked of 'things and persons that I did not understand' during the commonwealth.[28] At first he shared an office with them, but in 1662 he insisted on a private office for himself, leaving the two Sir Williams to share.

While Pepys was head of the family at Seething Lane, he remained a member of another family in which he felt almost equally at home, but where the role he had to play was quite different. When 'my Lady', countess of Sandwich, arrived in town in October 1660, he naturally called on her at once. He found her alone at supper in the Whitehall lodgings, and she pressed him to sit down with her and to stay on afterwards, 'she showing me most extraordinary love and kindness' and talking to him about his uncle Robert at Brampton, known to her for many years at Hinchingbrooke.[29] She was now thirty-five and mother of eight children, all alive and well including the twin boys – a rare record of success at that date. Her life had been distinguished by courage and discretion, since she had been more often than not in charge of her husband's house and estate in his absence, and supported him through difficult and dangerous times year in, year out. Entering the new and transformed London society for the first time as a countess and preparing to appear at court, she may have been a little nervous of what she would find and what was expected of her, not least by her husband. And indeed nothing in her life till then had prepared her for the court of the new king, with its pursuit of pleasure, its nights spent in gambling, its showy, competitive beauties; her beauty lay in a gentle face, thoughtful eyes and a tranquil mind. Pepys, whom she had known for years, could still be talked to in the old way; they could gossip, and she could trust him.

Two days after her talk with Pepys she invited him to bring Elizabeth to supper with her, Lord Sandwich being absent at the chancellor's; and, on Sandwich's going to sea a few days after that, Pepys became a regular visitor at the Whitehall lodgings. He had after all lived there and knew all the servants as well as the children; and although no longer exactly a servant himself, something of the role remained, and he made himself generally obliging and useful. When a French maid arrived, Elizabeth went along to interpret, because Lady Sandwich knew no French, a language not much studied in puritan families during the civil war and commonwealth period. Pepys noted that it was on this occasion, in November 1660, that Lord Sandwich, for the first time ever, took notice of Elizabeth 'as my wife'. For five years she had been invisible; now suddenly he could see her.[30]

Lady Sandwich did nothing to discourage Pepys from considering himself as one of the family, and he felt free to turn up for meals either at Whitehall or at the Wardrobe, where she moved in May 1661, whenever he felt like it. Sometimes he ate with the servants, sometimes with my Lady and sometimes, when he was there, with my Lord. For instance, Pepys noted the excellent quality of the food when he dropped in casually with Creed in May 1661 and 'we, with the rest of the servants in the Hall, sat down and eat of the best cold meats that ever I eat on in all my life'.[31] A week later he enjoyed a venison pasty for dinner with Lord Sandwich and all the officers of the Wardrobe. He also noted how the food deteriorated once Sandwich went to sea again in June and his wife economized: 'went and dined with my Lady; who now my Lord is gone, is come to her poor housekeeping again'.[32]

The Diary provides a marvellously detailed study of this near-feudal arrangement prevailing in the middle of the seventeenth century and of its slow shift into more modern attitudes. In 1660 Pepys still took his membership of the Sandwich household absolutely for granted; for years he had eaten and slept among the Sandwich servants whenever he chose to, and he still indulged in casual sexual familiarities with the housekeeper Sarah. He also knew that he owed duty, deference and practical assistance to Lady Sandwich, especially in the absence of her husband; both of them enjoyed his attentiveness to her. For instance, in January 1661 he promised to accompany her to Chatham to show her over the ships, my Lord having been much too busy to do so and now gone to sea. As the agreed time approached, Pepys had to spend three nights at Deptford inspecting the yard and forgot his promise. He arrived home from Deptford to be told that she had already set off by coach, expecting to meet him in Rochester; and, tired as he was, he at once put on his boots, hired a horse and a guide, and covered the thirty miles to Rochester in a speedy four hours.[33] There he found 'my Lady and her daughter Jem and Mrs Browne and five servants, all at a loss not finding me here', but 'at my coming she was overjoyed'.[34] Pepys liked to emphasize her expressions of affection in the Diary, but there is no reason to doubt she made them.

She had planned to make her visit incognito, but, unsurprisingly, the captain of the *Charles* recognized her, and there was a cheerful supper party. Pepys shared a bed with her page and breakfasted with her. The whole group was then taken by barge, first to the biggest ship in the fleet, the *Royal Sovereign*, built before the war, in 1637; it had six lanterns in the stern, and everyone managed to squeeze into one of them. Then on to the *Charles*, on which Pepys had sailed to Holland when it was the *Naseby*; he was delighted to revisit 'the ship that I begun my good fortune in', and she to hear him describe how everything was arranged for her Lord when he was aboard. Another breakfast was served, and there were gun salutes; then Pepys, always the eager teacher, insisted on showing her a small ship, so that she might appreciate the difference. He carried out his role to perfection, handing out tips and escorting her back to her coach. The weather turned so bad on the return journey to London that they were forced to spend the night at a Dartford inn, where, over dinner, Pepys and Lady Sandwich amicably argued the rights and wrongs of primogeniture. Afterwards he went off with the captains, looking for a pretty girl they had heard about who played a guitar; but they failed to find her. In the morning they all went back separately to London in the rain. She was in early pregnancy; he went straight to consult his doctor about the 'decay of my memory' that had made him forget his appointment with her, for which Hollier advised him to cut down his drinking.[35] The trip had turned out an undoubted success, a little interlude of pleasure for them both; and there were to be more.

She sometimes gave him advice, telling him he should be more generous to Elizabeth, of whom she became particularly fond. She was not narrow-minded but ready to chat and joke, and enjoyed gossiping about the scandals at court, especially the king's mistress Lady Castlemaine – admired by Pepys – and what would happen to her when he married. Pepys was especially helpful to her in the eleven months in which Sandwich was away at sea fetching the new queen from Portugal, during which Lady Sandwich gave birth to her daughter Catherine in London. The Diary records seventy-five visits to her over this period. 'Shows my wife and me the greatest favour in the world,' he writes; 'my Lady very merry and very handsome methought'; 'an hour or two's talk with my Lady with great pleasure'; 'stayed talking with my Lady all the afternoon, till late at night'; 'stayed all the afternoon with my Lady alone, talking'; 'an hour to two's talk in Divinity with my Lady'. After this particular talk, Elizabeth arrived, and they were 'very merry; and my Lady very fond, as she always is, of my wife'.[36] In common with all mothers, Lady Sandwich was especially grateful for his attentions to her children. He took the older girls to the theatre, to Islington to eat cheesecake and to Bartholomew Fair; and the younger children to see the lions in the menagerie at the Tower. He and Elizabeth offered to have the three little boys, Oliver, John and Charles, to stay, and they came to Seething Lane in August when Lady Sandwich was about to give birth. After the birth, her friend Mrs Crisp told her she would get the king to be godfather to the baby Catherine, which embarrassed her so much, she told Pepys, 'that she sweat in the very telling of it'. No sweat was needed, as the king did not become godfather.[37]

She invited both Pepyses to go with her to Hampton Court and showed them over the palace. He took the children to see the king's yacht, the *Catherine*, and later escorted her aboard it. This was the occasion of her first visit to Seething Lane, and she allowed him to lead her through the courtyard by the hand for everyone in the office to see, in her fine clothes and with her page holding up her train. After this they took a boat to Greenwich and walked to the top of the hill together – a considerable feat in a dress with a train – then returned on the water, 'she being much pleased with the ramble – in every perticular of it. So we supped with her and then walked home.'[38]

Pepys's attachment to 'my Lady' was a little like Will Hewer's to Elizabeth, a devotion to a woman who could safely be admired, even adored, because she was sexually inaccessible. For Pepys, she existed on a different level from the generality of her sex, and he never had a bad or seriously disrespectful word to say about her. When she made an unannounced visit to his house, and he, hurrying over from the office to greet her because Elizabeth was out, found her sitting on a chamber pot in his dining room, she blushed and he talked hastily to cover his embarrassment; but they both had enough aplomb to go on to discuss a debate in the House of Commons about a Dutch war before she made her dignified departure. The episode is surprising; she was in advanced pregnancy, with her last child, and it is her only other recorded appearance at Seething Lane. It clearly shook him somewhat: 'mightily taken with her dear visit' is what he wrote in the Diary.[39] His visits to her had few constraints. He saw her when she had just given birth and was also recovering from measles; the measles worried him so much that when he called and found the children and my Lord had fled the house he thought she might be dead: 'it will be a sad hour to that family should she miscarry'.[40] He stood by her bedside on another occasion when she was ill; he admired her sangfroid as she waited for news of her husband after a sea battle, 'in the best temper, neither confident nor troubled with fear, that I ever did see in my life'.[41] He helped her to organize her daughter Jem's wedding in the absence of Lord Sandwich and listened sympathetically to her fears that Jem might not like the match arranged for her. He lent her money, albeit reluctantly: even Lady Sandwich could not make him free with his money, and he charged her 6 per cent.[42] He admired her unworldliness, which made her so different from himself and which he called her innocence. To him she was 'My best Lady Sandwich', in the phrase that discreetly singles out those who are especially loved.[43]

Despite all this, time and circumstance changed their friendship. The quasi-feudal household ceased to attract him once he had established himself as a powerful and successful man in his own right, and he did not like it to be known that he had formerly been a servant. Once or twice she reproached him for not visiting her, and once she pressed him to come to Hinchingbrooke. She was much less in London after 1665, and Pepys was increasingly busy and preoccupied with war, work, the fire, his eye trouble and other worries. He managed to visit her briefly at Hinchingbrooke in the autumn of 1667, when they had long talks and she told him she looked on him 'like one of her own family and interest'.[44] He also wrote to her from time to time but may not have expected or got answers; writing was not her best accomplishment, as the few surviving letters to her husband show. This one went to him in Spain in the summer of 1668: 'I weare in great straiths for money . . . and can get none from Mr More, and therfor am forsed to borow of my cosen Pepys, a 100 pound, which I doubt will not serve till you com. I pray God send us a happy and spedy meeting, if it be his wille. Hinchbrok much want your selfe although it now is plesent.'[45] Her marriage suffered strains as well as long separations, but to Pepys she remained always 'the same most excellent, good, discreet lady that ever she was'.[46]

★

Pepys was not enthusiastic about many of his blood relations. Like most people, he preferred the ones who did well in life. His favourite London cousin was Jane Pepys, later Turner, whose parents had taken him to Surrey as a child, who had made a good marriage and continued her parents' kindness when she offered her house to him for his operation. He also got on well with the son of his Cambridge great-uncle Talbot, Roger Pepys, the lawyer. After this, there was a first cousin, Charles Pepys, who became a master-joiner at Chatham and referred to himself as 'your honnor's poor kinsman' when writing to him in later life; Pepys kept up a kindly distant interest in him.[47] Uncle Wight, his father's half-brother, a London fishmonger and general merchant who did well and lost all his children, had an obvious claim on Pepys's attention; his remarkable attempt to unite the two families is told in Chapter 13.

He found his mother's family more of a trial. Her nieces, Mary and Kate Fenner, married brothers, William and Anthony Joyce, sons of a rich tallow chandler but 'dull company and impertinent' in Pepys's view.[48] They called on him more often than he liked and took their cousinship seriously, commenting freely on family matters; for instance they laughed at the idea that Pepys might be knighted by the king when he came ashore in 1660; and they hurried round to tell Pepys that his brother Tom had the pox – falsely, as it turned out.[49] Neither of their own marriages was happy, but they enjoyed suggesting wives for Tom and husbands for Pall. In the course of the Diary, Pepys had to help William when he got into trouble for trying to arrest a peeress for debt, and to lend money to Anthony after his house was burnt in the great fire; and when Anthony tried to drown himself in a fit of depression, dying shortly afterwards, Pepys helped his widow Kate to secure the estate. Even with these troublesome cousins, although he grumbled, he had too strong a sense of the obligations of blood not to do his duty.

He showed less kindness to his own sister Pall than to many of his cousins. The attempt to make her into an extra servant at Seething Lane was not a success, and by the summer of 1661 he had decided to be rid of her. Following uncle Robert's death, the Pepys parents were moving to Brampton, leaving the Salisbury Court house and the tailoring business to Tom. Sam's plan was to send Pall to live with them in Huntingdonshire; he did not expect her to welcome the idea.

First he informed his father; then he set up a great scene in which both men declared they wanted nothing to do with Pall; and only when they had 'brought down her high spirit' – a phrase reeking of a sour and bullying morality – did they relent and say she might at any rate go to Brampton. Poor Pall had lived in London all her life and hated the idea of the country, but a few days later she was put into the slow carrier's wagon with her mother and went into exile in floods of tears.[50]

Her future was a worry to him. 'God knows . . . what will become of her, for I have not anything yet to spare her, and she grows now old and must be disposed of one way or another' – this in 1663, when she was twenty-three.[51] He set aside £500 as a dowry and over the next years made several attempts to find her a husband, all of which failed. As we have seen, in 1667 he offered her to Will Hewer, who explained politely that he planned to remain a bachelor.[52] He then tried to interest his school and college friend Richard Cumberland, with no more success; he was on his way to a bishop's throne. In the end she may have found her own husband, since he was a Huntingdonshire lad, John Jackson, 'a plain young man, handsome enough for her; one of no education nor discourse, but of few words . . . I shall have no pleasure nor content in him, as if he had been a man of breeding', wrote Pepys when he met him.[53] Neither he nor Elizabeth attended the wedding, which took place at Brampton on 27 February 1668. Pepys merely noted the news of it a few days later and wrote to congratulate his father, not Jackson or Pall herself.[54] The Jacksons settled down to farm at Ellington, not far from Brampton, and old Mr Pepys went to live with them; and when Pepys visited he observed that she had grown comelier, 'but a mighty pert woman she is, and I think proud, he keeping her mighty handsome, and they say mighty fond'.[55] The three mightys showed he was not going to warm to his sister even as a bride enjoying her brief season of dignity and joy. It did not occur to him for a moment that pert Pall and her ill-bred husband were going to produce a son who would win his love, accept his guidance, act out his dreams, serve his projects and contribute largely to his own family happiness.

9. Work

Pepys's office, the centre of his working life, was across the courtyard from his house. In a few steps he was at his desk, and in another few he was home again, and he went to and fro from early morning until midnight and after. There were no fixed working hours for the officers of the Navy Board, although their meetings were held twice weekly at Seething Lane, and they attended the duke of York as lord high admiral in Whitehall once a week on a Monday morning – sometimes they found he had gone hunting instead. Pepys's duties took him out of the office a great deal, but when he wanted to leave town for any reason, he applied to the duke for permission. Taking time off to enjoy himself in London was his own affair; he took plenty, but sometimes worried about being seen idling in the company of women or at the theatre, by courtiers who might report him to the duke – not that there is any evidence that they ever did.[1] Like almost everything connected with the navy, arrangements were informal, flexible, ad hoc and dependent on personal contacts. Pepys is often spoken of as an early civil servant, but there was no civil service as we know it: no career structure, no examinations for entry, no clear path of promotion and no pension system.[2] However, if things went wrong, those held responsible were liable to censure or the sack, and sometimes arrest and imprisonment.

The members of the Navy Board were appointed by the king and whoever he chose to listen to. In 1660 Sandwich, as vice-admiral, was one adviser, alongside the duke of York and his secretary, William Coventry. They agreed that the board should consist of four principal officers, as it had done under Charles I – treasurer, comptroller, surveyor and clerk of the acts – and three commissioners, a system that had worked well under the commonwealth. Sir George Carteret, an impeccable royalist whose service at sea had begun under Charles I and who had held Jersey for him, was appointed treasurer. He had official lodgings at Whitehall, a house in Pall Mall, another at Deptford and a country mansion near Windsor, and he was the highest paid, with £2,000 a year and the right to three pence in every pound he handled – this was a remnant of the old way of doing things. He was well disposed to Pepys, and Pepys knew he must cultivate him. The comptrollership went to two still more aged cavaliers, first Sir Robert Slingsby, who died within a year, then Sir John Mennes, whose naval career went back to the 1620s. He had fought at sea with Prince Rupert and no doubt against William Penn; and he was an educated man, a wit and a poet who had published imitations of Chaucer and encouraged Pepys to appreciate *The Canterbury Tales* and *Troilus and Criseyde*.

The surveyor, with particular responsibility for the dockyards and the design, building and repair of ships, was Sir William Batten, a professional who had served on both sides during the civil war. Of the commissioners, Penn, who was given a brief to take an interest in every aspect of the board's work, also owed his appointment to his years of experience as a naval commander; both men made a useful practical link with the commonwealth regime. Another commissioner, Peter Pett, the master-shipwright at Chatham, had nothing of the cavalier about him and had served Cromwell zealously; but no change of government could unseat him, because the Pett family had a virtual monopoly of shipbuilding in the Thames yards, and he moved smoothly to work for the restored monarchy. In May 1660 he had been summoned on board the *Naseby* to prepare it for the king, and later in the year he started to build a royal pleasure yacht, the *Catherine*, greatly admired by Pepys.[3]

These were the men with whom Pepys chiefly had to work; Lord Berkeley, the third commissioner, was appointed purely as a sign of royal favour; nothing was expected of him. There were further officers working at the more distant dockyards, Harwich and Portsmouth, some with histories of service to the commonwealth.[4] Other minor officials left over from commonwealth days contrived to hang on in lesser jobs: Thomas Turner, clerk-general of the Navy Office from 1646, was disappointed in his hope of getting the job that went to Pepys, although he was allowed to remain as purveyor of petty provisions and kept a lodging at Seething Lane. Pepys did not care for him but enjoyed gossiping with his wife.

Each officer of the Navy Board was served by his own two clerks, chosen by himself and usually owing their jobs to personal connections, just as their master did. Pepys was quick to defend his two, Tom Hayter and Will Hewer, against any criticism and to attack inefficiency among the others. The rest of the staff served everyone: two messengers, a doorkeeper, a porter and a couple of watchmen; and there were boatmen ready to take all the board officials up or down river at all times.

Pepys started work with more doubts than zeal as he sorted and made inventories of the papers of the outgoing regime. He began to realize how much technical and procedural knowledge he would need to master if he were to be an effective member of the board. His function, as clerk of the acts, was to act as secretary, keeping minutes and records; and he was not at all certain he wanted the job. He learnt that there was another claimant to it, an old man called Thomas Barlow who had held it under Charles I and needed to be bought out with an annuity. Pepys was tempted by another man who offered him £500 for the job and then, as he hesitated, doubled his offer to £1,000. Sandwich had to explain to him that it was not the salary that made a man rich, but the 'opportunities of getting money while he is in the place'.[5] He appreciated the point as gold pieces, silver tankards, barrels of oysters and presents for Elizabeth came in. It took him much longer to start to enjoy his work. Only when he saw that he could extend it far beyond his official function and take an active part in policy-making did it become really interesting to him.

During his first eighteen months at the board nobody was doing much beyond paying off ships as they came in from their voyages. By July 1661 the Cromwellian navy no longer existed, and it seemed unnecessary to maintain so large a fleet.[6] London was still in a celebratory mood, cheerful enough to overcome a few alarms from religious anti-monarchists who took up arms believing that Christ's Kingdom was coming and were ferociously put down; and there was the coronation to be attended to in April 1661. Pepys reported on it with all his bravura, from a 4 a.m. climb to perch on the scaffolding in the Abbey to waking in a pool of his own vomit the next morning – another set-piece. There were also the newly opened theatres, which he found irresistible, with their repertoire of Elizabethan and Jacobean masterpieces, their many adaptations from the Spanish and the French, new works by Dryden and D'Avenant, and ambitious scenery. Throughout 1661 he went two or three times a week to either the King's Company, managed by Thomas Killigrew, wit and courtier, or the Duke's, under D'Avenant. In January he saw a woman on stage for the first time, and may have thought of his own boyish attempt at Arethusa. In August he was at *Hamlet* with Thomas Betterton and found it 'beyond imagination': Betterton, 'the best actor in the world', was taught the part by D'Avenant, who had studied it with Shakespeare himself.[7] Other pleasures associated with his new position led to him being too drunk to conduct family prayers with the servants on a Sunday evening.[8] After this had happened twice, he was ashamed enough to take a vow at the end of December to avoid plays and wine; and at least partly as a result of this 1662 became the year in which he learnt to love his work. He saw that it gave him the chance to prove his capacity, and he realized that, whatever superiority his fellow officers at the board possessed in rank and experience, in intellect and application he surpassed all but one of them.

This one was William Coventry, the duke's secretary. Coventry was replacing Pepys's friend Blackborne, the commonwealth's secretary to the Admiralty; but he quickly became Pepys's hero, for his brains, his efficiency and his cool.[9] In 1662 he joined the Navy Board, remaining secretary to the duke, and he was also in parliament, where he was an admired speaker. Five years older than Pepys, he was a gentleman born and socially far above him, the son of a high official of Charles I; after Oxford he had fought for the king before retreating into private life, making at least one visit to the Continent to assert his loyalty to Charles II in exile. At the Restoration the royal brothers chose him to head their procession into London. He had a reputation as 'a wise and witty gentleman' and also as one 'void of religion'; and he had political ambitions.[10] From the start of his acquaintance with Pepys he liked his intelligence and efficiency and made sure that he had 'good access' to the duke.[11] He was also amused by his younger colleague and took an interest in his tastes; noticing his taste for gadgets, he presented him with a silver fountain pen. He wrote him personal letters; one of them specified charmingly, 'This is not an answer to you the office but you as Mr Pepys.' He listened to him singing. He accepted a spur of the moment invitation to dine at his home after they had been working together.[12] On the river one broiling August day, he put the skirt of his own coat over Pepys to protect him from the sun, an oddly intimate and touching gesture. Pepys trusted and relied on him in return. When his clerk Hayter was in trouble for attending a Quaker meeting, he went straight to Coventry, who in turn spoke to the duke of York and brought back his verdict that, so long as Hayter did his work well, his religion did not bother him. Hayter kept his job, and Pepys thought the better of the duke.

Pepys appreciated Coventry's conversation enough to write some of it down. There was his 'rule of suspecting every man that proposed anything to him to be a knave, or at least to have some ends of his own in it'. Another maxim was 'that a man that cannot sit still in his chamber . . . and he that cannot say no . . . is not fit for business' (to which Pepys added, 'The last of which is a very great fault of mine, which I must amend in'). He believed that Coventry could do more to reform the abuses he found in the shipyards – among them badly made contracts, poor regulation of repairs, the disastrous system of paying seamen by ticket – than the rest of the board put together and wrote to him early in their association, in 1662, urging him to give more time to its work: 'Would to God you could for a while spare 2 afternoons in a week for general debates.' Although there is no sign that this happened, the two men discussed office business and public affairs together regularly throughout the years of the Diary. Their private lives remained in strictly separate compartments: Coventry did not meet Elizabeth; and, while Sir William Penn made a toast to Coventry's nameless mistress, she makes no appearance in the Diary, and he never took a wife.[13]

Pepys enjoyed Mennes's literary conversation, his stories and his mimicry, but saw that he was too old to work and useless as comptroller.[14] He threw many a 'dotard' and 'old fool' at him in the Diary, and after two years of his incompetence told Coventry he intended to take over a good part of Sir John's work, without of course saying anything to him. 'I thought the Comptroller would not take it ill,' said Pepys, to which Coventry 'wittily replied that there was nothing in the world so hateful as a dog in a manger'.[15] Mennes was past the age of ambition and no doubt happy to have his work taken over by his junior. Other officers were not so acquiescent, and there was a nasty scene when Penn checked Pepys as he began to make out a contract and 'most basely told me that the Comptroller is to do it'. It was done in the presence of Coventry, and Pepys argued with Penn and lost the argument. The humiliation angered him so much that he wrote down that Penn 'did it like a base raskall, and so I shall remember him while I live'; and so he did. Pepys had a long memory for both favours and slights.[16]

All the officers made visits to the shipyards at Deptford, Woolwich, Chatham and Portsmouth, to inspect ships and pay off the seamen as they came in from their voyages. It was work, but there were some trips that combined pleasure with work, as Pepys shows in the Diary. In Chatham he flirted with the pretty daughter of the official in charge of the ropeyard. On another occasion Elizabeth and Creed went with him to Portsmouth, and he allowed Hayter to bring his wife along too, making it into a short holiday; they had their wives shown over a ship, took a walk on the walls of the town and saw the sights, including the room in which the duke of Buckingham had been murdered in 1628.[17] For the nearer yards, Pepys could travel up and down the Thames by boat, charging expenses of seven shillings for every visit to Deptford or Woolwich.[18] Rather than taking a boat, he very often walked along the south bank of the river, into Redriff (now Rotherhithe), and on through the orchards and meadows to Deptford, Greenwich and even Woolwich. He enjoyed walking, and the river bank and adjacent countryside were so little frequented that he often read a book as he followed the familiar grassy footpaths, breaking off to climb stiles. You can take his route today through housing estates, past grimy churches and scraps of garden and over the foully polluted River Ravensbourne, your imagination struggling to clean up and empty the world as you go. The river was unembanked then, and at low tide a wide beach appeared. There is still a Cherry Garden Pier marking where he bought cherries in the orchards close to the river, and an inn at the water's edge between Southwark and Rotherhithe on the spot where he often stopped for a drink. The fifteenth-century tower of St Nicholas's Church also remains at Deptford, where skulls grin over the churchyard gate. The green hill of Greenwich, rising solidly before you as you round the loop of the river, has changed little in three hundred years, and for Pepys this was one of the most familiar views in his working life. He described walking in Greenwich Park in the spring of 1662 with Penn, seeing the young trees newly planted by the King and the steps just made up the hill to the castle, 'which is very magnificent' – Wren's observatory, built in the 1670s, now stands on the site. From the top of the hill he could look back across the loops of the river, crowded with sails, and the miles of green country, back to London's spires and smoke; whether he walked or took a boat home would depend on the tide.

The board made contracts with suppliers of shipbuilding material – timber, hemp, tar, canvas, resin, nails – and with victuallers, who provided the food and drink served on board. These were primarily the responsibility of Batten as surveyor, but Pepys took to watching closely and critically, and very soon he was making contracts himself. His own account reveals him as too inquisitive, too clever, too ambitious and pretty soon too conscientious not to interest himself in the detail of everything he saw and heard, and shows him embarking on systematic studies of each area of supply and administration. His zeal was altogether admirable and exceptional, and greatly to the benefit of the navy; and it did not take him long to realize that understanding the procedures, as well as benefiting the navy – the king's good, as he put it – would also allow him to make profits for himself. Indeed he was quickly targeted by suppliers who saw him as a valuable ally. William Warren, the biggest of the timber merchants, with his houses and yards in Essex, Rotherhithe and Wapping, came to him with friendly offers of financial advice, backed by presents indistinguishable from bribes, as Pepys was well aware: for example, a pair of gloves containing forty gold pieces. By such means Warren won a virtual monopoly, beating Batten's candidate for timber contracts in the process. Pepys claimed he was serving the king's interest by choosing the best supplier, but he would hardly say otherwise, and he defended himself stoutly when Pett challenged him.[19] The duke's official 'Instructions' to the Navy Board urged complete disinterestedness in purchasing goods, but they were not taken too literally by anyone. Pepys and Batten were often at loggerheads, each with his own reasons for backing a particular supplier.[20]

The sums of money involved were huge, because the navy was the biggest industrial concern and the biggest employer in the country. It spent more than any other department in the state, and even in peacetime needed £400,000 a year to maintain it.[21] Tens of thousands of men were on its payroll as officers, sailors, victuallers and slop-suppliers, 'slops' being the clothes worn by the common sailors, the red caps, canvas suits and blue shirts; there was no uniform. There were also the shipbuilders, rope-makers, sail-makers, mast-makers and suppliers of everything that went into building and repairing ships. The life of a ship was reckoned at three human generations: it took about eight months to build and was expected to outlast its builders' children. A mast, on the other hand, lasted for only ten years. England did not produce enough wood, and much of it was shipped in from the Baltic countries; there were running arguments about the quality of the wood supplied. The legacy of the commonwealth in 1660 was a fleet of 157 ships, the largest number ever yet in service in England; one reason for Cromwell's high reputation at home and abroad had been the size and effectiveness of his navy.[22] The safety and prestige of the nation remained deeply involved with its successful running, but, while the duke and the king were eager to maintain its reputation and showed great interest in shipbuilding, they had no proper plan for funding it; and parliament was not inclined to vote money, at least not in peace time. After a year in his job, Pepys observed that 'the want of money puts . . . the navy out of order; and yet I do not see that the King takes care to bring in any money'.[23] It was to be his refrain throughout his years of service.

He began to dream of the rewards his application would bring him. Lying late in bed with Elizabeth on a Sunday morning in March 1662, he talked of becoming a knight and keeping a coach, once he had saved £2,000 by frugal living.[24] At that moment, his whole fortune stood at a quarter of that, £530. He began to do monthly accounts and worked out some strict spending rules for himself, swore to God to observe them and set himself penalties for failure to do so. By now he was confident he would become rich, it was more a matter of how soon.[25] As he began to enjoy his work he worked harder. He rose early, usually at four in the summer months; he dined at about noon, either at home or out with friends, then went back to the office and might be still there at midnight. 'My business is a delight to me,' he wrote; and it 'has taken me off from all my former delights'.[26] Again, 'I find that two days' neglect of business doth give me more discontent in mind than ten times the pleasure thereof can repair again, be it what it will.'[27] Elizabeth approved of this new sobriety and application.

He gave up the Privy Seal job, and by the end of the year heard with satisfaction that the world said he and Mr Coventry 'do all the business of the office almost; at which I am highly proud'.[28]

There was sometimes a price to be paid. For instance, in May 1662 he was asked to find and hand over papers relating to Sir Henry Vane, the ablest and most important naval commissioner under the commonwealth, who was being tried for his life. Vane was not a regicide, but an idealist who believed in religious toleration. His ideas were far ahead of his time, and their eccentricity had made him many enemies. In 1660 he refused to submit himself to the king and was perceived as dangerous; parliament and the king both wanted him dead. He defended himself bravely and was condemned on a single piece of evidence, his signature on a Navy Committee letter, written on the day of Charles I's execution: it was taken as proof that he had not opposed the execution, on the grounds that he would have stayed away from work if he had. It was a slender thread on which to decide a man's life, and Pepys, whether he knew it or not, must have supplied the fatal letter. He went to see Vane executed on Tower Hill on 14 June, the anniversary of Naseby – this was a royal public relations exercise – and wrote a long account of the condemned man's courage and dignity in the Diary, as well as a letter to Lord Sandwich, who, like Penn, Batten and Blackborne, had worked with Vane.[29] A few days afterwards Pepys dined with the Crews, and they spoke of Vane's courage as miraculous; another old Treasury clerk he met in the street called him a saint and martyr, and accused Pepys of wickedness: 'At all which, I know not what to think.' But he passed on the comments to Sandwich; and, reading about Vane some months later, declared that he had been 'a very wise man'.[30] Vane's last words, deliberately made inaudible to the crowd by drumbeats from the attending soldiers, have passed into history: 'It is a bad cause which cannot bear the words of a dying man.'[31]

Like the well-trained scholar he was, Pepys had embarked on the study of everything he needed to know to carry out his service to the navy, from its early records to its recruiting methods, from the multiplication tables and the use of the slide rule to the best methods of timber measurement, from rope manufacture to victualling and ships' pursers' accounts, from sea charts to tide tables, from flag-making to the language of sailors. To learn about shipbuilding he had himself taken round by a shipbuilder, going into every hole and corner of as many vessels as possible. He took lessons in how to draw ships. His programme still inspires awe for its thoroughness, and through it he began to identify with the navy, and to take a personal pride in its history and organization. He was not the sort of man who could have commanded a ship or fought a sea battle; he had been to sea only on his Baltic trip and the crossing to Holland, and in the whole course of his career added only another Channel crossing, a coastal voyage to Scotland and the Tangier expedition, made at the king's behest. The romance of the navy came to him not through wind, water and tides but through papers, contracts and ledgers, rows of figures and dockyard visits; but it cast its spell over him as strongly as over any of the fighting officers who sailed the oceans. It is one of the reasons that he is revered by naval historians.

His growing feeling that it was his navy, and that he knew best how things should be done, made him impatient with his colleagues, proprietorial and jealous. From very early in the Diary, he expressed his contempt for their professional failings. Only Coventry was entirely exempt from criticism. Batten and Penn came in for perpetual attacks, and we have seen how he insisted on a private office away from them. His jealousy of their experience and status, and his many quarrels with them, drove him to malice, sharpened by his determination to prove his own superiority and to be in control of what happened at the office and in the yards, and to be seen to be in control.[32] Mennes might have been a dotard, but he did not threaten Pepys; whereas Penn, friendly and generous as he was in their private dealings, was prepared to take him on and invoke precedents when Pepys exceeded his appointed powers, as he did over the drawing up of contracts in front of Coventry. Pepys never forgot or forgave that. 'Strange to see how pert Sir W Penn is today, newly come from Portsmouth with his head full of great reports of his service and the state of the ships there. When that is over, he will be just as another man again, or worse. But I wonder whence Mr Coventry should take all this care for him . . . when I am sure he knows him as well as I do, as to his little service he doth,' he wrote in the summer of 1664.[33] A few months later Pepys attacked Mennes too, for a poor report he had drawn up, speaking to him in front of Batten and his lady: 'I was in the right, and was the willinger to do so before them, *that they might see that I am somebody.*'[34] Pepys's absolute determination to impose himself on the men placed above him, but inferior to him in ability, is all in the phrase.

Rude and belittling remarks about Penn and Batten become a tetchy leitmotif, so predictable that rather than convincing they sometimes encourage you to sympathize with the men he is attacking. As Batten is repeatedly accused of corruption in his dealings with timber, hemp and tar merchants, flag-makers and rope-makers, you ask yourself, are these not the very groups of men with whom Pepys himself is engaged in profitable negotiations? Hard as it is to be categoric about the financial details of the contracts made by either Batten or Pepys, it seems likely that both were offered and both accepted the sweeteners that were standard for their time. If Batten was a rogue, then so was Pepys.

Still he called Batten and Penn rogues, accusing them of idleness, avarice, incompetence and hypocrisy, mocked their minor mistakes and gathered impressive quantities of evil gossip about them. Batten's young second wife was a whore and he was a cuckold.[35] Penn, for all his active service, was a coward.[36] In the real world, Batten, though neither saintly nor brilliant, was hospitable, friendly and capable of sustained hard work, for instance during the Second Dutch War when he was in charge at Harwich; and Penn was clever, competent and brave, going to sea to fight the Dutch again in 1665.[37] But Pepys had decided they were his enemies and was not amenable to reason. His hostility and aggression take on particularly dark colours when he describes himself making sexual advances to Penn's daughter Pegg. To attack the honour of a rival family through a sexual assault on one of its women is a primitive ploy, and it is clear that for Pepys it was a matter of power and humiliation of his enemy rather than attraction – he had described her as unattractive, and even suspected her of having the pox – and that he was more interested in slyly humiliating Penn than in gratifying himself when he fondled Pegg's breasts or thighs. He also claimed that she was compliant and even enthusiastic (*'fort* willing'); it does not absolve him from setting out to defile the daughter of a colleague and neighbour whose hospitality he regularly accepted. He had bouts with her both before and after her marriage to Anthony Lowther, a respectable MP and founding fellow of the

Royal Society, where Pepys too was a fellow from 1665. Had he not supplied the information himself, it would be hard to believe; but there it is, set down in his own words, with the same admirable exactitude he would have used in describing the process of rope-making.[38]

As clerk of the acts, Pepys could hardly fail to acquire rich and powerful friends, and the Diary charts his social and professional rise among ambitious men jostling for positions and property. He was invited to join bodies like the Trinity House, an organization that controlled pilots' licences and navigation on the Thames, made appointments and ran seamen's charities, as well as acting as a gentlemen's club – something between a Freemasons' Lodge and the Garrick Club – with regular and carefully planned gastronomic dinners for its members, in the course of which much business must have been discussed, all the more effectively for being unofficial. Pepys became a 'Younger Brother' in 1662, when Sandwich was master, progressed to 'Elder Brother' and rose to be master himself in 1676, and again in 1685. In 1662 he was also appointed to the Tangier Committee, set up by the king to run the new colony brought as a dowry by his Portuguese bride. This was another Sandwich concern: he had made a survey of Tangier for Cromwell and declared it could provide something the English had long wanted: a base for their fleet in the Mediterranean, despite the fact that it was entirely en-circled on the land by hostile Muslim tribes. He was there again for the king when the Portuguese handed it over in 1661. A garrison was installed and the building of a huge breakwater, or 'Mole', under-taken by English engineers: these were the business of the Tangier Committee.

  Pepys became increasingly impatient with the way in which the Tangier accounts were mismanaged by its treasurer, Thomas Povey, a rich man with an interest in foreign trade but little head for figures; and in 1665, by mutual agreement between the two, Pepys took over the treasurership. The appointment was a lucrative one, and there was a private clause to the agreement, which later led to a dispute. Meanwhile Povey, friendly and hospitable, also introduced Pepys into the Royal Society, where he could meet the most intelligent company in the land. This was in 1665 – its president was Lord Brouncker, who had become an active Navy Board commissioner in 1664 and worked closely and on the whole amicably with Pepys. Brouncker was a ship designer, a mathematician with an interest in musical theory and a freethinker.

In October 1665 Pepys put his own name forward to be surveyor-general of victualling for the navy, a post he had invented and to which he was duly appointed in December with the support of Coventry.[39] He held it for eighteen months and resigned it at the end of the Second Dutch War, in July 1667; by now he had increased his capital to about £7,000. In 1667 and 1668 Pepys defended the Navy Board in the House of Commons, where it was under attack for mismanagement; it was a culminating point of his career during the Diary years, when he addressed a full House for three hours to the admiration of all who heard him. Later that year he submitted his report on the state of the navy to the duke of York and began to make plans to enter parliament – an idea first suggested to him in 1661.[40] Although he did not succeed in being elected until 1673, the year in which he also became first secretary of the Admiralty Commission, the trajectory of his career, briefly indicated here, shows just how astonishing he was in his energy, his ambition and his range of abilities. He had a realistic grasp of what he could hope to achieve, how he could use one job to support another and how he could turn friendship to account. He encouraged and promoted able men, binding them to him and building up a body of loyal followers: for instance, he recommended Richard Gibson of Yarmouth as a local officer for victualling in 1665, then took him on as his chief clerk at Seething Lane; he trusted him to carry his gold out of town during a crisis two years later; he listened attentively to Gibson's views on the navy and used them in his memoranda to the duke.

Pepys could also be pitiless when he knew he could get away with it. The Diary records his admiration of Povey's house in Lincoln's Inn Fields, to which he was invited to sample the fine wines and admire the pictures; it also gives many rude comments on Povey's intellectual failings. What it does not set out are the details of the private pact Pepys made with Povey when he took over the Tangier treasurer's job in 1665: the terms, which we know from other papers, were that he would pay Povey four sevenths of all 'rewards & Considerations' received through the job within three days of receiving them.[41] The treasurership, like Pepys's clerkship at the Navy Board, brought unofficial offerings from contractors on top of the official salary. For instance, the Diary shows Pepys making £222 of personal profit from his services to Tangier contractors in August 1665; he was given £500 by a Tangier victualler on 30 December in the same year and another £200 on 15 June 1666 – totalling nearly £1,000 in under a year.[42] Yet it appears that he passed not a penny on to Povey, who complained, nine years later, that he had received nothing – nothing, that is, except Pepys's 'sullen and uncomfortable return, that you have made no other profits, than from the bare salary'. Povey found it impossible to believe this, as well he might, and said so. It was an 'improbable thing that what afforded in my unskillful hands some measure of honest advantage, should yield nothing, being transferred to yours . . . which I may believe have seldom had so ill success in other cases'.[43] Povey wrote again on 23 February 1674 complaining that Pepys had broken their agreement. Pepys put him off again.

Povey persisted with more letters: 'I do therefore still imagine (a word you are pleased to use in contempt of that ignorance I am kept in) that you cannot but have received some benefit at least, from the gratitude of such as you have had opportunities to oblige, seeing I found the same persons civil.'[44] Still Pepys denied making any profits as treasurer, the tone of his letter one of injured innocence and magisterial dignity: 'Pray therefore let us have no more of this sort of correspondence between us, for as I am one too stubborn ever knowingly to endure being imposed upon, so shall I with much less willingness be ever provoked to violate the known simplicity of my dealings, especially with one from whom I have always owned my having received such civilities as may challenge and shall meet with all expressions of gratitude on this side admitting of a manifest wrong.'[45] The ornate prose in which he chooses to tell his lies makes an interesting contrast to the concise language of the Diary.

Pepys was playing a shameful charade, treating Povey as a gull, confident that nothing could be proved. Povey tried writing to Sir Denis Gauden, for many years chief victualler for Tangier, to ask about his accounts with Pepys, and got nowhere with him. But Povey was not an entire fool, and when Pepys told him he had never asked Gauden for anything, he answered that *he* had never asked him either, because they both knew that Gauden gave without being asked. There the matter remained; Pepys was unbudgeable. In 1685, twenty years after the gentleman's pact had been drawn up between them, a period during which Povey performed several acts of notable kindness towards Pepys, he was still getting nothing but 'Contempt, Neglect, or Superficial Evasions, or Obstinate or affected Silence'.[46] By then Tangier had been given up, the great Mole knocked back into the sea again and the Moors left in possession.

His formidable way of dealing with officials he found wanting appears on many pages of the Diary. A striking instance is his tersely written account of a row he had with a dilatory assistant to Sir Anthony Ashley Cooper, the commissioner of prizes. The man kept Pepys waiting, couldn't find the necessary papers and said it was too late in the day. Pepys cowed him by referring to the man's political past. 'We then did our business without the order in less then eight minutes.' You can see why Pepys got where he did. He knew how to insist and how to threaten, scaring the man he was dealing with by telling him he knows that he worked for the commonwealth. Although Ashley Cooper and Pepys himself had both done as much, the threat worked. Pepys expected and got others to go at his pace and with his commitment.[47]

Yet he had his own times of inefficiency and disorder. After taking over the Tangier treasurership from Povey, he found himself in an alarming muddle with his accounts in October 1665, 'where I have had occasion to mix my monies, as I have of late done my Tanger treasure upon other occasions, and other monies upon that'.[48] He had contrived to mix up his private accounts with the public ones and got into such a state that he was 'ready to break my head and brains'. 'I never was in such a confusion in my life, and that in great sums.' Night after night he sat up to master them and still could not. Under the circumstances it has its funny side, but for Pepys it was humiliating and dismaying. The misery went on for months, made worse by a new anxiety about his eyesight, until the following July, when at last he sorted something out.[49]

This was an exceptional episode. He was as a rule a superb organizer, able to see the importance of getting the details right, and then looking beyond them to a larger vision. He prided himself on his orderliness and efficient running of his office. He was the first to keep written records of both officers and ships, and you can still admire the tidily ruled and written lists turned out by his clerks. When he wanted to prove a point – say, about the costliness of buying shipbuilding supplies on credit – he could ask one of the clerks to produce the evidence, as Hayter did in the winter of 1668, listing every item bought from the ironmonger, the chandler, the turner, etc. – double-spring locks, single-spring locks, door handles, scuttle hinges, table screws, sail needles, fire shovels, scrapers and much more – and giving for each the price paid first by the king and then by the ordinary merchant; and so showing what might be saved in every £100. It must have been a nightmare to compile, and Pepys gave Hayter full credit, submitting his work to the commissioners with his name upon it.[50] Sadly, it did no good. All such efforts were useless as long as the finances of the navy remained subject to the caprices of the king and the suspicions of parliament. All the same, Pepys was right to establish how much money was being wasted and in what fashion. In this as in many other ways he was a link between the efficient administrators of the commonwealth and the future, as he pressed for efficiency in the dockyards and a well-ordered, educated, professional body of officers. No wonder he became the hero of the navy that evolved in the nineteenth century, in which everything was docketed and everyone examined.

The Diary sends a beam of light into the way in which government officers and businessmen worked together, through clubs, through hospitality, through trips that mixed business and pleasure, through well-chosen and discreetly given presents and through cultivating the friendship of those in a position to be helpful in giving contracts or licences. The circumstances were different, but there is something eerily familiar about it too: today's arms and building contracts, entertainment of clients, quiet words at the club, conferences in luxury hotels, boardroom rivalries and contributions to favourite charities are all in the same tradition. Pepys was, among other things, mapping a recognizably modern world.

10. Jealousy

Elizabeth always blamed Pepys's jealousy for making her walk out on him in the early months of their marriage. She may have been justified, although we have no way of knowing; but we do know almost everything there is to know about a second jealous crisis in 1663, because it is covered in the Diary. The episode lasted for months and began with a case of dancing mania.

Pepys came to dancing late. He was invited to a dinner at the Dolphin by a sail-maker who wanted to soften him up in order to win contracts with the Navy Board. This was in March 1661, soon after his twenty-eighth birthday. The party included the Penns and the Battens, with their servants. They were given such a good time that they all stayed on into the evening. Elizabeth was not with them – she was at home in bed, suffering from her period – and Pepys did not feel inclined to hurry back to keep her company. He was persuaded to sing and to play his fiddle with a group of musicians who turned up at the Dolphin. Then the dancing began, and to his own surprise he found himself joining in. It was the first time he had ever attempted to dance. Dancing was not something a scholarly boy of his generation was brought up to; during the interregnum it was associated with the court, with masques and plays, and also with semi-pagan country celebrations, and mostly disapproved of as a form of self-display and sexual provocation. With the return of the king things changed. Charles was a dancer and had brought over French dances with him; although what most struck Pepys that first evening was not any display of French dancing, but the skill of Batten's black servant, Mingo, invited to show what he could do.[1]

Pepys made a second attempt a few weeks later, this time during a working trip to Rochester. Elizabeth was again absent. John Allen, the clerk of the ropeyard there, had two pretty daughters, and after a dinner of wine and oysters there was music, and the young women took the floor. Pepys felt impelled to join in, and although he was uncomfortably aware of his own deficiencies – he said he made 'an ugly shift' of it – he was also game. This was partly because he had developed a crush on Rebecca Allen, and he was rewarded for his efforts by being allowed to escort her home.[2]

So the bait was taken. Still he remained cautious for a long time after this. Later in the year Captain Robert Ferrer, Lord Sandwich's master of horse and a dashing fellow, talked him into visiting a dancing school in Fleet Street to see the girls. Pepys was intrigued but felt he had to express disapproval of their being encouraged to vanity.[3] Soon after this Elizabeth joined in some dancing at Lady Sandwich's, at the Wardrobe: Captain Ferrer seems to have been the instigator again, and he danced with Elizabeth. Then the subject of dancing seems to have lapsed until the following year, when Elizabeth announced to Pepys that she wanted to learn to dance 'against her going next year into the country'.[4] By the country she meant Brampton, and she can hardly have expected old Mr and Mrs Pepys to arrange dances; it looks as though she and Ferrer had talked it over and planned to dance at Hinchingbrooke. He had been there at the same time as her that summer of 1662, and he and Lord Sandwich had both been attentive to her.[5]

Pepys humoured her by buying a book of country dances – this was in December 1662 – and when, after their great quarrel about her loneliness, a companion was found for her, she turned out to be a keen and practised dancer. Elizabeth's brother, Balty, discovered the companion, Mary Ashwell; she was his landlady's niece, and he began his recommendation of her to Pepys by saying she was pretty and could sing. Pepys found out that she was a girl of good family, her father working in the Exchequer, and that she was teaching in a school in Chelsea. He was in no hurry to settle anything, and there were several visits by her parents as the two families sized one another up. Her wages were discussed with her father; they would be very small. But when Balty brought her to dinner, Pepys took to her at once; he liked her looks and her witty conversation. She agreed to come to them in a few weeks' time, and meanwhile invited Elizabeth to visit the school at which she taught, where the children were appearing in a play and she was taking part in another. Everyone was happy, and she arrived on 12 March. Pepys expressed the hope that, although she would cost him something, she would also be a cause of content. They were missing their maid Jane, who had left them in February.

Now Elizabeth could no longer complain of loneliness, and the whole family would feel the benefit. He could not have been more mistaken. Ashwell, as she was always known to them, was charming – a 'merry jade', he called her – and hardly put a foot wrong. She played the virginals and taught them card games. But her presence in the house turned out to be a catastrophe, precipitating domestic turbulence worse than anything the Pepyses had gone through since their separation in the 1650s.

It began when Pepys incautiously expressed his admiration of Ashwell's 'very fine carriage'. This immediately prompted Elizabeth to say she was 'almost ashamed' to see herself so outdone and to add that she must have dancing lessons to put the situation right. Slightly rattled, Pepys refused Ashwell permission to go out to the ball she wanted to attend with some old friends, and gave way about the lessons for Elizabeth. Wayneman Birch, the boy whom Pepys had just beaten for staying out for longer than he should in the streets, was sent out again to inquire for dancing masters in the locality. He came back with two names. Even before one could be decided on and summoned, Pepys obligingly took out his fiddle and played for Ashwell to dance in the room above, 'my best upper chamber'.[6]

The chosen dancing master was a Mr Pembleton, and the lessons began the very next day, while Pepys was out struggling with a particularly demanding session at the office, imposing his will on Batten over the appointment of a ship's mate. But in the evening he again played for the two women to dance, only commenting with husbandly wisdom in the Diary that he doubted Elizabeth would be much good as a dancer because she was too sure of herself. The next day, a Sunday, the family went for a picnic – Pepys, Elizabeth, Ashwell, Wayneman and the dog – taking pieces of cold lamb to eat. They gathered cowslips along the south bank of the river, and Ashwell entertained them with stories of the masques in which she had performed at Chelsea. But already on Monday Pepys was beginning to worry that he had made a mistake in letting Elizabeth learn to dance. He feared that she now expected to have more pleasures than he could give her. And what were these pleasures? He broke off from his office work the next day to go home 'to see my wife and her dancing-maister at it'. What he saw partly reassured him: 'I think after all she will do pretty well at it.'[7] This was his first meeting with

Pembleton, whom he later described as 'a pretty neat black man' – black, as usual in Pepys's time, referring to the colour of his hair.[8]

Having got her way did not improve Elizabeth's housekeeping or her temper. When Pepys scolded her for neglecting the house she became angry, and soon they were exchanging insults. He called her 'beggar', just to remind her that she had brought no dowry, and she answered with 'prick-louse', i.e., son of a tailor. The next day, a Sunday, she stayed in bed sulking, and Pepys took Ashwell to church and then gave her a music lesson, which both of them enjoyed. Elizabeth objected to his staying with Ashwell instead of coming up to talk to her, and Pepys saw she was jealous, and that he must be careful.[9] Suddenly jealousy was in the air. On the Monday he was due to go to Woolwich; he set off, then made an excuse to turn back and go home to take another look at Pembleton. The dancing master responded to this display of interest by persuading Pepys to take a lesson himself, suggesting he should start with the Coranto. This was the favourite dance of Louis XIV of France and the first to be learnt by a nobleman, as Pembleton no doubt explained. It was performed on tiptoe, with slight jumping steps and many bows and curtsies. Pepys decided it would be 'useful for any gentleman and sometimes I may have occasion of using it'.[10]

From this point the Diary has almost daily references to dancing lessons. On 5 May Pepys tried out his Coranto after dinner. On the 6th Pembleton arrived at supper time, and they all went 'up to our dancing room' for three or four country dances. After that another 'practice of my coranto . . . Late and merry at it.' On the 8th Pepys took both ladies to the theatre, Pembleton came round after supper, and they danced again, 'and they say that I am like to make a dancer'. Everyone was cheerful, and there was more dancing on the 11th. Then on the 12th clouds began to form once more, because Elizabeth decided that it was not enough for Pembleton to attend her once a day, he must come twice. Perhaps she did not like sharing her lessons with her husband; and for his part he felt she was 'minding nothing now but the dancing-maister'. On the 13th they all fell out because she would not listen to any criticism of her dancing from either Pepys or Ashwell.

Seething Lane was not the only place where there were problems. Pepys was told that Lord Sandwich had lost £50 playing cards with the king at Lady Castlemaine's; he was currently living in Chelsea, hoping to recover from a recurring fever in the country air. Lady Sandwich's father Lord Crew complained to Pepys at length of the dissolute life of the court and about Lady Castlemaine keeping the king in thrall with erotic tricks. He had perhaps heard rumours of Sandwich also being ensnared by a girl in Chelsea, although they had not yet reached Pepys; in any case Crew had a good deal to say about sexual misbehaviour, and he quoted the Italian proverb *Cazzo dritto non vuolt consiglio* ('You can't argue with a standing cock'). That evening Pepys arrived home late and found Elizabeth and Pembleton alone upstairs, 'not dancing but walking. Now, so deadly full of jealousy I am, that my heart and head did so cast about and fret, that I could not do any business possibly, but went out to my office.' After fuming in the office for a while he returned home and tried to find out whether his wife had been wearing drawers.[11]

Jealousy gripped him. He did his best to distract himself with work. He blamed himself, and attempted to control what he realized was a form of madness that threatened to render him ridiculous; but he was unable to prevent it. He ascertained that Pembleton was a married man, but that did not prevent the jealousy flaring up again and again, like a running fire that resists all attempts to stifle it. Anyone who has ever been jealous recognizes the horrible truth of his account. Pepys's sense of the absurdity involved, his candour and insight into himself, make it appallingly entertaining, as good as scenes from Molière or Shakespeare. Pepys had seen and admired *Othello* and noticed a woman in the audience crying when Desdemona was smothered. Perhaps he thought of that now.[12]

Making a noble effort, he invited Pembleton to join a family expedition to play ninepins on the south bank; the flames of jealousy leapt up again at the sight of his taking Elizabeth's hand, even 'in play'. They had reached the middle of May. The next provocation came when he found she had invited the dancing master to dine with her at home, without bothering even to mention the matter to her husband first. A suspicion arises in the reader at this point that Elizabeth was enjoying her power to upset him almost as much as she enjoyed the dancing. There was more that evening, and in the morning Pepys lamented that he could not 'get up so early as I was wont, nor my mind to business as it should be and used to be before this dancing'.[13]

An infection had taken over the household. More angry words were exchanged between husband and wife. He went into his study and made a vow to himself not to oppose her until the course of lessons was over, fixing a fine of two shillings and sixpence for himself every time he failed. Elizabeth raised the stakes. Pembleton was there again when Pepys arrived home, and at supper she quarrelled openly with him, using the word 'Devil' in front of Ashwell and the dancing master. Had they been alone, Pepys would have struck her.

He calmed down listening to the nightingales as he walked with Creed from Greenwich to Woolwich, and at home to a caged blackbird with a fine song, given him by a Deptford carpenter. But not for long. At church on Sunday Pepys watched Pembleton 'leer' at his wife throughout the sermon and realized that she had become uncharacteristically eager to attend both services at St Olave's. She was also asking for a second month of dancing lessons. 'I am loath to think the worst; but yet . . . it makes me curse the time that I consented to her dancing,' he wrote. Two days later he sat brooding at the office, went home and found Pembleton, now convinced 'by many circumstances . . . that there is something more than ordinary between my wife and him; which doth so trouble me that I know not, at this very minute that I now write this almost, what either I write or am doing nor how to carry myself to my wife in it'. In the afternoon he discovered she had sent everyone in the house out and suspected her of summoning Pembleton. Suffering 'a very hell in my mind', he slipped home yet again and indeed found the two of them alone, 'which made me almost mad'. 'And Lord, to see how my jealousy wrought so far, that I went saftly up to see whether any of the beds were out of order or no.'[14]

They were not. But his jealousy does not seem unreasonable. Unlike Othello, even in his rage he never stopped wanting to believe in his wife's innocence; but, while she was not going to bed with Pembleton, she was certainly flirting for all she was worth and deliberately provoking Pepys in the process. It looks like another campaign to keep the balance of power level between them, or even simply to attract his attention. He was always busy, rising at four in summer and often working at the office until midnight; he made frequent trips to Deptford, Woolwich and Chatham, and devoted most of his spare time to technical study of naval matters, learning arithmetic, sail-making, timber measurement, how to draw ships and going through the old records of the Navy Office. She had married at fourteen, she knew herself to be attractive, and she liked to be admired. Better perhaps a jealous husband who noticed her than one so absorbed in his duties and studies that he hardly did.

That night, husband and wife talked and she accused him of his 'old disease of Jealousy'. He countered by saying her behaviour was indiscreet. They argued for an hour, she cried and he caressed her; she remained upset. The 27th of May was the last day appointed for her lessons, and Pepys had not agreed to any extension. He invited the dancing master to supper and was polite to him; but in the course of the meal he became aware that Elizabeth had inflicted more humiliation on him by telling Pembleton about his jealousy.

At least the lessons were now over. But at once Elizabeth's jealousy of Ashwell flared up, and she complained that Pepys neglected her for the girl. He did his best to reassure her. At the end of May he expressed relief in the Diary that there was no more dancing – his Coranto was forgotten – and that he could fall to 'quiet of mind and business again'. But it was too soon to relax. Elizabeth accused Ashwell of stealing a piece of ribbon. Pepys noticed Elizabeth putting on drawers before going out and suspected her of meeting Pembleton. She made it obvious that she no longer enjoyed Ashwell's company, although the two of them were about to go to Brampton together. Shortly before they were due to leave, Pembleton called and the women went up to the dancing room with him. Pepys did not join them, but he could not help listening; he put his ear to the door and fretted when he could hear no sound of dancing.[15]

On the day before the women were to leave for the country, he and Elizabeth stayed at home while everyone else went to church and had another serious talk. And while he inwardly cursed ever taking on Ashwell or agreeing to the dancing lessons, and greatly resented Elizabeth's view of him as a jealous husband, they managed some sort of reconciliation, on the surface at least. She put on her riding suit and called on the Penns with him, and in the morning gave him her keys and set off for the coach while he was out on business; and he followed her to the coach and was there in time to kiss her often 'and Ashwell once'.[16]

He was invited that same day to a dinner at Trinity House, the shipmasters' association. There the talk presently turned to pretty women, and Lord Sandwich asked Sir John Mennes what he thought of his neighbour's wife, looking at Pepys as he did so: 'Why, Sir John, do you not think that he hath a great beauty to his wife? Upon my word he hath.' Pepys was proud to hear her praised, and it did not occur to him to feel jealous that Elizabeth should have caught his patron's eye. In the evening he went into her closet and played his violin there, going to bed without any supper, missing her sadly and feeling that he loved her with all his heart in spite of everything that had happened.

This was not the end of the drama. Pepys consoled himself for Elizabeth's absence by meeting Betty Lane in a wine house, where they indulged in lobster and petting, and were observed through a window by a man who shouted and threw a stone; Pepys was so worried by this that they left through separate doors. He had another bad moment when he saw a man who looked like Pembleton, and even though he didn't really think it was the dancing master, 'my blood did rise in my face and I fall into a sweat from my old Jealousy and hate, which I pray God remove from me'.[17] On a happier day he saw the ladies of the court walking through Whitehall, laughing and trying on one another's hats and feathers, on their way to attend the queen, and was so taken with them that he fancied himself sporting with the most beautiful, Frances Stuart, in his lonely bed that night. Two nights later he chose the queen as his dream bedmate.[18] Captain Ferrer was quite ready to discuss the court ladies with him and, in the course of his gossip, revealed the real reason that kept Lord Sandwich at Mrs Becke's house in Chelsea: 'whether he means one of the daughters of the house or no, I know not; but hope the contrary', wrote Pepys, but this was what Ferrer meant, and it was soon con- firmed by another of Lord Sandwich's servants. Will Howe knew that Lord Sandwich doted on Mrs Becke's daughter Betty and spent his time and money upon her, and that she was a woman of bad reputation 'and very impudent . . . And that the world doth take notice of it.' This was why Sandwich was not at Hinchingbrooke for the summer: 'in fine, I perceive my Lord is dabling with this wench, for which I am sorry; though I do not wonder at it, being a man amorous enough and now begins to allow himself the liberty that he sees everybody else at Court takes', wrote Pepys. He was deeply shocked.[19]

His news from Huntingdonshire was not encouraging. Elizabeth wrote of quarrels at Brampton between Pall, Ashwell, herself and her father-in-law. Then she described how she had boxed Ashwell's ears for lying 'to her teeth', and Ashwell had struck her back; things were so bad that Pepys's parents had talked to Lady Sandwich about the situation. After this his father wrote to say Elizabeth was returning to London early, and that they had all 'lived very ill together'.[20] He arrived in town at the same time but would not come to Seething Lane with her, choosing to stay with Tom instead. Pepys had to hear Elizabeth's and Ashwell's different versions of what had happened. He found Ashwell's the convincing one, an exact listing of the angry words and blows she had received, and he did not believe Elizabeth's denials; he was particularly ashamed that she should have made scenes at Hinchingbrooke, among my Lady's people. When Ashwell had gone to bed, he told Elizabeth what he felt, soberly and quietly.[21] Since Elizabeth could not control her fury against Ashwell, Pepys said he thought it best for her to leave, simply for the sake of peace. She agreed. Meeting him later in the street, Ashwell told him that Elizabeth had explained to her that it was his wish that she should leave, not hers – 'which was not well', as Pepys observed. Ashwell would go back to teaching, and for her last few days at Seething Lane she kept out of everyone's way.

The house was now nearly empty. Wayneman had run away and then been dismissed. The current cookmaid walked out on the day Ashwell was sacked, leaving no one to help them but a former maid, Susan. They had forgotten she was a drinker, and she made things still worse. On 19 August the Pepys household had a particularly difficult day. He had forgotten he had arranged for the joiners to start laying more new floors in the house, and they arrived first thing in the morning. He took himself to Hollier, his doctor, for some pills to treat a bad attack of wind. Elizabeth sacked Susan, who walked out leaving the house dirty and full of wet clothes. The Pepyses were reduced to a takeaway dinner ('fetched from the Cookes'). Pembleton called, 'which begun to make me sweat'; he was told that no more dancing lessons were wanted and took a short leave. And Pepys had two long talks with Lord Sandwich's man of business, Henry Moore, and one with Will Howe, about their master's folly at Chelsea: 'I find that my Lord is wholly given up to this wench, who it seems hath been reputed a common Strumpett.' Howe urged Pepys to speak to Sandwich, but Moore feared it would do no good and only harm Pepys, and for the moment he decided to 'let it alone and let God do his Will'.[22]

Ashwell left on 25 August. Things were not entirely restored to calm. Elizabeth accused Pepys of indulging in his perpetual building and works and interior decoration as a way of keeping her busy inside the house. Pepys went through more sweaty moments at sightings of Pembleton, each time suspecting him of plotting to call on Elizabeth while he was out. Pepys's brother John came to stay and complained in strong terms of Elizabeth's behaviour at Brampton and general rudeness towards her in-laws; Pepys made soothing replies. He was determined to keep her happy. He took her to Bartholomew Fair. He took her to dinner with Mr Povey in his magnificent house in Lincoln's Inn Fields. He took her shopping to buy expensive chintz with which to line the walls of her room. When in September he had to go to Huntingdon to sort out some legal matters, he was inspired to invite her to join him with the gallant words, 'Well, shall you and I never travell together again?' and she agreed to ride with him. As soon as they arrived at Brampton, he took her to spend the day with Lady Sandwich.[23] Later they rode into the woods to gather nuts, and he showed her the river – 'the first and only hour of pleasure that ever I had in this estate', wrote Pepys; and although this was not strictly true, it expressed his sense of the idyllic nature of their afternoon together in the autumn sunshine.[24]

The problem of Lord Sandwich remained. 'I am ashamed to see my Lord so grossly play the beast and fool, to the flinging off of all Honour, friends, servants and every thing and person that is good, and only will have his private lust undisturbed with this common whore . . . his carrying her abroad and playing on his lute under her window, and forty other poor sordid things . . . but let him go on till God Almighty and his own conscience and thoughts of his Lady and family do it.'[25] Pepys's fine words lose a little of their force coming immediately after his own foray to find Betty Lane ('God forgive me

. . . but she was not there'), but in his mind his own case bore no relation to Sandwich's. One was a small private transgression by a private man, the other a scandal involving a public figure whose behaviour was flagrant and causing widespread comment, and keeping him from his proper way of life and his home. And although Sandwich was at Hinchingbrooke briefly in September, where Pepys saw him, he was not his usual self, and Will Howe said he was hurrying back to Chelsea.

In November Pepys decided he must speak to Lord Sandwich. He went to his lodgings and waited for him; but when he came in, Pepys lost his nerve. He feared Sandwich would not take it well; he did not seem in the mood to talk, his manner was odd: perhaps he sensed he was about to be read a lecture. Pepys withdrew and told Howe he would write a letter instead.[26] It took him a few days to draft; among other distractions, Elizabeth was ill with her old complaint, the abscess on her vulva so bad now that it might require surgery. He read the draft of his letter to Moore, who approved it warmly. Pepys made two fair copies and gave one to Will Hewer to deliver personally into Lord Sandwich's hand. The letter appears in full in the Diary.[27] It is written with signal courtesy and tact, expresses Pepys's sorrow at the talk in the City and the court and from people of all conditions about Sandwich's absence from court and his failure to keep up his service to the king and the navy; goes on to mention his living in a house in which one of the daughters is known as 'a common Courtizan' and to say 'how much her wantonness occasions (though unjustly) scandal to your Lordship'. It ends by saying he finds 'a general coldness' towards Sandwich, such as he has never known before; and assures him that no one else knows what he has written. Pepys took the trouble to enclose the letter in another asking his Lordship not to open it unless he were alone and at leisure.

It was an extraordinarily bold move for Pepys to make. He was not Sandwich's social equal; he was his junior by eight years; he had been his servant and owed his present position to him. True, they were related by blood and on friendly terms, but Pepys had never yet presumed even to invite Sandwich to his house. Sandwich had not raised the subject of the letter with Pepys or invited his opinion. The society in which they were living was one in which adulterous affairs were openly carried on by the highest in the land. What made Pepys,

normally a cautious man, act as he did? He does not offer any
explanation, and we are left to guess.

He makes it clear that Moore, Howe and he were all straightfor-
wardly shocked by the change in their master and fearful of the
resulting scandal getting worse, with consequences that might affect
them all. But there was more to it than that. They had served
him since the days when public men were not expected to behave
licentiously. I believe Pepys was bitterly disappointed that Sandwich,
who had represented the old cause and its values for so long, should
be so easily corrupted by the new regime. The political change was
one thing and might be justified in the light of all that had happened;
Pepys himself had accepted and benefited by it. It was quite another
to see the rot go right through the man, making him frivolous and
self-indulgent, taking him away from his work, his duty and his home,
neglecting and humiliating his innocent Lady. And all for a naughty
Chelsea girl – it was not as though this were some great love. Until
now Pepys had been unfailingly deferential towards Sandwich; but
now his sense of family, and of what the members of a family owed
to one another, became stronger than his deference.

When Sandwich spoke to Pepys, his first question was to ask who
were his informants. Pepys gave him a curious list: James Pearse the
surgeon, Mary Ashwell, Sandwich's nephew Pickering and John Hunt
of Axe Yard, near whom Betty Becke had lodgings. He added that
the whole City spoke of his neglect of business. He did not mention
Sandwich's employees, Moore, Howe or Ferrer, who were his chief
informants, according to the Diary, no doubt to protect them. Sandwich defended the Becke family, then said he was intending to 'live
in another manner'. He went on to challenge Pepys's claim that
nobody else knew what he had written in the letter; Pepys kept quiet
and hoped to get away with it. He thought Sandwich was troubled,
but it was Pepys who wept, and Sandwich who moved the conversation on to a cheerful discussion of the king's picture collection at
Whitehall.[28]

The letter may have had some effect; or Lord Sandwich may have
been planning to bring his summer romance to an end; or possibly
not. He had sexual relations with his wife in October, as the birth of
a tenth child the following July testified, but that does not rule out
Betty Becke continuing to be his mistress.[29] Pepys went on worrying

about Sandwich's displeasure for weeks and months, noting every cool encounter and treasuring more cordial ones. He rejoiced when my Lord asked after 'his Cosen (my wife)' at the end of the year, the first time he had done so since the letter.[30] In the new year of 1664 Pepys wondered whether he dared to invite him to dinner and decided it was not possible. Sandwich continued to visit Betty Becke in Chelsea, and even arranged for his older daughters to lodge there for a while in the summer, allegedly sending them out when he made his visits; and Pepys saw and spoke to Betty, who impressed him with her fine figure and conversation: 'I warrant she hath brains enough to entangle him,' he wrote, pleased to have seen my Lord's mistress.

There was no more talk of sexual scandals involving Sandwich, who was in any case soon at sea again. Pepys's sexual conduct, on the other hand, took a sharp turn for the worse, as though his effort to set my Lord right had drained him of his own virtue. What neither of them could know was that five years later Elizabeth, in a Proustian moment of revelation, was going to confess to Pepys that Lord Sandwich had solicited her to be his mistress, sending Captain Ferrer as his go-between.[31] The likeliest time for this to have taken place was during the late summer of 1662, when she was at Brampton while Sandwich and Ferrer were at Hinchingbrooke. She came back full of talk of Captain Ferrer, enough to give Pepys a twinge of jealousy, and of Lord Sandwich's having drawn up some proposed alterations for Brampton while she was there; and Pepys wrote in his summary at the end of September, 'My Lord Sandwich has lately been in the country, and very civil to my wife.'[32]

His approach had been a temptation, Elizabeth said when she made her confession, but she had refused him out of faithfulness to her husband. Had she succumbed, there might have been no Betty Becke in Chelsea, no dancing lessons with Pembleton and a very different letter of reproof from Pepys to his Lordship. The comedy of errors that filled the year 1663 could have turned into something more like *Othello*, and the whole course of the Diary been diverted into another direction.

11. Death and Plague

Pepys grew up with death at his elbow. Against the odds, he became a survivor, outliving all his brothers and sisters. In the Diary his responses to death vary from the briskly matter of fact on learning of the passing of his uncle Robert, whom he had known since he was a boy – 'Sorry in some respect; glad in my expectations in another respect' – to a mournful meditation on hearing the church bells toll for a dark-eyed girl he knew only from seeing her in church.[1] He liked to call her 'my Morena' – my Moorish girl – to himself, and he learnt that she was suffering from a wasting illness. When she died he honoured her with a gracefully turned elegy: 'This night was buried, as I hear by the bells at Barking church, my poor Morena – whose sickness being desperate did kill her poor father; and he being dead for sorrow, she said she could not recover nor desire to live, but from that time doth languish more and more, and so is now dead and buried.'[2] Another local girl he observed, 'crooked' but not ugly, killed herself by taking poison, saying before she died that she did it 'because she did not like herself, nor had not liked herself nor anything she did a great while'.[3] Pepys had a writer's response to these stories: their subjects lived in his imagination, and in that private place he allowed himself to be melancholy or appalled by their fates. Yet when his cousin Anthony Joyce was thought to have killed himself, he was chiefly concerned to find out what might happen to the property, which the law assigned to the king if suicide were established.[4]

As a survivor himself, he was generally more interested in the survivors than the dead. When the earl of Southampton died, Pepys's first reaction was to describe the porter at the great man's gate in tears; he felt sorry for him and tipped him on the practical grounds that he was not now likely to pick up many more tips: 'he hath lost a considerable hope by the death of this Lord, whose house will be no more frequented as before'. Later he reported on the remarkable self-control shown by the earl, and how he had prepared himself to die by 'closing his own eyes and setting his mouth, and bidding Adieu with the greatest content and freedom in the world'. Southampton had died in the agonies of the stone, so Pepys had particular reason to admire this stoicism; he had nothing to say about his spiritual condition.[5] Another case, in which a colleague who was also a courtier died suddenly in the prime of life, led him to look at the court's response: 'I find the sober men of the Court troubled for him; and yet not so as to hinder or lessen their mirth, talking, laughing, and eating, drinking and doing everything else, just as if there was no such thing – which is as good an Instance for me hereafter to judge of Death, both as to the unavoydablenesse, suddenness, and little effect of it upon the spirits of others, let a man be never so high or rich or good; but that all die alike, no more matter being made of the death of one then another; and that even to die well, the prise [worth] of it is not considerable in the world.'[6] What interested him was not the dead man and his possible after-life, but the reactions of the living and his reputation in this world.

Pepys was not given to repining over the dead himself, but the precariousness of life sometimes caught at his imagination. We have seen how, saying goodbye to his mother in 1660, he was suddenly frightened that he might never see her again, because she was ill with a cold.[7] In October 1662 he arrived at Brampton to find father, mother, sister and two brothers Tom and John all assembled, and the thought came to him, 'So now we are all together, God knows when we shall be so again': and, as it turned out, they never were.[8] When Elizabeth was taken ill after drinking cold beer at an inn one day while they were riding to Brampton on another occasion, he was suddenly terrified: 'I thought she would have died, and so in great horror (and having a great trial of my true love and passion for her) called the maids and mistress of the house.' It turned out to be nothing serious, and she was better the next morning, but for a moment he had seen the abyss.[9]

When his mother was really dying, at Brampton in 1667, he made no attempt to visit her; instead, like Proust with his grandmother, he contented himself by dreaming of her. On the day she died, which was two days before he got the news, he dreamt he was at her bedside and 'laying my head over hers and crying, she almost dead and dying . . . but which is strange, methought she had hair on her face, and not the same kind of face as my mother really has; but yet did not consider that, but did weep over her as my mother'. When the news came, he did not go to Brampton for her funeral or to comfort his father but put his entire household into mourning, proud of cutting a fine figure when he went to church in his black clothes. He must be the first writer to take note of the vanity of the well-dressed mourner in his own person.[10] He dreamt of her again, coming to him and asking for a pair of gloves, and in the dream 'thinking it to be a mistake in our thinking her all this while dead' – 'this dream troubled me and I waked'.[11]

This mixture of tough in practice, tender in imagination, ran through all his dealings with death. His account of the last weeks of his brother Tom is particularly disconcerting in the way it alternates between callousness and sorrow. In the summer of 1663 Tom was 'a very thriving man', and the following Christmas he seemed well and cheerful, but ten weeks later he was dead. Tom had taken over their father's tailoring business in Salisbury Court in 1661, but he was not much interested in the work and let out rooms to supplement his meagre earnings. Pepys made strenuous efforts to find him a wife with a dowry but without success, partly because Tom's speech impediment worried prospective brides, and also because he lacked any of Pepys's dynamism. He muddled along, was known as a good fellow, ran up debts and made just enough to send a small allowance to his sister. There is a letter to 'sister Pal' in his neat small hand and terrible spelling, dated 16 January 1664, which he signed off in words that suggest he was fond of her and may have had an inkling of what lay in store for him: 'Your truly Loving Brother till Death'.[12] The letter was written a few weeks after Pepys had heard that Tom was unwell, called on him and decided he was 'not ill'. But from then on, he sank rapidly.

Pepys did nothing for him. He did not send for a doctor or a nurse, and he visited Tom no more than once a week, even though their cousin Jane Turner, who was Tom's neighbour in Salisbury Court, told Sam that he had less than two months to live. He seems to have refused to believe what he was told, perhaps because he found it too upsetting, and distanced himself from what was happening. He had the excuse of his office work, as always, and just then his troubled relations with Lord Sandwich; still, he found time to walk in the park on Ash Wednesday and to see D'Avenant's new play, *The Unfortunate Lovers*. When he did visit Tom on 8 March, he realized he was very ill, but then kept away again until the following Sunday, when other cousins, the Joyces, came to him and suggested he should find a woman to look after his brother. They added that they had heard, through an indiscreet doctor, that Tom had the pox, meaning gonorrhoea. At this Pepys hurried round to Salisbury Court. He found Tom delirious and 'with the face of a dying man'. By now a neighbour had engaged a nurse. Pepys, dismayed at the trouble he saw looming, whether his brother died or merely continued ill, talked anxiously with Tom's maidservant, who had stories to tell of his inefficient ways as a businessman and of his disquieting sexual practices – although sitting up at night 'doing something to himself' does not sound very bad. The news that Tom had the pox spread around the family, followed by talk of his being in debt, and Pepys was in an agony of shame on his behalf. When another doctor declared Tom had not got it after all, Pepys was so relieved that he sent for oysters and enjoyed a celebratory dinner; afterwards he himself, together with the doctor, inspected Tom's by now only intermittently conscious body and found no trace of any shameful disease. The truth was that he was dying of tuberculosis of the lungs, then called a consumption; it was often associated with venereal disease – Pepys talks of one of Batten's clerks dying of consumption 'got, as is believed, by the pox' – but wrongly both in general and in the particular case of poor Tom.[13]

Pepys did not summon the local clergyman to pray over him or administer the sacrament, but his scepticism was not quite proof against his brother's deathbed, and, as the end approached, he himself questioned Tom about where he thought he might be going. Tom's answer, although given in a distracted manner, was a good one, and Pepys wrote it out: 'Why, whither should I go? there are but two ways. If I go to the bad way, I must give God thanks for it. And if I go the other way, I must give God the more thanks for it; and I hope I have not been so undutiful and unthankful in my life but I hope I shall go that way.' As Tom's breath began to rattle in his throat, Pepys's nerve failed him. He went out until he could be sure Tom was dead, then came back to cry at the sight of the 'poor wretch, lying with his chops fallen'. After this his efficient self moved into action. He collected all Tom's papers, took them to Seething Lane, wrote to his father and returned in the darkness to Salisbury Court, where Elizabeth had taken refuge at Jane Turner's.

She invited them to stay overnight 'in the little blue chamber. And I lay close to my wife, being full of disorder and grief for my brother, that I could not sleep nor wake with satisfaction.' It would be hard to better Pepys's words here. They take us into the room and the bed, where the warm body of Elizabeth is both a comfort and a reminder of the body of his brother, with whom he must have bedded down many times when they were children – now lying alone and cold not far away.[14] This is where the immediacy of the Diary is supreme. If Pepys had written about his brother's death later, he would have been tempted to smooth and tidy the sequence of events to make it into a more seemly story; improved the number of his visits to Tom, cut out the theatregoing and oyster dinner, called a doctor and nurse earlier rather than relying on neighbours, omitted the rumour of the pox. Instead we get his jumble of reactions: yes, he loves his brother and sorrows for him, but he is also embarrassed by him and resents the interruption of his own activities. In describing Tom's last hours, he reverses the order of events in the Diary, writing of Tom dead and laid out, then remembering and recording his earlier solemn questioning of his still living brother.

His first thought was to have Tom buried in the churchyard among their brothers and sisters, but he changed his mind and decided to pay the extra to have him put inside the church, close to their mother's pew. A Shakespearean scene over the crowded vaults followed, the gravedigger telling a shocked Pepys that he would, for sixpence, 'justle them together but I will make room for him'.[15] The mourners, invited to Tom's house for biscuits and burnt claret, arrived hours late and in larger numbers than expected; and only after they had eaten and drunk did they walk with the coffin to the church. Then Pepys, Elizabeth, Jane Turner and her family went back to one of the lodger's rooms in Tom's house and cheered themselves up with oysters again, and cake and cheese, 'being too merry for so late a sad work'. Writing it up that evening, Pepys confessed that once his brother was dead he felt very little more grief.

But there was further trouble brewing. A few weeks later Pepys heard from an old servant of their father's, John Noble, that twin daughters had been born to Tom's maid Margeret, 'an ugly jade', of whom one survived. The baby, born as a parish pauper, was named Elizabeth Taylor and attributed to 'John Taylor', a fabricated name that at least suggested Tom's trade. He had acknowledged that the child was his and paid out various small sums of money for her care. He had also planned to get rid of her by handing her over to a beggar woman, until Noble warned him he might be suspected of murder if she should be asked for later and he were unable to trace her. Tom's next move was to give her to a local man with a lump sum of £5; this only led to the man being sent to prison for bringing a pauper child into the parish. The wretched baby was handed about further, and, when Tom died, Noble turned to Pepys and his father for money. Pepys declared there was no proof at all that Elizabeth Taylor was Tom's child, although he referred privately to 'my brother's bastard' and indicated he might do something for her; and the midwife testified that Tom had confessed to being the father and told her he had got the child on Bonfire Night, 5 November, a statement so ingenuous it sounds like the truth.

Tom's daughter was the only grandchild the Pepys family had yet produced. There was plenty of room for a little girl at Seething Lane or at Brampton, and either of the two childless young women, Elizabeth and Pall, might have been willing to supervise her care. Nothing of the sort happened – the idea that the little girl was his niece seems not to have occurred to Pepys – and her disappearance from the Diary suggests she was dead before the end of 1664. Would Pepys have been more interested in his brother's child if she had been a boy? Perhaps the taint of bastardy would still have been more important than the blood link; bastards were more readily accepted in the higher social circles than at Pepys's level. Yet his absolute rejection of Tom's offspring is faintly surprising, at a time when he had pretty well given up hope of ever having a child of his own.[16]

The next year, 1665, was, as everyone knows, the year of the great plague in London. Pepys had heard rumours of its approach; it was in Amsterdam in 1664. Plague was in any case endemic in London, and severe outbreaks were expected every few decades: 1592, 1603, 1625, 1636 had all been bad years. In 1625, 40,000 Londoners died, and a look at the parish registers shows deaths attributed to plague in almost every year of the century up to 1665. The rich could not count on being spared, but they usually left London when the plague was virulent; and since it was carried by a particular flea and fleas proliferated in town, getting away was certainly the best move. This is what the court and almost everyone else who could afford to do so, including many doctors and clergymen, did. The poor were the expected victims, squashed into their low-ceilinged, unaired rooms, their meagre, piled-up lodgings, narrow courtyards, alleys and streets. For most of them it was impossible to give up their occupations and move away. The plague was thought to be contagious, but no one knew how it actually arose or spread, which meant that none of the measures taken to control it, such as marking with a red cross and locking up houses where someone was known to be infected, were effective. In 1665 those who went to fight the Dutch at sea were preserved because the plague never reached the fleet: for once the sailors had a clear advantage over landsmen. For Pepys, who did not leave town until the end of August, the spaciousness and good condition of his house told in his favour. He may even have had a natural immunity. Some people's blood is unattractive to fleas, and he observed when he shared a bed with a friend in Portsmouth in 1662 that 'all the fleas came to him and not to me'. What seemed a trivial piece of good luck at the time may have had a much greater significance.[17]

The severity of the 1665 plague did not become apparent until June, and during the first five months, when it was no more than a threat, life in the Pepys family continued as usual. Towards the end of 1664 he noted with satisfaction the good state of his household consisting of Elizabeth, her new companion Mercer, three maids and Tom Edwards, who had been with them for six months. Mary Mercer was the daughter of a neighbouring widow who took in lodgers, among them Will Hewer, and it was Will who had recommended Mercer to the Pepyses; she was a merry, pretty seventeen-year-old, a good singer too, and Pepys was charmed by her.[18] 'And a pretty and loving quiet family I have as any man in England,' he wrote in his Diary.[19] This was not entirely true, since he had just blacked Elizabeth's eye during a quarrel about her failure to control her servants properly; and she had attempted to bite and scratch back. Throughout the Christmas period Pepys and Elizabeth were running separate lives, not least because she felt unable to go out with her black eye. She stayed in bed during the day and rose to play cards and games with her servants at night, without Pepys. On New Year's Eve he kissed her in the kitchen, and on New Year's Day 1665 they celebrated together, but the next day he went out looking for other women. He had recently started a carefully planned affair with the wife of a Deptford ship's carpenter, William Bagwell. The name Bagwell seems too good to be true, but it is there in the Deptford registers; and when Mrs Bagwell offered herself to Pepys, she was acting under her husband's instructions. Pepys expresses no feelings for Mrs Bagwell and never gives her first name. He sometimes reproached himself for his own 'folly', but he enjoyed the sexual thrill of having her, sharpened perhaps by her reluctance. The story is a shameful one of a woman used by two bullies: her husband, hoping for promotion, and Pepys, who was to arrange it. Pepys did not present it in quite those terms, but it is clearly how it was. He shows it was furtive and squalid, and he even makes us see the funny side of his own behaviour, but it can't have been funny, or fun, for Mrs Bagwell.

All through January he was like a tom cat. He laid siege to his barber's pretty servant, Jane Welsh; he hung about and kissed Sarah, the girl at the Swan Inn; he had Betty Martin, at this point seven months pregnant, afterwards reproaching her for her impudence; and he visited Mrs Bagwell, and was struck by her protestations that she loved her husband. He made a vow to 'laisser aller les femmes', but within days broke it; and he remained on bad terms with Elizabeth. Two of their maids left, one accusing Elizabeth of favouring Tom Edwards and quarrelling with everyone else in the house.[20] Pepys made another vow to leave women alone, and this time kept it until it ran out on 15 May. His working life during these months was arduous enough for several men, and he was busy at the office, often till late at night, and in the yards, as another war with the Dutch became imminent. Men had to be prevented from leaving their ships and more men pressed – 30,000 were needed to make up the necessary crews; merchant ships had to be hired to supplement the naval force, and the entire fleet prepared for battle. He was also struggling to sort out the accounts for Tangier, which he took over in February. By the end of March the duke of York and Lord Sandwich were both at sea, and Pepys was dealing with the problem of financing the fleet.

The plague did not deter his mother from coming up from Brampton to stay in May, and she enjoyed herself so much in town, shopping with Elizabeth, going out on the river and revisiting old haunts in Islington, that he had difficulty in persuading her to leave at the end of June, when the city suddenly and spectacularly emptied itself. She 'had a mind to stay a little longer', she said.[21] On 5 July Pepys moved his family to Woolwich. The king and court went first to Hampton Court, then to Salisbury and from there to Oxford. For the rest of the year Pepys travelled up and down the Thames even more than usual, visiting his wife when he could, but effectively leading a bachelor life, which may have contributed to his unusually high spirits.

Because the most notable fact about Pepys's plague year is that to him it was one of the happiest of his life. It was also among the busiest. He worked long hours, profited by every opportunity to make money, and quadrupled his fortune. He sought and was given two appointments that extended his power and earning capacity, treasurer to the Tangier Committee and surveyor-general of victualling for the navy. This was the year of his election to the Royal Society; he attended some lectures and acquired his own 12-foot telescope.[22] He continued his sexual rampages. He enjoyed a series of experiences that filled him with excitement and delight, from the wedding of the Sandwichs' daughter Jemima, which he helped Lady Sandwich organize in the absence of her Lord at sea, to the autumn evenings when he was living in lodgings at Greenwich, made music with friends and composed his own best-known song. There was a period during the same autumn when he found the energy to keep two diaries, the second entirely concerned with his negotiations to buy prize goods from the trading ships captured by Lord Sandwich from the Dutch. The year was so packed with events that the plague was largely relegated to the background in the Diary as Pepys pursued his activities with triumphant energy. When the death figures were at their worst, he wrote that 'everything else hath conspired to my happiness and pleasure, more for these last three months then in all my life before in so little time'. A few weeks later, 'I do end this month with the greatest content, and may say that these last three months, for joy, health and profit, have been much the greatest that ever I received in all my life.'[23] And at the end of the year he summed up 1665 with the words: 'I have never lived so merrily (besides that I never got so much) as I have done this plague-time.' The parallel is obvious with men and women at war or under bombardment who have found themselves living on an adrenalin high that gives extra intensity to every experience; so Pepys, while something like a sixth of the population of London died around him, experienced months of euphoria, revelling in his own success and pleasures.

Jemima Montagu's wedding was a high point, giving him the chance to be in control of a social event, to adopt the role of mentor to the young couple and to serve Lady Sandwich. His part in the wedding preparations brought him a pleasure so intense that the terrors of the plague receded into the background of his consciousness. He was in on the arrangements from the start. Lord Sandwich, briefly returned from one naval engagement and about to go to sea again, charged him at the end of June with proposing a match between Jemima and the eldest son of Sir George Carteret. It was a task very much to Pepys's taste, to be entrusted with an intimate affair between two noble families, acting for one and courteously received by the head of the other, who also happened to be his superior at the Navy Board. A good career move, clearly, but something much more: it put him in the know and virtually in charge. And indeed, hardly were the financial arrangements agreed and royal approval gained for the match than Sandwich departed suddenly with the fleet, leaving Pepys to take over. At this stage Jemima had not even met Philip Carteret; it was not a matter of concern to either of the fathers. Later, Sir George told Pepys that he would not have let his son have Lady Jem if he had been a debauch, as so many of the young men at court were, and Lady Sandwich expressed a mother's anxiety to Pepys as to whether her daughter would like the match.[24] But by then everything was settled.

The Carterets were living at the treasurer's house in Deptford because of the plague, and Lady Sandwich came to stay with them from Tonbridge, where she had been taking the waters, which, rather than doing her good, had made her ill. She was forty that summer; Pepys was in and out of the Carterets' house, sitting in her room to talk everything over, 'she lying prettily in her bed', still unwell.[25] Lady Jemima was sent to her aunt's house, Dagenham in Essex, across the river; the marriage was to be celebrated there, not at Hinchingbrooke. Pepys met the 24-year-old bridegroom and found him modest and intelligent but awkward in his manner; he said he liked his first sight of Jemima – Pepys elicited this by eager questioning – but he did nothing to show it. Pepys felt moved to give him a little instruction in how to take a lady's hand and lead her about the room, then the couple were left on their own for an hour in the gallery, and later in the garden. The weather was sweltering. Both appeared serious and shy. What they had in common as well as their rank was a physical disability, she her crooked neck, which had not been quite cured, he a limp, something their parents may have considered when they planned the match. Pepys was told she must be seen again by the doctor who had tried to straighten her neck before the wedding and that she needed new clothes, so he busied himself with these matters. He also questioned her on her reaction to her future husband and was pleased when she blushed, hid her face and said she could readily obey her parents' wishes. Lady Carteret sent her jewels, beautiful bedding and presents of all kinds, 'as if they would buy the young lady', he wrote, 'which makes my Lady and me out of our wits almost, to see the kindness she treats us all with'.[26] Pepys shows himself responding as one with Lady Sandwich: he is taking all the roles, as father, brother, teacher and indispensable cousin.

During the last days before the wedding, he continued to work at the office at Seething Lane, to visit the king and duke at Hampton Court and Greenwich to keep them informed; and to walk the city streets and the river banks much as usual. He advised his Joyce cousins to leave London for Brampton, 'using all the vehemence and Rhetoric I could', but they were unwilling to abandon their shop; and he heard that his old clerking friend Robin Shaw was a plague victim. Yet on this same day he declared he had enjoyed four days of 'as great content and honour and pleasure to me as ever I hope to live or desire or think anybody else can live'.[27] He caught up with his accounts, assisted by Will, and with his journal; and he travelled tirelessly between Seething Lane, Deptford and Dagenham, with a few quick forays to Woolwich to see Elizabeth. Once again, his energy appears more godlike than human. Twice he and the Carterets were held up by the tide in crossing the Thames with the ferry; they had to sleep in their coach on the Isle of Dogs one night, and on the day of the wedding itself, 31 July, they were again delayed and missed the ceremony. Sir George charmed him by remaining 'so light, so fond, so merry, so boyish' throughout; the practical Lady Carteret supplied Pepys with a bottle of plague water, one of the many concoctions made up by physicians to ward off the disease.[28]

In the confusion over the day and time of the wedding, the bride and groom did not put on their finery and wore ordinary clothes. Pepys, resplendent in a new silk suit with gold buttons and broad gold lace, thought Jemima looked sad and sober, and the day passed quietly, with dinner, cards, supper and prayers, but after this Pepys made a merry visit to the bridegroom as he undressed in his room, and then kissed the bride in bed and saw the curtains drawn. 'The modesty and gravity of this business was so decent, that it was to me, indeed, ten times more delightful than if it had been twenty times more merry and Joviall,' he wrote. Both in his Diary and in a letter to Lord Sandwich he expanded on the great joy and satisfaction afforded by the whole process; 'thus end we this month . . . after the greatest glut of content that ever I had' – adding, 'only, under some difficulty because of the plague', as though it were a minor inconvenience.

He was now called 'Cousin' by the Carterets, and, in the absence of Lord Sandwich or any of his sons, Pepys became the chief male representative of his family.[29] It was a sort of apotheosis. In the days before the wedding his feelings had been stirred so deeply that he was driven to thank God for having arranged the whole thing: 'For methinks if a man could but reflect upon this, and think that all these things are ordered by God Almighty to make me contented, and even this very marriage now on foot is one of the things intended to find me content in my life and matter of mirth, methinks it should make one mightily more satisfied in the world than he is.'[30] Neither the language nor the ideas are quite clear, but the general sense is unmistakable: Pepys was pleased with his destiny.

The marriage was made in spite of the plague, but the young couple did not have many years together. They settled in Bedfordshire at Hawnes, a large house with a deer park, purchased for them by Sir George Carteret. Three sons were born to them, and the birth of the third proved fatal to Jemima. She died in November 1671, aged twenty-five. Philip survived her by only a few months. After her death he took up the naval career he had abandoned when he married, only to be killed fighting the Dutch alongside his father-in-law Lord Sandwich the following May. The redeeming part of the story is that Sir George and Lady Carteret moved to Hawnes to care for their orphaned grandsons and raised all three successfully.[31]

★

After the wedding, Pepys's habits of hard work and careful planning continued as usual. He put all his papers in order and rewrote his will, acknowledging that he might become a victim himself. He chewed tobacco against the plague and worried in case wig-makers might be using the hair of victims. He had a moment of 'extraordinary fear' in July when he heard that Will Hewer had come in to work with a headache and gone to lie down on Pepys's bed. Pepys set his people very smartly to get him out of the house, although, he instructed them, 'without discouraging him'.[32] Will got over his headache. Early in August Pepys himself suggested the Navy Office should move from London to Greenwich, asking Coventry for the king's permission, although he volunteered to 'trust God Almighty and stay in town' himself.[33] Orders came for the move on 16 August, and, after making his gallant remark to Coventry on 25 August, 'You, Sir, took your turn at the sword; I must not therefore grudge to take mine at the pestilence', Pepys in fact immediately left town.[34] Yet he sometimes behaved as though he were invulnerable. He was driven by curiosity, making a quite unnecessary visit to the plague pits in Moorfields, for instance, because he wanted to see a burial there; and even after the removal of the office he continued to go into London to look after his private business or fetch things he wanted from Seething Lane.[35] He did not keep away from Westminster, though he knew it was badly affected, until he learnt of the death of 'poor Will that used to sell us ale at the Hall-door – his wife and children dead, all I think in a day'.[36] At the end of August he walked through the City to visit a goldsmith and remarked that the people he passed were 'walking like people that had taken leave of the world' – one of the few phrases in the Diary that gives a suggestion of the eeriness of the scene.[37]

When the fathers of both Will Hewer and Tom Edwards died of the plague in one week in September, Pepys kept the young men busy working at Greenwich; it was probably the best way to treat them. He showed a fatherly concern for Tom, sharing a lunch of bread and cheese in the office with him when the other clerks went home for their dinner, and taking him on a trip to Gravesend and back on the office yacht. He believed it was better for everyone if he himself 'put off the thoughts of sadness as much as I can; and the rather to keep my wife in good heart, and family also'.[38] Keeping your spirits up was thought to be a way of fighting off infection. On the day Elizabeth told him she feared her father was ill, and he answered that he thought it was the plague, because Mr de St Michel's house was shut up, he also got the news of Lord Sandwich capturing the Dutch trading ships and celebrated with colleagues and friends, Lord Brouncker and his mistress Mrs Williams, Sir John Mennes, Captain Cocke and John Evelyn, all in 'an extasy of joy', telling one another funny stories that 'did make us all die almost with laughing'. To die of laughter was the best alternative to thoughts of dying any other way, and 'in this humour we sat till about 10 at night; and so my Lord and his mistress home, and we to bed – it being one of the times of my life wherein I was the fullest of true sense of joy'.[39] He could not pretend to be much troubled about Elizabeth's father. In any case, old St Michel recovered from his illness.

Pepys knew he had earned the right to be proud of his courage in remaining at his post in town as long as he did. He made as much clear in a letter to Lady Carteret in which he spelt out some of his experiences in a very different tone from anything in the Diary:

I having stayed in the city till above 7400 died in one week, and of them above 6000 of the plague, and little noise heard day nor night but tolling of bells; till I could walk Lombard Street and not meet twenty persons from one end to the other, and not fifty upon the Exchange; till whole families (ten and twelve together) have been swept away; till my very physican, Dr Burnet, who undertook to secure me against any infection . . . died himself of the plague; till the nights (though much lengthened) are grown too short to conceal the burials of those that died the day before, people thereby constrained to borrow daylight for that service; lastly, till I could find neither meat nor drink safe, the butcheries being everywhere visited, my brewer's house shut up, and my baker with his whole family dead of the plague. Yet, Madam, through God's blessing and the good humours begot in my attendance upon our late Amours [he means the recent wedding] your poor servant is in a perfect state of health.[40]

Again, the suggestion is that his good spirits have contributed to his immunity.

Pepys's journal of the plague year is above all an account of one man's capacity to detach himself from disaster and rise above the horrors.

Plague takes its place alongside, but never in front of, office work, naval battles and their consequences, Jemima Montagu's wedding, family quarrels, music-making, sexual conquests and all the private interests and obsessions that made part of his daily life, more minutely chronicled than ever. Every month offers surprises and insights, some political, some personal, that are quite unconnected with the plague, and noted in detail and at length. For instance, at a council meeting to raise funds for the war, in April, the earl of Southampton, then in charge of the Treasury, asked, 'Why will people not lend their money? Why will they not trust the King as well as Oliver? Why do our prizes come to nothing, that yielded so much heretofore?' – questions no one present was able to answer.[41] In November he was faced with rioting seamen, unpaid and starving, breaking the windows of his Greenwich office and threatening more violence. He took the view that 'only money and a rope' could deal with them, but chiefly money; and in December he complained that the office had not received so much as a farthing for the men's payment for two months.[42]

There were other lighter moments. In June, for no fathomable reason, he adopted a fanciful vocabulary to describe an assignation, choosing to call the young woman 'fairest flower' and 'the rose'. He takes 'fairest flower' to Tothill Fields in a coach for the air, and when it is dark they go in 'to eat a cake, and there did do as much as was safe with my flower'. It is his only venture into the language of romance, altogether different from his usual foreign phrases, and he never repeated it; you wonder if it harked back to the novel he wrote at Cambridge.[43] In September he had a business meeting near Ewell in Surrey, at Nonsuch Palace, semi-derelict and with a ruined garden, which he observed with pleasure; and in this romantic place, while conducting his financial dealings, he spoke to a little girl and heard her sing. Her singing impressed him so much that he decided he would offer her employment when he next needed a girl in his household; and, more than a year later, he remembered her and did so.[44]

One more episode from the plague year concerns Pepys's old friend from his clerking days, Peter Luellin, who had visited him aboard the *Naseby* in 1660. They had written to one another, agreed how their lives would be improved if they only had private incomes and spent evenings swapping stories over drinks. After a spell in Ireland, where he failed to make his fortune, Luellin was back in England in 1663, working for a timber merchant called Edward Dering. What made him useful to Dering was his friendship with Pepys, who was in a position to give contracts to timber merchants, and soon Luellin was offering Pepys £200 a year for his good offices and fifty gold pieces for taking immediate goods. Pepys explained he was not to be bribed, but was prepared to accept an 'acknowledgment' of his services.[45] He repeated this more formally: 'I told him that I would not sell my liberty to any man. If he would give me anything by another's hand, I would endeavour to deserve it, but I will never give him himself thanks for it, nor acknowledge the receiving of any . . . I did also tell him that neither this nor anything should make me to do anything that should not be for the King's service besides.'[46] It is Pepys's central statement of his position on accepting presents from interested parties, and he reverted to it when he was challenged on this point in 1670.

For now, he took a £50 bill of exchange from Dering, 'the best New Year's gift I ever had', cashed for him by Luellin, to whom Pepys gave £2 for his trouble. After this Luellin was a frequent caller at Seething Lane, dining and taking Elizabeth to the theatre, even setting off a twinge of Pepys's jealousy.[47] But Luellin's target was always Pepys. The Diary sets out Pepys's moral juggling, now hoping for money from Dering, now complaining that Luellin is trying to force him to take some. Luellin continued to visit Pepys in Greenwich when the Navy Office moved there, bringing more proposals from Dering, and Pepys accepted twenty gold pieces, 'yet really and sincerely against my will'.[48] Luellin was becoming an embarrassment to him, and Pepys wrote him off as a lightweight, too keen on his pleasures to do well in business. A few weeks later Dering told Pepys that Luellin had died of the plague in St Martin's Lane, 'which much surprised me'. This was all the epitaph he got from his old friend. Pepys had moved on.

He was less eager to return to Seething Lane at the end of the year, when the danger had abated, than Elizabeth, who went home first with Mary Mercer and their maids, and had to make a special trip to Greenwich to urge Pepys to follow suit. When he did get back in January 1666, he was frightened by the sight of the churchyard at St Olave's, in which the graves were piled high; more than three hundred burials had taken place during the previous six months. A covering of snow in February made it look less ghastly, but he discussed spreading lime over it with a local merchant. Their clergyman, Mr Mills, also crept back to his parish in February – first to go and last to return, jeered Pepys – and delivered a sermon blaming the plague on the sins of the nation, which Will Hewer took down in shorthand.[49] Everyone kept a nervous eye on the plague figures; people were still dying, and the fear that it might increase when the hot weather started again could not be dismissed. 'If the plague continues among us another year, the Lord knows what will become of us,' wrote Pepys.[50] Another 2,000 Londoners died in 1666; the theatres were not reopened until November, and there was no public thanksgiving for the end of the plague until then. We know that the last recorded case was in 1679, at Rotherhithe; but neither Pepys nor anyone else could possibly know that the plague was making its final appearance and would never return to England.[51]

12. War

England was at war during two and a half years covered by the Diary – from May 1665 until August 1667 – but it is often easy to forget this as you read. Since those years also encompassed the plague and the fire of London, war is sometimes upstaged by the great domestic disasters, as well as by Pepys's private preoccupations and adventures. These were years in which he was spectacularly busy on many fronts, and his narrative grows fuller and longer every day: 1667 is the fattest year of the Diary. But he never saw action, and his pages offer no heroism and little violence. What he gives is a backstage view of war. There is confusion, jealousy, backbiting and greed; blame is laid, loyalties are divided; there is rejoicing – sometimes premature – as well as panic and despondency. The sound of guns is heard in the distance several times, and more immediate turmoil is produced by rioting, unpaid sailors and the weeping wives of pressed men. His job throughout was to supply and maintain the fighting force, and many of his associates were at sea during the summer months when the fleets expected to confront one another: Sandwich, Coventry, Penn, the duke of York all went off in the spring of 1665, alongside Monck, now duke of Albemarle, Prince Rupert and a mixture of sober, tough old Cromwellian captains like Lawson and light-hearted young gentlemen inclined to see war as a glorious game and surprised to find themselves spattered with blood and brains.

The Second Dutch War, like the first under Cromwell, was a commercial conflict. Pepys predicted and feared it as early as 1662.[1] It was meant to ensure English supremacy in trade with the Baltic, the East and West Indies and the African coast. The king and the duke of York, as well as Sandwich and Pepys's colleague Povey, were all investors in the slave trade; even the Royal Society invested some of its funds in Africa Company Stock in 1676, and again in the 1690s.[2] No one raised any objection to seizing and selling human beings until the Quakers began to do so in 1671, and Aphra Behn published her anti-slave trade novel *Oroonoko* in 1688; neither had any effect on the trade. We have seen that Lord Sandwich brought 'a little Turke and a negroe' as presents to his family in 1662, and Pepys himself owned and sold two slaves in the 1670s and 1680s.[3] The duke was president of the Royal Africa Company, which saw its business of supplying slaves to the West Indian sugar and tobacco industries threatened by the Dutch. The other trade routes were equally important and equally disputed. The king expected the war to be popular with the English merchant classes, and he was right. Parliament gave its blessing by voting two and a half millions towards its cost.

The fighting was almost entirely at sea, with great set battles in which the fleets faced and bombarded one another in ships that have been well described as floating abattoirs.[4] Apart from guns, the other weapons were fireships, launched as torpedoes, uncertain but often lethal. On the English side many of the men were pressed, meaning they were rounded up and forced to serve against their will. The Dutch never pressed – they had no need to – and there were English and Scotsmen who preferred to fight with the Dutch during this war, for political reasons and because they knew they were more likely to be paid. The English sailors were given vouchers, known as 'tickets', instead of money; the system was a bad one because proper payment was too often delayed, and men, desperate for ready cash, sold their tickets below value. When the Dutch attacked the Medway in 1667, Pepys was told that English voices were heard among the attackers, shouting that they were now fighting for money instead of tickets; and Esther St Michel, his sister-in-law, told him she heard both seamen and soldiers swearing they would rather serve the Dutch than the king, 'for they should be better used'.[5]

The work of paying, supplying and maintaining the navy fell heavily on Pepys. He went at it energetically, patting himself on the back in a letter to Coventry: 'had the hire of my labour been £10,000 per annum, I could not be possessed of a more hearty intentness in the early and late pursuance of my duty than I have been hitherto . . . I have heard no music but on Sunday these six months.'[6] This was in May 1665, before the first battle. He was hampered by lack of money and inefficiency in the yards, and acknowledged to himself that his office bore some blame for leaving the fleet short of clothing and provisions.[7] Coventry, aboard the *Royal Charles*, wrote asking for shirts for the men, turning his phrases with a smile but making a serious point: 'I do not intend to buy any of those shirts for my own use yet I am much concerned for them, because I think the health of the men concerned in their clothes, and men are so hard to get that I should be sorry to lose them.'[8] He also complained of the lack of essential provisions: 'Many ships have been on short allowance, some have drunk water, and some been in danger of neither having beer nor water.'[9] Less urbane grumbles came from Prince Rupert, who accused the navy commissioners of 'intolerable neglect'.[10]

Well supplied or not, the English fought the Dutch at the battle of Lowestoft on 3 June and beat them. Everyone in London went out to the park or the riverside to listen to the sound of the guns.[11] Pepys's old employer George Downing, ambassador in the Hague, also heard a 'continued terrible thunder from about 2 of the clock in the morning upon Saturday till between 11 and 12 at night'. When the news of the English victory came, he prudently fortified his house with stones and barrels of earth at the top of the stairs, fearing retaliation for the 5,000 Dutchmen dead.[12] Coventry had already decided that one victory would avail the English little, since the Dutch would be out again, and he was right. It was in any case a very partial victory, because fears for the safety of the duke of York, narrowly missed by a cannon ball that knocked off the head of the friend standing beside him on the deck, led to the pursuit of the Dutch being called off. It was not his decision but done while he was sleeping; still, the royal admiral had proved a liability. In spite of this, when the news of victory reached London five days later, Pepys lit a bonfire at his gate and distributed money to the local boys; and when the sunburnt officers arrived back in London, Coventry was rewarded with a knighthood and made a privy councillor. Sandwich protested that he had received no acknowledgement for his part in the fight, and told Pepys that he blamed Coventry, who was responsible for the official accounts of the battle.

Sandwich's next triumph proved still more bitter in its effects. He went to sea again – this was when he left Pepys in charge of his daughter's wedding – and captured two Dutch East Indiamen with cargoes worth hundreds of thousands of pounds. The news reached Pepys in September and produced an 'extasy of joy' in him – ecstasy on behalf of Lord Sandwich and the nation but also on his own behalf, since he was confident he could expect some share in the prize.[13] The distribution of prize treasure was subject to special commissioners. Officially the bulk of it was always meant to go to the state, with some allowed to the officers who took the prizes. The arrangement did not work out as it should, and in the time of Queen Elizabeth officers had on occasion shared out virtually the whole of the cargo among themselves; things were better controlled in the next century, but even under the commonwealth treasure sometimes disappeared mysteriously, as happened when Sandwich brought in his prize ships in 1656. Perhaps with that occasion in mind, he now called a council of his officers to consider what to do, and a majority agreed to start distributing part of the treasure among themselves before receiving any authorization. This was called 'breaking bulk', and Sandwich may have reckoned that, if the treasure was going to be plundered by others, he might as well get in first; he was also confident that the king would give his formal approval when asked. It was an arrogant assumption, and four officers refused to join in the distribution. Sandwich had made many enemies during his career; he was both envied and mistrusted.

He let Pepys know that he had taken £3,000 of goods for himself and offered him the chance to buy another £5,000 worth. Pepys went into partnership with a friend, Captain George Cocke, an old royalist now a merchant and navy contractor, and they prepared to move cartloads of goods to a lock-up found for them in Greenwich by John Tooker, the Navy Board messenger. This is when he started a second diary for his dealings in the prize goods, as though he felt he had to split off this part of his life.[14] Sandwich wrote a letter authorizing him to remove 'Several parcells of spirits, Silks and other Goods taken out of the two East India Prizes'; but even as the goods were being moved, Pepys began to have doubts.[15] Sandwich was attracting criticism on all sides: some of his own flag captains declared their opposition, Sir Christopher Myngs complaining that he had been kept waiting '3 or 4 hours together at that Earle's Cabin door . . . and at last foiled of admittance' – this was Pepys's report.[16] Albemarle spoke of 'embezzlement', and both he and Carteret wrote to Sandwich advising caution. So did Coventry, who asked coolly on 3 October for a list of the prizes 'with some account of their qualities . . . it might be of some use, for satisfying the nation, that their money hath not been thrown away'.[17] The warning tone from the man he now considered an enemy did nothing to stop Sandwich. On 14 October he wrote to Pepys again, assuring him the king had confirmed his right to what he had taken, 'so that you are to own the possession of them with confidence; and, if any body have taken security from them upon seizure, remand the security in my name, and return their answer. Carry it high; and own nothing of baseness or dishonour, but rather intimate, that I shall know who have done me indignities.'[18]

Sandwich's advice to 'carry it high' was meant to encourage Pepys. It failed to do so, because he had other plans afoot that depended on the goodwill of Coventry and Albemarle. On 19 October he asked Coventry to back him for the new position he had thought up for himself, as surveyor-general of victualling for the whole navy; on the same day he applied to Albemarle to give Balty a job as one of his guards. Albemarle agreed, and when Coventry consulted him about the victualling job for Pepys he agreed to that too.[19] Pepys wrote to thank the duke of York for confirming that the job was his and sent Albemarle a list of names he wanted appointed as his assistants. He was building up his own web of patronage and influence.

Meanwhile he made an attempt to restore friendly relations between his two warring patrons, Sandwich and Coventry. But Sandwich, proud and injured, told him reconciliation was impossible and accused Coventry of stirring up the trouble over the prizes. At this Pepys gave up. 'So I stopped,' he wrote flatly, and on 13 November he extricated himself from any further involvement with the prize business, selling his share to Cocke, and closing his second diary with the words, 'Ended all with Captain Cocke.'[20] Three days later he visited one of the prize ships with the other commissioners. He went into the hold and was overwhelmed by what he saw there, 'the greatest wealth lie in confusion that a man can see in the world. Pepper scattered through every chink, you trod upon it; and in cloves and nutmegs I walked above the knees, whole rooms full. And silks in bales, and boxes of copper-plate, one of which I saw opened . . . as noble a sight as ever I saw in my life.' It is a magnificent moment, showing us the inside of the great trading ship, packed so full the spices crunched underfoot; and an emblematic scene, as he surveys the riches of commerce and the spoils of war, now in his official capacity. There is some rich irony about too, since he has only just withdrawn from involvement in what some judged to be plundering it for private profit.

This was not the only irony. Shortly after the visit to the prize ships, he observed to Commissioner Pett at Chatham that 'It is now 2 months within 2 days since this Office hath felt one farthing of money for any service, great or small, though to save the life of a man by paying a ticket. We are in hopes of a little in a little while.'[21] While the wealth of the East Indies lay piled up in the prize ships, unpaid sailors were rioting outside his office, breaking the windows, cursing those inside, beating the unfortunate messengers, assaulting Batten and threatening to come back and pull the whole place down. 'What meat they'll make of me anon, you shall know by my next,' wrote Pepys to Coventry.[22] But Pepys remained unharmed, and on 4 December he received his official appointment as surveyor-general of victualling. It gave him another salary – he now had three – and the chance to make more on the side. At the end of the year he recorded the biggest increase yet in his personal fortune.

Sandwich would have been impeached had the king not given him immunity by quickly appointing him ambassador to Spain. Pepys, at his most sanctimonious, wrote in his end-of-year summary, 'The great evil of this year, and the only one indeed, is the fall of my Lord Sandwich, whose mistake about the prizes hath undone him, I believe, as to interest at Court . . . and endeed, his miscarriage about the prize-goods is not to be excused.' His own quick thinking had extricated him from being associated with Sandwich's mistake, and even improved his position with those in power. He rose as Sandwich fell, and his Lordship was left with a shadow over his reputation: 'it is scarce possible to tell you the public scandal and wound I have received', wrote Sandwich.[23] He was obliged to seek an official pardon, which was granted, but was slighted at a council meeting just before his departure for Spain and not even offered a seat. Pepys gave up his stool to his old master; but that evening abased himself to Coventry, 'desiring he would do the last act of friendship, in telling me of my faults'.[24] And when Pepys clashed with Prince Rupert in a council meeting a few months later, he was still worried that he might be regarded as 'a creature of Lord Sandwiches'. He made no effort to keep in touch with him, and in September 1667 observed that he had not written him a single letter since he left for Spain.[25]

★

Sandwich's departure as ambassador to Spain followed the entry of the French into the war as allies of the Dutch. In June 1666 the English, this time with Albemarle and Rupert in command, fought an extended battle known as the Four Days' Fight, in which they lost twenty ships and 6,000 men and the Dutch emerged as victors. Again Pepys heard the guns, this time from Greenwich, where he was overseeing the embarkation of 200 soldiers to help out at sea. He saw that most of them were drunk by the time they were shipped off. The following day, Whitsunday, he celebrated with Betty Martin after church ('did what he voudrais avec her, both devante and backward', he boasted to himself). After this he heard the first news that things were going badly at sea, and he and Creed shared their relief that Sandwich at least was no longer involved.

Monday brought a visitor to Seething Lane, 'black as the chimney and covered with dirt, pitch and tar, and powder, and muffled with dirty clouts and his right eye stopped with Okum'. This was Lieutenant Daniel of the *Royal Charles*. He had been put ashore at Harwich with a group of wounded men, and, in this state, the filth of battle on him and his injured eye untended, he rode with a friend to London. Pepys knew Daniel because he had lodged with his mother-in-law at Greenwich. He appreciated the drama of the situation and bore both men off to Coventry's lodgings, then hurried into the park to find the king, who caught Pepys's excitement and asked him to bring the men to him at once; and, standing in the park, Daniel gave his account of the battle so far: 'what the consequence of this day will be, that we hear them fighting, we know not'. With the gesture of a king in a folktale, Charles pulled twenty-odd pieces of gold out of various pockets for the men, and gave orders that they should be cared for by a surgeon.[26]

More seemingly good news came on 6 June, and bonfires were lit to celebrate victory; but the next morning contrary reports arrived, saying that the English had suffered a defeat. Pepys was plunged into despondency. He cheered himself by keeping 'little Mrs Tooker' – daughter or niece of his official messenger – in his chamber all afternoon 'and did what I would with her' while his family went out to see the launching of a new ship at Woolwich. That evening, after more grim accounts of the battle, he sat down to write to Lady Sandwich, giving her the latest bad news. She remained at Hinching-brooke, and he kept up his correspondence with her.[27]

Another aftermath of this battle was the funeral of Admiral Myngs at Whitechapel. He was killed but accorded no great honours, and Coventry was the single 'person of quality' present at the modest ceremony at Whitechapel church, to which Pepys also went. Myngs was only eight years older than him, another of the commonwealth stalwarts who had gone to sea as a boy and become a captain at twenty; now he was dead at forty-one, shot through the face. After the funeral a group of seamen approached Coventry's coach, tears in their eyes, and told him they would like to avenge the death of their commander by taking a fireship against the enemy. 'We are here a Dozen of us that have long known and loved and served our dead commander, Sir Chr. Mings, and have now done the last office of laying him in the ground. We would be glad we had any other to offer after him, and in revenge of him – all we have is our lives. If you will please get his Royal Highness to give us a Fireshipp among us all, here is a Dozen of us . . . that shall show our memory of our dead commander and our revenge.'[28] It was the grandest possible gesture of courage, offered out of loyalty and selfless love, and it came from a world whose values were remote from those prevailing in the circles about the king. According to Pepys, Myngs was a shoemaker's son who had by his own efforts 'brought his family into a way of being great' but had 'not had time to collect any estate'; he must also have been aware that Myngs had been one of the four officers who refused to take treasure from Sandwich's prize ships nine months earlier. By dying now, Myngs would be 'quite forgot in a few months, as if he had never been, nor any of his name be the better by it' – so Pepys predicted. He admired Myngs, but he may have been thinking of his own future at the same time. Would he have time to collect an estate? And would he be quite forgotten a few months after his death, leaving no one of his name?[29]

The funeral took place in the early evening of a long summer day, one in which long hours of light and sunshine kindled extra energy in Pepys. He had started with a board meeting in Whitehall with the duke of York, a cancelled Tangier Committee, a visit to the Exchequer with Balty, whom he then took to the studio of Hayls, the painter, currently working on a portrait of Pepys's father; after this he bought two lobsters and proceeded to lose them, leaving them in the hired coach that took him home for dinner, still with Balty. Then he was off to a meeting at the Excise Office in Bartholomew Lane, behind the Exchange; from which he went on to the funeral in Whitechapel.

For many this would have been a taxing day already, but Pepys kept going. He made his way to Deptford through the dusk and, once it was dark, at about ten o'clock, he presented himself at Mrs Bagwell's and 'went into her house and did what I would'. She then told him her servant had just died of the plague; and though she had disinfected the place by whitewashing the downstairs walls, he became extremely eager to leave. He bought himself a pint of sack, hailed a boatman and sat drinking as he was rowed upstream. At the end of the trip he handed over to the man what was left of the sack; and finally, almost at midnight, he called on a fisherman as he walked the last part of the journey home and paid the man three shillings for three eels. It was an impressive day's activity, and the next day, and the next, were almost as busy. During these summer months he also reports, among his other doings, looking at Jupiter and its satellites through the telescope he has acquired; composing and music-making; scientific conversations with Royal Society colleagues about teeth and optics and the nature of sounds; and commissioning some specially made glass-fronted bookcases, because, he wrote, his books were 'growing numerous, and lying one upon another on my chairs'. He helped to design them, they were built by a naval joiner, and they are the first-known purpose-built bookcases in England, and still in use.[30]

The Dutch celebrated their success by displaying the embalmed body of a fallen English commander in a sugar chest in the Hague and parading a captured living officer through the streets.[31] Two further military engagements that summer shifted the balance away from them again. On 25 July, St James's Day, Albemarle and Rupert engaged them in another battle. Again the guns were heard, and Pepys went up on to the Whitehall roof with the king and duke to listen to them; afterwards he dined off some of the food left over from the royal dinner table, called on two of his regular women on the way home and went out again to look at a print of the crucifixion he intended to buy, and some optical instruments that interested him. Again, there was no firm news for four days; then it came, and again, although the Dutch were beaten, the victory was only partial. Pepys's verdict was that there were 'no great matters to brag on, God knows'. Nevertheless he celebrated on the day of the public thanksgiving in

August with fireworks and the wildest party recorded in the Diary. There was drinking, daubing of faces with black from the spent fireworks, dancing and cross-dressing. At last Pepys had his chance to be a girl, as planned at Durdans many years before. He and two other men changed into women's clothes, Mercer became a boy and performed a jig in a suit borrowed from Tom, and Elizabeth and Pegg Penn, whose father was away fighting, put on periwigs. No one went to bed until past three in the morning. Meanwhile in Holland the formidable Sir Robert Holmes destroyed much of the Dutch East India fleet as it lay at anchor, using fireships, and followed this up by landing a force on the island of Schelling, where he plundered and burnt the small civilian town to the ground.[32]

The autumn of 1666, both before and after the great fire, brought complaints from Rupert and Albemarle, couched in 'plain and sharp and menacing' terms, about their fleets being inadequately supplied. Pepys was worried, Coventry resentful, and there was much discussion of accounting and shortfalls; the Navy Board warned that they could not execute their orders to man, supply and send out ships without being provided with more funds. A crucial meeting on 19 October led Coventry to tell the duke he would rather give up his commission than go on serving 'in so ill a place, where he cannot do the King service', and Pepys backed him up; the duke promised to pass on the message to the king.[33] But the king remained unforthcoming. Pepys noted how, after he had spoken on the affairs of Tangier at a council meeting, the king sat 'like an image' and 'could not speak one word'.[34]

In November Pepys wrote to the duke warning him to expect 'total and imminent miscarriage': the navy was without the means to repair ships, the men were unpaid, the officers forced to waste their time pressing, the workmen in the yards starving, 'walking like ghosts'.[35] John Evelyn, royalist to the core as he was, deplored the king's inattention to affairs of state. The merchant family of the Houblons predicted disaster for trade if things went on as they were. At the end of the year Pepys characterized the court as 'sad, vicious, negligent'.[36] The new year produced a long litany of warnings to the king and bitter complaints by his subjects. In March Pepys made a speech before Charles, telling him yet again that failure to fund the navy would lead to disaster. In April Pepys noted that Coventry was again threatening to 'abandon the King's affairs and let them sink or swim'.[37] In May Carteret told Pepys he feared the ruin of the state unless the king would 'mind his business', and in June Evelyn said the reputation of the kingdom was likely to be lost by the king's behaviour and boldly contrasted him with Cromwell – 'so much reputation got and preserved by a Rebell that went before him'.[38]

These complaints preceded the Dutch attack on the Medway in June 1667, and it proved the point the Navy Board had been making by bringing the worst humiliation the nation had suffered for six centuries. Panic hit London as the Dutch sailed up the Medway, destroyed the fort at Sheerness, broke the defensive chain across the river, burnt several important ships, including the *Royal James*, and bore off the *Royal Charles* itself. Pepys's Diary for the month of June gives what must be the most candid account ever written of the behaviour of a senior civil servant during a period of national crisis. On Sunday, 9 June, the day the Dutch landed on Canvey Island and the Kent militia were called out, he visited Coventry, eager that the world should see on what close terms he was with him; mocked at the 'young Hectors' setting off for Harwich to keep the Dutch at bay there and supposed they would debauch the countrywomen; went to church with Creed, left during the dull sermon and dined at home with his wife and father; returned to Whitehall and, after admiring Betty Michell in church, visited Betty Martin and 'haze what yo would' with her; took a boat for Barn Elms, alone, with a book; and finally got back to Seething Lane to find an order for fireships to be sent out, and Penn and Batten both arrived from their country places. On the Monday, with the news that the Dutch were now at the Nore, he set men to work at Deptford and went on to Greenwich, Woolwich and Gravesend, where he heard the Dutch guns and sneered at Albemarle, just arrived 'with a great many idle lords and gentlemen with their pistols and fooleries'. In truth Albemarle, now in his late sixties, was on his way to fight. Pepys went home by boat, passing many boats laden with the goods of the frightened citizens of Gravesend.

Evelyn reported general panic in 'County and City' on Tuesday, with everybody flying, 'none knew why or whither'.[39] Pett, in charge at Chatham, sent a message to the Navy Board reporting the loss of Sheerness and asking for assistance; Pepys described him as being 'in a very fearful stink'.[40] Brouncker and Mennes set off to help him, while Pepys, after going to Deptford to dispatch fireships, made sure his wages were fully paid up to date, and then amused himself by stalking Mercer through the streets for some time before returning to the matter of fireships. In the evening he heard that the City trained bands were being prepared to fight, so great was the fear that the Dutch would make an attempt on London.

Pepys's first thought when he got the news that the Dutch had broken the chain across the Medway and taken the *Royal Charles* on 12 June was that he must do what he could to secure his personal savings. His second thought was that the Navy Board might well be made scapegoats; but the money demanded immediate action. He sent Elizabeth and his father to Brampton with £1,300 in gold, and Richard Gibson after them with more, under the pretence that he was carrying an official message to the north. He contrived himself a belt in which he could carry another £300 in gold, sent for a poor cousin and entrusted her with his journal and some papers, and dispersed his more valuable pieces of plate among other cousins.[41] Around the office the wives of seamen shouted, 'This comes of your not paying our husbands.' There were other cries that the country was being bought, sold and governed by papists; Tom Hayter took this seriously enough to tell Pepys that he, like other Nonconformists, was thinking of moving to Hamburg. Elizabeth's parents actually left London for Paris.[42] A gibbet was set up in front of Chancellor Clarendon's great new house in Piccadilly: he had opposed the war, but he was to be one of the scapegoats for it. In fact the Dutch withdrew, in good order, and on 16 June celebrated their success with a service of Thanksgiving at home.

In almost any other country, Pepys reflected, he would probably have had his throat cut by now.[43] Even in England it was as well to prepare for trouble, and he began to prepare a defence of his office by assembling his correspondence with the duke of York. When news came that Commissioner Pett had been taken to the Tower he feared for himself again. On 19 June he joined in the attack on Pett at the council meeting, 'for which God forgive me, for I mean no hurt to him', and the following day he heard that people were reporting that he too was in the Tower. Henry Oldenburg, secretary to the Royal Society, was imprisoned there, for corresponding with a French scientist. Carteret resigned from his job as treasurer of the navy. With

Elizabeth still away, Pepys launched himself into some private sallies, on his cookmaid Nell and the Penns' maid Nan, and another attempt to get Pegg Penn on her own; in the office he fondled Mrs Daniel's pregnant belly. On the last day of the month he and Creed set off before dawn for Rochester and Chatham and took a barge to visit the site of the battle, seeing the wrecks of their own ships and a few dead bodies beside the water. Pepys remarked on the honourable behaviour of the Dutch in neither killing civilians nor plundering.

Pepys's account of himself at the fringes of war is as unheroic as Shakespeare's portraits of Falstaff and companions, or his Greeks and Trojans, and there are moments when he rivals Falstaff and Thersites as clown and rogue. As it happens, there is another, separate version of Pepys at war, also compiled by him, in which he figures as a diligent and blameless worker. This official face can be found displayed in his 'Navy White Book', in which the scope and scale of his preparations for the war are laid out in pages devoted to timber, sail-making, pitch, tar, ropes, contractors' prices, problems of recruitment and food supplies for ships, attempts to deal with inefficiency and corruption in the yards, and exchanges and wrangles with his fellow officers.[44] Here he appears as the impressive administrator he was, with every reason to be proud of what he did, and the 'Navy White Book' is an important and serious part of the record. But no one could call it a work of genius, whereas the Diary is just that.

One reason is that Pepys found himself so entertaining that he did not want to miss anything out. His self-portrait, warts and all, is compelling enough to draw us in and makes us live uncritically inside his skin. Moving so fast through the events of each day and the crowds of people with whom he had dealings, his energy burns off blame, making it surprisingly hard to disapprove of him. Pausing for a moment to make a few vows intended to curb his own behaviour, he remarks that 'my love of pleasure is such, that my very soul is angry with itself for my vanity in so doing'. He means, I think, that it is moral vanity in him to be making vows that aim above his real level, and that in his soul he thinks it might be better to remain his authentic, pleasure-loving self.[45] More than once he says in the course of the Diary that it is right to enjoy the world while you can, because there will be times when you will not be able to.[46] His authentic self is always so taken up with the immediate that he is quite unconcerned with glorifying his part in defending his country, and much more interested in conveying the texture and character of the world in which he is perpetually meeting new and exciting people and hearing and doing surprising things.

The peace treaty with the Dutch was signed at Breda at the end of July and ratified at the end of August, giving little pleasure and some shame to the English. In the same week *Paradise Lost* was put on sale at three shillings a copy; it is one of the few disappointments of the Diary that Pepys neither mentioned nor acquired it.[47] But he did read the work of Milton's friend and fellow poet Andrew Marvell that made its appearance in September, *Directions to a Painter, for Describing our Naval Business,* satirical verses on the war. Marvell took on the scapegoating of Commissioner Pett, still under threat of impeachment:

> After this loss, to relish discontent,
> Someone must be accused by punishment.
> All our miscarriages on *Pett* must fall:
> His name alone seems fit to answer all.
> Whose counsel first did this mad war beget?
> Who all commands sold through the navy? *Pett* . . .
> Who all our seamen cheated of their debt,
> And all our prizes who did swallow? *Pett.*
> Who did advise no navy out to set,
> And who the forts left unrepairèd? *Pett.*
> Who to supply with powder did forget
> Languard, Sheerness, Gravesend and Upnor? *Pett.*
> Who all our ships exposed in Chatham's net?
> Who should it be but the *Fanatic Pett?*
> *Pett,* the sea-architect, in making ships
> Was the first cause of all these naval slips:
> Had he not built, none of these faults had been;
> If no creation, there had been no sin.
> But his great crime, one boat away he sent,
> That lost our fleet and did our flight prevent.[48]

Not surprisingly, Pett's impeachment was adjourned until February and never revived. You could say he sank into obscurity except that he lives for ever in the lines of Marvell's scintillating defence. Pepys said it 'made my heart ache to read it, it being too sharp and so true'.[49]

The chancellor, Clarendon, was successfully scapegoated because he was distrusted by parliament, unpopular with the people and detested by Lady Castlemaine; and the king, to whom he had been a wise adviser for so long, was tired of being advised wisely. He let him go into banishment. Attempts to make Coventry another of the scapegoats for the failure of the war did not succeed, but he had had enough, and he left the Navy Board, telling Pepys that 'the serving a prince that minds not his business is most unhappy for them that serve him well'. Pepys found board meetings 'flat and dull' without him.[50] Coventry also gave up his position as secretary to the duke of York, who resented his criticisms of Clarendon, his father-in-law.[51] Both Penn and Batten told Pepys that they had 'cut him out' to take over as the duke's secretary, but he was not asked, and stoutly maintained that he would not have liked the disruption of his family life that the job would have brought with it.[52]

The end of the war meant he had to give up his position as surveyor-general of victualling – losing £300 a year – and lay off the extra clerks he had acquired. Penn faced worse: he was impeached for his part in the prize ship affair. There were also renewed attacks on the absent Sandwich. Parliament set up a committee to look into what had gone wrong in the war; Pepys was amused to find that it was to be chaired by an old commonwealth official, Colonel John Birch: 'it is pretty to see that they are fain to find out an old-fashion man of Cromwell's to do their business for them'.[53]

His eyes were giving him trouble, but he did not slacken his pace, and in March he spoke for three hours before the whole House of Commons in defence of the Navy Board. He was sick with nerves the night before and had to fortify himself with sack and brandy in the morning, but he made such an impression with his speech that he received compliments for weeks afterwards; even the king and the duke came up to him in the park to congratulate him.[54] This was the high point of his professional life so far, and it encouraged him to think of going into parliament. And so the war, which had brought shame and disaster to England and finished the careers of many of his colleagues, turned almost miraculously to his advantage. It was an outcome no one could have predicted.

13. Marriage

The Diary starts and ends in considerations of marriage. Pepys marks it as the central fact of his life at the beginning, and on each of the last two days he records being 'called by my wife'. The nine and a half years between give as good an account of the married state as has ever been written, its struggles, its woes, its pleasures and its discontents. You might put the Diary into the hands of a Martian to explain the institution and its workings, at least as it existed for the middle classes for three centuries, from the seventeenth until the twentieth, when men held economic and intellectual sway over their wives; and in many aspects it is still perfectly relevant, because its great achievement is to map the tidal waters of marriage, where the waves of feeling ebb and flow from hour to hour and month to month. The Pepyses were always moving between dependence and resentment, protectiveness and impatience, pride and shame, jealousy and anger, complicity and indifference, love and hate. They were capable of low abuse and physical violence towards one another, and also of delicacy, tenderness and forbearance. Whether it was a happy or an unhappy marriage is as difficult for us to pronounce now as it was for them at the time – everything depends on where you happen to be looking – but no one could accuse Pepys of not being in touch with his feelings about it at any given time.

The Diary describes long-running battles and sudden flares of rage. There were nights when she kept him awake with her complaining, others when he sulked. But 'And so we went to bed and lay all night in a Quarrell' is followed in the next sentence by 'This night I was troubled all night with a dream that my wife was dead, which made me that I slept ill all night.'[1] He was capable of blacking her eye, or twisting or pulling her nose, thoroughly nasty behaviour though casual violence, like a boy's angry lashing out, rather than calculated brutality; Pepys did not go in for husbandly beatings, and he and Elizabeth, like most couples, agreed that his blows were a private matter, shameful to them both and best kept concealed from the world. Jealousy, as we have seen, ran through their lives, binding them in a tormenting double chain. Elizabeth always wanted more of his time and attention than he gave her, as the letter of reproach with which this book began made clear. As head of the household, he wanted docility from her, and was disturbed and upset by her perpetual rows with the servants. After a quarrel with one departing maid, the girl went on to gossip about Elizabeth, suggesting she sat too long in the dark with Pepys's boy Tom Edwards, and kept him idle; Pepys expressed his anger in the Diary 'that all my trouble in this world almost should arise from . . . the indiscretion of a wife that brings me nothing almost (besides a comely person) but only trouble and discontent'.[2] He worried too that his rising prosperity would make her careless with his money: 'I fear she will forget by degrees the way of living cheap and under a sense of want,' he wrote in 1664.[3]

He could be blisteringly rude to her face too; as they walked to church one Sunday he was so critical of her clothes that she went home again, and then took herself to a different church. Another day he called her a whore for wearing ill-matched ribbons.[4] But she was not easily crushed. After a row over her kitchen accounts he wrote, 'I find she is very cunning, and when she least shows it, hath her wit at work; but it is an ill one.'[5] She learnt how to bargain with him, offering to give up the false hair she liked, and he hated, on condition that he stopped seeing his actress friend Mrs Knipp. Criticism of clothes and hair was strictly one-sided, and nowhere in the Diary is there any mention of Elizabeth commenting on his appearance. Even when he decided, in November 1663, to let his barber cut his hair and sell him a periwig, and reports his anxiety about the response of his neighbours, colleagues, bosses and even maids, he says nothing about what she thought of the change, although for her it meant that the man she had married was transformed into a quite different creature, who went to bed with a shorn head and put on by day the sign of power and status.[6] The fashion for periwigs came from France – the word is an Anglicized *perruque* – and Pepys was one of the first to adopt it in England. A wig declared your social standing at first glance. It was expensive to maintain, you needed several, and they were made of hair bought from someone poor enough to be prepared to sell theirs – Pepys also had one made from the first cropping of his own hair, which is how we know it was dark brown. He had enough doubts to grow his own hair long again, but in May 1665 'I find the convenience of Perrywiggs is so great, that I have cut off all short again, and will keep to periwigs.'[7] A wig meant that you need never go grey or bald in public; you appeared more of an icon, less of a person. This is why wigs had such a deadening effect on portraiture, stifling individuality under those great cushions of curls. Sadly all the portraits of Pepys show him as a wig-wearer; you have only to look at the few wigless representations of his contemporaries to see how much livelier they are: Evelyn old and grey, Newton's little bust with thin hair drawn back, Dryden in a rare wigless portrait.[8]

There were as many good times as quarrels in the marriage, when he confided in her and delighted in her company. The Sunday mornings when they lay late in bed, talking of his hopes and plans, were a particular pleasure and comfort to him; probably to her too, although we have to guess about that. Both enjoyed expeditions to theatres and shops together, as well as summer outings – on the river to Vauxhall or Barn Elms, or by coach to the country inns of Islington and Hackney. In October 1662 he reflected on how they have been 'for some years now, and at present more and more, a very happy couple, blessed be God'.[9] There were days when they cherished one another's ailments sympathetically, she advising him to sit 'long and upright' when he tried to empty his bowels, often a problem for him; and he hurrying home from the office to comfort her when she sent a message to say she was 'in great pain of those'.[10] When he was exasperated by his colleagues or troubled about the office, he dreamt of enjoying life with her away from the Navy Board: 'my wife and I will keep to one another and let the world go hang'.[11] The afternoon might go to a mistress, but the evening talk was with Elizabeth, 'with whom I have much comfort'.[12]

When things were easy between them, she happily took lessons from him: in music, arithmetic and astronomy. He prided himself on his teaching, and her eagerness to acquire knowledge and skills also tells us how she had been starved of education: to be a bright girl in that century was more frustration than joy. She took up painting and worked hard at it, turning out some work Pepys admired. What schooling she had enjoyed was in France, and part of her always yearned towards the country of her childhood and her convent teachers. The wandering habits and decayed gentility of her parents gave her the exotic aspect he was proud of but did not make her into the orderly housewife he also wished for: *bœuf en daube* and general resourcefulness, excellent; household accounts and discipline of servants, not so good. She liked long mornings in her dressing gown; when she passed an old gown on to her mother, Pepys remembered fondly that she had called it 'her Kingdome, from the ease and content she used to have in the wearing of it'. It is one of the few Diary entries in which we hear her actual words.[13]

Like her husband, Elizabeth had a thorough appreciation of the pleasures of ordering and appearing in new clothes. She was a beauty – luscious and responsive in the Hayls portrait – and she cared for her appearance. As well as acquiring hairpieces, she had her teeth scraped by the royal dentist, wore patches and collected dew for her complexion. She was noticed with admiration by many men, including the duke of York, who eyed her 'mightily' in the park.[14] She flirted with her admirers, capturing Will Hewer's heart, enjoying herself with her handsome dancing master and disquieting her father-in-law by her receptiveness to an attentive Guards officer who shared a London coach with them.[15] She appreciated the attentions of her Axe Yard neighbour John Hunt, and of Captain Robert Ferrer, both of whose names she put forward to be her Valentines in the year Pepys perversely chose to veto such expensive foolishness.[16] Later he noticed her *tendresse* for one of the engineers of the Tangier breakwater, the charming Henry Sheeres, and suffered a jealous twinge. Sheeres offered to teach her the rules of perspective, and Pepys observed that he became even more attractive to her when he revealed that he was a poet as well as an engineer.[17] She may have hoped for more poetry in Pepys, and in their life together.

What he called her vixen's temper frightened him, and he was sometimes cowed by it. When she scolded him one day for not dining at home and he gave her 'a pull by the nose and some ill words' and left the house for his office, she followed him; and, fearing that she would carry on the quarrel in the hearing of his clerks, he diverted her into the garden to calm her down and 'prevent shame'.[18] She made scenes in public when she was infuriated by his attentions to their friends Mrs Knipp and Mrs Pearse. Pepys's brother John was upset by her rudeness when he stayed at Seething Lane, and Pepys noticed her 'carrying herself very high' towards his father and sister at Brampton.[19] She flew into a tremendous fury against old Mr Pepys after he told Pepys about her flirtatious behaviour in the coach; she held him in 'absolute hatred', she said, and would not consider having him to live with them after Pall married. 'Very hot work a great while,' wrote Pepys as she boiled up to deliver threats that she would also refuse to live with Pepys and shame him 'all over the City and the Court' with complaints about his meanness and her lack of freedom.[20] He is unlikely to have felt too vulnerable to her accusing him to either the Court or the City, but she did know how to shake him. And about his meanness she was right, because he consistently spent more on his clothes and pleasures than he allowed her. About her freedom, less so: the Diary records her going out with friends, attending dancing parties and even staying out all night. At the same time he always felt it was bad for her to be away from his control, and that her character changed when he was not with her to keep her in order. When he visited her at Woolwich, where he took her during the great fire, he found her 'out of humour and indifferent, as she uses upon her having much liberty abroad'.[21] Another time, after she had stayed at Brampton for a long spell without him, he reflected on 'my wife's neglect of things and impertinent humour got by this liberty of being from me which is never to be trusted with for she is a fool'.[22]

The cycle of their relationship is established in the opening pages of the Diary, when she was twenty to Pepys's twenty-seven, and they had been married for five years of poverty, illness, quarrels, separation and reconciliation, as political storms raged and their future was quite uncertain. Five years into the marriage he has not yet introduced her to his patron, Edward Montagu; her place is necessarily in the background of his narrative and he does not even give her name – 'my wife' was always enough for Pepys. Their social life is markedly with his family, not with hers: a visit to his parents, a Twelfth Night party with his cousins. She runs a race in the park with his cousin Jane Turner's daughter Theophila, and borrows her mother-in-law's woollen mantle and her brother-in-law John's hat for Pepys to walk home in when it comes on to rain after their regular Sunday dinner *en famille*. She goes alone to visit her parents, and when her brother brings her a present of a dog, Balty is not named by Pepys either; he is pleased with the dog, but the pleasure does not last long, and soon he is telling her he intends to fling it out of the window 'if he pissed the house any more'.[23] It is her family's fault. The first quarrel in the Diary comes when he goes out without her in the evening and she, objecting, follows him along the street. He escorts her firmly home, then sets out alone again and appears to have won the argument, but she has the last word, because she goes to her neighbours the Hunts and contrives to stay out later than he does.[24] A fortnight into the Diary her fighting powers are well established.

Within the first month we are given a clear impression of how she lives, and indeed to women readers she starts as Everywife when on New Year's Day she burns her hand doing up the remains of the Christmas turkey. We hear of her going to market to buy food, and preparing the dinner they give in the Montagu lodgings in Whitehall Palace, working late into the evening to make tarts and lard the chickens and larks. She cooks well and is practical, killing a turkey sent by Lady Montagu with her own hands. She sometimes gets lost in a book, like her husband, staying up at night after he has gone to bed because she can't tear herself away from her French novel, *Polexandre*, about a beautiful queen who inhabits an inaccessible island and sends her knight to punish the royal suitors who aspire to her hand.[25] But she is also a hard worker, up all through a frosty night doing the monthly wash with Jane. She takes a sisterly interest in Jane's looks and does up her hair for her, to Pepys's admiration. She and Pepys are more often comfortable together than not: lying in bed on a cold morning, she reads aloud to him while he is getting up. On another evening she watches as he writes, while a drum beats a single stroke outside, and they ask themselves what it can mean in those troubled times.

This ordinary life makes the backdrop to Pepys's activities and the political events of the early months of 1660 – Monck's arrival in London with his troops, Montagu and Downing each holding his breath for the right moment to make his submission to Charles. Elizabeth stayed at home with Jane in Axe Yard when Pepys rode off intending to see Montagu at Hinchingbrooke; but as soon as he knew he would be going to sea for an indeterminate period, he made arrangements for her to leave London. There was no question in his mind of her being with either her parents or his in town, and he took the trouble to ride out again, this time to Buckinghamshire, on a borrowed horse, through the darkness and with a severe cold in the head, to settle proper lodgings for her with trusted friends, the Bowyers, where she could take Jane and her dog. Then he arranged a treat before their parting. They went to Fish Street together and bought eightpence worth of salmon – a substantial piece – and had it cooked in the Sun Tavern; and there, over dinner, 'I did promise to give her all that I have in the world but my books, in case I should die at sea.'[26] A few days later she was in Buckinghamshire, and he made his will as he had said he would, with the afterthought that the French books were to be hers. This was Pepys at his most tender and thoughtful. During his absence, they both wrote letters as often as possible, but on his return he was too busy to give her much attention until they settled in Seething Lane and took up a new pattern of life. From then on he fulfilled the primary duty of a husband, to be a good provider; they rose steadily up the social scale, and she no longer had to labour in the house but lived the life of a lady.

A wife was expected, in return for her husband's support and protection, to supervise household matters and to provide regular sex. The early years of the Diary have little to say about this last point, but we know he expected it because he complained when the service failed. On 2 August 1660 she had a pain – 'her old pain in the lip of her *chose*, which she had when we were first married', so a recurrence of the cyst in her private parts – and by the 6th he was 'not a little impatient'. He was allowed access again on the 8th. Even this short interruption gave him licence to look elsewhere, and within days he recorded an encounter with Betty Lane, his old flame from Westminster Hall. She had several admirers, among them John Hawley, Pepys's friend, whom he sometimes urged her to marry. He encouraged Hawley to the marriage too, 'God knows I had a roguish meaning in it', he explained to himself in the Diary.[27] Roguish seems a mild term for such behaviour; and there was no marriage between Hawley and Betty. She might have hoped to marry Pepys himself had he not already been taken, because she enjoyed herself with him. He would supply a bottle of wine and perhaps a lobster, and she brought unabashed enthusiasm to their love-making. Later he describes an athletic performance under a tavern chair, and how he was disconcerted by her showing her own enjoyment; on another occasion she left him 'almost defessus [exhausted] of the pleasure'.[28] Unlike her, he felt guilty about what they did together, and about what people would think if they knew. He could not resist what she offered, but it made him anxious: 'my mind un peu troublé pour ce que j'ai fait today. But I hope it will be la dernière de toute ma vie,' he wrote after the session under the chair; but it was not the last.[29]

Three weeks after seeing Betty Lane there was another episode, this time with Diana Crisp. As we have seen, he bought Elizabeth a pearl necklace the day after this. She did not know why then, but the sex–money equation continued to the end of the Diary, when her discovery of his gross misbehaviour won her the annual dress allowance she so much wanted at last. From her point of view, she accepted that he had a right to her body and saw his demands as a sign of her hold over him; she withheld herself only when she was ill, and she became anxious when he left her alone for months at a time. Not that there was much physical enjoyment for her. Only when she was roused to passionate fury, fourteen years into the marriage, did something approaching pleasure stir in her body. He improved on this by chance when, for the first time, he 'poner my digito [put my finger] in her thing, which did do her much pleasure; but I pray God that ella doth not think that yo [I] did know before – or get a trick of liking it'.[30] His anxiety that she might 'get a trick of liking' what he had done to her shows how strongly the stern tradition in which he was reared, which saw sex as intrinsically sinful, kept its hold over him. Men could hardly help desiring and enjoying it, but for a virtuous woman to share the pleasure was so disconcerting that he actually preferred her not to.

None the less he expected her to be available and complained when she was 'so ill of late of her old pain that I have not known her this fortnight almost, which is a pain to me'.[31] To his credit, he also took a practical interest in helping to deal with her complaint. In May 1661, for instance, he was tending her himself, under the advice of her physician, Dr Williams: the treatment involved putting a 'tent' into the cyst, which had now become an infected abscess, to try to drain out the infection. This did not end the trouble, and two and a half years later they had to call in his surgeon, Hollier, for what had by then become an abscess three inches deep. Hollier recommended cutting it. Elizabeth was insistent that no one could nurse her but Pepys, because she feared her maids might think she had a shameful

disease. Hollier then decided they would try to treat her with fomenta-
tions only; this appeared to ease things but could not cure the underlying condition.[32] Both Elizabeth and Pepys believed, wrongly, that
the trouble was brought on by sexual activity: 'we fear that it is my
matter that I give her that causes it, it never coming but after my
having been with her'.[33] It made a depressing situation for them both,
he with his boisterous appetite, she tormented by secret, painful and
humiliating sores. In the later years of the Diary he records long
periods when he did not make love to her at all – more than half a
year, he says, in August 1667.[34] The most enjoyable night they ever
spent together could be one they spent at a Hertfordshire inn – it was
in Welwyn – where they found two beds in the room and slept single:
'of all the nights that ever I slept in my life, I never did pass a night
with more epicurisme of sleep – there being now and then a noise of
people stirring that waked me; and then it was a very rainy night; and
then I was a little weary, that what between waking and sleeping
again, one after another, I never had so much content in all my life.
And so my wife says it was with her.'[35] The description is so delicious
it makes you want to find just such an inn, such beds and such a rainy
night to sleep and wake through; and it must be said that Pepys
conveys delight here as he never does when writing about sexual
activities.

There was also the question of children. Pepys never shows Elizabeth grieving over their childlessness and does not appear to have
talked the matter over with her or with their doctors. The Diary gives
no clue about what she felt. Whether he was too self-absorbed to
notice, or whether she concealed her feelings of sadness from him,
they are not in evidence. Her habit of taking to her bed with every
period may have been a signal of disappointment, but it could just as
easily have been physical pain or a cultural pattern learnt from her
mother. It is even possible that she did not mind too much about
the lack of children. She saw other women perpetually pregnant,
undergoing the ordeal of childbirth, losing their looks and their babies
too, since more children died than survived; while she remained
relatively free, young-looking and pretty. At least no little Pepyses
were fathered on anyone else, and she learnt to fill her days with
activity, with lessons, painting, dancing, house decorating, shopping
and sewing. Occasionally she told her husband she thought she was

pregnant, and he duly noted it down. The impression given by the Diary is that he was the one to brood. In January 1662 he was 'considering the possibility there is of my having no child'. A few weeks later, at a shipboard dinner, where men's tongues were loosened, he had to accept being linked with another man who could give his wife no children, both called 'fumblers'. In November 1663 Elizabeth said she was certain she was pregnant, 'which if it be, let it come and welcome', he wrote; but she was not.[36]

Early the next year came the bizarre incident of his uncle Wight, the rich fishmonger who was half-brother to Pepys's father, and with a wife past childbearing. Pepys had hopes of becoming his heir and consequently saw a good deal of him. But instead of writing a will in his favour, uncle Wight privately declared his love to Elizabeth and proposed that he should father a child on her: 'he would give her £500 either in money or jewel beforehand and make the child his heir. He commended her body and discoursed that for all he knew the thing was lawful. She says she did give him a very warm [i.e., angry] answer.' Pepys remained admirably calm when she reported this unusual suggestion to him. She had sent the lecherous old man packing after all; and he decided it was best to say nothing. He did not even break off relations with the Wights, and the two couples continued to dine together from time to time as though nothing had happened; it must have posed one or two problems for Elizabeth, but Pepys was still hoping for a legacy.[37] The equanimity with which he took other men's passes at her suggests he thought it normal for men to try their luck, as he tried his, and that as long as she fended them off no harm was done. It was only when she showed active interest in another man that he became agitated.

Uncle Wight's behaviour did at least stir Pepys into seeking advice. In July 1664, when Elizabeth was away at Brampton, he attended a christening party given by his Joyce cousins in London, contributing half a dozen bottles of wine to the occasion because he went with a purpose, which was to ask advice of the older women. It must have made a striking moment as Pepys rose with the ladies, leaving the men to their after-dinner talk: 'when the women were merry and ris from the table, I above with them, ne'er a man but I; I begin discourse of my not getting of children and prayed them to give me their opinion and advice; and they freely and merrily did give me these ten among them'. Pepys listed and numbered their suggestions with the same efficiency that he practised at his office, adding a note on which they considered the most important. These were: that he should drink sage juice; take wine and toast; keep his stomach warm and his back cool; make love when he felt like it rather than at a particular fixed time; and change the level of the bed so that his and Elizabeth's feet were higher than their heads. The ladies also advised cool drawers for him and not too much tight-lacing for her. Some of their advice is still given to couples with fertility problems; but it did nothing for him.[38]

That September Elizabeth again believed for a few days that she was with child.[39] Pepys's comment by then was that he neither believed nor desired it, and after this both seem to have given up; they had been married for nine fruitless years. Pepys embarked on more involvements with other women, and the crises of the war with the Dutch, the plague and the fire of London kept them both busy and on the move. There is some indication that he thought she rather than he was barren, because in July 1667 he expressed relief when Betty Martin gave him 'the good news que esta no es con child . . . the fear of which . . . had troubled me much'.[40] Later in the same month, when his brother John fell down in a mysterious faint while staying with them, Pepys suddenly wondered if he might be 'left without a brother or son, which is the first time that ever I had thoughts of that kind in my life'.[41] A few weeks later, seeing a pretty little boy, the child of cousin Sarah Giles, who had lost several in the plague, he wished he was his own.[42] He kept his liking for children but never fathered one, neither by Elizabeth nor anyone else, and had to settle for being a conscientious godfather and uncle.

One of the principal themes of the Diary is the classic conflict between his practical, sensible self and his romantic and erotic impulses, between prudence and order on the one hand and following free-ranging sexual impulses on the other. A marriage begun in romance and without reference to money is one of the curious anomalies of his life, because it cut across so many of the values in which he was reared. Even lower-middle-class families expected their children to marry in consultation with their parents, who would ensure that there was some financial advantage for them; and if Pepys, as a young graduate, felt he had outstripped his parents' advice, he could have set out to find himself a rich young widow or a City heiress. When his colleague John Creed wooed and won Lord Sandwich's niece Elizabeth Pickering, daughter of Sir Gilbert and cousin of Dryden, Pepys professed himself shocked on the grounds that they were too unequal in rank, but his outrage was really jealousy of Creed's success in carrying off such a coup.[43] Pepys knew he had wasted his own chance to better himself, and there are moments in the Diary when he blames himself for his folly, blames Elizabeth for having no dowry and reminds her of this by calling her a 'beggar'. At other moments he looks back fondly and approvingly at their courtship as an example of true love. Then again, when it came to the other members of his family, he did everything he could to ensure that none deviated from the path of prudence and proper financial settlements; we shall see that at the end of his life he disinherited his elder nephew for entering into exactly the sort of rash marriage he had made himself.

The character of Charles II set up another conflict for him. As a young man Pepys lived in a society in which two cultures coexisted: the sexually liberated low life found among the Whitehall clerks, tavern and shopkeepers of Westminster Hall, and the puritan culture in which he was brought up, with its ideal of continence and perpetual wrestling to resist temptation. You can see Pepys aligning himself firmly with the puritan ethos when, for instance, he expressed his shock and shame at the discovery of his brother Tom having fathered a child outside wedlock; and again in his response to hearing of Lord Sandwich's adultery. The same attitudes were still at work when, on Lord Brouncker becoming a navy commissioner in 1664 and moving into Seething Lane with Abigail Williams, the woman who shared his life but not his name, Pepys could hardly contain his disapproval and rarely missed a chance to abuse her in the Diary, calling her 'whore', 'painted lady', 'lady of pleasure' and 'doxy'. At the same time he had for years been aware of, and tempted by, the other, low-life culture that, during the commonwealth years, maintained itself underneath the public life of high moral tone. With the return of the monarchy a dramatic change came about, as high life rapidly outdid low life in its freedoms. The example of king and court, described by Pepys as 'nothing almost but bawdry . . . from top to bottom', could hardly fail to make a young man who had a struggle to keep his own libido under control ask himself why he should bother.[44] The king's disregard for the institution of marriage was flagrant; he kept a virtual harem, he ennobled his mistresses and his children by them, he presided over a court given over to pleasure, in which great lords consorted with actresses and great ladies were said to be infected with the pox and to abort their unwanted babies. The duke of York behaved no better, and Lord Brouncker was said to pimp for him. Pepys heard much of the court gossip from his friend James Pearse, Montagu's surgeon on the *Naseby*, who became surgeon to the duke in 1660 and picked up all the hot stories; although he hardly needed inside information, because everyone knew what went on at court. Pepys discussed Lady Castlemaine, the chief royal mistress, even with Lady Sandwich. His friend Povey entertained him with prurient accounts of the king's sexual practices.[45] More scabrous stuff came through his colleagues in the Navy Office. When Mennes and Batten gave him a robust commentary on the indecent pranks of the poet and courtier Charles Sedley, he confessed in the Diary that he did not know what buggery was: 'But blessed be God, I do not to this day know what is the meaning of this sin, nor which is the agent nor which the patient,' he wrote.[46] Pepys was thirty at this point, but we are hearing the voice of the puritan boy.[47]

Pepys's own adventures, so frankly recorded, have given him a great reputation with posterity, but the truth is he had not much sexual confidence. Consider this: 'walked (fine weather) to Deptford and there did business and so back again; walked, and pleased with a jolie femme that I saw going and coming in the way, which yo could aver sido contented para aver stayed with if yo could have ganar acquaintance con ella; but *at such times as those I am at a great loss, having not confidence, ni alguno [nor any] ready wit*. So home and to the office, where late; and then home to supper and bed.'[48] The italics are mine: he is making a central statement about himself here. You see why he listened with such fascination to the flirtatious and worldly exchanges of Sedley and a court lady when he sat close to them in the theatre – it was because he longed to emulate their sophistication and ease in the game of courtship, and did not know how.[49] Elizabeth had been an easily impressed child when he wooed and married her. Betty Lane, jolly and coarse, came out to meet him. Lady Sandwich was an untouchable ideal. He yearned for something else, something more –

to be a charmer of witty ladies, to exchange badinage while he won their sexual favours.

But he never achieved anything like this during the Diary years. Instead there are entirely down-to-earth encounters with shop girls, tavern girls and simple young women he picked up on out-of-town trips, like the silly shopkeeper's wife of Rochester whom he met in a cherry garden, kissed and took into the fields in June 1667.[50] Young girls were his regular targets, some apparently pre-adolescent, like 'little Mrs Tooker', the 'very pretty child' he made free with in his lodgings during the plague winter of 1665. She seems to have been accustomed to such treatment; there was no age of consent, and her mother was perfectly willing to hand her over and she to cooperate with Pepys; but to us she appears as a child victim, and by today's standards what he did would have earned him a prison sentence.[51] In his own household he launched himself routinely on the young women who served as his wife's companions and maids. In 1666 he said he felt himself beginning to love Mary Mercer too much 'by handling of her breasts in a morning when she dresses me, they being the finest that I ever saw in my life; that is the truth of it'.[52] In her case, and in Jane Birch's too, his advances were so habitual that they did not require many mentions in the Diary; occasional references make clear what went on. Girls in service must have been so used to being manhandled that they learnt to defend themselves, with threats to tell the mistress or laughter; or else they simply accepted that this was part of the scheme of things, as the cookmaid Nell Payne did.[53] He extended his attempts to the Penns' maid Nan, whom he also accused of being Sir William's whore. Among married women he picked out those whose husbands could be rewarded for their complaisance with promotion or financial help, like Daniel, the naval lieutenant, and Bagwell, the shipyard carpenter. Mrs Knipp, the actress, was an exception; she was another strong-minded woman who did as she pleased, defying her horse-dealer husband, and she flirted, romped and exchanged kisses with Pepys on terms of perfect equality, sometimes accepting his caresses and sometimes pushing his hands away; no doubt her independent behaviour was sustained by her ability to earn her own living.

By his own account, most of Pepys's stories of women are stories of pursuit and sexual failure. In the course of the Diary he has designs on something like twenty but succeeds in seducing only three or four.[54] John Donne's lines 'Whoever loves, if he do not propose/The right true end of love, he's one that goes/To sea for nothing but to make him sick' suggested that nothing would do except penetrative sex, but Pepys knew otherwise, and Povey's account of the king's enjoyment of non-penetrative sex must have reassured him that it was not to be undervalued.[55] He got pleasure from the chase itself, stealing a kiss, touching a breast or a thigh, getting his hand under a petticoat. He also did his best to persuade women to caress him; most resisted, and he makes clear many times in the Diary how much he wanted more. He encourages himself by insisting that he could have a particular woman – Pegg Penn, Rebecca Allen, the shopkeeper's wife at Rochester – if only the circumstances were more propitious. We don't believe him, and he probably doesn't really believe himself, but it looks good on the page and cheers him up.

When it comes to what actually did happen between him and a particular woman on a particular occasion, he provides what has all the signs of being a fair record: there is no boasting about the facts. Hope, excitement, satisfaction, humiliation or failure may be involved, and his tone may be eager, comical or mortified; the setting is always real, often uncomfortably so, and he is always recognizably himself, the man who was taking part in a committee meeting in a previous paragraph, and a page later will be planning his house improvements. Every episode is set firmly in the context of his life and other preoccupations. There were days when he went out on his rounds like an animal, going from one fancied girl to another, getting what satisfaction he could from each – a kiss here, a squeeze there – and ending up with the reliable Betty Lane or at least compliant Mrs Bagwell, with whom he could take liberties he would not dream of doing with Elizabeth, such as taking a good look at all parts of her naked body.[56] On other days he might wait for three hours in the cold outside Westminster Abbey on a Sunday for a shop girl he had arranged to meet. Or he could be crudely aggressive towards a stranger, such as the girl who defended herself with a pin in church.[57]

Fantasy and private pleasure was the simplest alternative to flesh and blood, and he writes of consoling himself with it, in church at the sight of another desired girl, or at home alone, calling up the image of a court beauty one night and boldly deciding to make it the queen the next.[58] In the real world, like Mozart's Don Giovanni, all his efforts left him with a low success rate. Perhaps this is why, however sorry you feel for some of the girls and women he pursued, you rarely lose all sympathy for him. He so often makes a mess of his attempts at wooing, and he does not attempt to justify his lewd and bungling behaviour. He had what may partly have provided an excuse, although he does not claim it as such, in his wife's medical condition. Above all, he tells his stories of failure with an energy that lifts them to a sort of sublimity, close to the sublimity of Shakespeare's (and Verdi's) Falstaff, or the erotic poems of Goethe.

Take for example the history of his infatuation with Betty Michell. This Betty, like Betty Lane, came from Westminster Hall, where her parents were shopkeepers and friends of Pepys and where she first caught his eye when she was still a child. He thought she looked like Elizabeth: 'a pretty girl and one I have long called wife; being, I formerly thought, like my own wife', he wrote in 1663. From then on he mentioned her often, reminding himself of how he used to call her his second wife, predicting that she would grow up into 'a mighty handsome wench' and 'a fine handsome woman' and declaring his love for her; he also pumped the older Betty for information about the younger.[59] To her he must have seemed a jolly uncle who hung about her parents' stall, liked and trusted by them both as customer and friend. After watching her in the Hall one day, he conducted an experiment that he noted down with scientific interest. He summoned a boat and 'lying down close in my boat, and . . . without use of my hand, had great pleasure, and the first time I did make trial of my strength of fancy of that kind without my hand, and had it complete avec la fille que I did see au-jour-dhuy in Westminster hall'.[60] By now she was about to be married to Michell, the son of one of Pepys's booksellers; this was after being betrothed to his brother, who died in the plague, 'which is a pretty odd thing', thought Pepys.[61] But he was pleased that the young couple was to move to his part of town, to run a shop selling spirits at the eastern end of Thames Street.

Up to this point Pepys's attitude to Betty was sentimental rather than rapacious. Now he became determined to have her. He embarked on a carefully thought-out campaign, described in all its deviousness in the Diary. He took Elizabeth to Westminster Hall to be introduced to Betty as a bride, daughter and daughter-in-law of long-established and friendly suppliers of his, and about to become a neighbour. Next he dropped in at the Michells' shop to buy himself a drink and followed this up by creating an opportunity to give both husband and wife a lift in his boat. Then he went out of his way to do Michell a financial favour in the matter of a seaman's ticket. So far so good, and, finding Betty alone when he called again, he decided the time had come to 'steal a kiss or two'. The next move was to suggest to Elizabeth that the Michells might be invited to a Sunday dinner, as an act of kindness to the deserving young couple. They came, and after dinner the Pepyses took them out into the country in a hired coach. He was suffering badly from wind, but in spite of this the expedition was a success, because Elizabeth took to the Michells. She found them an attractive and innocent pair, and they were grateful for the Pepyses' condescension and kindness. More invitations to dinner followed and were accepted.

The great fire of September 1666 interrupted the progress of his plans, but not for long. The Michells' house was destroyed, and they moved to Shadwell, still close enough to be dinner guests. Betty was now pregnant, and her mother had confided in Pepys that young Michell was not as kind to her as he might be, and suggested that he, as a wiser and older man, might 'appear a counsellor to him'.[62] Delighted by this licence to interfere, what he actually did was to give Betty a lift home in a coach and succeed in getting her hand under his coat 'and did tocar mi cosa con su mano [touch my thing with her hand] through my chemise, but yet so as to hazer me hazer la grande cosa [make me make the great thing, i.e., orgasm]'.[63] Here was a new game, and he was so taken with it that he proceeded to set up shared trips whenever he could, persisting even when her husband was with them and against her pleas that she had a headache. After a theatre and shopping trip together he made Elizabeth change places with him in the coach so that he could get hold of Betty's hand. The Sunday before Christmas he went to church with the Michells; there was snow on the ground, and he kindly offered to collect them from her parents later in the day. This time he had to use 'some little violence' to get hold of her hand 'contra su will' and force it to where he wanted it, 'she making many little endeavours para oter su mano [to remove her hand] still'. Once at Seething Lane, Betty 'did seem a little ill'. But Pepys kissed her goodnight blithely and went into his chamber, where 'with my brother and wife did Number all my books in my closet and took a list of their names; which pleases me mightily, and is a job I wanted much to have done'. Comic, if you put aside thoughts of Betty, feeling rotten, pregnant and at a loss how to deal with an old family friend who was in a position to do her and her husband good.[64]

The climax of the affair came in February 1667. Pepys called on Michell and left an invitation to Betty to join Elizabeth and him that afternoon for some more shopping at the New Exchange. She turned up at five to find only Pepys, who made an excuse and insisted on buying her an expensive dressing box. It would take an hour to be prepared. He suggested a drink. She said she preferred to spend the hour visiting relatives near by and would return to the shop later. There they watched the work on the box being finished together. The next part of the story is one of Pepys's virtuoso narratives. He mixes Spanish and French words into the English as he moves from delight to eroticism to fear, sweaty panic and relief:

the mistress of the shop took us into the kitchen and there talked and used us very prettily; and took her [Betty] for my wife, which I owned and her big belly; and there very merry till my thing done, and then took coach and home, in the way tomando su mano and putting it where I used to do; which ella did suffer, but not avec tant de freedom as heretofore, I perceiving plainly she had alguns [some] apprehensions de me, but I did offer natha [nothing] more then what I had often done. But now comes our trouble; I did begin to fear that su marido [her husband] might go to my house to enquire por ella, and there trovando mi moher [finding my wife] at home, would not only think himself, but give my femme occasion to think strange things. This did trouble me mightily; so though ella would not seem to have me trouble myself about it, yet did agree to the stopping the coach at the street's end; and yo allais con ella home and there presently hear by him that he had newly sent su maid to my house to see for her mistress. This doth much perplex me, and I did go presently home (Betty whispering me, behind the tergo [back] do her mari, that if I would say that we did come home by water, ella could make up la cosa well satis [enough]. And there in a sweat did walk in the entry antes my door, thinking what I should say to my femme; and as God would have it, while I was in this case (the worst in reference a my femme that ever I was in in my life), a little woman comes stumbling to the entry-steps in the dark; whom asking whom she was, she enquired for my house; so knowing her voice and telling her su dona [her mistress] is come home, she went away. But Lord, in what a trouble was I when she was gone, to recollect whether this was not the second time of her coming; but at last concluding that she had not been here before, I did bless myself in my good fortune in getting home before her, and do verily believe she had loitered some time by the way, which was my great good fortune; and so I in a-door and there find all well. So, my heart full of joy, I to the office a little and then home.[65]

Pepys wrote up the episode twenty-four hours later, after a busy day, morning at the office, afternoon attendance at a recital of Italian songs and a long talk with Thomas Killigrew about the state of the theatre. During those hours his imagination worked on the material, and the chronicler became the writer, so that his adventure with Betty has a fast-moving plot and dramatic asides: 'now comes our trouble', 'Betty whispering me', 'the worst in reference a my femme that ever I was in'. The foreign phrases are transparent as the narrator's emotions shift from pleasure at being taken for the father of Betty's child, to a complicit thrill at her whispering behind her husband's back, to his moment of terror at the idea of being found out at his own house, to the near-miraculous reprieve when he meets the old woman. As in a comedy, all ends joyfully – at least for the time being. Pepys the man has provided Pepys the writer with his material, and he knows exactly how to handle it.

Elizabeth never found out. A week later Betty told him she did not like 'touching', and he resolved to 'mind my business more', although he still loved her – 'I aime her de todo mi corazon' ['I love her with all my heart']. Betty's baby was born, a daughter, named after Elizabeth, who assisted the midwife and stood as godmother. Both Pepyses attended the christening, although he turned up his nose at the poor company. In the summer the baby died, and the Michells came and sat with the Pepyses in their garden to mourn the child. Betty became pregnant for a second time. Pepys did not get hold of her hand again, but he still yearned after her from time to time, even though he fell in love with another girl. Once he saw her in church and commented on how her looks had deteriorated, but on the last page of the diary he called at the Michells and found her with her mother, her husband being away: 'And here yo did besar ella, but have not opportunity parar hazer mas with her as I would have offered if yo had had it.' What he expressed in his Diary was what many – perhaps most – men feel at some time in their lives, when success is within their grasp and their energies are running high: that they would like to possess every pretty girl in the world, or at least to make love to every girl who catches their eye as she passes by in the street.

But Betty Michell, unpossessed, disappears into the darkness of unrecorded history, with her fading childish beauty, her dressing box, her sullen husband in his spirit shop beside the Thames and her second baby girl, whose fate we shall never know; having freed herself of uncle Pepys and sublimely unaware of the literary honour bestowed on her by him.

As to why he set down his own behaviour in all its shameful detail: no doubt it was partly to prolong the enjoyment, where there was enjoyment, and to give himself the chance to revisit it, with an extra gloss added by the exotic language. But also, and perhaps chiefly, for the reason that he was more interested in observing and recording his own actions than in presenting an immaculate or even favourable image of himself. So we have the spectacle of someone carefully noting down what any one of us would hide, from ourselves if we could and certainly from posterity. Lecher and liar as he knew himself to be, Pepys was a sceptic and a humanist as well; he was not confessing his sins here but setting down the facts of his experience as a man living in a complex environment. Only when you have taken in the least attractive bits of his behaviour in the Diary can you fully appreciate what a triumph of humanism it represents.

He is of course the hero of his narrative, painting himself in the brightest colours and finest details. In the background Elizabeth is a fainter, simpler figure, and voiceless since none of her letters survive. Robert Louis Stevenson, who found Pepys irresistible, called her vulgar, and twentieth-century feminist attempts to give her a voice have been unconvincing. Her failure to get on with any of her companions does not speak in her favour, although Lady Sandwich's affection for her does. She could be generous to her servants, joining in Christmas parties and celebrations below stairs with them; and she would go to help other women in childbirth. The deepest bond in her life may well have been with her brother, Balty; it was reciprocal, and each is shown looking out for the other in the pages of the Diary. She persistently and successfully urged Pepys to help him; decades after her death he still took her wishes to heart. She had a lot to put up with in being married to Pepys, but on balance more to enjoy than not. She did not give up easily when she wanted something, and she held her own in argument. Wives of greatly energetic men can be cowed by them, as Catherine Dickens was. Not so Elizabeth. She never sank into inertia or depression, and she refused the role of victim. By the last page of the Diary the reader has lived through high drama, witnessing a tremendous power struggle between husband and wife, closely matched and fought to a bitter and surprising finish. We shall come to that later.

14. The King

In September 1665, when Lord Sandwich brought in the prize ships he had taken from the Dutch, he was offered a 'handsome supper' by Sir John Mennes at Woolwich, together with Lord Brouncker, Pepys, Evelyn and a few more friends. It was a convivial gathering, and one of the stories told by Sandwich was about Pepys. He described how overjoyed he had been, back in May 1660, at the sight of a letter from the king, then still in Holland. The royal letter had come to them at sea, and Sandwich told the party that Pepys had kissed it, adding that 'whatever he was', Pepys had always loved the king. Sandwich was harking back to his own Cromwellian past, still held against him, and at the same time giving Pepys a testimonial. At this Lord Brouncker announced that 'he could not forbear kissing me before my Lord, professing his finding occasion every day more and more to love me'. They were all drinking freely, and perhaps Pepys was being teased by Lord Brouncker. But Pepys did not take it as teasing, and, when Captain Cocke mentioned the incident later, he thought it might turn out to be 'of good use to me'.[1]

Pepys's position at the Navy Board meant he owed direct duty and loyalty to the king, and the mass of his naval papers that survive in the shape of rolls, minute books, letters and memoranda all bear witness to his zeal in the royal service. His official letters are full of 'the King's service', 'the King's yards', 'the King's security' and 'the King's ships'. From 1665 he was known by name to Charles, who came to appreciate him as a useful officer and an outstanding speaker on naval affairs; and in due course he rose so high in royal favour that he was appointed secretary to the Admiralty in 1673.[2] The king thought well of Pepys. Pepys's real response to the king, in spite of Lord Sandwich's testimony and Lord Brouncker's kiss, was something different.

In 1660 he had gone with the tide of national enthusiasm for the Restoration. Everyone felt Charles's charm then, and Pepys was no exception, the more so since he received rich rewards through Sandwich's role in the king's return. Pepys was genuinely moved by the tale of his suffering as a youth, his poverty, courage and adventures after Worcester, and impressed by his energy – 'very active and stirring' – and easy, open manner.[3] The pageantry of the Restoration pleased him, as did the coronation, with its processions through the streets, its triumphal arches and gorgeous costumes, its ceremonial and feasting. Pepys responded to everything that was picturesque. He was not going to complain that the court was peopled by beautiful women who paraded glittering clothes, feathered hats and jewels, providing a rich source of gossip and enriching his dreams. The king's patronage of theatre, painting and music was unequivocally welcomed, and the Diary is full of the pleasures offered by the revival of church music, the reopening of the theatres and visits to the studios of painters where court beauties were being immortalized.[4]

The soap opera aspect of royal family life also appealed to him. He quivered with pleasure and excitement at being taken into Somerset House to observe the king and his new queen, Catherine, paying a visit to the queen mother, Henrietta Maria, in 1662, 'such a sight as I could never almost have happened to see with so much ease and leisure'. He reported a snatch of royal conversation. The king told the queen mother that the queen was with child. The queen answered 'You lie' – the first English words Pepys heard her speak – and the king teased her, saying he would teach her to say 'Confess and be hanged'. Pretty witty for a king, and Pepys went away very contented at having seen and heard this 'greatest rarity'.[5] He remained a curious spectator at other royal rituals, public dinners and the queen's birthday ball, which he watched from the loft above.[6] And his friend Pearse, surgeon to the duke of York and privy to every love affair, abortion, duel and case of pox at court, took the part of the tabloid press of today and fed him with scandalous tales, rather too many of which Pepys wrote out in the Diary.

None of this meant he set aside his sceptical intelligence. When he first went to court with Sandwich, he noted 'Court attendance infinite tedious'.[7] After seeing the king gravely laying hands on the sick who came to the Banqueting House to be healed by the royal touch, he wrote down his unhesitating opinion that it was a foolish activity.[8] Visiting the Tower with a royal group, he commented on 'the poor discourse and frothy that the King's companions . . . had with him'.[9] The arrival of the new queen prompted Pepys to point out that the people were not overjoyed but rather 'much discontented at the pride and luxury of the court, and running in debt'.[10] It was not long before he was shocked by what he heard of the swearing, drinking and whoring at court, and still more appalled by the extravagance and expectation of unlimited credit that prevailed there. Everyone spent, nobody paid.[11] Pepys set down the story of the king's stationery supplier to demonstrate what this meant to those who served and supplied him. Seven years after taking the throne, Charles went into his council meeting one morning and found no paper on his table. When he complained, he was told that the man who provided it 'was but a poor man, and was out 4 or £500 for it . . . and that he cannot provide it any longer without money, having not received a penny since the King's coming in'.[12] Pepys added, 'Many such Mementos the King doth nowadays meet.' No amount of hardship endured in his youth, no amount of present charm, could justify such treatment of his subjects.

Charles's openly displayed adultery, though good for gossip, also seemed to Pepys 'a poor thing for a Prince to do'. What he objected to was not so much the fact of the adultery as the absence of any decent discretion – a king should at least appear to set an example – and he spoke so freely to Creed on the subject in 1663 that he became anxious afterwards and wondered whether he could count on Creed's silence – a whiff of the fear always lurking in a state with an absolute ruler.[13] Soon after this Lady Sandwich's father, Lord Crew, talked even more indiscreetly to Pepys about the behaviour of the king, his refusal to attend to matters of state, his enslavement to Lady Castlemaine, his readiness to be swayed by favourites and neglect of the chancellor's advice, his hatred of 'the very sight or thought of business'.[14] Pepys wrote down Crew's words and pondered them. No one of his generation could fail to make mental comparisons between Cromwell and Charles, both as private men and as leaders. When Pepys attended a parade of the King's Guards in Hyde Park not long after his talk with Crew, he responded to the magnificence of the show with words that verged on the treasonable: 'methought all these gay men are not the soldiers that must do the King's business, it being such as these that lost the old King all he had and were beat by the most ordinary fellows that could be'.[15]

The word 'ordinary' is used here in praise of the parliamentary army. It crops up more than once in relation to the king with a very different significance: 'seemed a very ordinary man to one that had not known him', 'talking methought but ordinary talk'.[16] Pepys is weighing the monarchy's exalted status against its reality, much as the generation before him had weighed Charles I and found him wanting. Nothing stirred Pepys to any enthusiasm for the old king. In 1669 he prepared a document for the duke of York on the history of the Navy Board in which he showed his view of the politics of Charles I by referring to 'the rupture between his late Majesty and Parliament'. The duke asked Pepys to strike out the words he had written and substitute 'the beginning of the late Rebellion', because any suggestion that the dispute had been between two equally valid forces was not politically acceptable to him.[17]

Pepys's first seriously rude comment on Charles II's capacity was written down shortly after the parade in the park, in July 1663; always eager for first-hand experience, he managed to squeeze himself illicitly into the House of Lords to hear the king's speech. He described Charles sitting on his throne and giving a dismal reading from a piece of paper in his lap from which he scarcely raised his eyes. 'His speech was very plain, nothing at all of spirit in it, nor spoke with any; but rather on the contrary, imperfectly, repeating many times his words, though he read all – which I was sorry to see, it having not been hard for him to have got all the speech without booke.'[18] Pepys's scorn was that of a man who had himself learnt to memorize and speak in public, and he was profoundly shocked that Charles could not be bothered to put on a proper performance in front of the assembled lords. His criticism was repeated the following year, when he again smuggled himself into the House for the king's speech: 'he speaks the worst that ever I heard man in my life – worse then if he read it all, and he had it in writing in his hand'.[19]

Yet Charles was beginning to appreciate Pepys. The Diary shows that on 17 April 1665, at Whitehall, he called him by his name for the first time and engaged in conversation with him about ships; naval architecture was a subject on which Charles was very well informed. Whatever Pepys's opinion of him, this was an important step forward, and he decided that from now on he would prepare himself to be questioned and be ready with good answers. There were more informal exchanges about navy business during the next weeks, and in July

Charles summoned him to Greenwich, where he and the duke of York were spending the day. The plague had driven them from London, and they came by barge from Hampton Court, with only a few attendants and the young duke of Monmouth jumping about at their side, to see the progress of the new palace being built in Greenwich Park and to inspect a ship under construction in the yard. Pepys was there to answer their questions and felt he put on a good performance; he was therefore mortified when he was not invited to dine with the royal party. But in the afternoon he joined them aboard their barge and sailed with them to Woolwich and back, sitting close enough all the way to observe the royal brothers and listen to their conversation. That evening he wrote an account of the impression they made on him: 'God forgive me, though I adore them with all the duty possible, yet the more a man considers and observes them, the less he finds of difference between them and other men, though (blessed be God) they are both princes of great nobleness and spirits.'[20] The 'adore' demonstrates the required reverence towards royalty; it was not a word Pepys brought out often, and here it is used as an emollient, softening his real point, which is that both king and duke strike him as pretty commonplace. Even buttressed with two invocations of God's name and praise for their nobleness and spirits – the duke had indeed just returned from fighting the Dutch at sea – his remark is not that of a devoted courtier.

In Pepys's eyes Charles threw away his advantages by not taking his kingly role seriously enough. Instead of hard work, dignity and glory he settled into a life devoted to amusement and pleasure: women, horse-racing, sports, drinking, theatregoing, sailing. He took little interest in travelling around his kingdom, no doubt thinking he had done enough of that in his youth. He was clever, but even his much mentioned interest in science was not seriously pursued. He was amiable, polite, fickle; rarely showing displeasure directly, quickly bored. He had favourites but, in the words of Bishop Burnet, who knew him well, had 'a very ill opinion both of men and women; and did not think there was either sincerity or chastity in the world out of principle, but that some had either the one or the other out of humour or vanity. He thought that nobody served him out of love: and so he was quits with all the world, and loved others as little as he thought they loved him.'[21]

Pepys's account of the great fire of London is discussed in another chapter. The most striking thing about his approach to the king then was that he unhesitatingly took it on himself to inform him of what was happening and at the same time to give him direct advice – you might say instructions – as to what he should do: 'that unless his Majesty did command houses to be pulled down, nothing could stop the fire'.[22] This must have impressed Charles, especially as it turned out to be the only good advice he got. In the months following the fire, Pepys piled on criticism of his ineffectiveness in the conduct of the war. During the autumn of 1666 and early months of 1667 the Navy Board warned that they could not execute their orders to send out ships without funds, but their pleas produced no results, and ships were laid up one after another.[23] Pepys set down his 'grief that the King doth not look after his business himself, and thereby will be undone'. He recorded the remarks of colleagues on 'The viciousness of the Court. The contempt the King brings himself into thereby.' John Evelyn was struggling to organize care for the sick, the wounded and prisoners, and he too was driven to deplore Charles's inattention to affairs of state. In his end-of-year summary for 1666 Pepys characterized the court as 'sad, vicious, negligent', and the 1667 Diary carried a litany of reported complaints and warnings to the king.[24] In March Pepys made a speech before him, telling him that his failure to fund the navy would lead to disaster. In May Carteret told Pepys that he feared the ruin of the state unless the king would 'mind his business', and in June Evelyn said the reputation of the kingdom was likely to be lost by the king's behaviour and compared Charles unfavourably with Cromwell.[25]

The Medway disaster followed. Pepys was informed that 'the night the Dutch burned our ships, the King did sup with my Lady Castlemayne at the Duchess of Monmouth, and there were all mad in hunting of a poor moth'.[26] His informant, the first engineer of the Tangier breakwater, Hugh Cholmley, pursued the subject of Charles's inadequacy, suggesting that he had 'not brains, or at least care and forecast enough' to rule as the king of France did. Pepys added his own view, 'strange how he and everybody doth nowadays reflect upon Oliver and commend him. [*sic*] so brave things he did and made all the neighbour princes fear him; while here a prince, come in with all the love and prayers and good liking of his people . . . hath lost all so soon, that it is a miracle what way a man could devise to lose so much in so little time'.[27] He thought of going to hear the king's speech in parliament again, but 'upon second thoughts did not think it would be worth the crowd'. He went even further in his disapproval and actually took to avoiding the king, 'whom I have not had any desire to see since the Dutch came upon the coast first to Sheerness, for shame that I should see him, or he me methinks, after such a dishonour'.[28]

Carteret, once so strong in defence of his royal master, now reproached him directly for his behaviour and repeated to Pepys what he had said to Charles of 'the necessity of having at least a show of religion in the government, and sobriety; and that it was that that did set up and keep up Oliver, though he was the greatest rogue in the world'.[29] The point about the show of religion was the same as Pepys's about his adulteries: the King might believe or not, might have mistresses or not, but a ruler must offer a good example. Pepys grew still more withering, writing of the king's conduct in his council chamber: 'All I observed there is the silliness of the King, playing with his dog all the while, or his codpiece, and not minding the business, and what he said was mighty weak'.[30] Another council meeting, at which Pepys presented a paper, provoked him to 'I could easily discern that none of them understood the business; and the King at last ended it with saying lazily, "Why," says he, "after all this discourse, I now come to understand it; and that is, that there can nothing be done in this more then is possible" (which was so silly as I never heard), "and therefore," says he, "I would have these gentlemen to do as much as is possible to hasten the Treasurer's accounts; and that is all." And so we broke up; and I confess I went away ashamed to see how slightly things are advised upon there.'[31] There was more to come about 'a short, silly speech' by the king, his 'short, weak answers', his 'sorry discourse' and his 'idle conversation', as well as the 'maudlin pickle' he got into when drunk.[32]

Coventry, like Carteret, lost all faith in the king's capacity to rule properly in 1667. When Pepys tried out a polite formulation to him, expressing sympathy for Charles's difficulties with his finances and with parliament – that it was 'a sorry thing, to be a poor King and have others to come to correct the faults of his own servants, and that that was it that brought us all into this condition' – Coventry burst out with a passionate expression of disgust at Charles's behaviour. 'He answered that he would never be a poor King, and then the other would mend of itself; "No," says he, "I would eat bread and drink water first, and this day discharge all that idle company about me and walk only with two footmen; and this I have told the King – and this must do it at last." '[33] In another conversation with Pepys, Coventry said frankly that 'serving a prince that minds not his business is most unhappy for them that serve him well'. Coventry was the man Pepys most respected, and he was openly giving him his poor opinion of the king.[34]

Charles did two things to please Pepys during this period: he granted him a small prize ship in October 1667 and praised him for his speech to parliament in 1668; but neither made any difference to Pepys's private opinion of him. He continued to comment on his 'silly discourse', his devotion to pleasure, his 'short and weak' responses and his shifty ways. In March 1669 Pepys had Evelyn to dine, who spoke 'openly to me his thoughts of the times and our approaching ruin, and all by the folly of the King'.[35] In April Pepys heard rumours of an impending agreement with the French that would give the king money that would release him from dependence on parliament, and wrote 'this is a thing that will make the Parliament and Kingdom mad, and will turn to our ruin – for this money the King shall wanton away his time in pleasures and think nothing of the main till it be too late'.[36] No such agreement was entered into openly, but Pepys's information was good, because Charles's secret treaty with Louis XIV, made in 1670, was what he described, and French money became his weapon against parliament for the rest of his reign.

The last part of the Diary tells the story of how Coventry, for years the loyal friend and adviser of the royal brothers, lost favour and was dismissed from all his public appointments through a Byzantine court intrigue. At the end of the Dutch war Coventry advised Charles to rid himself of his ageing chancellor, Clarendon, whom he thought too set in his ways and becoming a liability. Coventry had in mind an honourable retirement for the man who had been chiefly responsible for Charles's return to the throne, but parliament was calling for Clarendon's blood, and Lady Castlemaine hated him because he did not conceal his disdain for her. In any case Charles was tired of being told what to do. He went further than Coventry intended, and, when Clarendon was threatened with impeachment by parliament, the king sent him into exile. It was an act of shameful ingratitude. There was now a cooling between Coventry and the duke of York, whose duchess was Clarendon's daughter; and Coventry left his position as secretary to the duke. He told Pepys it was at his own wish, and he remained a privy councillor and a member of the Treasury Commission.

Coventry could be a little heavy-handed in advising the king, as Pepys tells us, reporting a scene in which Coventry suggested some small economy to the king, who said it was a matter of indifference to him; to which Coventry responded, 'I see your Majesty do not remember the old English proverb, "He that will not stoop for a pin, will never be worth a pound."'[37] This tone, precise and preacherly, was exactly the wrong one to adopt with Charles. He had wittier advisers to turn to, among them his boyhood friend, George Villiers, duke of Buckingham, ambitious, unreliable but fascinating to men and women alike: it was said that every head turned when he walked by. Buckingham decided to tease Coventry, and for that purpose wrote an additional scene for a new comedy about to be played. It was called *The Country Gentlemen* and featured, among other characters, Mistress Finicall Fart, a landlady, and Sir Cautious Trouble-all, a high government official; Buckingham's scene poked fun at Sir Cautious demonstrating the desk at which he worked, a specially made round one with a passage into a central hole in which he could enclose himself and so easily turn round to look at his many papers. It was well known that Coventry had such a desk and was proud of it; he had in fact demonstrated it to Pepys. In Buckingham's scene Sir Cautious became a figure of ridicule, whizzing round on his revolving stool like a clown as he turned busily from one set of papers to the next.[38]

Coventry's sense of humour did not extend to putting up with Buckingham's satire. He was so angry when he heard of the play that he complained to the king, who asked to see the text. He was given a copy from which the key scene had been removed. Coventry then told Killigrew, the theatre manager, that he would have the nose of any actor who appeared in it slit; he also sent a challenge to Buckingham. Buckingham, who had recently engaged in a duel with the husband of his mistress that led to the man's death, was anxious to avoid another bloody encounter and leaked the news of the challenge to the king. At the next council meeting Coventry was arrested and sent to the Tower, on the grounds that a challenge to a fellow member of the Privy Council constituted a felony because it might result in his death – a long-forgotten statute of Henry VII being invoked for this unusual step.

The news of Coventry's arrest 'did strike me to the heart', wrote Pepys. He hurried to the Tower and visited him regularly during his detention. He was not the only one – on one day there were sixty coaches lined up at the Tower. The patent injustice of his punishment was obvious. But the king departed nonchalantly for Newmarket and wrote to his sister, 'I am not sorry that Sir Will. Coventry has given me this good occasion . . . to turne him out of the Councill. I do intend to turn him out of the Tresury. The truth of it is, he has been a troublesome man in both places, and I am well rid of him.'[39] Coventry had to sue for pardon before he released him.

As Pepys was sitting with him in the Tower one day he saw that he was writing a journal, and Coventry told him he kept one regularly. Pepys returned the confidence, 'and he is the only man that I ever told it to I think, that I have kept it most strictly these eight or ten years; and I am sorry almost that I told it him – it being not necessary, nor may be convenient to have it known'.[40] He might well have worried, given what he had written about over the years; but Coventry was not a man to intrude on or betray a friend. He had, however, become a dangerous friend, in Pepys's view; after his release from the Tower, but before he had been allowed into the royal presence again, Pepys became afraid of being seen with him in public; and when Coventry proposed a stroll in St James's Park, as of old, Pepys made an excuse and left. He had to think of his own position, and Coventry was no longer someone to be seen with.[41] Pepys might protest to himself in his own Diary, 'to serve him, I should I think stick at nothing', but he was not prepared to take any risks.

Coventry performed one more service for Pepys, by telling a government adviser that it would cost the king £10,000 to get anyone as good as the present clerk of the acts; and Pepys kept his job.[42] But Coventry's official career was finished, although he continued to sit in parliament.[43] Pepys was now in effect an orphan professionally, with Sandwich in Spain and Coventry out of power. Each had helped him into the sunshine of royal favour, and from each he had learnt about its unreliability; from now on he would have to stand on his own feet and deal directly with the royal brothers. Sadly for us, his indiscretions about the king ceased with the end of his Diary.

15. The Fire

At three on a Sunday morning, 2 September, Pepys was woken by Jane, who had got up early to cook for a dinner party. From her window she noticed a fire to the south-west, in the region of Billingsgate. It was enough to make her rouse Pepys. He put on his dressing gown and went to her window to see for himself, and, having done so, he decided the fire was not near enough to cause concern and returned to his bed. Jane went downstairs to start her cooking on their own kitchen fire. The great fire had started in Pudding Lane, in the house of a baker who had failed to extinguish the fire under his oven, and from his house the flames spread.

Pepys woke again at seven. This time he looked out of his bedroom window and decided the fire seemed smaller and even further away than he had at first thought – no doubt because it was moving west, away from Seething Lane, blown by a powerful east wind. He went into his closet, the small side room where he kept some of his treasures, pictures and books, intending to rearrange it after the efforts of the cleaners the day before, because he was expecting to show off its contents to one of his dinner guests. Then Jane reappeared and said she had heard that 300 houses had been burnt down and that the fire was now close to London Bridge. At this he decided to dress himself and walk over to the Tower, intending to use one of its high windows as an observation point. The lieutenant of the Tower's small son went up with him. What they saw was enough to start him worrying. His first fears, as he set them down, were for two of the girls he was fond of, Betty Michell, who lived close to the bridge, and his former maid Sarah, who now lived on the bridge.

He realized that there was more at stake than the girls, and without returning home he went down to the river, got himself a boat and had himself taken westwards, passing under the bridge. The Michells' house, he saw, was already burnt, and people along the river bank were bringing out their goods and throwing them into lighters or even into the water. He noticed that some of them were so reluctant to leave their houses that they put off going until the last possible moment, and that the pigeons behaved in exactly the same way, hovering about their familiar roosting spots until some had their wings burnt – one of his most vivid and telling observations. Looking about him in this way, and thinking over what he saw, he stayed on the water for an hour. He saw that the fire was being driven by the strong easterly wind, and that the dry summer weather had made everything combustible; and he decided to take action. This is when he instructed his boatman to take him to Whitehall, where Sunday service was in progress in the chapel. He went straight up to the king's closet and started telling people about the fire. It seems that no one had yet heard of it, and word was quickly taken to the king, who sent for him. Pepys told him what he had seen and advised him and the duke to order the blowing up of houses to stop it spreading further, telling them that the destruction of houses in the path of the fire was the only way to stop it.

This was his key role in the great fire of London, as the first to inform the king and the giver of sound advice. The king told Pepys to go to the lord mayor with the command to have houses pulled down and the promise of soldiers to help. Pepys set off back towards the fire in a borrowed coach, joined by Creed. They drove as far as St Paul's, then walked on eastwards along Watling Street, meeting crowds of refugees, among them sick people being carried on their beds, and into Canning (i.e., Cannon) Street, where they found the mayor, Sir Thomas Bludworth, in a state of exhaustion: 'he cried, like a fainting woman, "Lord, what can I do? I am spent! People will not obey me. I have been pulling down houses. But the fire overtakes us faster then we can do it."' He had been up all night and now intended to take a rest. Instead of returning to Whitehall for more instructions, Pepys simply walked on, fascinated by the strangeness of everything, seeing what he could see. This became his other great service, as a reporter to posterity. His description of the fire is one of the most famous set pieces in the Diary, and deservedly so. Most of it was written on loose sheets of paper, quite literally in the heat of the moment, and only copied into the journal proper later, and it follows his experience hour by hour.

People were putting their goods into the churches for safety, and the great merchant family, the Houblons, were removing their goods from their houses; all but one of the brothers lost their homes. By now it was noon, and he remembered he was expecting dinner guests. It did not occur to him to do anything but hurry home to greet them. A newly married couple had been invited, the Woods, Barbara Wood being a friend of Elizabeth and niece of the family in whose house she had lodged at Woolwich during the plague; he was the son of a rich mast-maker. There was also Moone, secretary to Lord Belasyse, whom Pepys knew through his Tangier business; Pepys had been hoping to show him his closet. Now that was put off, and the dinner party was not prolonged; all the same, 'we had an extraordinary good dinner, and as merry as at this time we could be'. Then Pepys walked through the City again with Moone, as far as St Paul's, before taking to the water once more. The king and duke were now on the river in their barge, and Pepys went with them to summon a colonel in the City militia to command him to pull down more houses below the bridge. It was too late. The wind was carrying the fire into the heart of the City.

Elizabeth meanwhile had gone to St James's Park with the Woods and Creed. Pepys went to meet them there and took them on to the river again. The air was hot and full of smoke and 'showers of Firedrops', the wind blowing as hard as ever. When they could endure no more of the heat, they steered for an ale house on Bankside and sat there till it was dark, watching the whole City burning, as far as they could see up the hill, 'a most horrid malicious bloody flame, not like the fine flame of an ordinary fire', and an arch of flame across the bridge. There was a terrible noise too, from the cracking of doomed houses and the sound the flames roaring before the wind. Pepys felt the horror of it – 'It made me weep to see it' – but he was also intent on recording the spectacle.

Back at home, Pepys found Tom Hayter arrived from his burnt-out house, and he invited him to stay at Seething Lane. They soon realized that they too must start salvaging what they could, because although the main movement of the fire was westwards, it was now such a huge conflagration that it was spreading slowly east as well. Hayter helped him drag his iron chests into the cellar and other goods into the garden, and Pepys got his bags of gold and his accounts into the office, ready to carry away. Batten had already most efficiently sent for carts from the country, expected to arrive during the night. Pepys went briefly to bed. He was up again at four on Monday morning, riding in one of Batten's carts in his dressing gown, with a pile of his valuables, to Bethnal Green, where a merchant friend of the Navy Office had agreed to take their possessions into his large house. This is where Pepys took his Diary for safety.

He got a navy lighter to take away more of his goods from Tower Dock. The duke of York called at the office. He had been put in command of the City and was riding about to maintain order. At home there were unfortunate scenes. Elizabeth, angry that Mary Mercer had gone to her mother's without asking permission, scolded her; her mother told Elizabeth that Mary was not a prentice girl to be so treated, and Elizabeth sacked her on the spot, to Pepys's considerable chagrin. But there was nothing he could do. Mercer left, and in the evening they ate leftovers from their Sunday dinner. The two junior maids seem to have gone to see how their own families were doing at this point, because no more is heard of them for the moment; and Will Hewer went to check how his mother was, found her burnt out and moved her to lodgings in Islington. There were now no beds to sleep on, because they had been dismantled and removed, and that night Pepys and Elizabeth lay on a little quilt of Hewer's on the floor of the office.

Pepys was up at break of day again on Tuesday, carrying more of his goods to another lighter. Then he and Penn went into Tower Street, took one look at the advancing fire and hurried home to dig a pit in the garden in which they laid their wine; Pepys famously buried his Parmesan cheese there as well. Both he and Penn now believed Seething Lane was lost, although Pepys proposed sending for work-men from Deptford and Woolwich to pull down more houses to save the Navy Office, and wrote off to Coventry for permission. And although no official answer came, Penn got hold of some men and they began blowing up houses. That night the Pepyses bought a roast shoulder of mutton from a cookshop for a picnic with some of their neighbours; after which he went out, first into the garden, then into Tower Street, to see how close the fire was. As well as threatening them, it was also advancing west along Fleet Street; Cheapside and St Paul's were now in flames. Pepys wrote a letter to his father and found he could not post it because the post office had burnt down.

On Wednesday, 5 September, after another few hours trying to sleep on the office floor, Pepys was woken at two in the morning by Elizabeth. She told him the fire was at the bottom of Seething Lane, by All Hallows Church, and he immediately decided to take her to Woolwich, where she had lived during the plague. They set off by boat with Jane, Will and another bag of gold, leaving Tom Edwards and Hayter. Pepys and Hewer hardly expected to find the Seething Lane buildings standing on their return, but they were. Penn had given good orders to the men blowing up houses, and the wind had dropped at last. All Hallows Church was also saved. Pepys climbed its familiar steeple 'and there saw the saddest sight of desolation that I ever saw'. There were fires burning all around, fuelled by oil and brimstone stored in cellars. He found the sight so frightening that he got down again fast.

Penn gave him some cold meat, and then he walked into the City, risking scorched feet from the hot coals underfoot everywhere, finding the main streets and the Exchange all destroyed, and Moorfields crowded with people camping out. He bought himself a drink and a plain penny loaf (observing that the price had gone up), picked up a piece of glass from a chapel window, melted and buckled by the heat, and saw a cat taken out of a hole in a chimney, still alive, with its fur singed off. Back at Seething Lane, fire watchers were installed in the office. It seemed so long since Sunday that he had almost forgotten the day of the week. There was, he noted, talk of the fire being started by either the Dutch or the French, rumours that grew and persisted. He snatched a little more sleep.

On Thursday morning he saw some looting, nothing serious, just people helping themselves to sugar from bags and mixing it with beer. He took himself to Westminster by boat, intending to buy himself a new shirt, but there were no stalls set up in Westminster Hall, which was being used as a deposit for the goods of the homeless. There was no one about in Whitehall either. He managed to get a shave, and went home again, to find his neighbour Sir Richard Ford giving an impromptu dinner of fried mutton served on earthenware platters. After this Pepys went off to Deptford to supervise his goods, which were being delivered at Carteret's house there, and returned to more male camaraderie. The fire was now burning itself out. He tried to sleep in the office again, but was disturbed by the labourers, who talked and walked about all night.

In the morning he made a melancholy survey of the landmarks of his life that had disappeared. St Paul's was gone, and his school with it. Ludgate and a good part of Fleet Street were destroyed, with St Bride's, the church in which he had been christened and had worshipped as a child, and 'my father's house' in Salisbury Court – also, although he did not say so, his cousin Jane's house in which he had been operated on for the stone. These were his immediate and most personal losses; around them more than 400 acres and 400 streets were reduced to smoking ruins. The medieval City no longer existed. He walked on to Creed's lodgings to borrow a shirt and to wash, then called on Coventry at St James's. He found him with a curtainless bed and all his goods removed; everyone at court had done as much. Coventry told him that he too had heard talk of the French being suspected of having had a hand in the fire.

Pepys ordered the cleaning of his house – the junior maids must have been back by now – and visited Elizabeth at Woolwich. Then he spent the evening with his neighbours, discussing house prices and rebuilding plans, and Penn good-naturedly offered him a curtainless bed in his house. After four nights on the floor he lay down comfortably in his drawers, worrying about the possibility of more outbreaks of fire as long as he was awake and dreaming of fire when he slept. The next day he got back to some work with Coventry – the country was in the middle of a war – and saw Albemarle, summoned back to London from his ship by the king to act as a reassuring and authoritative presence.

Pepys's brother John turned up from Huntingdon to see how things were. Pepys was touched but didn't know what to do with him. He took him to Bethnal Green when he went to collect his Diary and shared his bed at Penn's with him that night; but he did not really want him around, and the next day he sent him to dine with Elizabeth at Woolwich and then back to the country, with forty shillings 'for his pocket'. This was Sunday again, a week after the outbreak of the fire. Pepys went to church twice and wrote up his Diary in the office; he noted that it was raining at last – bad for John's journey but 'good for the Fyre'. Tom read him to sleep at Penn's.

On Monday he cleared out the cellar, belatedly thinking the old lumber he kept in it might constitute a fire risk. Everything was returning slowly to its usual order. Jane arrived back, and he set off

for Deptford, wanting to see Mrs Bagwell. Failing in that, he went on
to Woolwich, where Elizabeth was annoyingly 'out of humour and
indifferent'. But he stayed overnight with her, and the next day set to
office work again with his colleagues, at Brouncker's house. The
pattern of work resumed as his own house was slowly restored to
normal. Sexual forays were also resumed: on 12 September he had a
morning encounter with Betty Martin and an afternoon in bed with
Mrs Bagwell, suffering from remorse and disgust afterwards. The next
night Elizabeth was home, and they slept on the floor, with Balty and
his wife Esther in another room. Only on the 15th were the beds
reinstalled with their hangings. Sleeping in his own bed again, Pepys
had terrifying dreams of fire and houses falling down. These dreams
continued for many months; the following February he observed that
he could not 'sleep a-night without great terrors of fire; and this very
night could not sleep till almost 2 in the morning through thoughts
of fire'.[1] The huge area of ruins continued to smoulder and smoke for
months, and was believed to harbour robbers; Pepys unsheathed his
sword as he was driven through the City in a coach at night.

The fire was a terrifying ordeal for all involved, and it left a legacy
of fear; but it was very different from the Blitz of 1941, to which it is
sometimes compared. There were the same flames, falling buildings
and noise, but fewer than ten people were known to have died – if
there were more, their deaths were unnoticed and unrecorded – and
the worst lasted for only a few days. Naturally it left a long train of
difficulties and huge financial losses. The greatest sufferers were the
booksellers, who kept their shops and also lived around St Paul's.
Pepys laments their fate in the Diary. His own bookseller Kirton lost
his dwelling, his shop and many thousands of pounds' worth of books,
and was ruined beyond recovery. When he died a year later, Pepys
believed it was 'of grief for his losses by the fire'.[2] Some of his fellows
had hoped to save stock by putting books into churches or their hall,
the Stationers', only to see hall and churches burnt with all the
books inside feeding the blaze. Pepys's one-time schoolmaster, Samuel
Cromleholme, who had helped to nurture his love of books, also lost
his private library, said to have been the best in London.[3] Pepys's
losses from moving his goods were negligible, just two small pictures
of ships and the sea, one gold frame and some chipping to another gilt
frame; the few books he thought he had lost turned up again. Once

again Fortune had favoured him. The Pearses profited from the fire by letting out Mrs Pearse's closet with a little windowless chamber and a garret for an inflated amount, £50 down and £30 a year, to a dispossessed silk merchant. Pepys and Elizabeth talked of taking in Hayter and Hewer permanently, but they did not pursue the idea, and Hayter had to look for a new place, his wife still away in the country at the end of October. Pepys's cousin Jane Turner came down from Yorkshire in November to survey the empty space where her house in Salisbury Court had stood. Old Mr Pepys also came to London in October to see the ruins, which had become a tourist attraction.

Plans to set up a modern city on the site of the ancient streets were immediately considered. Three different proposals were prepared at great speed by three members of the Royal Society: John Evelyn, Robert Hooke and Christopher Wren. All had visions of broad and beautiful avenues replacing the old narrow muddled streets. The House of Commons discussed the matter before the end of the month, but any major changes to the street pattern were given up because every householder understandably wanted to rebuild on his own site. A few streets were widened, the riverside was opened up, and an attempt was made to improve the Fleet River into a something like a canal, with wharves. It was decreed that buildings had to be brick-built and flat-fronted; and in due course Wren's churches arose on the sites of the many lost medieval ones. The new St Bride's was built during the 1670s, although its enchanting steeple, the tallest of Wren's, did not appear until the beginning of the next century. St Olave's still stood, modest and reassuringly the same, but the backcloth and scenery against which Pepys had played out his life so far was gone for good. Hardly surprising that he had nightmares; and fire continued to cause havoc in his life, because seven years later it broke out in Seething Lane itself and destroyed another part of his life.

The political aftermath of the fire was almost as alarming as the fire itself. There were so many rumours of arson that parliament could not ignore them, and in late September Catholics were told to leave the City unless they had special permission to remain. Pepys, no bigot, was perfectly happy to stand godfather to the son of his Catholic picture varnisher, Lovett, in October. He had just acquired a fine picture of the crucifixion, or possibly a crucifix, from him. A Capuchin, one of the queen mother's priests, conducted the ceremony; he was wearing lay clothes, Pepys observed, considerably smarter than his own outfit.

His easy tolerance was not the norm. In October there was alarm when a collection of daggers was found in the ruins of a house reputedly owned by papists, and in November there was talk of a Catholic plot to poison the king; and when Pepys visited the Crews on 5 November, Sir Thomas told him the fire had been plotted and bragged about by papists.[4] In January 1667 a book appeared with what it claimed to be the evidence given to the House of Commons about the fire, saying it was started by French Catholics, Jesuits and the duke of York himself; Pepys was shown a copy but had nothing to say about it.[5] In May 1668, when a meteor was seen in the sky, his clerks Hayter and Gibson reported that people feared it was a sign that the rest of the City would be burnt, and the papists would cut all their throats.[6] The charge that they had been responsible for the fire came up again at the time of the Popish Plot in 1678, and in January 1681 parliament used it as part of the argument for the Exclusion Bill, intended to prevent the duke of York from succeeding to the throne. In the same year an inscription was added to the monument commemorating the fire, stating that it was caused by 'the treachery and malice of the popish faction . . . to introduce popery and slavery'.[7] By then religious tolerance like Pepys's had become dangerous in itself.

16. Three Janes

There are many Janes in the Diary, and three of them are distinctive characters, brought to life in Pepys's scattered comments. Of these the slightest is Jane Welsh – worth noticing for her cussedness and his curious obsession with her. She caught his eye at Jervas's, his barber and wig-maker, another establishment in New Palace Yard; and he first mentions her in July 1664 as a 'pretty innocent girl' who has been in service there for some time. Elizabeth was in the country, and he invited Jane to an ale house, 'sported' with her briefly and felt encouraged to pursue her. For six months after this her name comes up regularly. First he hoped Jervas would send her to Seething Lane to deliver his newly cleaned wig but was disappointed. Further attempts to get her to talk to him in the shop got nowhere. When he managed to suggest a meeting outside the shop, she told him that her master and mistress did not allow her out without them, adding that they were trying to find her a husband. Pepys decided he would like to find her one himself, because she was such a good-natured, attractive girl; he saw no inconsistency between this and chasing her himself. At last she agreed to meet him, on a Sunday when the Jervases were due to be away; the appointed place was outside Westminster Abbey, but when the day came she failed to turn up. He kicked his heels from three in the afternoon to six o'clock, and the next Sunday he waited again, and again she did not come. When he called at the shop she was cool, and for the rest of the year she remained unresponsive.[1] The effect of this marked indifference to his attentions was that by 9 December, when she again refused to have a drink with him at the Trumpet in King Street, he had developed 'grand envie envers elle [desire for her], avec vrai amour et passion'.

So far this was a straightforward Pepys pursuit. But in the new year Mr and Mrs Jervas told him they were worried about Jane because she now told them she had promised herself to a penniless fiddler and would not consider any other husband; and when Pepys volunteered to give her some good advice they were grateful. Several more of his attempts to meet her failed. Then, out of the blue, she suddenly turned up at his office one morning of her own accord, wanting to talk to him and announcing she had left her job with the Jervases for her violin-playing sweetheart. Without pausing to ask himself why she had come to tell him this, Pepys took her to a house in the fields on the south bank and gave her good advice just as he had promised the Jervases he would: she should return to them and to her job, and forget the fiddler. At the same time the opportunity for seduction was too good to miss. She let him launch himself on her, enjoyably enough for him, but she stopped him when he tried to go further than she thought right and 'would not laisser me faire l'autre thing, though I did what I pouvais to have got her à me laisser'. Letting him go as far as she did was perhaps the price she had decided to pay for his attention, because she needed someone to talk to; and perhaps she liked him well enough for his patient pursuit over many months. But chiefly she wanted him to know that she was going to marry the fiddler, and why. She said it was because she 'believed it was her fortune to have this man, though she did believe it would be to her ruin'.[2]

This is what fixes Jane Welsh in the mind: her oddity, her stubborn insistence on doing something she believed to be against her own interests but for which she was destined; and her need to explain this to someone who would listen and just possibly understand. Pepys, even in the grip of his carnal desires, had the grace to grasp that she wanted to give an account of her sense of her own fate; and foolish, even self-destructive as he thought her, he took the trouble to write down her explanation.

His portrait of Jane Welsh goes little further. Weeks later the Jervases told Pepys that Jane was 'undone', just as she had predicted she would be. She had been sleeping with her fiddler, they said, and now found out that he had a wife and child; and she was therefore leaving London for Ireland – why is not explained, but she may have had family there.[3] This was almost but not quite the last word on her. Leaving when she did she had the good luck to miss the plague, and a year later, in April 1666, she was back in London safe and sound. Pepys caught sight of her near Westminster jetty and carried her off for a drink across the river again, this time not to the fields but to Lambeth. Under questioning she confessed that her lover had been

married, and claimed she had not slept with him; but Pepys's interest
had waned and he was not curious enough to ask her anything more
about her current circumstances. 'There I left her, sin hazer alguna
cosa con ella,' was all he had to say. No longer in pursuit of her, he
went on to treat some other young women to prawns and lobsters in
Fish Street and finished the evening happily feeling Mary Mercer's
breasts at home.[4] Jane Welsh, who for a few months had danced in
his imagination, unpredictable and exasperating, disappeared back
into an unchronicled life. From what he has told us she had a good
chance of holding her own in the rough and tumble of London: she
was good-looking, she was tough, and her fate was better than she
had expected, since she had survived not only her false fiddler but also
the plague.

Jane Turner – 'Madam Turner' as Pepys sometimes called her – is a
much more substantial case. She comes out of the Diary as the strongest
character among the Pepys clan after Sam himself. They had known
one another from his infancy and her childhood, because her father
John Pepys was third cousin to his father and owned a large house in
Salisbury Court; it may indeed have been part of the reason why his
father set up his tailoring business there in the first place. These were
the affluent cousins who took Pepys as a boy to Ashtead and Durdans,
and Jane was the youngest of their three children, ten years or so older
than Sam and plainly fond of him and interested in his progress long
before he became a successful man. She was always well supplied with
money. She married her lawyer husband John Turner, a York-
shireman, around 1650: twenty years older than her, he was educated
at Cambridge, at the Middle Temple in 1634, kept his head down
during the civil war and became recorder of York in 1662. He wished
to live in his native Yorkshire but she preferred London; and, although
she bore him four children, she was able to defy his wishes over
considerable periods of time because she had inherited her father's
house in Salisbury Court. The ownership of this house was the crucial
factor in her independence. When Turner bought an estate in the
north, she preferred to be parted from him and even from some of
her children; for instance in 1662 the Diary tells us that her two sons
('very plain boys') had spent the last three years in Yorkshire in the
care of their father.[5] He appears in Pepys's pages only when he is

consulted for a legal opinion and is described as 'a worthy, sober, serious man' – rather too sober, it appears, for Mrs Turner.[6]

Careless as she seems to have been of her sons, to her cousin Sam she showed affection and generosity. She was the one who volunteered to look after him when he had the operation for the stone, a kindness that must have totally disrupted her household for two months. Six years later, when his brother Tom was dying, she again showed concern beyond the call of duty, sending notes to Sam urging him to visit Tom, sitting with him and dealing with doctors, giving a bed to the Pepyses on the night of his death and taking part in the funeral.[7] Like Pepys, she enjoyed being busy and in charge of arrangements. He expressed his gratitude for her care during his operation by planning the annual 'stone feast' at which she was always to be the guest of honour. Like many such plans, this one lapsed: in 1660 he was away, and after 1666 there were other reasons – plague, pressure of work, his mother's imminent death, Jane's absence – to prevent it. There were, however, other parties and outings the cousins enjoyed together; and she was sometimes flirtatious. They went to Greenwich and Hyde parks, they indulged in a play-reading, and in 1669 he gave a great Twelfth Night dinner for her, after which she chose him as her Valentine.[8] One day when he called as she was dressing by the fire she showed him her legs, of which she was proud. He duly admired them, without being stirred or tempted by the sight: she was too safely an elder sister figure. Still, when he came to choose her Valentine gift he bought her, as well as gloves and garters, some fashionable green silk stockings in delicate allusion to those fine legs.[9]

She assembled her own London household around her at Salisbury Court, which included her widowed sister and cousin Joyce Norton as well as her team of servants; and there were usually other women friends in attendance.[10] The next formidable member of the family was her daughter Theophila, known as 'The' and, unlike her brothers, always kept with her.[11] 'The' makes her first appearance in the Diary on 1 January 1660, supping with Pepys's father; she was a precocious, indulged and confident child and something of a brat. At nine she was ordering her own harpsichord and refusing to give Pepys a lesson on it when he asked her (although he could play several string and wind instruments, he never mastered a keyboard). When Elizabeth sent her a gift of doves, 'The' distinguished herself by writing her a rude letter, complaining that they had come in an inadequate cage; she grumbled about not having a good place for the coronation; and she forced herself on Pepys as his Valentine.[12] She did offer to play her harpsichord to him to console him after the death of his brother Tom, after which he wrote that 'the Musique did not please me neither'.[13] Her mother trusted her with commissions, and at the age of ten she was sent to ask Pepys to find their serving man John a place at sea; in her teens she was capable of escorting her two brothers and little sister Betty from Yorkshire to London and installing them in their schools in Putney. Mother and daughter made a remarkably strong-minded pair.

Jane was also close to another Pepys cousin, Roger, the Cambridge MP, and interested herself in his children and his marriages. You can see in the course of the Diary how she and Roger appreciated Sam's steady social rise as he made money and acquired power and influence – he was becoming one of them. And he enjoyed demonstrating that he was no longer among the poor Pepyses. In 1663 he was able to send her a present of wine and venison; when her brother died he was helpful about the funeral arrangements; and by 1669 he could lend her his own carriage horses. He showed off his grand new friends to her, taking her to Povey's house to see his perspective paintings and 'volary' (birdcage).[14] The benefits went both ways, her wealth and connections helpful to him; he wrote after one outing with her, 'I think it is not amisse to preserve, though it cost me a little, such a friend as Mrs Turner'.[15] He also knew he could count on her affection. When he had failed to call on her for six months while establishing himself at Seething Lane, he remarked that she was a good woman and 'could not be angry with me'; yet he was genuinely fond of her and worried about her when she was ill.[16]

When, however, her husband came to town to organize some Middle Temple dinners and expected Pepys to help with the food through his navy victualling office, he let him down and failed even to attend any of the dinners. She accused him of growing proud.[17] She scolded him again in November 1666 when, after a long exile to Yorkshire during the period of the plague and the fire, she came south to look at the spot where her house had stood, now nothing but ashes. 'She was mighty angry with me, that in all this time I never writ to her; which I do think and take to myself as a fault, and which I have promised to mend,' wrote Pepys. The loss of her house and all its contents was a disaster that meant she could no longer insist on living in London. Pepys soothed her with a 'noble and costly dinner' and listened to her complaints about the dullness of Yorkshire: 'She is quite weary of the country, but cannot get her husband to let her live here any more, which troubles her mightily . . . We sat long; and after much talk of the plenty of her country in Fish, but in nothing also that is pleasing, we broke up with great kindness.'[18] A few days later she told him she was forced to leave London again: 'She is returning into the North to her children, where, I perceive, her husband hath clearly got the mastery of her, and she is likely to spend her days there, which for her sake I am a little sorry for, though for his it is but fit she should live where he hath a mind.'[19] A husband's right to control his wife was not something Pepys would argue against. In fact within months 'The' brought the younger children to school in London, and in 1668 Madam Turner herself was back in high spirits; Betty, her second daughter, promised to be a beauty, and they were all as merry as ever in lodgings. There were theatre parties, dinners, suppers, music and visits to Mulberry Gardens. One night they danced until two at Seething Lane and slept there afterwards, all fifteen of the party, which included Roger Pepys and his wife and daughters. To accommodate them all Pepys and Elizabeth moved into the maids' bedroom, the maids slept in the coachman's bed and the coachman with the boy in his settle-bed. This high point of cousinly hospitality and pleasure comes almost at the end of the Diary, which gives a last glimpse of 'my cousin Turner and The and Joyce in their riding clothes' preparing to travel north again.

They must have been in London again in subsequent years. 'The' married a Devon baronet and became Lady Harris in 1673; but there are no further signs of them among Pepys's papers, and, if he kept his promise to write to Jane, none of their correspondence has survived. A pity, because she would be worth knowing through her own words as well as his. She was a fine example of a woman whose natural liveliness and independence were given rein by her father's legacy of a house. To her husband it may have been a nuisance, but to her it was an act of wisdom. John Pepys of Ashtead knew that economics determine social arrangements, and gave his daughter the means to live her life as she pleased.[20]

★

One of 'The' Turner's last appearances in the Diary was as bridesmaid to the Pepyses' maid, Jane Birch, when she married Pepys's clerk Tom Edwards. Jane Birch is the most important of the Janes and the only one whose story can be taken from before the start of the Diary to the end of Pepys's life. Within the Diary she appears on the first page already well established at Axe Yard at fifteen; at the end as a married woman and set to remain a family friend; and in the years between he tells us a great deal about her character and still more of what she had to put up with. Pepys once called her 'harmless', a word he also applied to Lady Sandwich, no doubt contrasting in his mind the natures of these two women with the more dangerous and unpredictable temperaments of his wife and his sister.[21] Will Hewer, another peaceable character, also had a high opinion of Jane. During one of her absences he was overheard telling the other servants how good she was and how the Pepyses would never have a better maid; and in later years he employed her himself.[22] Harmless as she may have been, she also kept on good terms with Pepys because, like Will, she learnt to resist his bullying.

Much of her story is given in asides, and sometimes she is not even named, just indicated as the girl, or the wench, and you have to work out if this is Jane, and the right Jane; all the same she emerges as one of the most interesting of the women who engaged his attention in the Diary. From our point of view she was also a representative of a vast and little documented group. Being a household servant was the commonest occupation by far for girls and women in the seventeenth century; there were very few other ways of earning anything – which is why Pepys took his own sister as a servant. But while every household had its maids, little information has come down to us about the detail of their lives. Through Pepys's account of Jane and her fellow maids a good deal can be gleaned. In his household, for instance, the maids slept sometimes in garrets, sometimes in cold weather by the kitchen fire and sometimes in other rooms, including his and Elizabeth's bedroom, which one girl found disconcerting, though Jane did not. They were recruited through friends and paid between £2 and £4 a year in addition to their board and lodging; and they appear to have had no formal holidays. They might be given cast-off clothes and taken on outings; and living close to their employers as they did, they generally knew everything that was going on in the family. The system was hierarchical and intimate at the same time, and the gap between maid and employer was an elastic one, which meant Jane was part slavey and part hairdresser, masseuse, secretary, even daughter. Not only might she sleep in her employers' bedroom, she also sometimes shared a bed with her mistress or sat beside the bed darning while her master was settling to sleep.

Perhaps because she was his first servant, Pepys did not take her for granted. From the start he was interested enough in her to note down some of the things he saw her doing, such as knitting stockings, possibly for herself, possibly for him. And he noticed too when she got up at two in the morning to start on the washing. He liked her well enough to take her along to Sunday dinner at his parents' house, and he trusted her with his books: she was given the job of carrying the ones he had left in his turret room in Whitehall Palace to his house in Axe Yard. Just before they moved to Seething Lane, she fell ill – the only time we hear of such a thing – and spent two days in bed with a bad leg. 'We cannot tell what to do for want of her,' he wrote despondently, but he worked it out and took on a second servant to help, a boy. Pepys and Elizabeth made the move to their new house by coach, overtaking the carts carrying their goods, and presumably Jane and the boy, in the Strand. On arrival she at once started washing the house while Elizabeth went to bed. Pepys writes of sporting with her and the boy in the kitchen while they combed his hair, his bedtime ritual: a little horseplay and some jokes. A few weeks later, when Jane was sleeping in their bedroom with them, the new boy was in trouble for stealing, and she fancied she heard a noise downstairs. Elizabeth was frightened that the boy was planning mischief – Pepys says she shook with fear – and it was intrepid Jane who went down to investigate, lit a candle, locked the door fast and reassured her employers. The boy was sacked, and Jane saw her chance and brought her younger brother Wayneman into the household in his place. She set about teaching him his duties: putting Pepys to bed, folding his clothes, presumably, as well as the hair-combing and making sure the chamber pot was in place.

December 1660 was a month of intimacies: on the 1st Pepys, finding the house untidy, let his anger rip and beat her with a broom until she cried 'extremely'. This upset him – can he have supposed she would take it as another bit of sporting? – and he felt obliged to appease her (his word) before he went out. Not long afterwards he describes the delightfully peaceful scene in which, while Elizabeth was away with friends, he lay in bed reading himself to sleep while Jane sat companionably beside him darning his breeches. Two days before Christmas she and Elizabeth struggled together to get a great turkey on to the spit; and after Christmas Pepys was ill in the night ('I think with eating and drinking too much'), called up Jane to bring a basin and recovered fast enough to be charmed by the innocent way she ran up and down in her night smock, presumably showing a good deal of arm and leg.[23]

Jane was not timid and she knew how to stand up for herself. When Pepys's or Elizabeth's treatment became too much for her, she either gave in her notice or refused to submit to their scoldings and drove them to dismiss her; then she insisted on taking the dismissal they clearly hoped to renegotiate. She wept when she left, but she went. Pepys too was reduced to the brink of tears on these occasions. She left for the first time after she had served the Pepyses for three years, two in Axe Yard, one at Seething Lane. This was in 1661, and she gave as her reason that her mother needed her in the country. Wayneman was now working for the Pepyses and he would remain in London. We are not told what part of the country they came from, but it must have been reasonably close, given that she and her two brothers all came to work in London, and her toings and froings. One possibility is that she was a Buckinghamshire girl recommended to Pepys by his fatherly friend at the Exchequer, Robert Bowyer, who had a house in Buckinghamshire where Elizabeth stayed with Jane in 1660.

When Jane decided to take herself home to her mother in 1661, Pepys said she had grown lazy, spoilt by having Pall to share the work with her, but he was still upset at losing her. It was especially annoying because he had just decided to get rid of Pall and send her to live in the country with their parents. Pall hated the idea of leaving London but was made to go; and, fortunately for the Pepyses, Jane enjoyed country life with her mother no more than Pall did with hers, and in the spring of 1662 she was back working for them again. In her absence Wayneman had got into trouble and been beaten for having gunpowder for Guy Fawkes' night in his pocket. When Pepys took him down to the cellar to beat him again shortly after Jane's return, she interceded for him, and Pepys called off the punishment. Later he felt obliged to explain to her that he was doing it for the boy's good.[24] Jane was tactful enough to accept this, but she was not happy about it. Wayneman got deeper into the Pepyses' bad books for misbehaving at Brampton when he was there with Elizabeth in August and September. She accused him of behaviour 'not fit to name', and old Mr Pepys complained too, saying he would not have him in the house again, so he must have done something pretty bad.[25] This was the summer when Ferrar and Lord Sandwich paid attention to Elizabeth, which may have preoccupied her so much that she allowed Wayneman to run wild. It was a complicated season for everyone.

Jane remained at Seething Lane with Pepys, helping to deal with the chaos caused by his building works there. The roof had to come off before the new storey could be added, and heavy rain made the whole process into a nightmare; fortunately the Penns were away for several weeks, and Pepys and Jane were able to move into their house while the worst part of work was carried out. Pepys speaks of her 'lying among my goods' at the Penns at the end of August. The Diary also says he is hoping for 'a bout' with her but is held back by his fears that she would prove honest and tell Elizabeth if he suggested such a thing. Then he wrote, 'I can hardly keep myself from having a mind to my wench, but I hope I shall not fall to such a shame to myself.'[26] Nothing happened, or at least nothing more appears from the text, which suggests that Pepys controlled himself; but Jane was no fool, and at eighteen she is likely to have been aware of her employer's interest.

Some time after Penn's return in September he told Pepys that Jane had attacked one of the carpenters working on the building site, cutting off his long moustache, a Delilah-like gesture that was probably self-defence. Girls in her situation needed to work out their strategies. The carpenter said his wife, when she saw the damage, assumed he had been 'among some of his wenches'.[27] After this there was another episode in which Lady Batten complained that Jane had insolently mimicked her way of calling her maid. Pepys felt he must 'school' her; but Jane knew he disliked Lady Batten and answered him 'so humbly and drolly about it, that though I seemed angry, I was much pleased with her'.[28] Then her combative spirit went too far even for him. At Christmas he scolded her for speaking saucily to Elizabeth and said she was growing proud and negligent. When he beat Wayneman again, for lying, in January 1663, she showed her anger, and at this Pepys told her to leave. She packed up her things to go. He 'could hardly forbear weeping', and she did cry, 'saying it was not her fault that she went away. And indeed, it is hard to say what it is but only her not desiring to stay, that she doth now go.'²⁹ She had effectively turned the tables on him.

With his sister gone, Wayneman grew wilder. He wanted to leave too, although his brother William urged him not to; but, when the boy saw Pepys preparing to beat him for not writing out his lesson in his copy-book, he ran away. No one knew where he had gone until Pepys saw him playing on Tower Hill several days later; he must have been living in the streets, and in his best suit too. Pepys sent the Seething Lane porter to fetch him, made him change into his old suit and sacked him on the spot. Jane and William Birch came round together to beg Pepys either to take him back or to send him to sea as a ship's boy. Pepys did neither. He took the whole episode seriously and was upset enough to describe his exchange with Jane in some detail: 'though I could yet be glad to do anything for her sake to the boy; but receive him again I will not nor give him anything. She would have me send him to sea; which if I could I would do, but there is no ships going out. The poor girl cried all the time she was with me and could not go from me, staying about two hours with me till 10 or 11 o'clock at night, expecting that she might obtain something of me; but receive him I will not. So the poor girl was fain to go away, crying and saying little.'³⁰ Pepys's language becomes almost biblical in this emotional passage with its short words, its repetitions ('the poor girl') and emphatic inversion ('receive him I will not'), also repeated; and its use of 'fain' in the sense of accepting the lesser of two evils – in this case, to depart unsatisfied rather than remaining to no purpose. He is trying to convince himself, and underneath the fine language he has doubts about what he is doing, punishing Jane, who is blameless and whom he loves, as well as Wayneman, who has disappointed him. Wayneman's next employer found him uncontrollable too and prepared to ship him off to Barbados as an indentured servant. Pepys was again applied to and asked to get a release for him, but he refused, 'out of love to the boy; for I doubt to keep him here were to bring him to the gallows'.³¹ He had decided Wayneman was past any help or discipline he could give him, and the boy disappeared into the harsh life of the plantations, only a small step up from slavery. After this Jane kept away from Seething Lane for more than two years.

It was Elizabeth who then sought her out in the spring of 1666, hoping to persuade her to return. Pepys almost babbled with delight in the Diary when she succeeded in weaning her away from her current employer. 'This day my poor Jane, my little old Jane, came to us again, to my wife's and my great content.'[32] By now he had known her for almost seven years. He had quite forgotten the pride, cheek and ingratitude he had accused her of, and become certain that she had 'all the marks and qualities of a good and loving and honest servant'. They decided to promote her to cook, which meant her wages would have gone up to about £4 a year. She had reached the age of twenty-one and done very well, rising from maid-of-all-work to this superior position in the household; there were now three other maids kept, as well as Tom Edwards from the Chapel Royal choir, who made music with Pepys, did some work as a clerk and lent a hand generally about the place. There were besides frequent visits from her old friend Will Hewer; and she was in high enough favour to be taken for outings on the river in a Navy Office boat on a Sunday afternoon, with Mrs Pepys and her waiting-woman Mary Mercer, and to walk on the lawns of Barn Elms on the Surrey bank. Some distinctions of rank were kept: for instance, she was never taken to the theatre by Pepys, although Elizabeth took her once, 'to show her the play', a new comedy called *All Mistaken; or, The Mad Couple*.[33]

It was Jane who, working late at night preparing a dinner party for the next day, roused Pepys at three in the morning on 2 September 1666 to tell him she saw a great fire in the City. She kept an eye on it while she continued with her cooking. And although she agreed to go to Woolwich with Elizabeth as the City blazed, she also, with characteristic enterprise, brought herself back of her own accord before Pepys fetched her mistress, and worked hard and late with him putting his books back on his shelves. She and Tom Edwards also helped him lug his iron chests out of the cellar and back into his closet in October.[34] Tom was a year younger than Jane and they became friends, living in the household together and sharing chores. Jane had no luck with her brothers – Wayneman was lost to her and in 1667 William died young, leaving a wife and two children – and she needed comfort. Pepys sympathized with her sorrow and gave her twenty shillings and wine for her brother's burial; but it was Tom who filled the emptiness left by their loss. At some point in 1667 the two of them agreed that they would marry when they could afford to. That summer Elizabeth gave Jane one of her lace neckerchieves, and Pepys thought she looked 'a very graceful servant' wearing it when he met them beside the Thames near Rotherhithe one afternoon; it was more formal praise than usual.[35] At this point he knew nothing of her engagement to Tom; they told Elizabeth first, and were so discreet in their behaviour that Pepys was unaware of it until she passed on the news in February 1668. Then he called Tom a rogue, because the story was that he had first wooed Jane, then slighted her, saying he was worried about displeasing Pepys. Tom understood how important it was to Pepys to be the dominant male in the household, and that his own position was a lowly one. All the same, Pepys wrote, 'I think the business will go on; which, for my love to her because she is in love with him, I am pleased with.' He took the view that Jane might have done better but decided he would give her £50, 'and do them all the good I can in my way'.[36]

The engagement did not proceed smoothly. In the summer Jane threw a hysterical fit, brought on by jealousy, it seemed. She had to be held down by five men for a good half hour. After this impressive display both Pepyses and Will Hewer questioned the lovers, and Pepys concluded that Tom had gone cold on the marriage project. He thought he would have to get rid of them both from his household; but his mind was on 'other greater things', and the whole matter was allowed to lapse.[37] Or at least lapse in one way. A few weeks later, as he was dressing, Pepys 'did begin para tocar the breasts of my maid Jane, which ella did give way to more then usual heretofore, so as I have a design to try more what I can bring it to'.[38] The way he puts this makes it clear that he has done as much before, and on a number of occasions, behaviour too unremarkable, it now appears, to be regularly mentioned in the Diary. Having a go at the household maids was, it seems, a standard activity; Pepys mentions trying it with Susan, the 'little girl', among others, and Tom Pepys, we remember, got his maid with child.[39] The scientist and architect Robert Hooke, secretary to the Royal Society and well known to Pepys, kept a diary in the 1670s, much briefer but in some respects as frank as Pepys's, which reveals that he regarded the young female inmates of his house as his

19, 20. Elizabeth and Samuel Pepys were painted by John Hayls in 1666; she was twenty-five, he thirty-three. Pepys complained of almost breaking his neck 'looking over my shoulder to make the posture' for his portrait. He had Elizabeth's hand and his music repainted, but the final results delighted him, and both pictures were hung in his house at the Navy Office in Seething Lane.

The portraits remained in the possession of Pepys's nephew's family until Elizabeth's was cut into strips some time around 1830 by a Scotch nurse shocked at the immodesty of the dress. Fortunately it had been engraved for the first edition of the Diary.

21. The first page of Pepys's Diary as he wrote it, showing the mixture of shorthand and longhand and the beautifully clear shaping and spacing. He put '1659/60' because the new year did not start until Lady Day, 25 March, according to the calendar then in use.

22. Will Hewer, nephew of a high commonwealth official dismissed in 1660, came to work for Pepys as a boy of seventeen. After a stormy start in which Pepys beat him, turned him out of the house and made Elizabeth give back a diamond locket he gave her, Hewer became a key member of the family and, as the years went by, Pepys's closest associate and friend.

23. There is no portrait of Jane Birch, the Pepyses' maid, whose life was interwoven with theirs from 1658 onwards. I have chosen this drawing from Charles Beale's 1670 sketchbook to stand in for Jane: it shows Susan Gill, a maid in his parents' London household. With her sweet face, short hair, simple clothes and broom, she rests on a kitchen chair, representing the great silent army of girls who cleaned, washed, scrubbed, swept, chopped, cooked, fetched water, emptied slops, carried coals and tended their masters and mistresses from early morning to late at night. She was paid £3 a year.

24, 25. Pepys decided to hate the brave Sir William Penn (*above*), his colleague at the Navy Office, jealous of his seniority and scornful of his intellectual powers. Thomas Povey of the Tangier Committee (*below*) suffered still worse: Pepys repaid his generosity by cheating him of money due to him.

26. Pepys's admired boss, William Coventry, secretary to the duke of York and navy commissioner, whose words of wisdom Pepys often noted in his Diary. A lifelong royalist who worked hard for Charles II, he warned Pepys that 'he that serves a Prince must expect and be contented to stand all fortunes and be provided to retreat'. So it happened: Coventry lost faith in the king's capacity to rule well, the king grew bored by the advice he offered, Coventry fell from favour and after a spell in the Tower retired from public life.

27. Charles II receiving the mapmaker Ogilby in Whitehall Palace with his queen, the duke and duchess of York, Prince Rupert and the duke's daughters, princesses Anne and Mary, beside him. The date is 1682, when the political whirligigs had put Pepys out of a job. The king found him another soon after this.

28. St Olave's, Hart Street, where the Navy Office went to church, shown here about 1670; it had been spared by the fire. Here Pepys buried his wife and his brother, and arranged to be buried himself.

30. Panoramic painting of the Great Fire of 1666 by an unknown Dutch artist. London Bridge appears on the left, St Paul's is haloed by flames in the centre, and the Tower is on the right. In the foreground crowds trying to save what goods they can are shown gathered on the river bank. Pepys watched the fire from a boat on the river on the first day, and observed how hot the air was, full of smoke and 'showers of Firedrops' blown by the strong east wind. There was also tremendous noise from the cracking of houses and roaring of the flames. 'It made me weep to see it,' he wrote, but he remained intent on recording the spectacle.

29. The most familiar of landscapes to Pepys, the view from Greenwich hill, showing the Queen's House astride the main road, John Webb's 1660s block, and behind them the ship-laden Thames winding its way from London past the Deptford shipyards and Rotherhithe.

31. When Elizabeth died suddenly at the age of twenty-nine, Pepys commissioned a memorial bust from the sculptor John Bushnell. Pepys judged well. Bushnell had studied in Rome and observed Bernini, who believed portrait busts should show the subject animated, as though in conversation; and this is how Elizabeth was treated, with striking results. The bust was placed high up on the wall of St Olave's and can be seen there today. A copy in the National Portrait Gallery allows a closer look but is not always on display.

natural prey; he expected to, and did, have sexual relations with several of his maids, and later also with his niece, who came to him as a schoolgirl and progressed to be his housekeeper. Hooke was a man with poor health and an unpleasing physical appearance, but that hardly explains away his domestic habits. Here are two contemporary records kept by very different men, both distinguished intellectually, both of whom persistently harassed the young women of their households. It is unlikely they were the only two.[40] It is also likely that Tom Edwards's hesitations were connected with anxieties about the relations between Pepys and Jane.

Elizabeth Pepys began to accuse her husband of being false to her with Jane. She alleged that Jane colluded by getting up late so that Pepys could watch her dress and allowing him into her room to do what he wanted – to be 'naught with her', a phrase indicating sexual misbehaviour. Jane must leave, she said. When Jane was summoned to their joint presence, she agreed to go at Easter but on condition that Tom could go with her.[41] A solution was slowly being reached, since now Pepys told Tom he would not keep him on after Jane left but would 'do well' by him. He kept his word and found him other work for the Navy Board.[42]

Elizabeth forgot her jealous rage at once and entered enthusiastically into the arrangements for the wedding of 'our young people', as they now became. She helped to get the licence, and the day was fixed for 26 March 1669, brushing aside the fact that it was in the middle of Lent and also the anniversary of Pepys's stone operation. She arranged for bridesmaids and bridesmen; two were Pepys cousins, 'The' Turner and Talbot, Roger's son, and another was Will Hewer; and she offered them a wedding dinner at the King's Head in Islington after the service and the use of the blue room for their wedding night. The blue room was one of the best bed-chambers in the house, in which she had spent ten days putting up the hangings herself and later had in upholsterers to make it more comfortable and complete the effect.[43] But while Elizabeth was busy with her plans for the festivities, Pepys sulked. Rather than presiding benevolently over preparations, he showed how much he resented what was happening, and how much he detested seeing his Jane handed over to another man. His feelings were so strong that he decided to take a trip to Chatham, arranging it so that he set off just before the ceremony, 'that I might be out of the way at the wedding and be at a little liberty myself for a day or two, to find a little pleasure and give my eyes a little ease'.[44] The pain in his eyes was a real anxiety, although he might have rested them at home. He preferred to stay away for four days, sightseeing in Kent and flirting with his old acquaintance Rebecca Allen, daughter of a Chatham official and now married. Pepys remembered dancing with her in 1661, before her marriage, and he now pressed his attentions on her again. Noticing that her hand was moist when he pulled off her glove and that her manners were 'mighty free', he concluded he could have anything he wanted of her if only time allowed. He also called her names in the Diary: 'ella is a whore, that is certain, but a very brave and comely one'.[45] This was Pepys at his angry and aggressive worst. Gradually he calmed down. He thought of Tom and Jane being put to bed on their wedding night, and also of his stone anniversary, left uncelebrated; and stayed away from home until everything was over. Then his good humour reasserted itself, and when he did return and was told how enjoyable the festivities had been, said he was glad and went with Elizabeth to pay the bill at the King's Head. He joked – at least you hope it was a joke – about how smug Tom and Jane both looked. Two days later they moved out into their own lodgings. That night Pepys cheered himself up in bed with a little fantasizing about the new maid, Jane's replacement.

This is almost the last of Jane in the Diary, which ends in May 1669. There are a few cheerful entries in April, when he took the newlyweds to a fashionable dining place, the Cock in Bow Street, and again noted his intention of giving them a wedding present, £40 for Tom, £20 for Jane from him and another £20 from Elizabeth. No doubt he carried out his promise. His other present may look symbolic to modern eyes, but to Pepys it must have been purely practical: he gave Tom a sword, with an old belt of his own to hang it on.[46]

After this he remained on good terms with Tom and Jane. He became godfather to their eldest son, Samuel, born in 1673. He saw to Tom's career, getting him appointed muster-master and navy agent at Deal five years later, in succession to Balty St Michel, so that the job was kept to all intents and purposes in the family.[47] When Tom died sadly young in 1681, leaving Jane with two children, she returned to work for Pepys, who was at that point sharing a house with Will

Hewer. Whether Pepys was less rampageous in his desires or not, she was by then a middle-aged widow and a mother, and his role was to act as an avuncular figure, full of benevolence and good sense. He did well, arranging for young Sam to be given a place at Christ's Hospital to study mathematics; and was rewarded by seeing him succeed. Sam was one of the pupils presented to King James at the beginning of 1688, and he grew up to become an officer in the navy, exactly as Pepys must have hoped. Jane remarried, a man called George Penny about whom we know nothing, and was soon widowed again. In 1690 Pepys settled an annuity of £15 a year on her.

Pepys loved Jane as you love someone who becomes a part of your life. His feelings for her were much warmer than anything he felt for his sister Pall, for instance, from the evidence of the Diary; and she appears as one of the most attractive figures in its pages. He shows her as affectionate, emotional, brave, stubborn, humorous, high-spirited, hard working and good at her work; loyal to her mother and brothers and faithful to her employers. Even Elizabeth had difficulty in picking quarrels with her. And he tells us what a hard time he often gave her and how stoutly she put up with his harshness, his unfairness and his general tiresomeness. When the day of Pepys's funeral came, her son was there to represent her, by then Lieutenant Sam Edwards. He and his mother each received a ring by Pepys's instructions, and she had an extra five guineas for mourning clothes in addition to the continued annuity 'Setled on my old and faithfull Servant Jane Penny' in his will.[48] Whatever scoldings, tears, beatings, fumblings in dark corners and other bad behaviour he had handed out to Jane were long forgotten; and in this case time allowed him to redeem himself doubly: by making the end of her life as comfortable as possible and also, though she never knew it, by leaving an admirable portrait of her to posterity.

17. The Secret Scientist

Pepys became a member of the Royal Society in 1665 and went on to become its president in 1684. As president his name appears on the title page of Isaac Newton's *Principia Mathematica*, linking him for ever with the great English scientist; but although Pepys was acquainted with Newton and had some correspondence with him, his own scientific credentials were almost nonexistent. He has been labelled 'almost comically an arts man' by a modern historian of science, and it is true that he was no chemist, physicist or astronomer.[1] Yet Pepys was a secret scientist of a kind, if only through his scrutiny of himself, and the candid, dispassionate, regular and detailed record he made of his own physical, moral and psychological state.

He was born at the same time as a generation of outstanding scientists, all of whom were prominent within the Royal Society and personally known to him. As well as Newton (born 1642) there was the chemist Robert Boyle (1627), Christopher Wren (1632), Robert Hooke (1635) and William Petty (1623); also the physician William Croone (1633), and the older mathematicians John Wallis (1616) and William Brouncker (1620). There were many other members who were linguistic scholars, antiquarians and mere gentlemen, with no more understanding of physics and chemistry than Pepys, and like him simply eager to be part of the most distinguished club in the country, where the scientifically gifted members showed experiments and led discussion, and everyone else came along to be diverted and instructed. What Pepys valued most was without doubt the sense of belonging to the group, hearing their exchanges of ideas and theories, and feeling he was at the forefront of progressive thought.

Pepys had what was considered a good education, but it did nothing to encourage him to think scientifically: the word 'science' in its modern meaning did not exist. The experimental scientists among his contemporaries all looked for encouragement and training from thinkers and teachers outside the conventional academic system, and set about creating new disciplines and new systems of thought. Boyle studied abroad and with private tutors after leaving Eton. Wren started as a boy making models of the solar system, left Westminster School at fourteen and acted as an assistant to Dr Charles Scarborough, a London lecturer in anatomy, before going to Oxford, where he worked with Boyle; at twenty-five he had a chair in astronomy, not in a university but at Gresham College in the City. Newton, intended for a farmer, and Hooke, intended for the Church, were both also dedicated model-makers as children; they made mechanical toys, Hooke produced a working wooden clock and Newton made dolls' furniture for the little girls of the village, and a model windmill with a mouse as miller.[2] Hooke studied with Boyle after Oxford and Newton did some of his best work away from Cambridge. Petty, with no schooling and no money, contrived to study medicine and chemistry abroad, had a chair in music at Gresham College and one in anatomy at Oxford by the age of twenty-eight, surveyed the whole of Ireland, designed ships and founded the science of political economy. These were not orthodox academic careers; some were facilitated by the civil war and commonwealth.

Wren particularly praised the encouragement given by the City of London in the speech he made on taking up his chair at Gresham College in 1657. The college, standing between Bishopsgate and Broad Street, was endowed in the 1590s by Thomas Gresham, City merchant and adviser to Queen Elizabeth; and he appointed professors who gave public lectures in English as well as Latin. It was in effect the first open university, and it is possible that Pepys went along to a lecture or two there when he was a boy. It established the first chairs of geometry and astronomy in England, and its activities were expanding during the later years of the Cromwells' protectorate, when Petty and Wren were there. Wren's speech paid particular tribute to the culture of the City. He praised it as the centre of mechanical arts and trade as well as liberal sciences, 'in such a Measure, as is hardly to be found in the Academies [i.e., Oxford and Cambridge] themselves'. Its citizens were 'the Masters of the Sea', the City itself another 'Alexandria, the established Residence of Mathematical Arts', and it was true that the City's long association with the navy had led to research on navigating instruments and shipbuilding.[3]

This intellectual liveliness of the City was part of Pepys's back-ground. He also read Bacon, who placed the study of the natural world above metaphysics, with enthusiasm. So he had heard and read enough to be eager for news of discoveries and inventions. As early as 1656 he attended 'magnetique experiments' with Montagu.[4] He haunted the shops of instrument-makers in Long Acre, Aldgate and Chancery Lane, men who made microscopes, slide rules, thermometers, telescopes and devices for drawing in perspective; he bought himself a microscope in 1664 and acquired scientific books. He watched private experiments undertaken by his friends Pearse, the surgeon, and Dr Clarke, who administered opium to dogs and dissected them.[5] He took himself to one of Dr Scarborough's dissections of a hanged man at the Surgeons' Hall and attended his lectures on anatomy.[6] He enjoyed conversation with men whose minds travelled along original lines: at the coffee house William Petty stirred his imagination with the suggestion that we cannot know for certain whether or not we are dreaming when we think ourselves awake and waking when we dream.[7] Petty was in his view 'one of the most rational men that ever I heard speak with a tongue, having all his notions the most distinct and clear'.[8]

The instrument-maker Ralph Greatorex took him to Gresham College in January 1661, where the Royal Society had just been set up. Among the founding members were his past and future bosses, Lords Sandwich and Brouncker and William Coventry; John Evelyn, destined to become a friend; Petty, Hooke and Wren; John Wilkins, whose plan for a universal language caught Pepys's interest; William Croone, who predicted the benefits of human blood transfusion; and John Wallis, mathematician. A year after this Dr Clarke talked of introducing Pepys to the Society, but nothing came of his proposal, and instead Pepys saw his rival, John Creed, introduced as a member in 1663 by Thomas Povey. Pepys records a conversation with Creed about duodecimal arithmetic, and another when Creed described experiments shown by Hooke at the Society.[9] Where Creed could go Pepys must follow, and it was again Povey who put up Pepys's name in 1665. He was elected, unanimously, on 15 February, and joined in a club supper afterwards with such worthies as Dr Goddard, who had been Cromwell's chief physician and now sold his famous 'Goddard's Drops' to the king: they contained crushed human bones and the flesh of vipers, and were good for lethargy.[10] Charles II was the Society's patron. He had some scientific curiosity and a laboratory of his own; and his protection was believed to be useful against those who might oppose the Society's activities. From time to time he sent along venison for the Society dinners, but he never chose to attend a meeting, and his interest dwindled with the years.[11]

The first weeks of Pepys's membership produced a rare occasion when we know something about him which he does not mention in his Diary. The Society's archives record that he was asked to question Captain Robert Holmes, returned from the African coast, about the action of some pendulum watches he had carried there for the Society. Holmes was in the Tower, accused of going beyond his orders in attacking the Dutch, and Pepys was reluctant to speak to him because they had clashed when Pepys appointed a master to Holmes's ship and Holmes sacked him and threatened Pepys with a duel – so Pepys chose to consult with the master of Holmes's ship, while Holmes was visited by Sir Robert Moray. Different accounts of the action of the pendulum watches came from the two men, and Pepys was then asked to procure the journals of ships' masters 'who had been with Major Holmes in Guinea, and differed from him in the relation concerning the pendulum watches'.[12] Pepys's silence in the Diary is puzzling. He may not have understood the point of the experiment with the pendulum watches; or perhaps he felt he was being used as a subordinate and resented the slight.[13]

In any case, the country was now at war, and in June the plague interrupted the Society's meetings and scattered the members. Some went abroad. Hooke, Petty and Wilkins retreated to Pepys's childhood paradise, Durdans, and worked there together on mechanical inventions.[14] Plague, fire and war meant there were several disturbed years, and when there were meetings Pepys's workload made it hard for him to attend. He sometimes managed to join the members afterwards, and in this way he heard of a blood transfusion performed on a dog by Hooke, and discussed it with him. A year later there was a human blood transfusion, after which he met the subject of the operation and found him 'cracked a little in his head, though he speaks very reasonably and very well'. Surprisingly, the man survived.[15] Pepys saw an experiment with an air pump and 'an abortive child, preserved fresh in spirit of salt'.[16]

An alertness to scientific matters is felt throughout the Diary. In the summer of 1666 he discussed with Brouncker whether Nature gave each creature teeth suitable to a particular food, or whether teeth adapted to the food available. He listened appreciatively to Hooke's account of sound being a matter of vibrations. He borrowed telescopes to set up on his roof, staying up till one to look at the moon and Jupiter.[17] He mentions a demonstration of refraction, using wax balls in water; and Dr Wilkins's book on universal language, which he acquired for his own library.[18] He also bought, read and reread Hooke's *Micrographia*; and acquired works by Boyle and Newton, which he found beyond him, as many of us do.[19] His respect for Hooke, a difficult man as well as a brilliant one, is to Pepys's credit, and Hooke mentions his kindness more than once in his own diary.[20]

Pepys became a useful member of the Society because he had a just idea of what he could and could not contribute, and remained interested. He paid his subscription regularly and gave extra money when asked; he raised funds and gave advice on how to invest money.[21] He served on the council over a period of twenty-seven years, elected for the first time in 1672 and for the last on 30 November 1699. He did not volunteer inappropriate statements at the meetings, unlike Povey, who described how the filing of one of his own slender teeth made it thicken, and offered his recipe for gooseberry wine.[22] Pepys said almost nothing at the meetings of the Society, confining his speech to the council meetings. The one time he came close to contributing was when Petty proposed that every member of the council should provide an 'experimental discourse' to be given at a public meeting within the year, or else pay a fine of forty shillings. Pepys offered to oblige and repeated his offer at another meeting, but never gave a discourse. This was in 1675, and he had the excuse that he was a busy man; he may also well have lost his nerve at the thought of addressing the best brains in the country.[23]

Isaac Newton became a member in the mid 1670s, and Christopher Wren was president for two years from 1680, when the Society was running into trouble, with a shrinking membership and many subscriptions in arrears. Pepys, elected president in December 1684, was one of a series of non-scientific presidents chosen for their administrative skills and influence. He got to work at once tidying up the affairs of the Society, ordering that names of all members in arrears with their subscriptions should be left out of the next list of members unless they paid up: sixty were got rid of, including the duke of

Buckingham. Pepys insisted on being provided with a written state-ment of the Society's cash position. Then, drawing on his own experience of training clerks in the Navy Office, he prepared orders for the Society's clerks. They must be single and childless, with good English, French and Latin and some mathematics. They might not be members of the Society while they served. They should be paid £50 a year at least. They must keep the minutes in books, not on loose papers, and index the books. Some of the good effects of these rules can be appreciated to this day in the neatly written records of the Society. On the other hand it is a relief to know that a rule was waived to enable Edmund Halley, the great astronomer, to serve 'notwithstanding his want of the fifth Qualification' – the one about being unmarried and childless.[24]

Pepys invited members to come to a council meeting with ideas for making experiments. He ordered that the Society's books should be searched 'to see what had been done towards the improvement of navigation'.[25] He communicated, via John Evelyn, his own observa-tions on the effects of thunder and lightning on two of the king's ships in Portsmouth Harbour during a storm in October 1685. He personally presented £50 to the Society, which was used to pay for the plates for a 'History of Fishes' it proposed to publish as a commercial venture. He is most famous for having ordered the printing of New-ton's *Principia Mathematica* for the Society, although he was not present at any of the council meetings at which the matter came up, nor did he order the Society to pay for the printing, which it failed to do. This glory belongs to Edmund Halley, at that time a mere secretary to the Society. The *Principia* did not actually appear until the summer after the end of Pepys's presidency, although he undoubtedly approved its publication and took pride in being associated with Newton.[26]

His interest in the Society was kept up to the end of his life. In 1694 he arranged for his nephew John Jackson to be elected a member.[27] In 1699 he encouraged the East India Company to make a donation.[28] Later that year his views were still being sought to suggest activities for the Society 'tending to the advancement of Natural knowledge'.[29] And in his last years he was attended by doctors who were fellow members, Hans Sloane and Charles Bernard; they also performed the autopsy on his body in just such a scientific spirit as he would have approved. It is a record that does credit both to the Society and to Pepys.

Yet his greatest achievement could not be known to his contemporaries in the Society. In 1664, the year before he was elected, it had set up a committee to consider how to encourage better use of the English language, Evelyn and Dryden being among its members. Their recommendation was that writers should aim to achieve 'a close, naked, natural way of speaking; positive expression; clear senses; a native easinesse, bringing all things as near the Mathematical plainnesse, as they can'.[30] It could almost be a description of Pepys's language as he arrived at it, privately and separately, when he embarked on the Diary. Had they been able to read his Diary, some at least would have marvelled at the achievement of a man observing himself with scientific curiosity, as he voyaged through the strange seas of his own life.

18. Speeches and Stories

On a Sunday afternoon in January 1667 Pepys met his cousin Roger, the lawyer and MP, in the park, and the two men walked along Pall Mall discussing parliamentary matters and the poll tax, for which Roger was a collector in Cambridge. When they reached Whitehall, Roger asked Pepys to take him into the rooms where various members of the court were to be seen, and to point out the beautiful and notorious Lady Castlemaine; and, as they stood gazing at her, her little black servant hurried by on an errand for his mistress. There was a dog in his way. Pepys adopts direct speech in the Diary at this point and writes: '"Pox of this dog!" said the boy. "Now," says he [Roger], blessing himself, "would I whip this child till the blood came if it were my child!" – and I believe he would.' It is a perfect piece of dialogue, letting us know in a few words that Roger was brought up as a good puritan, and in another four, spoken by the boy, informing us of the style of speech and manners of the court. Pepys's ear was so good he could have been a better playwright than many whose plays he sat through in the theatre. He knew exactly how to extract and present the dramatic kernel of a situation.[1]

Another dramatic sketch is made of a row with an official who objects to Pepys's insistence that he should search for some missing papers after hours: 'he told me I ought to give people ease at night, and all business to be done by day. I answered him sharply, that I did not make, nor any honest man, any difference between night and day in the King's business . . . he answered me short; I told him I knew the time (meaning the Rump's time) when he did other men's business with more diligence. He cried, "Nay, say not so," and stopped his mouth, not one word after.'[2] The four words tell us how frightened the man is that his political past will be brought up against him; Pepys has him by the throat, and he does as he is asked.

Pepys, unlike Evelyn, never writes a formal character sketch. He is a *pointilliste*, building up his impressions with small touches. He shows friends, enemies and celebrities in action and allows them to reveal themselves: for instance, Lady Castlemaine simply going 'puh' when the king said he had not fathered her child, and the next day telling him, 'God damn me! but you shall own it.'³ Or a story about George Downing, freshly brought to Pepys by his old neighbour John Hunt, now an excise officer in Cambridgeshire where Downing has acquired a country estate. On becoming the squire, Downing learns that it is customary to entertain the poor of the parish at Christmas. Sir George instructs his mother accordingly to prepare a meal for them; but instead of the traditional dinner of roast beef, she gives them only 'beef porridge, pudding, and pork . . . and nothing said all dinner, but only his mother would say, "It's good broth, son." He would answer, "Yes, it is good broth." Then his lady confirm all and say, "Yes, very good broth." By and by he would begin and say, "Good pork;" "Yes," says the mother, "good pork." Then he cries, "Yes, very good pork." And so they said of all things; to which nobody made any answer . . . and with this he is jeered now all over the country.' The father of Downing Street is nailed for ever in his meanness and hypocrisy.⁴

  It is a scene good enough for Ben Jonson, whom Pepys idolized, and he has shaped it himself, since it came to him at second-hand. There is a different sort of dramatic splendour about the rhetoric of the old lord treasurer, Southampton, son of Shakespeare's patron, whose questions were put directly to Pepys after hearing his account of the money needed by the navy: 'Why, what means all this, Mr Pepys? This is true, you say, but what would you have me to do? I have given all I can for my life. Why will not people lend their money? Why will they not trust the King as well as Oliver? Why do our prizes come to nothing, that yielded so much heretofore?'⁵ I am inclined to think this is a verbatim record, noted down as soon as heard, partly because he judged Southampton's words politically important and also because he responded to their dramatic, quasi-Shakespearean ring. Diary readers have to be cautious, but Pepys paraphrases so much more often than he offers a direct transcription that it seems reasonable to trust him when he does; another example is his brother Tom's deathbed words, given in Chapter 11. Getting the words down as they were spoken interested him more as time passed and his feeling for what he could do with his Diary grew; in 1667 there was something like five times as much direct speech as in the first three years put together. After that it diminishes again, possibly because his painful eyes made it harder for him to make shorthand notes on the spot.

What is striking about his use of direct speech throughout is the way he catches the different cadences, flavours and rhythms of individual speakers. Here is the combative Carteret, who cries out '*Guarda mi spada*' ('Watch out for my sword') when he is angry and boasts to Pepys of his nearly fulfilled ambitions: '"By God," says he, "I will, and have already almost brought it to that pass, that the King shall not be able to whip a cat but I must be at the tayle of it."'[6] The duke of York's impatient pride surges up in his words to the Tangier Committee: 'All the world rides us, and I think we shall never ride anybody.'[7] The duchess of Albemarle, coarse, loyal to her husband and effective in making her point, attacks Sandwich after he has left his naval command under a cloud and been given a royal appointment as ambassador: 'If my Lord had been a coward he had gone to sea no more it may be; then he might have been excused and made an Embassador [meaning my Lord Sandwich]' – 'cursed words' writes Pepys, but he sets them down.[8] Batten, much as he disliked him, sometimes pleased him with his seadog's turn of phrase: '"By God," says he, "I think the Devil shits Dutchmen."'[9] Even a puritanical passer-by who noticed Pepys fondling Betty Martin in a Westminster window and alarmed him by shouting, 'Sir! Why do you kiss the gentlewoman so?' was put on record – hard to think anyone but Pepys would have done as much.[10] Penn's coachman shocked him by complaining of being sent out to fetch Lady Penn with the words, 'A pox of God rot her! Can she not walk hither?', but he wrote them down too.[11] He liked his own 'Cuds zookes! . . . What is become of my lobsters?' when he found he had left them behind in a hackney coach.[12] And his brother Tom's description of their Joyce cousins: 'they are sometimes all honey one with another and then all turd'.[13]

He lets us hear Prince Rupert's voice as he argues with the duke of York about whether naval officers should lose their command for being found drunk: 'God damn me, if they will turn out every man that will be drunk, he must out all the commander in the fleet. What is the matter if [he] be drunk, so when he comes to fight he doth his work?'[14] Batten, declaring his scorn for a boastful gentleman captain, Sir Frescheville Holles, dismisses him as 'a wind-fucker'.[15] Lord

Sandwich gives Pepys his melancholy advice, four years after the Restoration: 'take it from me never to trust too much to any man in the world, for you put yourself into his power; and the best-seeming friend and real friend as to the present may have or take occasion to fall out with you; and then out comes all'.[16] And an exchange between Pepys and Coventry gives the tone of their private conversation as they consider their future prospects in the light of the failures of the Dutch war. Coventry says he is tired of his job, and that if there were to be another war, 'they should not find a Secretary; "Nor," said I, "a Clerk of the Acts, for I see the reward of it; and thanked God I have enough of my own to buy me a good book and a good fiddle, and I have a good wife;" – "Why," says he, "I have enough to buy me a good book, and shall not need a fiddle, because I have never a one of your good wifes." ' Coventry can be imagined allowing himself a very slight smile as he delivers his double entendre at the end of this perfect passage.[17]

Coventry is quoted more than anyone else, and he gives some striking comments on the administration he served. Staunch royalist as he was, he told Pepys he knew the navy could not be run without its old officers from the commonwealth period. ' "Why," says he, "in the sea-service it is impossible to do anything without them, there being not more then three men of the whole King's side that are fit to command almost." '[18] He offered a warning before retiring himself, 'that he that serves a Prince must expect and be contented to stand all fortunes and be provided to retreat'. They were words Pepys must have called to mind more than once in his own later career.[19]

We can see, as Pepys could not, that Lord Sandwich's remark, 'Why, Sir John, do not you think that he hath a great beauty to his wife? Upon my word he hath', was a tease, not an innocent compliment.[20] Pepys claimed to be offended by the 'loose expression' of Lady Robinson, wife of the lieutenant of the Tower: 'Look, there is a pretty man; I could be contented to break a commandment with him,' but to us she sounds like a Congreve heroine.[21] One of his second-hand stories has the duke of Buckingham also talking like a character in a play as he takes his mistress, the countess of Shrewsbury, to his house and finds the duchess, his wife, at home. The duchess was born Mary Fairfax, daughter of Cromwell's general and a pupil of Andrew Marvell – not, you would think, a woman to be trifled with – and she tells Buckingham it is not for her to share the house with his mistress. To which he replies, '"Why, Madam, I did think so; and therefore have ordered your coach to be ready to carry you to your father's;" which was a devilish speech, but they say true,' wrote Pepys. Only hearsay, but too sophisticated and too vile not to be recorded.[22] Another piece of sparring between wife and mistress was told him of Lady Castlemaine addressing the queen, '"I wonder your Majesty," says she, "can have the patience to sit so long a–dress-ing." "Oh," says the queen, "I have so much reason to use patience, that I can very well bear with it." '[23]

A quarrel with John Creed about what he should pay Pepys for passing his accounts with the Navy Office was moved towards a solution by a metaphysical conceit from Creed. 'Says he, "After all; well," says he, "I know you will expect, since there must be some condescension [i.e., giving way], that it doth become me to begin it; and therefore," says he, "I do propose (just like the interstice between the death of the old and coming in of the present king, all that time is swallowed up as if it hath never been), so our breach of friendship may be as if it hath never been." '[24] The idea that the eleven years from January 1649 to May 1660 had been wiped out by God in sympathy with the royalist cause was so ingenious, particularly coming from an old puritan zealot, that Pepys agreed the quarrel was over and accepted a lower payment than he had hoped for; but he liked Creed no better for his cleverness.

Pepys enjoyed the gossip of high life, politics, drama and wit, but simplicity of speech caught his fancy almost as often. The shepherd on Epsom Downs answered his question about the iron toes and heels of his shoes on a hot July Sunday with '"Why," says the poor man, "the Downes, you see, are full of stones, and we are fain to shoe ourselfs thus; and these," says he, "will make the stones fly till they sing before me." '[25] This was natural poetry, and to Pepys the shepherd was a reminder of the Patriarchs, surrounded by his sheep and with his son at his side to read aloud to him from the Bible. The same plainness pleased him in the words of the gravedigger at St Bride's preparing to bury Tom and finding the chosen space crowded, already quoted but worth repeating here: 'I will justle them together but I will make room for him.'[26] The Quaker woman who addressed the king, 'replying still with these words, "O King!" and thou'd him all along', earned her place in his gallery, and the small girl keeping cows beside the Dartford road who thought Pepys must be her godfather when he spoke to her, and promptly kneeled down 'and very simply cried, "Pray, godfather, pray God to bless me"'.[27]

With Lady Sandwich he had many conversations, on subjects ranging from primogeniture to religion, but he never gives her exact words. For instance, 'with my Lady Sandwich (good lady), talking of innocent discourse of good housewifery and husbands for her daughters, and the luxury and looseness of the times and other such things, till past 10 a-clock at night'. Was her speech too inconsequential and rambling, or did he think it might be disrespectful? He was not so inhibited with her husband. A fortnight later, when Lord Sandwich has returned from sea and is addressing his wife in Pepys's presence, he does give his exact words: '"How do you do, sweetheart; how have you done all this week?" – himself taking notice of it to me, that he had hardly seen her the week before.' Pepys was troubled by Sandwich's question to his wife because he blamed him for neglecting her since his return, but Sandwich's perfectly easy tone, with the endearment dropped in to sweeten his neglect, suggests his charm, and Lady Sandwich was content with it.[28]

Pepys's exchanges with Elizabeth were differently conducted, and although there is no direct speech from her either, during the period of their worst falling out he comes close to giving her exact words when he writes that she calls him 'a dog and a rogue', 'and that I had a rotten heart', and a few days later again, 'a false, rotten-hearted rogue'; and 'she swore . . . that she would slit the nose of this girl, and be gone herself this very night from me'.[29] It sounds authentic enough. And just once we hear him speak to her in the gallant voice of a wooer when, as he is planning a trip to Brampton on legal business, he turns to her with the words, 'Shall you and I never travel together again?', and she at once agrees to ride with him.[30]

The most eminent figure Pepys had dealings with was Clarendon, the great lord chancellor, who first spoke to him 'very merrily' in the Hague in 1660, from his bed, where he was suffering from gout. During the next years Pepys sometimes felt the sting of Clarendon's criticism, and observed him sleeping and snoring through committee meetings; he also admired the ease and authority of his public speaking so much that he talked of being 'mad in love' with him because of it. When Sandwich sent Pepys to the chancellor to apologize for the navy having marked for felling some of the trees on his Wiltshire estate, Pepys felt such 'horror' at what had happened that he cringed. 'I was the unhappy Pepys that hath fallen into his high displeasure, and came to desire him to give me leave to make myself better understood to his Lordshipp – assuring him of my duty and service.' Clarendon decided not to be angry and told him to come back after dinner, then invited him briskly, 'Come, Mr Pepys, you and I will take a turn in the garden.' He told Pepys to keep his hat on, treating him as an equal, and the two men walked together for an hour while others waited, and they parted with 'kindness and respect'.[31] The Diary also gives Clarendon's withering remark to the king during a discussion of the Dutch attack on the Medway: '"Treachery?" says he, "I could wish we could prove there was anything of that in it, for that would imply some wit and thoughtfulness; but we are ruined merely by folly and neglect."'[32]

It also shows Clarendon's gentleness and humanity. Pepys heard him making a private inquiry about his grandsons, the children of his daughter Anne who were princes of the blood and in line for the succession through their father, the duke of York. In the spring of 1667 both little princes were ill, and Clarendon sent for news of them from an official meeting at which Pepys was present: 'and it was pretty to observe,' he wrote, 'how . . . my Lord did ask (not how the Princes or the dukes do, as other people do) but "How do the children?" which methought was mighty great, and like a great man and grand-father'.[33] Everything about this pleased Pepys, who had a tenderness for children himself and liked to see a man of state behave simply, on the pattern of the Roman senators Clarendon and he both admired.

As for the king, we have already noticed that he did not impress Pepys as a conversationalist. On seeing his own officials arrive at Whitehall, '"Oh," says he, "here is the Navy Office."' Like his praise of Pepys's speech to the House, 'Mr Pepys, I am very glad of your success yesterday', the words earn their place only because they came from the king.[34]

Speaking for himself, he has a whole range of voices. One is as rude and alive as the language of the Jacobean playwrights, with their homely imagery of dogs and food, their double negatives and stark affirmations. 'I shall be revenged of him,' he writes, like a shout on the page.[35] About an office enemy in trouble, 'but all will not nor shall not do, for out he shall go'.[36] Of Luce, an unsatisfactory cook-maid: 'She was a very drudging, working wench; only, she would be drunk.'[37] Worrying about plans that may miscarry, he fears that 'All my cake will be doe still.'[38] After a naval disaster, as allegations are made: 'Out of all this, a great deal of good meat will be picked.'[39] The mighty Carteret, brought low, 'is now as supple as a spaniel'.[40] Someone returns from France 'an absolute Monsieur'.[41] Pepys drives into town after the plague in Lord Brouncker's coach: 'But Lord, what staring to see a nobleman's coach come to town – and porters everywhere bow to us, and such begging of beggars.'[42]

He has the trick of switching from ornate to simple language in a sentence: 'Took a turn with him in the Pell Mell, talking of the melancholy posture of affairs, where everybody is snarling at one another.'[43] Another passage moves from light fantastic to basics: 'It being a fine clear day I did *en gayeté de Cœur* propose going to Bow for ayre sake and dine there . . . They being come, we to Oysters and so to talk.'[44] At other moments his delivery is entirely staccato, rattling off like gunshot as he sums up the bad state of things for the Navy Board: 'And thus ends the month – with an ill aspect. The business of the Navy standing wholly still. No credit. No goods sold us. Nobody will trust us. All we have to do at the office is to hear complaints for want of money.'[45] And there are odd flashes of poetry, as when 'the City had a light like a glory round about it, with bonefyres'.[46]

The garbled foreign phrases he often used for sexual incidents had something to do with concealment perhaps, much more with his pleasure in marking off sexual experiences through special words and so heightening the excitement of reliving them. Some words pleased him especially: 'tocar' ('to touch'), 'ella' ('she') and 'su' ('her'), 'abaxo' ('below'), 'douce' ('soft' – as in 'skin very douce'), 'mamelles'. He will use a single word that pleases him for its own sake: 'formosa', of the new maid at the Harp & Ball: 'the maid, Mary, is very formosa'.[47] He produces some delightful jumbles: 'ella con the Roman nariz and bon body which I did heretofore like'.[48] And when things are good with Elizabeth, she is treated to the special vocabulary too: 'Waked betimes, and lay long hazendo doz vezes con mi moher con grando pleasure to me and ella; and there fell to talking, and by and by rose.'[49] It is the clever schoolboy as lover, showing off to himself in two ways at once.

Jonson's satire on the sanctimonious puritan whine may have amused him, but he was not immune from it himself: 'Lord, to see how unhappily a man may fall into a necessity of bribing people to do him right in a thing wherein he hath done nothing but fair, and bought dear.'[50] '. . . reading a little of *L'escolle des Filles*, which is a mighty lewd book, but yet not amiss for a sober man once to read over to inform himself in the villainy of the world.'[51] At dinner with a City merchant who is making up to him, 'and Lord, to see how I am treated, that come from so mean a beginning, is matter of wonder to me'.[52] He reaches out for standard formulations using God's name when he feels guilty ('God forgive me') or grateful ('ought to be thankful to God Almighty') or wants to add emphasis, 'I pray God to make me able to pay for it' when he buys an expensive new suit or 'I pray God keep me from setting my mind too much upon it' when he improves his house. There is a residue of childhood belief, the fear that some sort of lottery system of rewards and punishments is being run by God, which sometimes drives him to stronger affirmations; when he is thinking of his health a note of real thanksgiving is heard, and when he is in bad trouble with his marriage he takes his anguish momentarily to God. But this is rare, and elsewhere he invokes God's name as non-believers and half-believers do, a figure of speech only.

Every reader notices the frequently repeated expressions, from the famous 'and so to bed' to 'mighty merry', 'with much content', 'But Lord', 'brave dinner', 'noble discourse', 'to my great Satisfaction', etc. They can become tedious, although most readers enjoy them as signature tunes, amusing and reassuring, evidence of the spontaneity of his writing – Pepys too could be lazy and fall back on cliché. Often he stands aside from himself: 'a great joy it is to me to see myself in a good disposition to business'; 'carried home £10 worth of book, all I hope I shall buy a great while': he is offering himself the joy and the hope.[53] His language is always close to speech. You can compare it with his laborious efforts for other writing by looking at the draft of a letter to a friend that appears in the Diary. It goes like this: '(God though God knows (though without vanity (though I thank God (though the world hath been p[retty favourable to myself (though I cannot complain of (though the world hath [not] been very unkind to me in this matter) that I have taken little joy in the notice of my [home] friends at home . . .'[54] And so on. The vitality drains out in the effort to be polite; just as indeed it did drain out of his language in later years, when Augustan prose overcame him. It makes you wonder all the more at the incomparable liveliness and variety of the language of the Diary.

19. Surprise and Disorder

Only one of the love affairs recorded in the Diary is painted with the true colours of romance and tragedy, perhaps because it was also the only one found out by Elizabeth. After her discovery Pepys's narrative takes on a desperate intensity as he struggles with his conflicting emotions, guilt towards both women, remorse and obsessive desire. There is no comedy in his account but tenderness and a great deal of pain. In certain passages he prefigures the great adulteresses of nineteenth-century fiction, alternating between ecstasy and torment like Bovary and enduring the punishment inflicted by an angry and virtuous spouse, like Karenina.

The girl who set him on fire was Deborah Willet. She was just seventeen when she came to be Elizabeth's companion in the autumn of 1667, a slight, pretty and respectable girl who had been at boarding school in Bow, a village on the River Lea a few miles north of the City, for seven or eight years. She had been sent there by her aunt, a woman of good education herself, who brought her from Bristol after her parents died young. Elizabeth chose Deborah, who was recommended by friends, and when Pepys first set eyes on her – 'our pretty girl' – he wondered if she were not 'a little too good for my family'.[1] Admittedly this was at the end of an evening out in which he had first flung down the barmaid at the Swan over a chair in order to fondle her thigh, and then called on Betty Martin for his usual entertainment. Deborah he thought very grave as well as pretty. Almost at once he and Elizabeth took her to the theatre, and then they all set off on a sightseeing trip to Audley End and Cambridge, with Will Hewer in attendance. For a girl who could scarcely remember her parents to find herself part of a family again must have been a powerful emotional experience. Suddenly she was the youngest, pet as well as servant, almost a daughter, with a jolly father and an elegant mother; and travelling with the Pepyses was as different from boarding school life as could be. They cannot have gone unnoticed, with their high spirits, their taste for good fare and comfort, and their plentiful spending money. At first Pepys sometimes forgot her name – for a few weeks he called her 'the girl' in his Diary – but she soon became Deb to them all, and she was included in everything. They visited King's College Chapel, Trinity, and the library of St John's (but not Magdalene, it seems); and they slept at the Rose Inn, where Elizabeth and Deborah shared a bed and Pepys took another in the same room, enjoying some merry night-time conversation with his two ladies.

Cambridge was a stop on the way to Brampton, where he intended to dig up the gold his father and Elizabeth had buried in June at the time of the Medway crisis. He had not been there since the death of his mother in the spring or indeed for nearly three years before that, and he was pleased with the way his father had maintained the place, although he found the roofs low after his London ceilings. But his first thought was to visit Lady Sandwich at Hinchingbrooke. He had not seen her for two years, since her daughter Jemima's wedding, and he found her the same as ever, excellent, good and discreet as they talked of her absent Lord, still in Spain. Elizabeth walked up the lane after him, bringing Deb with her; and that night in the Brampton house Deb took a trundle bed next to the high one shared by Pepys and Elizabeth.

In London she had her own room. The other members of the household were Jane Birch, Tom Edwards and two more maids. Mary Mercer, although no longer officially part of the family, was an established friend, often with them and joining in many of their outings, and Will Hewer was also constantly in and out of the house. Elizabeth showed no sign of falling out with Deb apart from one frisson of jealousy Pepys observed when she noticed that he seemed fond of the girl. He resolved not to stir things up in any way.[2] They were both old enough to be sensible now – Pepys was thirty-four – and he would treat Deb like a daughter. She joined in card games with Mercer and Will in the evening, she was included in parties, taken to the theatre and on shopping expeditions, and went with Elizabeth on her many visits to her tailor John Unthank. Nobody seems to have warned her to watch out for the master, not Jane or Mercer and certainly not Elizabeth herself; after her one jealous twinge she appears to have become sublimely unaware of any possibility of trouble. Pepys was working harder than ever, dealing with the parliamentary attacks on the Navy Board, and on top of that he had problems with his eyesight: enough to worry about.

The Diary has not a word of warning, nothing to suggest any desires or plans he may have had. He simply lists a slow sequence of events, as though they came about without any volition on his part. There was nothing unusual about expecting Deb to comb his hair or help him prepare for bed, because these were both normal functions for one of the family, as she was. The combing began in November, and in January 1668 he mentioned his pleasure in having his head combed, 'as I do now often do, by Deb, whom I love should be fiddling about me'.[3] You can breathe the comfortable smell of hair, warm flesh and body linen arising from these words. He had given her his first paternal kiss when Elizabeth was ill and spending Sunday in her bed, three days before Christmas. No doubt Jane was preparing pies and puddings down in the kitchen, and Elizabeth needed bowls of water and chamber pots carried up and down stairs, and her bed tidied; everyone moved about the dark house from one patch of firelight to the next candle's ring of brightness. Pepys approached Deb so carefully that there was no good moment to start resisting or objecting to him; besides, she had every reason to like him for his kindness. It was the end of March before he took her on his knees, after scolding her for failing to write down something correctly: reduced to tears, she could be comforted like a child. His description is pitched between the erotic and the sentimental: 'I did give her good advice and beso la [kissed her], ella weeping still; and yo did take her, the first time in my life, sobra mi genu [on my knees] and poner mi mano sub her jupes and toca su thigh, which did hazer me great pleasure; and so did no more, but besando-la [kissing her], went to my bed.'[4]

Elizabeth and Deb left for the country together the next day, so things remained as they were until August, when Pepys made his first unequivocally sexual attack. He managed 'first with my hand tocar la cosa [thing, i.e., sexual parts] de our Deb in the coach – ella being troubled at it – but yet did give way to it'.[5] After this he used the hair-combing and bedtime sessions to advance his caresses. By day Deb and Elizabeth occupied themselves with various pleasures, going with Mercer to have their fortunes told by gypsies, to the theatre and to Bartholomew Fair, and in September they travelled together to Cambridge again, this time without Pepys and at the invitation of cousin Roger, who wanted to show them Sturbridge Fair. They seem to have got on very well. During their Cambridge trip Pepys had a go at Jane Birch, standard stuff. When they returned he took Elizabeth and Deb with him to look at bed-hangings and beds, because he was planning a fine new bedroom and wanted to have an exact copy made of the bed belonging to the duke of York's secretary, Matthew Wren, who obligingly allowed it to be viewed.

Then one evening Elizabeth, 'coming up suddenly', found him embracing Deb 'with my main in her cunny. I was at a wonderful loss upon it, and the girl also.'⁶ It was, wrote Pepys, 'the greatest sorrow to me that ever I knew in this world'. Understandably, it also drove Elizabeth into a state of frenzy; because, although we, as readers of the Diary, know that there is nothing new happening here, for her it is the first and devastating discovery of his infidelity. Also, it was happening directly before her eyes, and with a girl who was her friend and companion. Her almost immediate reaction was to tell him she was a Catholic, perhaps because it was the worst thing she could think of to frighten him; and maybe too distress drove her to her girlhood pieties, and she knew it was true. She said she would turn Deb out, of course. She also threatened to shame him publicly, although it seems unlikely that a wife's revelations of her husband's infidelity would interest anyone else. Pepys kept his head down and admitted to nothing; Deb did likewise, and very little was said in the house for several days by anyone except Elizabeth. She kept Pepys awake every night as she raged at him. She also expressed her anger and sorrow by giving up any attempt to wash herself.

Bad as things were, it looked as though they might yet be smoothed over. Deb's aunt visited Elizabeth and discussed her parting 'in kind terms', and Deb went out to look for another place. But a worse storm was on the way. Halfway through November Elizabeth somehow extracted a 'confession' from Deb, poor child. Whatever she confessed, the effect was to send Elizabeth almost mad. This was when she told Pepys about Lord Sandwich's attempt on her virtue; and she now insisted that Pepys must sack Deb and tell her that he disliked her. For three weeks Elizabeth had kept him from sleeping; he realized Deb had to go, but he feared becoming 'a slave' to his wife, still longed to 'have the maidenhead of this girl' and at the same time reported greatly increased sexual activity and pleasure with his wife. On 14 November Deb did leave, Elizabeth preventing him from going down to the kitchen to speak to her and telling him he was a dog and a rogue and that he had 'a rotten heart'. The next day, a Sunday, he wrote up his journal, reflecting that he would be glad to find Deb, 'though I fear it would be my ruin', an expression of almost feminine despair. But on Monday he put his fears aside and did go out to find her.

Two days later he tracked her down and persuaded her to meet him in a coach. A scene of passionate embraces and promises followed, in which he succeeded in making her 'tener mi cosa [my thing] in her mano, while mi mano was sobra su pectus [under her breast], and so did hazer with grand delight'; and afterwards made her vow not to let any other man do what he had done to her. He gave her twenty shillings and a contact address at one of his booksellers and went home happy. But Elizabeth was too alert to his movements and moods not to guess what had happened. The next day she exploded with rage again, made him confess his latest exploit, cursed and threatened him, and said she was quite prepared to leave him if he would supply her with a few hundred pounds. For good measure she offered to slit Deb's nose. At his wits' end, he sent for Will Hewer, told him the story and asked him to intercede. Will cried like a child and Pepys swore to see Deb no more; but he wrote down that he had no intention of keeping the vow. To make things bearable at home he agreed to an arrangement whereby he would not leave the house except in Will's custody. A sort of peace was made. Pepys made love to Elizabeth to placate her – he seems not to have minded her rank state – and then, alone in his bedroom, he prayed to God on his knees, asking Him to keep him true to 'my poor wife'. He also noted that the upholsterers had just finished work on the splendid new best bedroom, but that he had not the heart to enjoy the effect.

I know of no other account of marital rage and jealousy to match this one. Anyone who has lived through anything similar, in whichever position of the triangle, will recognize its truth and force, even though it is told entirely from one point of view. Pepys shows himself divided between sympathy for his wife, whom he acknowledges he has wronged, pity and grief for Deb, whom he has also wronged, and a profound pity for himself. And on the whole he is fair to everyone. On it went, as such things do. On 22 November, a Sunday, he tells us that Elizabeth at last decides to wash and 'cleans herself, after four

or five weeks being in continued dirt'. The following Sunday, Pepys
reports that he cannot help thinking of Deb. Elizabeth forces him to
write a letter to her telling her she is a whore. Will, also wanting to
be fair to everyone, winks at him to indicate he will deal with this,
and does so by removing the offensive part of the letter before he
delivers it to Deb. One day in January, Pepys manages to go out
without Will, and that night Elizabeth, as terrifying as Lady Macbeth,
arrives at the bedside carrying a pair of tongs heated red hot.[7] Pepys
talks his way out of this tricky situation, and things quieten down for
a time, though there are bumps, as when Elizabeth hears that Deb is
living in fine style, wearing fashionable black spots and speaking ill of
her. He reflects mournfully that he knows nothing of what has become
of her, although 'my devil that is within me doth wish that I could'.[8]
The more he suffers, the more he returns to the religious lessons of
his childhood.

At the end of March, after Jane's wedding, he is pleased to think
that there is now no servant left living in the house who remembers
the Deb affair. His self-esteem is returning. Everything is over, he
goes to Betty Martin in the old way – and then, on 13 April, he is in
Whitehall with Will and

as God would have it I spied Deb. which made my heart and head to work;
and I presently could not refrain, but sent W. Hewer away to look for Mr
Wren (W. Hewer, I perceive, did see her, but whether he did see me see
her I know not, or suspect my sending him away I know not) but my heart
could not hinder me. And I run after her and two women and a man, more
ordinary people, and she in her old clothes; and after hunting a little, find
them in the lobby of the Chapel below-stairs; and there I observed she
endeavoured to avoid me, but I did speak to her and she to me, and did get
her para docere me ou she demeures [to tell me where she lives] now. And
did charge her para say nothing of me that I had vu elle – which she did
promise; and so, with my heart full of surprize and disorder, I away.

He went into the park with a colleague, returned to Whitehall to
look for her again, worried in case Will should read his face. Pepys
went home with him, where he agonized over whether God would
let him see Deb, 'whom indeed I love, and with a bad amour' – a
refinement, this. But whatever God intended he had her address

safely, and two days later he was with her in an ale house, struggling to overcome her modesty, with only partial success, and giving her another twenty shillings.[9]

This was their last rendezvous. Although she agreed to meet him in Westminster Hall the following Monday, she failed to appear. He walked up and down for two hours, and afterwards consoled himself with Betty's sister, Doll Lane. Whether Deb let him down deliberately or was prevented we shall never know. Another unanswered question is whether she was in love with Pepys, as she might well have been; or had simply been unable to deal with his attentions. But although what happened may have shaken her faith in families and fathers, it was not the tragedy it might have been. She was not pregnant, and still technically a virgin. She could start her life again, and did so. There was a surprising moment when Pepys saw her in the street at the end of April, she with another gentlewoman and he with Elizabeth, who did not see her; and Deb winked and smiled at him. The next thing he heard was that she had moved to Greenwich, which set him longing to look for her again. The love affair seems to have left him more scarred than her, and he returned to it on the last page of the Diary, which speaks of 'my amours to Deb' as past.

Elizabeth embarked on a flirtation of her own with Henry Sheeres. Pepys suffered a jealous spasm or two, but Sheeres was on the point of leaving England for Tangier, and in any case Pepys regarded him as a friend. The whole business has no clear conclusion, partly because such episodes rarely do, and also because the Diary came to an end on 31 May. Pepys had responded to Elizabeth's anger because it revived his sense of the strict moral discipline in which he had been brought up, with its Christian basis, that decreed sex to be wrong and shameful outside marriage, and he saw the justice of her objection to what he had done in their home. But his response went only so far. He felt guilty when he was found out, but the power of his passion for Deb allowed him to believe he still had a right to her. It was the attitude of a romantic long before romanticism was thought of. And then outside the house, which could not be considered Elizabeth's domain, he failed to change his ways at all. He continued to have sexual relations with Betty Lane and Doll, to call on and dream of conquering Betty Michell, to keep things going with Mrs Bagwell, to look out for meetings with 'Mrs Tooker's daughters' and to flirt lewdly with an out-of-town dancing partner. Even at home, he began to fantasize about the new maid Elizabeth had taken on, Matt.[10] But none of this was perceived by Elizabeth; and, Christian ethics apart, what had made him give in to her about Deb was above all his desire for a quiet life. As a disincentive to adultery it is likely to be stronger than any moral teaching.

PART THREE
1669–1703

20. After the Diary

The Diary ended. Fear for his eyes silenced Pepys, and the unique process of self-examination and revelation closed down for good. Giving it up was, he wrote, like a form of death, 'almost as much as to see myself go into my grave'. This was not rhetoric but a serious statement. He was killing off a part of himself, the self created daily in his narrative, a creature more complete than he could ever allow himself to be again, complete as no fictional, dramatic or historical portrait had ever been. The loss for his readers is brutal as they find themselves suddenly stranded, the brilliant, troubling intimacies of the Diary replaced, for those who want to know more of his life, by official papers, parliamentary records, letters and scatterings of notes. A triple line has been drawn under his youth, and nothing he wrote later revived that voice or that person. Once the form he had created was abandoned, he and the world stood in a different relation to one another; and, as well as losing him, we are losing an unequalled record of the events of the time. No one else took up the chronicle of public events, and the 1670s seem a less lively time than the 1660s as a consequence.

He gave it up because he feared he was going blind. His eyes had started to be painful when he did close work or reading by candlelight as early as 1663 – 'and so to bed, being weary, sleepy, and my eyes begin to fail me, looking so long by candlelight upon white paper' – but over the next few years he mentioned the problem very rarely, and it was only from 1667 that it became a frequent complaint.[1] By then his eyes were suffering from his years of close work; increasingly they hurt if he read for too long, they reacted badly to bright light, and they felt sore and watered. None of the remedies he tried – spectacles, lotions, eyedrops, pills, purges, the use of a paper roll when reading – did much to help. Modern medical opinion is that he had long sight (hypermetropia), which made reading difficult, and some astigmatism. But he was not going blind, and his eyes deteriorated no further.² Whether they were helped by giving up the Diary or not, they served him adequately for the rest of his life.

This piece of good fortune apart, the year that followed the end of the Diary was catastrophic: a few months of grace, then the blows began to fall. In July 1669 his ambition to enter parliament looked as though it would soon be fulfilled when the duke of York recommended him for a parliamentary seat at Aldeburgh. Letters of support went off from Sandwich, Coventry, Povey and other influential men. A small cloud appeared when Pepys's opponents suggested that he, like his patron the duke, was a Catholic. James was in the process of converting to Catholicism, but this was not known to Pepys, and he expressed amazement at the idea that he should be under suspicion, 'my education at the University . . . the whole practice of my life, both past and present, giving testimony of my being no Papist'.³ The cloud did not go away, but grew larger and darker over the next years; but he supposed it was dealt with, and at last he and Elizabeth were free to take the holiday in France for which she had yearned for so many years.

The duke had given Pepys permission for three or four months' leave, with the idea that a long break gave a better chance of his eyes recovering. Tom Hayter was to take over his duties at the Navy Office. This should have been a perfectly satisfactory arrangement, but Pepys could not resist suggesting to the king that he might make himself useful on his trip by collecting information on foreign naval affairs. Charles took up his proposal eagerly. It meant the tour began in Holland with a look at the shipyards there, which can hardly have been what Elizabeth had in mind.⁴ Then Pepys became uneasy at the idea of being away from work for so long and cut the holiday down to two months; like many men, he found office life sustaining.

They set off in late August. He had applied to John Evelyn for advice on France and received a long letter of kindly, fussy recommendations. Evelyn suggested that they take a '*chambre garnie*' when they reached Paris, to be found for them by a friend of a friend in the Faubourg St Germain whose name he supplied; this, he explained, was the suburb favoured by Persons of Quality and so most suitable for the Pepyses.⁵ He went on to compare France with England, mostly to the detriment of the French. The Luxembourg Palace resembled Clarendon House, so much admired by Pepys. Notre-Dame was

infinitely inferior to St Paul's or Westminster Abbey. The Place
Royale 'is our Piazza of Covent Garden'. At the Sorbonne they should
attend a 'public Scholastical Exercise, and love our own Universities
the better after it'. Fontainebleau 'you will not judge comparable to
Hampton Court; nor can the French monarch shew such a Castle,
Palace, and Church, as our Windsor in all his wide Dominions'. Only
the Pont-neuf surpassed its English equivalent and would make them
'wish ours of London had no more houses upon it'. (The Pont-neuf
had none.) 'By some especial Favour you may be admitted to take a
View of the Bastille (which is their Tower).' He especially recommended climbing to the top of the Tour St Jacques, from which the
whole city could be seen, and visiting the Louvre to attend a public
audience of King Louis XIV and his queen; and there was a great deal
about libraries, galleries, engravers and print shops, botanical gardens,
hospitals and excursions out of Paris – far more than they could hope
to see in the few weeks at their disposal. Elizabeth may have wanted
to show her husband the streets she remembered from her childhood,
even perhaps the convent where the nuns had done their best to make
her into a good Roman Catholic; and Balty, who was with them for
at least part of the trip, may have had his suggestions. But the truth is
we have almost no idea what they did apart from shopping for precious
stones and embroidery wools for her, and books about Paris for him;
Elizabeth also may have sat for Pierre Lombart, famous for his female
portraits.[6] Paris was prospering, with solid private mansions going up
along the Île St Louis, and old churches such as St Sulpice being
rebuilt; and Pepys wrote afterwards that it was 'a voyage full of health
and content'.[7] They visited Rouen on their return journey, and
Elizabeth sent a thank you present of a mirror to the wife of a merchant
there as they travelled on to Brussels and so back to England.[8]

On the journey home, Elizabeth was taken ill. They reached
Seething Lane on 20 October, and she went straight to bed.[9] Hollier,
who knew her well, was doubtless called, as well as her physician. She
was running a fever that did not respond to treatment. As Pepys
struggled to understand and deal with this alarming situation, he was
also brought bad news from the office. It came in the shape of a
formidable list of questions from a parliamentary committee that had
been sitting at Brooke House for several months now, looking into
alleged abuses in the Navy Office; they wanted prompt and detailed

answers, and his fellow officers relied on him to provide them. With all this on his mind, he nevertheless sent a punctilious note to Evelyn, thanking him for his helpful advice on France. It is dated 2 November and said they had been back for ten days, and that his wife had been 'from the first day of her coming back into London . . . under a fever so severe as at this hour to render her recovery desperate'. Desperate as her condition was, his tone was stately and his sentences ornate. He went on, 'Which affliction hath very much unfitted me for those acts of civility and respect which, amongst the first of my friends, I should have paid to yourself, as he to whom singly I owe the much greater part of the satisfaction I have met with in my late voyage. Next to you, I have my acknowledgments to make to Sir Samuel Tuke, to whom (when in condition of doing it) I shall beg your introducing me, for the owning of my obligations to him on the like behalf.'[10] This is an admirable piece of politeness towards his distinguished friend, to whom he naturally wrote with the elaborate ceremoniousness used among gentlemen: and so remote from the voice of the Diary that it seems to come from a different man.

Eight more days went by, days without any proper structure, elastic in their hours and minutes, depending on the arrival of the doctor with his guarded face and careful words; on precious snatches of speech from the patient; on the smallest changes in her breathing; days when the watcher hardly dared to sleep himself and yet grew increasingly exhausted; days that must have carried Pepys back to the bedside of his dying brother Tom, and to even earlier sickbeds in which his young brothers and sisters had sweated and strained to keep the flame of life flickering. A fever could snuff out a life in days, as had happened to Cromwell, but at twenty-nine Elizabeth was young and strong and her body fought for her. And while he watched, he had at the back of his mind both his parliamentary agent in Aldeburgh, waiting for him to come and ingratiate himself with the electors, due to vote on 9 November, and the Brooke House commissioners' accusing questions. On the first he gave up; the second he had to think about, planning rebuttals in his head.

Elizabeth's struggle lasted for three weeks. Two desperate remedies for severe illness were to cut off the hair and to put pigeons at the patient's feet, and both had been used for the queen in 1663. She had recovered, but if they were tried in Elizabeth's case they did her no good.[11] On 9 or 10 November Pepys sent for Daniel Mills, the vicar of St Olave's, to whose child Elizabeth had stood as godmother in happier days, and he came to give her the sacrament. As far as we know, it was the first time she had received it for many years; her religious loyalties were in any case uncertain. The intense interest Pepys displayed fifteen years later in the king's deathbed return to the Catholic faith may hark back to Elizabeth's last hours, when he had to decide what to do. He must have remembered her saying, after the death of his brother Tom, that she intended to die a Catholic, and how she repeated that she was a Catholic at another time of stress, over Deb, in October 1668. Pepys chose to put aside this knowledge, and, although he rather liked Father Fogourdy and rather disliked Mills, he did what convention and prudence dictated.[12] By then she was no doubt past making any request or decision for herself.

We do not know whether her father and mother came face to face with their son-in-law for the first time in years over her deathbed, but it seems possible, and from then on Pepys contributed to their support.[13] No doubt Will Hewer came to weep his farewell, and Jane and Tom Edwards; cousin Jane Turner, Mary Mercer and her mother, Tom Hayter and his wife, whom Elizabeth had helped in childbirth, and their old friends and neighbours from Axe Yard, John and Elizabeth Hunt, may be imagined, a trail of mournful figures making their way to the house. Lord Sandwich was in London, which he rarely left these days; he knew the taste of grief himself from the death of his daughter Paulina earlier in the year, and surely dispatched a servant – Robert Ferrar perhaps – for news of his beautiful cousin. Pepys would have sent word of what was happening to Lady Sandwich at Hinchingbrooke, as well as to his father, brother and sister; and, even as Elizabeth lay dying, a new generation was launched at last in Huntingdonshire, where Pall – Mrs John Jackson – was about to give birth to her first child. This was a son and, somewhat surprisingly, she named him Samuel and invited her brother to stand as godfather.[14]

Elizabeth died on 10 November and Pepys fixed the funeral for the evening of the 13th at St Olave's. Night-time was the preferred time for the fashionable, and John Evelyn's diary tells us that he stayed in town and travelled home the next day after being present 'the night before at the funeral of Mrs Pepys'. Otherwise there is no account of the ceremony. The church bell would be tolled, the house draped in black and all the family servants given their mourning. Inside the church, faintly lit with candles, Mr Mills read the appointed words for the burial of the dead, and Elizabeth's comely body was laid under the floor of the chancel. Although there is a note of his brother Tom's funeral expenses among Pepys's miscellaneous papers, there is none of Elizabeth's. At this last he was generous to her memory. He composed a Latin epitaph, praising her knowledge and her beauty and perhaps overpraising her lineage. He also commissioned a memorial bust from a brilliantly inventive and original sculptor, John Bushnell. He had studied in Rome when Bernini was working there and went on to make great Baroque statues of Charles II, Charles I, and Sir Thomas Gresham for the Royal Exchange building, as well as memorials of Albemarle and the poet Abraham Cowley for Westminster Abbey.[15] Pepys could not have chosen better, and Bushnell produced a triumphant result. There is no suggestion of heavenly piety or submission to God's will about his bust of Elizabeth. Instead she is shown as though in mid conversation, slightly smiling, her mouth open and her eyes wide, still intent on the comedy of the world. Somehow he has given her more of a French than an English air; and you ask yourself what you would have to say to this lively young matron who looks as though she might speak sharply at any minute. The bust was set high up on the wall of the church and makes a very striking, speaking, humanist representation to match the portrait in the Diary. When the memorial was put up, the Navy Office gallery in which Pepys and his colleagues sat allowed a much closer view, but that has gone and it is now difficult to appreciate her properly from the floor of the church; but she has weathered the centuries well and survived being taken down when the bombs of the Second World War threatened.[16]

There were letters of condolence on the 'decease of your Deere & vertuous Lady' to be answered, and for months Pepys sealed his own letters with black sealing wax.[17] The surest distraction from grief was work, and there was no shortage of that. Two weeks after the funeral, he had written out his answers to the Brooke House Commission, which he then delivered in person. Even there he was reminded of his loss. It happened that the clerk was his one-time friend Will Symons; they had been married in the same place and within months of one another. Pepys had seen him soon after Will lost his wife, and noted disapprovingly how inappropriate his conversation was for a bereaved man. Now they were both young widowers.

On Monday, 2 December, Pepys was officially back in his office, and the following Monday he attended the duke of York in Whitehall with the whole board. The next morning he was in Whitehall early to confer with the duke's secretary.[18] On 14 December he signed papers that gave him a power of attorney for Sandwich, on whose behalf he could now demand and receive payments; his old patron remained confident of Pepys's financial skills.[19] His other former employer, Downing, also wrote to him from the Treasury, asking him to help elucidate the claims of Carteret as treasurer of the navy, which ran to more than £500,000, not all of which they believed to have been spent on the war: a delicate situation for Pepys, who was 'cousin' to Carteret since his son's marriage to Jemima Montagu.[20]

January and February were fully occupied with almost daily sessions at Brooke House before the commission. Their accusations were essentially parliament's way of expressing its dissatisfaction with the handling of the Dutch war and disgust at what had happened on the Medway. Corruption and incompetence were their theme, and they accused just about everyone from the treasurer of the navy down to the lowest purser and dockyard worker of one or the other, and often of both. Pepys himself was accused of various wrongful dealings, including private manufacture of flags, which he had indeed gone in for five years before. Coventry warned him over a dinner that he must expect rough handling, and for a few hours he brooded over the idea of giving up his job, in which he was 'yoked' with colleagues he knew to be incompetent and required to defend them from blame for failures of which he was all too aware.[21] But as soon as he came face to face with the accusers, his natural robustness and combativeness returned, and he launched into powerful, indeed bruising, counter-attacks.

His private and general defence was that the navy could not be properly run unless it was properly funded, which was true. The defences he put up in particular cases were made with bounding energy and skill in deploying his detailed knowledge of his own archives. He conceded nothing. As Richard Ollard has demonstrated, the daily record kept by Pepys of the two months' investigation was a public document, dictated to his clerks, and setting out the official defence of the Navy Office, and did not by any means represent his private view of things. For instance, he had a high regard for one of the commissioners, the old Cromwellian Colonel George Thomson, but was obliged to spar with him in public because Thomson was putting the case against the management of the recent war. Pepys knew perfectly well it had been badly managed, but he was bound to defend the Navy Office; and, in making his case for the defence, he was effectively defending the king and his policy also, which he had deplored in private so often. He carried out his difficult task with admirable skill. He was not required to be sincere.

His skill did him no harm with the king. Charles sat in on most of the meetings and saw what a well-equipped and loyal champion he had found. A new relationship blossomed. On Pepys's side the disapproval and scorn for the king expressed in the Diary appear to melt away. They were soon laughing together and supporting one another's jokes. When Charles remarked that people in the coffee houses were always saying how much things were better done in the navy during the commonwealth, '"those pure angelical times" (saith the King)', Pepys chimed in with 'those times concerning which people discourse in matters of the Navy as historians do of the primitive times in reference to the church'.[22] Pepys's own view of the commonwealth navy and its officers was almost exactly the one satirized by Charles, but an exchange of jokes with the king was too good an opportunity to be missed. Power and truth make different demands.

And Pepys was a performer, as he had already proved when he addressed parliament in 1668. Now he delighted in tripping up his opponents and rose almost friskily to a challenge. When Lord Brereton, whom he knew and liked well enough, accused him of dealing in seamen's tickets and asked, 'How, Mr Pepys, do you defy the whole world in this matter?', he answered 'Yes, that I do defy the whole world and my Lord Brereton in particular if he would be thought one of it.' You can hear the relish as the words came off his tongue. He could silence everyone with the flow of his eloquence, and was happy to go on for hours. Lord Arlington, having listened to him, felt it wise to recommend plainness and 'the least show of rhetoric' when he came to write his speeches down because, although the king was pleased, he was also easily bored.[23]

The oddest performance of the whole affair was Pepys's letter to the commissioners in which he laid out his own defence. It began in a perhaps justifiable display of self-righteousness and self-congratulation and ended in bare-faced lies. His diligence during the plague, his frequent Sunday work and late hours, often until midnight, the greatness of the burden that he had shouldered and the damage to his eyes were all listed. What he said was undeniable, although it might have come better from someone else; but no one else could have been called as a witness in the tricky matter of corrupt dealings. Pepys claimed he had never asked for any fee, gratuity or reward, and that anything offered to him was accepted only if he believed the affair was to the advantage of His Majesty; he insisted that he was owed £400 in expenses – a fine counter-attack – and roundly asserted that his ten years of service had not bettered his estate by so much as one thousand pounds.[24] Even Bryant, for whom Pepys could do little wrong, called this last statement a 'daring lie'.[25] He must have felt so secure in his accounting methods – and in Hewer's support – that he could defy all questions. Referring obliquely to his Diary, he also boasted that he was 'able upon oath' to give an account of his daily employment during his entire time of working for the Navy Office; here too he was confident he could keep his documents to himself.[26]

By the end of the Brooke House sittings, which lasted for two months, everyone must have felt that, whatever criticisms might be levelled against Pepys, he was a good man to have on your side. He ended his own report by declaring that 'the whole business of these Observations ended, with a profession of all satisfaction on his Majesty's part in reference to every particular'.[27] Of his fellow officials at the Navy Board during the war, Batten was dead and Penn close to death – he died in September 1670. Coventry and Carteret had left the board in 1667, Pett had been pushed out, and Sir John Mennes was not held responsible for anything – he died in February 1671. Only Brouncker and Pepys remained of the old guard to take the blame. Neither lost his job. Pepys's retirement to the country could be postponed.

So, for the time being, were his hopes of entering parliament. He had lost the by-election at Aldeburgh, not surprisingly, given that he had been unable to visit the town. Now he returned to the routine of the office and the comfort of working with his chosen clerks, Hewer,

Hayter, Gibson and Edwards. Will was the most intimate, trusted like a second self; with Tom he could make music as well as keep the shipping lists up to date; Hayter had been solidly with him from the start, and Gibson too was a man of his own age who knew the history of the commonwealth navy from his own experience, and besides could quote John Donne.[28] They made an orderly, hard-working, intelligent and loyal team, the nearest thing to a family of sons and brothers. It was his real brother John who was a problem, kicking his heels at the Jacksons' in Huntingdonshire. When Pepys heard in March of a clerkship going at Trinity House, the seamen's foundation, he urged John to come to London at once, and on the same day wrote to the duke of York, to Sandwich, to Evelyn's father-in-law Sir Richard Browne and to other worthies, asking them to support John Pepys for the post. He described John to them as a sober and diligent scholar whom he had long intended for such a position and coached personally with it in view; never mind that the truth was that he had been on poor terms with John, who was unemployed at twenty-nine and had never had a job.[29] Pepys's mighty effort on his behalf was successful, and John moved to the Trinity House in Water Lane. He worked there unobtrusively under his brother's directions; his tobacco and wine bills have survived, as well as evidence that he sent gifts to old Mr Pepys and to Pall and her son – a little boy's hat, some oysters, claret, a bottle of spirits and boxes of sweetmeats.[30] Only a year before Pepys had launched a furious memorandum complaining of the way clerks were appointed, 'chosen for the sake of acquaintance, kindred, or some other ground in which their present qualifications bore no part.' He had forgotten his own start and failed to foresee his brother's.[31]

The pattern of his life re-established itself. The minute books of the Navy Board show meetings starting at 8 a.m. every Monday, Wednesday and Friday. There were the usual contracts to be dealt with and visits to be made to Deptford, Woolwich and Chatham, though perhaps he went less often on foot now that he had his own coach, and was less inclined to walk through the fields between Rotherhithe and Deptford with a book to read. In May 1670 he prepared a summary of the financial state of the navy to present to the king. He calculated that £900,000 were needed to pay off last year's debts and to repair and supply the ships and dockyards.[32] In June he wrote a much fuller paper 'for my own satisfaction', showing how much more money was needed for the navy than the £200,000 projected for its maintenance this year: his estimate of the real cost was over twice that sum.[33] Nothing like this was found. The king could never be trusted to follow a straight path, and he was busy with more thrilling projects. That same May he sent Sandwich to fetch his sister Henriette, wife of the brother of Louis XIV, from Dunkirk and went to meet her at Dover. She came with a secret treaty by which France offered Charles £150,000 to declare himself a Catholic and provoke a war with Holland when Louis was ready; there was to be more money – £225,000 a year – while the war lasted. Charles did not make any public declaration of his Catholic faith, but he was set on course for confrontations with parliament, and for a third Dutch war.

The tragedy of Pepys's career is that it was spent serving masters, first Charles and then James, who wanted to build up their personal power and defeat parliament. For twenty-eight years they replayed the struggles of the 1640s, and took their French cousin, the absolute monarch Louis XIV, as a model; and in the long run they were bound to lose. By temperament and upbringing a parliamentarian, Pepys found himself trapped on the wrong side, professionally bound to kings whose ambition was doomed and patronage poisoned.

The Diary tells us enough about Pepys's sensibility to suggest how, at Elizabeth's death, he must have suffered, wept, recalled her beauty and his love for her, and reproached himself for his failings and bad behaviour. It also tells us that he was quick to recover from grief, and too interested in the world and his role in it to turn away from his busy life, so much of which had in any case been led apart from her. While she was alive, his entertainments had been the theatre, shopping and making improvements to the house; the Royal Society meetings; walks and excursions on the river; reading and music, whether listening or making it himself: he had written in the Diary on a cheerless day that 'music is the thing of the world that I love most, and all the pleasure almost that I can now take', and this remained true for him through good and bad times.[34] There was also dining with friends and inviting them to the house, gossiping and pursuing women. None of these activities required the presence of a wife, and he was fully capable of ordering his own household, with some assistance at first no doubt from Mrs Edwards, his 'little old Jane', and then from a housekeeper.

The only entertainment he is known to have attended in January 1670 was the hanging of the highwayman Claude Duval at Tyburn, a very popular event; if he felt up to that, you have to hope he found better distraction in the theatre. That spring, Dryden made Nell Gwyn get up from her stage deathbed for a witty ending to his play *Tyrannic Love*. 'Hold! are you mad? you damned, confounded dog!' she scolded the stage hands preparing to carry her offstage. 'I am to rise, and speak the epilogue.' She went on to offer to haunt the beds of the men in the audience: 'And faith you'll be in a sweet kind of taking/When I surprise you between sleep and waking.' Perhaps Pepys dreamt of Nelly, as he had dreamt of other ladies who took the king's fancy. Waking, a determined man might have traced Deb, but a remorseful one, remembering Elizabeth's rage, was likely to have felt such a search would border on sacrilege; besides which, Deb herself could have other ideas even if he did succeed in finding her. There were still Betty Martin, her sister Doll and Mrs Bagwell to minister to one sort of itch, and Knipp for a glamorous fumble, and there is no reason to think he gave up their company. He may even have kept up his hopes of Betty Michell, with her baby and her cross husband in the spirit shop by the river. He also found, with impressive speed, a new mistress, young and an undoubted lady; her story will have to wait for another chapter.

Pepys was an intensely sociable being, and he had friends for every occasion, the Pearses for gossip and good company; the Crews for serious conversation; the Hunts for talk of old times; Anthony Deane, the shipbuilder, when he was in London, for shop; Povey, a fool maybe, but good-hearted, rich, another gossip and a generous host. The playwright and poet Thomas Shadwell and his actress wife became close enough friends to ask him to be godfather to their son John.[35] Brouncker was a colleague with whom he shared other interests than work, notably the Royal Society, of which Brouncker was a long-serving president; and Coventry was happy to talk politics with him. His cousin Barbara, daughter of Roger Pepys, married Dr Thomas Gale in 1674, bringing him a new friend both learned and convivial. Gale was a scholar of distinction and high master of St Paul's

School; and the youngest Gale boy became another godson to Pepys. The City bankers such as Sir Robert Vyner and Edward Backwell were well disposed to Pepys, who had nearly £7,000 on deposit with Backwell in 1671; and the hugely wealthy Sir John Banks of the East India Company, ennobled by the king for lending him money in 1661 and a steady supplier of loans to the navy, found Pepys a congenial companion. Creed, an irritant throughout the Diary, had leapt ahead with his marriage and was preparing to leave London to live as a country gentleman in Oundle, where he fathered eleven children and became high sheriff of Northamptonshire.[36]

The best of Pepys's friends in the City were the Houblon clan, French Protestants who had brought their business skills to London from Lille in the 1590s, fleeing religious persecution. The older James Houblon was well established as a merchant by the time of the civil war and gave his support to the parliamentarians, to whom he supplied horses and arms, and probably money too. He reared seven sons, of whom five became merchants. Their trading and shipping business covered the world, and the origins of their friendship with Pepys lay in business connections, since a member of the Navy Board had obvious uses for merchants who depended on their ships getting about freely. So they cultivated him; he expected to benefit financially, and he did. The second James Houblon became his particular friend. Pepys dined with him in 1665 – a masculine dinner, although he was taken afterwards into another room to hear Mrs Houblon sing – and the Diary records a 'present' of £200 to Pepys in 1666, for licensing two voyages at a difficult time for shipping.[37] They talked business and politics from time to time in the late 1660s. Five of the brothers supped with Pepys together on one occasion, on another he dined with them at a tavern without Elizabeth, and when James Houblon called he left his wife waiting outside in the carriage with a companion.[38] So it was only after Elizabeth's death that the relationship developed into an intimate family one. The younger James and his English wife Sarah were of an age with Pepys and had been married in 1658; and they welcomed him warmly into their home, a fine large house, formerly the Spanish ambassador's, in Great Winchester Street, close to London Wall and between Moorgate and Bishopsgate. There the business was conducted and the four children brought up, and there they also entertained in splendid style. Evelyn described James

Houblon as living '*en prince*' when he dined with him, and Pepys, after another dinner, said none of the food or wine came from anywhere nearer than Persia, China and the Cape of Good Hope.[39] Sarah appears from her portraits to have been a beauty, dark eyed and dark haired, dressed and bejewelled as sumptuously as a court lady.[40]

Many of Pepys's friends in the post-Diary years were rich, and the Houblons were among the richest; and, while money spoke to Pepys, his friendship with them developed into something true and deep, involving the women of the family as well as the men. They found Pepys delightful, and he reciprocated. In December 1670 he wrote sending a 'hand kiss' to Madam, telling them to expect a Christmas visit and hoping they would make a return one to him.[41] After this there were theatre trips and outings to Chelsea; Pepys and Sarah took to singing together, and in later years they all shared a holiday cottage at Parson's Green. He called them 'cousin' and took an avuncular interest in the next generation, 'my sweet W[ynne]' and 'little Jemmy'.[42] Sarah told him that the children of the family were born with the instinct to wish him well, and Pepys lavished on them the affection he might have given his own children, had there been any.[43] They had fun together, and exchanged intimate letters; Pepys sent a 'merry, roguish, mysterious letter to S. H.' – presumably Sarah – on his way to Tangier in 1683, and his letters to James are affectionate and witty.[44] Because the Houblons had never known him young, poor, a servant, one who sat half tongue-tied and envying the talk of gallants in the theatre, he could be at ease with them and confident as the man of the world he had become; and they satisfied a yearning in him to be part of another, ideal family, a new version of the once idealized Montagus.

He may well have kept in touch with his various poor cousins, but almost nothing more is heard of them. In their place more recently discovered family connections appear on the scene.[45] They were Lady Mordaunt and her sister Mrs Steward, cousins by marriage through Jane Turner's husband – the Ashtead connection again – and they lived elegantly in Portugal Row, on the south side of Lincoln's Inn Fields. Betty Mordaunt, twice widowed, still young, lively and sociable and with her own income, was happy to have Pepys as an escort to the theatre and a dinner guest; a little light, risk-free flirting took place.[46] They were a far cry from Pepys's Joyce cousins, also sisters, who had caused him trouble in the past. These two new-found connections were presentable enough to be introduced into the circle of John Evelyn, with whom Pepys dined for the first time early in 1671; and the growing friendship with Evelyn, gentleman-scholar and courtier, was another sign of his rising status in society.

He watched his finances as carefully as he had always done. In June 1670 he made a note that he was charging 6 per cent on the £100 he had lent Lady Sandwich two years earlier and the same on the £500 lent to Lord Sandwich; he did not consider waiving his interest.[47] When the king, in one of his most unscrupulous acts, put a stop on the Exchequer in January 1672, which meant that no one who had lent money to the government could withdraw it, many of his subjects were ruined, and the big bankers put into severe difficulties, among them Pepys's banker Backwell; but Pepys himself was unscathed. He had moved his savings elsewhere and converted his credit with Backwell to an overdraft, almost certainly because he had advance warning of the Stop.[48]

With a keen eye out for chances of promotion he gave dinners for important people. Baron Ashley Cooper, soon to be lord chancellor and earl of Shaftesbury, with whom he had dined in 1667, made at least one social visit to Seething Lane at this time.[49] Pepys reacted speedily when he heard of a chance of advancement. As Sir John Mennes lay dying in February 1671, he sent off a letter to the duke of York stressing the importance of appointing a man of proven ability to succeed him in charge of the Navy Board. It was not the first time he had made the point, and he was careful to disclaim any ambition to be given the job himself, but he was positioning himself. Sir Thomas Allen would be appointed this time, but next time, who knows?[50]

Another letter about promotion went off the following year when England was at war with the Dutch, in alliance with the French as the king had promised. The war was unpopular in England, and Lord Sandwich himself declared that he neither understood the reason for it nor approved of it. All the same, as vice-admiral he went to sea in the spring of 1672, with the duke of York in command of the fleet again. Sandwich was in a melancholy state of mind. He told friends he expected to die, and in so doing retrieve his reputation. He still resented the accusations of greed and cowardice that had been made against him in 1665, and may have felt his commonwealth past was not entirely forgotten or forgiven.[51] When the Dutch fleet was known to be threatening the east coast in May, he advised caution and sensed that the duke suspected him of cowardice.

If so, the duke was wrong. Sandwich dined gloomily with a younger officer on the evening of Whit Monday, 27 May, and early the next morning, when news came that the Dutch were approaching, he had his valet tie back his long hair and dress him in his full regalia as a knight of the Garter, with jewelled collar and star on breast, a black plumed hat on his head. After this ceremonious preparation, he commanded his flagship, the *Royal James*, so that it bore the brunt of the battle fought off the Suffolk coast, in Sole Bay, on 28 May. He was the first to engage the Dutch. The fighting was savage on both sides; Sandwich destroyed several enemy ships, but by nine in the morning his own hull was badly damaged by shot and many hundreds of his crew were dead or wounded. Still he drove off fireships and the *Groot Hollandia* when it came alongside, tangling the rigging of the two ships so that they had to cut themselves free. Then, in the dense smoke of the battle, another fireship set the *Royal James* ablaze. With most of his men and officers dead, and no help forthcoming from any other English vessel, Sandwich knew he could not save his ship.

There have been many conflicting accounts of what happened. Captain Richard Haddock tried to persuade Sandwich to leave his ship and failed; wounded himself, he slipped through a porthole and swam until he was picked up by an English boat. He was almost the only officer to survive; Sandwich's son-in-law, Philip Carteret, did not. A few of the men got away in 'the jolly-boat'. Some reported that Lord Sandwich was dead on board. Another said his body had been seen in the water but not moving. There was a suspicion that the men who got away in the boat had abandoned him, and the Dutch alleged that he was smothered in the boat by the crew jumping on him. Yet another story was that he 'did endeavour to save himself by swimming, and perished in the attempt'. The sea was 'as calm as a milk-bowl' under a bright sun, and people watching from the coast had a clear view of the ship as she burnt all through the afternoon. By six she was reduced to embers. Sandwich's fate, the subject of many rumours, remained unknown for twelve days.[52]

During this anxious period, Pepys heard that the duke of York's secretary, Matthew Wren, had been wounded in the battle, and he wrote to Coventry asking him to support his application to take over Wren's job. In terms of career, Pepys was right to seize the moment, and Coventry was the man he felt he could rely on. If Pepys hesitated at all out of respect and grief for his old Lord, lost somewhere at sea, and well aware that Sandwich regarded Coventry as his enemy, his hesitation was shortlived. He delivered his letter to Coventry in person on 3 June, spent the evening with him, got his promise to speak for him and went home happy. Early next morning a note arrived from Coventry withdrawing his support on the grounds that his nephew Henry Savile wanted the job. Both Coventry and Pepys knew that his abilities were greater than Savile's, but Pepys was not part of the charmed circle of the aristocracy, and even Coventry was not prepared to back him against one of his own family. Savile got the job: it was a cruel lesson.

Sandwich's body was found in the sea off Harwich on 10 June, by sailors dragging for lost anchors. He was still wearing his Garter ribbon, jewel and star. Lady Sandwich was given the news at Hinchingbrooke. After this Pepys spent five days with the fleet, an unusual move for him, which he may have combined with a visit to Hinchingbrooke to pay her his respects. He did not forget to do his bit for his own family, pressing the duke to make Balty's position at Deal permanent.[53]

The king ordered a state funeral for Sandwich, and on 3 July his embalmed body was borne along the Thames at the head of a procession of barges draped in black and carrying most of the leading men of the state – women did not attend such occasions. The guns fired from the Tower and Whitehall, and drums and trumpets added their solemn noise. From Westminster stairs the mourners followed the body on foot into the abbey, to be buried in Henry VII's chapel, where Albemarle already lay: so the two men chiefly responsible for restoring Charles to his throne were placed beside one another. Pepys had charge of one of the great banners displaying the dead man's arms, carried alongside the coffin and then laid over his resting place.[54]

Sandwich was only forty-six. Pepys was thirty-nine; it no longer seemed such a gap as it had been when he was a poor boy and his cousin a statesman and soldier. While there had been no total breach between the two men, they had been on cooler terms with the passing of the years. Gratitude can grow irksome, and there were reasons for resentment on both sides. Sandwich did not mention Pepys in his will, and Pepys may have felt liberated as well as bereaved. Yet he owed Sandwich too much, and their lives had been too closely linked, for him not to feel the shock of the loss of the man who had dominated his youth and given him his chance in life. Sandwich bequeathed the Manor of Brampton to his Lady, which suggests she felt an attachment to the place; but as dowager she had to leave Hinchingbrooke, which had been her home for nearly thirty years. Since she had lost her two eldest daughters, she took herself to live close to her third daughter, Anne, who had just married Sir Richard Edgcumbe and gone to live on his estate on the River Tamar, in Cornwall.[55] It is unlikely she and Pepys met again. In his will, Sandwich spoke of her as 'my dear and loving wife (to whom I cannot express kindness enough)', spelling out at the end his love and respect for the patience, innocence and loyalty of the woman he had married when they were both seventeen.[56] She was no Lucy Hutchinson or Anne Fanshawe, and never thought of putting down any account of her life – her few letters show she was a barely literate – so that hers remains a sadly untold story.[57] Bred in a family of the puritan gentry, bride of one of the youngest officers in the parliamentarian army, she had known Charles I, Cromwell and Charles II, presided over a great country house, borne ten children and conducted herself with exemplary discretion throughout civil wars and many changes of government; supported her husband through danger and long periods of separation, as well as ennoblement and favour at a court that had nothing to offer a woman of her breeding and character. She lived only two years after her husband's death. The warmth of Pepys's admiration and his unwavering affection for her in the Diary make up a rare tribute, and, although her name appears no more among his papers, he took the trouble to visit her daughter Anne in Cornwall, where Lady Sandwich had ended her days, as he sailed for Tangier in 1683. Whether he stood beside her grave then or not, he cannot have failed to think of her.[58]

There were two more deaths in Pepys's family circle in 1672. In August his father-in-law, Alexandre de St Michel, died in Deal, where he and his wife were living with their son. It made little difference to Pepys, who continued to be the chief support of all the remaining St Michels, including another nephew and godson, 'Litell Samuell'. In September uncle Wight, who had once hoped to impregnate

Elizabeth on Pepys's behalf, also died, leaving no living children and no will. Some good came of this to Pepys's father, who was able to make a successful claim on part of the estate.

A further break with the past came in January 1673. The Navy Board minute book for 30 January gives its own account: 'Yesterday between 3 and 4 a Clock in the morning happened in my Lord Brouncker's lodging at the Navy Office in Seething Lane an unhappy fire, which in six hours time Laid in ashes the said office, with Severall of the houses about it.'[59] Abigail Williams, Lord Brouncker's mistress, was credited with starting the blaze in her closet. Pepys had time to save his books, including the six volumes of his Diary, otherwise very little. His house and more than twenty others round about were entirely destroyed as well as the offices. The nightmares he had suffered after the great fire had come true, and the house into which he had put so much of himself and that enshrined the memory of his years with Elizabeth was gone as though it had never been. Financially, he lost only the contents, since it belonged to the crown, and the crown was obliged to rehouse him; but for a man who set so much store by the choice and placing of his possessions, and who cared about the shape and meaning of life, it must have acted as an after-shock to the loss of his wife. His goods, his clothes, his pictures, his living habits and arrangements and all the rest of his physical connections with the past were gone.

21. Public and Private Life

Pepys went into lodgings. 'Fusty lodgings', according to Sarah Houblon, but he had not much choice after the fire. The Navy Office had to be kept running. They continued to deal with their business, three times a week at 8 a.m., now on Tuesday, Thursday and Saturday, without a break, re-establishing themselves in Mark Lane, a block west of the old site; and his lodgings were close by, provided by the crown.[1] Here he lived out the rest of 1673; and in the course of the year good fortune returned to him. In June he was appointed secretary to the Admiralty Board, and by January 1674 he achieved his ambition to enter parliament, taking his seat in the House of Commons alongside his old masters William Coventry and George Downing. In that same month he moved, after thirteen years in the City returning to the west end of his youth. He did not take a house this time but moved into the new Admiralty headquarters, Derby House, between Whitehall and Westminster, installing himself and his servants in airy rooms above the offices. He had become, in modern terms, a flat dweller, enjoying a view over the river for the first time. His salary and fees were increased, and, as he went up the ladder, he took his own people with him. Will Hewer now became chief clerk to the Admiralty, and within a year he took a lease on a very large new house in a smart terrace, York Buildings in Buckingham Street, which ran from the Strand down to a terrace walk over the river and the water gate built for the newly demolished York House.[2] Tom Hayter and John Pepys were given Pepys's old job as clerk of the acts to share between them, and Pepys also saw to the advancement of his brother-in-law St Michel, Tom Edwards and Richard Gibson.[3] Coventry sent congratulations on the secretaryship and, with a neat touch of flattery, asked Pepys to exert his powers of patronage to find a purser's job for the brother of one of his servants.[4]

Whatever Pepys's private opinion of the king, he owed all his advancement to royal favour. Charles and his parliament were on bad terms. The country was edgy and suspicious of the intentions of the royal family, fearing it was moving towards despotism and Catholicism under the influence of the French. Anti-Catholic feeling became so strong that a Test Act was passed in the spring of 1673, obliging all office holders to affirm their loyalty to the Church of England. It was now generally known that James, duke of York, had converted to Catholicism, as had the duchess before her death in 1671. Like Pepys, James had just lost his wife, and he was preparing to marry again, a Catholic-born princess of fifteen who could be expected to bring him sons. Since the king had no legitimate children, the prospect of a Catholic inheritance to the crown loomed, unacceptably. Charles seems to have had little faith, and, if he had Catholic leanings, he was prepared to dissemble rather than lose his crown, and he avoided confrontation even when exasperated by his parliaments, so that when his brother refused to conform, or even to pretend to conform, as the Test Act required, he accepted that James must lose his office as lord high admiral. This was when he promoted Pepys to the new post of secretary to the Admiralty.

He replaced the duke with a group of Admiralty commissioners made up of favourite courtiers, strengthened by Prince Rupert, experienced in command at sea, and the earl of Shaftesbury, who was keen on the war against the Dutch. The king himself took the chair. Pepys's job was purely administrative, and, while he made himself felt in matters of naval discipline, he had no say in policy; but he and his royal patrons believed he might become an influential spokesman for the navy in parliament.[5] This was the reason for finding him a safe seat at a by-election. The duke of York still had enough power of patronage to get Pepys nominated and, it was hoped, elected without trouble. As it turned out, his patronage also meant that when Pepys presented himself at Castle Rising in Norfolk in the autumn of 1673 he was accused of being 'a Bluddy Papist' and jeered at by the crowd. Shaftesbury, fiercely anti-Catholic – he had personally tried to persuade the duke to return to the Church of England – gave secret support to the rival candidate, and Pepys had to submit testimonials to his own Anglican faith to the voters. He won the election, but the papist mud stuck.[6]

As soon as Pepys took his seat in the House of Commons he felt the hostility. First he was attacked on naval matters, which he could deal with well enough, but then came the personal accusations. That he was a Catholic. That he had an altar and a crucifix in his house. That he had broken his wife's heart by trying to convert her to Catholicism, an allegation that must have amused and enraged him privately. Someone remembered him saying that the Anglican religion 'came out of Henry VIII's codpiece'.[7] The tone and level of the attack was disconcerting, especially for a new MP, unfamiliar with the ways of the House and not yet part of the club. One of his accusers, Sir Robert Thomas, said he was ready to produce witnesses. Coventry, coming to Pepys's aid, said it would be hard for anyone to defend themselves against the remark about Henry VIII's codpiece; to him, as to us, it seemed likely enough that Pepys had made the joke, and perfectly ridiculous to raise it against him in the House. Coventry then challenged Thomas to name his witnesses. He was reluctant. The speaker insisted, and Lord Shaftesbury was named. Sensation in the House.

Shaftesbury, known to the king and his brother as 'Little Sincerity' in sardonic reference to his small stature and many changes of allegiance, was a man of ideas, clever, rich from birth, interested in power, popular in parliament and at this point embarked on a campaign to exclude the duke of York from the succession to the throne. Any ammunition that came to hand was useful, and, if he could show that the new secretary to the Admiralty and MP was a covert Catholic, it would serve his purpose well. The fact that he had known Pepys personally for years through Sandwich – whose colleague he had been under Cromwell and through all the changes since – and also through the Tangier Committee did not trouble him. The House appointed a group of MPs to go to him; the earl was not someone you sent for. Pepys, who had until now admired Shaftesbury for his brains and wit, asked to go with them.[8] Coventry supported Pepys's application. Meanwhile a message arrived at the House from Shaftesbury, saying 'he hath some imperfect memory of seeing somewhat, which he conceived to be a Crucifix . . . could not remember whether it were painted or carved, or in what manner the Thing was; and, that his Memory was so very imperfect in it, that, if he were upon his Oath, he could give no Testimony'. Face to face with Coventry and Pepys, he decided he had *not* seen an altar but still thought he *had* seen a crucifix. As they left, he could not resist teasing his victim: 'Mr Pepys, the next time we meet, we will remember the Pope!'

On 10 February Pepys stood up in the House and 'did heartily and flatly deny, that he had any Altar, or Crucifix, or the Image of a Picture of any Saint whatsoever in his House, from the Top to the Bottom of it'. Coventry pointed out that a great many would be found to be Catholics if ownership of a picture of the crucifixion were taken as evidence. Pepys asked Shaftesbury to see him alone. He refused, and Pepys then wrote inviting him to declare himself unequivocally either for or against having seen a crucifix, and reminding him of their twenty years' acquaintance.[9] It did him no good. He also wrote to St Michel, requesting support for his claim to being a good Anglican; Balty obliged at length, throwing in a paragraph on Elizabeth's convinced Protestantism for good measure.[10] In the House, Sir John Banks, the financier, declared he had known Pepys for years and visited him at home without ever seeing either altar or crucifix or thinking he was a Catholic.

Pepys then spoke in his own defence. He went back to his Cambridge years and his early service as secretary to Lord Sandwich. He said he had attended church twice every Sunday and taken communion seven or eight times a year, and never in his life been at mass. He spoke of how he had embellished his home with paintings because his work prevented him from going out much; and described the small table in his closet with the Bible and Book of Common Prayer on it, a basin, a cushion and his wife's picture above – this, he thought, might be the supposed altar. He was angry, frightened and sorry for himself, and he did what Englishmen are not expected to do, showed his feelings.[11] More testimony was produced, none of it decisive, and he declared himself ready to submit to the judgement of the House. The debate was adjourned for two weeks. Before they were up, the king prorogued parliament, meaning that its sittings were discontinued, until November. Without this intervention, Pepys would almost certainly have lost his seat. It was the worst start anyone could have had in the House. Royal favour had raised him and at the same time exposed him to entirely unforeseen dangers.

Did 'Little Sincerity' really believe Pepys was a Catholic? Something that suggested a shrine had clearly caught his attention at Seething Lane, possibly the painting of the crucifixion Pepys had bought in the days of the Diary. He may also have heard gossip about Pepys attending mass. We know that what took Pepys to mass was curiosity and a liking for the music, not religious faith; and in private, among equals, Shaftesbury might well have accepted that his interest was aesthetic and anthropological, and nothing to do with religion. He himself, when asked about his religion by a lady, answered that 'wise men are of but one religion', and when pressed as to which religion this was, said 'wise men never tell'; and Bishop Burnet declared that he was 'a deist at best' where religion was concerned.[12] But even if Shaftesbury's allegiance to the Church of England was more political than spiritual, he had marked Pepys in his mind as vulnerable to attack and so potentially useful to his cause.

Curiously, Pepys failed to take warning from the clash with Shaftesbury and parliament. You might have expected him at least to burnish his credentials as a member of the Church of England. Instead he proceeded to send for and install in his house a Roman Catholic musician, Cesare Morelli, recommended to him by a friend in Lisbon.[13] Morelli, fluent in Latin and several modern languages, and a fine singer and performer on the lute, had lived in Flanders, Rome and Lisbon, but longed to return to England, which he had once visited. He was to be Pepys's luxury, someone of his own with whom he could make music whenever he chose; having abased himself to the House, he became defiant and proud and felt he had a right to this pleasure. He made the arrangement with Morelli in November, about the time parliament met again, and Morelli arrived in the spring of 1675. In the increasingly hysterical anti-Catholic climate he was a risky luxury.

All the same, Pepys bounced back with characteristic verve after his difficult start in the House. He was always an effective speaker on naval matters and he soon showed himself a brilliant one again, as he had done in 1668. In April 1675 he gave an account of the state of the navy, and in February 1677 made a speech urging that money should be voted for the building of thirty new ships; he succeeded in winning over an initially suspicious House to vote the necessary £600,000.[14] It was a triumph but did not prevent him from being regularly sniped at on smaller matters, especially where he was suspected of less than pure financial dealings, over fees received for granting passes to ship-owners, for instance. Even without the testimony of the Diary, we can believe that there was still a Pepys who made money on the side, as well as the other Pepys who stunned everyone by his grasp of naval matters and authority of exposition. And even this Pepys could be resented in the House; he was accused of speaking 'more like an admiral than a secretary'. No doubt he did. The French ambassador reported that he was one of the best speakers in England.[15] Few MPs had any knowledge of the navy, and the secretary of the Admiralty had made up his mind to educate them.

He still consulted with the duke of York about naval appointments, and worked closely with the king. He was with him at Chatham and Spithead in the summer of 1674, and at Portsmouth in the summer of 1675. He was also invited to a mock siege set up by the duke of York in the meadows at Windsor in 1674, where the duke and Monmouth showed off their tactical skills together with guns, mines and pretend prisoners, all lit by fires in the darkness. Evelyn was also present among the thousand spectators and found it 'very divertisant'; and he and Pepys travelled back to London together in the small hours.[16]

Games apart, Pepys was pushing through his own ideas for the navy. In December 1677 he put forward the most notable of these. It was a proposal that no one should be appointed as lieutenant until he had served for three years, received a certificate from his captain and passed an examination in navigation and seamanship at the Navy Office. Prince Rupert opposed it, but the flag officers and the king supported Pepys, and the first examinations took place early the next year. Pepys had made history at a stroke, bringing about a revolution in the way the navy was run, fired by his belief that education and intelligence were more useful to the nation than family background and money; and that however gallant and courageous 'gentlemen' captains might be, the service needed to be professionalized. It was a very natural idea for one who had received his own education in Cromwell's England. It was also to the king's credit that he saw the point and accepted Pepys's proposal.[17] The same faith in education led him to persuade the king to give money to Christ's Hospital School to endow a mathematics department where boys could be prepared for the navy; and Pepys was able to turn to friends at the Royal Society for advice, asking Robert Hooke to recommend a suitable mathematics teacher for the boys.[18]

He became a governor of Christ's Hospital, and also of Bridewell Prison, where for the first time a schoolmaster was installed for child inmates in the year of his appointment, 1675. Honours came in plenty now. In 1676 he was master of Trinity House. His eloquence was not found up to scratch by Robert Hooke, who observed that 'Mr Pepys master of the Trinity House made a long speech to no great purpose', but no one else found fault.[19] The next year he was master of the Clothworkers' Company, following in the footsteps of Joseph Williamson, another self-made man he had long admired. His old college tutor, Samuel Morland, asked him to stand as godfather to his daughter.[20] Like anyone seen to be doing well, he was invited to contribute to a new building at his old college, and did so.[21] In his mid forties, Pepys appears a formidable figure, sure of himself, known to have the king's ear, with rich friends in the City and clever ones at the Royal Society, and a substantial and growing fortune.

Shaftesbury's sally could surely be forgotten. Pepys also felt he could brush aside Povey's pleas to honour their old agreement about sharing the profits he received as treasurer from the Tangier victualling. A file of letters exchanged between them in 1674 and 1675 shows Pepys at his cheating and bullying worst.[22] At the same time other friends benefited from Pepys's powerful position. When Sir Denis Gauden, the Tangier victualler, was arrested for debt in 1677, Pepys was able to call off a creditor by putting Admiralty pressure on him. Gauden proved to be beyond rescue and became bankrupt, and at this point Will Hewer bought the lease of his country house in Clapham, allowing him to go on living in part of it.[23] At a more modest level William Bagwell of Deptford, carpenter of the *Resolution*, was promoted by the Navy Board to be overseer of the *Northumberland* in 1677; and Tom Edwards was appointed muster-master and navy agent at Deal in 1678.[24]

In Huntingdonshire, old Mr Pepys lived quietly with Pall, her dull husband and their two little boys, Sam and John. Pepys kept in touch, sent his father medical advice from Hollier, made sure he had wine to drink and received him as a visitor in London in 1675. In March 1677 Pepys's last surviving brother John died suddenly. He was only thirty-six. Pepys took out his Diary for 1664, in which he had entered the names and birth dates of his brothers and sisters, and added the single word 'mort'. Morelli composed special mourning music that he and Pepys sang together.[25] Pepys also had to sort out his tangled financial affairs; and he was led to think about the future of the family. He knew now there would be no Pepys descendants – he told his

father he did not expect to have children of his own – and he began
to take a greater interest in his sister's sons. The Jacksons and old Mr
Pepys moved back to the Brampton house later in the year.[26] Pepys
was also spurred to sit down and write a long, careful and fascinating
account of his own health.

It makes you wonder how he ever got out of bed at all, let alone
ran and reformed a government department, addressed parliament
and attended the king wherever he happened to be. His words reveal
his body as a rickety and uncertain machine with trouble in almost
every part: shortness of breath, pains in the hip and knee joints, the
back, shoulders, fingers and wrists. He is liable to allergic swellings,
prickings and itchings all over, and loss of voice in wet weather. He
experiences severe pain in his eyes every morning until he has 'drained'
his head by spitting and blowing his nose, as well as pains in the bowel
and bladder, sometimes spreading all over the body and dealt with by
frequent use of suppositories, which he finds painful to insert. This
might seem enough, but is by no means all. He goes into the history
of his stone – a success story – and the trouble with his eyes. Until
eight years ago they had worked perfectly, but ever since, looking at
any near object, especially books and papers, has meant bad eye pain,
with no relief from spectacles or any other device; he is obliged to use
his clerks to read to him and write for him. 'Other evils than these
with reference to my bodily health (either chronical or other) I thank
God I never knew,' he concludes. Even by the standards of the time,
when people had little choice but to accept pain, his refusal to let it
interfere with his work is striking. Physical suffering may even have
been a spur to activity for some. Shaftesbury also suffered chronic pain
and recurrent jaundice for years from a cyst on the liver, for which he
had surgery in 1668, and he lived thereafter with a tube in his side
that was used to drain the wound.[27]

Among his symptoms, Pepys throws in a few details of his daily
life. He never eats much when he is alone and gets small pleasure
from eating at all because he has 'very little taste' – sad for the man
who had once tucked so eagerly into anchovies, lobsters, oysters,
venison pasties and the first peas of the season. He finds the coarser
wines – claret, Italian, Portuguese, Spanish and Greek – more agreeable than light French ones, but in any case drinks little, and has
altogether given up late suppers, which had made him 'dizzy'. At sea,

he is subject to violent seasickness; but then he is not often at sea. And he is bled in the arm once or twice a year but takes no regular courses of medicine. His condition is partly a tribute to Hollier's skill and advice; his stoicism is all his own.

There was one other element in his life that goes unmentioned here. Like many successful men, Pepys had a secret. There are a few clues, one in the diary of Robert Hooke, who saw a good deal of Pepys in 1676 and noted in his diary for Friday, 15 December, that he 'gave Mrs Pepys' a recipe for making varnish. Who was this Mrs Pepys? A better clue appears in a letter to Pepys from Daniel Skinner, a young fellow of Trinity College, Cambridge, in July 1676, asking for his help in finding work. Skinner was the eldest son and namesake of a neighbour and fellow parishioner of Pepys, a merchant with a house in Mark Lane and a large family. Daniel's letter is in Latin and is not entirely clear at all points, but it does refer unambiguously to Pepys's declared love for his sister some years back, and his kindness to young Daniel himself at the time; also to angry accusations made by their parents against Pepys and to the breach this produced between the two families. A third clue was provided by Pepys himself in a codicil made to his will in May 1703, less than two weeks before his death, which speaks of the 'Excellent Lady Mrs Mary Skyner' and her 'Steddy friendship and Assistances during the whole course of my life, within the last thirty three years'. This puts the start of their relationship in 1670, probably before Elizabeth's monument was up in its place in St Olave's.

Mary Skinner was the eldest daughter of Daniel Skinner Snr, a merchant from Braintree in Essex who had been living in Mark Lane and worshipping at St Olave's since the 1650s, and his wife, Frances. But Mary was not brought up in the city. Because the Skinners had a growing family, and Frances's sister Elizabeth was childless, Mary was sent as a child to live with her aunt in Hertfordshire. There Mary grew up as a cherished foster daughter ('whom I have brought up as my own', her aunt wrote in her will) to aunt Elizabeth and her husband, Sir Francis Boteler. They lived in a handsome Elizabethan manor house, standing in its estate of Woodhall, Hatfield, just north of Hatfield House and adjoining the Cecil lands; the River Lea, with its idyllic green banks and small watermills, marked part of the boundary. The famous Hatfield vineyard and gardens, visited and admired by Pepys in 1661 and again in 1667, adjoined the Boteler lands, and both Cecils and Botelers worshipped at St Ethelreda's, the parish church of Hatfield, where Pepys admired the many 'handsome faces and gentile persons' of the congregation in 1667.[28]

Sir Francis had two daughters from his first marriage, Isabel and Julia, about ten years older than Mary, who grew up under their protective wing; Julia and Mary were especially close, and remained friends for life.[29] The household was a cultivated one. Among their good friends were Sir Richard Fanshawe, who preceded Lord Sandwich as ambassador to Spain, and his brilliant wife, Anne, the memoirist.[30] Both Sir Francis and Dame Elizabeth, as his wife was addressed, were well educated – he had been to Cambridge in the 1620s, and she had her own collection of books – and he was known for his courtesy and kindness to his children, and as a good neighbour and a churchgoer, hospitable to friends and charitable to the poor. She endowed a charity for five poor widows of Hatfield and Tewin in 1678.[31] He liked to spend some of the winter months in London; she owned the lease of a house in Crane Court, off Fleet Street, although this was not necessarily where they stayed in town. In the 1680s he went into parliament. His daughters, Mary's foster sisters, married local gentry, settled in nearby Hertfordshire villages, Tewin and Digswell, and started families of their own. You can judge something of the ease of life at Woodhall, and the position of Mary within the family, from Dame Elizabeth's will, in which she bequeathed to Mary many jewels (including 'my great jewel'), a 'Picture Case set round with diamonds' and 'all my books in my closet', as well as £1,000; and appointed her one of the trustees of her charitable endowment for poor widows.[32]

In this way Mary grew up comfortably, away from her real parents, and with different expectations from her younger sisters'. No doubt she appreciated the difference between life at Woodhall and at Mark Lane; but she remained no less dear to her mother and became an admired figure to her siblings. Her brother Daniel was closest in age; he was born in 1651, which makes it likely she was born about 1653, since the rest arrived at intervals of about two years between 1655 and 1668: Elizabeth, Frances, Robert, Obrian, Frederick, Corbet and the baby Peter.[33] The Skinner family was large, and they fell into financial difficulties, but they were neither destitute nor ignorant. Daniel the younger wrote of the 'disasters on land and sea' and 'heavy and bitter blows' of fortune that reduced his father to comparative poverty in the 1670s; but he had kept Daniel at Westminster for seven years and sent him on to Trinity College, Cambridge, and Mary's sister Frances married Sir William Buck, a well-connected Lincolnshire baronet. The younger children, however, did not have the same chances.[34] It must also be said that neither Skinners nor Botelers did much for Mary's formal education. Whereas Mrs Skinner wrote a perfectly decent letter, Mary's spelling, like that of so many of her female contemporaries – and some males too – was of the picturesque school: 'plaine inglish', 'mountianes', 'aplycasion' and 'afectionat unkle'.[35]

How did Mary and Pepys meet? Her parents attended the same church, so they may have met when she was visiting them at Mark Lane. Or he could have noticed her at the church in Hatfield, where he sometimes stopped on his way to and from Brampton; but St Olave's is more likely. Churches acted as dating agencies: people stood about after the service and talked to their neighbours, and Pepys might easily invite Mr and Mrs Skinner to taste a glass of wine and a slice of cake and to view the treasures of his house – in 1670 he was still living in Seething Lane – and to bring their visiting seventeen-year-old daughter with them. And since young Daniel says he met Pepys through Mary – 'long ago I first entered with happy omen into your grace through my sister' – there must have been a reasonably long period of general family friendship. Pepys's wooing techniques were likely to have been much the same as they were in the days of the Diary, and may have included offers to take her out on the water in a smart Navy Board vessel – at first with a younger brother or sister – and to Vauxhall or Greenwich; or for a coach trip, to enjoy cheesecakes and ale in the country. She liked him, and he seized his chance.

Seductions usually came to light when the girl found herself pregnant, and in this case there was no risk of that, although Pepys may still have thought of it: his joking reference to becoming a father in one of his speeches in the closing days of the Brooke House Commission in 1670 suggests as much.[36] For a time the lovers enjoyed an entirely secret affair, while Pepys took a kindly interest in Daniel – he was friends at Cambridge with the Montagu twins, Oliver and John – and remained on cordial terms with the Skinner parents. Their discovery of what was going on between Pepys and Mary angered them so much that there was a total breach, and the Skinners may have succeeded in separating them for a period. Daniel refers to Pepys's professions of love for his sister and to his estrangement from the family: 'whether you can have been guilty of the charge my parents are so ready to make against you, is certainly not for me to examine or pursue . . . your friendship, which I counted among my greatest distinctions, and which I valued so highly, was broken and ruined'.[37]

Daniel's letter is our only source, and those are all the details he gives. What happened after the discovery and breach is unclear. Mary may have retreated to Woodhall. What she told the Botelers, and what their attitude was, we don't know, any more than whether she simply defied her parents' anger and continued her affair with Pepys in the face of it or brought them round slowly. She could have chosen to settle in lodgings in London. The fire at Seething Lane meant he was in lodgings too, both uprooted creatures free to be together as they chose. There was nothing to prevent them marrying, but there was no marriage. Why not? Pepys may have felt he had experienced all he wanted of the married state. He may have vowed at his dying wife's bedside that he would never take another bride. He was also a man for whom the double standard went unquestioned – friendly as he was with Lord Brouncker, he unhesitatingly labelled his much loved living-in mistress a whore – and he may have felt disinclined to marry a young woman who had already succumbed to him. Lord Sandwich's warning story of the man who shits in his hat and claps it on his head comes to mind.

Pepys knew he was in a strong position, and he made the most of it. He could love Mary on his own terms. A semi-secret, unofficial love affair kept its erotic thrill and also left him free, allowing him to maintain his independent, unembarrassed bachelor social life with friends like the Houblons and Lady Mordaunt. Yet Robert Hooke's assumption that Mary was Pepys's wife in 1676 suggests that she was installed with him in Derby House at that point, and he seems to have been tending her health there two years later, as the next chapter will show.[38] There were later periods when Mary lived in lodgings of her own, although this was when he was in difficulties and without a home himself; and it was not until the late 1680s that there was a general acceptance that she was his consort. Pepys always liked to compartmentalize his life, and Mary was able to look after herself when she had to. She may have possessed the same charm, cheek and enterprising spirit as her brother Daniel, allied to more patience. There was money about to ensure that her life was comfortable, from her Boteler aunt and uncle, and no doubt from Pepys too. Woodhall plainly remained her second home.

Over time her parents came to accept the arrangement and friendly relations were re-established between all concerned. There was the further consideration that Pepys was a rich and influential man who might help the Skinner boys as their father's fortunes waned. As the years went by, Mary's mother corresponded with him affectionately and asked his help in finding her younger sons careers; and Pepys wrote warmly to her, sending greetings to the Botelers.[39] He records calling on Sir Francis in London about 1678 and in 1680.[40] Mary's father agreed to testify to Pepys's irreproachable attendance record at St Olave's when he needed a certificate to that effect in 1681.[41] Mary was plainly in high favour when Dame Elizabeth drafted her will in the same year, and Mary was also a witness to Sir Francis's will – her aunt died in 1684, he in 1690. She always had her own maid and in due course what looks like her own bank account; and her position within his household was in later years acknowledged by even Pepys's most pious and discerning friends.

What we should most like to know about Mary Skinner would be Pepys's account of her; but that is what we don't have. In writing his Diary he was inspired by the condition of marriage itself; Elizabeth can be seen as its muse, without whom it might not have been written. It had been a glorious process but demanding and painful, and he was not going to repeat it. Mary was never allowed so close: neither wife nor muse. But she fought for her own place beside him, and she had the character to make their unconventional arrangement work in the long run. Without being wife or muse, she remained his companion for thirty-three years.

22. Plots

In 1676 Mary's brother Daniel got into difficulties. He had gone up to Trinity College, Cambridge, in 1670, just about the time Pepys first met the Skinner family, taken his degree in 1673 and been awarded a junior fellowship in the autumn of 1674. In the intervening year he found himself a job in London working for the poet Milton, then living in Artillery Row, by Bunhill Fields.[1] Daniel was enterprising, clever, charming and something of a chancer: Milton was a great and learned man, but he was still *persona non grata* to the rulers of the nation. He was also blind, poor and failing in health, and in the last months of his life; he died in November 1674. Daniel made copies of some of the official letters he had written for Cromwell and took them away, together with a manuscript of a theological work, his *De Doctrina Christiana*. Later, he told Pepys the works were ones 'Milton left behind him to me', which may have been true; or he may simply have helped himself.[2] If any inkling came to Pepys through Mary of Daniel's connection with Milton in 1674, he would not have wanted to know, given the poet's disgraced condition as a radical and republican, and his own dependence on the crown for advancement.

In 1675 Daniel was at Trinity as a junior fellow. He sent his Milton manuscripts to the Dutch publisher, Elsevier, but before the rejection letter arrived he had left Cambridge again, finding the pace of life there too slow. In July 1676 he wrote to Pepys asking him to recommend him for a diplomatic post in Holland – this was in the letter mentioned in the last chapter. It was written in Latin and veered between ornate compliment and intimate allusion to Pepys's love for Mary, the accusations the Skinner parents had made against him and the breach this had produced between the two families. Although he was at pains to say he did not know whether Pepys was 'guilty of the charge my parents are so ready to make against you' or not, it was a bold approach, and Pepys must have been relieved that it came decently obscured in Latin.[3] Whatever his private feelings, he responded as Daniel hoped and sent off a reference to the chief English diplomat at Nijmegen, stretching the truth somewhat by saying he himself had been 'privy to every part of the Gentleman's education, from his Father's house through Westminster School to Trinity College in Cambridge' and praising Daniel's 'Sobriety, Parts and Learning', with particular mention of his fine Latin.[4] Daniel was offered a secretarial job at the embassy; but before he could take it up the offer was withdrawn. The secretary of state, Sir Joseph Williamson, well known to Pepys and respected by him, having heard from Daniel himself of his connection with the Milton papers, vetoed his appointment, describing him as 'a very pretty young man' but one who must 'air himself from such infectious commerce' as friendship with Milton. Daniel's offer to burn the Milton papers did not mollify Williamson. Warnings against young Skinner and condemnations of Milton and his political ideas circulated for some time.

Before leaving for Holland Daniel had borrowed £10 from Pepys. He wrote again from Rotterdam, this time in English, 'with tears instead of ink', apologizing for failing to visit him or return the loan and begging him to intervene with Williamson again; and he explained that although he 'happen'd to be acquainted with Milton in his lifetime', he shared none of the poet's dangerous opinions. He was now stuck, jobless, in Rotterdam: 'I am here just a person without a soul,' he wrote, but what he lacked was not so much a soul as a patron. Pepys replied in his most ponderous style, warning him that 'some time must be suffered to pass before you can reasonably look to have this unfortunate concernment of yours with Mr Milton and his Writings forgotten'. He advised him to stay abroad and study languages. Daniel took his advice and got his father to fund him as far as Paris, where he was confident he could perfect his French in six months; after that he meant to go to Italy. He was not yet out of trouble, because in 1677 the master of Trinity ordered him to return to college and warned him not to seek to publish 'any Writing mischievous to the Church or State'. Daniel was now regarded as 'a wild young man' as well as a clever one. It was not the last time he asked for help from Pepys, who may well have reflected that he was destined to take up with young women with needy brothers. As for Milton's papers, they were sent back to England, conveyed to Williamson by Daniel's father and consigned to a cupboard at Whitehall where they lay gathering dust until 1823.[5]

Daniel's knowledge of Pepys's private relations with Mary made it possible for him to ask for help, but it was Pepys's position as a public figure that made him worth asking. In the mid 1670s he was as well established professionally as a man can be. His letters breathe assurance and dignity. He was on easy terms with the richest men in the City. He could hold his own when he was sniped at by fellow members of parliament, and had become a formidably effective spokesman for the navy in the House. He attended the king regularly at Whitehall, Hampton Court and Windsor, and was often summoned to join him and the duke of York at Newmarket; and, however ordinary or despicable they had seemed to him in the past, he gave them his loyalty. Lord Shaftesbury, their enemy and his, was locked away in the Tower from February 1677, when the king had sent his secretary of state, the same Sir Joseph Williamson who had scuppered Daniel's diplomatic career, to order him to leave town, and Shaftesbury had refused. Pepys may have been among the crowds who went to hear his unsuccessful appeal against this imprisonment at Westminster Hall in June; he could also have enjoyed a satirical play aimed at him, *Sir Popular Wisdom; or, the Politician.*

But Shaftesbury was not to be laughed at. His long political career had taught him how to wait, how to manoeuvre and how to organize. In February 1678 he was fifty-seven and could not walk without the help of sticks, but he was as determined as ever to pursue his policies. He humbled himself just enough to be released from the Tower and emerged unrepentant, set on course to save England from 'Popery and slavery'. His chief aim now was to exclude the Catholic duke of York from the succession to the throne, and in the House of Lords in May he pointed him out in person as the main danger to the country. He had already warned the House (in January 1674) that there were more than 16,000 Catholics in the London area, ready for desperate measures and threatening a massacre. The claim was absurd, but fear and hatred of Catholicism meant that such warnings were taken seriously. Folk memory kept fresh Catholic Queen Mary's burnings at the stake, the Spanish Armada and the Gunpowder Plot, and in France the St Bartholomew's Day Massacre, and there were still many who believed the fire of 1666 had been started by papists. The kings's policy of alliance with Catholic France was generally disliked. So was the fact that he had not only a Catholic wife but Catholic mistresses; some of Nell Gwyn's popularity came from her supposed merry declaration, 'I am the *Protestant* whore.' Shaftesbury may have suspected that Charles was close to being a Catholic himself, although if he was he had no intention of revealing or imposing his faith on anyone else; but his heir, the duke of York, had a Catholic wife who would give him Catholic children. Too many Irish priests were seen at court, too many Catholics had commissions in the army. The combination of arbitrary rule and religious persecution practised by Louis XIV in France showed what Protestants could expect from a Catholic ruler. Shaftesbury's detestation of such a prospect drove him to action.

A weapon was put into his hands when rumours of a Catholic plot to murder the king and take over the country were started in the summer of 1678. He was not responsible for inventing the Popish Plot, as it became known, or for the grotesque fabrications of Titus Oates and his fellow informers, but he saw at once what he could do with such material and encouraged them for his own purposes. Like the anti-Communist frenzy spirited up by Senator McCarthy in the United States in the 1950s, the Plot caused normally reasonable people to lose their judgement, and before the hysteria wore itself out thirty-five men had been unjustly put to death, many more imprisoned, threatened and falsely accused, and scores of informers paid and fêted for their fictions. When Oates addressed the Commons in October 1678, Pepys's friend Sir Robert Southwell, usually a level-headed man, considered his deposition a 'loose and tottering fabric which would easily tumble if it stood alone', yet he decided to believe it because he felt that papists were too much indulged and had become dangerous; two months later the madness had increased to the point that Southwell was as convinced of the reality of the Plot 'as of my creed'.[6]

On 2 November Shaftesbury proposed a resolution in the Lords that there was a 'damnable and hellish plot contrived and carried on by the Popish recusants for the assassination and murdering the King, subverting government and rooting out the Protestant religion', and that the duke of York must be removed from the king's presence.[7] Two days after this Pepys and all his clerks attended St Margaret's, Westminster, and took the sacrament together. It was a precaution, meant to show they were good members of the Church of England.

But although Pepys was not a Catholic, his political loyalty was to the duke of York, whom he found a supportive master, and if the country was to be divided between the duke's supporters and Shaftesbury's, he was unhesitatingly on the side of the duke.

Both Pepys and Shaftesbury had made long political journeys, Shaftesbury from royalist to parliamentarian, back to royalist at the Restoration and now prepared to take on a royal family that had, in his view, become disastrous for the country. Pepys's journey took him from the boy who exulted at the execution of Charles I to the junior administrator stingingly critical of Charles II during the 1660s, and on to the senior servant of the crown, proud of the trust placed in him by his royal masters in the 1670s. Shaftesbury, an aristocrat, brilliant, subtle and arrogant, became the founder of the Whig Party. Pepys, who had risen from nothing, knew he owed his rise to Charles and James Stuart as much as to his own brainpower; as soon as the label 'Tory' was heard in English politics, he applied it to himself: 'we Tories', he wrote.[8] When Shaftesbury compiled a list of MPs in February 1679, marking his supporters with a *w*, meaning worthy, and his opponents with a *v* for vile, Pepys was marked with a *v*.[9]

The panic engendered by the Plot led to absurdities as well as cruelties. The queen was accused of encouraging the murder of her husband. The discovery of gunpowder on the premises of a Frenchman living near the palace caused a frenzy until it was noticed that he was the royal fireworks-maker. When a noise of 'knocking and digging' in Old Palace Yard put the House into a state of alarm – was this another Gunpowder Plot? – Christopher Wren was called in to investigate and found that the roof was so rotten the building might fall down in the next high wind. Chains were fixed across the streets of the City against a Catholic rising. Small wonder that Pepys, working flat out to ensure the navy was not infiltrated by papists, wrote of 'the whole government seeming at this day to remain in such a state of distraction and fear, as no history I believe can parallel'.[10] One of the Jesuits arrested was Fogarty, surely the same 'Fogourdy' whom he remembered as an agreeable visitor to Elizabeth at Seething Lane.[11] Because his own resident musician, Morelli, was a Catholic, and Catholics were banned within a thirty-mile radius of London, he asked James Houblon to attempt a rapid conversion; when, predictably enough, that failed, he spirited Morelli away – by the back water gate, according to his butler – sending him to Brentwood in Essex and paying him a small retainer.[12]

As Morelli left, the attack on Pepys began. Since he had already been accused of Catholicism in the House, he offered an easy target. It is likely that Shaftesbury ordered it and certain that his associates carried it out, revealing themselves as unprincipled thugs in the process. They began with the arrest of one of Pepys's clerks, Samuel Atkins, accused of being an accessory to the murder of a magistrate, Sir Edmund Berry Godfrey, whose body had been found, strangled and stabbed, on Primrose Hill in mid October: it is one of the most famous murder mysteries in English history, and still unsolved. Godfrey, a Protestant of austere habits, had taken a deposition from Titus Oates in September, and his murder was construed as part of the Catholic Plot. London boiled with rumour and panic. Daggers were sold inscribed 'pro religione Protestantium' and 'Memento Godfrey 12 Oct 78'; they were supposed to be used against the expected Catholic massacre.[13] Atkins was arrested on false evidence on 1 November and examined in Newgate Prison on the 6th. He was kept in isolation, sometimes in irons, without pen and paper and allowed no contact with anyone outside; it was an exceptionally bitter winter, and prisoners were lucky if they had fires in their cells. 'That we have no rack in England, and this is true, and a great blessing surely, but I am told Captain Richardson hath a hole in Newgate which never any man could endure two days without confessing anything laid to his charge,' wrote a respectable MP.[14] But although Atkins was not a favourite clerk of Pepys, he was stubbornly loyal to his master and to the truth. He refused to be intimidated even when Shaftesbury personally threatened him with hanging if he did not 'make some discovery'.[15] The plan was that he should incriminate Pepys indirectly, because Pepys happened to have an unbreakable alibi for the time of Godfrey's murder – he had been at Newmarket with the king. Meanwhile Pepys was questioned about Atkins in the House; outside it, he busied himself establishing Atkins's alibi.

The news got about enough for his sister Paulina Jackson to write to him anxiously from Brampton. His answer shows that their relations had improved with the years, because he addresses her as an intelligent person, sends his 'kind love' and urges her to write to him weekly. He explains about the 'manifest contrivance' against his clerk Atkins, 'which (though most untrue) cannot be thought to pass in the world at so jealous a time as this without some reflections upon me, as his master, and on that score does occasion me not a little disquiet. But I thank God I have not only my innocence to satisfy myself with, but such an assurance of his also as that I make no question of his being able to aquit himself with advantage to him and infamy to his accusers'.[16] At this stage Pepys believed himself unassailable; and indeed his detective work on behalf of Atkins came up with a complete alibi. There were witnesses who had been with him at a drinking party of friends of both sexes aboard the yacht *Catherine* at the time of Godfrey's murder, after which Atkins, 'very much fuddled', needed to be rowed home. The case against him was destroyed. Atkins had to endure four months in prison, but when the trial came in February 1679 he was acquitted and released. The other three accused, who were equally innocent, were not so lucky. They were hanged.

Atkins's trial coincided with an election. Castle Rising did not want Pepys, but Harwich, which had him to thank for recent shipbuilding contracts, duly elected him and Anthony Deane, his shipbuilder colleague and friend. This was when Shaftesbury marked his list of members and saw that he had twice as many supporters as opponents elected.[17] The king appealed for a 'healing parliament' and national unity and, failing to get them, bowed to pressure and sent the duke of York abroad. Although Charles never believed in the Plot, he did not want to lose his crown, and followed the advice of Lord Halifax, 'that the Plot must be handled as if it were true, whether it were so or not'.[18] Innocent people continued to be imprisoned and executed, and James left for Brussels in March.

His departure was bad news for Pepys. Life upstairs at Derby House was upset at the same time, because Mary was ill with attacks of fever that failed to respond to her ordinary doses of Jesuits' powder, or quinine, regarded with suspicion by some staunch Protestants, because it was brought by the Jesuits from Peru. Pepys was worried enough about her to consult a surgeon he knew in Chatham, who sent bottles of stronger medicine, though still containing quinine. She recovered.[19] Daniel was in trouble again too, ordered by the master and seniors of Trinity to 'come home to the College to clear himself from suspicion of being a papist' – a change at least from being suspected of republicanism. He complied and, surprisingly, was appointed a major fellow.

Then he got himself a passport testifying to his Protestantism and prepared to go on his travels again.[20]

Shaftesbury's position looked so strong that the king gave ground, sacked his existing council and revived the old title of lord president of the council for Shaftesbury. At the same time he appointed a new commission for the Admiralty. This meant that Pepys was thrown to the lions, because the new commission was made up of men hostile to him. Almost at once he was attacked in the House, while a parliamentary committee was appointed to inquire yet again into the failings of the navy. On 6 May he wrote to the duke of York, 'your Highness was pleased to foretell me at your going hence what I was soon after to look for; and it is come to pass. For, whether I will or no, a Papist I must be, because favoured by your Royal Highness.' He went on to ask the duke to get him named as a commissioner. There was no chance of this, but James wrote to the king at once with the impossible request. He let Pepys see the letter, and, while it did him no good, it bound Pepys to the duke for life.[21]

Pepys's opponents had got hold of three men prepared to incriminate him. They were a sorry lot, the first a disgruntled sea captain with a story that Pepys, along with Deane and St Michel, had allowed a privateer they ran as a consortium to prey on English shipping. The second was his ex-butler, John James, who bore a grudge for his dismissal – Morelli had found him in bed with a woman servant – and was ready to swear Pepys was a Catholic and Morelli a Jesuit. The third was a swaggering villain calling himself Colonel John Scott, just arrived in England from the Continent, who accused him of sending Deane to France to supply coastal maps and information about the fleet to the French government, with much circumstantial evidence; and Scott's paymaster appears to have been the duke of Buckingham, who was doing dirty work for Shaftesbury. With this material the parliamentary committee declared there was a 'Sea-Plot' and Pepys was formally accused of 'Piracy, Popery and Treachery'. The leading spokesman against him was William Harbord, as it happened the brother of Sandwich's protégé who had died with him at the battle of Sole Bay: 'Mr Pepys is an ill man, and I will prove him so,' announced Harbord on 20 May. Pepys rose to defend himself on the spot. You can catch his indignant amazement in the repeated 'But, Sir!'s that pepper his speech, of which a verbatim version is preserved among his papers:

'Mr Speaker – It must be a great misfortune to have so many things cast upon me at once, and all by surprise . . . But, Sir! pray allow me to say this . . . But, Sir! I don't expect to be acquitted by any profession of mine here . . . at a time so dangerous, Sir! that I would with all my heart contribute to my own prosecution . . . But, Sir! this I am . . .'[22] He was wasting his words. Later that day he was committed to the sergeant of arms, on the next he resigned as secretary to the Admiralty and as Tangier treasurer, and on the third day he was taken to the Tower. His rooms in Derby House were shut up. If Mary had not already gone, she must now have taken herself to Woodhall. One consolation for Pepys was that his work was given to his old protégé Tom Hayter, who had once been in such trouble for being caught at a Nonconformist meeting: at least he could not be accused of being a papist.

He may have expected the king to rescue him from the Tower as he had done Sir Joseph Williamson, who had been extracted by royal command within hours when he fell foul of parliament; but nothing like this happened to Pepys. He could console himself only with the sound of the familiar bells of All Hallows and St Olave's and his memories of how, as a young man, he had brought the Sandwich children to see the lions at the Tower, looked out at the fire from one of its high windows, escorted Mrs Knipp and a party of ladies to view the crown jewels and visited Coventry during his detention in 1669. Now it was his turn to receive visitors: James Houblon, John Evelyn and his lawyers. He began to organize his own defence at once. Since he was accused of selling secrets to the French, it occurred to him that his French-speaking brother-in-law could be put to work on his behalf. He applied to the king for permission to send St Michel to Paris, and Balty set off, only too pleased be crossing the Channel with all expenses paid and taking with him his eldest son, who can't have been more than eight years old; Pepys sent a steady stream of letters after him, giving detailed instructions for searching out and preparing witnesses against Scott.[23]

His stay in the Tower was not long. On 20 June he and Deane were moved to the King's Bench in Southwark, and on 9 July they were released on bail. Pepys had to give £10,000 of his own and Houblon and three other City friends put in £5,000 each. Pepys remained a rich man – he kept his coach and continued to employ several clerks – but he had lost his income and he was homeless. Will

Hewer now showed the 'care, kindness and faithfulness of a son' and invited Pepys to move into his Buckingham Street house, where he gave him a suite of rooms.[24] Esther St Michel was already installed there with four small children; Will had also advanced money to Balty, perhaps the only imprudent financial measure of his life. All this says much for his good nature; and Pepys too, at this juncture, was meticulous in keeping Balty informed about the health of his wife and infants, without a single word of impatience at their presence.[25]

He was out of prison but not free, and still facing the prospect of a trial for capital crimes.[26] But the political tide was just beginning to turn. In July Oates's testimony against the queen's doctor, whom he accused of planning to poison the king, failed to convict. In August Charles was ill, and the duke of York returned to England to be with him. Recovering, Charles appointed James high commissioner to Scotland. Pepys accompanied him as far as Hatfield on his journey north in October. Hatfield meant a possible visit to Woodhall; he was now on cordial terms with both Skinners and Botelers.[27] He also made a trip into Oxfordshire, possibly to consult with Coventry, who had retired to Minster Lovell. Back in court on the first day of the law term, he found his 'old prosecutor, Harbord' failed to put in an appearance.[28] In October Charles felt strong enough to dismiss Shaftesbury, and parliament too; he ruled without it for a year, while he negotiated for another handout from Louis XIV. Anti-Catholic agitation continued, with the usual autumn street processions featuring Jesuits with bloody daggers, popish bishops, the Pope's chief physician with Jesuits' powder and a urinal, and an effigy of the Pope stuffed with live cats, to be burnt at Smithfield. There was punishment for Pepys too, in the form of two savagely satirical pamphlets, also attacking Hewer. *Plain Truth or Closet Discourse Betwixt P. and H.* accused them both of coining money by selling jobs and licences, cheating seamen and taking bribes, with Hewer doing the dirtier work to allow Pepys to maintain an innocent front. They were given Punch-and-Judy style dialogue:

H. Sir, you know I have never failed hitherto in my management of your affairs . . .

P. I thank thee, good H. It was strangely our good fortune that we ever met together. (Then they hug and kiss one another.)

Pepys was reminded that he was the son of a poor tailor, mocked for the ostentatious decorations on his coach and barge, and for his friendships with well-to-do women like the Houblon ladies and Lady Mordaunt. In *A Hue and Cry after P. and H.* humiliating details of his health problems were given. There was also a list of presents he was said to receive from favour-seekers, captains, consuls, carpenters and their wives, and it must be said that some have a familiar ring: pots of anchovies, butts of sherry, barrels of pickled oysters, Parmesan cheeses, hogsheads of claret and fine Spanish mats. Houblon commiserated, Pepys put a brave face on it, and other friends may have smiled; some of the jokes cut uncomfortably close to the truth. Later, he learnt that his ex-butler James had provided information.[29]

But Pepys was too busy to brood. For six months he kept dictating instructions to 'Brother Balty' in Paris, telling him precisely how he must proceed and proving amazingly successful at such long-distance detective work. Balty was sent to men and women of all classes, from ambassadors to servants, in the quest for witnesses against Scott; he had to question and listen, assess the value of what he was told, persuade witnesses to make formal statements before notaries and in some cases agree to travel to England to testify at a trial for which there was as yet no date fixed. He must never offer money, and he must reject Catholic witnesses, because they would not be trusted in England; it meant excluding Monsieur Pelletier, a friend from the Paris trip of 1669, when 'your poor Sister and we were in France', as Pepys reminded him.[30] St Michel worked enthusiastically, although he spent too much and had to be told he could not afford to hire a private French tutor for his son; nor was he allowed home for a summer break. No one expected to stay in Paris in August, but Balty was made to. Pepys sent out an assistant in September, and Balty was back in England in January 1680. He had helped to establish Scott's low reputation among the French, his loose, boastful talk and history of fraudulent behaviour, and presently Scott was complaining of Balty 'tampering with everybody he thought fit for his turn'.[31] There could have been no better tribute to his work.

As the evidence to disprove Scott's stories piled up, and witnesses arrived in England for discussions with Pepys, Scott simply disappeared abroad again. Without him there could be no trial; yet the court did nothing to resolve the situation. Pepys raged: 'taking in all the circumstances of scandal, expense, trouble and hazard, no innocent man was ever embarrassed as I have been, and remain at this day, from the villainy of one man of no acquaintance with myself nor credit with any honest man that knows him. The thoughts of which, should I give much way to them, would distract me. But God is above all.'[32] God was Fate or Fortune, all-powerful and unreadable, and Pepys knew he had to fight his own fight. It meant getting involved with characters he would normally have kept well clear of. John Joyne, an English watch-maker Balty found in Paris and an old friend of Scott now happy to testify against him, arrived early to see Pepys on 27 November and, according to his own account, 'being very dirty and so observed to be by Mr Pepys went home to shave and shift myself [i.e., change his clothes]'.[33] Joyne kept notes of his meetings with both Scott and Pepys in London that autumn that give a vivid picture of all their activities, Scott slouching round London streets and taverns, Pepys decorous in his coach but sometimes reduced to accepting an invitation to eavesdrop on his enemies. Also among Joyne's notes is a letter to Pepys written on 31 December which begins, 'I went to Mr Skinner's Daughter in the Haymarket, I left word with her that I should come again on Wednesday night to see her father,' and ends, 'Mr Hewer told me that you were gone out of Town . . . am now going to Mr Skinner's.'[34] What was Joyne's connection with the Skinners? His letter suggests that her father was helping Pepys, but, as this is his only surviving reference to them, it remains tantalizing. What it does tell us is that Mary was living in the newly built and fashionable Haymarket, not far from Buckingham Street; and that she remained there while Pepys was away.[35]

Meanwhile Pepys's other accuser, the ex-butler John James, was having further thoughts about his evidence; he was dying of tuberculosis and feared for his soul. He approached Pepys in January 1680, coming to Hewer's house to tell him 'that he has from the beginning been employed by our Enemies to gather witnesses against us . . . that he was pressed twenty times by a person of quality to give information against me in Parliament . . . that he had not much regard to what he said, but was drawned in to say whatever they had a mind he should say . . . that he did not swear to it, and was not much rewarded . . . and that he knowed Scott and has enough to stop his mouth'.[36] This was promising stuff, but James wanted money to talk more. Pepys knew he must not risk appearing to bribe him, and sent him away. Within days he was back again.

Pepys needed a record of their conversations, and this inspired him to start another diary. It was nothing like the great Diary – it was dictated and written out in longhand, and without set pieces or indiscretions – but still from 27 January until 10 April there is a glimpse of his daily activities again, with even one nostalgic 'and so to bed'. The first thing it tells is that Pepys's life was as firmly compartmentalized as it had ever been. There was Buckingham Street, where Will's widowed mother presided, Elizabeth's portrait hung on the wall, and Balty's children flourished.[37] There was his circle of well-to-do friends of both sexes, who made a fuss of him in their homes and went with him to the theatre or on the river. He saw an Etherege farce, *She Would if She Could*, with young Mr Wynne Houblon. He drove Wynne's mother Sarah – 'Cousin Houblon and children' – to Chelsea. He supped with Lady Banks; he escorted Lady Mordaunt and her sister to Vauxhall, and to Putney and Wimbledon by barge. Lady Mordaunt fed him nobly – her lobster pie gets a mention – and he was also a regular dinner guest at the Houblons. The diary shows he was assiduous in his church attendance; and that he visited his stationer in Cornhill and Harford the bookseller. He was at St James's to greet the duke of York on his return from Scotland, and made his farewells to the duke and the king at court before they left for Newmarket in mid March. He called on Mary's foster-father, Sir Francis Boteler, between attending Covent Garden Church and driving in the park on 21 March. It also tells us that Mary went to Knightsbridge in March, probably for her health; he visited 'MS' in this quiet rural spot where the London road crossed the River Westbourne.[38] She does not seem to have been taken to the theatre or to Vauxhall.

The chief theme of this diary is in any case Pepys's dealings with witnesses, some arrived from France, but principally James the butler. James's moods fluctuated alarmingly. When he was disposed to talk it was of meetings at the Mitre in Fenchurch Street with Harbord and other grandees, who had given him money. As he grew weaker he became anxious about his burial arrangements. Pepys was anxious too, because he needed to extract a formal confession before James died, and in the presence of an independent witness, that he had lied and taken money for lying. Pepys arranged for a clergyman and reassured him about the funeral, but James resisted being visited by any 'person of quality' – meaning the required witness – because he was ashamed of his poverty and the fact that there was only one bed for himself, his sister and mother in their lodgings. At last he agreed to speak. Pepys, amazingly, asked Povey to be the independent witness; and Povey, amazingly, consented, perhaps his pleasure in being involved in so notorious a case outweighed his displeasure with Pepys. On 2 March Povey took a statement from James. Word got out of this development – Pepys saw to that – and Harbord hurried round to try to get James to change his story again. Some blackly farcical hours followed as rival groups crammed into the dying man's room, on the one hand Pepys, Povey, Hewer and their lawyer, with James's sister and mother, urging him to stand firm; and on the other Harbord with two justices, two clergymen, two political associates and a clerk, pressing him to sign a paper denying that he had ever been bribed. Harbord then proposed that they should each give two guineas towards his care, 'and accordingly we did so,' recorded Pepys, 'Mr Povey lending each of us two Guinnys'.[39] Whether Povey saw any of his guineas again is not part of the story. Harbord knew when he was beaten, and began to talk to Pepys as though the whole episode had been something of a joke; he 'declared openly that he did not believe me to be a Papist or Popishly inclined, and so did all the Company'.[40]

Pepys did not forgive him, but the successful outcome with James made him cheerful enough to order his coach for his first drive of the year in Hyde Park; and he picked up a couple of bottles of champagne to take to the Houblons for a celebratory drink. Another sign of good spirits was his summoning of the joiner to help him move his furniture about, 'shifting my Bedchamber and Study', an activity he always enjoyed. James died on 20 March. If his conscience troubled him as he lay dying, his explanation for switching sides was simple: 'Mr Pepys had used him unkindly . . . [but] Mr Harbord had taken away his allowance.'[41] Pepys behaved decently to his womenfolk, inviting them to dinner and paying what they owed in rent; or rather he got Hewer's clerk to supply them with the money and take a receipt.

Things continued to improve. The king summoned him to Newmarket, which allowed him to visit his father, sister and her family at Brampton on the way; he set off on 29 March and was in London again on 3 April, having called on Morelli on the return journey.[42]

But not until the end of June did Pepys and Deane hear that the attorney-general, unable to muster a single credible witness against them, was giving up on the case. On 1 July Pepys wrote to Mrs Skinner announcing his 'full discharge from the bondage I have, from one villain's practice, so long lain under', and thanking her and her family for their support throughout the year.[43]

With hindsight it is easy to think that Pepys had never been in danger of his life. But there were certainly those who expected him to lose his head, and there must have been moments when he was afraid. Other innocent men had after all gone to the scaffold. His work on his own defence distracted him from such fears and kept him almost as busy as usual. The result of these labours was never needed in court but remains a testimony to his cool courage under attack, his ability to think through tangled masses of evidence and impose order upon them, and his skill in deploying others to carry out his plans. It was a colossal task. It was also responsible for a colossal book, one that has never been printed and still sits in manuscript in the Pepys Library, leather bound and gilded, in two volumes of 1,338 pages and something like 400,000 words.[44] The volumes make up one of the oddities of literature. They contain a collage of documents, letters, journals, verbatim statements and accounts of court proceedings. Some are in foreign languages, with translations provided; most are copies of originals made by Pepys's clerks.[45] Assembled, they bring us face to face with crooks and informers, men and women, victims and decent witnesses, allowing us to hear their words as they spoke them and to follow them on their travels. Colonel Scott, with his boasts, his fights, his swearing, his false names and disguises – now burnt-cork eyebrows, now a milliner's dress – his selling of non-existent property, his desertion of his American wife, his preying on widows and their children, his composition of vile love poems, his claim to alchemical powers, his travels, his boasting of grand connections and his cowardice in battle, his court-martialling at Nevers and spreading of mischief wherever he travelled, in America, England, Holland and France, swells into a ludicrous but still alarming scoundrel. And however Pepys suffered from Scott's accusations, he became fascinated by him – just how fascinated appears in the fact that he named the book he made after one of Scott's fantasies.

Among his extravagant lies, Scott laid claim to the ownership of an estate that he called Mornamont, and in France he was sometimes known as 'Seigneur d'Ashford et de Mornamont'.[46] In the real world there was no Mornamont, just as there was no case against Pepys; but the name, and Scott's myth-making, appealed to him so much that he enshrined it in his work by naming the whole thing Mornamont – 'my book of Mornamont', he called it, or 'my two volumes of Mornamont'. It was a title fit for a romance, and a reminder that the young Pepys who wrote 'Love a Cheate' had not been entirely swallowed up in the administrator. 'Mornamont' speaks of things Pepys understood very well, ambition, fantasy and the eternal human ache to get your hands on some money. It has all the raw materials for a novel by Defoe, and it is Pepys's most surprising legacy.

23. Travels for the Stuarts

In June 1680 Pepys was out of danger but he was also still out of work. Whatever personal favour the king showed him, he did not offer him a job. When the royal summons to Newmarket came that September, Pepys went determined at least to put in a claim to arrears of payment owing to him. Charles had other ideas and asked him to take down his account of his escape after the battle of Worcester in 1651. Pepys, flattered, did so, using his shorthand. He did not get his arrears. A touch of his old sharpness about the king appeared in a letter to James Houblon from Newmarket, saying there was 'nothing now in motion but dogs, hawks, and horses; so that all matters look as they were left to God Almighty to look after, and much more happy it might have been for us all had they been long ago so'.[1]

As he wrote this letter, his father was dying at Brampton. John Pepys had reached eighty and Sam, now forty-seven, could be said to be his one success in life; the two men lived in different worlds, but the son had never failed to treat his father with respect. His death signalled a general change at Brampton. Pall's husband, Jackson, had died a few weeks before, Pall herself was ill, the estate had to be sorted out, the house needed repairs, and Pepys's nephews Sam and John had reached the age when they must be educated if they were not to be bumpkins like their father, a man 'of no education nor discourse'.[2] Pepys hurried back to London and returned in his own coach to take charge, bringing with him Paul Lorrain, a young French Protestant who had been clerking for him for three years, and bundles of paperwork, including the half-completed 'Mornamont'. Many bits of legal business had to be dealt with, and a schoolmaster sought; happily the current headmaster of the grammar school, John Matthews, was a distant cousin and prepared to take the Jackson boys as boarding pupils.[3] There was not much joy for anyone at Brampton. Hinchingbrooke stood across the meadows unchanged, but no longer to be visited as family; Pepys's families were all in London now. He sent off letters to Hewer, to the Houblons, to Lady Mordaunt, to the Skinners.

Houblon and Hewer kept him informed of what was happening in the reconvened parliament, where Harbord and Shaftesbury's party were keeping up their call for the duke of York to be excluded from the succession and for driving Catholics out of public life.

December saw Pepys back in Buckingham Street, leaving Lorrain at Brampton to supervise the building work. Pall came to London for medical advice. Sometimes Pepys thought of disposing of Brampton, sometimes he revived his old idea of retiring to live the life of a modest country squire. In the spring he worried about the pasture and how the maid he left there should deal with the two cows and a calf; and he took himself back in June and stayed for another six weeks of summer weather.[4] While he was there he went into Cambridge and considered a proposal that he might become provost of King's. The offer was tempting enough to allow him to dream of being installed there and settling to write the great naval history Evelyn was urging him to take on; but he hesitated, and lost his chance.[5] London was in any case too strong a draw. Should he find a town house of his own? Hewer refused to allow the idea, protesting that he had never been so happy as he was with Pepys in his house: 'if I know my own heart, I am much more contented in my present condition, then I ever was in any'.[6] They were joined by shared ambitions and labour, by twenty years of memories in common and by their beloved dead. It is possible that Will felt himself to be Pepys's guardian, as he had once been appointed by Elizabeth; then against Deb, now against Mary. Will could be prim. He referred to Lord Brouncker's consort Abigail Williams as 'the Lady belonging to the . . . family', as though he could not bring himself to name the shocking creature; but he could be trusted with Pepys's petty secrets, like the volume of Rochester's rude poems kept in the right-hand drawer of his desk.[7] Pepys remained in Buckingham Street.

At Brampton he had builders working on a new staircase. Now the idea came to him that the place could become a temporary solution to the problem of St Michel's family. He had arranged a posting in Tangier for Balty, and Esther was as usual unprovided for. Pepys dispatched her to Brampton with her five children and an allowance of a pound a week. There she remained for a year, complaining, not unreasonably, that this was not enough to live on. Pepys insisted that he and Elizabeth had lived on no more for several years in London, adding that he still had her accounts to prove it.[8] Esther explained that food was more expensive in the country: 'All Gardinage is derer here A peny in too pence,' she wrote. She also passed on a message from his builders: 'the worke men which were Imployed About your honers stare Case are in great distres for want of there mony and desiers to be remmebred [*sic*]'.[9] Although she failed to move Pepys on the matter of her allowance, to the impartial reader she makes her point. Pepys need not have done anything at all for the St Michels, and he had many calls on his charity, but Balty had done well for him in Paris, and Esther was not a countrywoman who knew how to grow her own vegetables; he could have spared a few extra shillings. She remained at Brampton throughout the winter, and Pall joined her in the spring of 1682; the two women came from different compartments in his life and did not make friends. Esther departed in August. Meanwhile Balty hated Tangier and was manoeuvring to return.

When Pepys wanted fresh air now he went with the Houblons to a villa they rented together at Parson's Green. He lived quietly, keeping his head down while Shaftesbury mounted a final attempt to defeat the duke of York in the spring of 1681. People were nervous of a return to the 'tumults, confusions and rebellions of 1641 and 2', although no one has left a description of the atmosphere to match his accounts of London in 1659 and 1660.[10] Pepys advised Morelli to stay out of town. Morelli, hearing Pepys had a fever, asked him to send nail clippings and hair, proposing a magical cure. Pepys applied to Mills, still vicar of St Olave's, for another sort of magic, a certificate of regular attendance at church, as well as one proving that Elizabeth died in the Protestant faith. They show how vulnerable he still felt, and Mills obliged, crediting him with an attendance record that owes more to his good nature than to the truth. Hewer was one of the signatories of the document, Mary Skinner's father another. Of Mary herself there is not a shred of news. She was still kept in her separate compartment; but her brothers did not hesitate to ask favours of Pepys. Between 1680 and 1683 he helped three of them, 'Little Obrian Skinner', Peter Skinner, who expressed a wish to go to sea and was found a place by Pepys, and Daniel, on his travels again, for whom he wrote a letter of introduction to an old friend, Will Howe from the Sandwich household, now a judge in Barbados.[11] Mary's mother told Pepys later that one of her husband's last wishes before he died in

1684 was that their son Peter should be 'brought up with you', which suggests a degree of intimacy.[12] Young Daniel did nothing in Barbados, and turned up in Cambridge again in 1681 to swear the oaths of allegiance and supremacy and to be seen taking communion as a good Protestant.[13]

Other old friends were given a helping hand. At a guess it was Pepys who put in a good word for Betty Martin when she was awarded a pension of £100 a year in the summer of 1680, on a Privy Seal warrant, two years after her husband died in a debtors' prison. Pepys did not forget personal favours. In December 1681 he wrote to Lord Brouncker recommending William Bagwell, master-carpenter of Deptford, for further promotion and praising his diligence, sobriety and fidelity in the service of the navy; whether Mrs Bagwell still had charms for him as she approached forty is not on record; six years later he wrote to her husband telling him to keep her away from his office.[14] The obliging Mr Mills's son-in-law was also found a place at the Navy Office.[15]

The political situation changed again in 1681 when the king summoned a parliament in Oxford only to dismiss it, depriving Shaftesbury of his power base; he was arrested and imprisoned, and, although no London jury would find him guilty of treason, he had come to the end of his career. Dryden, at the king's suggestion, immortalized him cruelly as the false Achitophel: 'In friendship false, implacable in hate: / Resolv'd to ruin or to rule the state.' Shaftesbury, broken and ill, took himself into exile and died in November 1683. The king ruled without parliament until the end of his reign, and the duke of York's succession seemed secure. Whatever this meant for the country, it made things easier for Tory Pepys. Still no job, but as soon as Shaftesbury's defeat was certain, he was invited to rejoin the governing board of Christ's Hospital. The school became a major interest, and when the death of Tom Edwards in December 1681 left Jane with two young children, he saw how he could help her. She returned to London to work at Buckingham Street – Hewer had always thought highly of her – and Pepys arranged for ten-year-old Sam Edwards to be admitted to Christ's Hospital, where he flourished.[16]

At the same time Pepys was engaged in commissioning a large painting for the school. Once again he chose to defy anti-Catholic prejudice, inviting Antonio Verrio, a Catholic painter from Naples, to carry out the work. He was favoured by the king, his 'antique and heroical' frescos adorning Windsor Castle, and the new work was intended to honour Charles's benefactions to Christ's Hospital. Pepys himself was to be one of the solemn figures standing alongside the king; he borrowed scarlet robes from a City alderman friend in which to be painted.[17] He was invited to Newmarket again in March 1682; Pearse the surgeon, still rich in gossip, was in attendance. Pepys sent off a skittish account to Lord Brouncker, saying the town was full and 'I have not yet been at Mrs Nelly's [Nelly Gwyn], but I hear Mrs Knight is better, and the King takes his repose there once or twice daily.' The once or twice is the point: Charles was fifty-two – three years older than Pepys – and Mrs Knight was the latest addition to the royal harem.[18]

The duke of York was also at Newmarket. He had come from Scotland, and was due to return to Edinburgh in May to fetch his duchess. He decided to make a sea voyage of it and gave Pepys a last-minute invitation to join his party. Pepys feared seasickness, and when he went aboard the duke's ship, the *Gloucester*, he found it crowded with courtiers and decided to move himself to a half-empty yacht, a decision that probably saved his life, because the weather turned fierce, a pilot made a misjudgement, and at dawn the next day the *Gloucester* hit a sandbank. The duke was escorted into a boat with John Churchill; his dog was also rescued. Apart from that, one other boat carried a few grandees to safety and a few more were taken up out of the water; two hundred courtiers and sailors drowned.

Pepys remained remarkably calm, sent reassuring letters to his friends, and once on dry land again did not allow the tragedy to interfere with his sightseeing. Glasgow was 'a very extraordinary town for beauty and trade', he noted, but the Scots in general he found short on hygiene, as he explained with Johnsonian candour to Hewer: 'a rooted nastiness hangs about the person of every Scot (man and woman), that renders the finest show they can make nauseous, even among those of the first quality'.[19] Travelling south again, he visited Berwick, Holy Island, Newcastle, Durham and Hull – and was then summoned home by what he took to be an urgent note from Hewer. In fact it was a hoax, written in a disguised hand by Lady Mordaunt, intended as 'a sportful revenge' for his having left London without telling her. There was a touch of spite about it, since it cut short his enjoyable tour; also a touch of possessiveness; but if Pepys resented it he was flattered too, because he copied it out into his letter book.

In his absence, Colonel Scott had reappeared in London, to crown his career by murdering a hackney coachman in a quarrel over the fare. He had to flee the country and did not trouble Pepys again, although word sometimes came of him from places as distant as Norway, where his fantastical boasts and stories of betrayal were brought out for wondering listeners. Morelli also left England; from Brussels he kept in touch with his old employer, but fell out of favour when he did not let him know he was getting married. Pepys never liked his servants or relatives to marry without consulting him.[20]

In other ways the years had changed him. The young man who wanted to know, do and conquer everything, and who could look into his own heart and write with so much fluency and freedom, had stiffened a little, and grown more cautious. His backbreaking service to the king and the navy had been rewarded neither with honours nor with a great fortune. His exertions and prudence meant he was comfortably established, but his fortune could not begin to compare with that of a James Houblon. He had no real home of his own, no place in which his taste and imagination could express themselves; no children to carry his name forward and keep his memory alive; instead, many dependants, most of them embarrassing ones. He had suffered wounds, private and public, of a kind that do not easily heal. One was the death of a wife whom he had partly loved and used ill: remorse and loss go badly together. Another was the attack from men he had expected to welcome him to the House of Commons and respect him as a colleague, and who had instead pitched him into a nightmare, unmerited and pointless. A third was the carelessness of the king, his failure to appreciate the value of Pepys's service or to help him. 'Most princes . . . think that they ought never to remember past services, but that their acceptance of them is a full reward,' wrote his contemporary Bishop Burnet, meaning Charles.[21] Pepys set down part of what he felt about his behaviour during the Popish Plot in his naval notes: 'No king ever did so unaccountable a thing to oblige his people by, as to dissolve a Commission of the Admiralty then in his own hand, who best understands the business of the sea of any prince the world ever had, and things never better done, and put it into hands which he knew were wholly ignorant thereof, sporting himself with their ignorance.'[22] The king's frivolity shocked him more than his ingratitude.

All these circumstances meant that life was a heavier weight on his shoulders than it had been. He did not know where he was going next. He had thoughts of writing, and had he felt less oppressed he might have turned the collection of documents that make up 'Mornamont' into the narrative version it cried out for. Or he could have embarked on an earlier plan for a history of the Dutch wars, originally suggested to him by Coventry; Pepys thought it should be written 'not in style of Panegyric or Apology, which sort of writing have seldom any great Authority or lasting reputation with Posterity', and that it should include proper praise of the Dutch leaders, 'by which the whole History will appear more candid and disinterested'. The work would have suited his intelligence and reporting skills; but he knew it required research in Holland as well as among English state papers, not something he could carry out at this point.[23] It would have been a much more feasible project for him than the one Evelyn was encouraging him to pursue, the 'General History of Navigation' from biblical and ancient times to the present. Evelyn wrote enthusiastically, intending to be helpful, his letters so erudite and discursive they can only have been daunting; still, Pepys borrowed papers from him and made notes.[24]

Suddenly, in August 1683, without any warning, the king found something for him to do. He was told to take himself, at two days' notice – Stuart style again – to Portsmouth, 'without any account of the reason of it', ready to embark for an unknown period and destination under the command of Lord Dartmouth, whom he hardly knew but had at least met on the Scottish trip. There was no chance to make any farewells face to face, and he had to send hurriedly written letters explaining what had happened to his closest friends, the Houblons, the Gales, Deane, Brouncker, Lady Mordaunt, Evelyn, even to Mary – we can take it that the word 'Woodhall' in his list meant Mary.[25]

He was at least to be paid, at a rate of £4 a day; and there were other congenial conditions. His one-time clerk Sam Atkins was appointed secretary to Dartmouth, and Pepys was also able to take his 'neerest friend', Hewer, with him, and to recommend the chaplain for the expedition, Dr Thomas Ken of Winchester: a good and amiable man, even if his sermons proved 'weak', 'unsuccessful' or even 'forced meat'.[26] Arrived at Portsmouth, he found they were to sail with a 'very fair squadron of ships' to Tangier, taking with them another old friend and charmer of Elizabeth, Henry Sheeres, the engineer responsible for the breakwater, or Mole, at Tangier. Pepys settled into his cabin aboard the *Grafton* and started a new diary; his eyes were good enough to allow him to write it himself in shorthand, but in every other way it is unlike the great Diary.[27]

What had happened? Life had bruised him, it's true. He had held a high position and hoped to do so again, and had perhaps come to think that discretion, even in communion with himself, was safer than fearless and brilliant self-exposure in one travelling as an official answerable to the crown. There is no zest in the Tangier Diary. The curiosity about himself and the world, the energy and stylistic inventiveness, are gone with the spring of his earlier prose. Nor is his heart what it was. Putting in to Plymouth Sound at the start of the trip, he calls on Anne, Lady Edgcumbe, whom he had known as a child, daughter of Lord and Lady Sandwich. She is now a mother herself, mistress of Mount Edgcumbe, and receives him 'extreme kindly'; he views her house, garden and beautiful park, but has nothing personal, no allusion to the past or her parents, to add, even though Lady Sandwich is buried on the estate. And after this the voyage is a flat record of meetings, sermons, seasickness, letter writing, variable weather and the other features of life at sea: porpoises swim alongside, the sailors make music and dance, one is punished for drunkenness and another, a Turk, for attempted buggery (Pepys now knows what the word means). He reads the Bible, stargazes on a fine, still night, makes another attempt at *Hudibras*, studies Hooke's *Micrographia* and argues against the existence of spirits with Dr Ken. It has period interest, naturally, but it could be almost anyone's diary. Even when he arrives at Tangier and comes face to face with his brother-in-law he only notes that St Michel is 'mightily altered in his looks, with hard usage as he tells me', and that is all he has to say of him.[28]

The object of the voyage was a strict secret until a week after embarkation, when Dartmouth told Pepys, but not the others, that the colony was being abandoned. They were going to evacuate it and blow the whole place up, including the Mole; and Dartmouth showed Pepys the detailed plans worked out in London. Sheeres was not

informed until they were about to anchor that he was to be in charge
of destroying his own work, a task so appalling to contemplate after
his years of effort that it is surprising he agreed to carry it out. Even
for Pepys, who dutifully wrote out a list of notes 'towards reasons for
justifying the prsent demolishing of Tangier' on the voyage, there was
an irony about the situation that may not have escaped the king. The
idea that Tangier could become a naval base for the English in the
Mediterranean had been Lord Sandwich's, and when Portugal made
it part of Queen Catherine's dowry in 1662 it was he who chose the
site for the Mole, which was to provide sheltered mooring. Through
Sandwich Pepys had been put on to the Tangier Committee. He
had worked closely with the engineers, first Hugh Cholmley, then
Sheeres, as they put their best energies and skills into constructing the
Mole that was now, after twenty years' work, nearly 500 yards long and
30 yards wide, with houses built along one side, gun emplacements,
moorings and huge arched cellars on the other. The expense had been
vast not only for the work but for the maintenance of a garrison in a
place encircled by hostile Moors. It was on the back of all this
expenditure that Pepys had made so much money during his fourteen
years as treasurer for Tangier; but, while it had brought wealth to him
and a few others, it had not proved its value to England, and by the
late 1670s questions were being raised about its future. Many naval
officers said they preferred Gibraltar; and early in 1681 Sheeres was
warned that parliament and some of the king's advisers would like to
see Tangier 'blown up in the air'. Having tried to sell it, first to France
and then back to the Portuguese, this is what the king was now about.

   There was a further irony for Pepys in that he longed to travel and
had been largely unable to satisfy his longing; but his ambition was to
visit the great cities of Europe, and instead he found himself dispatched
to a place that had almost nothing to interest and much to disgust
him. He was allocated the job of assessing the value of the property
of the about-to-be dispossessed residents; he formed a poor opinion
of them and was shocked by the behaviour of the garrison. Under the
Portuguese Tangier had been beautifully laid out and maintained, its
castle, churches and narrow streets of whitewashed and flat-roofed
houses provided with well-tended gardens and orchards; the English
and Irish soldiers of the garrison, hard drinkers and badly disciplined,
neglected and spoilt the place, even burning down the trees – olive,

lemon, mulberry and fig – planted by their predecessors. On arrival
Pepys wondered that anyone had ever thought it could be defended
against the Moors encamped all round it, and expressed his amazement
'that the king has laid out all this money upon it'.[29] He was tormented
by bed-bugs and mosquitoes, caught a cold that would not go away
and was frightened by 'old swimming in my head at my rising and
most of the morning, which makes me melancholy, and a fear also of
my right foot being lame'. When he felt better he washed his feet and
thighs in brandy.[30] Letters from England took a month. Pepys was
disgusted by the sexual licence of the garrison. At the end of November
he abandoned his diary.[31]

The separate miscellaneous notes he kept include accounts of the
dissolute habits of Colonel Percy Kirke, the governor, and Admiral
Arthur Herbert, promiscuous and pox-ridden, of whom Pepys particularly disapproved. He detested everything about Herbert, a Shaftesbury
supporter, very popular in the navy, surrounded by cronies and known
to ill-treat his Turkish prisoners. Pepys also considers more general
matters of naval discipline in a way that suggests he was hopeful they
might become his province again, with the Whigs out of power; and
notices how the attitude of officers towards him improves as the political
situation shifts. The relative merits of gentlemen officers and those 'tarpaulins' who rose through the ranks comes up, and he criticizes Dartmouth for letting the gentlemen captains get away with things: ' 'Tis
pretty to how my lord himself can pass by anything in a gentleman
captain and let it be made a jest, let it be never so clear a breach of
order.'[32] Pepys the meritocrat claims he could find in any gentleman's
family, if you looked back over three generations, evidence of 'bastardy,
disloyalty, knavery, mechanicry [working-class origins] or poverty'.

He discusses whether captains should be allowed the 'Good
Voyages' that earned them personal profits, paid by merchants
whose money, plate and goods they agreed to carry while officially
on duty serving the king. He considered it an abuse, while noting the
view that employment was so uncertain for officers that they needed to
make money whenever and however they could. He was also sternly
critical of the king for undermining good naval discipline by favouritism
and light-heartedness, and records disapprovingly how Charles had
laughed at an officer and called him a fool for his correct behaviour in
refusing a 'Good Voyage' and losing £4,000 for his own pocket.

Many of Pepys's virtues appear in these notes – his open-mindedness, for instance, as he insists on the superiority of the diet of the Turkish navy, almost meatless and rich in water, oil, olives and rice, over the beef-and-beer-obsessed English. We see the genesis of what became the Navy List as he jots down the idea of a list of all captains, to be drawn up: he saw that proper list-making was an essential adjunct to discipline. He was also insistent on the importance of captains keeping proper journals of all voyages, which many simply did not bother to do. He broods on the education of officers, and remembers Penn, who went to sea as a boy with his father before he was set to any formal study of navigation, and is now surprisingly elevated to the status of a model by Pepys.

You sense that he is in his element here, practical, authoritative, ready to listen to captains and clerks but sure of himself when he delivers his own view of how things should be done in his beloved navy. Then, suddenly, in the middle of these busy notes, he describes taking a boat, going out rowing alone and experiencing a moment of sublimity: 'I know nothing that can give a better notion of infinity and eternity than the being upon the sea in a little vessel without anything in sight but yourself within the whole hemisphere.'[33] The lines tell us that a spark of the younger diarist who felt the beauty and strangeness of the world is after all still alight.

Pepys had never thought of visiting Africa. What he had dreamt of was travelling in Europe, further than his brief trips to Holland and northern France, south to Italy and the great cultural meccas; so a visit to Spain had been in his mind from early in the Tangier expedition. He gave up any idea of being home by Christmas and asked Dartmouth if he and Will Hewer might be ferried across the straits when he had finished his work in the colony. Dartmouth agreed but wanted them back in three weeks; and they were taken to Cadiz aboard the *Montagu* at the beginning of December.[34] They embarked in a downpour, and their bad luck was that the worst winter for decades had settled on Europe. In London the Thames was frozen thickly enough for carriages to cross the ice and stalls to be set up, and even in southern Spain there was steady, torrential rain and flooding. The two men struggled as far as Seville, where they were stuck for six weeks as rivers burst their banks and any further progress became impossible. Pepys jotted down a few terse, impersonal notes about Spanish life: 'Won't piss in the streets, but doors.' 'Rare to see a Spaniard drunk.' 'A ploughman, or even a beggar that has not shoes to his feet, will have slashed sleeves and his laced band sewed to his shirt.' He managed to satisfy his curiosity about some celebrated miraculous cures, extracting a confession that they were faked to impress simple people, not aimed at clever ones like him. Pepys the sceptic was pleased with this piece of research; but the Pepys who went to Spain to store up impressions and add to his store of knowledge, to visit remarkable cities and admire renowned picture collections, was bitterly disappointed by the trip.[35] As they returned to England with the fleet they were held up for further weeks by continuous storms that kept driving them back. His fifty-first birthday and the anniversary of his stone operation were both spent at sea; and, having expected to be away for two months when they set sail the previous summer, he and Will did not reach England until the end of March 1684.

24. Whirligigs

He was in London at the beginning of April 1684 to find everything changed. The Stuart whirligig was bringing in its revenges again, and its rewards too, and the king had resolved at last not only to rid himself of the Admiralty commissioners Pepys despised but to create a new position for him, restoring him to his official life. His five years in limbo were over. He was in effect given ministerial powers, as secretary for the affairs of the Admiralty of England, and in May he was back at Derby House as though he had never left, signing orders, sending for reports from the yards, reprimanding officers for slackness, drunkenness or failure to keep proper records and accounts, and finding jobs for the deserving. His salary came to £2,000 a year, with the usual extra payments for passes and appointments; on top of that he had nearly £1,000 due to him for the Tangier trip. The duke of York was now working closely with the king again; Pepys conferred with his royal masters at least once a week, and resumed his visits of inspection to the yards at Deptford, Chatham and Portsmouth. He expected to find signs of neglect and did: toadstools 'as big as my fists', he wrote, were growing in the unaired holds of some of the ships he had caused to be built five years before. He began to prepare one of his reports on the state of the navy and the 'disorders and distresses' into which it had fallen.[1]

The king's enemies were being punished vigorously. He had decided to abolish the ancient charters of city and trade corporations, known strongholds of Whig opposition. Even – and especially – the City of London, so proud of its power and independence, was to lose its charter. Pepys was called on to demonstrate his Tory loyalty by rewriting the charter of the Trinity House, on whose board he had served for many years; and, when he was appointed to its mastership by royal command, he felt obliged to take immediate steps to remove 'dissenters from the Church' and any suspected of disaffection to the government from its membership. It was not the action of the old tolerant Pepys, but times had changed.[2]

His new eminence attracted other honours. In December 1684 he was elected president of the Royal Society. He may have been chosen, like Joseph Williamson before him, for his influence and administrative skills, but he was also friendly with many of the scholars and scientists who met at Gresham College. In the same month he became president he was engaged with an ex-president, Christopher Wren, in putting up a gilded statue of the king's grandfather, James I, at the Royal Exchange, commissioned by the Clothworkers' Company and carved by Grinling Gibbons. Pepys's own face, in the Godfrey Kneller portrait painted for the Royal Society in 1684, shows the same fleshy lips and nose as in earlier portraits, but the eyes more knowing: this is a man who has seen a great deal and has few illusions about the world, pleased as he is with his position.

Behind the triumphant public foreground his domestic life was also changing discreetly. He arrived back from Spain to find that Mary's father had died and that her foster-mother Dame Elizabeth Boteler was also on her deathbed at Woodhall. She died in April, leaving Mary enough to make her financially independent, but deprived of one she loved and relied on.[3] At the same time Lord Brouncker, Pepys's old Navy Board colleague and friend, died, and Pepys was executor to his will, which left his entire estate to his 'beloved friend', Abigail Williams. Pepys had always disliked and disapproved of her ('doxy', 'whore', 'prating, vain, idle woman'), and even prevented Elizabeth from calling on her.[4] Yet here he was faced with a striking example of a mistress allowed her dignity, fully acknowledged and made secure by her aristocratic lover, a man he respected. Whether or not this caused him to reflect that Mary had now been his mistress for fourteen years, and to take stock of their situation, by the following year she seems to have moved into Buckingham Street, and from this point Pepys and 'Madam Skinner' presided over a single household in something like a dignified partnership. Tactful Evelyn was soon referring to him as 'so long the Master of a Familie, the Husband of so excellent a Lady'.[5] Mary was never an intellectual companion, and he complained bitterly of boredom and loneliness when he did not see his men friends; they, however, found her an agreeable hostess. And he enjoyed teaching her and encouraging her artistic interests, as he had encouraged Elizabeth's. Among his notes is a list of educational visits to be made with her, including one to show her Gresham

College. Others are to see processes such as enamelling, copper and gold work, wire-making, ribbon and stocking weaving, gilding and founding of letters used for printing. Evelyn refers to her adorning a cabinet that he compares to those at Versailles in its beauty: Evelyn was a flatterer – he goes on to suggest there is no need to go to France for one who can see Mrs Skinner's cabinet – but it shows she took her artistic work seriously.[6]

Her installation may have been partly responsible for Will Hewer giving up his lease on the Buckingham Street house and moving out. He acquired another in the neighbourhood and took Jane Edwards to be his housekeeper there, while his mother settled in his country house in Clapham.[7] In the summer before he moved there was nearly another fire disaster, with more panicky packing up of books, papers and household goods, and No. 12 was saved only at the last minute when troops were brought in to blow up its neighbour. In spite of this, Pepys asked permission to transfer the Admiralty Office from Derby House to Buckingham Street. So high was he in favour that it was granted, in what must be the only instance of a civil servant being allowed the privilege of bringing his place of work into his home. The office went with them when he and Mary moved three years later into a larger house at the end of the street, facing directly on to the river and with a strip of garden in front, planted with trees.[8]

In January 1685 Pepys presented the king with his paper on the state of the navy. Charles did not read it because on 1 February he had a stroke. He lingered for a few days while his doctors tried their remedies, painful and distressing ones that he bore gallantly, and Dr Ken – now a bishop – offered him the sacrament according to the Church of England. This he refused, and his current French mistress, helped by the duke of York, smuggled in a priest to allow him to make his peace with the Catholic Church. It was a shifty arrangement, but he accepted it, and so he died in his mother's faith. Charles was laid in his grave with little ceremony for fear of disturbances. Pepys soon heard a rumour of the Catholic deathbed. He was bold enough to question the new king, James II, and had it confirmed by him. He passed the information on to trusted friends, and Evelyn's opinion was that James's open Catholicism was preferable to Charles's concealment.[9] It was not a view shared by the nation.

Having worked devotedly with James when he was duke of York,

Pepys could count on a continuation of royal favour. He walked prominently in the coronation procession, and was returned to parliament in the first election following it, for Harwich; Hewer also became an MP, as did Mary's foster-father, Sir Francis Boteler. Pepys was invited to become deputy-lieutenant for Huntingdonshire. He had James's support for his plan for a special commission to restore the navy to efficiency, and he had every reason to expect to be in charge of naval affairs until he chose to retire in a glow of success and splendour, ten years or more in the future. This did not happen for one reason only: whereas his agenda was the navy, the king's was the restoration of the Catholic faith in England. It brought disaster to both of them in rather less than four years.

The character of James II has not found much favour with posterity. His childhood began in the impersonal splendour that was the lot of royal babies, and became uncertain and frightening as the civil war started when he was nine; at thirteen he was handed over to the parliamentary forces and imprisoned in London, and two years later he escaped in disguise. The happiest years of his life were almost certainly those in which he was a professional soldier, serving with the French and then the Spaniards, and distinguishing himself by his bravery and dash. He showed the same energy and courage when he was given the chance to fight at sea after the Restoration. Otherwise the way of life at his brother's court was enough to undermine any but the strongest character: lechery, intrigue, gambling, hunting and horse-racing. James did not resist the temptations on offer. He was not stupid, but his view of the world was narrow, as so easily happens with royalty, and he was without subtlety in his dealings with people. Like Pepys, he kept some sort of diary; unfortunately it did not survive, and the biography based on it and published in the nineteenth century is essentially political, self-justifying and without self-awareness or original insights.[10] Whereas Charles had learnt to charm and prevaricate, James expected immediate compliance with his wishes; when he was opposed he became more rigid, and when the opposition threatened to succeed he was thrown into panic. His decision to become a Catholic seems to have been a quest for something serious and stable in his life; it was unfortunate that it was combined with the belief that he was entitled to absolute power when he became king.

Pepys liked and trusted his new master, but he had no intention of converting to Catholicism himself, as his friend Dryden and some others did. He trod carefully. He contributed to funds to help Huguenot refugees driven out of France by Louis XIV's Catholic persecution; but when Dr John Peachell, master of Magdalene and vice-chancellor of Cambridge University, wrote to tell him he feared he was going to lose his position for opposing the king in the granting of a degree to a Benedictine monk, there is no record of Pepys's reply, and more than a year elapsed before he tried to help Peachell, who was indeed dismissed.[11] Pepys naturally kept quiet when James talked about miracles enacted in Spain, which rested on the cheat Pepys himself had discovered; but he could not resist telling Evelyn the whole story.[12] He was often at court, and sometimes privately satirical about aspects of what went on there: 'Tonight we have had a mighty Music-Entertainment at court, for the welcoming home of the King and Queene. Wherein the frequent Returns of the Words Arms, Beauty, Triumph, Love, Progeny, Peace, Dominion, Glory &c had apparently cost our Poet-Prophet more paine to find Rhimes than Reasons.'[13]

James made greater demands on him than Charles. Notes by clerks for the summer of 1686 show Pepys attending Hampton Court or Windsor seven times in June and seven in July, four times in August and five in September; the following summer it was worse, ten times in June, thirteen in July, and a summons to accompany a royal progress in the West Country in August.[14] However tiring, it was the price for being allowed to push through his programme of naval reform, and James agreed to all Pepys's suggestions, allowing him to appoint his own special commissioners and to fix the rules for serving officers. Pepys set out to change the system of payments in the yards under which he had suffered so much in the 1660s, so that everything would be settled on the nail, clearly accounted for, with no accumulation of debts on which interest must be paid. Hewer was made responsible for this, and did as well as could be hoped, although many of the problems remained. Pepys called a conference of shipbuilders, put Anthony Deane in charge, and made plans to repair the yards as well as the ships, build two new frigates a year and improve the supply system. In this he was notably successful. Sir John Berry, a friend from Tangier and Cadiz, advised on discipline at sea, and the king put out a proclamation intended to end 'Good Voyages' and all the corruption and uncertainty that went with them; officers were to be compensated for giving up this source of income by increased allowances. It was an excellent reform in principle but it did not actually happen, because the new allowances were never paid, and 'Good Voyages' continued as before.[15] A striking omission from Pepys's reform programme was his failure to address himself to the worst abuse of all, the pressing of men: it was something he had defended in the past and which he saw no way of bringing to an end, and it remained a blot on the navy until 1815.[16] His insistence on the importance of discipline, planning and the keeping of proper written records at sea and in the yards did, however, produce permanent benefits.

The name of the fourth special commissioner appointed to reform the navy comes as a surprise. It was 'Mr St Michel'. Finding Balty recommended by Pepys to the king for his vigour of mind, zeal and readiness to give his 'whole time to this Your Service, without liableness to Avocation from other Business or Pleasure' makes you wonder for a moment if this can be the same St Michel to whom Pepys so often preached financial prudence and diligence. But Balty was still Elizabeth's brother, and Pepys still felt he must look after him. It was not what a hard-headed administrator would have done, as he knew very well, but he went so far as to get him installed in what had been the Treasurer's House at Deptford.[17] This was the high point of Balty's career, and at the end of 1686 Pepys urged him to take responsibility for his own future, warning him that he himself had lost strength and was suffering from a new kidney stone and an ulcer.[18] Esther was expecting her seventh child at this point, and she died giving birth in February; Balty, left with so many children, showed no sign of giving up his dependence on Pepys. It was not in his nature to plan or save.

Paulina still lived at Brampton, where Pepys's deputy-lieutenant-ship of the county must have taken him from time to time. Judging that Sam, her elder son, was 'heavy and backward in his learning', he sent him to sea at fifteen. The Huntingdon schoolmaster gave better hopes of the younger, and eighteen months after Sam's departure, in June 1686, John Jackson was entered as a pensioner at Magdalene. Well aware of what was expected of him, the thirteen-year-old sent off his first Latin letter to his uncle from his old college, and worked hard for his degree.[19] Jane's son Sam Edwards turned out to be another good boy, not surprisingly given his parentage, and in January 1688 Pepys saw him presented to the king and the lord mayor with the other boys of the mathematics department. Another figure from the past, John Creed, wrote to remind Pepys of their 'long and very singular friendship': he called him cousin, regretted that he himself was still only a Younger Brother of Trinity House, and made it clear he thought he should be made an Elder Brother – what are old friends for? But Pepys was no more disposed to like him than he had been before and did not oblige.[20]

Then there were the deaths of friends. William Coventry, the man he had most respected in public life, with his dry wit, sharp mind and occasional tenderness, died at fifty-eight; he was quite withdrawn from politics and the world, but sharp in mind as ever.[21] Betty Martin, who had cheered Pepys with her appetite for pleasure, departed in the same year. So did the flirtatious Lady Mordaunt, who had cheered him in a different fashion through some difficult years. His pretty Cambridge cousin Barbara, daughter of Roger Pepys and wife of Dr Gale, high master of St Paul's School, died at forty, leaving a large family.[22]

Two weeks after a Royal Society dinner in November 1687, at which Pepys must have spoken with the formidable William Petty, he too died, at his house in Piccadilly. He had been intellectually active to the last, recommending a university for London, a new bridge at Lambeth and the embankment of the river from Lambeth to Rotherhithe.[23] He believed women should be properly educated and made sure his daughter was: 'one day Arithmetick and Account-antship will adorn a young woman better than a suit of ribbands'.[24] He thought the state should support illegitimate children.[25] He proposed decimal coinage and a national health system. He suggested punishing thieves by labour rather than imprisonment. He scorned a peerage – 'I had rather be a copper farthing of intrinsic value, than a brass half crown' – and at the end of his life was advising William Penn the younger how to run his colony.[26] Pepys had eleven of Petty's books in his library, and not long before his death asked him to write an essay for him, a 'Dialogue on Liberty of Conscience', in which Petty was a passionate believer; he obliged, and Pepys kept the essay among his papers. Petty wrote in his will that he was content to die 'in the profession of that faith, and in the practice of such worship, as I find established by the Law of my country, not being able to believe what I myself please, nor to worship God better than by doing as I would be done unto'.[27]

Such views were unusual. Most people in England were thoroughly opposed to liberty of conscience, particularly now they saw their king celebrating mass in public, ignoring the Test Act and putting Catholic officers into the corporations, the army and the navy. His appointment of the Catholic Sir Roger Strickland as commander of the fleet in the Narrow Seas was deeply resented by officers and seamen. He went so far as to sack some high officials who refused to convert, among them his brothers-in-law, Henry and Lawrence Hyde, earls of Clarendon and Rochester respectively, now among Pepys's friends; both were turned out of their government jobs. He began to build up a standing army. He intimidated certain judges and corrupted others. He dismissed his parliament and ruled without it; and he interfered in the universities. A crisis was reached in the spring of 1688 when he ordered his new 'Declaration of Indulgence', which allowed complete freedom of worship, to be read in all the churches in the country. On the face of it this looked like a fair promise of tolerance for all, but this was not how it was interpreted. Seven bishops refused and were imprisoned in the Tower, among them Pepys's friend from the Tangier trip, Bishop Ken. Pepys was present when they were brought to be questioned by the king and Judge Jeffreys, and was called as a witness at their trial in Westminster Hall in June. He managed to say nothing that could help either side; here, as with the navy, he had to tread a most delicate path. The jury was in any case going to find the bishops not guilty, and when it did so the bonfires were lit in the streets, an effigy of the Pope was burnt in front of St James's Palace, money was thrown to the crowds by various noblemen, and the soldiers camped on Hounslow Heath – supposedly there to enforce the king's will – cheered the verdict.

Pepys had seen London boil up regularly throughout his life – in the forties, the fifties, the sixties and the seventies – and now it was boiling again. What made the whole country turn against James was the birth of a son; there were allegations, quite unfounded but widely believed, that the baby was an impostor, smuggled into the queen's delivery room in a warming pan. This coincided with the trial of the bishops, and since the little prince had two Catholic parents and would be brought up a Catholic and take the throne as one, he proved the last straw. A group of politicians was already in touch with William of Orange, husband of James's Protestant daughter Mary, and the people were ready and eager to attack 'Jesuits', 'papists' and Irishmen. Admiral Herbert, whom Pepys had so detested in Tangier, travelled in disguise to Holland carrying a formal invitation to William from leading statesmen and peers to come and take the throne of England; and Herbert, popular as ever among seamen, offered his services to the Dutch fleet to bring him over.[28]

When news came that the Prince of Orange was indeed fitting up his fleet, Pepys went to Chatham to see to the defences and the manning of the ships. He found things in good order technically; the morale of officers and men was less certain. The king appeared calm, as though determined not to take the threat seriously; he had turned down an offer of help from Louis XIV, and when he began to think he might need it after all the French were busy with their own concerns and no ships were available. At the end of September William put out an address to the officers and seamen of the English fleet, naming Herbert as his man, warning them of James's intended destruction of their religion and liberties, and promising favour to 'all who deserve well of Us and of the Nation'.[29] This did make James remove his Catholic commander-in-chief at sea, Strickland, and replace him with Dartmouth, another close friend but a Protestant and so less obnoxious to the men. Pepys drafted the king's instructions on 1 October, requiring him 'to use his utmost endeavours with the Fleet to prevent the Fleet of War expected from Holland from approaching or making any Descent [i.e., landing]'.[30] In October Pepys punctiliously closed his special commission at the end of its two years' work and prepared to support Dartmouth as best he could. Both men were in agonizingly difficult positions, their personal loyalty to James demanding that they support him against his son-in-law, while London, the country and the navy were clearly turning to Protestant William as their saviour.

The king, realizing at last that he had to appease the angry nation, promised an election, restored the City's charter and privileges and the heads of colleges he had sacked. By now William's fleet was about to set sail. It was driven back by a storm. Dartmouth was off Harwich with the English fleet; Pepys suggested he should sail towards the Dutch coast to inspect the damage inflicted by the storm. Dartmouth declined. Pepys's intelligence led him and the king to expect the Dutch to attempt to land in the north-east of England, but, when on 1 November the Dutch embarked again, an east wind sent them along the south coast. The brightly decorated fleet, 200 troop transports escorted by 49 fighting ships, sailed as blithely as though on a pleasure cruise. The country's loyalties were so completely reversed that they were not perceived as a threatening enemy, and the sea battles of the Dutch wars, even the attack on the Medway, were forgotten. With the wind against him, Dartmouth was unable to get his ships out; in any case his captains were reluctant. On the day William landed at Torbay, the English fleet reached Beachy Head and was again becalmed. It was clear they were not going to attack the Dutch. William came ashore peacefully, bringing with him the biggest army that had ever landed in England.

He proceeded adroitly, announcing nothing, asking James only for a free election. James reviewed his troops at Colchester and then set off for Salisbury, first arranging that his infant son should be taken to Portsmouth and conveyed to France; Dartmouth refused to hand over the prince to a foreign power, and the baby was returned to London. At Salisbury James's senior officers, led by John Churchill, began to desert him for William. Pepys's friend Sheeres, still loyal and in command of the dwindling artillery, wrote to Dartmouth to say that the king was almost deserted: 'The King is very ill . . . I am at my wits' end, and you will forgive me, my good Lord, while you know what an aching heart I have for you.'[31] In various parts of the country there were risings in favour of William, and only two military encounters took place between his soldiers and James's, both insignificant.

Strong as Pepys's personal loyalty to James was, he had to think of his own position, and at this stage his behaviour was not quite that of a hero. On 17 November he accompanied James, who was on his way to Salisbury, as far as Windsor, and presented him with an IOU for a sum agreed by Charles II in March 1979, plus further sums due to him as treasurer for Tangier. The king signed, a striking testimonial at such a moment to his friendship for Pepys, and perhaps his view of what was going to happen.[32] As the situation deteriorated for him, Pepys struggled to keep afloat, uncertain what he should do. The letter he sent off to the mayor and Corporation of his constituency at Harwich shows him straining to adopt an acceptable position, loyal to James, but also loyal to the Church of England and prepared for the revolution: 'not but that I do still firmly hope (as Cloudy as things do at this day look) that God Almighty has it yet in his Gracious purpose to support the King and his Government, and strongly protect the Church of England . . . but that hope not being entirely void of some apprehension that things may possibly end otherwise'.[33]

His apprehension was justified. When the king reached London again he found his second daughter, Princess Anne, had fled and put herself under the protection of his opponents. A modern historian has suggested that James suffered a nervous breakdown at this stage, brought on by stress and memories of his boyhood and the fate of his father; certainly from now on there is no sign of the brave young soldier he had been. His behaviour became confused and he was plainly frightened.[34] He agreed to William's terms to remove Catholics from all offices and assign revenues to support the invading forces until an election could be called; he then disbanded his own army without paying it. Pepys signed his orders for the use of a yacht to carry the queen and prince to France, and on 12 December James took flight himself. He was captured by fishermen and held humiliatingly at Faversham while London erupted into riots, and he wrote to William asking to be rescued. A rescue party was sent, and on his return to London the volatile crowds cheered him – the *mobile vulgus*, or the mob, as it was beginning to be known.[35] William was now at Windsor, where he received assurances that the English fleet would submit to him, as he informed Herbert in a note: assurances that can have come only from Dartmouth.[36] The next day William held a council and his troops reached London. James was invited to go to Ham House, on the Thames between Richmond and Hampton Court, but chose to take flight again, to the general relief, and this time it was made sure that he should reach France without hindrance. His flight was not announced for several days, during which London was without any controlling force; a group of peers met and offered to keep order until William arrived in town. On 18 December he was in Whitehall. Pepys was summoned to him the following day. He was not deprived of his office, although his friends expected him to be.

On the same day Hewer wrote to him to say, 'You may rest assured that I am wholly yours, and that you shall never want the utmost of my constant, faithful, and personal service; the utmost I can do being inconsiderable to what your kindness and favour to me has and does oblige me to. And therefore as all I have proceeded from you; so all I have and am, is and shall be at your service.' Pepys inscribed it with the words 'a letter of great tenderness at a time of difficulty', and kept it carefully. It is the nearest thing to a love letter among his papers.[37]

He continued to work throughout the Christmas season, sending William's orders to the fleet on Christmas day itself and attending him again on 12 January, two days after the formal dismissal of Dartmouth. This meant that Pepys had to appear alongside the hated Admiral Herbert to receive instructions for preparing naval defences against any intervention by the French. He gritted his teeth and did so. By now he had decided to stand again in the parliamentary election due to be fought in February. On New Year's Day he wrote again to the mayor of Harwich to sound him out: 'upon so great a Revolution as we are now under, it may very well be that the Corporation may at this Conjuncture think of some Person that may be more useful for them'.[38] He was right to be cautious, but he went ahead, and the old stories were brought out against him. A friend wrote to tell him that a Captain Hugh Ridley of the *Antelope* had declared at a coffee house in Harwich 'that Pepys was a Papist and went to Mass and he had several times observed you at the King and Queen's chapel'. The last part was probably true. There were also cries of 'No Tower men, no men out of the Tower'. He can't have been surprised to lose the election.[39] On 13 February William, who had negotiated firmly for the crown and nothing less, was declared king alongside Queen Mary, with the succession to her sister Anne.

The overwhelming majority of the nation, including high government officials, welcomed the new regime with relief. But there were a few, including the archbishop of Canterbury, who considered themselves bound by their earlier oaths of allegiance to James and refused to take a new one. They were known as nonjurors, and among this small band was Pepys. A week after the proclamation of the new monarchs he resigned his secretaryship. The changes he saw coming in the Navy Office were one reason. There was also his personal loyalty to James, which now became more important to him than any principle involved – for Pepys was a parliamentarian and no believer in absolute monarchy. But where Joseph Williamson was able to move coolly from court supporter under Charles and James to privy councillor under William and continue his career as a diplomat, Pepys could not bring himself to make the necessary adjustments. Memories of the accommodations of 1660 surely made their contribution. He was not going to turn his coat again. Hewer resigned his position alongside him; so did Deane and Pearse; and St Michel lost his. The new secretary to the Admiralty wrote requiring Pepys to hand over his official papers and furniture, and, since his house had been used as a government office, he was also required to vacate it. He dug in his heels at this point and made so many difficulties that the Admiralty gave up and decided in April that it would be easier to set up their offices somewhere else. Pepys remained at the end of Buckingham Street with his household, his books, his pictures, his papers and his view over the Thames, paying his own rent, stubborn and, for the first time in his life, a hero.

25. The Jacobite

Pepys faced an unhappy prospect. His loyalty to King James put him under suspicion, and although he was still a rich man, he was to earn nothing more. There was no pension, and no more contact with his beloved navy. He was harassed by the government, and James's attempts to win back the crown made things worse for him. He could not travel. His domestic life was made awkward by competing claims for his favour. Mary would be forty as he reached sixty, a mistress preparing for her next role as nurse, and not always well herself. Other friends sickened and died, among them his cousin Roger Pepys, who died at the height of the crisis, in October 1688; and his own health deteriorated from year to year.[1] He was used to physical pain but also to physical pleasure; now it was pain on the menu most days. Yet, when you look at his and his friends' letters from the years after 1689, there are few signs of self-pity or failure of nerve, and many of a man busy with plans and projects, determined to think, to act and to renew himself. He had the sustaining force of the love of old friends, and he never stopped making new ones, including younger men whose promise he saw and did what he could to help along. He valued his doctors as much for their conversation as their skills. He gave substantial help to Protestant refugees from France. He took up fresh interests. Unable to travel himself, he made a surrogate of his nephew and through him gloried in the Grand Tour he had dreamt of making. His library became at once his obsession and his comfort. He wrote some magnificent letters. He planned treats for his protégés, commissioned portraits and gave musical parties. He encouraged Dryden to make his version of some of *The Canterbury Tales* and lent him his own early edition; an invitation to discuss Chaucer over a meal of cold chicken and salad is among his letters.[2] There were philosophical exchanges with Evelyn. He never lost the will to squeeze every drop from every day.

He had lost his job before, and knew roughly what to expect in 1689. Many of the men now in power had been Shaftesbury's allies;

they took their old enemy seriously enough to pursue him. On 4 May he was arrested with Hewer and Deane, all three accused of 'dangerous and treasonable practices against his Majesty's government'. They were held in the Gatehouse Prison, in Tothill Street, close to Westminster Abbey. King William was about to declare war on France, as part of a grand alliance against the ambitions of Louis XIV, who, among his other interests, upheld the claim of his cousin James Stuart to the English crown; and James had already left Paris for Ireland to drum up support. Pepys's imprisonment may have been a purely precautionary move, or he may have been suspected of communicating with his old master; and, guiltless as he and his friends appear to have been, in prison they remained until 15 June.

He was bailed, but this was not the end of his difficulties. In July he was formally accused over an incident of 1685 involving an East India ship for which he was in no way responsible; Houblon, a committed Whig himself but staunch as always, intervened to clear the matter up. Then, as James left Ireland for France again, Pepys was hauled in front of a parliamentary committee to be interrogated about the condition of the English fleet currently in Bantry Bay. He dealt easily with this, and returned to sorting his papers and considering how much further he might have to withdraw from public affairs if he were to have any hope of being left in peace. In August he resigned from his position as Elder Brother of Trinity House, ending an association of many years. At the end of the year he responded to a request for his presence at Christ's Hospital on the occasion of a visit by the new king and queen by writing 'Went not' on the invitation; but he did not sever his links with the school.[3] When Deane wrote to him saying he expected nothing more now than 'the old soldiers request, a little space between busines and the grave', Pepys replied robustly, telling him to cheer up, and that for himself 'the worse the world uses me the better I think I am bound to use myself; nor shall any solicitousness after the felicities of the next world . . . ever stifle the satisfactions arising from a just confidence of receiving . . . the reparations due to such unaccountable usage as I have sustained in this'.[4] A man of this world Pepys had always been, and remained; righteous indignation buoyed him up, and he was not going to turn his face to the wall. He continued to attend the meetings of the Royal Society, to entertain, to buy books for his library, to work on its catalogue and to make plans for the future.

When the last of his siblings, his sister Pall, died in November, he had a memorial stone put up in the aisle of Brampton Church – it can still be seen there – and let out the house. He had never cared much for her and had no time at all for her lumpish husband, but she had redeemed herself by giving him nephews. Sam Jackson left the navy and returned to Huntingdon, where he began to behave as though he were entitled to the Brampton rents, and had to be made to understand he was not.[5] John, once he had taken his degree at Cambridge, was invited to move into Buckingham Street and set out to make himself agreeable. He was diligent and a decent scholar; otherwise no nephew could have been less like his uncle. He had a pert, pretty child's face that survived into adult life, when Kneller painted him in a large pale wig. He was not a chancer like his brother, and had none of Pepys's enterprise, originality or charm. Cautious and polite, he was proud of his education and of his status as a gentleman, and knew his future prospects depended on pleasing. The surprise is that Pepys was so very pleased with him. Mary was not, and she and Jackson viewed one another with suspicion.[6]

She had a way of dealing briskly with demands on Pepys she disapproved of. St Michel gives a glimpse of a scene of raw emotions that took place when he called at Buckingham Street and found himself face to face with her. Pepys was absent – in prison – where he received a furious letter of complaint from 'brother Balty': 'I understand that by the malicious inventive ill Offices of a female Beast, which you keepe, I am like allsoe to lye under your Anger and disgrace . . . but I hope, and humbly pray (though she told me impudently, and arogantly, you Scorned to see me) that with your Generous Usuall goodnesse, wisdome, manhood and former kindnesse you will not damn him Unheard whoe Shoold Joy to hazard . . . his dearest Bludd for your Service.'[7] St Michel had just married again, and he must have been desperate for whatever help he could extract from his benefactor. In Mary's eyes he was a scrounger who would never stand on his own feet and whose only claim was through Elizabeth Pepys, dead these thirty years. To Balty Mary was, as well as a female Beast, a kept woman, supplanting his sister and standing between him and his brother-in-law. His rudeness shocked Pepys, who was in any case no longer in a position to fix jobs for Balty. At least his St Michel godson, little Samuel, was already at sea. So was Mary's twenty-year-old brother Peter, also helped by Pepys and also in trouble. Peter Skinner's letters were as grovelling as Balty's, and they came now seeking pardon for his faults, telling Pepys that Mary was 'the Darling of my Repose, the Center of all my Happiness and all my Earthly Felicity' and expressing himself eager to make 'some Retaliation of all past kindnesses which I have received both from you and my Deare Sister'.[8] If this were not enough, Pepys had difficulties with his housekeeper, whose 'bitterness and noise of tongue' he found insupportable; but Mary was her friend and twice saved her from being sacked.[9] The competing claims continued.

Pepys's necessary retreat was his library, and there, or in an adjacent room, high up in the house where the light was good, he sat, alone or with one of his assistants to bring him the books he wanted, to replace them on the right shelf, sometimes to read to him and take dictation. Paul Lorrain had served him for many years, John Jackson was learning to perform some of the same functions, and there came a time when Mary also helped out as a scribe. Two other young men also worked intermittently in the library, David Milo and Thomas Henderson. Apart from this the house was run by a stately staff of nine servants, housekeeper, cook, two footmen, laundrymaid – did he ever recall to himself that this had been his mother's profession? – and housemaid; with a coachman and a porter, and Jones, his personal attendant, who was assigned his own little house in Buckingham Street's York Buildings. Pepys's physical comfort was as well seen to as possible; and Mary was free to follow her own interests as she chose and to make visits to her family, her foster-sister Julia Shallcross in Hertfordshire and her blood sister Frances, Lady Buck, with whom her mother went to live at Hanby Grange, near Grantham in Lincolnshire.[10] In 1690 her foster-father Sir Francis Boteler died, leaving Woodhall to Julia, now a widow.[11]

In 1690 Pepys thought boldly of returning to parliament. Although he had suffered some bad hours in the House, there had been triumphs too, and he was proud of his skill and reputation as a speaker. He wrote to two former colleagues asking if they would help him find a seat in the coming election; if he had any answers – there are none in his files – they were discouraging. He had to accept that his parliamentary career was over. Then in June he was again arrested and imprisoned

in the Gatehouse as 'a suspected Jacobite', this time during an invasion
scare caused by the French fleet, sighted off the Isle of Wight. Again
he was bailed. Will's uncle, Robert Blackborne, whose friendship
went back to 1660, put up part of the money; he had remade his
career and was now secretary to the East India Company, the value
of whose stock had risen spectacularly.[12] James Houblon put up
another part; he was knighted in 1691, and three years later, when the
Bank of England was founded, he sat on the board alongside two of
his brothers.

  Pepys was cleared of the charges against him in October. Things
could have been much worse: his old colleague Dartmouth was
charged with high treason and died in the Tower, aged forty-three.
Another friend, Dr George Hickes, ejected from the deanery of
Worcester for refusing the oath of allegiance to the crown, escaped
arrest only by going into hiding and had to live under assumed names
for years; even so his house was attacked by a mob after an assassination
plot against King William was discovered in 1696. Henry Sheeres was
arrested as a Jacobite at the same time.[13] Pepys had to suffer nothing
more severe now than double taxes for continuing to refuse the oath,
and the consciousness that William III's surveillance system kept an
eye on him. In 1697 he wrote of 'my infirmitys of age and Jacobitism'
to a Huntingdon friend, and when he was preparing to send John
Jackson abroad he provoked a flurry of interest and a suspicion that
the young man might be conveying a message to Pepys's one-time
royal master. Although the matter was not pursued, the suspicion
was not entirely surprising.[14] Hickes had made a dangerous trip to
St Germain to visit James II in 1693; his object was to get his blessing
for the consecration of new, nonjuring bishops who rejected King
William and asserted their loyalty to James; and in 1694 Hickes was
secretly consecrated, along with others, in a private house in London,
in the presence of Lord Clarendon. There was clearly a political
agenda here alongside the religious one, and some inkling of it is likely
to have reached Pepys, who was close to both men; Clarendon dined
with Pepys not long after the consecration.[15] His views were in any
case well known in his own circle; on the accession of Queen Anne
in 1702, the keeper of the Cottonian Library, Thomas Smith, another
nonjuror, sent Pepys a highly indiscreet political letter enclosing 'an
epitaph upon the late high and mighty Dutch hero [William III] as

also some few heroic lines upon *Sorrell* [the horse whose stumble had killed the king]; which after a single reading I presume you will throw into the fire'.[16]

Pepys himself did not cross the Channel again. In 1690 his doctors testified that he had a life-threatening ulcer on one of his kidneys; they must have intended to speed his release from prison and the danger was not immediate, but it was a warning. He knew his own nature well enough to remain active. He still visited and wrote to Lady Mordaunt's sister, Mrs Steward, in Lincoln's Inn. He gave dinners and the occasional musical party, and kept open house on Saturday evenings, gathering friends for conversation, Evelyn, of course, and other botanists, book lovers and scholars, several from the Royal Society. One regular was Captain Charles Hatton, a Jacobite who had been imprisoned in 1690, accused of handing a treasonable paper to the press and held in the Tower.[17] Another was Thomas Gale, drawn closer by the death of his wife Barbara, Pepys's cousin. These Saturday evenings became the high point of his week, and when they lapsed in the summer months he complained of loneliness.[18]

He continued to collect, discard and lend books, and to assist others with their collections; there are sums in his bank account paid to his French bookseller in London, Caillou, and many letters about acquisitions. The Houblons were helpful in getting their dealers to pick up rare volumes around the Mediterranean. He acquired manuscripts, including autographs of Queen Elizabeth, Mary Queen of Scots and Charles I. He also started new collections, one of 'heads', engravings of the famous. He began to bulk-buy collections of old ballads, the crudely printed songs that were sold in the streets, and had them sorted by subject and bound into volumes: 'Devotion and Morality', 'Tragedy', 'Love, pleasant', 'Love, unfortunate', 'Humour, Frolic and Mirth' and so on. His eclecticism made his library unlike any other; it occurred to no one else to preserve so much popular and ephemeral material, and the ballads proved their value within half a century, when Bishop Percy drew on them for his *Reliques of Ancient English Poetry*.

Evelyn was still urging him to write his naval history, and at last he made a gesture and produced a slim volume. *Memoires Relating to the State of the Royal Navy* was more polemic than history, an attack on the navy commissioners of 1679–1684 and a defence of his own work, largely drawn from the paper he had submitted to the king in 1685.

It is passionately self-justifying, the language is unwieldy (probably because it was dictated), and it is bulked out with too many lists of names of ships and officers.[19] Pepys was so uncertain about what he had produced that he read it to Evelyn, whose loyalty to his friend brought his enthusiasm to a rolling boil:

When I Reflect (as who can but Reflect) upon what you were pleas'd to communicate to me Yesterday; so many, and so different passions crowd on my thoughts, that I know not which first to give vent to: Indignation, pitty, Sorrow, Contempt and Anger: Love, Esteeme, Admiration, and all that can expresse the most generous Resent'ments of One, who cannot but take part in the cause of an Injur'd and worthy Person! With what Indignation for the Malevolence of these men, pitty of their Ignorance and Folly, Sorrow and Contempt of their Malice and Ingratitude, do I looke upon and despise them! On the other side, In what bonds and obligations of Love, Esteeme, and just admiration, ought we to Reguard him who dares Expose himselfe to all this suffering with so intrepid a Resolution . . .

It is not a literary judgement, but it is a vintage piece of Evelyn, and was enough to persuade Pepys to publish.[20]

The *Memoires* appeared in 1690, and their subsequent history is more interesting than the book itself. Until the 1980s its arguments were held to be indisputably true; but when the naval historian J. D. Davies took the trouble to research the background, what he found led him to doubt some of Pepys's assertions. Davies believes that Pepys's determination to damn the commissioners of 1679–84 made him less than truthful, and that they did not perform anything like as badly as he said they did. He also points out Charles II's arbitrary and capricious behaviour made difficulties for even the most diligent naval administrators, and that the necessary funding for the navy was rarely made available by the Treasury.[21] Pepys's private notes tend to agree with these points, but he did not choose to make them publicly: in 1690 he put his loyalty to the Stuarts first. Copies of the book were sent out to friends and compliments received; and although he said he planned to publish more naval history, nothing else appeared. He must have seen that his skills did not lie in that direction.[22] Instead, he used some of his notes on naval history to contribute to the work of a young scholar, Edmund Gibson, who was preparing a new edition of *Britannia*, the great popular guide to the British Isles first published a century earlier. Gibson acknowledged that 'the account of the Arsenals for the Royal Navy in Kent with the additions to Portsmouth and Harwich so far as they relate to the Royal Navy were communicated to me by Mr Pepys'.[23]

In January 1692 he was not well enough to attend the funeral of Robert Boyle with his fellow members of the Royal Society, but he invited Evelyn, Gale and Isaac Newton to dine with him to talk over Society matters. Henry Sheeres, also struggling with poor health, sent him a present of a turkey, eggs and bacon from the country; thanking him, Pepys wrote, 'I have missed seeing you or your hand a great while, a welcome visiter being become a great dainty, at least to mee.' A less welcome visitor, St Michel, wrote to thank him for his 'generous goodness, favour, kindeness, and charity' and begging for any old morning gowns, wigs or cloaks he had to spare.[24] The spring was late, and there were fears of invasion by James, supported by the French. A naval battle off the Normandy coast at La Hogue in May gave the English their biggest victory for years. The French were humiliated, fifteen of their ships destroyed, and James abandoned his invasion plans. The navy's triumph in such circumstances stirred complicated feelings in Pepys. One of the victorious English admirals was Clowdisley Shovell, with whom he had clashed on matters of discipline during the 1680s; yet Shovell had learnt his seamanship from Christopher Myngs, a hero of the 1660s much admired by Pepys. Now Shovell was getting medals from William III.

Pepys knew his days of power would not return. He had problems to resolve. In the summer of 1692 he told all his friends he was going to the country. Mary had left town, perhaps for Woodhall, perhaps Lincolnshire. Meanwhile he stayed put and shut himself up in his library for over three months, in order to deal with papers 'that I have so many years been tumultuously gathering and laying by, without a vacancy or hand or head ever to garble, sort, or putt in order for use either to myselfe or any that come after mee'.[25] Only in September did he confess his deceit to Evelyn and Gale, and then he had also to admit that his months of confinement indoors had caused his left leg to swell so badly that he was now unable to put on a shoe or get downstairs, let alone out of the house. What was the 'small peece of Worke' that demanded such absolute and uninterrupted solitude for a man who normally craved company? No explanation was offered, and the state of Pepys's papers as they were left to posterity does not suggest that he spent the time in filing. A guess is that he was reading through his Diary, slowly, as his eyes required, and considering its future and his own. He knew now that he was not going to achieve literary immortality by writing naval history. To leave a book behind you is the surest form of afterlife, as Pepys, reader and collector of books, knew well. He had remarked years before on the death of an eminent doctor that he was a man of good judgement, 'but hath writ nothing to leave his name to posterity by'.[26] Pepys, however, had. There were six volumes, still decently veiled in shorthand, that might one day speak for him to posterity, if he had the courage to allow them to survive. Some time during the last years of his life he thought the matter over, and this mysterious solitary summer stands as a likely moment for him to have done so. The volumes of the Diary were replaced on the shelves and renumbered in the new catalogue he made in 1693.[27]

26. A Journey to be Made

On 29 September 1693, the feast of Michaelmas, Pepys was driven by his coachman out of London and into the country towards the riverside village of Chelsea; they may have been on their way to dine with friends, or simply going to take the air. With him in the coach were some ladies and his nineteen-year-old nephew John, who was sporting a silver-hilted sword. The road ran through meadowland and past isolated farms and a few large villas. When three men on horseback, armed and wearing masks, appeared and put one pistol to the breast of the coachman and another to Pepys, there could be no thought of putting up a fight. The men asked what he had, and he handed over his purse with about £3 in it and the various necessaries he carried with him, his silver ruler, his gold pencil, his magnifying glass and five mathematical instruments. It made an impressive collection, and when he asked to have back one particular instrument he was told that, since he was a gentleman, as his assailant claimed to be also, if he sent to the Rummer Tavern in Charing Cross the following day he should have it. John gave up his sword and hatband. Pepys asked the highwaymen to be civil to the ladies and not to frighten them; and some of the ladies were frightened, but one kept her wits about her: 'My Lady Pepys saved a Bag of Money that she had about her.'[1] So read the law report from which this story comes, because two of the men were tried for the crime at the Old Bailey in December. The men, Thomas Hoyle and Samuel Gibbons, were found guilty partly through the evidence of a witness who saw their faces as they pulled off their masks, and partly because Hoyle was taken at the Rummer Tavern with Pepys's pencil in his possession. Pepys gave evidence at the trial but he would not swear they were the men concerned because he had not seen their faces. Both, however, were found guilty of felony and robbery, condemned to death and hanged. The most quick-witted member of the party seems to have been Mary Skinner – Lady Pepys for the occasion – who managed to keep her money safe under her skirts. She was not asked to be a witness, but she was clearly a force to be reckoned with.

Pepys did not learn to like King William any better as the years went by, but a moment came when he consented to act as an adviser to the regime. It was through Evelyn, a good fixer, who suggested to a friend in government that Pepys was the man to be consulted about the project to build a hospital for sick and wounded seamen at Greenwich. Since it was something Pepys had discussed already with James II, he agreed to go to Greenwich again with Christopher Wren in November 1694 to consider what might be done. He was impressed by the ingenuity and splendour of Wren's proposals, and wrote to Evelyn of 'an *Invalides* with us for the sea, suitable in some degree to that of Paris for the land'. Practical as ever, he also pointed out that the scale of the plans meant the building would need parliamentary funding; and he was proved right, because the work suffered many delays through money running out. Clearly he was pleased to be offering advice once more; and the visit to Greenwich must also have sent his mind back to many earlier occasions – a ramble to the top of the hill with Lady Sandwich; a stroll with the king and the duke on a July morning, young Monmouth running and jumping in circles around them; and the winter of the plague, when he had lived in Greenwich lodgings, riotously. Now, thirty years later, the November afternoon closed the scene fittingly; it was the last official outing he was to make.[2]

Evelyn was feeling his age – he was after all thirteen years older than Pepys – and this year he gave up his Deptford house and moved to Surrey. He still visited London, but occasions for meeting were fewer, and he was not at the council meeting of the Royal Society to which Pepys went soon after his Greenwich visit, to make sure that John Jackson was elected. All went well, and 'Mr Jackson nephew to Mr Pepys and Mr Bridges son to Lord Chandos were ballotted and approved.' Among those present were his old rival John Creed, up from Oundle; his old friend Robert Hooke; and a newer one, the widely travelled young doctor, naturalist and collector, Hans Sloane, acting as secretary of the society and just appointed physician in charge at Christ's Hospital.[3]

Sloane attended Pepys and Mary professionally, getting Mary to go horseback riding for her 'dropsy'. Pepys lent the doctor books and borrowed some in return, enjoying his conversation so much that he wrote to him on one occasion 'almost wishing myself sick, that I might have a pretence to invite you for an hour or two to another [visit] by yourself'.[4] He and Sloane both did their best to encourage a still younger scholar, Humfrey Wanley, who had been a Coventry draper's apprentice until his genius for deciphering and dating almost any piece of writing set before him was noticed by the local bishop, who sent him to Oxford. Pepys's Oxford friends sent him with an introduction in 1695 when Wanley wanted to visit the celebrated Cottonian Library. Pepys arranged this, and showed him his own for good measure.[5] Wanley became deputy librarian at the Bodleian; soon he was writing to the bookdealer John Bagford asking him to help in the pursuit of acquisitions from 'any noble spirited and Worthy Gentlemen, who are Masters of any Curiosities which we want, and are or may be willing to part with to our Library . . . send me word in your next what may be done with Mr Pepys'.[6] Wanley's letters to Pepys are flattering, as the manners of the age required from a poor scholar to a potential benefactor, but they suggest real affection too. In one he assured Pepys that his conversation was 'more nearly akin to what we are taught to hope for in Heaven than that of anybody else I know.'[7] Wanley was on good terms with Mary and with Jackson too; as a palaeographer in constant quest of manuscripts he envied Jackson his chance to travel in Europe, and drafted a long letter to him with questions and suggestions. He also asked Pepys to support his own application to Oxford for funding to visit libraries on the Continent, and Pepys and Sloane both wrote testimonials for him.[8] In such ways Pepys kept in touch with the most advanced scholars and scientists, refusing to allow age or illness to close his mind or dull his curiosity.

He also kept up his interest in Christ's Hospital. The mathematics department was his particular concern, and he was eager to see good results, often asking how the boys fared when they went to sea and sending directives to the staff. When at his request a group of the boys came to his house in 1695 for him to assess their progress, he was disappointed, diagnosed a general slackness in the organization of the school, started a row with the treasurer and wrote to Isaac Newton, no less, asking him to put up the name of a new mathematics master. Newton recommended a young graduate called Sam Newton – not a relation – for his good character and abilities; and after a few months in the job Sam Newton complained to Pepys that the children were being taken out of his hands too young. The school had been set up to educate the boys until they were sent to sea as apprentices at sixteen – but with the proviso 'or if the Master of Trinity House sees fit earlier'. This was the problem, that they were being hauled off to sea before they had a chance to do any serious study by the master of Trinity House, Sir Matthew Andrews, who was also a governor of the school. Sam Newton laid out the situation in a letter to Pepys:

comes Sir Matthew for a Boy, to be putt out the next week. I told him I had none ready, so he replied if there were none ready he must have one unready because he had promised one to a Sea Capt. and that hee would answer (I think he said excuse) the Boye's unpreparedness to the Trinity House. It grieves me to my very Soul when I reflect upon such inconsiderate Actions, and that the most famous Mathematics School . . . should be thus torn in pieces by one man . . . [Such] proceedings will bring down the Honour & Reputation of the Famous Nursery to the level of an Abcdarian, and every common Tarpaulin who never knew either the usefulness or sweetness of Mathematical learning will run down our poor Children . . .: and in time this School which was created on purpose to improve our English seamen in Arts & Sciences (part. Navigation) will fall under the lowest degree of contempt.

It was a brave letter, and it ended with a plea to Pepys to 'find out some Expedient to stop this injurious Career'.[9]

Pepys's answer shocked Newton, because instead of standing up for the boys' right to an education he insisted that he must give way to Sir Matthew, 'not only your Superiour, and so not decently to be contended with by you, but the Person whom you find in a special manner depended on by the House on business of the disposing of the Children'. Pepys had worked with Sir Matthew for years at Trinity House and was simply not prepared to take him on. Newton must apply himself to improving each child 'in the little time allowed you for it', he wrote, and give Certificates 'in the decentest Terms you are able of the several heads of Science wherein you can safely assert the Child's being instructed'.[10] Here their exchange ends, leaving a dismal picture of boys being sent to sea untutored and too young to protest or escape, rather than receiving the education and care Christ's Hospital had promised. Some may have preferred life at sea to lessons, and some ran away, but it was not what their families or benefactors expected. Pepys's capitulation is the sadder because he believed so strongly in the need for education and its importance in raising standards in the navy; had he been younger and more fit, you feel, he would have taken up Newton's cause.

He was ill in both the spring and the autumn of 1697, and retreated to Will Hewer's house at Clapham for several weeks in the summer. Clapham was then a mere scattering of village houses round a small church, and the house was one Pepys had visited and admired more than thirty years before.[11] The departure of Thomas Gale to the deanery at York in the inaccessible north left him living almost like a monk, he grumbled when he got home to London. Yet at this same time he received a visit from his old college tutor Joseph Hill, now resident in Holland; he came with a daughter who made friends with Mary and proposed to take her back with her for a visit. Whether Mary went to Holland is uncertain. No letters of hers have survived, and none from Pepys to her. We know that she could write, since she took his dictation, but like Elizabeth she was made into a silent woman. There was a courtly letter from Pepys to her foster-sister Julia this year in which he assured Julia that he would never be guilty of neglecting her, but that 'Indeed Madame the World and I have been strangers a great while'; and he goes on to quote verses on political melancholy, a veiled allusion to his Jacobitism.[12]

The war against France ended in September 1697, and Louis XIV recognized William III as king of England. Then, in January 1698, the last great fire of Pepys's lifetime reduced the whole of Whitehall Palace to ashes, leaving only the Banqueting Hall standing. It marked the end of the world in which he had lived and worked, where the royal family, courtiers and officials lived in sets of rooms, some hardly grander than those of college heads, and an intimacy developed among those who knew their way about that made it almost like a village. Now this way of life and all that went with it passed into history. Queen Mary had died in 1694, King William disliked Whitehall, and Wren's plans for rebuilding were set aside. In the City at least his work was advancing, although neither the dome nor the towers of St Paul's were finished during Pepys's lifetime; but he must have admired the transformation of his boyhood territory, where Wren built wharves on both sides of the Fleet River and crowned the new St Bride's with his most perfect spire. Pepys was given the Freedom of the City in 1699 for his services to Christ's Hospital, which may have given him his last close look at once familiar streets.[13]

He had a specially designed book desk built for his library and another of the great matching bookcases in 1699; now he had left the service of the navy he had to pay for them out of his own funds. The bookcase was the eighth, and some time before it was installed he had two drawings made of the library in York Buildings.[14] They give a good impression of the arrangement of the furniture and pictures, and they also offer a glimpse into an adjoining room, where a small painting set in a gilt frame and showing the king of France on horseback can just be glimpsed, hung low on the wall above a leaf table with curly legs.[15] The painter was Mary, and here was her mark on the house, and as an artist, for all to admire. After many years in the shadows she had at last become visible, and not only visible – she was mentionable, admired even. Evelyn's grandson praised her as the mistress of the house, presiding like a Muse or Athene among the guests, in some Latin verses he sent to Pepys complimenting him on his Saturday gatherings. Pepys himself wrote of her making a call on his behalf to invite a friend to visit if he could 'still afford an hour for Philosophy and a tansey'.[16] Gentlemen sent her their wives' compliments alongside their own, a significant sign of social accept-ance. So respectable did she now appear that a French Protestant pastor, a refugee whom Pepys had assisted to a living in Ireland, invited her to be godmother to his child. Greetings came to her in letters from the good Dr Hickes and from Wanley, who took her position and influence to be such that '2 words from You Sir, Madam Skinner, or Mr Jackson' would help him to a fellowship to which he aspired.[17] Most strikingly of all, when Pepys gave £10 towards repairs to the old building of his college in Cambridge, she also sent her own donation of five guineas. It is marked in the college records as from 'Mad^m Pepys', and it speaks eloquently of her wish to support her companion of so many years in his interests and loyalties.[18]

Early in 1698 an official pass was issued for John Jackson, Mary Skinner, Julia Shallcross and another woman friend to travel to France with two servants: a little holiday in which Pepys was not included. Instead he was busy planning a more ambitious project for his nephew, nothing less than a Grand Tour.[19] The Houblons helped him prepare every step, with itineraries, introductions and arrangements to draw money, and Pepys appointed one of his servants, appropriately named Paris, to go with him. He was to travel through France, Switzerland, Italy, Spain and Portugal, seeing the sights and learning the languages, and reach Rome in time for the celebrations of the new century. Never was a young man sent off with so many instructions; Pepys kept the reins tightly in his hand, and his nephew responded to every twitch. He was to carry out commissions for Pepys, Mary and many others, and to write regularly detailing his experiences. When Pepys told him he must not omit the names of any friends from the greetings at the end of his letters, which he intended to pass round for all of them to see, Jackson did exactly as asked. He was not going to put a foot or a word wrong.

Once he had left, his uncle fell into gloom, and his first letter to Jackson was a lament. Paul Lorrain, he said, was less willing than he had been. 'I had rather (you know) beare with things not being done at all, or do them myself where I can (which truly now grows too much for me, especially as to copying) than see them done with reluctancy. Nor is this a small difficulty with me, as knowing too well my having no choice towards the solving it, there being no body but he that knows my business and manner of working, and at the same time qualifyd in every respect for doing it. So that the only true and adequate solution to it is, to knock quite off.' That was not all: 'add my having ¾ or more of my whole time to spend without anybody near me, to read or write word for me, or know how to fetch me a book out of my library or put it in its place again when done with; and this, as I grow older, growing less supportable'.[20] No doubt Lorrain did want freedom to do his own work – he was preparing for ordination – and Pepys, always a demanding master, was made more so by increasing infirmities. Mary was able to step into the breach; many letters after this are in her hand and in her picturesque spelling.

Pepys's gloom was tied up with the state of his ulcerated kidney. Early in 1700 he wrote of being 'unable to bear the stone in a coach', and by March 1700 he was so ill that Lorrain sent a secret letter to Jackson, warning him how bad things were. The wound of the old stone operation had broken open, and three surgical interventions were necessary before it was more or less successfully stitched up. Pepys had the best surgeon in London, Charles Bernard, and the most fashionable doctor too, John Radcliffe. He showed his usual courage, and against the odds he recovered, after three weeks in bed, and characteristically wrote a detailed account of his symptoms and treatment to Jackson.[21] In May the household moved to Hewer's Clapham house. It was comfortable and airy, and Evelyn described it as 'a very noble, and wonderfully well furnished house . . . the Offices and Gardens exceedingly well accommodated for pleasure and retirement'; but, as another friend, Henry Hyde, understood, Pepys was not a countryman by inclination. 'I hope your being thus long at Clapham (for I thinke you were never soe long in the countrey before since you knew the world) will make you relish the pleasure of a garden,' he wrote, not too hopefully.[22]

Mary had been tending Pepys, but now she too fell ill again. She thought of taking herself to Paris for a cure – a little rivalry with Jackson perhaps. We know of her plan through Dr John Shadwell, Pepys's godson, now the English ambassador's physician in Paris, who kept up a skittish correspondence with Jackson: Mrs Skinner, Shadwell wrote, was thinking of trying the air of Paris 'for her dropsy'. In his next letter he said the news from Clapham was good, 'since it brings no account of the motions of your evil genius this way'; and in July he assured Jackson that 'The Lady at London is at present so indisposed that she has wholly laid aside her thoughts of crossing the sea, so that there's one exception the less to the place [Paris].'[23] Clearly there was no love lost between Jackson and Mrs Skinner. Pepys meanwhile was pressing Jackson to buy some Spanish leather, a fan and an illuminated book for her, a commission he carried out carefully: pleasing Mary was a necessary part of pleasing his uncle.[24]

Although the new century started so painfully for Pepys, it still allowed him his moments of grace and eloquence. '"What then," will you say' – he was writing to Evelyn – '"are you a doing?" Why truely, nothing that will bear nameing, and yet am not (I think) idle; for who can, that has so much (of past and to come) to think on as I have? And thinking, I take it, is working.' And although he had few books at Clapham and missed his library, his thinking reminded him of his scientific interests, and in September he was sprightly enough to set up his own Newtonian experiment in optics, 'collecting the Rays of light in a dark Room; I having done it to a degree of pleasure and Ease in its Execution as much exceeds what I have ever seen'.[25] The summer was unusually warm and sunny, which meant not only that he could collect rays of sunlight indoors but also make expeditions into the country, to Windsor, Hampton Court, Richmond and as far as Epsom – with what pleasure and what memories of his service to two kings, and further back to his childhood visits to Durdans, can be imagined.[26]

In Buckingham Street Lorrain was recataloguing the library, and Mary was getting the house ready for his return. Pepys was impatient to be back among his books but was persuaded to remain at Clapham until the late autumn. Another thought of the past came to him, and he wrote to Jackson, now in Cadiz, suggesting he should visit 'my once Royal Mistriss our Queen Dowager' in Lisbon: Catherine of Braganza had returned to her native country, and Pepys, attached to his memories of a queen he had found modest and innocent, wished to present his 'profoundest duty'.[27] After this came more sorrow, with the death of James Houblon, 'one of the longest as well as most approved friends till now left mee in the world'; Sarah had died earlier, and James had been ill for months, but Pepys had hardly expected to outlive them both.[28] Nor was he well enough to attend the funeral in the City. Even in his grief Pepys worked on one of his great letters, a disquisition on the place of music in education, 'a science peculiarly productive of a pleasure that no state of life, publick or private, secular or sacred; no difference of age or season; no temper of mind or condition of health, exempt from present anguish, nor, lastly, distinction of quality, renders either improper, untimely, or unentertaining. Witness the universal gusto we see it followed with, wherever to be found.' No education should be without music, he believed. Here too he looked back and invoked his old master, Edward Montagu, earl of Sandwich, for whom music had been a daily pleasure, right up 'to that very hour wherein through a sea of blood and fire in the service of his Prince and country, he exchanged it for that of a State of Harmony more unspeakable and full of glory'. Pepys's own love of music and profound belief in its importance were woven into memories and attachments, and further into his thoughts about a future state of unspeakable Harmony.[29]

He had signed off the *Memoires* with a declaration that did not name God but attributed power and mystery to 'Something above' and 'Incomprehensible', 'to which alone be Glory'; and it may be in these formulations of unspeakable Harmony and incomprehensible power that we should look for Pepys's faith. It was certainly no ordinary or conventional one. Once, when asked to provide a reference, he wrote, 'what his Religion or Creed is I neither know concerning him, nor ever thought worth enquiring after any other man's; provided his Conversation be sober and honest'.[30] And the motto he adopted in the last years of his life was essentially a humanist one, taken from Cicero, meaning 'the mind is the man'.[31] His charitable work for French Protestants fleeing persecution was surely inspired more by dislike of intolerance than zeal for their creed. His early scepticism about religion, his anthropological and aesthetic curiosity about other sects, his lack of interest in doctrine, Christ or the Bible, his indifference to regular church attendance allied to a perfect readiness to conform to the rites practised by his fellow citizens when convenient or expected, all suggest that he stood close to William Petty's broadly based tolerance: happy to follow the conventional religious practice of his society but reserving the right to think for himself.[32] He had many friends who made careers in the Church, but religion was not a topic of his correspondence with them, rather books, manuscripts, libraries, history, handwriting, even tales of second sight. Still, as he aged and saw his friends die one by one, there were more references to prayer, faith and the afterlife in his letters, and Evelyn's gentle piety, often interwoven with classical references, touched and interested him as the two men prepared for what they both imagined as a voyage. 'Pray remember what o'clock it is with you and me,' wrote Pepys, and Evelyn replied that 'an easy, comfortable passage is that which remains for us to beg of God, and for the rest to sit loose to things below'.[33]

Sitting loose did not come easily to Pepys. In January 1701 he wrote to his cousin Matthews in Huntingdon about his nephew Sam Jackson, whom he imagined to be still under Matthews' guidance: 'And a very unwelcome surprize it is, to understand from you now that 'tis otherwise; as suspecting his being guilty of something worse on this Occasion, than (for his sake) you have thought fitt to tell me. Which however I shall at present forbear any further Enquiry after.'[34]

Throughout the first six months of 1701 he was in Buckingham Street, but so unwell that he could not go out of doors. No doubt his legs were too swollen, and it is likely that continence had become a problem. In his wretchedness he wrote to John Jackson asking him to return, knowing that the journey from Spain was likely to be slow, and in June he himself returned to Clapham. In August he wrote a will, leaving Brampton to Samuel and the rest of his fortune to John. Will Hewer, 'my most approved and most dear friend', was his executor, and was to have £500. Apart from an annuity to 'my old and faithful Servant Jane Penny' – who must be Jane Edwards, remarried and widowed again – that was all. The £28,007.2s.1¼d. owed to Pepys by the state, if paid, should be put into land and divided between his nephews (it never was paid). He urged them not to be disappointed with what they got but to remember that it was more than he or they had been born with. A few days later, John arrived back in England.

The circle at Clapham now consisted of Pepys, Will Hewer, John Jackson and Mary. Pepys longed to see Evelyn, preferably in this world, he joked, and before the winter was over; at Christmas he sent greetings from his three companions to all the Evelyns. There was never anything to tell of Hewer, always his quiet and peaceable self and always mindful of Pepys's comfort. Mary was having her portrait painted, either by Kneller or his brother Zacharias, and, as well as going for sittings, she acted for Pepys, fetching from Fleet Street one of the boxes wrapped in sacking he had deposited at his banker's in June: 'Dl^d back one of them to Mrs Skinner' entered the clerk in the ledger on 10 December.[35] If John Jackson paid a visit to his brother Sam at Huntingdon, as he might well have done after so long an absence abroad, he must have learnt that Sam was married, and without consulting their uncle. Pepys soon heard of the marriage and sent off an angry letter. In April he wrote to Matthews complaining of the young man's 'Folly, Undutifulness & Obstinacy'. 'As to whom, I protest to you, Sir,' he went on, 'that when I reflect upon the Perverseness as well as Stupidity legible in what he writes, I think it were best both for you and me, to ridd our hands of him.'[36] But he took no further action as yet.

He knew death could not be far off, but resisted it at every step. He was sixty-nine in February 1702, and it was only his body that was failing him; the mind was still the man, the wits were still sharp, and he continued to set himself new tasks that absorbed and satisfied him. One was the commissioning of a portrait of the mathematician John Wallis to present to the University of Oxford. This kept him in close touch with Kneller, with Wallis and the Royal Society, and with scholarly Oxford, which he jokingly called his aunt, Cambridge being his academic mother. And rather than accepting his separation from his books, he now had his entire library moved from York Buildings to Clapham. It was a sign that he did not expect to return to London; it was also a very big operation, although happily he had thought of how they were to be moved from the start and designed the bookcases to be taken apart easily. The cornices were made to lift off, the central sections divided in two and the bases provided with carrying handles. Hewer prepared a large and splendid wainscotted room for their installation. As well as the bookcases and desk, double-sided pictures were set in the panels of the room, the two globes were installed on pulleys, and Pepys's model ships were displayed in their glass cases.[37] He could feel pretty well at home.

He was reading the first part of Clarendon's history of the 'Great Rebellion', newly published by his friend the second earl, with the pleasure that comes from finding the events of your own life transformed into official history; and he wrote to compliment Henry Hyde and to urge him to speed the publication of the further volumes.[38] Compliments came to Pepys too, but he could still make fun of flattery. When young Evelyn's Latin verses proclaimed there was no need to travel to Rome now that its pleasures could be enjoyed in the Pepys household, where Jackson's loot was on display, Pepys remarked that Evelyn had 'long since taught him to make all Mr Pepys's Geese Swans'. And when the orator of Oxford University eulogized him following his gift of the Wallis portrait, he thanked him for raising 'a new world of glory to me out of nothing'.[39]

Two kings, both his juniors, his master James II and his enemy William III, died within six months of one another in 1701 and 1702, and Queen Anne was crowned in April. In June William Nicolson, a scholar with a particular interest in libraries, was called to London to be consecrated bishop of Carlisle by the new queen. He had borrowed books from Pepys earlier, and during his short stay in town he made a point of visiting him in Clapham, 'in the pleasant House of Mr

Hewer, formerly Mr Pepys's Clerk'.[40] Nicolson was a friend of Hickes and of Edmund Gibson, who went to Clapham with him; Evelyn was also there to meet them, and Nicolson wrote a description of the place and the occasion in his diary:

In the House mighty plenty of China-ware and other Indian Goods, vessels of a sort of past[e]; harden'd into a Substance like polish'd Marble. Pictures in full pains of wainscot; wch (by haveing one moveable, painted on both sides) admits of three several Representations of the whole Room. Models of the Royal Sovereign & other Men of War, made by the most famous Master-Builders; very curious and exact, in glass Cases. Mr Pepys's Library in 9 Classes [?Cases], finely gilded and sash-glass'd; so deep as to carry two Rows . . . of Books on each footing. A pair of Globes hung up, by pullies. The Books so well order'd that his Footman (after looking the Catalogue) could lay his finger on any of em blindfold. / Misscellanies of paintings, cutts, pamphlets, &c in large & lesser Volumes . . . A contracted Copy of Verrio's Draught of King Ja. the II. and the blew-coats at Christ-Church Hospital (wth the Directors and Governours of the place, Lord Mayor & Aldermen &c) suppos'd to be one of the best Representations of the various Habits of the Times, postures, &c, that is an where extant . . .

Nicolson also admired the 'Gardens, Walks and Bowling-Green, Ponds, &c answerable to the House', and the hedges of different heights and woods, bay, yew, holly and hornbeam; and he noted that Evelyn 'own'd himself the causer of a deal of Luxury in these matters'.[41]

In July Mary had to go to Lincolnshire, where her mother was dying. Mary and her sister Frances, Lady Buck, were joint executrices of Mrs Skinner's will, chosen as the 'beloved daughters', and shared the largest part of their mother's estate; it cannot have amounted to much.[42] Pepys was soon making inquiries of a legal acquaintance about Mary's duties and whether one executor could proceed without another.[43] Mrs Skinner left him 'two broad pieces of gold to buy him a ring', which was more than went to some of her children; her daughter Elizabeth, working as a servant, got £100 on condition she did not marry a certain Thomas Byutt.[44] Parents found it irresistible to try to control their children after death, and both Mrs Skinner and Pepys used their wills as a means of maintaining their power.

He reached his seventieth birthday in February 1703. By now his bad kidney had reduced his strength to its lowest ebb yet: he was frail, emaciated and in pain. Urinary infections are acutely painful, and there was no effective treatment, where today antibiotics or surgical removal of one kidney might have saved him. Mary was dealing with the household finances, paying out money from her account at Hoare's. She confided her worries about Pepys to a cousin, Mary Ballard, who wrote to him saying that 'Madam Skynner' thought he did not take care of his health as his condition required and offering to prepare for him some of the 'odd things which I now and then used to make which were not only healthfull but pleasing to your stomack', such as 'jelly broth, hartshorn jelly, sego'.[45] The gesture was kindly meant, but he was hardly able to eat. His last-known letter was written on behalf of his brother-in-law, a plea for a pension for St Michel to the commander-in-chief of the Fleet. It was, he said, the only request he had made since retiring from the navy.[46]

In March he sent a message to Dr Hickes, who knew the Clapham household from earlier visits – one in the summer of 1700 – and he agreed to come when Pepys felt he was approaching his end. In April he was told he had no hope of recovery, after which John Jackson composed a careful letter to Hewer, asking him to assure Pepys that his nephew counted on nothing from him: its intentions were probably the opposite of its assertions, and he was in any case sure of Pepys's affection.[47] For Pepys, there was just enough time and energy left for a last dramatic stroke. Once he heard he could not recover, he set about a complete revision of his will, dictating two enormous codicils on successive days, 12 and 13 May. In the first he took away the Brampton estates from his nephew Sam, allowing him no more than an annuity of £40 a year. Brampton went to John with the major part of the estate.

He was also given the library in trust, charged with joint responsibility with Hewer for finding the best means for preserving it 'in one body, undivided unsold and Secure against all manner of deminution damages and embesselments; and finally disposed . . . for the benefit of posterity'. Two further sets of instructions specified what they were to do. All his books were to go to 'one of our Universities', and rather Cambridge than Oxford; to a library, preferably that of Magdalene, with Trinity as a fall-back; and the collection must be kept entire and separate, in a room to be chosen by Jackson in the new building, no one allowed to remove any books except the master, and he only as far as his lodge. He proposed a system of annual visitation by Trinity to check that his instructions were being obeyed in perpetuity, giving them the right to the library if they found any infringement by Magdalene. Everything about his instructions indicates that Pepys had prepared them with the greatest care and must have thought and planned the disposal of his library over a considerable period before it made its last-minute appearance in his will. They are also so idiosyncratic that he may have modelled the conditions on those of another Cambridge college library, that of Matthew Parker at Corpus Christi, which had been similarly protected to good effect.[48]

This was not the only striking last-minute addition. Mary, not so much as mentioned in the earlier will, makes her first appearance in the 12 May codicil. 'Whereas I hold myself obliged on this occasion to leave behind me the most full and lasting acknowledgment of my esteem respect and gratitude to the Excellent Lady Mrs Mary Skyner for the many important Effects of her Steddy friendship and Assistances during the whole course of my life, within the last thirty three years; I doe give and devise unto the said Mrs Mary Skyner One Annuity or yearly payment of Two hundred pounds of Lawfull money of England for and during the terme of her natural Life.' That he should want to provide for her and to acknowledge that she had been an intimate part of his life for so long is understandable: but why only at this very last moment? The best explanation may be that he had intended some discreet private arrangement, worked out and agreed with his executor, Will Hewer; and that either he himself realized this was not good enough, or that Will tactfully suggested it would be wiser to put things in writing. Mary's family and friends may have made representations, but more likely Mary herself inquired and then insisted on her right to be acknowledged and provided for. If she did, you can only admire her spirit in the face of Pepys's persistent tendency to exclude women from the masculine world of the written word. However it came about, it was a just decision, allowing her some dignity, ensuring her a comfortable independence when she should lose her home with him and informing posterity of the place she had filled at his side.

As the end approached, Pepys began to think of more he could do for Mary. He may have been growing light-headed; she may have been putting on pressure. There is a lot of curious behaviour round deathbeds when there is money in question, as Pepys knew from his favourite playwright Ben Jonson. Another codicil assigned £5,000 of the £28,000 owed him by the government to Mary, and a verbal request, carefully noted down, stated his wish to give £50 of plate each to 'Mrs Skynner, Mr Hewer, and J.J.', as well as 'Pictures and Goods to Mrs Skynner'.[49] Whatever the final value of the estate that went to John Jackson, it was enough to ensure that he never had to work, although not enough to make Evelyn accept his proposal of marriage to his granddaughter. Family friendship or no, Evelyn turned him down on financial grounds.[50]

On 14 May 1703 Evelyn, himself recovering from a broken leg, called to see Pepys and found him '[l]anguishing with small hope of recovery which much affected me'. The weather, he noted, was lovely, fair and temperate, the summer conditions Pepys had always delighted in. The two friends did not meet again, and it was left to John Jackson to give an account of his uncle's last days.[51] He did well. On Monday, 24 May, Dr Hickes arrived and found Pepys lying on a couch. He prayed by him and then, taking his hand and finding his pulse very weak, told him he should simply say, 'Come Lord Jesus, Come quickly.' Pepys, practical to the last, asked him to pray to God to shorten his misery. That evening he fell into convulsions, trembling and breathing with difficulty. At four in the morning he showed more signs of distress, and asked for the curtains and windows to be opened; no doubt Pepys wanted to see the light of dawn and feel the summer air. 'Whilst lying on the couch he beckoned me to him, – took me by the hand, – the same by Mrs Sk, and speaking to me (as well as he could) said, "Be good friends; I do desire it of you"; in conclusion of which I offered to kiss his cheek; he turned his mouth and pressed my lips with an extraordinary affection. / Dr Hicks coming, Mr Hewer told him; upon which he ordred himselfe to be raised up in his bed, and the Doctor coming-in performed the Office for the Sick, and gave him the Absolution, laying his hand on his head. The Service done, U[ncle] said, "God be gracious to me"; blessed the Dean and all of us, and prayed to God to reward us all, and M.S. then appearing, said, "And thee in particular, my dear child."'

During the next hours Pepys thanked all his servants and kissed

Earl of Sandwich

32, 33. Edward Montagu (*below*) as earl of Sandwich, splendid in his Garter robes and looking every inch the great servant of the Stuarts he became: privy councillor, naval commander, ambassador to Spain. The countess, her features regularized by the painter into an approximation of a court beauty, remained unchanged in character, the same 'excellent, good, discreet lady that ever she was', as Pepys wrote. She complained neither of her husband's infidelity nor his long enforced absences when she was left short of money to maintain Hinchingbrooke and bring up their ten children.

Montagu died nobly and unnecessarily at sea in 1672, fighting the Dutch off the Suffolk coast at Southwold. The widowed countess left Hinchingbrooke and survived him by only two years.

34, 35. James Houblon was the son of a Huguenot refugee who settled in the City and raised his seven sons to successful business careers. His mercantile interests led him to cultivate Pepys at the Navy Office in 1665, and after Elizabeth's death he and his English wife, Sarah, welcomed Pepys into their family circle. They gave princely dinners, and Pepys records dropping in on them with two bottles of champagne on one occasion. He and Sarah had musical tastes in common, they went to the theatre together, and shared a summer villa at Parson's Green. When Pepys was in the Tower in 1679, Houblon stood £5,000 bail for him, repeating the gesture in 1690. Houblon was knighted in 1691 and sat on the board of the newly founded Bank of England in 1694. Although he was a Whig and Pepys called himself a Tory, their friendship transcended such labels.

36. A copy of this portrait is in the Witt Library. It is described as 'Mrs Pepys' and attributed to Kneller, but it does not look like the work of Kneller, is clearly not Elizabeth Pepys, and the original has disappeared since it surfaced among Pepysian material in 1931. Might it be the young Mary Skinner, known on occasion as Mrs Pepys? She was painted by Kneller, although this could not be the portrait he made in the 1690s – hair and dress suggest the 1670s.

37, 38. Anthony Ashley Cooper, earl of Shaftesbury, brilliant and subtle founder of the Whig party, persecuted Pepys because he was a loyal servant of James, duke of York and lord high admiral. To Shaftesbury, the duke's Roman Catholic faith made him ineligible to be king; and Shaftesbury suspected Pepys of being a Catholic. In fact Pepys cared little about religion. What bound him to James (*below*) was that James defended, promoted and relied on him. Pepys survived Shaftesbury's attacks as well as Shaftesbury himself, who died in exile in 1683. Yet James, who succeeded to the throne in 1685, lasted only three years as king before he too was driven into exile by Shaftesbury's political heirs. Pepys lost his position under the new regime and remained hostile to it.

39, 40, 41, 42. Pepys cultivated the company of learned men, among them John Evelyn (*top left*), diarist, maker of gardens and town planner, and William Petty (*top right*), anatomist, economist, social theorist and free thinker. Pepys corresponded with Isaac Newton (*bottom left*) and sought his advice; and he accompanied Christopher Wren (*bottom right*) to Greenwich to consider the planning of the Royal Naval Hospital. Robert Hooke, experimental scientist and architect, was another friend who should be here, but there is no portrait in existence.

43, 44. Two contemporary views of Pepys's airy library as he arranged it on an upper floor of his Buckingham Street house facing the river. It shows seven of his bookcases, portraits and a map. A later inventory mentions 'The miniature K: of France on horseback by Mr Skyner', just seen hanging outside the open door. I believe 'Mr Skyner' is Mary Skinner, whom we know to have been an artist.

James R

Wee doe hereby graciously declare our continued sense of ye long & faythfull services performed to our late dearest Brother & our selfe by Mr Pepys our Secretary for ye Affayrs of our Admiralty of England, & that his long want of Satisfaction to his just pretensions attested by our selfe when Duke of Yorke, & confirmed by our sayd dearest Brother in a state thereof bearing date ye second day of March 167 8/9 shall bee noe impediment to his receiving ye same from us; wee hereby earnestly recommending him to ye Lords Commissrs of our Treasury for theyr doeing him full right on our behalfe therein, & in what is further due to him on his Account as late Treasurer for Tangier. Given at our Castle of Windsor this 17th day of November 1688. J R

45. The IOU letter presented by Pepys to James II and signed by James on 17 November 1688, acknowledging Pepys's 'just pretentions' to money owed to him by the Treasury, with the docket and tracing of the watermark.

46. (*below*) Lines from Pepys's account with Hoare's Bank. This entry notes that he deposited two boxes 'Rapt up in Sacking' on 23 June 1701 and that Mrs Skinner collected one of them on 10 December 1701.

Novr 17. 1688.

His Majesty's Confirma=tion & Recomendation of ye arrear due to Mr Pepys upon his Service in the Navy & Admty & as Treasr for Tangier to the Lords Commrs. of the Treary.

Samll Pepys Esqr 2 boxes Rapt up in Sacking June 23: 1701
Decr. 10. 1701 ...Putting ye Cubbard in my fathers Closet
deliverd one of them to Mrs Skinner   8 292

47. The pert face of Pepys's nephew John Jackson, son of his unloved sister Pall and her bumpkin husband. John became his uncle's favourite, was sent to Pepys's college, Magdalene, at thirteen, taken into Pepys's London household, introduced into the Royal Society and dispatched on the Grand Tour that Pepys had longed in vain to make himself. He pleased his uncle and became his principal heir, but remained undistinguished; only his account of Pepys's last hours rises to its subject.

48. Pepys as an old man in the 1690s, by Closterman. Neither political misfortunes nor failing health kept him from intellectual interests or from keeping up old friendships and making new ones. His library was his passion and was moved with him to his last home, Will Hewer's country house in Clapham, where, sustained by the love of Hewer, Mary Skinner and John Jackson, he died in 1703.

49. Profile of Pepys carved on a small ivory medallion in 1688 by Jean Cavalier, a Huguenot artist, signed and dated on the back. It remained in the Pepys Cockerell family until 1931.

50. The first page of John Smith's transcription of the Diary, begun in the spring of 1819. The task took him three years and fills fifty-four notebooks. He had no key to the shorthand and was paid a flat £200. He made a good job of it, but his work was handed over to Lord Braybrooke, who cut about three quarters and rewrote a good deal. Not until 1970 was an edition printed with the first page as Pepys wrote it and John Smith transcribed it.

some of them; and as night fell again, 'M.S. and I stole up to his bed to see him and shook him by the hand, he not discerning who it was. Dr Shadwell coming, was stoln in to feel his pulse, which [was] quite gone. / About 1 on Wednesday morning, Paris crossed the room. U[ncle] called him and ask for me, where I was. "In bed; shall I call him?" "No." By and by again asked for me. "Shall I call him?" "Yes." He did so, and I came and found him lying on the bed ratling in the throat and breathing very hard.' He had taken no nourishment for two days, and he died, according to his own reliable watch, at 3.47. The sun was about to rise in the summer sky.

Epilogue

Later on the day of his death, John Shadwell, Hans Sloane and the surgeon Charles Bernard performed an autopsy on the body of their friend. Shadwell and Sloane were fellow members of the Royal Society, and they were following Jackson's wishes, 'for our own satisfaction as well as public good', he explained to Evelyn. Pepys himself would undoubtedly have approved, both because he valued scientific research and because he believed his case to be of interest. What they found makes his stoicism over the last years the more impressive. The left kidney contained seven irregular stones joined in a mass adhering to his back, the surrounding areas including the gut much inflamed, septic and mortified, the bladder gangrenous and the old wound from the stone operation broken open again. The lungs were full of black spots and foam, the guts discoloured, flaccid, empty and inflamed; but the heart and the right kidney were sound. Jackson sent his own account of their report to Evelyn.[1]

Evelyn immediately wrote his tribute to his 'particular friend' of forty years.

This day dyed Mr. Sam: Pepys, a very worthy, Industrious & curious person, none in England exceeding him in the Knowledge of the Navy, in which he had passed thro all the most Considerable Offices, Clerk of the Acts, & Secretary to the Admiralty, all which he performed with greate Integrity: when K: James the 2d went out of England he layed down his Office, & would serve no more: But withdrawing himselfe from all publique Affairs, lived at Clapham with his partner (formerly his Clerk) Mr Hewer, in a very noble House & sweete place, where he injoyed the fruit of his labours in greate prosperity, was universally beloved, Hospitable, Generous, Learned in many things, skill'd in Musick, a very great Cherisher of Learned men . . .

The funeral was held on 4 June, at St Olave's and at nine o'clock at night, as decreed by Pepys, who chose to be buried in a vault below Elizabeth's monument. The coffin was brought from Clapham 'in a very honourable and solemn manner'.² Dr Hickes took the service. There is no mention of music, although it is hard to imagine Pepys going to the grave without any. The long list of those Pepys wished to have mourning rings included friends from Cambridge, Oxford and the Royal Society, from the Admiralty, the Navy Office and the established Church, including the archbishop of Canterbury; not all were present. Political divisions were laid aside, since four of the pall-bearers were nonjurors and two were Whigs. The nonjurors were three close friends, the earl of Clarendon, Anthony Deane and Charles Hatton, and they were joined by the earl of Feversham, known as a personal friend and supporter of James II. Feversham was perhaps standing in for Evelyn, whom Pepys had wanted but who felt unable to be there – he was, after all, eighty-three. The other two were Sir Thomas Littleton and James Vernon, both connected with Mary Skinner and surely chosen for that reason. Littleton was a family friend of the Botelers and Vernon connected by marriage, his wife the sister of Sir William Buck, husband of Mary's sister Frances.³ Since women were not expected to attend funerals, Mary was not present, but she could feel she was represented.

Jane Penny, 'little old Jane', who was given five guineas for her mourning as well as her ring, would have been represented by her son Lieutenant Edwards, unless he were at sea. Roger Pepys from Cambridgeshire was the only Pepys to have a ring; his Gale grandson, Pepys's godson, had another. Others in the family were both Jackson nephews and John Matthews, the cousin who had raised them; St Michel and his daughter Mary; and the current earl of Sandwich and his brother John, both known to Pepys from their childhood. There were rings for various other godchildren, clerks, servants and professional advisers, for Will Hewer and many of his family, for Henry Sheeres, for the two sons of James Houblon. William Penn the younger was another, and Dr Thomas Smith, the nonjuring keeper of the Cottonian Library.

After the funeral Dr Hickes wrote of Pepys that 'The greatness of his behaviour, in his long and sharp tryall before his death, was in every respect answerable to his great life; and I believe no man ever went out of this world with greater contempt of it, or more lively faith in every thing that was revealed of the world to come . . . I never attended any sick or dying person that dyed with so much Christian greatnesse of mind, or a more lively sense of immortality, or so much fortitude and patience.'[4] It is a deserved tribute to Pepys's courage and testifies to his readiness to receive the Christian rites gratefully at the end; but it is hard to believe that he felt even a moment's contempt for the world in which he had gloried, and to whose future inhabitants he left his greatest legacy.

John Jackson remained at Clapham with Will Hewer, continuing work on the library, adding books and compiling a new catalogue with Lorrain. It was valued at £4,000. Three months after Pepys's death he wrote to the master of Magdalene to say that he and his fellow executor intended to carry out Pepys's scheme for its final disposal to the college. The following summer he visited Cambridge and chose two central rooms in the new building at Magdalene for its reception. He was not put off by the fact that all the books in the existing college library were entirely overgrown with mould; or perhaps he was not shown them.[5] During 1705 the catalogue was completed, the last bookcases installed, and the whole of Pepys's collection, including his model ships, portraits and some of his furniture, put on display at Clapham.

Mary returned to Westminster to live in lodgings. She kept a portrait of Pepys on her wall, and many mementoes of her life with him, and she had a diamond heart mourning ring made for herself. Her rooms were furnished with two well-filled bookcases, a great Indian screen of six leaves and an Indian cabinet, a good deal of plate and a number of other pictures, including her own portrait, which she described as being by Godfrey Kneller; she also owned a gold Tompion watch.[6] She remained close to her foster-sister Julia, and it is likely that she visited her at Woodhall from time to time. She also took an interest in the children of her sister Frances, Lady Buck; and her relations with John Jackson seem to have become more friendly. When he married Hewer's cousin Anne and started a family, she became godmother to their daughter Paulina. But she survived Pepys by only twelve years, dying in her early sixties in 1715; Jackson was her executor and she bequeathed almost everything Pepys had left her to him and his family.[7] To Julia Shallcross she left her silver gilt perfume bottles; her bookcases and books went to her nephew Charles Buck, and her 'new clothes' to his sisters. A few pictures and the residue of her estate went to her nephew Daniel Skinner, probably

Corbet's son, and his daughter. Her wish to be buried close to her foster-mother Elizabeth Boteler in St Ethelreda's, the Hatfield church, was carried out; she left the substantial sum of £300 for her funeral, and the burial register for 18 October 1715 has her name, 'Mrs Mary Skinner, of St Martin's in the Fields, London'.[8] A few weeks after her death Will Hewer also died; his memorial is in Clapham Church.[9]

Apart from carrying out Pepys's instructions Jackson did nothing more with his life beyond marrying and begetting children. In July 1724, following his death, the library of 3,000 leather-bound books was transferred from Clapham to Cambridge with their cases.[10] The removal was paid for by Lord Anglesey, son of Pepys's one-time colleague; it cost £23 to pack everything up and move it from Clapham to London, and another £18 to take it on to Cambridge.[11] Anglesey also provided enough to pay the library keeper '£10 per annum for ever'. Neither the Magdalene librarian, Samuel Hadderton, nor anyone else there knew that among the books to be unpacked in the new library was the Diary, its six volumes clad in the same brown leather bindings as the other books. Their presence was, however, clearly indicated in Jackson and Lorrain's catalogue, which also listed Pepys's collection of shorthand primers, among them Shelton's *Tachygraphy*, the system he had used. Four years after the books were installed, in May 1728, a Peter Leycester visited the library and noticed in the catalogue a book on shorthand, in which he was interested, 'but the gentleman who showed us the library being a stranger, and unacquainted with the method of the catalogue, we could not find it'. Still, in searching for the shorthand book they found five (not the six you would expect) volumes written in shorthand, 'being a journal of Mr Pepys; I did not know the method, but they were writ very plain, and the proper names in common characters . . . I had not time, and was loath to be troublesome to the library keeper, otherwise I could have deciphered some of the journal.' Leycester wrote to his friend John Byrom, who was also interested in shorthand, and who was in Cambridge at various times over the next two decades; but he did not follow up the information about the Diary.

Elsewhere there was interest in Pepys, although not in his Diary. A mountain of papers had been acquired from his estate by a collector called Richard Rawlinson, and in 1749 he asked Thomas Bowdler for information about the man; Bowdler got most things wrong, confidently asserting that Pepys was the son of a clergyman, and a considerable landowner. When Rawlinson died in 1755 he left the papers to the Bodleian Library in Oxford; in 1778 another haul of papers, taken from the Sandwich family by Thomas Carte, were also deposited in the Bodleian. A few forays were made into Magdalene, for Pepys's ballad collection – Percy's *Reliques* appeared in 1765 – and for his account of Charles II's escape after Worcester, published in 1766. In 1805 the first lord of the Admiralty, Sir Charles Middleton, wrote of Pepys as 'a man of extraordinary knowledge in all that related to the business [of the navy], of great talents, and the most indefatigable industry'.[12] But he was hardly a household name.

In 1812 a Scottish historian, David Macpherson, included a few words from the Diary to illustrate the growth of the tea trade in Europe – Pepys had his first cup of tea and recorded the fact on 25 September 1660, writing the words 'Cupp' and 'Tee' in longhand. No one knows how Macpherson came on the reference, but his book, *History of the European Commerce with India*, was noticed in the *Quarterly Review*. The following year a very young Master, the 24-year-old Revd and Hon. George Neville, was appointed to Magdalene by the hereditary visitor of the college, who happened to be his father. The Master's uncle, Thomas Grenville, was a remarkable man, friend of Charles James Fox, a first lord of the Admiralty and a trustee of the British Museum, to which he bequeathed his personal collection of 20,000 books; and it is likely that he encouraged his nephew to have the Pepys Diary looked at. The publication of John Evelyn's diaries in 1818 acted as a spur, and Thomas Grenville – breaking Pepys's condition that no book should be removed further than the Master's lodge – took the first volume to his brother, Lord Grenville, who knew some shorthand. He failed to realize that it was written in a known system, but declared that it could be easily and quickly transcribed and should certainly be published.

What followed was tragi-comedy. The Master found an undergraduate prepared to take on the task. John Smith was twenty, the son of a schoolmaster and desperately poor as a result of an unwise marriage in his teens; he was already the father of a child. So he was glad to have the task and kept at it for three years, sometimes working more than twelve hours a day, from the spring of 1819 until 6 April 1822, when he completed his transcription of Pepys's 3,102 pages on to 9,325 of his own, filling 54 fat notebooks with his flowing, legible hand, covering the right-hand pages only. He carried out the entire task without knowing that the key to the shorthand was in the library. He made a few misreadings, but left out very little, only a few sexually frank passages, usually noted on the left-hand page as 'Obj.' – 'objectionable' – although occasionally omitted without comment. For 'bloody' he wrote 'b. . . .y' and for 'yard' (penis) 'y. .d'. Notably, he transcribed the opening page exactly as Pepys wrote it. For this labour of three years he was paid a flat £200.

Smith's transcript was handed to yet another member of the Master's family, Richard Neville (shortly to inherit a title and become Lord Braybrooke), who became its official editor. Braybrooke bowdlerized, cut the transcript by three quarters and rewrote substantial amounts in his own words, producing what its modern editor, Robert Latham, has called a travesty of the original. He did, however, employ assistants who collected hundreds of letters to and from Pepys, to print alongside the Diary.[13] His acknowledgement to Smith was short and cool, merely saying that he was not personally acquainted with him but that he appeared to have performed his task with diligence and fidelity. Smith remained aggrieved for the rest of his life. He saw a rich aristocrat taking all the credit while his essential work was glossed over. In 1842 the Master of Magdalene told a visitor to the library that the transcription had taken 'about a twelvemonth'. Smith meanwhile scraped a meagre living as a curate in Norfolk, paid £100 a year by the 'rich Pluralist' whose work he did. His wife was an invalid and he said he was kept out of the debtors' prison only by the help of friends; and it took many pleas to the lord chancellor's office before he was given his own parish at Baldock in Hertfordshire, with £130 a year, in 1832.[14]

John Murray, publisher of Byron and Jane Austen, turned the Diary down, but Henry Colburn published Braybrooke's edition – two thirds Diary, one third letters – in two large volumes with engravings at six guineas in the summer of 1825.[15] There was great interest. *The Times* hailed it, and Jeffrey called it 'a treasure box of new detail' in the *Edinburgh Review*. Walter Scott found Evelyn superior to Pepys because of his higher social standing and moral tone; Pepys's Diary was more various and amusing, but 'inferior in its tone of sentiment and feeling'. 'Early necessity had made Pepys laborious, studious and careful', he wrote, but his 'natural propensities were those of a man of pleasure'. Scott was critical of Braybrooke for inaccuracies in editing and expressed a wish for the complete text to be published.[16] There was no question of that, although there were two reprints in 1828. Sydney Smith told Lady Holland it was nonsense, and Thomas Creevey, a diarist himself, much preferred Pepys's collection of prints to the Diary, which he pronounced 'almost trash compared to the other contents of the library'.[17] More significantly, Macaulay enthused, saying he felt he knew every inch of Whitehall from the diaries – 'I go in at Hans Holbein's gate and come out through the matted gallery' – and he used Pepys as a source for his *History of England*.

In 1833 Granville Penn, a descendant of Admiral Sir William Penn, published a memoir of his ancestor in which he attacked Pepys as the son of a low-born tailor for traducing him. You can hardly blame him. In 1841 John Smith published his transcription of the Tangier Diary and some more Pepys letters together with a brief biography. In 1842 Magdalene was visited by a scholar, Frederic Madden, who questioned the Master, the Hon. George Grenville, about the so-called 'objectionable passages', which he supposed could be read in John Smith's transcript. Grenville told him that the transcript was in his possession and added with sublime hauteur 'that only *two* persons had applied to him for permission to read it, and these were George the Fourth and Lady Holland! Both applications he had *refused*.'[18]

Meanwhile the library itself was moved, first into a dining room in the Master's lodge, then into the new lodge, and then back to another room in college.[19] An expanded edition of the Diary appeared from 1848 to 1849, from which Braybrooke cut any acknowledgement to Smith. This too sold out, and a still fuller edition appeared in 1854. John Smith died in 1870, without publishing the 'History of the Diary' he said he had written. Then in the 1870s, after Braybrooke's death, an invalid fellow of Magdalene, Mynors Bright, made a new transcription of the Diary from the original. Again John Murray turned down the chance to publish, and it went to a firm called Bickers & Son, who published four fifths of the text in six volumes between 1875 and 1879.[20] It was a small printing and provoked some hostile criticism for its inclusion of details considered unsuitable for publication, but also the most perceptive essay ever written on the Diary, from Robert Louis Stevenson. Stevenson disagreed with the prevailing view that

Pepys had not intended his Diary to be seen one day and insisted that on the contrary he meant it to survive – 'Pepys was not such an ass, but he must have perceived, as he went on, the extraordinary nature of the work he was producing.' He spoke of his romantic passion for his own past, and compared him with Rousseau and Hazlitt; and he called him 'an unparalleled figure in the annals of mankind' for three reasons. First, that he was 'known to his contemporaries in a halo of almost historical pomp, and to his remote descendants with an indecent familiarity'; secondly for his honesty about himself; and thirdly for his ability to place himself before us with 'such a fullness and such an intimacy of detail as might be envied by a genius like Montaigne'.[21]

Further printings of the Braybrooke version appeared, and Henry Wheatley, who published the first general book about Pepys in 1880, *Samuel Pepys and the World He Lived In*, edited and published an extended eight-volume edition using Bright's transcription between 1893 and 1896. It was agreed, by Leslie Stephen among others, that some passages were too indecent ever to appear; and although there were many more reprints and selections, it was not until 1970, when Robert Latham and William Matthews made a third complete transcription for a new edition, that the whole Diary, including the opening page, was printed as Pepys had written it three hundred years earlier, and as he left it to the world.[22]

Pepys's life was a drama from start to end. It had its ordeals by sickness, passion, fire, bereavement, imprisonment, false accusation and revolution, and it was played out against the most disturbed years in England's history, a period as intellectually thrilling as it was dangerous and bloody. From his republican boyhood he kept a belief in a meritocratic system, and did much to promote it within the navy; yet the young Pepys who rejoiced at the execution of Charles I became the Tory and Jacobite who would not turn against James II when the whole country, navy included, rejected him. The sorriest aspect of his career is that it attached him to kings he could not respect but to whom he felt he must give personal loyalty. But he had too much energy to let tragedy be the mode of his life for long; and he was too much of an individualist, with a sense of his own destiny to pursue. He knew how to deal with bad luck, just as he knew how to seize the good luck when it came his way. He was brave in taking risks – the stone operation could have killed him – and rose gloriously to challenges such as his great speech in the House, his battle with the Brooke House Committee and his defence against the accusation of treason. He was a good and well-liked master to his clerks. He had the gift of making friends with the many outstanding men he encountered, winning their love and respect by his charm, his curiosity and mental agility, his conversation and hospitality. Men of state, shipbuilders, engineers, merchants, scholars, physicians and writers all cheered his later years. Women he did not see as friends, even when he loved them. Both Elizabeth and Mary had to fight his crushing egotism with whatever weapons they could find. Lady Sandwich was an exception to this rule, his cousin Jane Turner another, and his maid Jane Birch, although she also had to put up a fight to keep her status. That he had no children of his own was a sadness he dealt with, characteristically, by providing himself with surrogate sons; and Fate played a sly trick by making his despised sister Pall the mother of his beloved nephew John Jackson.

The most unlikely thing at the heart of his long, complex and worldly life is the secret masterpiece. Nobody knew, and nobody could have imagined, that a young man in his twenties and thirties, building his career and pursuing his pleasures with unbounded appetite, should have found the energy and commitment to create a new literary form, and that it should become a work of genius. The Diary carries him to the highest point, alongside Milton, Bunyan, Chaucer, Dickens and Proust, although he was unlike them in that he does not seem to have started out with conscious dedication. Rather it grew within him. He felt its demands and was enlisted in its cause. So he came to render a whole society and at the same time to present himself as a hero of an altogether new kind. And as he did so he forged a language – vigorous, precise, enchanting – in which to do what had not been done before, revealing discoveries as curious in their way as any of those of his scientific and philosophical colleagues, discoveries of the complex relations between the inner and outer worlds of a man. The achievement is astounding, but there is no show or pretension; and when you turn over the last page of the Diary you know you have been in the company of both the most ordinary and the most extraordinary writer you will ever meet.

Notes

Prologue

1. Diary, 13 Nov. 1662, where Pepys says he intends to burn it unread 'before her face', but does not actually describe doing so.
2. J. R. Tanner, *Samuel Pepys and the Royal Navy*, lectures published in 1920. Tanner lived from 1860 to 1931 and devoted much of his life to researching and writing about Pepys.
3. See Chapter 25.
4. Diary, 3 Nov. 1661, a Sunday that he spent reading and trying 'to make a Song in the prayse of a Liberall genius (as I take my own to be) to all studies and pleasures'. The 'Song' may have been a poem, 'but it not proving to my mind, I did reject it and so proceeded not in it'.
5. The 1680 fragments of diary, written in longhand, are found in the manuscript of 'Mornamont', held in the Pepys Library and never printed; see Chapter 22. The Tangier Diary, written in shorthand and first printed in a bad version, should be read in Edwin Chappell's edition of 1935, published by the Navy Records Society; see Chapter 23.
6. Robert Louis Stevenson in his essay 'Samuel Pepys', first printed in the *Cornhill* for July 1881, p. 36.

Part One: 1633–1660

1. The Elected Son

1. Diary, 17 Mar. 1664. The house lay 'neere the churchyard door', and when in 1663 Pepys's brother Tom rebuilt part of the top floor he had permission to 'lay and frame his timber in the churchyard'. Diary, 21 July 1663, and note in Latham and Matthews.
2. The Thames came up a good bit higher before embankment in the nineteenth century, not much below today's Tudor Street. Salisbury Court was a house belonging to the Bishop of Salisbury in the sixteenth century, which then passed into secular hands and was from 1568 until the 1590s the residence of the French ambassador. East of it was another large dwelling, Dorset House. Both had gardens on the slope towards the river, and the name 'Salisbury Court' transferred itself to the whole complex of large and small houses around the open area. Information from John Bossy.

3. There are ruins of a Roman villa under the church.

4. There were another 100,000 in the larger area of London. The figures are taken from an estimate of 1631 made in connection with the corn supply and given by G. N. Clark in *The Later Stuarts* (1934), p. 40, footnote. Clark says 'most modern historians adopt the estimate of three quarters of a million, or about one seventh of the population of England and Wales'; he is referring to 1660.

5. The information about the contents of the house is taken from an inventory made when Tom Pepys took over the tailoring business from his father in 1661 printed in *The Letters of Samuel Pepys and His Family Circle*, ed. H. T. Heath (1955) pp. 13–15. The family possessions may have changed, increased or decreased, but since there had been no major events in the family beyond the deaths of children and the marriage of Samuel, and no change in the status of the Pepys parents, I think it fair to assume there had not been too much change in their goods and chattels either. Trundle (or truckle) beds were made to be pushed under the high beds when not in use. The 'little chamber, three storeys high' is mentioned in the Diary, 21 June 1660, when several members of the Pepys family were forced to sleep together in it, the house being overcrowded with lodgers.

6. The bass viol is also known as the viola da gamba and looks something like a cello. It was the most important of the viols, and the English were considered the best players of it in the seventeenth century. It fell out of favour at the end of the eighteenth century. The virginals was the earliest form of harpsichord, usually an oblong box that was placed on a table. It was popular in the sixteenth and seventeenth centuries, when much music was composed for it by leading English composers such as Gibbons and Byrd. It was thought especially suitable for young women.

7. *The Diary of Bulstrode Whitelocke 1605–1675*, ed. Ruth Spalding (1989), p. 74. The masque, called *Cœlum Britannicum*, was performed on the night of Candlemas, 2 Feb. 1634 (dated 1633 old style, the new year beginning at the end of Mar.). See also Ruth Spalding's *The Improbable Puritan: A Life of Bulstrode Whitelocke* (1975). Thomas Carew's text and a description of the masque are printed in his complete works, ed. J. W. Ebsworth (1893).

8. *The Diary of Bulstrode Whitelocke*, ed. Ruth Spalding, p. 76. I have modernized spelling.

9. Robert Hooke observed such a cloud from the Banstead Downs and recorded it in his diary for 28 Sept. 1676, *The Diary of Robert Hooke 1672–1680*, eds. H. W. Robinson and W. Adams (1935). See also John Evelyn's *Fumifugium* of 1661, in which he describes the atmosphere of London and its effect on inhabitants.

10. Browne, *Religio Medici* (1642), Part II, Section 9.

11. Dates are a nightmare in this period, because the 'new year' was on 25 Mar. ('Lady Day', or the Feast of the Annunciation). It means that the period from 1 Jan. to 25 Mar. is usually, although not always, dated as the previous year. Pepys is not entirely consistent in his own Diary, sometimes writing 'January $\frac{1661}{62}$' at other times 'January 1665/6', which is the form he favours in his letters.

Bulstrode Whitelocke, on the other hand, sticks to the old year's date until the end of Mar. Pepys's godparents are not known.

12. See Kenneth H. D. Hayley, *The First Earl of Shaftesbury* (1968), p. 142. The young Anthony Ashley Cooper lived as an orphan with his guardian, Sir Daniel Norton, who was in London during the law terms, from 1631, when he was ten, until he was fourteen.

13. See *The Life of Milton* by Edward Phillips, his nephew (1694), printed as an appendix to William Godwin's *Lives of Edward and John Philips, Nephews and Pupils of Milton, including Various Particulars of the Literary and Political History of Their Times* (1815). '[In 1640] he took him a lodging in St Brides church-yard, at the house of one Russel, a taylor, where he first undertook the education and instruction of his sister's two sons' (p. 362 in Godwin).

14. John Brinsley's *Ludus Literarius* of 1612, a dialogue (in English despite the title) between two schoolmasters, makes this sensible suggestion.

15. For the backyard sports, Diary, 25 Dec. 1663; for the Temple Hall visit, Diary, 1 Jan. 1668; for 'beating the bounds', Diary, 25 Mar. 1661.

16. Taken from a 1619 reprint of *The Schoole of Vertue*, printed 'next to the Globe' and sold 'at the sign of the Bull, by St Paul's Churchyard'. It was first published in 1577 and went on being reprinted until 1626.

17. Pepys noted the birth dates of all his brothers and sisters at the end of his Diary for 1664, but not the dates of their deaths. These are to be found in the parish records of St Bride's, held at the Guildhall.

18. Tom's speech impediment was bad enough to deter a possible bride when he came to look for one.

19. Bodleian Library, Rawlinson MSS, A 185, fols. 206–13, 7 Nov. 1677.

20. In the Diary Pepys revisits Kingsland on 25 Apr. 1664 and recalls 'my nurse's house, Goody Lawrence, where my brother Tom and I was kept when young'. He says his mother's unmarried sister, Ellen Kite, was living in a Mrs Herbert's house at Newington Green near by. He also says he was boarded at Hackney – still close to Kingsland – as 'a little child'. On 12 May 1667, however, he recalls being boarded at Kingsland and shooting with his bow and arrow in the fields. There seem to have been fields all the way between Kingsland, a mere roadside hamlet, and Hackney, which was more of a village. Perhaps he was sent to one or another family in that direction for several summers.

21. Diary, 27 Mar. 1664. Pepys saw *Twelfth Night* twice, in Sept. 1661 and Jan. 1663, but failed to enjoy it on either occasion and thought it 'a silly play', in spite of Sir Toby Belch and his cakes and ale.

22. See Diary for 11 Mar. 1668, and Pepys's wish to avoid speaking to Colonel Cocke, 'formerly a very great man and my father's customer whom I have carried clothes to'.

23. Coke said this to Bulstrode Whitelocke's father in 1615: see Ruth Spalding, *The Improbable Puritan*, citing James Whitelocke's memoir, p. 29.

24. Diary, 30 May 1668.

25. The two Diary entries are for 1 Sept. 1662 and 26 July 1663. Evelyn listed the

gardens of Durdans among the English ones he most admired in a letter to Sir Thomas Browne, 28 Jan. 1658. Information about house and garden from John Harris's article on Durdans in *Country Life*, 8 Sept. 1983, in which he discusses Jacob Knyff's 1673 view of the house Pepys visited, which was pulled down in the 1680s and replaced by an entirely classical house. Note also Pepys's remark on 3 Dec. 1668 about the greatness of John Pepys of Ashtead in the world; and that his daughter Jane, who became Mrs John Turner, named one of her daughters Theophila (after Lady Theophila Coke) – she was usually known as 'The' to Pepys. The Berkeleys came to Durdans in the mid 1630s and added the new Hall in 1639. Their own children died at birth, which may have prompted their interest in a visiting child.

26. Diary, 25 July 1663. John Pepys of Norfolk and then Ashtead (1576–1652) was third cousin once removed of Sam Pepys's father. He married Anne Walpole of Houghton in 1610, both regarded with great warmth by the Cokes, she for particular kindness to the women of the family during illness. Their son was named Edward, no doubt for Coke. For their daughter Jane, see Chapters 4 and 16 below. In 1642 Robert Coke was imprisoned in the Tower as a royalist, and John Pepys and his family moved back to London, where he was also imprisoned for four months for his failure to contribute money demanded for the war chest. Lady Theophila visited her husband in the Tower until her death from smallpox in 1643. Sir Robert returned to Surrey on his release and died there in 1653, bequeathing the books in the library at Durdans – 300 folios and many smaller books – to the City clergy at Sion College, 'whom the iniquity of the time had stripped of everything but (what could not be taken from them) their Religion, Loialty & Learning'. Information partly from unpublished paper by F. L. Clark in Bryant archives, Liddle Hart Centre, King's College, London.

27. Robert Pepys was Sam's uncle, his father's eldest brother, who seems to have inherited what little land there was in the family. Robert and John Pepys's father was Thomas Pepys, an elder brother of Paulina (Lady Montagu). See Family Tree.

28. See F. R. Harris, *The Life of the First Earl of Sandwich* (1912), vol. I, p. 19.

29. Richard Baxter in *The Holy Commonwealth* (1659), ref. from Christopher Hill's *The Century of Revolution 1603–1714* (1974), p. 110.

30. Edward Hyde, earl of Clarendon, *The True Historical Narrative of the Rebellion and Civil Wars in England* (1888), vol. III, p. 264.

31. Maurice Ashley, *The English Civil War* (1980), p. 50. Ashley suggests on p. 51 that these armed men were better-off citizens, merchants and shopkeepers, organized by City members of parliament.

32. C. V. Wedgwood, *The King's Peace* (1983), p. 422. You can see women in the crowd watching the execution of Strafford in Hollar's engraving of the scene.

33. See Diary, 18 Mar. 1664, where Pepys arranges to have his brother Tom buried inside St Bride's and 'as near as I can to my mother's pew'. But see too 4 Mar. 1660, when Pepys and his mother 'talked very high about Religion, I in defence of the Religion I was born in', i.e., the established Church of England.

34. David Masson, *The Life of Milton* (1859–94), vol. III, p. 147.

35. Quotation from Ruth Spalding, *The Improbable Puritan*, pp. 82–3.

36. See Christopher Hill, *The Century of Revolution*, p. 167.

37. Information about the building of the defences of London in 1642 and 1643 mostly from N. G. Brett-James, *The Growth of Stuart London* (1935), who quotes Bulstrode Whitelocke's *Memorials of the English Affairs* ('it was also wonderful to see how the women and children and vast numbers would come to work digging and carrying of earth to make the new fortifications'), p. 268; and report of Venetian ambassador, p. 270; and from Samuel Butler's *Hudibras* – he recorded that the women, 'From ladies down to oyster-wenches/ Labour'd like pioneers in trenches'; and from other contemporary reports such as the newssheet *Perfect Diurnal* for May 1643 and William Lithgow's *Present Surveigh of London and England's Estate &c.*, also of 1643. John Evelyn inspected the 'so much celebrated line of communication' in Dec. 1642. The defences were largely razed in 1647, partly because they took up so much land.

38. State papers listed reasons for fortifying the City: 'There is terrible news that Rupert will sack it, and so a complete and sufficient dike and earthern wall and bulwarks must be made which will render ample recompsense for trouble. The fortifications will discourage foes and encourage friends to come and inhabit by multitude, whereby London will grow famous and rich even in time of War . . .' Cited in N. G. Brett-James, *The Growth of Stuart London*, p. 273.

39. See Diary, 26 July 1663. The name of Heale appears on the map of the manor of Ashtead made in 1638, on two small holdings not far from John Pepys's land. Information from F. L. Clark's unpublished paper.

40. John Pepys travelled to Holland again much later, in 1656, when Cromwell was protector, Montagu a high official with Sam working for him; on this occasion Sam applied for the pass for his father. On 7 Aug. it was granted to 'John Pepys and his man with necessaries for Holland, being on the desire of Mr Samll Pepys'. H. B. Wheatley, *Pepys and the World He Lived In* (1880), p. 9, giving as source Entry-Book No. 105 of the protector's Council of State, p. 327; also footnote to Diary, 24 Jan. 1666, Latham and Matthews edition, which gives source as *Calendar of State Papers, Domestic Series*, 1656–7, p. 582.

　　For Dutch engineers advising on fortifications, N. G. Brett-James, *The Growth of Stuart London*, p. 274. Montagu took minutes at a meeting of the East Anglian Association at Bury St Edmunds, 9 Feb. 1643, raised support in Huntingdon and was made a deputy-lieutenant by parliament in June. Clarendon said 'he was so far wrought upon by the caresses of Cromwell that, out of pure affection for him, he was persuaded to take command in the army'.

41. Letter of the Venetian ambassador, 15 May 1643.

42. On the 1625 outbreak, Nehemiah Wallington, *Historical Notices of Events Occurring Chiefly in the Reign of Charles I*, ed. Rosamond Webb (1869), vol. I, p. xvii.

2. A Schoolboy's War: Huntingdon and St Paul's

1. Pepys mentions 'Beard' as the carrier in a letter to Montagu, 22 Oct. 1659, 'old Beard' on 14 Mar. 1660 and 'Bird the carrier' in 1661, when his mother travelled with him on 3 Jan., and both his parents and his sister Pall on 5 Sept. By then Pepys himself either rode or took a coach.

2. Montagu's involvement is my guess. The only evidence that Pepys attended the school is in his remark in the Diary, 15 Mar. 1660, when he meets Tom Alcock, 'one that went to school with me at Huntington, but I have not seen him this sixteen years'. This is good evidence, and seems to establish that he was there in 1644 (although Pepys is not always reliable in his recollection of dates). Pepys mentions 'my shee-cousin Alcock' in a letter of 5 Dec. 1657 to Montagu. Elizabeth Pepys, sister of Paulina Montagu, another great-aunt of Sam, married a Henry Alcock. For information about the Free Grammar School, see Philip G. M. Dickinson's *History of Huntingdon Grammar School* (1965).

3. A note in Sir Sidney's hand in vol. III of the Sandwich Papers at the National Maritime Museum records that he 'gave up house-keeping to my Son Edward' in 1643. He moved to Barnwell in Northamptonshire.

4. The conjecture that Sam lodged with his uncle is supported by the fact that he became his heir, which suggests approval at least. Robert Pepys appears to have been employed as a bailiff by the Montagus and was described as 'of Hinchingbrooke' in a bond signed by Sidney Montagu in 1630. In the same year Robert married a widow, Anne Trice, at All Saints', Huntingdon, and moved to the house at Brampton. (Information from the *Companion* to the Latham and Matthews edition of the Diary.) He was probably born in the mid 1590s. His two stepsons were some years older than Sam.

5. The house belongs to the Pepys Association. It is a private residence, but permission to view it may be obtained. It has doubled in size, with an eighteenth-century addition behind the original Tudor house. The windows have been enlarged, and the staircase moved from where it probably was in Pepys's day, next to the central chimney stack.

6. It is now called the Black Bull. In Pepys's time the alternative drinking place was Goody Gorrum's ale house, which has disappeared.

7. Pepys mentions Thomas Taylor, Diary, 10 Oct. 1667. He was master at Huntingdon for nearly forty years, from 1641 to 1679.

8. The parents' complaint is mentioned in John Brinsley's *Ludus Literarius*, a dialogue between two schoolmasters published in 1612.

9. Information from Philip G. M. Dickinson's *History of Huntingdon Grammar School*. Cooke was appointed in 1625 by his predecessor, Dr Thomas Beard, who had taught Cromwell. So Cooke must have taught Edward Montagu before retreating from the job in 1639. He remained the official headmaster until 1655 and was succeeded by the Revd Francis Bernard, who belonged to

a family Pepys knew well. Sir Robert Bernard, mentioned in the Diary in 1661, was a lawyer and the son-in-law of a Cromwell-appointed peer, Oliver St John. William Bernard, one of his sons, was a grocer in London whom Pepys entertained to dinner and who returned the invitation, serving an excellent pie. Francis may have been another. There were still Bernards living in the house in which Cromwell was born as late as 1897.

10. Diary, 15 Mar. 1660.
11. Quoted in Michael McDonnell's privately printed *History of St Paul's School* (1959), p. 224. Langley made the comment at the end of his high mastership, in the 1650s, so it may not have applied in Pepys's time.
12. The house has changed, of course. Edward Montagu himself made improvements in the 1660s; a fire in 1830 led to a great deal of rebuilding; and in 1970 the Sandwich family sold it and it became Huntingdon Comprehensive School. Since then much more of the early structure has been uncovered, revealing features of the original abbey and some of Richard Cromwell's work.
13. Horace Walpole's later description, cited in Latham and Matthews's *Companion*, p. 186.
14. This was William Camden's description in his *Britannia* (1607).
15. The school buildings were probably more extensive than what is now known as the school, currently a small museum dedicated to Cromwell.
16. Diary, 14 July 1661, 13 Oct. 1662.
17. Cardinal Mazarin, after dining with Montagu aboard the *Naseby* in the spring of 1658, described him as 'un des gentilhommes du monde le plus franc et mieux intentionné et le plus attaché à la personne de M. le Protecteur'. Richard Ollard, *Cromwell's Earl: A Life of Edward Montagu, First Earl of Sandwich* (1994), p. 61.
18. See F. R. Harris, *The Life of the First Earl of Sandwich* (1912), vol. I, p. 28.
19. Much quoted exchange, here taken from Samuel Rawson Gardiner, *History of the Great Civil War 1642–1649* (1893), vol. II, p. 59.
20. Samuel Rawson Gardiner, *History of the Great Civil War*, vol. II, p. 196.
21. There are many authorities for Charles I's occupation of Huntingdon, 24 Aug. 1645. He is reputed to have made the George Inn his HQ, and there is a letter from him dated 'Huntingdon 25th August'. Gardiner mentions the episode. I quote from the parliamentarian Nehemiah Wallington's account in his contemporary *Historical Notices of Events Occurring Chiefly in the Reign of Charles I*, ed. Rosamond Webb (1869), vol. II, pp. 267–70. Richard Symonds's *The Diary of Marches Kept by the Royal Army During the Great Civil War*, ed. C. E. Long (1859), gives an eyewitness account – he says the king moved on to Woburn on Tuesday – and Alfred Kingston's *East Anglia and the Great Civil War* (1897), p. 196, gives a contemporary letter about the exchange of prisoners.
22. F. R. Harris, *The Life of the First Earl of Sandwich*, vol. I, pp. 71–2.
23. Diary, 24 Jan. 1669: Pepys recalls how he 'saw my old Lord lie in state when he was dead'. Essex was fifty-five; he made a better end than his father, the first

earl, who had died at thirty-five on the scaffold, for treachery towards Queen Elizabeth.

24. See Chapter 14, and especially Diary, 27 July 1663, when Charles II addressed parliament formally: 'the King, sitting in his throne with his speech writ in a paper which he held in his lap and scarce looked off of it, I thought, all the time he made his speech to them'.

25. Michael McDonnell, *History of St Paul's School*, pp. 223–4.

26. Michael McDonnell, *History of St Paul's School*, p. 205.

27. The school's anti-royalist tradition appears in Gill, who was arrested and imprisoned in 1628 for attacking the royal favourite, the duke of Buckingham, and 'the old fool and the young one', meaning James and Charles. He was sentenced to two years in prison and to have his ears cut off, this last part being remitted.

28. When Tom was delirious on his deathbed, he spoke in French: 'A great deal of French, very plain and good,' wrote Sam of Tom's ramblings, of which he gives an example, 'quand un homme boit quand il n'a point d'inclination à boire il ne lui fait jamais de bien.' I can't think of a more plausible explanation than a French lodger in the Pepys household when they were children, from whom the boys picked up the language together; Tom must have become fluent for his French to emerge as it did when he was dying.

29. See Diary, 22 Jan. 1661, when Pepys visits the Mercers' Great Hall: 'It pleased me much now to come in this condition to this place, where I was once a peticioner for my exhibicion in Pauls school. And also where Sir G. Downing (my late master) was chaireman, and so but equally concerned with me.'

30. F. R. Harris, *The Life of the First Earl of Sandwich*, vol. I, pp. 73–4, citing Sir Thomas Herbert (Harleian MSS, 7396), and M. Noble's *Memoirs of the Protectoral House of Cromwell* (1787), vol. I, p. 44, footnote: 'K. Cha. I . . . on his way from Holmby was very magnificently and dutifully entertained there by lady Mountagu . . .'

31. Information about London in this chapter from many sources including Samuel Rawson Gardiner, *History of the Great Civil War*, and David Masson, *The Life of Milton* (1859–94).

32. George Downing in Islington to Winthrop, 8 Mar. 1648, cited in John Beresford, *The Godfather of Downing Street: Sir George Downing 1623–1684* (1925), pp. 49–51.

33. Samuel Rawson Gardiner, *History of the Great Civil War*, vol. IV, pp. 99–101.

34. Samuel Rawson Gardiner, *History of the Great Civil War*, vol. IV, p. 129.

35. F. R. Harris, *The Life of the First Earl of Sandwich*, vol. I, p. 75.

36. Samuel Rawson Gardiner, *History of the Great Civil War*, vol. IV, p. 299.

37. According to Locke, then a schoolboy of seventeen at Westminster: information from Conrad Russell's *The Crisis of Parliaments* (1971), p. 383.

38. *The Diaries and Letters of Philip Henry, MA, of Broad Oak, Flintshire 1631–1696*, ed. M. H. Lee (1882), p. 12. Henry became a Nonconformist preacher and suffered much as a result under Charles II's legislation against Nonconformity.

39. Diary, 1 Nov. 1660.

40. Diary, 13 Oct. 1660.

41. *The Diary of John Evelyn*, ed. E. S. de Beer (1955), 30 May 1649.

42. Talbot Pepys is on record as having been one of the commission that raised taxes to support the parliamentary army in 1643, 1645, 1648 and again in 1657 (for the war against Spain). See Charles Henry Cooper, *Annals of Cambridge* (1842–53), vol. III, pp. 354, 384, 420, 466.

43. E. K. Purnell, *Magdalene College* (1904), p. 115.

3. Cambridge and Clerking

1. Sept. 1654, *The Diary of John Evelyn*, ed. E. S. de Beer (1955).

2. Pepys accepted a description of himself as 'a low, squat man': Pepys Library, Mornamont MSS, p. 41, 'I asked him what was that Pepys, he said he was a low squat man.' See also his own statement (Diary, 4 Jan. 1669) that he could stand under the arms of 'the great woman' of 6' 5", which would make him about 5' 1". (Evelyn said she was 6' 10" but I'm inclined to trust Pepys here.) It must be remembered that the general height of the population was lower – for instance, William III was described as tall at 5' 6". The many portraits of Pepys, although they were all made later in life, give a consistent picture of his facial features – see also L. Cust, 'Notes on Some Distinctive Features in Pepys's Portraits', *Occasional Papers Read by Members at Meetings of the Samuel Pepys Club* (1917), vol. I, pp. 38–9.

3. These figures are in Samuel Morland's accounts for his time as a sizar in 1644. They are taken from p. 122 of E. K. Purnell, *Magdalene College* (1904).

4. Charles Henry Cooper, *Annals of Cambridge* (1842–53), vol. III, p. 366. Scobell's ordinance of Nov. 1643 ordered the heads of the colleges to remove all images and pictures in the chapels, but nothing was done until William Dowsing arrived in Dec. and set to work. He kept a record of his destruction.

5. J. E. B. Mayor (ed.), *Cambridge under Queen Anne* (1911), p. 245.

6. See Diary, 7 Oct. 1667, when Pepys stays at an inn in Bishop's Stortford with all his family and finds the landlady is his old friend Mrs Aynsworth. Her version of 'Full Forty Times Over' must have been lewder than the one printed as 'A Song' in *Wit and Drollery, Jovial Poems Never before Printed*, ed. John Phillips (1656), although you can imagine how it might be made ruder:

> Full forty times over, I have strived to win
> Full forty times over neglected have been,
> But it's forty to one, but I'll tempt her again:
>   For he's a dull lover,
>   That so will give over
>   Seeing thus runs the sport,
> And assault her but often you'll carry the fort.

> There's a breach ready made, which still open hath bin,
> And thousands of thoughts to betray it within,
> If you once come to storme her, you're sure to get in,
> > Then stand not off coldly,
> > But venter on boldly
> > With weapon in hand,
> If you do but approach her, she's not able to stand,
> > With weapon in hand
> If you do charge her, but home she's not able to stand. &c – three more
> stanzas

7. See Diary, 30 Jan. 1664.

8. Diary, 25 June, 7 and 11 Nov. 1660 for references to Elizabeth Whittle; there are many more to her husband Stephen. He became the grandfather of Charles James Fox, but she was not his grandmother, as Arthur Bryant states; this was Fox's second wife, Christian.

9. In the 1650s Sir Ralph Verney complained about girls learning Latin and shorthand: 'the difficulty of the first may keep her from that Vice, for so I esteem it in a woman; but the easiness of the other may be a prejudice to her; for the pride of taking Sermon notes, hath made multitudes of women most unfortunate . . . Had St Paul lived in our Times I am most confident he would have fixed a Shame upon our women for writing (as well as for their speaking) in the Church.' Ralph Verney to Dr Denton, n.d. but 1650s, cited in *Memoirs of the Verney Family during the Civil War*, eds. Lady Frances Parthenope and Lady Margaret M. Verney (1892), vol. III, p. 72. *Tachygraphy* is rich in symbols relating to biblical names and religious terms.

10. See William Matthews's essay in the *Companion* to the Latham and Matthews edition of the Diary, pp. xlviii–liv.

11. This is what Samuel Morland did in 1644: see p. 121 of E. K. Purnell, *Magdalene College*, citing his own account.

12. Oliver Heywood was up immediately before Pepys. He named the divines whose works he enjoyed as Perkins, Bolton, Preston, Sibbes, and the titles given in the text are from their works. See J. B. Mullinger, *Cambridge in the Seventeenth Century* (1867), p. 181.

13. W. T. Costello, *The Scholastic Curriculum at Early Seventeenth-Century Cambridge* (1958), gives a good account of the curriculum, with many examples drawn from commonplace books, etc.

14. Dryden was a very distant connection of Pepys, because his mother was a Pickering, cousin to Gilbert Pickering, Edward Montagu's brother-in-law.

15. Diary, 8 Oct. 1667, and note by Latham on the Saunders family; and Diary, 26 June 1662.

16. Pepys to Dr Arthur Charlett, 5 Nov. 1700, *Private Correspondence and Miscellaneous Papers of Samuel Pepys*, ed. J. R. Tanner (1926), vol. II, p. 109. He calls music 'a science peculiarly productive of . . . pleasure . . . Witness the universal

gusto we see it followed with . . . by all whose leisure and purse can bear it' and suggests its teaching could be simplified 'were the doctrine of it brought within the simplicity, perspicuity, and certainty common to all the other parts of mathematick knowledge'.

17. See Diary, 25 May 1668.
18. This was in Oct. 1645. Sir Henry Vane and Gilbert Pickering served on this body with him. See Charles Henry Cooper, *Annals of Cambridge*, vol. III, p. 398.
19. Cromwell's letter is given in Charles Henry Cooper, *Annals of Cambridge*, vol. III, p. 452.
20. Charles Henry Cooper, *Annals of Cambridge*, vol. III, p. 461. All three were also to act as visitors to Eton, Winchester, Westminster and Merchant Taylors' schools.
21. Diary, 30 Mar. 1662, which was Easter Sunday, records that he did not take the sacrament, 'which I blame myself that I have hitherto neglected all my life, but once or twice at Cambridge'.
22. Sawyer became a barrister and rose to be attorney-general in 1681. Pepys heard him pleading a case 26 Nov. 1666 (Diary).
23. David Masson, *The Life of Milton* (1859–94), vol. IV, p. 602.
24. Charles Firth, *The Last Years of the Protectorate* (1909), vol. II, pp. 133–5.
25. King Street was narrow and 'better inhabited than built, the Houses being generally built after the old way, with Timber and Plaister, and the street somewhat narrow', according to John Stow, *A Survey of the Cities of London and Westminster . . . And the Survey and History Brought Down from the Year 1633 to the Present Time by John Strype* (1720), Book VI, p. 63.
26. Pepys uses the words 'our old house for clubbing' in Diary, 26 July 1660, when he revisits Wood's in Pall Mall with his old friends. On 5 July 1665, during the plague, he walks to Whitehall round the locked-up park and observes 'a house shut up this day in the Pell Mell, where heretofore in Cromwells time we young men used to keep our weekly clubs'.
27. Diary and note for 23 Aug. 1660.
28. Edward Phillips went on to become tutor to John Evelyn's son. His brother John Phillips was also publishing work that Milton would not have approved; he edited in 1656 *Wit and Drollery, Jovial Poems Never before Printed*, a collection including work by Pepys's future colleague Sir John Mennes as well as Suckling, D'Avenant and one poem by Donne, 'Love's Progress'. John Phillips dedicated the book 'To the TRULY NOBLE Edward Pepes, Esq.'. This must be the lawyer son of John Pepys of Ashtead and Salisbury Court, born in 1617 and admitted to the Middle Temple 1636, and evidently rich enough to be a patron. Edward Pepys was of course known to Samuel Pepys, who attended his funeral in 1663.
29. Samuel Rawson Gardiner, *History of the Commonwealth and Protectorate* (1897), vol. III, pp. 318, 325.

4. Love and Pain

1. Diary, 27 Feb. 1668.
2. For most of the play the angel appears as a page-boy, 'Angelo', sustaining his Christian mistress in the face of persecution by the Romans. The descent from heaven in Act V was the invention of the Restoration stage manager, the text simply requiring the angel to enter with a basket of fruit and flowers, though sporting 'a pair of glorious wings'. Massinger and Dekker's *The Virgin Martyr* was first published in 1622, reissued in 1631, 1651 and 1661. J. Harold Wilson in *Notes & Queries* for 21 Feb. 1948 points out that Pepys first saw the play in Feb. 1661, and that after seeing it for a second time in February 1668 – this was when he was so transported by the music – he went again on 6 May. On 7 May he did not attend the performance but went backstage after it ended and met Nell Gwyn 'in her boy's clothes, mighty pretty', as well as Knipp, the actress he was trying to seduce, and was impressed by the confident talk of the actresses.
3. A note by H. M. Nixon, in vol. VI of the Pepys Library Catalogue (1984) states that a 1647 edition of the *Nouveau Testament* inscribed 'S. Pepys 1654' is now in the Pierpont Morgan Library. It adds that it was given to Mary Skinner later.
4. See Diary, 31 May 1666, for Pepys's mostly unflattering description of Pall's physical appearance. He does allow that she is 'a pretty good-bodied woman and not over-thicke', although by this time Pall was in her mid twenties.
5. Pepys destroyed some of his love letters during the quarrel of Jan. 1663, the others presumably after the death of Elizabeth. The letter quoted is from the mid 1650s and is by his contemporary Oliver Heywood, who was already ordained when he wrote; it is not surprising that Heywood won his 'Mrs Betty'. Like Pepys, he lost her early. From the *Autobiography 1630–1702* of the Revd Oliver Heywood (1937), vol. I, pp. 131–2.
6. For Act of 24 Aug. 1653 on civil marriage ceremonies, see Samuel Rawson Gardiner, *History of the Commonwealth and Protectorate* (1897), vol. II, p. 292.
7. He noted the anniversary in the Diary in 1661, 1664, 1665 and 1666. He also put on the monument to Elizabeth that she died in the fifteenth year of marriage. She died on 10 Nov. 1669, so if they counted the marriage from Oct. 1655, she had been married for fourteen years, and was indeed just into the fifteenth year of the marriage; whereas if they counted from Dec., she had been married only thirteen years and eleven months, and was still in the fourteenth year.
8. Legally, men were allowed to marry at eighteen and women at twelve. An attempt to raise the age to fourteen in 1689 failed. David Ogg, *England in the Reigns of James II and William III* (1955), pp. 75–6.
9. See Diary, 3 Sept. 1660.
10. Diary, 10 Feb. 1664, for the gold lace, and 5 July 1663 for the bridal respect.
11. Diary, 6 Aug. 1666.
12. Arthur Bryant, *Samuel Pepys: The Man in the Making* (1933), p. 28. The inversion is so curious that it is tempting to think it is Bryant's way of expressing emotion.
13. Diary, 25 Feb. 1667.

14. Diary, 2 Aug. 1660, 'my wife not very well of her old pain in the lip of her *chose*, which she had when we were first married'.

15. Accounts of the sufferings of those with bladder stones are found in medical manuals of the time and make unpleasant reading. See notes on surgery below. Elizabeth probably was suffering from Bartholin's abscess or cyst, a relatively common condition treated today with antibiotics and, if necessary, surgery; in the seventeenth century there was no effective treatment, and the condition tended to recur, as it clearly did in Elizabeth's case. Although it was not caused by venereal infection but by bacteria living on the skin, Elizabeth may have suspected her husband of infecting her. It does not begin until puberty because it is the action of the glands that produces it, and in Elizabeth's case puberty probably coincided more or less with her marriage. I am indebted to Patrick French for the medical information. Her condition continued to cause trouble, for example when Pepys refers to 'her old pain', Diary, 29 Oct. 1660, which prevented sexual intercourse for two weeks. By the autumn of 1663 she had an abscess three inches deep ('a pain in the place which she used to have swellings in; and that that troubles me is that we fear that it is my matter that I give her that causes it, it never coming but after my having been with her', Diary, 24 Oct. 1663) and their surgeon, Hollier, considered operating; but she was so upset by this suggestion that he settled for a fomentation.

16. Diary, 15 Nov. 1660.

17. Diary, 3 Sept. 1660, when Pepys again sees him off and recalls the earlier occasion.

18. Sir d'Arcy Power, *Occasional Papers Read by Members at Meetings of the Samuel Pepys Club* (1917), vol. I, pp. 78–93: he blames Hollier for dividing an ejaculatory duct. Milo Keynes, 'Why Samuel Pepys Stopped Writing His Diary: His Dimming Eyesight and Ill-health', *Journal of Medical Biography*, vol. v, Feb. 1997, p. 26, suggests a secondary infection or a stricture resulting from damage during the removal of the stone. Keynes dismisses d'Arcy Power's suggestion that his sexual activity was stimulated by the irritation to which his genito-urinary system was subjected. Keynes is altogether more convincing than Power on the subject.

19. Diary, 4 July 1664, 13 Aug. 1661.

20. It may have been during the separation that Pepys went to Fleet Alley. Looking – and only looking – at a pretty prostitute there on 29 July 1664, he recalled earlier visits: 'there saw what formerly I have been acquainted with, the wickedness of those houses and the forcing a man to present expense'. During the Diary period he avoided prostitutes entirely for fear of infection.

21. Elizabeth's birthday was on 23 Oct. 1640: Pepys gave the date and place, which he put down as Somerset, in his memorial inscription to her. When Balthasar married on 3 Dec. 1662, he gave his age as twenty-two. He may have got it wrong, or they may have been twins, or just possibly born within a year of one another, in which case he must have been born in Jan. 1640. He writes that 'my sister and wee all ware borne' in Bideford, which suggests other children were born who did not survive.

22. Balthasar de St Michel to Pepys, 8 Feb. 1674, in *The Letters of Samuel Pepys and His Family Circle*, ed. H. T. Heath (1955), pp. 25–8, and Diary, 29 Mar. 1667.

23. Diary, 2 Nov. 1660. Elizabeth sometimes spoke of becoming a Catholic to Pepys; and she and her mother were friendly with a Jesuit called Father Fogourdy in Paris, who visited her in 1664 (6 Feb. and 28 Mar.), which Pepys found disquieting, although he liked the man. Fogourdy's name comes up during the Popish Plot: see Chapter 22.

24. Diary, 4 June 1663: 'I did employ a porter to go, from a person unknown, to tell him that his daughter was come to his lodgings. And I at a distance did observe him; but Lord, what a company of Questions he did ask him; what kind of man I was and God knows what.'

25. Diary, 22 Nov. 1660. Lady Sandwich (as she then was – at this date Lady Montagu, and always known to Pepys as 'my Lady') asked the question, after Elizabeth acted as interpreter between her and her newly acquired French maid, who seems to have raised the subject.

26. The debates about Naylor are found in *The Diary of Thomas Burton*, ed. J. T. Rutt (1828), vol. I, p. 154 *et seq.*, and in Charles Firth, *The Last Years of the Protectorate* (1909), vol. I, pp. 87–102. Gilbert Pickering, Thurloe, Whitelocke and Cromwell were for a more merciful treatment.

27. A. G. Matthews, *Mr Pepys and Nonconformity* (1954), p. 36.

28. Quoted in Granville Penn, *Memorials of Sir William Penn* (1833), vol. II, p. 159.

29. Quoted in F. R. Harris, *The Life of the First Earl of Sandwich* (1912), vol. I, p. 97.

30. Charles Firth, *The Last Years of the Protectorate*, vol. I, p. 55.

31. Pepys in a letter to Edward Montagu, 9 Dec. 1656, writes 'your Honour may remember present at Sir W.P.'s magnetique experiments'. W.P. suggests William Petty, physician, statistician and founding member of the Royal Society, later a friend of Pepys, although he was not knighted until 1661. Montagu was also a founding member of the Royal Society.

32. Pepys to Edward Montagu, 8 Jan. 1657, *Letters and Second Diary of Samuel Pepys*, ed. R. G. Howarth (1932), pp. 5–6.

33. Pepys to Edward Montagu, 8 Dec. 1657, *Letters and Second Diary of Samuel Pepys*, p. 7.

34. See among many accounts David Masson, *The Life of Milton* (1859–94), vol. V, p. 148, and Richard Ollard's *Cromwell's Earl: A Life of Edward Montagu, First Earl of Sandwich* (1994), p. 54, with its admirable description of the occasion as 'a kind of laicized Coronation'.

35. Pepys to Edward Montagu, 26 Dec. 1657, *Letters and Second Diary of Samuel Pepys*, p. 11.

36. Pepys to Edward Montagu, 22 Dec. 1657, *Letters and Second Diary of Samuel Pepys*, p. 9.

37. Pepys's own description, Diary, 26 Mar. 1664, when he writes thanking the Lord God for raising him from his sickness and poverty.

38. *Lithotomia Vesicae* (1640), English translation from the Dutch, pp. 49–50.

39. There were specialist surgeons all over Europe, where the operation had been

practised since ancient Egyptian times. In Ralph Josselin's diary he mentions two men from his Essex village who went to London to be cut for the stone, one in July 1649, the other in Apr. 1665. Both returned cured, and the first of the two lived another thirty-three years. *Diary of Ralph Josselin 1616–1683*, ed. Alan MacFarlane (1976).

40. Diary, 30 May 1663, mentions this aunt James and her account of John Pepys seeking prayers for his son.

41. You can read the prescription, given in Latin by Dr J. M., probably James Moleyns of Bart's, for 'Mr Pepes . . . before he was cut for the stone by Mr Hollyer' in a notebook kept by a contemporary physician. British Library, Sloane MSS, 1536, fol. 56.

42. *Lithotomia Vesicae*, pp. 81–4.

43. A contemporary description of the operation was made by John Evelyn, who saw it performed on five patients at the La Charité Hôpital in Paris in May 1650. This is his account of one:

> The sick creature was strip'd to his shirt, & bound armes & thighes to an high Chaire, 2 men holding his shoulders fast down: then the Chirurgion with a crooked Instrument prob'd til he hit on the stone, then without stirring the probe which had a small channell in it, for the Edge of the Lancet to run in, without wounding any other part, he made Incision thro the Scrotum about an Inch in length, then he put in his forefingers to get the stone as neere the orifice of the wound as he could, then with another Instrument like a Cranes neck he pull'd it out with incredible torture to the Patient, especially at his after raking so unmercifully up & downe the bladder with a 3rd Instrument, to find any other Stones that may possibly be left behind: The effusion of blood is greate. Then was the patient carried to bed, & dress'd with a silver pipe accommodated to the orifice for the urine to pass, when the wound is sowed up: The danger is feavor, & Gangreene, some Wounds never closing.

Surely Evelyn was wrong about the incision being through the scrotum? *The Diary of John Evelyn*, ed. E. S. de Beer (1955).

44. A second prescription, this time by two doctors, Moleyns and Dr G. Joliffe, 'for Mr Peapes who was cut for the Stone by Mr Hollier March the 26 [1658] and had a very great stone taken this day from him'. British Library, Sloane MSS, 1536, fol. 56v.

45. See Diary, 27 Feb. 1663, and Pepys's mention of Dr Jolly (George Joliffe) who had cared for him and answered his questions in 1658.

46. Pepys preserved his stone and showed it to Evelyn on 10 June 1669. *The Diary of John Evelyn*, ed. E. S. de Beer.

47. He did not order the case until 20 Aug. 1664, when he notes in the Diary that it will cost him twenty-five shillings. See also Diary, 3 May 1667, where he describes taking it to be shown to the earl of Southampton to encourage him to be operated upon, unavailingly; he died two weeks later, unoperated. Also Evelyn's mention of it in his diary for 10 June 1669.

48. Diary, 5 Dec. 1660.
49. Richard Ollard, *Cromwell's Earl*, p. 61, for Mazarin quote; Morland was one who testified to Montagu being 'wholly devoted to old Noll, his country man [i.e., Oliver Cromwell]', F. R. Harris, *The Life of the First Earl of Sandwich*, vol. I, p. 137. For Cromwell's letter to Edward Montagu, dated 2 Oct. 1657, National Maritime Museum, Sandwich Journal, vol. I, X98/065.

5. *A House in Axe Yard*

1. It can be seen clearly in Roque's map of 1746, which shows it as starting close to where the Cenotaph now stands. Andrew Davies's *The Map of London from 1746 to the Present Day* (1987) is helpful.
2. A letter from Downing to General Monck in 1654 is dated 'Axeyard 7ber 30th, 54', cited in John Beresford, *The Godfather of Downing Street: Sir George Downing 1623–1684* (1925), p. 64. For Downing's mention of Hawley, and his move into another house in Axe Yard, Major Greenleaf's, in 1658, see the *Companion* to the Latham and Matthews edition of the Diary, p. 170.
3. Diary, 18 Feb. 1660, 'went to my Lord's lodgings to my turret there, and took away most of my books and sent them home by my maid'.
4. So Pepys said in a letter of 1 Oct. 1681 to his sister-in-law Esther St Michel, printed in *The Letters of Samuel Pepys and His Family Circle*, ed. H. T. Heath (1955), p. 188, in which he urged economy on her. He claimed they lived on this income 'for several years' and added that he still had Elizabeth's household accounts at the time of writing. Unfortunately they have not survived to the present.
5. For cake-making, Diary, 6 Jan. 1668; for refusal to kill turkey, Diary, 4 Feb. 1660; for possession of book, Pall accused of stealing hers, 24 Jan. 1660. Female literacy increased steadily during the seventeenth century, from 10 per cent at the start to 55 per cent at the end, according to Tim Harris, *London Crowds in the Reign of Charles II* (1987), p. 27.
6. Since Jane refused to come for less than £3 a year when the Pepyses asked her to return to their service, 26 Mar. 1662 – see Diary – it is unlikely she was paid this much in 1658.
7. Diary, 18 Feb. 1662, when Pepys wrote that the wind was 'such as hath not been in memory before, unless at the death of the late Protector'; and 19 Oct. 1663, when he remarked to his wife, 'I pray God I hear not of the death of any great person, this wind is so high'. Marvell, 'Poem upon the Death of His Late Highness the Lord Protector', lines 117–19, 131–2.
8. For Newton's response to the storm, see David Masson, *The Life of Milton* (1859–94), vol. V, p. 358.
9. Cited in John Beresford, *The Godfather of Downing Street*, p. 100.
10. Bernard Capp, *Cromwell's Navy* (1989), p. 149. See also Godfrey Davies's *The Restoration of Charles II* (1955), pp. 10–11.
11. See Diary, 28 Nov. 1660, when Pepys describes the disbanding of the regiment,

receives his pay of £23.14s.9d., and regrets that he won't be getting any more
in this easy fashion.

12. See Bernard Capp, *Cromwell's Navy*, p. 332.

13. Dryden's presence is disputed by one of his biographers, Charles E. Ward, but
accepted by most other authorities, and certainly seems likely.

14. Evelyn mistakenly gave the date as 22 Nov. 1658, *The Diary of John Evelyn*, ed.
E. S. de Beer (1955).

15. Information about Cromwell's funeral from the contemporary account by the
Revd John Prestwich, fellow of All Souls, printed as Appendix VII in *The
Diary of Thomas Burton*, ed. J. T. Rutt (1828), vol. II, pp. 516–30. Among those
he listed as present were a Mr Ewer, comptroller of the clerks, possibly
connected with Will Hewer, as well as Robert Blackborne, secretary to the
Admiralty commissioners and Hewer's uncle; also Francis Willoughby, the
Admiralty commissioner whose house in Seething Lane was taken over by
Pepys. More information about the ceremonial from Antonia Fraser's *Cromwell,
Our Chief of Men* (1973), pp. 680–85, and from Godfrey Davies's *The Restoration
of Charles II*, pp. 40–44.

16. For the vulture and the titmouse, James Heath's *A Brief Chronicle of the Late
Intestine Warr*, edition of 1676, cited in F. R. Harris, *The Life of the First Earl of
Sandwich* (1912), vol. I, p. 115.

17. Pepys's care for the Montagu children begins with the operation on their eldest
daughter, Jemima, in London in the winter of 1659/60, and continues with many
other instances. For Lady Montagu's affectionate behaviour to him, see the first
entry about her in the Diary, 12 Oct. 1660, when Pepys, hearing she has arrived
in town, immediately calls on her: 'found her at supper, so she made me sit down
all alone with her; and after supper stayed and talked with her – she showing most
extraordinary love and kindness'. After this they are numerous.

18. So he told Pepys: see Diary, 21 June 1660.

19. *The Diary of John Evelyn*, 5 May 1659. De Beer (vol. III, p. 229, footnote 2)
gives the Cockpit in Drury Lane.

20. Bernard Capp, *Cromwell's Navy*, p. 335.

21. For Captain Country, see Diary, 27 Sept. 1661. The footnote in the Latham
and Matthews edition points out that Pepys conferred a sinecure on Country
in 1676, as a gunner on the *Royal Charles*. For Pepys to find him 'little' he must
have been very short, given his own height.

22. For Lieutenant Lambert, Diary, 4 Oct. 1660, where Pepys calls the ship by its
new name, the *Charles*.

23. Morland to Charles, 15 June 1659, cited in F. R. Harris, *The Life of the First
Earl of Sandwich*, vol. I, p. 138.

24. National Maritime Museum, Sandwich Journal, 47,60ff.

25. Diary, 15 May 1660: 'he told me that his conversion to the King's cause (for so
I was saying that I wondered from what time the King could look upon him
to be become his friend), from his being in the Sound [i.e., Baltic], when he
found what usage he was likely to have from a Comonwealth'.

26. F. R. Harris, *The Life of the First Earl of Sandwich*, vol. I, pp. 156–7.

27. Pepys to Edward Montagu, 20 Oct. 1659, *Letters and Second Diary of Samuel Pepys*, ed. R. G. Howarth (1932), pp. 11–12.

28. Pepys to Edward Montagu, 6 Dec. 1659, *Letters and Second Diary of Samuel Pepys*, p. 15. All following quotes from Pepys to Montagu in this chapter from this source, spellings modernized.

29. F. R. Harris, *The Life of the First Earl of Sandwich*, vol. I, pp. 165–6. Lawson's proclamation also suggested some radical reforms: no more pressing, abolition of the Excise and pensions for men no longer able to serve.

6. A Diary

1. Montaigne was born exactly a century before Pepys, in 1533, and died in 1592. He also suffered from the stone. An English translation of his essays by Florio appeared in 1603, another by Charles Cotton in 1685, and he was greatly admired in England throughout the century. Pepys bought a copy of the Florio translation ('Montagne's *essays*') in 1668 – see Diary, 18 Mar. 1668 – and later acquired the Cotton version, which remained in his library (Pepys Library 1018–20).

2. Francis Bacon, 'Of Travel', *Essays* (Everyman ed., 1994), p. 54.

3. Will Hewer, for example, learnt and used tachygraphy. The diaries themselves are on display at the Pepys Library at Magdalene College, Cambridge. The introduction to vol. I of Latham and Matthews's edition gives a great deal of information about their physical characteristics and about the shorthand, including the fact that Pepys adapted it slightly for his own use.

4. Diary, 11 Apr. 1660, when he shows it to Lieutenant Lambert at sea; and 9 Mar. 1669, when he tells William Coventry of its existence.

5. Diary, 5 Feb. 1660.

6. Diary, 24 Jan. 1664, suggests as much, when he describes 'entering out of a by-book part of my second Journall book, which hath lay these two years and more unentered'.

7. Diary, 10 Nov. 1665.

8. For Downing's journal, see John Beresford's *The Godfather of Downing Street: Sir George Downing 1623–1684* (1925). Beresford was able to track down only part of it (in a country house in Norfolk); he points out that there was a tradition of diary-keeping in his family, since Downing's East Anglian grandfather, Adam Winthrop, kept a journal between 1597 and 1622, from which he prints a few entries. The first volume of Montagu's journal has been published by the Navy Records Society in 1929, edited by R. C. Anderson; the manuscripts of the rest are owned by the present earl of Sandwich.

9. Nine years later, William Coventry told Pepys he was keeping a journal – see Diary, 9 Mar. 1669 – and Pepys returned the confidence, less than three months before he abandoned his. Coventry's has not survived.

10. See William Haller's *The Rise of Puritanism* (1938), p. 99.

11. For diaries mentioned in text, see Bibliography.

12. 'A Journal kept by me, George Carteret, in His Majesty's ship the *Conventive*, being bound for the coast of Barbarie, 1638'. See G. R. Balleine, *All for the King: The Life Story of Sir George Carteret* (1976), p. 15 and notes p. 167, which say the journal had been privately printed in Philadelphia by B. Penrose.

13. Evelyn's remarks in his diary, 4 Oct. 1680, *The Diary of John Evelyn*, ed. E. S. de Beer (1955). For the information about Evelyn senior, I am indebted to Frances Harris, who believes he is likely to have made his entries in the pages of an almanac, as an aide-mémoire in his business affairs. None of his diaries appear to have survived.

14. The philosopher John Locke, another close contemporary, kept a diary during his travels in France in the late 1670s and 1680s. From what I have seen of it, it was a record of his journeys, the sights he saw and notes about agriculture, manufacturing, tax, religious questions, notably the condition of the Protestant population in France: highly interesting and quite impersonal. See *The Life and Letters of John Locke*, ed. Lord King (1858).

15. 'Samuel Pepys', *Cornhill* magazine, July 1881.

16. Diary, 4 Mar. 1660, for argument with mother, and 14 Dec. 1663 for his objection to Montagu's swearing 'Before God' and other oaths.

17. For Pepys's religious attitude, see Chapter 26. Diary, 15 May 1660.

18. Diary, 2 Oct. 1660.

19. Wheatley's 1893 edition makes the sentence on p. 1 'My wife . . . gave me hopes of her being with child, and on the last day of the year [the hope was belied].' As already noted, Bryant did give the complete text of the opening passage in the first volume of his biography in 1933. But when Edwin Chappell gave the tercentenary lecture that same year at the Clothworkers' Hall, he felt he could not quote it, explaining satirically that 'I cannot take the responsibility of corrupting your innocence'. The standard editions of the Diary, including J. P. Kenyon's abridged version of 1963, remained bowdlerized, and Latham and Matthews's 1970 edition was the first not to cut Pepys's opening paragraph.

20. For Lawson, see Bernard Capp's *Cromwell's Navy* (1989), particularly Chapters 10 and 11.

21. Bernard Capp, *Cromwell's Navy*, p. 357.

Part Two: 1660–1669

7. Changing Sides

1. See the royalist John Lane's complaint of Downing to Sir Edward Nicholas, 30 Mar. 1658, cited in John Beresford, *The Godfather of Downing Street: Sir George Downing 1623–1684* (1925), p. 93; and p. 97 for attempt to assassinate him in summer of 1658.

2. The details of Downing's behaviour are mostly in John Beresford's *Sir George Downing*, pp. 92–122.

3. Harrington's *Oceana*, published in 1656, laid out a plan for a republic with a rotating senate, votes for all freemen (servants were not enfranchised), partial religious toleration (Jews and Catholics were excluded from it) and restrictions on property owning. Henry Neville was another republican and atheist member of the Rota. Others were Roger Coke, a grandson of the great Sir Edward Coke, and the republican and Leveller John Wildman. According to John Aubrey, the club was formed in 1659 and 'The Doctrine was very taking, and the more because, as to human foresight, there was no possibility of the King's return.'

4. Pepys put a portrait of Harrington in his collection in the Pepys Library. *Oceana* was reissued in 1887 and is still discussed to this day. Harrington is now considered a forerunner of Adam Smith and the science of political economy. See Christopher Hill, *The Century of Revolution 1603–1714*, p. 161. Harrington's theories also had an influence in the future United States: see Godfrey Davies, *The Restoration of Charles II* (1955), p. 291.

5. F. R. Harris, *The Life of the First Earl of Sandwich* (1912), vol. I, p. 171; Richard Ollard, *Cromwell's Earl: A Life of Edward Montagu, First Earl of Sandwich* (1994), p. 77.

6. *The Diary of Bulstrode Whitelocke 1605–1675*, ed. Ruth Spalding (1989), p. 574.

7. Richard Creed eventually moved to Monmouthshire, where his father-in-law, Walter Cradock, had been a puritan divine and a leading Propagation commissioner in the county, responsible for ejecting royalist clergy. Creed had clerked for him in the 1650s and also acted as parliamentary surveyor. Cradock died in 1659, but Creed was specifically named in the Act of Indemnity as one excluded from ever holding public office again, and he ended his days as a humble schoolmaster in Llangwm Uchaf. He died in 1690 and his memorial tablet recorded that he had served admirals Blake and Sandwich, but nothing about Harrison. Information from Julian Mitchell's unpublished essay 'Monmouthshire Politics 1660–1706'.

8. Diary, 12 Apr. 1664, for Pepys plotting to get Will Howe Creed's job with Lord Sandwich: 'And I would be glad to get him secretary and to out Creed if I can – for he is a crafty and false rogue.'

9. Diary, 12 May 1661.

10. Diary, 18 Jan. 1665, where it is Edward Montagu's wife, by then Lady Sandwich, who has heard this bad report of John Creed. 'I told her I thought he was as shrewd and cunning a man as any in England, and one that I would fear first should outwit me in everything – to which she readily concurred.'

11. Diary, 8 Mar. 1660. This was Captain Philip Holland, a good fighting officer, who later defected to the Dutch and then returned and got his pardon by giving information about them: see Bernard Capp, *Cromwell's Navy* (1989), pp. 388–9, 391.

12. Diary, 19 Mar. 1660. For details of Blackborne's career, see George Aylmer, *The State's Servants: The Civil Service of the English Republic* (1973).

13. Diary, 16 Mar. 1660.

14. Diary, 17 May 1660.

15. Robert Blackborne to Edward Montagu, 7 May 1660, National Maritime Museum, Sandwich Journal, vol. III. fol. 213. The figure of Cromwell on the prow appears not to have been removed until 1663, when Pepys reports a conversation about its being pulled down and burnt, and deplores 'the flinging away of £100 out of the King's purse to the building of another – which it seems must be a Neptune'. Later on the same day he makes the point about the waste of money again, and says that it has in any case been forgotten whose head it was. Diary, 14 Dec. 1663.

16. Godfrey Davies, *The Restoration of Charles II*, p. 349. Thurloe was arrested a fortnight later for high treason, but released six weeks later.

17. Diary, 3 May 1660.

18. Pepys heard of it in advance, Diary, 13 May 1660: 'I heard . . . how Mr Morland was knighted by the King this week, and that the King did give the reason of it openly, that it was for giving him intelligence all the time he was clerk to Secretary Thurloe.' Morland, when he engaged to work for Charles, made it a condition that he would not bear witness against his old colleagues 'if upon his restauration they should happen to bee arraigned at the barr of justice'. H. W. Dickinson, *Sir Samuel Morland: Diplomat and Inventor* (1970), p. 21.

19. Diary, 4 May 1660. Montagu told Pepys he feared Crew's support for Presbyterians would damage his chances, but Charles accepted Montagu's plea and made Crew a baron.

20. Diary, 20 May 1660. Until the Reformation, 'a month's mind' meant the period of commemorative masses for the dead. It was then mysteriously transmuted into the sense of having a liking or fancy for something or someone, as in Shakespeare, *Two Gentlemen of Verona*, I.ii.133, 'I see you have a month's mind to them'. Congreve uses it in this sense in *The Way of the World*, III. i: 'She has a Month's mind; but I know Mr Mirabell can't abide her.' Pepys's usage possibly also suggests that he has endured a month – actually two months – of sexual abstinence.

21. Diary, 17, 19 May 1660.

22. Diary, 15 May 1660.

23. Years later, in Oct. 1680, he took down in shorthand, at Charles's request, a narrative of his adventures and escape from England after the battle of Worcester.

24. See Diary, 25 May 1660.

25. Given as direct speech in the Diary, 2 June 1660.

26. Diary, 18 June 1660.

27. See Diary, 15, 19 June 1660.

28. When Lady Pickering called on the Pepyses on 14 July 1668, Pepys was too busy to see her. 'But how natural it is for us to slight people out of power, and for people out of power to stoop to see those that while in power they contemned,' he wrote in his Diary.

29. Edmund Ludlow, John Carew, Thomas Scott, Sir Hardress Waller and Adrian Scrope were some who gave themselves up, believing the promise of pardon.

Waller was a friend of Montagu, and all of them known to him. Ashley Cooper was responsible for saving Haslerig from being tried, but he died in the Tower during the winter of 1660/61.

30. Information from *The Diary of Bulstrode Whitelocke* and from Ruth Spalding's *The Improbable Puritan: A Life of Bulstrode Whitelocke* (1975).

31. Diary, 21 June 1660, and footnote for information. Note too a petition to Lord Sandwich from the governors of the 'Hospital' installed in the Wardrobe not to have it taken from them.

32. George Aylmer, *The State's Servants*, p. 337. For Pepys's objections, see his memo of 3 Apr. 1669, in his 'Navy White Book', printed in *Samuel Pepys and the Second Dutch War*, ed. Robert Latham, transcribers Robert Latham and William Matthews (1995), p. 196.

33. There is no picture of Seething Lane and it is not possible to construct any plan, but the whole complex must have been vast and each house substantial, with up to ten rooms apiece and two or three storeys high, with cellars. The existence of the 'leads' that means so much to Pepys – areas of flat roofing covered in lead that would be used as a terrace – suggests that there was a narrower upper storey that left roof space over the one below.

34. See Bernard Capp, *Cromwell's Navy*, pp. 280–81 and pp. 290–91 for his good work as navy commissioner, p. 371 for his leaving England.

35. National Maritime Museum, Sandwich Journal, vol. I, item 27.

36. Charles's remark cited in Godfrey Davies, *The Restoration of Charles II*, p. 353.

37. Diary, 10 Aug. 1660.

38. Diary, 15 July, 7, 22 Oct. 1660.

39. Diary, 7 Nov. 1660.

40. Diary, 22 Oct. 1660, and note by Latham.

41. Diary, 3 Oct. 1660.

42. Diary, 7 Oct. 1660.

43. See M. Noble, *Lives of the English Regicides* (1798), p. 332.

44. Diary, 16 Oct. 1660.

45. Diary, 20 Oct. 1660.

46. Diary, 20 Oct. 1660.

47. Diary, 6, 7 Nov. 1660.

48. Diary, 19 Nov. 1660.

49. Diary, 4 Dec. 1660.

50. For the payment to see the body, *Diurnal of Thomas Rugg 1659–1661*, ed. W. L. Sachse (1961), p. 143, and for the placing of the head, note by Latham to Diary, 5 Feb. 1661, the day Pepys saw it. Cromwell's head remained unburied until 1960, when a head believed to be his was laid to rest at his old college, Sidney Sussex, in the ante-chapel.

51. George Downing to Sir Edward Nicholas, 17 Mar. 1662, cited in John Beresford, *Sir George Downing*, pp. 146–7, from British Library, Egerton MSS, 2538, fols. 37–8.

8. Families

1. Diary, 1 Jan. 1661.
2. Diary, 8 Feb. 1662.
3. Diary, 26 May 1663. Pepys is frank about the contents of the chamber pot: solid and liquid.
4. Diary, 3 Nov. 1661, and alluded to earlier in the Prologue.
5. Diary, 22 Sept. 1660.
6. Diary, 14 Mar. 1661.
7. See Diary, 28 June 1661.
8. Diary, 12 Nov. 1660.
9. Diary, 2 Jan. 1661. Compare Ralph Josselin, East Anglian clergyman, writing in his diary in 1644, when his sister Mary arrived 'under my Roofe as a servant, but my respect is and shall be towards her as a sister, god might have made me a waiter upon others'. *Diary of Ralph Josselin 1616–1683*, ed. Alan MacFarlane (1976).
10. Diary, 18 July 1660.
11. Diary, 11 Aug. 1660, for Will's tears.
12. Diary, 8 June 1662: 'observe my man Will to walk with his cloak flung over his shoulder like a Ruffian; which whether it was that he might not be seen to walk along with the footboy, I know not, but I was vexed at it; and coming home, and after prayers, I did ask him where he learned that immodest garb, and he answered me that it was not immodest, or some such slight answer, at which I did give him two boxes on the ear; which I never did before, and so was after a little troubled at it'.
13. Diary, 24 Feb. 1662.
14. Diary, 8 Jan. 1662. Sir George Carteret, the treasurer, made the accusation and expressed his anger against Will to Sir William Penn, who advised Pepys to sack him. Pepys questioned Will without revealing the source of the accusation, saw that he understood and did nothing more. Pepys himself saw less of Blackborne after this.
15. See, for example, Diary, 18, 28 Jan. 1664, and again 19 Oct. the same year.
16. Information about variant spellings of Hewer from Dr Charles Knighton. The variants on Pepys I have taken from the ledgers of Hoare's Bank, where he had an account from the 1680s, except for the last, which is found in a document describing Pepys's collection shortly after his death, Bodleian Library, Rawlinson MSS, D 396, fol. 35. Also Pyppes in Rawlinson MSS, A 180, fol. 406, and Phips in another, fol. 369.
17. For sale of the lease, Diary, 17 Sept. 1660. For Betty Lane at the house, 12 Aug. 1660, and for Diana Crisp, 4 Sept. 1660.
18. Pepys is sworn in as JP 24 Sept. 1660. For Sherwyn's fall, see George Aylmer, *The State's Servants: The Civil Service of the English Republic* (1973), pp. 253–4, and later references in Diary, for example, 17 Jan. 1665, when Pepys finds it

'mighty strange' to sit with his own hat on 'while Mr Sherwin stood bare as a clerk'.

19. Diary, 22 Nov. 1660.
20. Diary, 9 Apr. 1661.
21. Diary, 24 July 1661.
22. Penn was close to Lawson and Fifth Monarchy men, just as Montagu was known as a religious radical. See Bernard Capp, *Cromwell's Navy* (1989), p. 294.
23. Diary, 2 Apr. 1661.
24. Diary, 9 Apr. 1661.
25. The Quakers were the first group to object to slavery on principle, in 1671. William Penn the younger, who became a Quaker leader, had of course experienced slave ownership in his father's house.
26. *DNB*, and *Calendar of State Papers, Domestic Series*, p. 407, letter from Sir William Coventry to the earl of Arlington, 4 June 1665, praising Penn's conduct in the battle of Lowestoft.
27. Diary, 27 Mar. 1661, 1 Nov. 1660. They were called servants, and seem to have been affectionately treated in the families they served, but they were really slaves, brought from Africa, without rights. Pepys saw the little Turk and Negro acquired by Lord Sandwich to be pages to his family on 30 May 1662. Note also a letter from Pepys to Sandwich, ?23 Oct. 1664 (National Maritime Museum, Correspondence of Samuel Pepys, LBK/8), about the Dutch success on the Guinea coast and 'defeating them in their great Contract with Spain for Blacks'. The slave trade had been going for forty years, and Bristol, home town of Batten and Penn, was one of the two chief ports in England used by the slaving ships, Liverpool being the other. Neither puritans nor cavaliers saw anything wrong in slavery. George Downing observed and approved slavery at Barbados, writing to his cousin John Winthrop on 26 Aug. 1645, 'If you go to Barbadoes, you shall see a flourishing Island, many able men. I believe they have bought this year no less than a thousand Negroes, and the more they buy, the better able they are to buy, for in a year and a half they will earn (with God's blessing) as much as they cost.' Later, on another island, he calls Negroes 'the life of this place'. John Beresford, *The Godfather of Downing Street. Sir George Downing 1623–1684* (1925), pp. 44, 45. Charles II encouraged the formation of the Royal Africa Company, which dealt in slaves. Pepys himself later owned two black slaves (see below, p. 180).
28. Diary, 28 May 1661.
29. Diary, 12 Oct. 1660.
30. Diary, 15 Nov. 1660.
31. Diary, 16 May 1661.
32. Diary, 22 May, 15 June 1661.
33. The London to Oxford coach took twelve hours. Pepys needed a guide because there were no road maps – John Ogilby's were the first to be published, at the request of Charles II, and appeared in 1675.
34. Diary, 16 Jan. 1661.

35. Diary, 18 Jan. 1661.

36. Diary, 24 July, 25 Oct., 1, 9, 24, 27 Nov. 1661.

37. Diary, 31 Aug. 1661.

38. Diary, 12 May, 30 June 1662.

39. Diary, 21 Apr. 1664.

40. Diary, 29 Apr. 1664.

41. Diary, 6 June 1665.

42. See his accounts with the Sandwiches dated 15 June 1670, in which he charges 'interest for two years at 6 per cent . . . £12' on the £100 'supply'd my Ladie'. Bodleian Library, Rawlinson MSS, A 174, fol. 437.

43. The only other example I know of is Shelley's, writing to his second wife, Mary – 'my best Mary'. Pepys uses it in his letter to Lady Carteret of 4 Sept. 1665, after the wedding of the two ladies' children. 'My Lord Sandwich is gone to sea with a noble fleet . . . My best Lady Sandwich, with the flock at Hinchingbrooke, was, by my last letters, very well.' *Letters and Second Diary of Samuel Pepys*, ed. R. G. Howarth (1932), p. 24.

44. Diary, 10 Oct. 1667.

45. National Maritime Museum, Sandwich Journal, Appendix, fol. 130.

46. Diary, 9 Oct. 1667.

47. For Charles's letter to Pepys, 15 Mar. 1697, *Private Correspondence and Miscellaneous Papers of Samuel Pepys*, ed. J. R. Tanner (1926), vol. I, p. 138. His spelling is wonderful, e.g., 'harrey caen' for 'hurricane', 'Scowayer' for 'squire'. But his status as a Pepys with sons meant he was a residual legatee in Pepys's will.

48. Diary, 8 Apr. 1662.

49. Diary, 1 June 1660 – Elizabeth writes to Pepys to tell him about the Joyces. For the story about Tom, see Chapter 11.

50. Diary, 26 Aug., 5 Sept. 1661.

51. Diary, 31 Dec. 1663.

52. Diary, 16 Jan. 1667.

53. Diary, 7 Feb. 1668.

54. Diary, 2 Mar. 1668, for news of wedding; for letter to father, Diary, 7 Mar. 1668.

55. Diary, 24 May 1668.

9. Work

1. See, for example, Diary, 1 Sept. 1666, when Pepys is 'horribly frighted' to see Henry Killigrew, son of the dramatist and groom of the Bedchamber to the duke of York, with his friends, at a performance of *Polichinelly* Pepys attended with Penn, Elizabeth and Mercer: 'we hid ourselfs, so as we think they did not see us'. Even Lord Brouncker, a personal friend of the royal family as well as a Navy Board official, was worried about being noticed at the theatre by the king, and when he and Pepys set out to see a play together they agreed to take a high box 'for fear of being seen, the King being there'. Diary, 29 Oct. 1667.

2. At Pepys's level he might be expected to save money, but the cases of two of his clerks illustrate how vulnerable they were: when Tom Edwards died young after an illness, Pepys saw personally to helping his widow and sons, otherwise destitute. Richard Gibson, who served the navy for more than five decades in various positions of trust and outlived Pepys, sent pathetic letters enclosing testimonials in 1712, begging to be given a post as a steward at Greenwich Hospital in order to support his family.

3. Diary, 8 Nov. 1660. The *Catherine* was finished in May 1661.

4. Colonel Thomas Middleton, appointed to the Navy Commission, Portsmouth, in 1664, had fought for parliament and sometimes compared the poor organization and discipline of the 1660s with the superior conditions prevailing under the commonwealth.

5. Diary, 16 Aug. 1660.

6. See Bernard Capp, *Cromwell's Navy* (1989), p. 375.

7. Pepys saw his first actresses on 3 Jan. 1661. He saw Betterton in *Hamlet* on 24 Aug. 1661 and again on 27 Nov. in the same year (and on 28 May 1663 and 31 Aug. 1668), and decided he was the best actor after seeing him in Massinger's *The Bondman*. He also saw him play Bosola in Webster's *The Duchess of Malfi* on 30 Sept. 1662 – 'to admiration'.

8. Diary, 29 Sept., 10 Nov. 1661.

9. For Coventry replacing Blackborne, George Aylmer, *The State's Servants: The Civil Service of the English Republic* (1973), p. 266.

10. Evelyn called him wise and witty in his Diary for 1659; H. C. Foxcroft (*The Life and Letters of Sir George Savile, First Marquis of Halifax*, vol. I, p. 29) says he headed the procession: Clarendon said he was void of religion; he was called 'Will the Wit' in hostile references by Andrew Marvell in his *The Last Instructions to a Painter* (1667), line 228; other information from the *DNB*.

11. Diary, 16 Mar. and 31 Dec. 1662.

12. Coventry to Pepys, 21 Apr. 1665, Bodleian Library, Rawlinson MSS, A 174, fol. 458.

13. For the gift of the pen, Diary, 5 Aug. 1663. For Pepys singing to Coventry on the barge, Diary, 16 Apr. 1661. For the boat trip in which Coventry shielded Pepys from the sun and told him his rules in life, Diary, 8 Aug. 1662. Dines with Pepys at home, 18 Dec. 1662. For the Hayter affair, Diary, 9, 10, 15 May 1663. For Pepys's letter to Coventry suggesting afternoon meetings for general discussion, Pepys to Coventry, 22 Aug. 1662, National Maritime Museum, Correspondence of Samuel Pepys, LBK/8. For Penn's reference to Coventry's mistress, Diary, 7 Jan. 1664.

14. Mennes conveyed his enthusiasm for Chaucer (Diary, 14 June 1663), and Pepys later acquired a Caxton edition of *The Canterbury Tales* and some fragments of Chaucer MS. He encouraged Dryden to make his versions of some of the *Tales*. See Chapter 25.

15. Diary, 25 Nov. 1663.

16. Diary, 3 June 1662.

17. For Chatham trip, see Diary, 8–11 Apr. 1661; for Portsmouth trip with Elizabeth, see Diary, 1–8 May 1661.

18. From the 'Navy White Book', printed in *Samuel Pepys and the Second Dutch War*, ed. Robert Latham, transcribers Robert Latham and William Matthews (1995), p. 68. Pepys records putting in 'My journeys and disbursements expressed in a bill' on 30 June 1664, and Sir John Mennes urging him to charge more, '"For," says he, "why will you have less than the clerks? And it is too little." But I would have it go as it was, saying it was as much as it cost me.' When he walked, it presumably cost him nothing.

19. Pepys to Pett, June 1665, cited in Arthur Bryant, *Samuel Pepys: The Man in the Making* (1933), pp. 255–6. Pett objected to the board's failure to look at other suppliers of masts, and Bryant praises Pepys for his tremendous putting down of Pett, although he elsewhere acknowledges that Pepys accepted bribes from Warren.

20. Pepys notes the arrival of the duke's 'Instructions' at the office, 5 Feb. 1662. They were based on earlier 'Instructions' of 1640.

21. See J. D. Davies, *Gentlemen and Tarpaulins* (1991), p. 15, and David Ogg, *England in the Reign of Charles II* (1955), p. 260.

22. The figure of 157 ships at the time of the Restoration is Pepys's own, given in a speech to parliament in 1675. Some of these were not in active service but laid up in dock, without officers or crew and stripped of rigging, guns and perhaps even masts: information from Professor Bernard Capp in private communication. He points out that the fleet the Navy Board actually had to deal with in 1660 was of 84 ships in service, with 25 waiting to be paid off; the others were laid up.

23. Diary, 30 Sept. 1661.

24. Something like £40,000 today, although all such equivalents are very approximate.

25. Diary, 2, 3 Mar. 1662. For the amount of his fortune, 30 May 1662.

26. Diary, 28 June, 1 Sept. 1662.

27. Diary, 30 Sept. 1662.

28. Diary, 23 Dec. 1662.

29. Diary, 14 June 1662. He mentions his letter to Lord Sandwich, who was at Hinchingbrooke seeing to his building works, but it has not survived. Samuel Morland, Pepys's old tutor, is said to have refused to testify against Vane and burnt some papers in his possession that might have incriminated him: see Violet Rowe, *Sir Henry Vane the Younger* (1970), p. 237, footnote.

30. Diary, 22, 27 June 1662, 11 Feb. 1663.

31. Given in Brewer's *Dictionary of Phrase and Fable*, centenary edition of 1970, among 'Dying Sayings'.

32. See, for example, Bernard Pool, *Navy Board Contracts* (1966), p. 2.

33. Diary, 18 June 1664.

34. Diary, 20 Nov. 1664.

35. Diary, 1 Aug. 1661, 3 May 1664.

36. Pepys gives Blackborne's hostile talk of Penn, including accusations of coward-
    ice, Diary, 9 Nov. 1663, and on 6 Nov. 1665 he gives Carteret's account of the
    duke of Albemarle saying Penn was a 'cowardly rogue' who had brought
    'roguish fanatic captains into the fleet', and of Coventry's defence of Penn. It
    appears from these two passages that Penn was attacked from both political
    sides.

37. Evidence for this is found in *Calendar of State Papers, Domestic Series* for 1665,
    where a great many dispatches from Batten in Harwich appear, as does William
    Coventry's commendation of Penn's behaviour in battle, dated 4 June.

38. For Pepys's attempts on Pegg, Diary, 28 Nov. 1666, 13 Apr., 23 May 1667, 10
    May 1668. For Pegg's suspected pox, Diary, 15 May, 13 Sept. 1667. Lowther's
    cousin, Sir John Lowther, became a commissioner of the Navy Board in 1689,
    and Pepys corresponded with him in that year asking for assistance on behalf of
    both his brother-in-law Balthasar St Michel and a cousin Charles Pepys: see
    The Letters of Samuel Pepys and His Family Circle, ed. H. T. Heath (1955), pp. 225,
    227 and 243.

39. See Diary, 19 Oct. 1665, and Pepys's letter to Coventry of same date, in which
    he says the duke of Albemarle has asked him to nominate candidates for the
    job:

    > which I desired a little time to do, being unwilling to make an over-sudden nomination
    > . . . as the rendering their service useful will principally depend upon his diligence and
    > care that hath the putting together and reporting what rises from the several informations
    > from every port, so I am at the greatest loss whom to pitch upon for that employment.
    >
    >   The truth is, I know one that if you shall think fit to have it propounded to, I dare
    > go far in assuring you the work shall be done to your mind . . .
    >
    >   His employment in another capacity I confess is very full, but half the trouble which
    > this will add will be saved by the ease it will bring him in the many letters, orders,
    > messages, and mental labours he now is exercised with.

    Further Correspondence of Samuel Pepys 1662–1679, ed. J. R. Tanner (1929),
    pp. 63–4.

40. It was suggested by Sir Robert Slingsby, the first comptroller.

41. The Diary merely mentions the drawing up of the agreement, 26, 27 Mar.
    1665. A copy of the 'privat pack' is in the Bodleian, Rawlinson MSS, A 172,
    fol. 102.

42. There is more: for example, on 11 Dec. 1665 Gauden allows Pepys £500 on a
    £4,000 transaction, and a year later, on 10 Dec. 1666, Gauden 'doth promise
    me consideration for my Victualling business for this year, and also as Treasurer
    for Tanger, which I am glad of, but would have been gladder to have just now
    received'. The first engineer of the Tangier Mole, Sir Hugh Cholmley (at
    St Paul's at the same time as Pepys) visited him on 23 Nov. 1665 and offered
    him £200 a year; on 19 Jan. 1666 he received £100, 'whereof Povey must have
    half', wrote Pepys in the Diary, but whether he did is not clear; from Povey's

letters, it would seem not. On 23 May 1666 Lord Belasyse, the governor of Tangier, 'promised me the same profits Povey was to have had'.

43. Povey to Pepys, 16 Feb. 1674, Bodleian Library, Rawlinson MSS, A 172, fol. 100.

44. Povey wrote to Pepys, 8 and 13 Mar. 1674. The words quoted are from 13 Mar., Bodleian Library, Rawlinson MSS, A 172, fol. 104.

45. Pepys to Povey, 15 Mar. 1674, Bodleian Library, Rawlinson MSS, A 172, fol. 107.

46. Povey to Pepys about Tangier profits, 3 Feb. 1685, Bodleian Library, Rawlinson MSS, A 179, fol. 38, and Povey to Anthony Deane, fol. 40, for the words quoted in the text.

47. Diary, 5 Dec. 1665.

48. Diary, 18 Oct. 1665.

49. Diary, 21 Dec. 1665, 4, 25, 27, 30, 31 Mar., 1, 2, 3, 11, 16, 23 Apr., 25, 29 June, 3 July 1666.

50. Hayter to Pepys, 31 Dec. 1668, and Pepys to the commissioners, 13 Jan. 1669, *Further Correspondence of Samuel Pepys*, ed. J. R. Tanner, pp. 207–13.

10. Jealousy

1. Diary, 27 Mar. 1661.
2. Diary, 10 Apr. 1661.
3. Diary, 11 Nov. 1661.
4. Diary, 5 Oct. 1662.
5. See, for example, 12 Sept. 1662.
6. Diary, 24 Apr. 1663.
7. Diary, 26–8 Apr. 1663.
8. Diary, 15 May 1663.
9. Diary, 2 and 3 May 1663.
10. Diary, 4 May 1663.
11. Diary, 15 May 1663.
12. He saw *Othello* with Creed at the Cockpit, Diary, 11 Oct. 1660.
13. Diary, 20 May 1663.
14. Diary, 26 May 1663.
15. Diary, 9 June 1663.
16. Diary, 15 June 1663.
17. Diary, 13 July 1663.
18. Diary, 13 and 15 July 1663.
19. Diary, 10 Aug. 1663.
20. Diary, 10 Aug. 1663.
21. See Diary, 12–25 Aug. 1663.
22. Diary, 19 Aug. 1663.
23. For Pepys's gallant invitation, Diary, 13 Sept. 1663.
24. Diary, 19 Sept. 1663.

25. Diary, 9 Sept. 1663.
26. Diary, 12 Nov. 1663.
27. Diary, 18 Nov. 1663.
28. Diary, 22 Nov. 1663.
29. This was the Hon. James Montagu, the last child in the family; Pepys records his arrival 15 July 1664.
30. Diary, 30 Dec. 1663.
31. Diary, 10 Nov. 1668.
32. Diary, 30 Sept. 1662.

11. Death and the Plague

1. For death of Robert Pepys, Diary, 6 July 1661.
2. The story is found in the Diary in 1662, 3, 22 Oct.
3. Diary, 27 Oct. 1662.
4. Diary, 21 Jan. 1668.
5. Diary, 16, 19 May 1667.
6. Diary, 19 Oct. 1663.
7. Diary, 20 Mar. 1660.
8. Diary, 11 Oct. 1662.
9. Diary, 14 Sept. 1663.
10. Diary, 25, 27 Mar. 1667.
11. Diary, 29 June 1667.
12. Tom Pepys to Pall Pepys, 16 Jan. 1664, *The Letters of Samuel Pepys and His Family Circle*, ed. H. T. Heath (1955), p. 6.
13. For Batten's clerk's illness, Diary, 14 July 1667.
14. Diary, 15 Mar. 1664.
15. Diary, 18 Mar. 1664.
16. Diary, 6 Apr., 4, 20, 27 May, 25 Aug. 1664.
17. Diary, 23 Apr. 1662. The point is made by Christopher Morris in the *Companion* to the Latham and Matthews edition of the Diary in a fascinating discussion of why the 1665 plague was the last great outbreak in England. He suggests that those susceptible to it may have virtually died out, leaving a population with natural immunity. He also suggests that some people are more attractive to fleas than others, something many have noticed.
18. Diary, 1 Aug., 8 Sept. 1664.
19. Diary, 31 Dec. 1664.
20. Diary, 31 Jan. 1665.
21. Mrs Pepys arrived 10 May, made many outings with Elizabeth and trips on the water with Pepys and 'had a mind to stay a little longer' on 22 June, the day after he saw coaches and wagons full of people leaving from Cripplegate. Like her son, she clearly much preferred town life to the country, even at the risk of the plague. This was her last visit to London.

22. Diary, 15 Feb. 1665. He met and was impressed by Robert Hooke; he had recently bought his *Micrographia*.
23. Diary, 24, 30 Sept. 1665.
24. Diary, 9, 23 July 1665.
25. Diary, 12 July 1665.
26. Diary, 14 July 1665.
27. Diary, 26 July 1665.
28. This was probably one of the plague waters made up by the College of Physicians, distillations of plant juices – tormentil, angelica, peony, salvia, pimpernel, scabious, calendula, juniper are all mentioned by Nathaniel Hodges in his *Loimologia* of 1667, translated 1720 by J. Quincy, pp. 170–215. Hodges thought sack was good, tobacco useless and the wearing of amulets had a purely psychological effect. Like Pepys, he believed that keeping cheerful was important: 'Fear or Sorrow . . . prepare the way for the Infection' (p. 62). He called it the 'Poors Plague' because the rich saved themselves by leaving town.
29. Diary, 31 July 1665.
30. Diary, 26 July 1665.
31. See G. R. Balleine, *All for the King: The Life Story of Sir George Carteret* (1976), p. 162 and genealogy.
32. Diary, 29 July 1665.
33. Pepys to William Coventry, 5 Aug. 1665, *The Further Correspondence of Samuel Pepys 1662–1679*, ed. J. R. Tanner (1929), p. 49.
34. Pepys to William Coventry, 25 Aug. 1665, *The Further Correspondence of Samuel Pepys*, ed. J. R. Tanner, p. 53.
35. Diary, 30 Aug., 9 Oct. 1665.
36. Diary, 8 Aug. 1665.
37. Diary, 28 Aug. 1665.
38. Diary, 14, 15, 17 Sept. 1666.
39. Diary, 10 Sept. 1665.
40. Pepys to Lady Carteret, 4 Sept. 1665, *The Letters and Second Diary of Samuel Pepys*, ed. R. G. Howarth (1932), p. 25.
41. Diary, 12 Apr. 1665.
42. Diary, 4 Nov. 1665; Pepys to Peter Pett, 2 Dec. 1665, *The Further Correspondence of Samuel Pepys*, ed. J. R. Tanner, p. 82.
43. Diary, 1 June 1665.
44. Diary, 21 Sept. 1665, 12 Oct. 1666. The girl was Barker, who succeeded Mary Mercer, but, although she sang well, she did not take to life with the Pepyses and they dismissed her.
45. Diary, 12 Dec. 1663.
46. Diary, 29 Dec. 1663.
47. The £50 bill of exchange was given on 1 Jan. 1664. Luellin took Elizabeth to the theatre 8 Mar. 1664, and dined several times with the Pepyses around this

time and in 1665. On 17 Feb. 1665, for example, Pepys came home and found Luellin with Elizabeth, provoking his jealousy.

48. Diary, 30 Sept. 1665.

49. Diary, 4 Feb. 1666, and Latham's footnote.

50. Diary, 13 Jan. 1666.

51. When Daniel Defoe, who was five or six in 1665, published his *Journal of the Plague Year* in 1722, it was meant as a warning of what might happen again.

12. *War*

1. Diary, 28 June 1662, 'Great talk there is of a fear of a war with the Duch . . . but I hope it is but a scarecrow to the world, to let them see that we can be ready for them; though God knows, the King is not able to set out five ships at this present without great difficulty, we neither having money, credit nor stores.'

2. See Henry Lyons, *The Royal Society 1660–1940* (1944), pp. 81, 105.

3. He was given a 'neager-boy' by Lieutenant John Howe of the *Phoenix* in 1675 (Bodleian Library, Rawlinson MSS, A 185, fols. 66, 70), probably the same one he sold in June 1680 (Bodleian Library, Rawlinson MSS, A 181, fol. 317). On 11 Sept. 1688 Pepys also asked Captain Stanley of the *Foresight* to sell his slave Sambo in the plantations, saying he was 'dangerous to be longer continued in a sober family' and beyond reform. Arthur Bryant, *Samuel Pepys: The Saviour of the Navy* (1938), p. 270. For Pepys's observation of Sandwich's present of slave children, see Diary, 30 May 1662.

4. Ronald Hutton, *Restoration* (1985), p. 221.

5. Esther St Michel was living on the Essex coast and saw much of the Dutch action. Her remarks to Pepys are recorded in the Diary, 17 July 1667.

6. Pepys to William Coventry, 20 May 1665, *Further Correspondence of Samuel Pepys 1662–1679*, ed. J. R. Tanner (1929), p. 45.

7. Diary, 22 May 1665.

8. William Coventry to Pepys, 21 Apr. 1665, Bodleian Library, Rawlinson MSS, A 174, fol. 458.

9. William Coventry to Lord Arlington, 24 May 1665, *Calendar of State Papers, Domestic Series*, p. 382.

10. Rupert's complaints are recorded in Milward's parliamentary diary, 31 Oct. 1667, *Diary of John Milward from September 1666 to May 1668*, ed. Caroline Robbins (1938), and in his and Albemarle's Letter Book, 9 Aug. 1667, etc., *The Rupert and Monck Letter Book 1666*, ed. J. R. Powell and E. K. Timings (1969).

11. Dryden wrote, 'the noise of the cannon from both navies reached our ears about the city, so that all men being alarmed with it, and in a dreadful suspense of the event which we knew was then deciding, everyone went following the sound as his fancy led him; and, leaving the town almost empty, some took towards the Park, some across the River, others down it, all seeking the noise

in the depth of silence'. *Essay of Dramatic Poesy*, cited in David Ogg, *England in the Reign of Charles II* (1955), p. 288.

12. John Beresford, *The Godfather of Downing Street: Sir George Downing 1623–1684* (1925), pp. 192–3.

13. Diary, 10 Sept. 1665.

14. The second diary, transcribed from Bodleian Library, Rawlinson MSS, A 174, fol. 299v.,r., is printed as Appendix IV to Edwin Chappell's edition of *The Tangier Papers of Samuel Pepys* (1935), pp. 335–7.

15. Sandwich's authorization for Pepys, 1 Oct. 1665, Bodleian Library, Rawlinson MSS, A 174, fol. 305.

16. Pepys to Lord Sandwich, 12 Oct. 1665, from Erith, National Maritime Museum, Sandwich Journal, vol. I, X98/065, fol. 63.

17. For Albemarle's letter of 19 Sept. 1665 to Lord Sandwich, Bodleian Library, Carte MSS, 75, fol. 363. For Carteret's letter of 28 Sept., National Maritime Museum, Sandwich Journal, vol. I, fol. 51. For Coventry's letter of 3 Oct., National Maritime Museum, Sandwich Journal, vol. I, fol. 54. Pepys reports Albemarle's remark about embezzlement in a letter of 25 Nov., National Maritime Museum, Sandwich Journal, vol. I, fol. 109.

18. Lord Sandwich to Pepys, 14 Oct. 1665, Bodleian Library, Rawlinson MSS, A 174, fol. 303.

19. Diary, 19 Oct. 1665, and Pepys to Coventry, *Further Correspondence of Samuel Pepys*, ed. J. R. Tanner, pp. 63–4.

20. Pepys to duke of York, 25 Oct. 1665, *Further Correspondence of Samuel Pepys*, ed. J. R. Tanner, p. 65. Pepys to Albemarle, 28 Oct. 1665, *Further Correspondence of Samuel Pepys*, ed. J. R. Tanner, pp. 67–8. Pepys talks to Lord Sandwich about Coventry, Diary, 25 Oct. 1665. Pepys said in a statement dated 12 Feb. 1668 that he ended up with nothing but one Indian gown for his wife and a nest of small Indian boxes worth £6 (Bodleian Library, Rawlinson MSS, A 174, fol. 301).

21. Pepys to Peter Pett, 2 Dec. 1665, *Further Correspondence of Samuel Pepys*, ed. J. R. Tanner, p. 82.

22. Pepys to Coventry, 4 Nov. 1665, *Further Correspondence of Samuel Pepys*, ed. J. R. Tanner, pp. 74–6, and Diary, 4 Nov. 1665.

23. Letter of 29 Dec. 1665, Lord Sandwich to Manchester and Clarendon, cited in F. R. Harris, *Life of the First Earl of Sandwich* (1912), vol. II, p. 29, who also reports that Sandwich sued for pardon before Christmas. Bodleian Library, Carte MSS, 75, fol. 422, and 34, fol. 514.

24. Diary, 29 Jan. 1666.

25. Diary, 7 Oct. 1666. Pepys wrote on 8 Sept. 1667 that he had not written to Lord Sandwich at all since he left for Spain in Feb. 1666.

26. Diary, with Daniel's account, 4 June 1666.

27. Diary, 7 June 1666. Also worth noting, Pepys refused a loan requested by the Sandwichs' son, Lord Hinchingbrooke, 17 June 1667, 'to teach him the necessity

of being a good husband [i.e., manager of his own affairs] and keeping money or credit by him'.

28. Diary, 13 June 1666.

29. Pepys states in the Diary that Christopher Myngs was the son of a shoemaker, but the *DNB* says Pepys's account of the poverty of his background was exaggerated, that he came of a reasonably well-to-do Norfolk family, and that he left £300 to a daughter and some land in Norfolk to a son who became a navy commissioner in the eighteenth century. It looks as though Pepys was at any rate partly misinformed, but whether he was or not makes little difference to the point of his musing on Myngs's fate.

30. Diary, 23 July 1666. I am indebted to Richard Luckett, Pepys librarian, for telling me that they are the first-known purpose-built bookcases in England. Pepys had them made by Thomas Simpson, a master-joiner at Woolwich and Deptford dockyards, and they are constructed to take to bits for easy carriage. These first two and the further cases he had made may be seen in the Pepys Library at Magdalene College, Cambridge.

31. Pepys mentions these details in Diary, 16 June 1666 – the dead man was Sir William Berkeley, the captured one Sir George Ayscue.

32. For the party, Diary, 14 Aug. 1666. For the news of Holmes's 'bonfire', Diary, 15 Aug., though it had taken place on 9–10 August.

33. Diary, 19 Oct. 1666; see also Pepys to duke of York, 17 Nov. 1666, *Further Correspondence of Samuel Pepys*, ed. J. R. Tanner, p. 147.

34. Pepys to William Penn, 19 Oct. 1666, *Further Correspondence of Samuel Pepys*, ed. J. R. Tanner, p. 144.

35. Navy Board to duke of York, 17 Nov. 1666, *Further Correspondence of Samuel Pepys*, ed. J. R. Tanner, pp. 146–54.

36. Diary, 15, 21, 31 Oct., 14 Nov., 14, 31 Dec. 1666.

37. For Pepys's speech before king, Diary, 14 Mar. 1667 and *Further Correspondence of Samuel Pepys*, ed. J. R. Tanner, p. 162. For Coventry and the king, Diary, 4 Apr. 1667.

38. For Carteret, Diary, 9 May 1667. For Evelyn, Diary, 3 June 1667.

39. 11 June 1667, *The Diary of John Evelyn*, ed. E. S. de Beer (1955).

40. Diary, 11 June 1667.

41. This was Sarah Giles, daughter of his mother's sister.

42. They remained in Paris for some months only and were back in England, living with Balty and his wife at Deptford, by the summer of 1668, when Pepys records Elizabeth visiting them there.

43. Diary, 13 June 1667.

44. The 'Navy White Book', kept partly in shorthand and partly written by Gibson, Hayter and Hewer, from the run-up to the war in 1664 until 1669, when it was the subject of investigation, was edited by Robert Latham, transcribed by Latham and William Matthews and published by the Navy Records Society in *Samuel Pepys and the Second Dutch War* (1995).

45. Diary, 6 June 1666.

46. For example, Diary, 20 May 1661, 'But though I am much against too much spending, yet I do think it best to enjoy some degree of pleasure, now that we have health, money and opportunities, rather than to leave pleasures to old age or poverty, when we cannot have them so properly.'
47. There is a copy of the fourth edition of 1688 in the Pepys Library.
48. From Andrew Marvell's *The Last Instructions to a Painter*, published 4 Sept. 1667, line 765, after description of Medway disaster.
49. Diary, 16 Sept. 1667.
50. Diary, 8 Dec. 1667, 10 Sept. 1667.
51. See Bernard Capp, *Cromwell's Navy* (1989), for attempts to scapegoat Coventry. The duke of York told him he resented his attitude on 30 Aug. 1667 and Coventry left on 2 Sept.
52. Diary, 2 Sept. 1667. Later he was eager to have the job, see pp. 294–5 below.
53. Diary, 22 Oct. 1667; 31 Jan. 1668, etc.
54. Diary, 5, 6 Mar. 1668, etc.

13. Marriage

1. Diary, 6 Nov. 1660.
2. Diary, 3, 4 Feb. 1665.
3. Diary, 29 Sept. 1664.
4. Diary, 15 June 1662, 19 Dec. 1661.
5. 'Cunning' has not the modern derogatory sense, but conveys something more like cleverness here: Diary, 28 Feb. 1665.
6. Diary, 3 Nov., and following days, 1663.
7. Diary, 5 May 1665.
8. See Lionel Cust's 'Notes on Some Distinctive Features in Pepys's Portraits' (1911), printed in *Occasional Papers Read by Members at Meetings of the Pepys Club* (1917), vol. I, p. 38, where he writes about the 'monstrous haycock of the periwig' and goes on 'a vast deal of the characteristic form of a man lies in the shape of his head, in the placing of his ear, and in the way in which his head is poised on his neck. All this disappeared under a periwig, and nothing of the upper part of a man differentiated him from his fellows except the actual features of his face.'
9. Diary, 24 Oct. 1662.
10. Diary, 9 Dec. 1663.
11. Diary, 5 Mar. 1667.
12. Diary, 1 Nov. 1666.
13. Diary, 28 Mar. 1664, where he calls it a morning-gown. Perhaps both of them knew John Donne's poem 'To his mistress, going to bed', with its line 'my kingdom, safeliest when by one man manned', although she called it *her* kingdom. Pepys acquired a copy of Donne's poems in 1669.
14. Diary, 11 Apr. 1669.
15. Pepys's father wrote to him about this, and about Elizabeth agreeing to travel

back to London in the same coach as the officer, a man called Coleman, Diary, 24 June 1667. She invited him to a lunch party after the journey, but he failed to turn up.

16. Diary, 13 Feb. 1663, the year Pepys decided against Valentines on grounds of expense. For Valentines, see Chapter 16, note 8.

17. Diary, 31 Mar., 26 Apr., 1 May 1669.

18. Diary, 12 July 1667.

19. Diary, 1 Sept. 1663, 9 Oct. 1667.

20. Diary, 12 Jan. 1668.

21. Diary, 10 Sept. 1666.

22. Diary, 17 June 1668.

23. Diary, 8 Feb. 1660.

24. Diary, 13 Jan. 1660.

25. Diary, 31 Jan. 1660. The idealized Alcidiane's story, a pseudo-historical romance, was told – in five volumes – in French, by an academician, Marin Le Roy de Gomberville (1600–1674). It is hard going.

26. Diary, 15 Mar. 1660.

27. Diary, 22 Dec. 1663.

28. See Diary for 16 Jan. 1664 for the encounter under the chair, and 16 Feb. 1667 for the encounter that leaves Pepys 'defessus'.

29. Diary, 16 Jan. 1664. This is the first time that he goes into French for such an episode, and interestingly he used it both for the sexual part and for the expression of remorse.

30. Diary, 7 Feb. 1669.

31. Diary, 31 Oct. 1660.

32. Diary, 12, 16, 17 Nov. 1663.

33. Diary, 24 Oct. 1663.

34. Diary, 2 Aug. 1667.

35. Diary, 23 Sept. 1661.

36. Pepys thinks he may have no child, Diary, 23 Jan. 1662; called a fumbler, 22 Mar. 1662 (note that the *OED* gives the sexual meaning of 'fumbler' as 'impotent', which Pepys would surely have resented). Elizabeth thinks herself with child, 6 Nov. 1663.

37. For uncle Wight, 21, 22 Feb., 11, 15 May.

38. Diary, 26 July 1664.

39. For Elizabeth thinking herself pregnant, 22, 27 Sept. 1664.

40. Diary, 6 July 1667.

41. Diary, 25 July 1667.

42. Diary, 19 Sept. 1667.

43. Diary, 29 July 1668, etc.

44. Diary, 1 Jan. 1663.

45. Diary, 16 Oct. 1663.

46. Diary, 1 July 1663, for the Sedley episode and Pepys's private response to hearing Mennes and Batten's account and their remark that 'buggery is now

almost grown as common among our gallants as in Italy, and the very pages begin to complain of their masters for it'.

47. Twenty years later he was better informed: see p. 334 below.

48. Diary, 1 Apr. 1667.

49. For Sedley in the theatre, Diary, 4 Oct. 1664.

50. Diary, 30 June 1667. Pepys was visiting the Medway with Creed in the aftermath of the Dutch attack.

51. Diary, 23 Nov. 1665, 4 Jan., 7 June 1666. The age of 'Mrs Tooker' is not given, but Pepys calls her a child. He seems to have just about stopped short of complete sexual intercourse with her, although only just. In Feb. 1667 Elizabeth told Pepys that the girl was said to have gonorrhoea, blaming it on her mother having her in bed with her when a man came to her, and in Mar. she said she had syphilis. No doubt she intended to warn him off. Pepys continued to find her attractive, 'grown a little woman', and kissed and fondled her. She dined with the Pepyses in Apr., and after this disappeared from the scene.

52. Diary, 19 June 1666.

53. See chapter on Jane Birch and Diary, 16 Sept. 1668. Nell Payne was much handled by Pepys in the summer of 1667 and dismissed by Elizabeth 5 Aug. 1667 for being a gossip and gadding abroad. When Pepys saw her on 4 Mar. 1669 she cried for joy, and he still had 'a month's mind' to her, and thought he might go back for a bout with her another time.

54. Betty Lane and her sister Doll, Mrs Bagwell and possibly Diana Crisp, given his '*nulla puella negat*'.

55. Diary, 16 Oct. 1665.

56. Diary, 1 Feb. 1667, 'Je besa also her venter and cons and saw the poyle thereof.'

57. Diary, 18 Aug. 1667. At St Dunstan's Church 'stood by a pretty, modest maid, whom I did labour to take by the hand and body; but she would not, but got further and further from me, and at last I could perceive her to take pins out of her pocket to prick me if I should touch her again; which seeing, I did forbear'.

58. For episode when he forces Betty Michell to touch him in coach, Diary, 27 Jan., and 5, 11 Feb. 1667. For fantasies about Frances Stewart and Queen Catherine, Diary, 13, 15 July 1663.

59. Diary, 13 July 1663, 8 Feb. 1664.

60. Diary, 16 Dec. 1665.

61. Diary, 23 Mar. 1666.

62. Diary, 12 Sept. 1666.

63. Diary, 2 Dec. 1666.

64. Diary, 23 Dec. 1666.

65. Diary, 11 Feb. 1667.

14. The King

1. Diary, 10 Sept. 1665. Pepys had nothing about letter kissing in the Diary for 1660.
2. Charles addressed him by name for the first time 17 Apr. 1665, and Carteret reported his appreciation of Pepys's abilities, Diary, 6 Nov. 1665.
3. Diary, 23 May 1660. He also reported his early rising habits, 15 Aug. 1660.
4. Peter Lely had in fact made his name under Cromwell and painted him and Edward Montagu. He simply changed his vein to become the supreme portraitist of the beauties at Charles II's court.
5. Diary, 7 Sept. 1662.
6. Diary, 15 Nov. 1666.
7. Diary, 16 June 1660.
8. Diary, 13 Apr. 1661.
9. Diary, 24 Nov. 1662.
10. Diary, 15 May 1662.
11. For the swearing, etc., Diary, 31 Aug. 1661. For the failure to settle bills, 15 May, 30 Nov. 1662.
12. Diary, 22 Apr. 1667.
13. Diary, 1 Feb. 1663.
14. Diary, 15 May 1663.
15. Diary, 4 July 1663.
16. Diary, 19 Aug. 1661, 2 Nov. 1663.
17. Pepys to duke of York, 17 May 1669, historical account of Navy Office duties cited in *The Further Correspondence of Samuel Pepys 1662–1679*, ed. J. R. Tanner (1929), p. 232.
18. Diary, 27 July 1663.
19. Diary, 5 Apr. 1664.
20. Diary, 26 July 1665.
21. Gilbert Burnet, *A History of My Own Time* (1818), vol. I, p. 168. Burnet was for a few years chaplain to Charles II and a hostile witness.
22. Diary, 2 Sept. 1666.
23. Diary, 19 Oct. 1666; Pepys to duke of York, 17 Nov. 1666, *Further Correspondence of Samuel Pepys*, ed. J. R. Tanner, p. 147.
24. Diary, 15, 21, 31 Oct., 14 Nov., 14, 31 Dec. 1666.
25. Diary, 9 May (for Carteret), and 3 June (for Evelyn) 1667.
26. Diary, 21 June 1667, Pepys reporting Hugh Cholmley.
27. Diary, 12 July 1667, for both Cholmley's and Pepys's views.
28. Diary, 29 July 1667.
29. Diary, 27 July, 8, 9 Aug. 1667.
30. Diary, 4 Sept. 1667.
31. Diary, 25 Sept. 1667.
32. Diary, 23 Sept. 1667.
33. Diary, 28 Oct. 1667.

34. Diary, 8 Dec. 1667.
35. Diary, 16 Mar. 1669.
36. Diary, 28 Apr. 1669.
37. Diary, 2 Jan. 1668.
38. Sir Robert Howard, an established playwright and a friend of Buckingham, was the author of the rest of the play, a comedy with a standard plot, apart from Sir Cautious's desk. See article in the *TLS*, 28 Sept. 1973, p. 1,105, by Arthur H. Scouten and Robert D. Hume.
39. Charles II to Henriette, 7 Mar. 1669, letter cited in article in previous note.
40. Diary, 9 Mar. 1669. Pepys forgot that he had told a naval lieutenant about his Diary, 11 Apr. 1660. Coventry's diary has not been discovered.
41. Diary, 30 Mar. 1669.
42. Diary, 30 Mar. 1669.
43. Diary, 3–20 Mar. 1669, covers Coventry's arrest, imprisonment and release.

15. The Fire

1. Diary, 28 Feb. 1667.
2. Diary, 11 Nov. 1667.
3. Diary, 26 Sept. 1666, for booksellers' losses and Cromleholme's, and 5 Oct. 1666.
4. Diary, 5 Nov. 1666.
5. Diary, 23 Sept. 1667. 'The examinations endeed are very plain' was all he wrote – the duke was, after all, his boss, and he had seen him working against the fire.
6. Diary, 21 May 1668.
7. Information from Nikolaus Pevsner, Buildings of England, *London 1: City of London* (1998), p. 322. The inscription was removed in 1685 when James II became king and put back in 1689. It was removed again in 1830.

16. Three Janes

1. Diary, 24, 28 July, 18 Aug., 3, 11, 18, 19 Sept. 1664.
2. Diary, 26 Jan. 1665.
3. Diary, 6 Apr. 1665.
4. Diary, 18 Apr. 1666.
5. Diary, 21 May 1662.
6. John Turner is mentioned as being in London in Nov. and Dec. 1661, when Pepys consults him for a legal opinion, and is briefly back in town in the spring and autumn of 1662; again early in 1665 when he is Lenten reader for the Middle Temple feasts, and in the spring of 1669 – Pepys's tribute to his character is made 27 Jan. 1669.
7. Diary, 27 Jan.–18 Mar. 1664.
8. The play-reading was 22 Apr. 1664, but the Diary disappointingly says 'part of a good play' without specifying which. For the Twelfth Night party, Diary, 6

Jan. 1669. During the seventeenth century it was customary to choose your Valentine from among your family, friends and neighbours, and a man who was chosen was obliged to give a present to the lady who chose him.

9. Diary, 3 Feb. 1665. Pepys gives 'leg' in the singular, and perhaps one leg was less improper than two would have been. For the Valentine gifts, Diary, 15 Feb. 1669.

10. Jane Turner's sister was Elizabeth Dyke, her cousin Joyce Norton, from the Norfolk branch of the family, both of whom appear as a sort of chorus accompanying Jane at dinners and outings with Sam.

11. 'The' was obviously named for Lady Theophila Coke of Durdans: see note 25 to Chapter 1.

12. For rude letter to Elizabeth, 18 Oct. 1660 ('The' can't have been more than eight or nine at this point); for chafing about coronation, 25 Mar. 1661; for harpsichord, 22, 26 Feb., 31 Mar. 1661; for Valentine, 3 Mar. 1663.

13. Diary, 16 Mar. 1664.

14. For wine, Diary, 17 June 1663; for brother's funeral, 17, 23 Dec. 1663; for horses, 21 Apr. 1669; for visit to Povey, 11 Aug. 1663.

15. Diary, 11 Aug. 1663.

16. Diary, 22 Feb. 1661, and for her illness, Diary, 14, 24 Nov., 5, 18, 23 Dec. 1661, 16 Feb. 1662 when Pepys attends service with special sermon at St Bride's on her recovery and escorts her home.

17. Diary, 3 Feb., 3 Mar. 1665.

18. Diary, 30 Nov. 1666.

19. Diary, 11 Dec. 1666.

20. Nothing more is known of Jane Turner except that all her four children married well and she predeceased her husband, in 1686 according to Wheatley's note; he died in 1689. Readers of the Diary have to distinguish carefully between her and Pepys's gossipy Navy Office neighbour, another Mrs Turner (Elizabeth), who also had a daughter called Betty. He sometimes calls Jane 'my cousin Turner', sometimes 'Mrs Turner', sometimes 'Madam Turner'. Neither Wheatley's nor Latham's index is entirely reliable on the Turners.

21. Diary, 26 Aug. 1661.

22. Diary, 11 Jan. 1664. For Jane acting as Hewer's housekeeper, see Arthur Bryant, *Samuel Pepys: The Saviour of the Navy* (1938), p. 228.

23. For Jane carrying books, Diary, 18 Feb. 1660; for dining with Pepys parents, 4 Mar., for knitting, 10 Mar., and for early rising for washing, 12 Mar. 1660. For her illness, 29 June, 2 July 1660. For move and house washing, 17 July, and more washing of house, 11 Sept. For hair-combing, 14 Aug. For sleeping in their bedroom, 29 Aug. For Pepys beating her, 1 Dec.; for sitting by his bed, 12 Dec.; for turkey cooking, 23 Dec., and for running about in her smock, 27 Dec. 1660.

24. Diary, 18 Apr. 1662.

25. Diary, 28 Sept. 1662. Old Mr Pepys said he did not want to have Wayneman back, 11 June 1663.

26. Diary, 1, 6 Aug. 1662.
27. Diary, 14 Sept. 1662.
28. Diary, 5 Nov. 1662.
29. Diary, 8 Jan., 2 Feb. 1663.
30. Diary, 28 July 1663.
31. Diary, 14 Nov. 1663.
32. Diary, 29 Mar. 1666.
33. Diary, 20 Sept. 1667. It was an early performance of a comedy by Dryden's brother-in-law, James Howard.
34. Diary, 20 Sept., 21 Oct. 1666.
35. Diary, 7 July 1667.
36. Diary, 11 Feb. 1668.
37. Diary, 19 Aug. 1668.
38. Diary, 16 Sept. 1668.
39. For little Susan, Diary, 6 Aug. 1665.
40. Robert Hooke (1635–1703) was an outstandingly able experimental scientist and architect, son of a country clergyman and, as well as being almost of an age with Pepys, inhabited the same world, that of professional men working in London, with friends in common such as William Petty, Lord Brouncker and Evelyn (see Chapter 17 below). He was an official of the Royal Society, a book collector, interested in a universal language. He was not religious, and his diary suggests he never went to church. Compared with Pepys's, Hooke's diary is exiguous, often no more than a few words to a day. He was unmarried, regarded as eccentric, difficult and quarrelsome, partly because he was reluctant to publish his results and then bitter when others claimed to have reached them ahead of him. He also suffered from poor health. Pepys admired him greatly as a scientist, and he figures in the Diary in 1665, 1666, 1667 and 1668. Pepys is also mentioned in Hooke's diary.
41. Diary, 7, 8 Feb. 1669.
42. Diary, 14 Mar. 1669.
43. Elizabeth put up the blue hangings in 1666 (Diary, 26 Feb.) and the upholstery work was done 6–17 Nov. 1668.
44. Diary, 22 Mar. 1669.
45. Diary, 24 Mar. 1669.
46. Diary, 12, 19, 30 Apr. 1669.
47. National Maritime Museum, Correspondence of Samuel Pepys, LBK/8, p. 809.
48. Information about Jane's later years and her son from Latham and Matthews's *Companion* to their edition of the Diary, text and notes, and from *The Private Correspondence and Miscellaneous Papers of Samuel Pepys*, ed. J. R. Tanner (1926), vol. II, p. 315.

17. *The Secret Scientist*

1. The remark about Pepys's lack of science is from A. Rupert Hall's essay in the *Companion* volume to Latham and Matthews's edition of the Diary, pp. 384–5.

2. Jeremy Bernstein in *Cranks, Quarks and Cosmos*, pp. 162–3, citing Newton's biographer Stukeley.

3. Wren's inaugural speech is quoted in Douglas McKie's essay 'The Origins and Foundations of the Royal Society' in *The Royal Society: Its Origins and Founders*, ed. Sir Henry Hartley (1960).

4. Pepys to Edward Montagu, 9 Dec. 1656, mentioning a visit they made together to see 'Sir W. P.'s magnetique experiments', *Letters and Second Diary of Samuel Pepys*, ed. R. G. Howarth (1932), p. 4. See note 31 to Chapter 4.

5. Diary, 16 May 1664.

6. Diary, 27 Feb. 1663.

7. Diary, 2 Apr. 1664.

8. Diary, 27 Jan. 1664.

9. For Creed's introduction by Povey, Thomas Birch, *History of the Royal Society* (1756–7), vol. I, pp. 340, 342. For Creed's scientific conversations with Pepys, Diary, 9 June 1663, 14 Apr. 1664.

10. Goddard's 'Drops' were made of spirits of hartshorn rectified with human bones well dried and broken into bits, together with two pounds of viper's flesh. All this was distilled into spirit, oil and volatile salt, set in earth for three months, then the oil separated off and kept for use. The drops were used for faintings, apoplexies, sudden and alarming onsets and lethargies, 20 to 60 drops in a glass of canary. They continued to be used long after Dr Goddard's death. Information from Douglas McKie's essay cited above, p. 74.

11. See E. S. de Beer's essay 'Charles II and the Royal Society' in *The Royal Society: Its Origins and Founders*, ed. Sir Henry Hartley, pp. 39–47.

12. Sir Robert Moray read Holmes's report, 'An Account of the Going of Two Watches at Sea from 28th April to 4th September 1663' to the Royal Society on 21 Oct. Richard Ollard, *Man of War: Sir Robert Holmes and the Restoration Navy* (1969), p. 84, and the whole of his Chapter 7, 'The Clash with Pepys'.

13. Thomas Birch, *The History of the Royal Society*, vol. II, pp. 21, 23, 24. Pepys was also asked to get hold of a diver from Deptford, which again goes unmentioned in the Diary.

14. Evelyn is our informant here – on 7 Sept. 1665 he called and found the three scientists staying there. *The Diary of John Evelyn*, ed. E. S. de Beer (1955).

15. Diary, 14, 16 Nov. 1666 for the dog; 21, 30 Nov. 1667 for the man.

16. Diary, 22 Mar. 1665, and 3 May 1665. He is wrong about the spirit of salt, which is hydrochloric acid, and would have destroyed the foetus.

17. Diary, 28 July, 7, 8 Aug. 1666.

18. Diary, 30 Nov. 1667.

19. For his reading of Hooke's *Micrographia*, Diary, 21 Jan. 1665.

20. Hooke's diary for 28 Aug. 1676, 'I was twice with Mr Pepys who was very

civill and kind.' Also for 3 June 1693, 'I called at Mr Pepys very kind.' Both examples quoted by A. N. Da C. Andrade's paper on Pepys in *Notes and Records of the Royal Society of London*, vol. 18, 1963, p. 86.

21. On 8 Feb. 1699 the Society ordered the treasurer to give Pepys five guineas 'to be distributed to the offices of the East India Company for the present lately received', which suggests Pepys had something to do with it, no doubt through Hewer. Secretary's minutes, MS at Royal Society, p. 145.

22. Thomas Birch gives the dates in his *History of the Royal Society*, 15 Jan. 1680 and 17 July 1679.

23. Information in this paragraph from Thomas Birch, *The History of the Royal Society*, vol. III, pp. 137, 178. Pepys volunteered to make his contribution on 14 and 28 Jan. 1675, came to one more meeting and then kept away for the rest of the year. He was elected to the council again in Nov. 1676.

24. Secretary's minutes, MS at Royal Society, 16 June 1686, p. 85.

25. Thomas Birch gives this on 3 Mar. 1686, the orders for clerks on 27 Jan. 1686.

26. For Halley's exemption from the rule governing the clerks, secretary's minutes, MS at Royal Society, 16 June 1686, p. 85. Pepys's name appears on the title page of the first edition of Newton's *Principia*, 'IMPRIMATUR/S. PEPYS, *Reg. Soc.* PRAES./Julii 5. 1686', and below it the date at which it appeared, Anno MDCLXXXVII (1687). Sir Joseph Williamson, Sir John Hoskyns and Thomas Gale took the chair at the meetings he missed in 1686. Halley wrote to Newton on 22 May 1686, after a meeting of the Society on 19 May chaired by Williamson, telling him that the printing of the *Principia* would be at the charge of the Society. At a council meeting of 2 June, where Thomas Gale was in the chair, it was again ordered 'that Mr Newton's book be printed', but instead of sanctioning the resolution of the general meeting that it should be printed at their charge, they added 'that Mr Halley undertake the business of looking after it, and printing it at his own charge, which he engaged to do'. Halley explained the delay to Newton by saying it arose from 'the president's attendance on the king' (James II was indeed absorbing Pepys's time), but it may have been more to do with the bad financial state of the Society. Information from the Journal Book of the Royal Society, the secretary's minutes and the detailed entry on Newton by Henry Taylor in the 11th edition of the *Encyclopedia Britannica*.

27. Secretary's MS minutes, for 21 Nov. 1694, p. 120.

28. ibid., 8 Feb. 1699, p. 145: 'It was ordered that five Guineas should be given to Mr Pepys by the Treasurer to be distributed to the officers of the East India Company for the present lately received.'

29. ibid., 8 Mar. 1699, p. 148.

30. Thomas Sprat's *History of the Royal Society* of 1667 reports this recommendation from the committee of 1664.

18. Speeches and Stories

1. Diary, 27 Jan. 1667.
2. Diary, 5 Dec. 1665.
3. Diary, 29, 30 July 1667.
4. Diary, 27 Feb. 1667.
5. Diary, 12 Apr. 1665.
6. Diary, 8 May 1662, 14 Aug. 1665.
7. Diary, 12 Aug. 1664.
8. Diary, 9 Dec. 1665.
9. Diary, 19 July 1667.
10. Diary, 29 June 1663.
11. Diary, 13 Sept. 1667.
12. Diary, 13 June 1666.
13. Diary, 13 Dec. 1663.
14. Diary, 2 Jan. 1668.
15. Diary, 17 June 1667. Batten's contempt for the swaggering captain, courtier and friend of the duke of Buckingham and critic of the Navy Board, is not entirely fair: he had lost an arm in the Four Days' Battle in June 1666, and he was to die in the battle of Sole Bay in 1672.
16. Diary, 13 July 1664.
17. Diary, 18 Feb. 1668.
18. Diary, 24 June 1663.
19. Diary, 2 Sept. 1667.
20. Diary, 15 June 1663.
21. Diary, 5 Nov. 1665.
22. Diary, 15 May 1668.
23. Diary, 4 July 1663.
24. Diary, 12 Feb. 1664.
25. Diary, 14 July 1667.
26. Diary, 18 Mar. 1664.
27. Diary, 11 Jan. 1664, 11 Apr. 1661.
28. Diary, 21 Feb., 5 Mar. 1665.
29. Diary, 19 Nov. 1668.
30. Diary, 13 Sept. 1663.
31. Diary, 14 July 1664.
32. Diary, 12 July 1667, Pepys setting down the words as Cholmley (reporting Clarendon) repeated them, fresh from the meeting at which they were spoken.
33. Diary, 14 May 1667.
34. Diary, 2 Nov. 1663, 6 Mar. 1668.
35. Diary, 13 June 1666.
36. Diary, 3 Apr. 1667.
37. Diary, 18 May 1667.

38. Diary, 27 Apr. 1665.
39. Diary, 1 Nov. 1667.
40. Diary, 23 June 1666.
41. Diary, 15 Nov. 1667.
42. Diary, 5 Jan. 1666.
43. Diary, 28 Feb. 1666.
44. Diary, 14 Mar. 1667.
45. Diary, 31 Oct. 1666.
46. Diary, 23 Apr. 1661.
47. Diary, 15 May 1665.
48. Diary, 19 Mar. 1667.
49. Diary, 25 May 1668.
50. Diary, 10 Oct. 1665.
51. Diary, 9 Feb. 1668.
52. Diary, 24 Nov. 1665.
53. Diary, 1, 2 Mar. 1666.
54. Diary, 13 June 1668 – during a period in which Pepys entered unfinished notes in the Diary while he was travelling. The laborious draft is all the more interesting in that the letter is not an official one but for a personal friend, Thomas Hill.

19. *Surprise and Disorder*

1. Diary, 30 Sept. 1667.
2. Diary, 12 Oct. 1667.
3. Diary, 11 Jan. 1668.
4. 31 Mar. 1668.
5. Diary, 6 Aug. 1668.
6. Diary, 25 Oct. 1668.
7. Diary, 12 Jan. 1669.
8. Diary, 12 Mar. 1669.
9. Diary, 15 Apr. 1669.
10. Diary, 9 Apr., 12 May 1669, for Betty Lane; 19 Apr. 1669 for Doll; 31 May 1669, for Betty Michell; 4, 29 Mar. 15 Apr. 1669, for Mrs Bagwell; for Mrs Tooker's daughters, 24 Mar. 1669, also dance with Rebecca Jowle, née Allen; for fantasy about new maid Matt, 29 Mar. 1669.

Part Three: 1669–1703

20. After the Diary

1. Diary, 19 Feb. 1663.

2. A clear account is given by Milo Keynes in his paper 'Why Samuel Pepys Stopped Writing His Diary: His Dimming Eyesight and Ill-health', *Journal of Medical Biography*, vol. V, Feb. 1997, pp. 25–9.

3. Pepys to Captain Elliot at Aldeburgh, 19 Aug. 1669, *The Further Correspondence of Samuel Pepys 1662–1679*, ed. J. R. Tanner (1929), pp. 256–7.

4. Pepys to Charles II, 8 Jan. 1670, a letter in which he refers to this. The 'Navy White Book' in *Samuel Pepys and the Second Dutch War*, ed. Robert Latham, transcribers Robert Latham and William Matthews (1995), pp. 330–32. And Pepys to John Evelyn, 24 Dec. 1701, *The Private Correspondence and Miscellaneous Papers of Samuel Pepys*, ed. J. R. Tanner (1926), vol. II, p. 242, for his recollection of going 'through Holland and Flanders to Paris and so home'.

5. John Evelyn to Samuel Pepys, 21 Aug. 1669, *The Correspondence of Samuel Pepys and John Evelyn*, ed. G. de la Bédoyère (1997).

6. The precious stones and embroidery wools are mentioned in a letter of 26 Oct. 1669, M. Peletyer, merchant of Paris, to Elizabeth, Bodleian Library, Rawlinson MSS, A 174, fol. 335. Pepys refers to his attempt to buy a history of Paris that was reprinting when he was last there, in a letter to Mr Brisbane in Paris dated 12 Mar. 1675, National Maritime Museum, Correspondence of Samuel Pepys, LBK/8, p. 705.

   Pepys referred to a portrait of Elizabeth by 'Lombard' when he was describing his closet under questioning in the House of Commons in Feb. 1674. Pierre Lombart (1620–81), known for his female portraits in the style of Van Dyck, worked in England under the commonwealth but was in Paris in the 1660s.

7. Pepys to Captain Elliot, 3 Mar. 1670, *Letters and Second Diary of Samuel Pepys*, ed. R. G. Howarth (1932), p. 37.

8. Marie Legendre to Elizabeth, n.d. but with letters in 'Private Papers' bundle dated late Oct., early Nov. 1669, Bodleian Library, Rawlinson MSS, A 174, fol. 341.

9. See Pepys's 'Brooke House Journal' in 'The Brooke House Papers', part of *Samuel Pepys and the Second Dutch War*, ed. Robert Latham, p. 334, where he gives this date.

10. Pepys to John Evelyn, 2 Nov. 1669, *The Correspondence of Samuel Pepys and John Evelyn*, ed. G. de la Bédoyère. Tuke was Evelyn's cousin.

11. Diary, 19 Oct. 1663, for the remedies used for Queen Catherine.

12. Elizabeth talked of 'being and resolving to die a Catholique' on 20 Mar. 1664, a few days after the death of Tom. She repeated this sentiment on 25 Oct. 1668, the day she found Pepys with Deb Willet. It was a Sunday, and she also said she had received the Holy Sacrament.

13. For a time the French Church gave them support, see Pepys's report in Diary, 29 Mar. 1667. They moved to Paris later in 1667 but were back in England in 1668, living in Deptford with their son.

14. By then not only old Mr Pepys but also his younger son John were living with the Jacksons. Pall's first child, Samuel, was born late in 1669, followed by a second son, John, who died in 1673, and a third son, another John, born in December 1673. There was another child who died, leaving her with two sons, Sam and John Jackson.

15. The magnificent larger than life statues of Charles I, Charles II and Gresham are now installed inside the Old Bailey building, well cared for but not seen to as much advantage as they might be. Another of Bushnell's memorials, done in 1675, shows Lord Ashburnham grieving for his wife and has been praised by Pevsner for 'new compositional freedom and a new possibility of inventiveness'. Dame Mary May, done in 1681 at Lavant, shows the dead woman 'apparently pock-marked as in life', 'capricious, but the portrait exact, and the execution good'. Bushnell is on record as having asked for pictures of his memorial subjects.

16. In 1970 the National Portrait Gallery had a cast made for its Pepys exhibition, and, although it is not on display as I write in 2001, it may well be shown to the public again.

17. The phrase is from the only such letter to survive among Pepys's private papers, from M. Legendre in Rouen. Bodleian Library, Rawlinson MSS, A 174, fol. 331. See his letter to his brother John dated 26 Mar. 1670, Bodleian, Rawlinson MSS, A 182, fol. 475, which is sealed with black.

18. See entry in Pepys's 'Navy White Book', *Samuel Pepys and the Second Dutch War*, ed. Robert Latham, pp. 250–52.

19. Document in Bodleian Library, Rawlinson MSS, A 174, fol. 446.

20. Pepys's note for 3 Jan. 1670 in 'Brooke House Papers', *Samuel Pepys and the Second Dutch War*, ed. Robert Latham, p. 336.

21. Entry for 7 Jan. 1670 in Pepys's 'Brooke House Papers', *Samuel Pepys and the Second Dutch War*, ed. Robert Latham, p. 341.

22. Pepys noted the king's remark and his own supporting addition on 24 Jan. 1670, *Samuel Pepys and the Second Dutch War*, ed. Robert Latham, p. 371.

23. 6 Jan. 1670, in *Samuel Pepys and the Second Dutch War*, ed. Robert Latham, p. 340.

24. For the expenses, see the 'Brooke House Papers' in *Samuel Pepys and the Second Dutch War*, ed. Robert Latham, p. 329.

25. Arthur Bryant, *The Years of Peril* (1935), p. 25.

26. He makes this claim in his letter to the Brooke House commissioners, 6 Jan. 1670, *Samuel Pepys and the Second Dutch War*, ed. Robert Latham, p. 326.

27. Words from final paragraph of Pepys's report, *Samuel Pepys and the Second Dutch War*, ed. Robert Latham, pp. 434–5.

28. For Richard Gibson's reference to Donne, his letter to Pepys, 17 Aug. 1671, after he had gone to serve with the Mediterranean fleet. He invokes Donne's

sermon in which he says the goodness of God is seen not so much in our creation as in our redemption, 'nor so much that we are his, as that nothing can take us out of his hands. In return of which I wish no longer to live than the Impress of your Favours may remain in my Heart.' Rawlinson MSS, A 174, fol. 372. Flowery language but suggests real affection. In a later letter he sends respects to Pepys's father and brother, and love to Mr Hayter, Mr Hewer and Mr Edwards.

29. Pepys to Sir Richard Browne, *Letters and Second Diary of Samuel Pepys*, ed. R. G. Howarth, pp. 38–9. H. T. Heath gives references for other letters of recommendation, footnote 1, p. 16, *The Letters of Samuel Pepys and His Family Circle* (1955).

30. The tobacco and wine bills are among Pepys's miscellaneous papers in the Bodleian. The gifts are mentioned in a letter from Pall to John, 5 Mar. 1672; from John to his father, 12 Mar. 1674, and from John Pepys Snr to his son, 18 July 1676, all printed in *The Letters of Samuel Pepys and His Family Circle*, ed. H. T. Heath, pp. 17, 29, 41.

31. The memo is printed in the 'Navy White Book', *Samuel Pepys and the Second Dutch War*, ed. Robert Latham, p. 196.

32. Paper by Pepys dated 9 May 1670, *The Further Correspondence of Samuel Pepys*, ed. J. R. Tanner, pp. 266–7.

33. It was £426,886. Bodleian Library, Rawlinson MSS, A 174, fol. 181.

34. Diary, 30 July 1666.

35. John Shadwell, Pepys's godson, born in 1671, grew up to become a successful physician (see Chapter 26), and also published an edition of his father's plays. Thomas Shadwell produced adaptations of Molière and Shakespeare and comedies mocking the manners of the court and City, including *Epsom Wells* (1672). He was a friend of Charles Sedley, whose wit Pepys admired in the Diary.

36. Information from Charles Knighton, who has kindly let me see his article on Creed for the new *DNB*, and from my own inspection of Creed's tomb, put up by his widow, in Titchmarsh Church.

37. Diary, 5 Mar. 1666.

38. Diary, 9 Feb. 1666, 14 Nov. 1666, 12 Feb. 1668.

39. John Evelyn, 16 Jan. 1679, *The Diary of John Evelyn*, ed. E. S. de Beer (1955), and Pepys to John Evelyn, 13 Nov. 1690, *The Correspondence of Samuel Pepys and John Evelyn*, ed. G. de la Bédoyère.

40. There are several portraits of Sarah Houblon. The one with the best provenance has been passed down through the family and was reproduced in Lady Alice Archer Houblon's *The Houblon Family*, where it was attributed to Mary Beale; but recently it has been thought to be by William Wissing. Another, attributed to Peter Lely, shows her in a pose and with a nose very like Lady Castlemaine's; it is currently displayed at Cannon Hall Museum, Barnsley, which acquired it from a private owner in 1956. I have seen a photograph of a third, head and shoulders only, sold through Sotheby's in 1931 and filed under Lely at the Witt Library, which shows a handsome face with a Roman nose and the same

jewellery as in the Cannon Hall portrait. All three give her dark curls and dark eyes, and the second and third show her richly and fashionably dressed and jewelled, with pearl necklace and large matching drop earrings.

41. A draft letter in Bodleian Library, Rawlinson MSS, A 180, fol. 244.

42. For the singing, letter from Cesare Morelli to Pepys, 4 Apr. 1681, *Letters and Second Diary of Samuel Pepys*, ed. R. G. Howarth, p. 112. Pepys to James Houblon, 19 Oct. 1683, *Letters and Second Diary of Samuel Pepys*, ed. R. G. Howarth, p. 161 (Pepys is writing from abroad).

43. For the instinctive feelings of a new Houblon baby for Pepys, Sarah Houblon to Pepys, 3 Dec. 1683, ibid., p. 163.

44. 30 Nov. 1683, ibid., p. 435.

45. Pepys first met Lady Mordaunt in 1666 (Diary, 11 Dec. 1666) at his cousin Jane Turner's, describing her as 'a most homely widow, but young and pretty rich and good-natured'. He met her again with Jane Turner in Feb. and Mar. 1667, the second time with her sister.

46. Evidence for the flirting is found in a letter from Thomas Hill, Pepys's friend whom he had known since January 1664, who wrote from Lisbon, 14 Apr. 1673, teasing Pepys about Lady Mordaunt and Mrs Steward: 'they are desperately in Love with you, and sigh out their Passions so charmingly . . . Your enjoyments in their Conversation, can no where else be found; theirs is so great, when you entertain them, that they all acknowledge your Humour the best in the whole world.' *Letters and Second Diary of Samuel Pepys*, ed. R. G. Howarth, pp. 41–3.

47. Bodleian Library, Rawlinson MSS, A 174, fols. 437–9, dated 15 June 1670.

48. See Bryant's account, *The Years of Peril*, pp. 65–6. Andrew Marvell called Charles's action 'Robbery at the Exchequer'.

49. Pepys had dined with Ashley Cooper at his house in the Strand, 23 Sept. 1667, and expressed admiration of his great abilities, displayed for instance at the Tangier Committee, several times in the Diary, for example, 15 and 27 May 1663, 16 Jan. 1665. Shaftesbury's belief that Pepys was a Catholic, which first surfaced in the election at Castle Rising in November 1673, was partly based at least on his having seen something like a crucifix at Pepys's house, i.e., at Seething Lane.

50. Pepys to duke of York, 17 June 1669, 18 Feb. 1671, *Further Correspondence of Samuel Pepys*, ed. J. R. Tanner, pp. 239, 268–9.

51. See note by John Evelyn, 16 May 1672, given in F. R. Harris, *The Life of the First Earl of Sandwich* (1912), vol. II, p. 248: 'Going to Whitehall to take leave of his lordship, who had his lodgings in the Privy Garden, shaking me by the hand he bid me good-bye, and said he thought he should see me no more, and I saw to my thinking something boding in his countenance. "No," says he, "they will not have me live. Had I lost a fleet I should have fared better; but be as it pleases God, I must do something I know not what, to save my reputation."' See also Pepys's account of Lord Clarendon's (Henry, the second earl) description of a meeting with Sandwich 'just before his last going to Sea; when their

discourse turning upon the preparations for that Summers Campaign and what was to be expected from it, his Lordship then walking with his hands upon the Shoulder of Charles Harbord and the other upon Cotterells (for his greater Ease being then grown somewhat Goutish and otherwise unwieldy) told the company by way of reflexion upon the then management of our Sea Affairs that though he was then Vice Admiral of England and Admiral of the narrow Seas, yet he knew no more of what was to be done that summer than any of them, or any other that knew nothing of it; this only I know that I will die and these two Boys [meaning Harbord and Cotterel] will die with me. Accordingly they did most honourably.' Pepys wrote this down in 1694; it appears as No. 138 among his naval papers, and a copy is attached to vol. X of the Sandwich Papers in the National Maritime Museum.

52. Various accounts of the death of Lord Sandwich are found in letters in the *Calendar of State Papers* for May and June 1672; in John Charnock's *Biographia Navalis* (1794–8), vol. I, pp. 42, 230; in John Campbell, *Naval History of Great Britain including History and Lives of the British Admirals* (1818), vol. II, pp. 295–6; in F. R. Harris, *The Life of the First Earl of Sandwich*, vol. II, pp. 265–78 (Harris cites various other sources); and in Richard Ollard, *Cromwell's Earl: A Life of Edward Montagu, First Earl of Sandwich* (1994), pp. 256–62. I am grateful to Dr Charles Knighton for help here.

53. Pepys to Balthasar St Michel, 22 June 1672, *Further Correspondence of Samuel Pepys*, ed. J. R. Tanner, p. 271, for both the five days spent with the fleet and the application to the duke on behalf of Balty.

54. A stone on the north side of the chapel marks the place.

55. Anne Montagu was married 5 Jan. 1671, aged seventeen.

56. The words of the will are given by F. R. Harris, *The Life of the First Earl of Sandwich*, vol. II, p. 288.

57. Lucy Hutchinson (1620–?) and Anne Fanshawe (1625–80) both wrote memoirs, officially of their husbands but containing much information about themselves. Anne Fanshawe's husband Richard preceded Lord Sandwich as ambassador to Spain, and unlike Lady Sandwich she accompanied him there.

58. Pepys's Tangier Diary, 22 Aug. 1683, *The Tangier Papers of Samuel Pepys*, ed. and transcriber Edwin Chappell (1935). Lady Sandwich died at Cotehele, the Edgcumbes' beautiful old manor house, on 17 July 1674; she is buried at Calstock. Cotehele is now open through the National Trust.

59. PRO, ADM 106/2887, unnumbered pages, but dated 30 Jan. 1672/3.

21. *Public and Private Life*

1. Arthur Bryant gives Sarah Houblon's remark in *Samuel Pepys: The Years of Peril* (1935), p. 91. The lodgings were in Winchester Street. The Navy Office went first briefly to Trinity House in Water Lane, then on 24 Feb. to a house belonging to a merchant family, the Blaynings, in Mark Lane. PRO, Navy Board minute book, ADM 106/2887, which gives dates and times of meetings

and initials of officers present. The volume of work recorded is impressive: questions and demands from shipyards and ships, instructions from the duke of York, letters from suppliers, etc.

2. Buckingham Street and some of the houses, including Hewer's No. 12, which has a plaque, are still there. So is the water gate, high and dry since the river was embanked, spoiling the charm of the area. Information from John Stow, *A Survey of the Cities of London and Westminster . . . And the Survey and History Brought Down from the Year 1633 to the Present Time by John Strype* (1720), Book VI, p. 76, and N.G. Brett-James, *The Growth of Stuart London* (1935), p. 328, who says the architect of York Buildings was Barbon, son of the Praisegod Barebones who preached in Fleet Street in Pepys's boyhood and later gave his name to one of Cromwell's parliaments. Hewer's house, now a language school, is six windows across and five storeys high plus basements, with a yard at the back in which stands a fine decorated water tank with his initials W.H. on it, and the date 1710 (five years before his death). The house also has the splendid original banisters and staircase.

3. For Hewer's shipbuilding activities in 1674, see Bernard Pool, *Navy Board Contracts* (1966), p. 14.

4. Coventry to Pepys, 25 June 1674, letter cited in *Letters and Second Diary of Samuel Pepys*, ed. R. G. Howarth (1932), p. 43.

5. He wrote to Coventry to say as much on 20 Aug. 1673, letter printed in *Further Correspondence of Samuel Pepys*, ed. J. R. Tanner (1929), p. 272. See also B. McL. Ranft, 'The Significance of the Political Career of Samuel Pepys', *Journal of Modern History*, vol. 24, pp. 368–75. Ranft believes the letter was to Savile rather than to Coventry.

6. Bodleian Library, Rawlinson MSS, A 172, fols. 141–6.

7. For parliamentary debates, A. Grey, *Debates of the House of Commons* (1769), vol. II, pp. 304–428.

8. Among several references in the Diary, Pepys called him, on 15 May 1663, 'a man of great business and yet of pleasure and drolling too'. Later Pepys wrote of his taking a bribe, but this is unsubstantiated and very unlikely to be true, if only because Shaftesbury was too rich to bother with the sort of bribes Pepys himself found attractive.

9. The letter, dated 15 Feb. 1674, is in the Bodleian Library, Rawlinson MSS, A 172, fol. 135, also quoted in full by Arthur Bryant, *Samuel Pepys: The Years of Peril*, p. 114.

10. Balthasar St Michel to Pepys, 8 Feb. 1674, letter printed in *Letters and Second Diary of Samuel Pepys*, ed. R. G. Howarth, p. 44, and *The Letters of Samuel Pepys and His Family Circle*, ed. H. T. Heath (1955), p. 25.

11. Obviously, he also lied about the church attendance and never having been present at a mass, as almost anyone under that degree of pressure would. It was not the real issue, and no one pressed him on it, but there may have been those who knew he was lying, which would not have helped his case.

12. Bishop Burnet in his *History of My Own Time* (1818), vol. I, p. 103.

13. The friend, whom Pepys met through the Houblons, was Thomas Hill. Pepys to Hill, 21 Nov. 1674, printed in *Letters and Second Diary of Samuel Pepys*, ed. R. G. Howarth, pp. 48–9. Pepys wrote defiantly 'nothing which has yet or may further happen towards the rendering me more conspicuous in the world, has led or can ever lead to the admitting any alteration in the little methods of my private way of living'.

14. Anchitel Grey, *Debates of the House of Commons*, vol. IV, pp. 115–18, and summary in Arthur Bryant, *Samuel Pepys: The Years of Peril*, p. 162.

15. For remark about speaking more like an admiral, Anchitel Grey, *Debates of the House of Commons*, vol. V, p. 388, and Arthur Bryant, *Samuel Pepys: The Years of Peril*, p. 167, footnote.

16. 21 Aug. 1674, *The Diary of John Evelyn*, ed. E. S. de Beer (1955).

17. In 1693, however, his one-time clerk Richard Gibson put in a memo on the state of the navy to William III in which he asked that 'the employment of lieutenants in your ships be vacated', i.e., abolished, in favour of a right of succession 'from a midshipman by seniority to the master's mate and master. This will encourage all chief officers and masters of merchant ships to come voluntarily into your sea-service.' A copy of Gibson's paper, which covered the question of gentlemen officers versus 'tarpaulins', the appointment of commissioners, the keeping and checking of ships' journals, treatment of sick and wounded, victualling, etc., was given to Pepys in 1696; by then he was out of office and does not appear to have commented. Gibson's proposal to abolish lieutenants was not adopted.

18. E. H. Pearce, *Annals of Christ's Hospital* (1908), p. 104. Also Pepys to Sir John Frederick, president of Christ's Hospital, 31 Dec. 1675, about his memo on scheme for apprenticing maths department boys, approved by order in council, 12 Nov. 1675, given in *Further Correspondence of Samuel Pepys*, ed. J. R. Tanner, p. 286. Also *The Diary of Robert Hooke, 1672–1680*, eds. H. W. Robinson and W. Adams (1935), 11 July, 28 Aug. 1676. Later Pepys applied to Newton for a recommendation: see Chapter 26.

19. 19 Dec. 1676, *The Diary of Robert Hooke*, eds. H. W. Robinson and W. Adams.

20. Bodleian Library, Rawlinson MSS , A 185, fols. 114, 116.

21. Pepys to Dr Burton, 9 Apr. 1677, *Letters and Second Diary of Samuel Pepys*, ed. R. G. Howarth, pp. 66–7.

22. For Pepys's behaviour towards Povey with regard to this agreement, see Chapter 9.

23. Pepys to Sir Denis Gauden, 31 July 1677, *Further Correspondence of Samuel Pepys*, ed. J. R. Tanner, pp. 302–3. For Hewer acquiring lease of Clapham house, see Will Hewer's letter of 14 Nov. 1678, British Library, Egerton MSS, 928, fol. 229, saying he has lease of Sir Denis Gauden's house, at a yearly rent, and for the goods and chattels, etc., all of which were in possession of the Sheriff upon a judgement by one Pilkington and others, to whom Gauden was indebted.

24. Reference from Bernard Pool, *Navy Board Contracts*, p. 14, citing National Maritime Museum, Sergison (4), Navy Board, 5 Sept. 1677.

25. Morelli's composition of 'new Psalms' when John died and the mournful

singing with Pepys come in the testimony of his butler John James, given to the parliamentary committee that accused Pepys of Catholicism. James's testimony contains lies, but there is no need to doubt this particular information. Pepys Library, Mornamont MSS, vol. II, pp. 1,181–7.

26. Pepys to his father, 20 June 1677, printed in *The Letters of Samuel Pepys and His Family Circle*, ed. H. T. Heath, pp. 51–4, and other family letters in Heath.

27. Pepys's paper, 'The Present Ill State of My Health', is in the Bodleian Library, Rawlinson MSS A 185, fols. 206–13, and was first printed by Arthur Bryant as an appendix to *Samuel Pepys: The Years of Peril*, pp. 405–13. For Shaftesbury's operation and health, Kenneth H. D. Hayley, *The First Earl of Shaftesbury* (1968), pp. 204–5.

28. Woodhall Mansion, an Elizabethan building standing north of Hatfield House, was pulled down shortly after the first marquess of Salisbury bought the whole estate from Revd Julius Hutchinson, grandson of Mary Skinner's foster-sister Isabel, in 1792. The Elizabethan doorway was re-erected as a landscape feature by a lake in the park of Hatfield House, where it can still be seen, although now much eroded. Some wrought-iron gates displaying Sir Francis Boteler's initials were also moved to Hatfield's East Garden, where they can also be seen. A cottage dating from the same period as the Woodhall Mansion remains, but some of the land is now covered by the southern districts of Welwyn Garden City. The handsome tombstones of Sir Francis and Dame Elizabeth Boteler in St Ethelreda's Church are unfortunately hidden by a carpet.

29. Sir Francis's first wife died in 1644, which means his daughters were a good ten years older than Mary. Mary's will of 1714 names Julia Shallcross (née Boteler) as 'my dearly beloved friend' and leaves her two 'Indian perfuming Bottles' and ten pounds for mourning.

30. Anne Fanshawe's memoirs for their visit to the Botelers at Woodhall in 1663. *Memoirs of Lady Fanshawe* (1829), p. 176.

31. Biographical information about Boteler from *The History of Parliament*'s first volume, *House of Commons 1660–1690*, ed. Basil Duke Henning (1983), pp. 691–2. I am grateful to Robin Harcourt Williams, archivist at Hatfield House, for drawing my attention to this. As a younger son, Boteler initially had a struggle. He enlisted to fight in Ireland under Strafford, was knighted by Charles I at York in 1642, and in 1649 owned nothing but his horse and clothes. He inherited the estate after this.

32. Will of Dame Elizabeth Boteler, dated 14 Jan. 1681, in Hertfordshire County Record Office.

33. Frances Skinner's affection for Mary is shown in her will of 1702, made at the home of her daughter Frances (Lady Buck), in which Mary and Frances are called 'well beloved' and made executrices. Seven of the Skinner children's baptisms were registered at St Olave's. The missing two, Daniel and Mary, are clearly the eldest. Obrian is given as Briant in the register, but both his mother's will and Pepys's reference give Obrian.

34. Daniel Skinner Jr to Pepys, letter received 5 July 1676, Latin text in *Letters and*

Second Diary of Samuel Pepys, ed. R. G. Howarth, pp. 53–5. I am indebted to Nicholas Monck for the English translation. For the marriage of Frances Skinner, see entry for Buck of Hanby Grange in Burke's *Extinct Baronetage*, also the wills of her mother (PRO, PROB 11 467) and Mary Skinner (PRO, PROB 11 548).

35. The examples are taken from letters taken down by Mary Skinner from Pepys's dictation in 1699, reproduced verbatim by J. R. Tanner in his *Private Correspondence and Miscellaneous Papers of Samuel Pepys* (1926).

36. *Samuel Pepys and the Second Dutch War*, ed. Robert Latham, transcribers Robert Latham and William Matthews (1995), p. 433: 'so as I plainly told his Majesty, my work must be to get a son and bring him up only to understand this controversy between Brooke House and us, and that his Majesty too should provide for successors to be instructed on his part in the state of this case, which otherwise would never likely be understood'.

37. Letter from Daniel Skinner Jr. to Pepys, op. cit.

38. 15 Dec. 1676, *Diary of Robert Hooke*, eds. H. W. Robinson and W. Adams. Pepys's concern for Mary's illness in Mar. 1679 is discussed in the next chapter.

39. For example, Pepys to Mrs Skinner, 24 Oct. 1680, *Letters and Second Diary of Samuel Pepys*, ed. R. G. Howarth, p. 89.

40. Note in Bodleian Library, Rawlinson MSS, C 859, fol. 56, 'Sir Fr. Boteler', probably about 1678. Entry in Pepys Library, Mornamont MSS, 21 Mar. 1680, vol. II, p. 1,228, 'to Covent Garden church, thence to Sir Francis Butler's, so to the Parks'.

41. Daniel Skinner Snr's name is among the signatories of the certificate of regular attendance by 'Mr Pepys and his whole family' at St Olave's provided by the Revd Mills on 22 May 1681. Bodleian Library, Rawlinson MSS, A 194, fols. 248v.–50.

22. Plots

1. It has been generally assumed that Daniel and Mary Skinner were related to Milton's old friend Cyriack Skinner, and that this led to Daniel becoming Milton's amanuensis. However, William Riley Parker's 1968 biography of Milton, revised by Gordon Campbell in 1996, says that, although a connection is possible, 'I have found no proof that Cyriack Skinner was a relative [of Daniel Skinner]' (p. 1,130). Cyriack's mother, Bridget, was a daughter of Sir Edward Coke; his father was William Skinner (1594–1627) of Thornton Curtis in Lincolnshire, son of Sir Vincent Skinner, who died in London 1616. Cyriack had a brother Edward who died 1657, leaving a son Edward, and a brother William, born 1626. None of these connect with Daniel Skinner, who came from Essex; and Skinner is a common name. Daniel's account of his academic career is found in his letter to Pepys, undated but received 5 July 1676, in which he says he spent seven years at Westminster and then six at Cambridge.

2. Some have seen Daniel's removal of the manuscripts as a laudable attempt to

---

preserve writings that might otherwise have been lost, others as cashing in on his privileged position. Milton's nineteenth-century biographer David Masson accepted that Milton gave them to Skinner, but more recent scholars point out that there is no proof of this and that he may have helped himself. See Gordon Campbell, John K. Hale, David J. Holmes and J. Tweedie, 'The Provenance of *De Doctrina Christiana*', *Milton Quarterly*, no. 31, 1997, pp. 67–93.

The absence of Milton's name from Pepys's Diary is its saddest omission and remains puzzling, given what else went in. The poet had preceded him at St Paul's, praised his cousin Montagu in verse, served as secretary on Cromwell's council when Pepys had friends clerking there and was a close friend of his Axe Yard neighbour Hartlib. The first edition of *Paradise Lost* was published in London in 1667, but the earliest dated edition of *Paradise Lost* in Pepys's library is from 1688.

3. Daniel Skinner to Pepys, n.d., received 5 July, *Letters and Second Diary of Samuel Pepys*, ed. R. G. Howarth (1932), pp. 53–5. English translation by Nicholas Monck.

4. Pepys to Sir Leoline Jenkins, 24 July 1676, cited in Gordon Campbell et al., 'The Provenance of *De Doctrina Christiana*', op. cit. Further quotations in this paragraph from same source, pp. 67–93.

5. They were published by order of George IV and reviewed by Macaulay in his essay on Milton (1825), which sings the praises of the puritans and defends the execution of Charles I.

6. Southwell's remarks cited in Kenneth H. D. Hayley, *The First Earl of Shaftesbury* (1968), pp. 469, 495.

7. ibid., p. 471.

8. Pepys to James Houblon (whom he addresses as 'Your Whigship'), 14 Mar. 1682, printed in *Letters and Second Diary of Samuel Pepys*, ed. R. G. Howarth, pp. 127–8. Richard Ollard suggests Pepys is joking in calling himself a Tory, but this is not borne out by subsequent events.

9. J. R. Jones in *Bulletin of the Institute for Historical Research*, vol. xxx, 1957, prints list of MPs taken from Shaftesbury papers in PRO, Via/348. Old members are marked with an *o*, new members are *H* = honest, i.e., pro-Shaftesbury, *B* = bad or base, or *D* = doubtful. Pepys and Deane are both marked *ov* (old vile), so are Sir Robert Southwell and Lawrence Hyde. Roger Pepys, however, is *ow* (old worthy). The great majority of those on the parliamentary committee that examined Pepys's case in Apr. 1679 are either 'old worthy' or 'new honest'.

10. Pepys to Sir Richard Beach at Chatham urging all imaginable vigilance against papist designs on the Fleet, 19 Nov. 1678, printed in Arthur Bryant, *Samuel Pepys: The Years of Peril* (1935), p. 240.

11. J. P. Kenyon, *The Popish Plot* (1972), gives Fogarty's name among Jesuits arrested, p. 68. Jane Lane in her *Titus Oates* (1949), pp. 99–100, says Oates accused Fogarty of being present when the plot to poison the king was laid and of offering to murder Ormonde himself, etc. Fogarty died in prison the same winter.

12. Pepys to James Houblon, 2 Nov. 1678 and 4 Nov. 1678, printed in *Further Correspondence of Samuel Pepys 1662–1679*, ed. J. R. Tanner (1929), pp. 326–7, 327–8. Morelli being sent away with his trunks by the back water gate comes from testimony of Pepys's butler John James, Pepys Library, Mornamont MSS, vol. II, pp. 1,181–7.

13. Kenneth H. D. Hayley, *The First Earl of Shaftesbury*, p. 495. Thousands of daggers were produced and had to be officially banned.

14. Sir Edward Dering, in draft speech *c.* 1681 referring to witnesses at defence trials, cited in *Parliamentary Diary of Edward Dering*, ed. M. Bond (1976), p. 214.

15. Atkins's own statement is in the Bodleian Library, Rawlinson MSS, A 173, fol. 113.

16. Pepys to Paulina Jackson, 5 Dec. 1678, *Further Correspondence of Samuel Pepys*, ed. J. R. Tanner, pp. 328–9.

17. The figures are 302 to 158, from J. R. Jones, *Bulletin of the Institute for Historical Research*, op. cit.

18. Halifax's advice was given in 1679. See J. P. Kenyon, *The Popish Plot*, p. 166.

19. Pepys to Mr Conny (or Coney), surgeon at Chatham, 20 Mar. 1679, *Further Correspondence of Samuel Pepys*, ed. J. R. Tanner, pp. 354–5. Mary Skinner is not named in his letter, but she is the most likely 'lady on whose behalf I solicited' the medicine, and who is now 'wearied out with the frequent returns of . . . fits' and expects another 'within a day or two'. He is writing from Derby House.

20. On 29 Mar. College Conclusion Book B, 148. Information from Gordon Campbell et al., 'The Provenance of *De Doctrina Christiana*', op. cit., p. 87.

21. Pepys to duke of York, 6 May 1679, *Private Correspondence and Miscellaneous Papers of Samuel Pepys*, ed. J. R. Tanner (1926), vol. I, p. 5, and duke of York to Charles II, 12 May 1679, and to Pepys, 13 May 1679, pp. 9, 10.

22. Bodleian Library, Rawlinson MSS, A 173, fols. 62f.

23. For Pepys getting permission from the king, Pepys to Tom Hayter, 11 Nov. 1679, *The Letters of Samuel Pepys and His Family Circle*, ed. H. T. Heath, pp. 131–2. Letters from Pepys to St Michel in Heath, pp. 64–90, 92–131, 132–51, 152–5. Little Samuel was said to be ten by his mother in the summer of 1681.

24. Pepys to Balthasar St Michel, 14 July 1679, ibid., p. 74.

25. St Michel writes of 'my five small babes', 24 Sept. 1680, ibid., p. 164.

26. So they were reminded again by the attorney-general in Jan. 1680. Pepys Library, Mornamont MSS, vol. I, p. 62.

27. Pepys wrote to Mrs Skinner, 23 Oct. 1679, sending greetings to the Botelers. *Letters and Second Diary of Samuel Pepys*, ed. R. G. Howarth, p. 89.

28. Pepys to Mrs Skinner, 24 Oct. 1679, ibid., p. 89.

29. James confessed just before his death in Mar. 1680. Pepys Library, Mornamont MSS, vol. II, p. 1,248.

30. Pepys to Balthasar St Michel, 29 Sept. 1679, *The Letters of Samuel Pepys and His Family Circle*, ed. H. T. Heath, pp. 104–6.

31. Pepys Library, Mornamont MSS, vol. II, p. 1,169.

32. Pepys to Balthasar St Michel, 26 Jan. 1680, *The Letters of Samuel Pepys and His Family Circle*, ed. H. T. Heath, p. 151.

33. John Joyne's statement for 27 Nov. 1679, from Pepys Library, Mornamont MSS, vol. I, p. 296.

34. ibid., p. 210.

35. Pepys wrote to Balthasar St Michel in Paris on 1 Jan. 1680 saying he had just returned to town. *The Letters of Samuel Pepys and His Family Circle*, ed. H. T. Heath, pp. 144–5.

36. Pepys Library, Mornamont MSS, vol. II, p. 1,189.

37. A note, undated but apparently from the late 1670s, reads 'WH – my Wife's picture', which suggests Pepys may have let Hewer have a portrait of Elizabeth to hang in his house. Bodleian Library, Rawlinson MSS, C 859, fol. 40.

38. The visit to Mary is on 10 Mar.

39. Pepys Library, Mornamont MSS, vol. II, p. 1,214.

40. ibid., p. 1,213.

41. 2 Mar. 1680, ibid., p. 1,240.

42. Pepys to his father, 27 Mar. 1680, Pepys to Morelli, 27 Mar. 1680, *Letters and Second Diary of Samuel Pepys*, ed. R. G. Howarth, pp. 92–4. The diary says nothing of Morelli, merely 'I returned to Town.'

43. Pepys to Mrs Skinner, 1 July 1680, ibid., p. 96.

44. Some pages are blank. I am indebted to Dr Charles Knighton for his estimate of the number of words.

45. Many of the originals are among the Rawlinson MSS in the Bodleian.

46. Pepys Library, Mornamont MSS, vol. I, p. 517, document dated 27 May 1675.

23. *Travels for the Stuarts*

1. Pepys to James Houblon, 2 Oct. 1680, printed in *Letters and Second Diary of Samuel Pepys*, ed. R. G. Howarth (1932), p. 102.

2. Diary, 7 Feb. 1668, on meeting Jackson before his marriage to Pall.

3. John Matthews, M.A., was the Huntingdon schoolmaster in 1680, and John Jackson is entered as a pupil there. *Victoria County History of Huntingdonshire*, vol. II, p. 109.

4. Pepys to Mr Loke, 23 Apr. 1681, *Letters of Samuel Pepys and His Family Circle*, ed. H. T. Heath (1955), pp. 180–81.

5. Evelyn suggested the naval history to Pepys first in a letter 30 Jan. 1680, *Correspondence of Samuel Pepys and John Evelyn*, ed. G. de la Bédoyère (1997), and see below. Letters about provostship in *Letters and Second Diary of Samuel Pepys*, ed. R. G. Howarth, pp. 115–18.

6. Will Hewer to Pepys, 16 Nov. 1680, *Letters and Second Diary of Samuel Pepys*, ed. R. G. Howarth, p. 109.

7. Will Hewer to Pepys, 15 Nov. 1680, ibid., p. 107, and Pepys to Will Hewer, 2 Nov. 1680, ibid., p. 105.

8. Pepys to Esther St Michel, 1 Oct. 1681, *Letters of Samuel Pepys and His Family Circle*, ed. H. T. Heath, p. 188.

9. Esther St Michel to Pepys, 24 Sept. 1681, ibid., p. 187.

10. The words are used by Dr John Peachell of Cambridge to Pepys, 11 Jan. 1681, *Letters and Second Diary of Samuel Pepys*, ed. R. G. Howarth, p. 110.

11. Will Howe had served Sandwich alongside Pepys from before 1660. Pepys to Howe, 8 July 1680, ibid., pp. 96–7, Howe's response, 15 June 1681, pp. 114–5.

12. Obrian Skinner applied to Pepys in Jan. 1682 and Pepys endorsed his letter 'little Obrian Skinner to Mr Pepys'. Cited in James Hanford, 'Pepys and the Skinner Family', *Review of English Studies*, vol. vii, July 1931, pp. 257–70. Peter was placed at sea in 1683, and Pepys wrote to his old friend Will Howe, by then a judge in Barbados, recommending Daniel, 8 July 1680, *Letters and Second Diary of Samuel Pepys*, ed. R. G. Howarth, pp. 96–7. Mrs Skinner's letters to Pepys about Peter are 25 Apr. 1683, ibid., pp. 149–50, and 10 June 1689, ibid., pp. 200–201. Old Daniel Skinner died 21 Jan. 1684 and is buried at St Olave's.

13. Trinity College. Conclusion Book B, 155, from Gordon Campbell, John K. Hale, David J. Holmes and J. Tweedie, 'The Provenance of *De Doctrina Christiana*', *Milton Quarterly*, no. 31, 1997, pp. 67–93.

14. Bodleian Library, Rawlinson MSS, A 194, fol. 261. The letter asking Mrs Bagwell not to 'lose time in attending, at least upon me' was written 7 Jan. 1687, printed in Arthur Bryant, *Samuel Pepys: The Saviour of the Navy* (1938), pp. 166–7. Pepys to Lord Brouncker, 17 Dec. 1681, cited in Arthur Bryant, *Samuel Pepys: The Years of Peril* (1935), p. 372.

15. Appointment of Mills's son-in-law, Arthur Bryant, *Samuel Pepys: The Years of Peril*, p. 372.

16. Her name appears in Pepys's poll tax returns as one of his servants between 1681 and 1689. His letter to Mr Parry, 7 Apr. 1682, recommending Samuel Edwards to Christ's Hospital is printed in *Letters and Second Diary of Samuel Pepys*, ed. R. G. Howarth, p. 110.

17. Evelyn's description of Verrio's Windsor frescos, 16 June 1683, *The Diary of John Evelyn*, ed. E. S. de Beer (1955). Verrio was a Catholic who had special permission to work in England, J. P. Kenyon, *The Popish Plot* (1972), p. 342.

18. Pepys to Lord Brouncker, 13 Mar. 1682, *Letters and Second Diary of Samuel Pepys*, ed. R. G. Howarth, pp. 126–7.

19. Pepys to Will Hewer, 19 May 1682, ibid., p. 139.

20. Morelli's letter of 16 Feb. 1687, 'excusing late marriage, and desiring re-admission' to the favour of his one-time employer, is his last appearance in Pepys's files. Bodleian Library, Rawlinson MSS, A 189, fol. 327.

21. Gilbert Burnet's *History of My Own Time* (1818), vol. II, p. 234. Burnet's account of Charles II's character is devastating, and of course drawn from personal experience. He likens him to Tiberius, but we must not forget that Burnet was the friend of William III.

22. Cited in J. R. Tanner, *Mr Pepys: An Introduction to the Diary together with a Sketch of His Later Life* (1925), p. 249, from the Pepysian MSS, no. 2866, Naval

Minutes, p. 76. Tanner remarks, 'The last phrase brings before us vividly Charles II's characteristic way.'

23. For Coventry's original suggestion, see Diary, 13 June 1664. Pepys's notes suggesting an account of 'both the Dutch wars' are undated but follow a copy of a letter from William Petty dated Apr. 1675, so they may have been written soon after the Third Dutch War ended in Feb. 1674. If this is so, Pepys is excluding the First Dutch War, fought under Cromwell, which again seems likely. His notes are in Bodleian Library, Rawlinson MSS, A 185, fol. 221.

24. Evelyn's letters to Pepys urging him to undertake a 'General History of Navigation' and supplying him with bibliographical and historical information are printed in *The Correspondence of Samuel Pepys and John Evelyn*, ed. G. de la Bédoyère, between pp. 94 and 140. They cover a formidable range, from ancient history and ancient Britain, naval architecture and engineering works, battles, fishing rights, trade, Anglo-French rivalry, Italian and French military studies, old coins marked with ships, drinking cups in the shape of ships, biblical references to ships, etc., etc.

25. The list of 'Adieus' is found among his 'Tangier Memoranda', Bodleian Library, Rawlinson MSS, C 859, fol. 151v.

26. Pepys to John Evelyn, 7 Aug. 1683, *The Correspondence of Samuel Pepys and John Evelyn*, ed. G. de la Bédoyère. For Pepys's comments on Dr Ken's sermons, see *The Tangier Papers of Samuel Pepys*, ed. and transcriber Edwin Chappell (1935), pp. 21, 30, 38.

27. The 'Journal Towards Tangier' is part of *The Tangier Papers of Samuel Pepys*.

28. ibid., p. 16.

29. ibid., p. 17.

30. ibid., pp. 56, 57.

31. ibid., 26 Nov. 1683, p. 56.

32. ibid., p. 213.

33. ibid., p. 224. It is not clear whether this is the same occasion as the one described in the journal for Monday, 22 Oct., when he rows in the bay at evening and observes the blueness of the remote hills 'as I have sometimes seen them painted but never believed it natural painted' (p. 47).

34. On 19 Oct. 1683 Pepys wrote to his cousins Barbara and Thomas Gale in London, still expressing the hope of 'eating brawn with you at Christmas'. *Letters and Second Diary of Samuel Pepys*, ed. R. G. Howarth, pp. 162–3.

35. Evelyn reports Pepys telling him about his investigation into the supposed miraculous cures, the contriver of which confessed to him that they were 'all a cheat, which he would easily discover, though the poore superstitious people were imposed upon: yet have these Impostors, an allowance of the Bishops, to practice their Juggleings'. 16 Sept. 1685, *The Diary of John Evelyn*, ed. E. S. de Beer.

24. Whirligigs

1. The toadstools are described in his *Memoires Relating to the State of the Royal Navy of England for Ten Years Determined December 1688*, published in 1690 from the report and recommendations he made from 1684 on.

2. The appointment was made by James II in July 1685, and celebrated by him personally at Deptford Church and at a dinner in London. Within days Pepys took steps to end the 'scandal' of Younger Brothers of Trinity House being 'dissenters from the Church and ill affected to the Government'. J. R. Tanner, 'Samuel Pepys and the Trinity House', *English Historical Review*, vol. xxxxiv, 1929, pp. 583–5.

3. Mary's own will asked that she should be buried as close as possible to her aunt Elizabeth, which I take to be an indication of her feeling for her.

4. For his rude references to her, Diary, *passim*; for his not allowing Elizabeth to call on her, 15 May 1668.

5. John Evelyn to Pepys, 3 Oct. 1685, *The Correspondence of John Evelyn and Samuel Pepys*, ed. G. de la Bédoyère (1997). Evelyn can hardly have been referring to Elizabeth, dead now for fifteen years.

6. Pepys's 'Home Notes for myself to attend to when able' are conjecturally dated 1698 by J. R. Tanner in *The Private Correspondence and Miscellaneous Papers of Samuel Pepys* (1926), vol. I, p. 167, and include the section 'Works to bee visited with MS'. John Evelyn to Pepys, 14 Jan. 1699, *The Correspondence of Samuel Pepys and John Evelyn*, ed. G. de la Bédoyère.

7. Pepys writes of making 'a visit to good Mrs Ewer at Clapham': Pepys to John Evelyn, 2 Oct. 1685, *The Correspondence of Samuel Pepys and John Evelyn*, ed. G. de la Bédoyère.

8. This house was demolished in 1791. You can still appreciate how good its position over the water gate must have been.

9. 15 Sept. 1685, *Diary of John Evelyn*, ed. E. S. de Beer (1955).

10. James Stanier Clarke was entrusted by the prince regent with the task of editing the 'Life' of James II and given access to the 'Private Manuscripts of James the Second' that had been smuggled out of Italy at Leghorn under the prince's instructions in 1810 and brought to the library at Carlton House. They consisted of a biography apparently based on James's own notes written from the age of sixteen, which he deposited in the Scotch College in Paris in 1701, only to be burnt in France during the revolution. The author is not known, but was thought to be Thomas Innes, a Catholic superior of the Scotch College. Clarke's two volumes appeared in 1816.

11. The Revocation of Edict of Nantes in France brought many Huguenot refugees. A commission headed by archbishop of Canterbury and lord chancellor was formed to assist them, and 'Saml. Pepys Esquire' was among its members. N. G. Brett-James, *The Growth of Stuart London* (1935), p. 488.

    Peachell wrote to Pepys in Feb. 1687 and was suspended from his mastership and vice-chancellorship of the university in May 1687. Pepys recommended him for a naval chaplaincy with Lord Dartmouth in Sept. 1688, which Peachell turned down. Letters in *Letters and Second Diary of Samuel Pepys*, ed. R. G. Howarth (1932), pp. 176–7, 194–5.

12. 16 Sept. 1685, *The Diary of John Evelyn*, ed. E. S. de Beer.

13. Pepys to Sir Robert Southwell, 10 Oct. 1685, last page of MS, British Library Add MSS, 12,907, fol. 31. Dryden was the laureate, but perhaps he was not on duty on this occasion.

14. Notes in the Bodleian Library, Rawlinson MSS, A 189, fol. 8, made by Josiah Burchett, Pepys's clerk.

15. See J. D. Davies, *Gentlemen and Tarpaulins* (1991), p. 184. 'Good Voyages' were still part of the naval system a century later.

16. Pepys has notes on the pressing of men in his 'Navy White Book' and prepared a paper for the duke of York in 1669, but he made no proposals to end it.

17. See pp. 353–4 in vol. V, covering modern MSS in the *Catalogue of the Pepys Library*, ed. Charles Knighton (1981), for MS 1490 concerning St Michel's appointment as commissioner of navy for Deptford and Woolwich yards (19 Apr. 1686) and his being given the Treasurer's House at Deptford, obliging a Mrs Gunman to leave. The house was the one in which Carteret had entertained Lady Sandwich and Pepys when his son married Jemima Montagu in the summer of 1665, and also where Pepys had attended a party at which the duke and duchess of York, Lady Castlemaine and the maids of honour played party games, sitting on the carpet because there were no chairs and being very witty in 'I love my love with an A because he is so and so; and I hate him with an A because of this and that', Diary, 4 Mar. 1669.

18. Pepys to Balthasar St Michel, 11 Dec. 1686, *The Letters of Samuel Pepys and His Family Circle*, ed. H. T. Heath (1955), pp. 205–6.

19. Letters from John Jackson (24 Feb. 1687) and Sam Jackson (at sea, 20 July 1688) in ibid., pp. 210, 173–4.

20. John Creed to Pepys, Feb. 1687, Bodleian Library, A 189, fol. 98.

21. He died 23 June 1686 at Tunbridge Wells, where he had gone saying, 'If the waters do not cure me, the earth must.' His dying was, according to his nephew, 'as regular and exemplary as his living; he had his senses to the last moment'. H. C. Foxcroft, *The Life and Letters of Sir George Savile, First Marquis of Halifax* (1898), vol. I, p. 465.

22. Pepys knew Barbara as pretty Bab when she stayed at Seething Lane in 1669 and joined in dancing, sightseeing to Bedlam, theatre parties and outings with Elizabeth, a few years before her marriage to Gale. One of her sons was Pepys's godson and the eldest, another Roger, became an antiquarian and a friend, so that he knew four generations of the family.

23. *The Petty Papers*, ed. Marquess of Lansdowne (1927), vol. II, p. 36. Other information from *DNB*, article by Irvine Masson and A. J. Youngson in *The Royal Society: Its Origins and Founders*, ed. Sir Henry Hartley (1960), and *Life of Sir William Petty* by Lord Edward Fitzmaurice (1895).

24. Petty regarding his daughter Anne to Sir Robert Southwell, 4 Dec. 1685, Lord

Edward Fitzmaurice, *Life of Sir William Petty*, p. 297. His advice to Penn, *The Petty Papers*, ed. Marquess of Lansdowne, vol. I, pp. 95–114.

25. *The Petty Papers*, ed. Marquess of Lansdowne, vol. I, p. 267.

26. Lord Edward Fitzmaurice, *Life of Sir William Petty*, p. 155.

27. Essay on God from MS copy made for Pepys of Petty's letter to earl of Anglesey of Apr. 1675, among Pepys's papers in the Bodleian Library, Rawlinson MSS, A 185, fol. 219. Petty's will dated 2 May 1685, printed in Lord Edward Fitzmaurice, *Life of Sir William Petty*, p. 324.

28. William of Orange was a Stuart through his mother, Mary, daughter of Charles I and sister of Charles II and James II. He was also married to a Stuart, James II's elder daughter by his first wife, Anne Hyde, another Mary, brought up as a Protestant at the insistence of Charles II. Her claim to the throne was good as long as James II did not have a son, which is why the birth of his son in June 1688 was a crucial factor in the opposition to him, and why William took seriously allegations that the baby was not the child of James and his queen but had been smuggled in.

29. 29 Sept. 1688, British Library, Egerton MSS, 2621.

30. Bodleian Library, Rawlinson MSS, A 186, fol. 470.

31. Henry Sheeres to Lord Dartmouth, 24 Nov. 1688, text given in Arthur Bryant, *Samuel Pepys: The Saviour of the Navy* (1938), p. 323.

32. J. R. Tanner, *Mr Pepys: An Introduction to the Diary, together with a Sketch of His Later Life* (1925), p. 246, footnote, states that James II wrote a letter on 17 Nov. 1688 recommending the lords commissioners of the Treasury to pay the sum of £28,007.2s.1¼d. owing to Pepys, as agreed by Charles II on 2 Mar. 1679. This is the amount given in Pepys's will as still owing. The letter does not, however, specify a sum, and Tanner appears to have incorporated the sum from his knowledge of Pepys's will.

Among Tanner's papers is a copy of the letter in a modern hand. This is now in Arthur Bryant's archives (N 10, Box 1, enveloped marked 1688). Below the text is added: 'Docketed Nov. 17, 1688. His Majesty's Confirmation & Recommendation of the Arrears [*sic*] due to Mr Pepys upon his Service in the Navy & Adm/lty & as Trea/r for Tangier to the Lords Comm/rs of the Trea/ry. (This letter, which is framed & was shown at a meeting of the S.P. Club, belongs to Lieut. Col. Frederick Pepys Cockerell, OBE, MC, 36 Kensington Square. He let me have a copy and said I could make what use I liked of it. The signature only appears to be written by the King.)' On his death, Tanner's papers went to Bryant, who gave the text in his *The Saviour of the Navy*, p. 312. He noted that Frederick Pepys Cockerell (born in 1876) was dead by the time he published this volume in 1938.

The records of the Samuel Pepys Club show that Frederick Pepys Cockerell brought the original letter to the club on 11 Dec. 1923. In Feb. 1925 he presented a facsimile of the letter to the National Portrait Gallery, along with a reproduction of the portrait of Pepys used on the cover of this book. Both appear to have remained in the family since Pepys's death. Frederick Pepys

Cockerell put other facsimiles on the market with reproductions of the portrait and advertised them in the *Burlington Magazine* for Jan. 1924, which stated that the originals were in his possession. This explains why there are so many facsimiles about.

The original was purchased – presumably after the death of Frederick Pepys Cockerell – by the collector André de Coppet, and at his death sold through Sotheby's (sale of 14 Mar. 1955) to Denys Bower, who kept it with other Stuart memorabilia at Chiddingstone Castle in Kent. Bower died in 1977. His collection remains at Chiddingstone, but the letter is not at present on display.

33. Pepys to the mayor, Captain Thomas Langley, and Corporation of Harwich, 27 Nov. 1688, Bodleian Library, Rawlinson MSS, A 179, fol. 264.

34. J. P. Kenyon, *Stuart England* (1978), pp. 248–53.

35. Compare 11 Dec. 1688, 'the mobile got together and attacked Popish chapels', Narcissus Luttrell, *A Brief Historical Relation of State of Affairs from September 1678 to April 1714* (1857).

36. William to Admiral Herbert from Windsor, 16 Dec. 1688, 'j'ai des assurances de la Flotte d'Angleterre qu'elle se soumet a mes ordres'. British Library, Egerton MSS, 2621, fol. 81.

37. Bodleian Library, Rawlinson MSS, A 179, fol. 39.

38. Pepys to Captain Thomas Langley, 1 Jan. 1689, Bodleian Library, Rawlinson MSS, A 179, fol. 142.

39. Bodleian Library, Rawlinson MSS, A 179, fols. 218, 223, filed by Pepys as 'Harwich Papers between SP & that Corporation . . . approaching election Jan. 22 1688/9'.

25. The Jacobite

1. Roger Pepys died at Impington on 4 Oct. 1688. His will is dated 31 Aug. 1688 and was proved 13 Oct. Information from Sheila Russell.

2. Pepys to Dryden, 14 July 1699, *Letters and Second Diary of Samuel Pepys*, ed. R. G. Howarth (1932), p. 281. The Fables, published in 1700, became Dryden's most popular work. The prefatory note to my nineteenth-century edition reads, 'The "Character of a Good Parson", one of the most delightful sketches in our language, was recommended to Dryden for *refacimento* by Pepys, the diarist, who was one of his intimate friends, and who to much simplicity of character seems to have united a good critical judgment, as well as a good business capacity.'

3. 30 Dec. 1689, Bodleian Library, Rawlinson MSS, A 170, fol. 180, among what Pepys labelled 'Promiscuous Papers Current'.

4. Anthony Deane to Pepys, 29 Oct. 1689, Pepys to Anthony Deane, 23 Nov. 1689, *Letters and Second Diary of Samuel Pepys*, ed. R. G. Howarth, pp. 211–12. I have omitted Pepys's parenthesis about the felicities of the next world, 'which yet I bless God I am not without care for'.

5. 11 Apr. 1693 Pepys learnt that £69.10s.1d. had been given to Sam Jackson out of the Brampton rents. He promised repayment, and on 24 June Matthews,

Pepys's cousin, the Jackson boys' one-time teacher and now agent for Brampton, sent £10 on behalf of Sam to Pepys, who was delighted and forgave the rest of the debt (*Sotheby's Sale Catalogue*, 1931, p. 23). But by Apr. 1702 Pepys was complaining to Matthews about Sam again.

6. Letters from Thomas Shadwell to John Jackson during his Grand Tour at the end of the decade refer to 'an enemy, female' of JJ, and to his 'evil genius', and the 'Lady at London' whom he is not eager to see, all of which appear to mean Mary: they are printed in *The Private Correspondence and Miscellaneous Papers of Samuel Pepys*, ed. J. R. Tanner (1926), 15 Mar. 1700, vol. I, p. 295, 20 May, 2 June 1700, vol. I, pp. 343, 349, 8 July 1700, vol. II, p. 10. By JJ's own account Pepys urged them to be friends on his deathbed, which suggests they were not.

7. Balthasar de St Michel to Pepys, 28 May 1689, *The Letters of Samuel Pepys and His Family Circle*, ed. H. T. Heath (1955), pp. 123–4.

8. Peter Skinner to Pepys, 27 Sept. 1689, Bodleian Library, Rawlinson MSS, A 170, fol. 42, and 8 Nov. 1689, fol. 30.

9. Letters in *Letters and Second Diary of Samuel Pepys*, ed. R. G. Howarth, show Mrs Fane was discharged in 1687 (p. 180, footnote) and interceded for by Mary; then, she was about to be discharged again in 1689, Pepys to James Houblon, 10 July 1689 (pp. 194–5). But Pepys's account with Hoare shows payments to Mrs Jane Fane in Dec. 1691.

10. J. R. Tanner, *Mr Pepys: An Introduction to the Diary together with a Sketch of His Later Life* (1925), p. 272, from a paper in the Pepys Library, dated 1697, listing his servants.

11. Sir Francis died 9 Oct. 1690. His will, held in the PRO, was written in 1684, the year of his wife's death. Julia Shallcross was mistress of Woodhall until her death in 1726, when it went to her sister Isabel Hutchinson, and it seems reasonable to think Mary sometimes stayed with Julia at Woodhall after 1690.

12. G. M. Trevelyan, *Social History of England* (1962): 'For 30 years after the Restoration the profit on the original stock averaged first 20 and later 40 per cent per annum. The market price of £100 stock touched £500 in 1685.'

13. For Hickes, J. H. Overton, *The Nonjurors* (1902), also *DNB*. For Sheeres, 3 Mar. 1696, Narcissus Luttrell, *A Brief Historical Relation of State of Affairs from September 1678 to April 1714* (1857), vol. IV, p. 24.

14. A tribute surely to William III's surveillance system. It looks as though Pepys was questioned about the proposed trip, because James Vernon wrote to Matthew Prior in Paris on 16 Aug. 1698, 'I hope you will have an eye upon Mr Pepys's nephew that he doth not go astray. I believe the old gentleman means fairly, and hath sent no underhand compliments to his old master, having professed the contrary; but young men and ladies may sometimes be libertines and forget good advice.' Information from J. R. Tanner, *Mr Pepys: An Introduction to the Diary*, p. 270.

15. Henry Clarendon was the second earl, son of Chancellor Clarendon; he had been arrested and sent to the Tower in 1690 and was not in favour with King William. Clarendon dined with Pepys on 27 Apr. 1694, as Pepys recorded in a

note pasted into vol. X of the Sandwich Papers (also no. 138 in naval papers in Pepys Library). George Hickes was known to Pepys from at least the 1680s when he was dean of Worcester.

16. Thomas Smith to Pepys, 16 Apr. 1702, *The Private Correspondence and Miscellaneous Papers of Samuel Pepys*, ed. J. R. Tanner, vol. II, pp. 259–62.

17. Narcissus Luttrell, *A Brief Historical Relation of State of Affairs from September 1678 to April 1714*, vol. II, p. 64, says Captain Hatton was arrested 25 Jan. 1690 and discharged 12 Feb. 1692. He was the younger brother of Christopher, first Viscount Hatton, a founder member of the Royal Society. Charles Hatton was born in the mid 1630s and became a close friend to Pepys in the 1690s.

18. For example, Pepys to John Evelyn, 8 Oct. 1691, *The Correspondence of Samuel Pepys and John Evelyn*, ed. G. de la Bédoyère (1997).

19. This is the beginning: ' 'Twas in April 1679, when (my unhappy *Master*, his then *Royal Highness*, having but newly been commanded abroad, and my self now shut up in the Tower) *His Majesty K. Charles the Second* was led to the exchanging the *Method* wherein the *Affairs* of his *Admiralty* had for some years before been manag'd under his own Inspection, for that of a *Commission*, charg'd with the *Execution* of the whole *Office* of his *High Admiral*.' (In fact it was not in April but in May.)

At the end he announces his intention of writing more naval history and continues:

In which consideration I shall (not gladly only, but) thankfully receive Intimation of any Matters herein calling for Amendment; as well-knowing how far from infallible his best endeavours must be, that has to do with a Subject so extensive, various, and complicate, as that of a Navy; and a Navy circumstanc'd as this happens to be within the limits of this Chapter.

But whatever (more or less) I may meet with from better Hands toward the improvement of this Schitz [i.e., sketch]: Somewhat (I trust) of present utility may (even as it is) be hoped for from it, in the som ample, fresh, and costly Experiment (and to England most instructive) which this Paper exhibits, of the Validity of these three Truths in its Sea Oeconomy, viz,

1. That Integrity, and general (but inpractic'd) Knowledge, are not alone sufficient to conduct and support a Navy so, as to prevent its Declension into a State little less unhappy, than the worst that can befall it under the want of both.

2. – That not much more (neither) is to be depended on, even from Experience alone and Integrity; unaccompany'd with Vigour of Application, Assiduity, Affection, Strictness of Discipline, and Method.

3. – That it was a strenuous Conjunction of all these (and that conjunction only) that within half the Time, and less than half the Charge it cost the Crown in the exposing it, had (at the very instant of its unfortunate Lord's Withdrawing from it) rais'd the Navy of England from the lowest state of Impotence, to the most advanced step towards a lasting and solid Prosperity, that (all Circumstances consider'd) this Nation had ever seen it at.

And yet not such; but that (even at this its Zenith) it both did and suffer'd sufficient
to teach us, that there is Something above both That and Us, that Governs the World.
To which (Incomprehen-
sible) alone be
GLORY.

20. John Evelyn to Pepys, 11 June 1690, *The Correspondence of Samuel Pepys and John Evelyn*, ed. G. de la Bédoyère. The letter continues to p. 218, and there is a second letter on 17 June 1690, p. 219, which is roughly the equivalent of a modern pre-publication puff.

21. J. D. Davies's 'Pepys and the Admiralty Commission of 1679–1684', *Bulletin of the Institute for Historical Research*, vol. lxii, 1989, pp. 34–53, makes the case that Pepys had the strongest political motivation for destroying the reputation of the commission and set out to do so; and that truth suffered. For instance, Pepys ignored circumstances when he compared the size of the navy in 1679 (76 ships) with 1684 (24 ships), because in 1679 the country had just mobilized a fleet for an intended war and been unable to pay off the men, lacking the money to do so; while in May 1684 there were in fact 39, not 24, ships in service, and they were the normal summer guard. Davies believes that some of the planking used for the ships built under Pepys's commission was unfit, and that some of the rotting vessels he found were a result of that unfitness as much as subsequent neglect. He suggests that the 1679 commission did all it could to combat 'Good Voyages' and found themselves hampered by the king, as Pepys himself observed in his Tangier notes; that the king in fact intervened arbitrarily in Admiralty affairs whenever he chose – the Admiralty was, for example, left entirely in the dark about the Tangier expedition until it was under way – and left it unsupported to struggle with the economic problems faced in day-to-day running. And so on.

22. When a life of James II was prepared from James's own notes by James Stanier Clarke, librarian to the prince regent (and friend of Jane Austen) and published in 1816, Clarke quoted chunks of Mr Secretary Pepys's account of the qualities needed by Navy Board officials. Clarke says James II approved and associated himself with Pepys's recommendations. He had of course read them in 1685, but it looks as though a copy of Pepys's *Memoires* may have found its way to him in 1690.

23. David Douglas, *English Scholars* (1951), p. 258.

24. Pepys to John Evelyn, 9 Jan. 1692, Pepys to Henry Sheeres, 29 Jan. 1692, Balthasar St Michel to Pepys, 20 Mar. 1692, all in *Private Correspondence and Miscellaneous Papers of Samuel Pepys*, ed. J. R. Tanner, pp. 51–2, 53–4, 55–6.
Sheeres, like Pepys, was kept under surveillance as a suspected Jacobite and was arrested on 3 Mar. 1696, when there were again fears of an invasion attempt by James from France. Narcissus Luttrell, *A Brief Historical Relation of State of Affairs*, vol. IV, p. 24.

25. Pepys to Thomas Gale, 15 Sept. 1692, *Letters and Second Diary of Samuel Pepys*,

ed. R. G. Howarth, pp. 230–32. He wrote to John Evelyn the following day, *The Correspondence of Samuel Pepys and John Evelyn*, ed. G. de la Bédoyère, pp. 235–6.

26. Diary, 24 June 1666, on hearing of the death of Sir Francis Prujean, one-time president of the Royal College of Physicians.

27. They were renumbered in 1693. Since they were arranged by size, they were kept in four separate places up to and after this date, and only in 1700, during Pepys's last supervision of the cataloguing and arrangement, were they put together – see Robert Latham's introduction to vol. I of the Diary, p. lxviii.

26. A Journey to be Made

1. From H. B. Wheatley's *Pepysiana* (1899), pp. 45–7, which prints the account of the trial given in the Old Bailey Session Papers for 6–9 Dec. 1693.

2. Pepys to John Evelyn, 7 Nov. 1694, *The Correspondence of Samuel Pepys and John Evelyn*, ed. G. de la Bédoyère (1997). The visit with Lady Sandwich was 30 June 1662, with Charles II and the duke, 26 July 1665.

3. Pepys outlived Creed, which must have pleased him – Creed died in 1701 and his widow put up a fine memorial stone in Titchmarsh Church, Northants. Secretary's minutes to Royal Society for 21 Nov. 1694, pp. 119, 120.

4. For advising Mary to ride, Pepys to Hans Sloane, 14 Oct. 1701, 'Your Patient is a Cock-horse every day, and I hope will have benefitt by it.' *Letters and Second Diary of Samuel Pepys*, ed. R. G. Howarth (1932), p. 334. For Pepys's wish to talk with Sloane, 31 July 1702, p. 348.

5. Humfrey Wanley to T. Tanner, 16 Apr. 1695, *Letters of Humfrey Wanley, Palaeographer, Anglo-Saxonist, Librarian 1672–1726*, ed. P. L. Heyworth (1989), pp. 12, 13. Humfrey Wanley to Smith, 23 Apr. 1695, when he saw 'Mr Pepyses noble Library', p. 16.

6. Humfrey Wanley to John Bagford, 24 May 1696, ibid., pp. 37–8.

7. Humfrey Wanley to Pepys, 15 Apr. 1701, *Letters and Second Diary of Samuel Pepys*, ed. R. G. Howarth, pp. 330–31.

8. For Pepys's and Sloane's testimonials, *Letters of Humfrey Wanley*, ed. P. L. Heyworth, pp. 473–5. Sloane also offered £100 towards the funding; also *Private Correspondence and Miscellaneous Papers of Samuel Pepys*, ed. J. R. Tanner (1926), vol. I, pp. 366–7. In spite of all this, Wanley failed to persuade Oxford to back him.

9. Sam Newton to Pepys, n.d. but 7 Aug. 1695, British Library Add MSS, 20,732, fol. 158.

10. Pepys to Sam Newton, 8 Aug. 1695, ibid., fols. 158v., 159.

11. Diary, 25 July 1663, when Pepys and Will called on Gauden there. Pepys found 'the house very regular and finely contrived, and the gardens and offices about it as convenient and as full of good variety as ever I saw in my life. It is true he hath been censured for laying out so much money.' He called again 27 July 1665 and found the gardens 'mighty pleasant'. In 1663 Clapham had 562 hearths

(*Victoria County History of Surrey*, vol. IV, p. 37) and in 1664 there were 92 houses. *Companion* to Latham and Matthews's edition of the Diary, p. 65.

12. The verses he quotes from memory run, 'When I see a Discontent/ Sick of the faults of Government/ Whose very Rest and Peace dis-ease him,/ 'Cause giv'n by those that doe not please him/ Mee thinks that Bedlam has noe Folly, "Like to the politick Mellancholly"'. Pepys evidently felt safe confiding his political feelings to Julia Shallcross.

All that is known of this letter is given by G. de la Bédoyère, *The Correspondence of Samuel Pepys and John Evelyn*, p. 235, footnote. It is taken from the *Rosenbach Company Catalogue*, Philadelphia 1937, Item 287, p. 102. Bédoyère was unaware of the existence of Julia Shallcross when he published it. Later, in Aug. 1700, Pepys wrote to thank Dr George Stanhope for his attentions to 'Mrs Shellcrosse and her party at Greenwich'. Stanhope was vicar at Tewin in Hertfordshire, close to Woodhall, and the home of Julia's sister Isabel.

13. He planned to visit the Houblon sons in the winter of 1700–1701, but it is not clear whether he managed to do so. *Private Correspondence and Miscellaneous Papers of Samuel Pepys*, ed. J. R. Tanner, vol. II, p. 124.

14. There were to be another four bookcases. The ninth was installed by 1702, and the last three delivered after his death. The drawings were done by Sutton Nicholls, folded and preserved in the catalogue. D. McKitterick, *Catalogue of the Pepys Library* (1991), vol. VII, p. xxxiii.

15. 'The Miniature K: of France on horseback by Mr Skyner – in gilt frame'. The attribution comes from the Houghton Library Harvard inventory made in the early nineteenth century, a transcription of a lost original. 'Mr Skyner' is surely Mary, whom we know to have been an artist.

16. Evelyn's grandson's poem is dated 12 July 1699 and printed in *Private Correspondence and Miscellaneous Papers of Samuel Pepys*, ed. J. R. Tanner, vol. I, p. 179. Pepys to Sir Littleton Powys, 20 Jan. 1697, vol. II, p. 137. Tansy is a herb whose juice, yellow and bitter, was used to flavour puddings for Easter.

17. P. P. Dégalénière to Pepys, 5 June 1701, ibid., vol. II, pp. 226–9, for reference to Mary being godmother to his daughter. Dr George Hickes to Pepys, 1 Sept. 1702, ibid., vol. II, p. 267. Humfrey Wanley to Pepys, 25 Sept. 1702, *Letters of Humfrey Wanley*, ed. P. L. Heyworth, pp. 193–4. For greetings from wives, Captain Charles Hatton to Pepys, 31 Aug. 1700, *Private Correspondence and Miscellaneous Papers of Samuel Pepys*, ed. J. R. Tanner, vol. II, p. 62, and Mrs Evelyn, 22 July 1700, *Letters and Second Diary of Samuel Pepys*, ed. R. G. Howarth, p. 304.

18. I am indebted to Charles Knighton for this information from the Magdalene College archives. It appears in a section covering the years 1690 and 1713, fol. 127. Pepys's donation, entered on the immediately preceding fol. 126v., was made 18 June 1694, and is entered in his account with Hoare's bank.

19. *Calendar of State Papers, Domestic Series*, 12 Feb. 1688/9. 'Pass for Mr John Jackson, Mrs Julia Shallcrosse, Mrs Mary Skinner, Mrs Ann Cherritt and Alice Edmonds and Conrad Bechsteiner, their servants, to go to France.'

20. Pepys to John Jackson, 19 Oct. 1699, *Private Correspondence and Miscellaneous Papers of Samuel Pepys*, ed. J. R. Tanner, vol. I, pp. 199–202.

21. For Pepys's remark about the pain of the stone in the coach, letter to John Jackson, 11 Nov. 1700, ibid., vol. II, pp. 123–4. Pepys to John Jackson (in Venice), 8 Apr. 1700, ibid., pp. 316–17. Tanner informs us that the letter begins in his own hand, Lorrain takes it up, and the postscript is in Mary's hand; and that Pepys's signature is 'in a very trembling hand'.

22. 23 Sept. 1700, *The Diary of John Evelyn*, ed. E. S. de Beer. Henry Hyde to Pepys, 1 July 1700, *Private Correspondence and Miscellaneous Papers of Samuel Pepys*, ed. J. R. Tanner, vol. II, p. 1.

23. Dr John Shadwell to John Jackson, 20 May, 2 June, 8 July 1700, *Private Correspondence and Miscellaneous Papers of Samuel Pepys*, ed. J. R. Tanner, vol. I, pp. 343, 349, and vol. II, p. 10.

24. Pepys to John Jackson, 13 June 1700, ibid., vol. I, pp. 358–9.

25. Pepys to John Evelyn, 19 Sept. 1700. Bédoyère does not give passage about optics (pp. 282–3) but Howarth and Tanner do, noting that it is deleted – Pepys evidently cut the part of the letter that included an invitation to Evelyn's grandson to come and see his experiment, perhaps because he no longer felt up to such a visit.

26. Pepys to Charles Hatton, 19 Sept. 1700, *Letters and Second Diary of Samuel Pepys*, ed. R. G. Howarth, p. 310. The weather records in Gordon Manley's essay 'Central England Temperatures: Monthly Means 1659 to 1973', *Quarterly Journal of the Royal Meteorological Society*, no. 100, 1974, pp. 389–405, indicate a warm July, August and September in 1700.

27. Pepys to John Jackson, 8 Oct. 1700, *Private Correspondence and Miscellaneous Papers of Samuel Pepys*, ed. J. R. Tanner, vol. II, p. 87. Diary, 7 Sept. 1662, for Pepys's remarks on the queen. John Jackson did not manage to deliver the message, but he did see the queen in Apr., after lingering in Madrid, where he was particularly keen to attend the 'Bull-Feast', 'the diversion very well worth the seeing, once; the worst of it is its barbarity'.

28. Pepys to Wynne Houblon, 30 Oct. 1700, ibid., vol. II, p. 105.

29. Pepys to Dr Arthur Charlett about Dr Gregory's educational proposals, 5 Nov. 1700, *Letters and Second Diary of Samuel Pepys*, ed. R. G. Howarth, pp. 317–20.

30. Pepys to his cousin Angier of Hawley, 14 Mar. 1695, British Museum Add. MSS, 20,732, fol. 85.

31. The whole passage in Cicero's 'Scipio's Dream' (Book VI, *On the Republic*) from which the motto is taken talks about the division between the mortal body and the soul, which is not mortal. 'Tu vero enitere; et sic habeto, non esse te mortalem, sed corpus hoc; nec enim tu is es, quem forma ista declarat, sed *mens cuiusque is est quisque*, non ea figura, quae digito demonstrari potest.' Richard Ollard's admirable translation reads, 'Fight the good fight, and always call to mind that it is not you who are mortal, but this body. For your true being is not discerned by perceiving your physical appearance. But *what a man's mind is, that is what he is*, not that individual human shape that we identify through our senses.'

Pepys explained to Will Hewer that Cicero had derived the idea from Plato, and that Saint Paul had 'wrought-upon' it afterwards; this is one of his rare references to the Bible, and suggests he was more interested in it as he grew older. The English version of the motto also recalls Oliver Cromwell's use of the phrase 'The mind is the man' in his speech to parliament in 1656, when he went on to say, 'If that be kept pure, a man signifies somewhat; if not, I would very fain see what difference there is between him and a beast.' For Cromwell's speech of 17 Sept. 1656 see *Speeches of Oliver Cromwell*, ed. Ivan Roots (1989), p. 98. Pepys was working for Edward Montagu and wrote his earliest surviving letter to him, about Cromwell and the question of kingship, in November 1656, so it is possible he got to hear something of the speech and remembered it.

32. Pepys's ownership of a book on deism, William Stephen's *An Account of the Growth of Deism in England*, published in 1696, still in the Pepys Library, is no evidence that he held deist ideas himself, but the simplicity of deist faith, and its emphasis on natural rather than revealed religion, does accord with his indifference to doctrinal questions. Deists believed in one God who requires worship, piety and virtue of mankind, forgives sins and punishes and rewards in the after-life; and that nothing more needs to be added. This is John Leland's account of seventeenth-century deist tenets in his *View of the Principal Deistical Writers that Have Appeared During the Last and Present Century*, a hostile account published in 1754.

33. Pepys to John Evelyn, 7 Aug. 1700, Evelyn to Pepys, 9 Aug. 1700, *The Correspondence of Samuel Pepys and John Evelyn*, ed. G. de la Bédoyère.

34. Pepys to Matthews, extract of unpublished letter printed from MS in *Sotheby's Sale Catalogue* of 1931, p. 24.

35. Mary mentions her portrait by Godfrey Kneller in her will; Kneller himself mentions 'Mrs Skinner's picture' in a letter to Pepys, 29 July 1702, saying it is 'lokt up with others by my brother', but this is ambiguous. *Private Correspondence and Miscellaneous Papers of Samuel Pepys*, ed. J. R. Tanner, vol. II, p. 265. Manuscript records of Pepys's account at Hoare's Bank, Fleet Street.

36. Pepys to Matthews, 21 Apr. 1702, *Sotheby's Sale Catalogue* of 1931, p. 25.

37. See description in diary of William Nicolson, Bishop of Carlisle, 17 June 1702, referred to below and printed in *Transactions of the Cumberland and Westmorland Antiquarian and Archaeological Society*, vol. ii, 1902, p. 155.

38. Pepys to Henry Hyde, 4 Aug. 1702, *Private Correspondence and Miscellaneous Papers of Samuel Pepys*, ed. J. R. Tanner, vol. II, p. 266.

39. Pepys to John Evelyn, 19 Sept. 1700, *The Correspondence of Samuel Pepys and John Evelyn*, ed. G. de la Bédoyère. Pepys to Dr Arthur Charlett, 14 Nov. 1702, *Private Correspondence and Miscellaneous Papers of Samuel Pepys*, ed. J. R. Tanner, vol. II, p. 286.

40. For Nicolson's borrowings from Pepys's library, 14 June 1700, and receipts Dec. 1700 and Jan. 1701, *Private Correspondence and Miscellaneous Papers of Samuel Pepys*, ed. J. R. Tanner, vol. I, pp. 362–3.

41. Nicolson's description of the library as it appeared at Clapham is unique. He had been advised to keep a diary by Sir Joseph Williamson when he travelled to Germany as a young man and kept up the habit; but, while it is a document of some social and considerable political interest – he became a hard-working member of the House of Lords – it has none of Pepys's genius, either in the writing or in the presentation of himself. The small version of the Verrio painting at Christ's Hospital is presumably the one sold in the sale at Sotheby's in 1931, described as 'watercolour sketch by Verrio', 17⅜ × 93¾ inches in size; its present whereabouts unknown to me.

42. I have been able to trace wills by Mrs Frances Skinner and by two Skinner daughters, Mary and Elizabeth, but none by Daniel Skinner Snr or any of the sons; the women appear to have been dominant in the Skinner family.

43. J. Glasier to Pepys, Dec. 1702, *Private Correspondence and Miscellaneous Papers of Samuel Pepys*, ed. J. R. Tanner, vol. II, p. 288.

44. Will of Frances Skinner in PRO, PROB, 11/467.

45. Mary Ballard to Pepys, 1 Mar. 1703, *Private Correspondence and Miscellaneous Papers of Samuel Pepys*, ed. J. R. Tanner, vol. II, p. 302. The Ballards appear to be related to Mary Skinner, who made a legacy of £10 to her 'cousin Samuel Ballard' in her will, presumably their son. Both Ballards received rings at Pepys's funeral, listed among 'Former Servants and Dependants', but the category was a broad one, including his physicians and surgeons and Sir Littleton Powys, a judge of the Queen's Bench.

46, Pepys to Sir George Rooke, Apr. 1703, *Letters and Second Diary of Samuel Pepys*, ed. R.G. Howarth, pp. 373–4.

47. John Jackson to Will Hewer, 20 Apr. 1703, printed in ibid., vol. II, pp. 309–10.

48. It seems likely that Pepys had heard from Wanley of similar ones set up by Archbishop Matthew Parker in 1575 for his valuable library at Corpus Christi College in Cambridge and taken them partly as a model in order to safeguard his own in the future. Humfrey Wanley worked at the Parker Library in 1699 and was aware of the restrictions Parker set in forbidding the removal of the books, as he makes clear in a letter to Arthur Charlett (also Pepys's friend) dated 17 Sept. 1699 from Cambridge, in which he says he can borrow what books he pleases, 'excepting those of Bennet College' (Bennet College being another name for Corpus Christi – *Letters of Humfrey Wanley*, ed. P. L. Heyworth, p. 138). Parker had left elaborate instructions to ensure that the books should not be removed. He also provided that, should Corpus Christi be negligent, the library must pass to Caius, and should Caius also fail, on to Trinity Hall. Parker was markedly successful in achieving his aims for his library. (So was Pepys.)

Pepys was also aware of the troubled situation of Sir John Cotton's library. In 1701, when Sir John's death seemed imminent, Wanley asked Pepys to support his application to become librarian; Pepys, after consulting with Dr Thomas Smith, the current librarian, who feared losing his position because he was a nonjuror, explained to Wanley that he felt he should support Smith. The Trustees of the library were too busy to meet, and Pepys died before they managed to do so; meanwhile the library was kept locked up and inaccessible to those who wished to consult it. See P. L. Heyworth's article in the *TLS*, 31 Aug. 1962, p. 660. Pepys may have wanted to avoid similar problems.

49. The verbal bequest appears at the end of the list of mourning rings bequeathed by Pepys, printed in *Private Correspondence and Miscellaneous Papers of Samuel Pepys*, ed. J. R. Tanner, vol. II, p. 318.

50. This was in 1705, the reason given by Evelyn that he was unable to make a large enough settlement on his granddaughter. It is possible too that he did not want Jackson on other grounds such as his humble origins or his character.

51. John Jackson's account is in *Private Correspondence and Miscellaneous Papers of Samuel Pepys*, ed. J. R. Tanner, vol. II, pp. 312–14.

Epilogue

1. The autopsy is printed in *Private Correspondence and Miscellaneous Papers of Samuel Pepys*, ed. J. R. Tanner (1926), vol. II, pp. 311–12. Jackson's letter to Evelyn is in the introduction to Wheatley's edition of the Diary, pp. xliii–xliv. Latham and Matthews's edition of the Diary suggests (vol. X, pp. 172–6) that Pepys was suffering from brain damage produced by high blood pressure secondary to the destruction of his left kidney. Milo Keynes's article in the *Journal of Medical Biography*, vol. v, Feb. 1997, pp. 25–9, corrects this: 'From the emaciation and post-mortem findings, the likely cause of death was from toxaemia secondary to intra-abominal sepsis' – which seems right, given that Pepys, though weak, showed no sign of brain damage.

2. From *Post Boy*, 5 June 1703, no. 1,257, given in Braybrooke's sixth edition of the Diary, p. xxxviii.

3. Dame Elizabeth Boteler's bequest of £1,000 to Mary Skinner was secured upon 'a mortgage of certain Lands of Sr Thomas Littleton Baronet in the County of Essex'. There were two Sir Thomas Littletons, father and son, and this was probably the younger (1647–1710), speaker of the House 1698–1700 and treasurer of the navy at the time of Pepys's death. James Vernon, principal secretary of state 1698–1702 (who had an eye on Pepys in Aug. 1698, see note 14 to Chapter 25), was married to Mary Buck, daughter of Sir John Buck, Bart., and sister of Sir William, who married 'Frances Skinner, daughter of Daniel Skinner, Merchant', and sister of Mary Skinner – see Burke's *Extinct Baronetages*.

4. Dr George Hickes to Dr Arthur Charlett, 5 June 1703, printed in Wheatley's introduction to the Diary, pp. xlv–xlvi.

5. According to Zach Conrad von Uffenbach, who visited Magdalene in 1710, *London in 1710* (1934); J. E. B. Mayor, *Cambridge under Queen Anne* (1911), p. 139.

6. Her will, from which this information comes, reads, 'my owne Picture and my

Neice Hores picture both drawn by Sir Godfrey Kneller'. The reference to her 'Neice Hores' is probably to Mary Buck, who married a Hoar.

7. For instance, she gave to John Jackson, executor, £30 'to make with the gilt cup and cover and salver which I took for £20 though value of £50 which I received in plate of his late uncle Samuel Pepys Esquire deceased which cup and cover and salver I have lately given to my God daughter Paulina Jackson daughter of the said John Jackson.' And, 'Whereas the said Mr Pepys made me a present of the Gold medall of the French King, the clock in my chamber, the great skreen of six leaves Indian all of which I give to Mr John Jackson and also my picture of his uncle's head which he desired me to give him, also I give to the said Mr Jackson my three books the Heathen Gods, the description of the Castle and Water Works of Versailles and a little French book of heraldry called Jendarinorer [? Gens d'honneur] all colored by myself. To Mr Jackson's wife she that was Mrs Anne Edgley my diamond heart ring it being a mourning ring which I made for her husband's uncle.'

8. Unfortunately her grave cannot be located now, and the Boteler gravestones are concealed under carpet in the church. Information about burial entry at St Ethelreda's from Henry W. Gray.

9. Hewer's cousin Blackborne, who kept a diary, went to Doctors' Commons in Feb. 1716 to read the wills of 'Mr Hewer, Mr Pepys and Mrs Skinner'. This entry in his diary appears in the *Sotheby's Sale Catalogue* of 1931.

10. The house at Clapham, which is thought to have been on the north side of the common, near what is now Victoria Road, was pulled down about 1760. In 1774 the old church was also taken down, but Clapham remained rural until the nineteenth century (*Victoria County History of Surrey*, vol. IV, p. 37). Samuel Pepys Cockerell, John Jackson's grandson, built himself a house at 29 Northside, Clapham Common, in the late eighteenth century.

11. Wheatley gives the figures in his *Pepysiana* (1899), p. 34: 'For Boxes, Workmen, Necessary Expences and Carriage from Clapham to London £22.18s.11d. Carriage to Cambridge £18.3s.10d.'

12. J. R. Tanner, *Samuel Pepys and the Royal Navy* (1920), p. 16.

13. The letters were gathered from Jackson's descendants, the Pepys Cockerells (see Family Tree), as well as from the Bodleian and the British Museum.

14. Smith's pathetic and indignant letters are in the Pepys Library at Magdalene.

15. Colburn paid £2,200, of which the Master's Rent Book says £1,200 was lent to the college at 3 per cent, while an annual sum of £50 was set aside to help a needy scholar chosen by the Master.

16. Scott was writing in the *Quarterly Review* for spring 1826.

17. Smith to Lady Holland, 20 June 1826. *The Creevey Papers: A Selection from the Correspondence and Diaries of the Late Thomas Creevey*, ed. Sir H. Maxwell (1903–5), vol. II, p. 280. This remark made in 1834.

18. *Sir Frederic Madden at Cambridge*, ed. T. D. Rogers (1980), p. 22.

19. The moves took place in 1834, 1847 and 1854. In 1879 it occupied the south-east room on the first floor of the second court, which was rendered fire-proof. It

was not restored to the room Jackson had chosen for it until 1956 – which is perhaps why I did not see it when I was an undergraduate in the early 1950s. See E. K. Purnell's *Magdalene College* (1904), pp. 128–36.

20. Bright presented his transcription to Magdalene, but it has been lost.

21. Robert Louis Stevenson, 'Samuel Pepys', *Cornhill*, July 1881, pp. 31–46.

22. The publishers sought the opinions of Gerald (later Lord) Gardiner and Professor C. S. Lewis on whether they were likely to be prosecuted. Both thought it was now safe (the Obscene Publications Act had been passed in 1959). It must be said that Bryant bravely quoted the opening passage in full in the first volume of his biography, which appeared in 1933.

Bibliography

The date given in each entry is that of the edition used rather than that of first publication.

1. Unpublished Material

The Bodleian Library: Rawlinson MSS, A 170–95 and D. Carte MSS.

The British Library: Add MSS, 22,183, Add MSS, 19,872, Add MSS, 32,094, Add MSS, 20,732. Egerton MSS, 928: William Hewer, Sir John Kempthorne and their lawyers' letters of 1678 about ownership of Clapham that Hewer has taken over from bankrupt Sir Denis Gauden, in debt to Kempthorne who proposes to seize goods and crops from Clapham. Hewer prevents this. Egerton MSS, 2621: Admiral Herbert papers include correspondence with prince of Orange during 1688 invasion. Sloane MSS, 2572, fols. 79–87: Richard Gibson's account of his career.

The National Maritime Museum: AGC/19, Miscellaneous Papers of Samuel Pepys. LBK/8, Correspondence of Samuel Pepys. Also X98/065, vol. I of the Sandwich Journal.

Further volumes of Sandwich Journal in possession of Lord Sandwich.

Hoare's Bank, Pepys's accounts 1680–1703; also the account of 'Ann Skinner'.

The Public Record Office: Admiralty papers relating to Pepys, ADM 106/2887. ADM 20/4, Tangier Roll AOI/310, 1220, 1221: accounts for 1665 and for 1667–71. Wills of Sir Francis Boteler, Mrs Frances Skinner, Mary Skinner.

Hertfordshire Record Office: will of Dame Elizabeth Boteler.

Pepys Library: Mornamont MSS in two vols. Magdalene College Letters. John Smith's transcription of Pepys's diary in 54 volumes. Correspondence of John Smith about promise of help made by Lord Chancellor Brougham, 1831–2.

Guildhall, parish registers of St Bride's and St Olave's, Hart Street.

Liddle Hart Centre at King's College, London, archives of Arthur Bryant, containing extensive MS research notes and correspondence of both Henry Wheatley and John Tanner, correspondence, as well as Bryant's research notes.

Julian Mitchell's unpublished essay, 'Monmouthshire Politics 1660–1706', for information about Richard Creed, brother of John.

The Royal Society: journal books and secretary's minute books 1670–1700.

National Portrait Gallery archives: notebook of Charles Beale for 1681, part diary, part account book, bound in with Lilly's astrological almanac.

2. *Contemporary Diaries and Memoirs*

Aylmer, George (ed.), *The Diary of William Lawrence*, 1961 (personal papers written 1657–84)

Beadle, John, *The Journal or Diary of a Thankful Christian*, 1656

Bond, M. (ed.), *Parliamentary Diary of Edward Dering (1644–84)*, 1976

Burnet, Gilbert, *Sermon at Funeral of J. Houblon*, 1682 (biographical, not entirely reliable)

——*History of My Own Time*, 4 vols., 1818

Coates, W. H. (ed.), *The Journal of Sir Simonds D'Ewes (1602–50)*, 1942

de Beer, E. S. (ed.), *The Diary of John Evelyn*, 6 vols., 1955

Denne, S. (ed.), *The Life of Phineas Pett of Deptford, Commissioner of the Navy*, 1796

Dick, Oliver Lawson (ed.), *John Aubrey's Brief Lives* set down between 1669 and 1696, 1958

Ellwood, Thomas, *Life of Himself (1639–1713)*, 1880

Fox, George, *Journal (1624–91)*, 1694

Henning, Basil Duke (ed.), *Diary of Edward Dering (1670–73)*, 1940

Fanshawe, Anne, Lady, *Memoirs (1625–80)*, 1907

Firth, C. H. (ed.), *E. Ludlow's Memoirs 1619–1692*, 1894. Now revealed to have been heavily rewritten after Ludlow's death for first publication in 1690s

Heywood, Revd Oliver, *Autobiography 1630–1702*, 2 vols., 1937

Hutchinson, Lucy, *Memoirs of the Life of Colonel Hutchinson*, 1906

Hyde, Edward, earl of Clarendon, *The True Historical Narrative of the Rebellion and Civil Wars in England*, 6 vols., 1888

Joyne, John, *A Journal*, 1959

King, Lord (ed.), *Life and Letters of John Locke, with Extracts from His Journals and Commonplace Books*, 1858

Lee, M. H. (ed.), *The Diary and Letters of Philip Henry, MA, of Broad Oak, Flintshire, 1631–1696*, 1882

Long, C. E. (ed.), *Richard Symonds's Diary of Marches Kept by the Royal Army during the Great Civil War*, 1859

Luttrell, Narcissus, *A Brief Historical Relation of State of Affairs from September 1678 to April 1714*, 1857

MacFarlane, Alan (ed.), *Diary of Ralph Josselin 1616–1683*, 1976

Morris, C. (ed.), *The Journeys of Celia Fiennes*, 1949

Nicolson, William, *Diary*, partly published in *Transactions of the Cumberland and Westmorland Antiquarian and Archaeological Society*, vol. ii (1902). Also Jones, Clyve, and Holmes, Geoffrey (eds.), *The London Diaries of William Nicolson, Bishop of Carlisle, 1702–1718*, 1985

Robbins, Caroline, *Diary of John Milward from September 1666 to May 1668*, 1938

Robinson, H. W., and Adams, W. (eds.), *The Diary of Robert Hooke 1672–1680*, 1935

Rutt, J. T. (ed.), *Diary of Thomas Burton (1656–9)*, 4 vols., 1828

Sachse, W. L. (ed.), *Diurnal of Thomas Rugg 1659–1661*, 1961

Spalding, Ruth (ed.), *The Diary of Bulstrode Whitelocke 1605–1675*, 1989

Teonge, Henry, *Diary 1675–1679*, 1825

Webb, Rosamond (ed.), Nehemiah Wallington's *Historical Notices of Events Occurring Chiefly in the Reign of Charles I*, 2 vols., 1869

William Haller's *The Rise of Puritanism*, 1938, has a good discussion of puritan diary-keeping. There is also W. Matthews, *British Diaries 1442–1942*, 1950. See too Mark Goldie, 'Roger Morrice's *Entring Book*' in *History Today* (Nov. 2001), p. 38. Morrice was Pepys's contemporary (1628–1702), a Cambridge graduate who used shorthand, but, according to Goldie's account, his book is not so much a diary as a newsletter for Whig politicians. It is currently being transcribed.

3. Other Contemporary Writing

Anon., *Plain Truth or Closet Discourse Betwixt P. and H.*, 1679, and Anon., *A Hue and Cry after P. and H.*, 1679

Bayley, Thomas, *The Wallflower*, 1650, and Gomberville, Marin le Roy de, *Polexandre*, 5 vols., 1638 (two novels read by Elizabeth Pepys)

Bédoyère, G. de la, *Correspondence of Samuel Pepys and John Evelyn*, 1997

Carkesse, James, *Lucida Intervalla* (poems), 1679. Carkesse, a Navy Office clerk, dismissed in 1667 for corruption, became mentally unbalanced. Pepys refers disparagingly to him in the Diary, and Carkesse's poems contain attacks on Pepys as well as accounts of his time in Bedlam.

Congreve, William, *The Complete Plays*, 1948

Dryden, John, *Poetical Works*, 1893

—*Plays*, 2 vols., 1949

du Bartas, Guillaume de Saluste, *La Semaine, ou la création du monde*, 1578, and English translation by William L'Isle, 1625 (Milton's French predecessor, plodding but popular)

Ebsworth, J. W. (ed.), *The Poems and Masque of Thomas Carew*, 1893

Etherege, George, *The Dramatic Works*, 1927

Keynes, Geoffrey (ed.), Sir Thomas Browne's *Selected Writings*, 1968

L'Estrange, R., *A Brief History of the Times*, 1687–8

Margoliouth, H. M. (ed.), *The Poems and Letters of Andrew Marvell*, 2 vols., 1927

Massinger, Philip, *The Dramatic Works of Massinger and Ford*, 1875

Phillips, John (ed.), *Wit and Drollery, Jovial Poems Never before Printed*, by Sir J[ohn] M[ennes], Ja[?ohn] :S[uckling], Sir W[illiam] D['Avenant] J[ohn] D[onne], 1656. A mixed bag of poems, literary, royalist, scatological. Donne's 'Love's Progress' is the last in the collection. It is dedicated 'To the TRULY NOBLE Edward Pepes, Esq.', who must be Samuel Pepys's cousin, son of John Pepys of Ashtead. Edward was born 1617, admitted to the Middle Temple 1636, died at his sister Jane Turner's in 1663; SP helped with the funeral arrangements

Phillips, Edward, *The Mysteries of Love and Eloquence; or, the Arts of Wooing and*

Complementing as They are Managed in the Spring Garden, Hide Park, the New Exchange and Other Eminent Places, 1658. Advice from Milton's nephew on how to succeed with girls

Shadwell, Thomas, *The Dramatic Works of Thomas Shadwell*, 4 vols., 1720

Shelton, Thomas, *A Tutor to Tachygraphy*, 1642. The shorthand used by Pepys

4. History and Biography

The *Dictionary of National Biography* and the *Oxford English Dictionary* have both been much used

HISTORY

Calendar of State Papers, Domestic Series for the relevant years

Grey, Anchitel, *Debates of the House of Commons from 1667 to 1694*, 10 vols., 1769

Macaulay, T. B., *History of England*, 1889, and his 1825 essay 'Milton'

Feiling, Keith, *British Foreign Policy 1660–1672*, 1930

Clark, G. N., *The Later Stuarts*, 1934

Ogg, David, *England in the Reign of Charles II*, 1955

— *England in the Reigns of James II and William III*, 1955

Henning, Basil Duke, *The History of Parliament. Vol. I: The House of Commons 1660–1690*, 1983

Hill, Christopher, *The Century of Revolution 1603–1714*, 1974

Kenyon, J. P., *Stuart England*, 1978

Kingston, Alfred, *East Anglia and the Great Civil War*, 1897

Stone, Lawrence, *The Family, Sex and Marriage in England 1500–1800*, 1977

Gardiner, Samuel Rawson, *History of the Commonwealth and Protectorate*, 4 vols., 1897

— *History of the Great Civil War*, 4 vols., 1893

Firth, Charles, *The Last Years of the Protectorate*, 2 vols., 1909

Russell, Conrad, *The Crisis of Parliaments: English History 1509–1660*, 1971

Roots, Ivan (ed.), *Speeches of Oliver Cromwell*, 1989

Zagorin, Perez, *A History of Political Thought in the English Revolution*, 1964

Aylmer, George, *The State's Servants: The Civil Service of the English Republic*, 1973

Godwin, William, *Lives of Edward and John Philips, Nephews and Pupils of Milton, including Various Particulars of the Literary and Political History of Their Times*, 1815

Noble, M., *Lives of the English Regicides*, 1798

Walker, John, *Sufferings of the Clergy during the Grand Rebellion*, 1862

Matthews, A. G., *Mr Pepys and Nonconformity*, 1954

Watkins, Owen C., *The Puritan Experience*, 1972

Hutton, Ronald, *Restoration*, 1985

Davies, Godfrey, *The Restoration of Charles II*, 1955

Davies, K. G., *The Royal African Company*, 1957

Richards, R. D., *Early History of Banking in England*, 1929

Marshall, Alan, *Intelligence and Espionage in the Reign of Charles II*, 1994

Houblon, Lady Alice Archer, *The Houblon Family*, 2 vols., 1907

Pearce, E. H., *Annals of Christ's Hospital*, 1908

Trollope, Revd William, *History of Christ's Hospital*, 1834

Wilson, John, *A Brief History of Christ's Hospital*, 1828

Routh, E. M. G., *Tangier: England's Lost Atlantic Outpost 1661–1684*, 1912

Christie, R. C., 'Sir William Coventry', *Saturday Review* (11 Oct. 1873)

Scouten, Arthur H., and Hume, Robert D., *TLS* (28 Sept. 1973), p. 1,105, article on *The Country Gentlemen* by Robert Howard, with inserted scene by duke of Buckingham

Archer, Ian, 'Social Networks in Restoration London: The Evidence of Samuel Pepys's Diary' in *Communities in Early Modern England*, Shepard, Alexandra, and Withington, Phil (eds.), 2000

Campbell, Gordon, et al., 'The Provenance of *De Doctrina Christiana*', *Milton Quarterly*, no. 31 (1997), pp. 67–93

Hanford, James, 'Pepys and the Skinner Family', *Review of English Studies*, vol. vii (July 1931), pp. 257–70

Wilson, J. Harold, 'Pepys and the Virgin Martyr', *Notes & Queries* (21 Feb. 1948)

Birch, Thomas, *History of the Royal Society*, 4 vols., 1756–7

Lyons, Henry, *The Royal Society 1660–1940*, 1944

Hartley, Sir Henry (ed.), *The Royal Society: Its Origins and Founders*, 1960

Andrade, A. N. Da C., on Pepys in *Papers of Royal Society*, vol. 18 (1963)

Lansdowne, Marquess of (ed.), *The Petty Papers*, 2 vols., 1927

Ranft, B. McL., 'The Significance of the Political Career of Samuel Pepys', *Journal of Modern History*, vol. 24, (1952), pp. 368–75

Kenyon, J. P., *The Popish Plot*, 1972

Tanner, J. R., 'Pepys and the Popish Plot', *English Historical Review*, vol. vii (1892)

Wilson, J. H., *The Ordeal of Samuel Pepys's Clerk*, 1972

Tanner, J. R., 'Naval Preparations in 1688', *English Historical Review*, vol. viii (1893)

Powley, E. B., *The English Navy in the Revolution of 1688*, 1928

Mitchell, A. A., 'The Revolution of 1688', *History Today* (July 1965)

Douglas, David, *English Scholars*, 1951

Overton, J. H., *The Nonjurors*, 1902

Heyworth, P. L. (ed.), *Letters of Humfrey Wanley, Palaeographer, Anglo-Saxonist, Librarian 1672–1726*, 1989

Sisam, Kenneth, *Studies in the History of Old English Literature*, 1962

O'Donoghue, E. G., *Bethlehem Hospital*, 1914

Parkes, Joan, *English Travel in England in the Seventeenth Century*, 1925

Speed, John, *The History of Great Britaine*, 1611

BIOGRAPHY

Hill, Christopher, *God's Englishman: Oliver Cromwell and the English Revolution*, 1970

Beresford, John, *The Godfather of Downing Street: Sir George Downing 1623–1684*, 1925

Harris, F. R., *The Life of the First Earl of Sandwich*, 2 vols., 1912

Ollard, Richard, *Cromwell's Earl: A Life of Edward Montagu, First Earl of Sandwich*, 1994

Ashley, Maurice, *General Monck*, 1977

Masson, David, *The Life of Milton*, 7 vols., 1859–94

Spalding, Ruth, *The Improbable Puritan: A Life of Bulstrode Whitelocke*, 1975

Balleine, G. R., *All for the King: The Life Story of Sir George Carteret*, 1976

Dickinson, H. W., *Sir Samuel Morland: Diplomat and Inventor*, 1970

Fitzmaurice, Edward, Lord, *The Life of Sir William Petty*, 1895

Lansdowne, Marquess of, *The Petty–Southwell Correspondence 1676–1687*, 1928

Pinto, Vivian de Sola, *Sir Charles Sedley*, 1927

Coleman, D. C., *Sir John Banks*, 1963

Muddiman, J. G., *The King's Journalist*, 1923

Rowe, Violet, *Sir Henry Vane the Younger*, 1970

More, Louis T., *Isaac Newton*, 1934

Hutton, Ronald, *Charles II*, 1989

Fraser, Antonia, *Charles II*, 1979

— *Cromwell, Our Chief of Men*, 1973

Chapman, Hester, *The Tragedy of Charles II*, 1972

Parker, W. R., *Milton: A Biography*, 1996

Verney, Lady Frances Parthenope, and Verney, Lady Margaret M. (eds.), *Memoirs of the Verney Family duirng the Civil War*, 4 vols., 1892

Foxcroft, H. C., *The Life and Letters of Sir George Savile, First Marquis of Halifax*, 2 vols., 1898

Winn, J. A., *John Dryden and His World*, 1982

Hayley, Kenneth H. D., *The First Earl of Shaftesbury*, 1968

Lane, Jane, *Titus Oates*, 1949

Turner, F. C., *James II*, 1948

Clarke, James Stanier (ed.), *Life of James II*, 2 vols., 1816. Compiled from James's lost diary by the prince regent's librarian and friend of Jane Austen

5. *London History and Topography*

Anon, *Rambles by a Pedestrian*, 1833

Bossy, John, *Giordano Bruno and the Embassy Affair*, 1991

— *Under the Molehill*, 2001 (both books elucidate the topography of Salisbury Court)

Bradley, S., and Pevsner, Nikolaus, *The City*, 1998

Brett-James, N. G., *The Growth of Stuart London*, 1935

Cherry, Bridget, and Pevsner, Nikolaus, *London 2: South*, 1990

Dews, Nathan, *History of Deptford*, 1883

Evelyn, John, *Fumifugium*, 1661

Harris, Tim, *London Crowds in the Reign of Charles II*, 1987

Kingsford, Charles Lethbridge, *Early History Piccadilly, Leicester Square and Soho*, 1925

Reddaway, T. F., *The Rebuilding of London after the Great Fire*, 1951

Steele, Jess, *Turning the Tide: The History of Everyday Deptford*, 1993
Sturdee, T., *Reminiscences of Old Deptford*, 1895

Other topography: *Victoria County History*, Huntingdonshire, Surrey and Hertfordshire volumes

6. *Childhood and Cambridge*

Harris, John, 'Durdans', *Country Life* (8 Sept. 1983)
James, Ch. W., *Chief Justice Coke*, 1929
Thorne, S. E., *Sir Edward Coke*, 1957
Seager, Francis, *The Schoole of Vertue, and Booke of Good Nourture for Chyldren, and Youth to Learne Theyr Dutie by*, 1619
Brinsley, John, *Ludus Literarius*, 1612
—*A Consolation for Our Grammar Schooles*, 1622
Hoole, Charles, *A New Discovery of the Old Art of Teaching Schoole*, 1660
Dickinson, Philip G. M., *Huntingdon Grammar School*, 1965
Mead, A. H., *A Miraculous Draught of Fishes: A History of St Paul's School*, 1990
McDonnell, Michael, *History of St Paul's School*, 1909
Ackermann, R., *History of the Colleges of Winchester . . . The Schools of St Paul's &c.*, 1816

Costello, W. T., *The Scholastic Curriculum at Early Seventeenth-Century Cambridge*, 1958
Heywood, J., and Wright, Thomas, *Cambridge University Transactions during the Puritan Controversies of the Sixteenth and Seventeenth Centuries*, 2 vols., 1854
Cooper, Charles Henry, *Annals of Cambridge*, 5 vols., 1842–53
Purnell, E. K., *Magdalene College*, 1904
Mayor, J. E. B. (ed.), *Cambridge under Queen Anne*, 1911
Mullinger, J. B., *Cambridge in the Seventeenth Century*, 1867
Uffenbach, Zach Conrad von, *London in 1710*, Quarrell, W. H., and Mare, Margaret (trs.), 1934
Benson, A. C., *Magdalene College: A Little View of Its Buildings and History*, 1923

7. *Medical*

The British Library, Sloane MSS, 1536, fols. 56v., r. These are the prescriptions 'for Mr peapes who was cut for ye Stones by Mr Hollier March ye 26 and had a very great stone taken this day from him.'
Power, Sir d'Arcy, 'The Medical History of Mr and Mrs Samuel Pepys', *Occasional Papers Read by Members at Meetings of the Samuel Pepys Club*, vol. I, 1917
Keynes, Milo, 'Why Samuel Pepys Stopped Writing His Diary: His Dimming Eyesight and Ill-health', *Journal of Medical Biography*, vol. v (Feb. 1997), pp. 25–9.
Lithotomia Vesicae, 1640 (English tr. from Dutch)

Tolet, F., *Traité de la Lithotomie*, 1693, and English ed. 1683

Nathaniel Hodges, *Loimologia*, Quincy, J., (tr.), 1720

Robinson, Nicholas, *A Complete Treatise of the Gravel and Stone*, 1734

Ellis, Harold, *A History of Bladder Stone*, 1969

8. Naval History

Anderson, R. C. (ed.), *Journal of Edward Montagu*, 1929

Campbell, John, *Naval History of Great Britain including History and Lives of the British Admirals*, 8 vols., 1818

Capp, Bernard, *Cromwell's Navy*, 1989

Chappell, Edwin, *Samuel Pepys as a Naval Administrator*, 1933

Charnock, John, *Biographia Navalis*, 6 vols., 1794–8

Davies, J. D., *Gentlemen and Tarpaulins*, 1991

—'Pepys and the Admiralty Commission of 1679–1684', *Bulletin of the Institute for Historical Research*, vol. lxii (1989), pp. 34–53

de Beer, E. S., 'Reports of Pepys's Speech in the House of Commons, 5 March 1668', *Mariner's Mirror*, vol. 14 (1928), pp. 55–8

Harris, G. G., *The Trinity House 1514–1660*, 1970

Ollard, Richard, *Man of War: Sir Robert Holmes and the Restoration Navy*, 1969

Padfield, Peter, *Maritime Supremacy and the Opening of the Western Mind*, 2000

Pool, Bernard, *Navy Board Contracts*, 1966

Powell, J. R., and Timings, E. K. (eds.), *The Rupert and Monck Letter Book 1666*, 1969

Rogers, P. G., *The Dutch in the Medway*, 1970

Tanner, J. R. (ed.), *Naval Minutes of Samuel Pepys*, 1926

—*Descriptive Catalogue of the Naval Manuscripts in the Pepysian Library*, 4 vols., 1903–23

Tanner, J. R., *Samuel Pepys and the Royal Navy*, 1920

—'Samuel Pepys and the Trinity House', *English Historical Review*, vol. xxxxiv (1929), pp. 583–5

Tedder, A. W., *The Navy of the Restoration*, 1916

Wilcox, L. A., *Mr Pepys's Navy*, 1966

9. The Diary and Pepys Material

The manuscript of the Diary is held at the Pepys Library, Magdalene College, Cambridge. Of the three transcriptions, John Smith's manuscript is also held at the Pepys Library. It was the basis of the first edition, Lord Braybrooke (ed.), *Memoirs of Samuel Pepys . . . Deciphered by the Revd John Smith . . . and Selection from Private Correspondence*, 2 vols., 1825. Mynors Bright's transcription, finished in 1875, has been lost; it was published 1875–9. Henry Wheatley's edition of 1893–9, which drew on both Braybrooke and Bright, has notes and a good index; I have found the 1926 edition useful. The complete and definitive edition, edited and transcribed by

Robert Latham and William Matthews (1970–83), is in 11 vols., one containing an index, vol. X a companion.

Pepys's *Memoires of the Royal Navy 1679–1688*, 1690; also Tanner's edition of 1906
Occasional Papers Read by Members at Meetings of the Samuel Pepys Club, 2 vols., 1917 and 1925
Smith, John, *The Life, Journals and Correspondence of Samuel Pepys*, 2 vols., 1841
Firth, C. H., 'The Early Life of Pepys', *Macmillan's Magazine*, vol. lxix (1894), p. 32
Wheatley, H. B., *Samuel Pepys and the World He Lived In*, 1880
— *Pepysiana*, 1899
Tanner, J. R., 'General Introduction to Pepys Library Catalogue' of 1903
— *Samuel Pepys and the Royal Navy*, 1920
— *Mr Pepys: An Introduction to the Diary together with a Sketch of His Later Life*, 1925
Tanner, J. R. (ed.), *Naval Minutes of Samuel Pepys* (from Pepys Library), 1926
— *Private Correspondence and Miscellaneous Papers of Samuel Pepys*, 2 vols., 1926
— *Further Correspondence of Samuel Pepys 1662–1679*, 1929
Whitear, W. H., *More Pepysiana*, 1927
Howarth, R. G. (ed.), *Letters and Second Diary of Samuel Pepys*, 1932
Chappell, Edwin (transcriber and ed.), *The Shorthand Letters of Samuel Pepys*, 1933
— *The Tangier Papers of Samuel Pepys*, 1935
Chappell, Edwin, *Samuel Pepys as a Naval Administrator*, 1933
— *Eight Generations of the Pepys Family*, 1936
Bryant, Arthur, *Samuel Pepys: The Man in the Making*, 1933
— *Samuel Pepys: The Years of Peril*, 1935
— *Samuel Pepys: The Saviour of the Navy*, 1938
Heath, H. T. (ed.), *The Letters of Samuel Pepys and His Family Circle*, 1955
Ollard, Richard, *Pepys*, 1974
Latham, Robert (ed.), *Catalogue of the Pepys Library*, 10 vols., 1978-94
Rogers, T. D., *Sir Frederic Madden at Cambridge*, 1980. Madden's account of his visit to the Pepys Library in 1831 and again in Nov. 1842, when he observed the wife of the master and other ladies 'all pulling down P's volumes, and doing just as they please, because *they* are *privileged persons!*'
Latham, Robert (ed.), and Latham, Robert, and Matthews, William (transcribers), *Samuel Pepys and the Second Dutch War* (containing Pepys's 'Navy White Book' and his 'Brooke House Papers'), 1995

CRITICAL ESSAYS

Scott, Walter, review of Diary, *Quarterly Review*, vol. xxxiii (Mar. 1826), p. 264
Jeffrey, Francis, review of Diary, *Edinburgh Review*, vol. xliii (Nov. 1825), p. 54
Review of Mynors Bright transcription, *Athenaeum* (29 Jan. 1876)
Stevenson, Robert Louis, 'Samuel Pepys', *Cornhill* (July 1881).

Text and Illustrations Permissions

The publisher would like to thank the following photographers, organizations and collections for their kind permission to reproduce the copyright material in this book:

Extracts from *The Diary of Samuel Pepys*, edited by Robert Latham and William Matthews (copyright © The Master, Fellows and Scholars of Magdalene College, Cambridge, Robert Latham and the Estate of William Matthews, 1983), are reproduced by permission of Peters Fraser and Dunlop on behalf of the Master, Fellows and Scholars of Magdalene College, Cambridge, the Estate of Robert Latham and the Estate of Lois Emery Matthews.

Front and end papers: From Hollar's long view of London, published in Amsterdam in 1647.

1. View of St Paul's and the City from rural Islington, by Hollar, 1665. Pepys Library, Magdalene College, Cambridge.
2. Detail of Milford Stairs, by Hollar, 1640s. Pepys Library, Magdalene College, Cambridge.
3. Durdans House, Epsom, oil painting by Jacob Knyff, 1673. Berkeley Castle Will Trust. Photo: Photographic Survey, Courtauld Institute of Art.
4. Destruction of Cheapside Cross, 1643. Pepys Library, Magdalene College, Cambridge.
5. The north-east view of Hinchingbrooke House, 1730. From *The Victoria County History of Huntingdonshire*, vol. II.
6. Jemima Montagu, *c.* 1646. Earl of Sandwich 1943 Settlement.
7. The young Edward Montagu, oil painting by Peter Lely, *c.* 1646. Earl of Sandwich 1943 Settlement. Photo: Roderick Field.
8. Pepys House, Brampton. From *The Victoria County History of Huntingdonshire*, vol. III.
9. Execution of the earl of Strafford on Tower Hill, 12 May 1641, by Hollar. Pepys Library, Magdalene College, Cambridge.
10. Oliver Cromwell. Pepys Library, Magdalene College, Cambridge.
11. Execution of Charles I at Whitehall, 30 January 1649. Private collection. Photo: The Bridgeman Art Library.
12. New Palace Yard looking towards Whitehall Palace, 1664. Pepys Library, Magdalene College, Cambridge.
13. Samuel Morland, by Peter Lely, 1659. In possession of the Gibbes Museum of Art, South Carolina, USA.

14. George Downing. By permission of the British Library.
15. Magdalene College in 1690 by David Loggan. Pepys Library, Magdalene College, Cambridge.
16. List of plate in Pepys's hand. Bodleian Library, University of Oxford, Carte MS 73, fol. 201r.
17. Frontispiece of Edward Phillips's *The Misteries of Love and Eloquence*, 1658. By permission of the British Library.
18. 'Extraction of the stone out of the bladder', print from François Tolet, *Traité de la Lithotomie*, English edition of 1683. Photo: Wellcome Library, London.
19. Elizabeth Pepys, engraving by T. Thomson after John Hayls's portrait of 1666. National Portrait Gallery Archive Engravings Collection.
20. Samuel Pepys, oil painting by John Hayls, 1666. National Portrait Gallery, London.
21. First page of Pepys's Diary, 1659/60. Pepys Library, Magdalene College, Cambridge.
22. Will Hewer, an engraving from vol. II of the first edition of Pepys's Diary, 1825. By permission of Robin Hyman. Photo: Nathan Kelly.
23. Susan Gill, red chalk drawing by Charles Beale, 1670. © The British Museum.
24. Admiral Sir William Penn, by Peter Lely, oil painting. Photo: © National Maritime Museum Picture Library, London.
25. Thomas Povey, by J.M. Wright. The Blathway Collection, National Trust. Photo: Photographic Survey, Courtauld Institute of Art.
26. Sir William Coventry, by John Riley, oil painting. Reproduced by permisssion of the Marquis of Bath, Longleat. Photo: Photographic Survey, Courtauld Institute of Art.
27. John Ogilby presenting to King Charles II and Queen Catherine the list of subscribers to the map he and William Morgan were preparing, 1682. Museum of London.
28. St Olave's Church, Hart Street, London, *c.* 1670. Reproduced by kind permission of the Reverend John Cowling.
29. 'Greenwich from the Park', by Hendrick Danckerts, mid 1670s. Photo: National Maritime Museum Picture Library, London.
30. The Great Fire of London, 1666 (Dutch, artist unknown). Museum of London.
31. Memorial bust of Elizabeth Pepys, attributed to John Bushnell, *c.* 1670. Photo: Fleming.
32. Jemima Montagu, countess of Sandwich. Earl of Sandwich 1943 Settlement.
33. Edward Montagu, earl of Sandwich, school of Peter Lely, *c.* 1670. Earl of Sandwich 1943 Settlement. Photo: Roderick Field.
34. James Houblon. Private collection. Photo: Richard Greenly.
35. Sarah Houblon. Private collection. Photo: Richard Greenly.
36. 'Mrs Pepys'? Reproduced by kind permission of the Witt Library, London.
37. Anthony Ashley Cooper, first earl of Shaftesbury, artist unknown, *c.* 1672–3. National Portrait Gallery, London.

38. James, duke of York, as lord high admiral, by Henri Gascar, *c.* 1675. Philip Mould, Historical Portrait Ltd, London/Bridgeman Art Library.
39. John Evelyn, print from the Kneller portrait, *c.* 1689. Pepys Library, Magdalene College, Cambridge.
40. William Petty, by Isaac Fuller, *c.* 1640–51. National Portrait Gallery, London.
41. Marble bust of Isaac Newton, by Louis F. Roubiliac. © The Royal Society.
42. Bust of Sir Christopher Wren, by Edward Pierce, Ashmolean Museum, Oxford.
43. and 44. Two views of Pepys's Library in Buckingham Street. Pepys Library, Magdalene College, Cambridge.
45. Letter by Pepys presented to James II and signed by James, 17 November 1688, with docket and tracing of watermark. The Denys Eyre Bower Bequest, Chiddingstone Castle, Kent.
46. Lines from Pepys's account with Hoare's Bank. By kind permission of C. Hoare & Co.
47. John Jackson, an engraving from vol. II of the first edition of Pepys's Diary, 1825. By permission of Robin Hyman. Photo: Nathan Kelly.
48. Samuel Pepys, by John Closterman, *c.* 1700. National Portrait Gallery, London.
49. Ivory medallion of Pepys, by Jean Cavalier, 1688. Courtesy of the Clothworkers' Company, London.
50. The first page of John Smith's transcription of Pepys's Diary, 1819. Pepys Library, Magdalene College, Cambridge.

Every effort has been made to trace the copyright holders. We apologize for any unintentional omission and would be pleased to insert the appropriate acknowledgement in any subsequent edition.

Index

'EP' indicates Elizabeth Pepys and 'SP' Samuel Pepys.

S. Dunston in the East

Magnes   2 Gray church   5 .. Billins Garke

Lyon kay   Billings gate

THE BRIDGE